Rules for Predicate Logic

Rule UI: $(u)(\ldots u \ldots)$ $/\therefore (\ldots w \ldots)$

Provided:
1. $(\ldots w \ldots)$ results from replacing each occurrence of u free in $(\ldots u \ldots)$ with a w that is either a constant or a variable free in $(\ldots w \ldots)$ (making no other changes).

Rule EI: $(\exists u)(\ldots u \ldots)$ $/\therefore (\ldots w \ldots)$

Provided:
1. w is not a constant.
2. w does not occur free previously in the proof.
3. $(\ldots w \ldots)$ results from replacing each occurrence of u free in $(\ldots u \ldots)$ with a w that is free in $(\ldots w \ldots)$ (making no other changes).

Rule UG: $(\ldots u \ldots)$ $/\therefore (w)(\ldots w \ldots)$

Provided:
1. u is not a constant.
2. u does not occur free previously in a line obtained by **EI.**
3. u does not occur free previously in an assumed premise that has not yet been discharged.
4. $(\ldots w \ldots)$ results from replacing each occurrence of u free in $(\ldots u \ldots)$ with a w that is free in $(\ldots w \ldots)$ (making no other changes) and there are no additional occurrences of w already contained in $(\ldots w \ldots)$.

Rule EG: $(\ldots u \ldots)$ $/\therefore (\exists w)(\ldots w \ldots)$

Provided:
1. $(\ldots w \ldots)$ results from replacing **at least one** occurrence of u, where u is a constant or a variable free in $(\ldots u \ldots)$ with a w that is free in $(\ldots w \ldots)$ (making no other changes) and there are no additional occurrences of w already contained in $(\ldots w \ldots)$.

Rule QN: $(u)(\ldots u \ldots) :: \sim (\exists u) \sim (\ldots u \ldots)$
$(\exists u)(\ldots u \ldots) :: \sim (u) \sim (\ldots u \ldots)$
$(u) \sim (\ldots u \ldots) :: \sim (\exists u)(\ldots u \ldots)$
$(\exists u) \sim (\ldots u \ldots) :: \sim (u)(\ldots u \ldots)$

Rule ID: $(\ldots u \ldots)$ $\qquad\qquad$ $(\ldots u \ldots)$
$u = w$ $/\therefore (\ldots w \ldots)$ $\qquad$ $w = u$ $/\therefore (\ldots w \ldots)$

Rule IR: $/\therefore (x)(x = x)$

Logic and Philosophy
A Modern Introduction
Tenth Edition

Alan Hausman

Hunter College, City University of New York

Howard Kahane

Late of University of Maryland

Paul Tidman

Mount Union College

THOMSON ™
WADSWORTH

Australia • Brazil • Canada • Mexico • Singapore • Spain
United Kingdom • United States

THOMSON
★
™
WADSWORTH

Publisher: *Holly J. Allen*
Philosophy Editor: *Steve Wainwright*
Assistant Editors: *Lee McCracken,*
  Barbara Hillaker
Editorial Assistant: *Gina Kessler*
Technology Project Manager: *Julie Aguilar*
Marketing Manager: *Worth Hawes*
Marketing Assistant: *Alexandra Tran*
Marketing Communications Manager:
  Stacey Purviance
Creative Director: *Rob Hugel*

Executive Art Director: *Maria Epes*
Print Buyer: *Karen Hunt*
Permissions Editor: *Bob Kauser*
Production Service: *Scratchgravel Publishing*
  Services/G&S Book Services
Copy Editor: *Linda Purrington*
Cover Designer: *Yvo Riezebos*
Cover Image: *Jay Corbett/Getty Images*
Cover Printer: *Phoenix Color*
Compositor: *Scratchgravel Publishing Services*
Printer: *Maple-Vail, Binghamton*

Thomson Higher Education
10 Davis Drive
Belmont, CA 94002-3098
USA

For more information about our products, contact
us at:
Thomson Learning Academic Resource Center
1-800-423-0563

For permission to use material from this text or
product, submit a request online at
http://www.thomsonrights.com.
Any additional questions about permissions can
be submitted by e-mail to
thomsonrights@thomson.com.

Library of Congress Control Number: 2006922155

ISBN 0-495-12844-9

Contents

Chapter Three: Truth Tables   55

Chapter Four: Proofs   88

Chapter Five: Conditional and Indirect Proofs   125

Chapter Six: Sentential Logic Truth Trees   150

Chapter Eleven: Rationale Behind the Precise Formulation of the Four Quantifier Rules

Chapter Twelve: Predicate Logic Truth Trees   269

Chapter Thirteen: Identity and Philosophical Problems of Symbolic Logic

Chapter Fourteen: Syllogistic Logic   316

Preface

This new edition of *Logic and Philosophy* has been quite extensively redone. More specifically, the first fourteen chapters, all of which deal with deductive logic, have been carefully re-edited. A *great* deal of effort has gone into ensuring the accuracy of the problems and exercises throughout the text.

I have provided much new content, mainly of a more philosophical nature. In Chapters Six and Twelve, which deal with sentential and predicate trees respectively, there has been a complete rewrite. Chapter Six now stresses, beyond the construction of the trees, the theoretical relationship to truth tables, demonstrated by the use of creative exercises. Chapter Twelve incorporates a flow chart for constructing trees, and a long section on metatheory. Much in the way of philosophical discussion has been added to topics such as existential import, the justification of truth tables, and the semantics of predicate logic, and exercises with a philosophical bent have been inserted after at least some of these discussions.

The purpose of this book is to provide students with a clear, comprehensible introduction to a complete system for sentential (Part One) and first-order predicate logic (Part Two). Included as well are a discussion of the relationship between traditional syllogistic logic and its modern expression, and a wealth of material in Part Three of a supplementary nature.

This text is designed for those who desire a comprehensive introduction to logic that is both rigorous and student friendly. In Parts One and Two, numerous exercise sets take the student from sentential logic through first-order predicate logic with identity. The rules are carefully motivated and compared to other systems of rules for sentential and predicate logic. Part Three includes a solid range of additional material, including chapters devoted to informal logic, inductive logic, and modal, epistemic, and deontic logics. Thus the text is designed to provide instructors with maximum flexibility in course design. This great variety of material enables instructors to choose topics of interest to them and best suited to the needs of their students.

Through all editions, the goal has been to make symbolic logic understandable for the typical student. Several features of the book contribute to this goal.

Help for the Mathematically Anxious or Averse

The symbols in a symbolic logic text and the rules for their manipulation are mathematical in character; the discussions of both are philosophical. *Logic and Philosophy* stresses the relationships between the mathematical and the philosophical in ways that are designed to engage student interest and at the same time to provide explanations of *why* the symbols work as they do. I know from sad firsthand experience how often both explanation and interest are missing in mathematics courses and texts, and it is such texts that most beginning students in logic have as their model of mathematical thinking. The result is all too often fear and loathing in mathematics courses. Students can overcome math anxiety once they see that logic is intelligible in a sense they can understand.

Many students who fear mathematics do not fear the learning of a language. Throughout, the learning of logical systems is treated like the learning of a foreign language, the happy difference being the absolute rigor of logic's grammatical rules (somewhat analogous to the once popular idea of a universal language to be spoken, Esperanto, which had completely regular grammatical rules). I have found in my own classes that this approach is helpful to many.

"Walk-Through" Sections

For crucial exercises there are "how-to" type sections where the student is carefully walked through a moderately difficult sample problem step by step.

Coverage of Basic Concepts

Beginning with the first chapter, attention is paid to such topics as logical form and the relationship between consistency and validity. The fundamental concept of a semantic interpretation is used to provide a unified explanation of such basic concepts as validity, consistency, logical equivalence, and logical implication in both sentential and predicate logic.

The changes in the Tenth Edition are built on this foundation. Some of these changes were of course motivated by errors in the previous edition. Obviously, logic texts cannot afford such mistakes. Every effort has been made to make the text and exercises accurate. Just as important, it is my intent in this and future revisions to restore much of the original philosophical purpose that Howard Kahane had when he wrote the book. Since I was a close friend and was intimately connected to the writing of the first edition, I feel uniquely qualified to undertake this task. Here are some of the highlights of these changes:

- Philosophical discussion and justification of basic concepts has markedly increased in many sections. For example, a section on the justification of the truth tables has been substantially revised. There is a discussion of the freeing of variables by existential and universal instantiation that does not occur in most logic texts, and there is an expanded look at the issues surrounding existential import.
- I have also added suggestions for philosophical discussions below some of the exercises. I must add that I do not envision these discussions as directed at philosophy majors alone. Many of them arise quite naturally from the material itself—questions, for example, that those fearful of math are so often afraid to ask but, if answered, replace anxiety with understanding. I, for example, was a mathematics major as an undergraduate; each year my puzzlement over what was going on in my math classes got worse and worse. When as a graduate student I took a symbolic logic class from Professor Gustav Bergmann, he carefully explained what a function was, and years of mystery dissolved overnight. The concepts of logic are far from cut and dried, and they need not ever be dry.

- Chapter Six has been rewritten. Exercises on how to construct the tree rules themselves show the relationship of the rules to truth tables.
- Chapter Twelve has been carefully revised so that the nature and structure of the construction of predicate trees is now much clearer. Metatheoretic results have been included as well.

Acknowledgments

I wish to express my thanks to the many teachers who sent in comments and suggestions about the Ninth Edition. Thanks especially to the following for their helpful comments: Nathan Andersen, Eckerd College; David Gibson, Pepperdine University; Robert Lane, University of West Georgia; Larry J. Waggle, Illinois State University; Nancy Brown, De Anza College; Alan Gorfin, Western New England College; Larry J. Kaye, University of Massachusetts, Boston; and Roderick M. Stewart, Austin College. Christopher Hom, University of California, Santa Cruz, checked Ninth Edition errata sheets. Jon Wulff, Bellevue Community College; Peter Horban, Simon Fraser University; Matthew Phillips, Rutgers University; Jeffrey Buechner, Rutgers University; Reina Hayaki, University of Nebraska, Lincoln; and Lisa Warenski, Union College, all helped with detecting and correcting errors. It is my hope that the Tenth will be a worthy successor to the editions edited by Paul Tidman, who took over from Howard Kahane after he fell ill.

Howard Kahane's *Logic and Contemporary Rhetoric*, a direct response to student cries for relevance in the late 1960s, was a groundbreaking work that has set a standard for all subsequent informal logic texts. *Logic and Philosophy*, although not revolutionary in that way, was unique in its informal pedagogical style. Both works typified the intense commitment Kahane had to his students and his work. He lived the life of an intellectually honest man. His death in 2001 deprived the world of a fine philosopher, a wonderful human being, and a dear friend.

Alan Hausman
Hunter College
City University of New York

Logic and Philosophy

Chapter One

Introduction

---

1 *The Elements of an Argument*

Consider the following simple example of reasoning:

> Identical twins often have different IQ test scores. Yet such twins inherit the same genes. So environment must play some part in determining IQ.

Logicians call this kind of reasoning an **argument.** (But they don't have in mind shouting or fighting. Rather, their concern is *arguing for* or presenting reasons for a conclusion.) In this case, the argument consists of three statements:

1. Identical twins often have different IQ test scores.
2. Identical twins inherit the same genes.
3. So environment must play some part in determining IQ.

The first two statements in this argument give *reasons* for accepting the third. In logic terms, they are said to be **premises** of the argument, and the third statement is called the argument's **conclusion.** An argument can be defined as a series of statements, one of which is the conclusion (the thing argued for) and the others are the premises (reasons for accepting the conclusion).

In everyday life, few of us bother to explicitly label premises or conclusions. We usually don't even bother to distinguish one argument from another. But good writing provides clues that signal the presence of an argument. Such words as *because, since,* and *for* usually indicate that what follows is a premise. And words such as *therefore, hence, consequently,* and *so* usually signal a conclusion. Similarly, such expressions as "It has been observed that . . . ," "In support of this . . . ," and "The relevant data . . ." generally introduce premises, whereas expressions such as "It follows that . . . ," "The result is . . . ," "The point of all this is . . . ," and "The implication is . . ." usually signal conclusions. Here is a simple example:

> *Since* it's wrong to kill a human being, *it follows that* abortion is wrong, *because* abortion takes the life of (kills) a human being.

In this example, the words "since" and "because" signal premises offered in support of the conclusion signaled by the phrase "it follows that." Put into textbook form, the argument reads,

1. It's wrong to kill a human being.
2. Abortion takes the life of (kills) a human being.
∴ 3. Abortion is wrong.

The symbol "∴." represents the word "therefore" and indicates that what follows is a conclusion. This particular argument has two premises, but an argument may have any number of premises (even only one!) and may be surrounded by or embedded in other arguments.

Not just any group of sentences makes an argument. The sentences in an argument must express statements, that is, say something that is either true or false. Many sentences are used for other purposes: to ask questions, to issue commands, or to give vent to emotions. In ordinary contexts none of the following express statements:

Open the door. (*command*)
Who's the boss here? (*question*)
Thank goodness! (*expression of emotion*)

Of course, sometimes nondeclarative sentences are indeed used to make statements. "Who's the boss here?" *can* be used to make a statement, particularly if the boss is talking. In this case the boss is not really asking a question at all, but rather is saying, "*I am the boss here*," thus declaring a fact under the guise of asking a question.

But even if every sentence in a group of sentences expresses a statement, the result is not necessarily an argument. The statements must be related to one another in the appropriate way. Something must be argued for (the conclusion), and there must be reasons for accepting the conclusion. Thus, mere bald assertions are not arguments, anecdotes generally are not arguments, nor are most other forms of exposition or explanation. It's important to understand the difference between rhetoric that is primarily expository or explanatory and rhetoric that is basically argumentative. A passage that contains only exposition gives us no reason to accept the "facts" in it other than the authority of the writer or speaker, whereas passages that contain arguments give reasons for some of their claims (conclusions) and call for a different sort of evaluation than merely an evaluation of the authority of the writer.

Examples

Two of the following groups of statements constitute arguments, and two do not. These examples also illustrate that although words such as "therefore" and "because" usually signal the presence of an argument, this is not always the case.

1. I believe in God because that is how I was raised. (This is biography, not an argument. "*Because*" is used here to indicate the cause of the speaker's belief—to give an explanation—not to signal a premise.)

2. I believe in God because life has meaning. If there is no God, life would be meaningless. (This is an argument. The speaker is advancing a reason to believe that God exists.) Here is the argument put into textbook form:

   1. Life has meaning.
   2. If there were no God, life would be meaningless.
   ∴ 3. God exists.

   (Notice that in this case the word "because" does signal that a premise is to follow.)

3. Biff was obviously afraid of making a commitment to a long-term relationship. Therefore, Susie was not surprised when they eventually broke up. (This is not an argument. This is an explanation of why Susie was not surprised.)

4. We'll get a tax break if we marry before the end of the year. Therefore, I think we should move our wedding date up and not wait until January. (This is an argument.):

   1. We'll get a tax break if we marry before the end of the year.
   ∴ 2. We should move our wedding date up and not wait until January.

Exercise 1-1

Here are twelve passages (the first six are from student papers and exams, modestly edited). Determine which contain arguments and which do not. Label the premises and conclusions of those that do, and explain your answers. Paraphrase if that makes things clearer. (Even-numbered items in most exercise sets are answered in a section at the back of the book.)

1. I don't like big-time college football. I don't like pro football on TV either. In fact, I don't like sports, period.

2. My summer vacation was spent working in Las Vegas. I worked as a waitress at the Desert Inn and made tons of money. But I guess I got addicted to the slots and didn't save too much. Next summer my friend Hal and I are going to work in Reno if we can find jobs there.

3. Well, I have a special reason for believing in big-time college football. After all, I wouldn't have come here if Ohio State's football team hadn't gone to the Rose Bowl, because that's how I heard about this place to begin with.

4. At the present rate of consumption, the oil will be used up in 20 to 25 years. And we're sure not going to reduce consumption in the near future. So we'd better start developing solar power, windmills, and other "alternative energy sources" pretty soon.

5. The abortion issue is blown all out of proportion. How come we don't hear nearly as much about the evils of the pill? After all, a lot more potential people are "killed" by the pill than by abortion.

6. I've often wondered how they make lead pencils. Of course, they don't use lead, they use graphite. But I mean, How do they get the graphite into the wood? That's my

problem. The only thing I can think of is maybe they cut the lead into long round strips and then cut holes in the wood and slip the lead in.

7. Punishment, when speedy and specific, may suppress undesirable behavior, but it cannot teach or encourage desirable alternatives. Therefore, it is crucial to use positive techniques to model and reinforce appropriate behavior that the person can use in place of the unacceptable response that has to be suppressed.
—Walter and Harriet Mischel, *Essentials of Psychology*

8. There was no European language that Ruth could not speak at least a little bit. She passed the time in the concentration camp, waiting for death, by getting other prisoners to teach her languages she did not know. Thus did she become fluent in Romany, the tongue of the gypsies.   —Kurt Vonnegut, *Jailbird*

9. The death of my brother was another instance in which I realized the inadequacy of the superstition of progress in regard to life. A good, intelligent, serious man, he was still young when he fell ill. He suffered for over a year and died an agonizing death without ever understanding why he lived and understanding even less why he was dying. No theories could provide any answers to these questions, either for him or for me, during his slow and painful death.   —Leo Tolstoy, *Confession*

10. To be sustained under the Eighth Amendment, the death penalty must "comport with the basic concept of human dignity at the core of the Amendment"; the objective in imposing it must be "consistent with our respect for the dignity of other men." Under these standards, the taking of life "because the wrongdoer deserves it" surely must fail, for such a punishment has as its very basis the total denial of the wrongdoer's dignity and worth.
—Justice Thurgood Marshall, Dissenting Opinion in *Gregg v. Georgia*

11. The electoral college should be abolished. Everyone's vote should count the same. With the electoral college the votes of those who live in small states count for more. That's how Bush won the election, even though Gore got more votes. So I think we should do away with it.

12. Every event must have a cause. Since an infinite series of causes is impossible, there must be a first uncaused cause of everything: God.

13. If God were all good, he would want his creatures to always be happy. If God were all powerful, he would be able to accomplish anything he wants. Therefore, God must be lacking in either power or goodness or both.

14. It is now some years since I detected how many were the false beliefs that I had from my earliest youth admitted as true, and how doubtful was everything I had since constructed on this basis: and from that time I was convinced that I must once for all seriously undertake to rid myself of all the opinions which I had formerly accepted, and commence to build anew from the foundation, if I wanted to establish any firm and permanent structure in the sciences.
—René Descartes, *Meditations*

15. If you can discover a better way of life than office holding for your future rulers, a well-governed city becomes a possibility. For only in such a state will those rule who are truly rich, not in gold, but in the wealth that makes happiness—a good and wise life.
—Plato, *The Republic*

2 *Deduction and Induction*

Deduction and induction are commonly thought to be the cornerstones of good reasoning. The fundamental logical property of a **deductively valid argument** is this: if all its premises are true, then its conclusion must be true. In other words, *an argument is valid just in case it is impossible for all its premises to be true and yet its conclusion be false.* The truth of the premises of a valid argument guarantees the truth of its conclusion.

To determine whether or not an argument is valid, one must ask whether there are any possible circumstances under which the premises could all be true and yet the conclusion be false. If not, the argument is valid. If it is possible for the premises to be true and the conclusion false, the argument is invalid. An **invalid argument** is simply an argument that is not valid.

The question naturally arises as to why it is impossible for the conclusion of a valid argument to be false if all its premises are true. Why do its premises, if true, "guarantee" the truth of its conclusion? Unfortunately, there is no simple answer to this question. A clear answer for some types of deductive arguments is given in this book. It is revealing to notice that in a typical case the information contained in the conclusion of a deductively valid argument is already "contained" in its premises. We tend not to notice this fact because it is usually contained in the premises implicitly (along with other information not contained in the conclusion). Indeed, cases in which the conclusion is explicitly mentioned in a premise tend to be rather trivial.

Examples

Here is an example of a deductively valid argument whose conclusion is implicitly contained in its premises:

1. All wars are started by miscalculation.
2. The Iraq conflict was a war.
∴ 3. The Iraq conflict was started by miscalculation.

Having said in the first premise that all wars are started by miscalculation and in the second that the Iraq conflict was a war, we have implicitly said that the Iraq conflict was started by miscalculation. And this is what is asserted by the argument's conclusion.

Here is another example:

1. If Bonny has had her appendix taken out, then she doesn't have to worry about getting appendicitis.
2. She has had her appendix taken out.
∴ 3. She doesn't have to worry about getting appendicitis.

The first premise states that if she has had her appendix out, then she doesn't have to worry about appendicitis, and the second, that she has in fact had her appendix out, which implicitly asserts the conclusion that she doesn't have to worry about appendicitis.

And here is a trivial case in which the conclusion is explicitly stated in the argument's premise:

1. Shakespeare wrote *Othello,* and Chaucer wrote *The Canterbury Tales.*
∴ 2. Shakespeare wrote *Othello.*

In addition to deductive arguments, there are also **inductive arguments.** Arguments of this kind differ from deductively valid arguments in having conclusions that go beyond what is contained in their premises. Good inductive arguments are said to be **inductively strong.** The crucial difference between inductive strength and deductive validity is that it is possible for the premises of a strong inductive argument to be true and yet the conclusion be false. Whereas true premises in a valid argument *guarantee* the truth of the conclusion, true premises in a strong inductive argument make the conclusion *likely* or *probable.* The basic idea behind inductive reasoning is that of *learning from experience.* We notice *patterns, resemblances,* or other kinds of *regularities* in our experiences, some quite simple (sugar sweetens coffee), some very complicated (objects move according to Newton's laws), and project them onto other cases.

We use inductive reasoning so frequently in everyday life that the inductive nature of this kind of conclusion drawing generally goes unnoticed. It's a bit like being told that we've been speaking prose all our lives to discover that we've been drawing perfectly good inductive inferences (and some stinkers) since an early age. By the age of five, the use of induction has taught us a great many of the basic truths that guide everyday behavior. We have learned, for instance, that some foods taste good and some don't, the sun is going to rise tomorrow morning and every morning after that, very hot things burn the skin, some people are good and some aren't, you can't hold your breath for more than a minute or two, and so on. Our reasoning for the belief that the sun will rise tomorrow, as an example, can be expressed in this way:

1. The sun has always risen every morning so far.
∴ 2. The sun will rise tomorrow (or every morning).

The great virtue of inductive reasoning is that it provides us with a way of reasoning to genuinely new beliefs, and not just to psychologically new ones that were implicit in what we already knew, as in the case of valid deductions. However, this benefit is purchased at the cost of an increase in the possibility of error. The truth of the premises of a deductively valid argument guarantees the truth of its conclusion, but a strong induction may contain all true premises and yet have a false conclusion. Even the best "inductive leap" may lead us astray, because the pattern noticed in our experiences may not turn out to be true in other cases. For example, in 1986 after the success of *Star Wars* and *Return of the Jedi,* it was a pretty safe bet that the next film produced by George Lucas would be a box office hit. So movie-goers in 1986 could have constructed the following inductively strong argument:

1. All of the movies produced in recent years by George Lucas have been successful.
∴ 2. The latest film produced by Lucas will be successful.

Unfortunately, the film turned out to be *Howard the Duck.*

Although an inductively strong argument does not guarantee that if its premises are true, then its conclusion also will be true, it does make its conclusion more probable (one reason why the expression "probability argument" is sometimes applied to inductive arguments). And, of course, the more and the better the evidence, the higher the probability that its conclusion will in fact turn out to be true. Unlike validity, inductive strength comes in degrees. It makes no sense to speak of one argument as being "more valid" than another. All deductive arguments are either valid or invalid. But it does make sense to describe one argument as being inductively stronger than another. This fact alone makes inductive logic controversial and much more complex.

3 *Deductive Argument Forms*

Consider the following argument:

    1. Art is an Ohioan, or he's a New Yorker.
    2. Art is not an Ohioan.
∴ 3. He's a New Yorker.

In this argument, if premises 1 and 2 are both true, then the conclusion must be true also. But are both premises true? We have no way of knowing, since, presumably, we don't know anything about Art and consequently don't know whether Art is or is not an Ohioan. Nevertheless, it is clear that if the premises are true (that is, if Art is either an Ohioan or a New Yorker, but he's not an Ohioan), then the conclusion must be true (that is, Art must be a New Yorker). We know this from the *form* of the argument and not because of its content; its form makes this argument a valid argument.* Any argument having the same form—that is, any argument of the form

    1. _____ or _____ .
    2. It's not the case that _____ .
∴ 3. _____ .

where each pair of similar lines (solid lines, dashed lines) is filled in with the same expression—is deductively valid.** (Of course, there are many other valid argument forms.)

Examples

Arguments (1) through (4) all have the same form. So do arguments (5) through (8), but the form they share is different from that of (1) through (4):

(1)   1. It will rain or it will snow.
        2. It's not the case that it will rain.
   ∴ 3. It will snow.

---

* You will see later that, in general, arguments have several forms; any argument with at least one valid form is valid.
** Notice we write "It is not the case that Art is an Ohioan" for "Art is not an Ohioan."

(2)   1. A Democrat will win or a Republican will win.
      2. It's not the case that a Democrat will win.
   ∴ 3. A Republican will win.

(3)   1. There's a devil or there's a God.
      2. It's not the case that there's a devil.
   ∴ 3. There's a God.

(4)   1. There's complete justice, or there's a devil.
      2. It's not the case that there's complete justice.
   ∴ 3. There's a devil.

(5)   1. If Art is an Ohioan, then he's a Republican.
      2. Art is an Ohioan.
   ∴ 3. He's a Republican.

(6)   1. If a Republican wins, then a Democrat loses.
      2. A Republican wins.
   ∴ 3. A Democrat loses.

(7)   1. If a Democrat wins, then a liar wins.
      2. A Democrat wins.
   ∴ 3. A liar wins.

(8)   1. If a Republican wins, then a thief wins.
      2. A Republican wins.
   ∴ 3. A thief wins.

Logic is concerned primarily with argument forms, and only secondarily with arguments, for *all arguments that have a valid argument form are valid.* The form, not the content, of the preceding arguments makes it impossible for them to have all true premises and a false conclusion. Thus, the principal task of deductive logic is to provide a method for distinguishing valid argument forms from invalid argument forms.

 Truth and Validity

It is important to realize that a deductively valid argument can have a false conclusion if one or more of its premises are false. However, an invalid argument can have both true premises and a true conclusion. In fact, every combination of validity–invalidity and truth–falsehood can occur, except one: *A valid argument with true premises cannot have a false conclusion.* The question of validity is the question of whether the conclusion follows from the premises, that is, whether it is *possible* for all the premises to be true and the conclusion false. So if all you know about an argument is that it is valid, that alone tells you nothing about whether the premises or the conclusion are *in fact* true.

Examples

Valid Arguments

(1) True premises and true conclusion:
1. If Ali beat Frazier, then Ali was heavyweight champion of the world.
2. Ali beat Frazier.
∴ 3. Ali was heavyweight champion of the world.

(2) True premises and false conclusion: (This cannot occur; an argument with true premises and a false conclusion must be invalid.)

(3) False premises and true conclusion:
1. Bill Clinton is a politician, and he once won a gold medal in the Olympics for the 200-meter hurdles.
∴ 2. Bill Clinton is a politician.

(4) False premises and false conclusion:
1. The moon is made of green cheese, and the planet Mars is made of milk chocolate.
∴ 2. The moon is made of green cheese.

Invalid Arguments

It is very easy to produce invalid arguments having any combination of truth and falsity with respect to premises and conclusion. Simply produce true or false statements that have no connection whatsoever to one another, such as the following:

(5) True premises and true conclusion:
1. Africa is a continent.
2. George Washington crossed the Delaware.
∴ 3. Broccoli is a vegetable.

Obviously, no one is going to fooled by this argument. But there is an important point behind this example. *From the mere fact that an argument is invalid you can draw no conclusion whatsoever about the truth or falsity of the premises or the conclusion.*

To make things more interesting, the remaining arguments will at least resemble valid arguments. Here's another invalid argument with both true premises and a true conclusion that at least looks like a valid argument:

1. If you are reading this book, then you are not asleep.
2. You are not asleep.
∴ 3. You are reading this book.

(6) True premises and false conclusion:
1. If Rhode Island is a small island in the South Pacific, then it is smaller than Texas.
2. Rhode Island is smaller than Texas.
∴ 3. Rhode Island is a small island in the South Pacific.

(7) False premises and true conclusion:
    1. If the duckbill platypus is a mammal, then the duckbill platypus does not lay eggs.
    2. The duckbill platypus does not lay eggs.
∴ 3. The duckbill platypus is a mammal.

(8) False premises and false conclusion:
    1. Either Dianne Feinstein is a senator representing the state of New York, or Hillary Rodham Clinton is governor of Ohio.
    2. Hillary Rodham Clinton is governor of Ohio.
∴ 3. Dianne Feinstein is a senator representing the state of New York.

Note that although all these examples have either all true premises or all false premises, it is also possible to produce both valid and invalid arguments that have a mix of some true and some false premises. Here are two examples:

(9) Valid:
    1. Either Newt Gingrich is a Republican or he's a Southerner. (true)
    2. It is not the case that Newt Gingrich is a Republican. (false)
∴ 3. Newt Gingrich is a Southerner. (true)

(10) Invalid:
    1. If the oboe is a brass instrument, then some brass instruments are played with a double reed. (true)
    2. Some brass instruments are played with a double reed. (false)
∴ 3. The oboe is a brass instrument. (false)

The only combination of truth and falsity it is impossible to produce is an argument that is valid and has all true premises and a false conclusion.

Although we can sensibly speak of valid and invalid arguments and argument forms, it makes no sense to speak of valid or invalid statements, premises, or conclusions. Nor does it make any sense to call an argument true or false. Validity and invalidity are properties of *arguments*; truth and falsity are properties of *statements*.

Exercise 1-2

1. Produce your own example of an argument that has the form

    1. _____ or _____ .
    2. It's not the case that _____.
∴ 3. _____ .

and whose conclusion is obviously false.

2. Produce an argument with the same form but whose conclusion is obviously true.

3. Produce your own example of an argument that has the form
    1. If _____ then _____ .
    2. It's not the case that _____ .
    ∴ 3. _____
    and whose conclusion is obviously false.

4. Produce an argument with the same form but whose conclusion is obviously true.

5. Is it possible to produce an example of an argument having the first form that also has premises that are all obviously true and a conclusion that is obviously false? If so, produce such an argument.

6. Is it possible to produce an example of an argument having the second form that has premises that are all obviously true and a conclusion that is obviously false? If so, produce such an argument.

7. Which of your arguments are valid, and which are invalid? Will everyone who followed the instructions have the same answer to this question? Explain.

5 *Soundness*

Obviously, an argument can be valid but have one or more false premises. Such arguments are said to be **unsound.** To be sound, an argument must meet two conditions: It must (a) be valid and (b) have all true premises. An **unsound argument** is any argument that fails to meet one or both of these two conditions. Thus, example (1) (following) is sound because it is valid and has true premises; the other examples are all unsound because they are invalid, have a false premise, or both.

In general, logic is not concerned with the soundness of arguments, because, with one exception, logic alone cannot determine whether the premises of an argument are true or false. (The one exception concerns premises that are logically true or false. See the discussion of tautologies in Chapter Three.)

Examples

(1) A sound argument:
1. Either a majority voted for Bush in 2004, or he received more votes than any other candidate.
2. It's not the case that a majority voted for Bush in 2004.
∴ 3. Bush received more votes than any other candidate.

(2) An argument that is valid, but clearly not sound:
1. If grapefruits are fruits, then grapefruits grow on trees.
2. It's not the case that grapefruits grow on trees.
∴ 3. It's not the case that grapefruits are fruits.

(3) A valid argument. The soundness of the argument is a question that falls outside the scope of logic:

1. Either an uncaused being exists, or an endless chain of beings has always existed.
2. It is not the case that an endless chain of beings has always existed.
∴ 3. An uncaused being exists.

6 *Consistency*

Logic can be used for other purposes than the evaluation of arguments. In particular, logic can be used to determine whether a set of statements is consistent. A set of statements is **consistent** if it is possible for all the statements to be true. If it is impossible for them all to be true, the set is **inconsistent.**

But what does "possible" mean here? This philosophical question has a long history. Although philosophers hardly agree, one point that has emerged from the debates is that there are many different senses of the word "possible," such as the sense in which it is not possible for pigs to (naturally) have wings is different from the sense in which it is not possible that $2 + 2 = 6$. We can see this a bit more clearly if we try to imagine pigs with wings—we can—and then try to imagine $2 + 2 = 6$—we cannot. What is important for our purposes is that we will develop a very precise sense in which it is impossible for the premises to be true and the conclusion false in a certain class of valid arguments and, along with this, a clear relationship between the ideas of possibility and necessity. Some logicians have developed what are called modal logics. These systems of logic deal with different senses of the words "possible" and "necessary." We will develop such systems in this book.

No one wants to be guilty of inconsistency. Indeed, it is an interesting philosophical question (not to be pursued here) whether it is even psychologically possible for humans to knowingly believe explicitly inconsistent statements.

Examples

Perhaps the most obvious examples of inconsistent statements are pairs of statements that explicitly contradict one another.

1. Ronald Reagan was one of our country's greatest presidents.
2. Ronald Reagan was not one of our country's greatest presidents.

Unfortunately, sometimes inconsistency is not so obvious. The inconsistency in the following is a little less obvious:

1. John F. Kennedy was a man of great moral character.
2. John F. Kennedy regularly committed adultery.
3. No one who regularly commits adultery has great moral character.

Here is a famous example of an inconsistent statement that is not at all obvious:

1. Harry, the barber, shaves all of those who do not shave themselves.

(*Hint:* Does Harry shave himself?)

If you have inconsistent statements, at least one of those statements must be false. Just as logic usually cannot tell us whether to accept the premises or conclusion of a valid argument, so logic is typically silent on which statements of an inconsistent set are in fact false. (Again, the exception is sentences that are logically true or false.) As you saw with validity, the question of whether a set of sentences is consistent does not depend on the actual truth-value of those sentences. A set of sentences can be consistent and all its members be true, and a set can be consistent but all its members be false. The only possibility that is ruled out is a set of sentences that is inconsistent and whose members are all true (just as with validity the only possibility that can be ruled out is an argument all of whose premises are true and whose conclusion is false). All the other possible combinations of truth and falsity, consistency and inconsistency are possible.

7 *Consistency and Validity Compared*

Consistency, like validity, is a matter of logical form. Surprisingly, validity and inconsistency have a lot in common. To say that an argument is valid is to say that something is impossible—it is to say that it is impossible for the premises of the argument all to be true and the conclusion false. Likewise, to say that a group of sentences is inconsistent is also to say something is impossible—in this case, that it is impossible for the sentences all to be true. Just as the form of a valid argument guarantees that it is not possible for the premises to be true and the conclusion false, so the form of a set of inconsistent sentences guarantees that they cannot all be true.

We explore the relationship between consistency and validity in some detail in the chapters that follow. For now we can summarize the relationship as follows: *An argument is valid if and only if it is inconsistent to say that all its premises are true and its conclusion is false.*

Example

The argument

1. If capital punishment is not a better deterrent than life imprisonment, it should be abolished.
2. Capital punishment is not a better deterrent than life imprisonment.
∴ 3. Capital punishment should be abolished.

is valid if and only if the following three sentences are inconsistent:

1. If capital punishment is not a better deterrent than life imprisonment, it should be abolished.
2. Capital punishment is not a better deterrent than life imprisonment.
3. *It is not the case that* capital punishment should be abolished.

This is a very useful relationship. It means that any procedure that can be used to test for consistency can be slightly modified and used as a test for validity (and vice versa). For example, suppose you had a computer program that could scan any group of sentences and tell you whether or not they were consistent. To use this program to check an argument for validity, simply attach the words "It is not the case that . . ." to the beginning of the conclusion and then scan the resulting statement along with the argument's premises. If the program informs you that these sentences are *consistent*, then the original argument is invalid (because this shows it is possible for the premises to be true and the conclusion false). However, if these sentences are *inconsistent,* then the argument in question is valid.

How to Use a "Consistency Checker" to Determine Whether an Argument Is Valid:

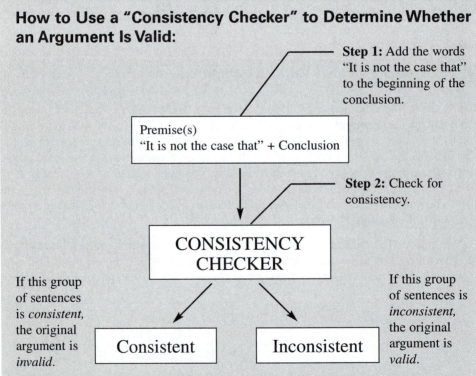

Step 1: Add the words "It is not the case that" to the beginning of the conclusion.

Premise(s)
"It is not the case that" + Conclusion

Step 2: Check for consistency.

CONSISTENCY CHECKER

If this group of sentences is *consistent,* the original argument is *invalid.*

Consistent

Inconsistent

If this group of sentences is *inconsistent,* the original argument is *valid.*

Why this is so: If the premises together with the claim that the conclusion is false form a consistent set, then it is possible for the premises to all be true and the original conclusion false. Thus the argument is invalid. However, if the premises and modified conclusion are inconsistent, then it is impossible for the premises to be true and the conclusion false, and the argument is valid.

8 *Contexts of Discovery and Justification*

When someone states that something is true, two important kinds of questions can be asked. First, what factors led that person to think of such a conclusion, and second, what reasons are offered for accepting it as true? Questions of the first kind are said to be in the area or **context of discovery,** and those of the second kind in the area or **context of justification.**

In general, logic does not deal with the context of discovery. The historical factors that lead to, or the mental processes used in thinking of hypotheses or conclusions are of interest to the historian or psychologist, not the logician. The logician is interested in reasons that are, or might be, presented in support of conclusions. In other words, the logician is interested in the context of justification.

The difference between discovery and justification is illustrated by the difference between the sometimes agonizing thought processes necessary to "figure out" solutions to difficult problems and the arguments we then present in their defense. The discovery process, the figuring out, often is long and involved, whereas the argument presented to justify the conclusion arrived at by this long process is elegantly simple.

For instance, a scientist may first think of a scientific theory in a dream. But the arguments presented to fellow scientists to support the theory would not refer to the dream. The dream and its contents are part of the process of discovering the theory, not part of the process of justifying it. (Of course, sometimes the processes of discovery and justification overlap.)*

9 *The Plan of This Book*

You have seen how the validity of an argument can be due to the form of the argument's premises and conclusion. Likewise, the consistency or inconsistency of a set of statements depends on the form of those statements. As you will see, there are a number of different ways of characterizing logical form. Indeed, this book provides an overview of leading systems of logic, each of which comes at the question of form a bit differently. Part One of the book looks at sentential (sentence) logic. Here the crucial bits of form are words such as "and" and "or" that can be used to connect sentences. Part Two covers predicate logic. Predicate logic extends sentential logic to include elements of logical form found *within* sentences. So whereas sentences form the basic units of sentential logic, the smallest units of predicate logic are individual things and their properties. Together sentential and predicate logic comprise what is commonly referred to as symbolic or formal logic.

---

* For a philosophically contrary view, see T. S. Kuhn's, *The Structure of Scientific Revolutions*. Kuhn's famous and influential work broadens the scope of what *counts* as a reason.

Exercise 1-3

1. Can an argument have all true premises and a true conclusion, yet not be deductively valid?

2. Can an inductively strong argument have all true premises and a false conclusion?

3. Can a deductively valid argument have false premises?

4. Can a deductively valid argument have a false conclusion?

5. Can a deductively invalid argument have a true conclusion?

6. Can a deductively valid argument have all true premises and a false conclusion?

7. Can an argument be sound but not valid?

8. Can a deductively valid argument be sound, yet have a false conclusion?

9. Have we proved that the conclusion of a deductively valid argument is true when we have established that its premises are all true?

10. Can all the members of a consistent set of sentences be false?

11. Can some members of an inconsistent set of sentences be true?

12. Can all members of an inconsistent set of sentences be true?

13. List two English words that commonly signal premises of arguments.

14. List two English words that commonly signal conclusions of arguments.

15. What is the difference between the context of discovery and the context of justification? Which one is the concern of logic?

Philosophical Discussions

1. See if you can think of some other senses of "possibility" that differ from the ones mentioned on p. 12.

2. What are the "intuitive" relationships between the notions of possibility, necessity, and contradiction? An easy example: a contradiction is impossible. Could we, for example, express the notions of contradiction and possibility just using the notion of necessity (and the notion of something not being the case)?

Key Terms Introduced in Chapter One

Argument: A series of sentences, one of which (the conclusion) is claimed to be supported by the others (the premises).

Argument form: Informally, the logical structure of an argument. (In Chapter Three we will introduce a more technical definition for this term.)

Conclusion (of an argument): The statement in an argument that is argued for on the basis of the argument's premises.

Consistent: A set of statements is consistent if and only if it is possible for all the statements to be true.

Deductively valid argument: (See *Valid argument*.)

Deductively invalid argument: (See *Invalid argument*.)

Discovery, context of: The thought processes or psychological processes that may lead to the finding of new conclusions or theories. (See also *Justification, context of*.)

Inconsistent: A set of statements is inconsistent if and only if it is impossible for all the statements to be true.

Inductive argument: An argument that is not deductively valid but whose premises provide some measure of support for its conclusion.

Inductively strong argument: An inductive argument such that if its premises are all true its conclusion is probably true.

Invalid argument: An argument that is not valid. An argument is invalid just in case it is possible for the premises of the argument to all be true and the conclusion false.

Justification, context of: The context in which we try to justify conclusions by means of rational argument. (See also *Discovery, context of.*)

Premises (of an argument): The reasons given in support of an argument's conclusion.

Sound argument: An argument that is valid and has all true premises.

Unsound argument: Any argument that is either invalid or does not have all true premises.

Valid argument: An argument is valid if and only if it is not possible for all of its premises to be true and its conclusion false. If all premises of a valid argument are true, then its conclusion must be true also. The conclusion of a valid argument follows logically from the premises.

Part One

Sentential Logic

Chapter Two

Symbolizing in Sentential Logic

We are about to embark on a project that many philosophers consider hazardous. Symbolic logic can be—and if you were taking this as a math class almost certainly would be—developed mathematically, like algebra with its own special symbols and rules for their manipulation. Indeed, when one realizes that mathematics *uses* deductive logic to get its results, one might think with good reason that deductive logic is an elucidation of mathematical thinking in terms of some sort of basic mathematical system.

But traditionally, logic has also been thought to have a close connection to natural language, in our case English. Some textbooks think of the symbols we will introduce as mere shorthands for English; others, as some sort of analysis of a basic structure of at least part of English—that is, the logic of English; still others, as translations of English into another, more precise, language. If you are bilingual, you may well wonder whether your other language would yield the same logic. Some philosophers and logicians have argued that any language *necessarily* (that word again!) has the logical qualities that we will discuss here. How they know this when they have not studied all the thousands of natural languages in the world is a question left to the exercises in this chapter.

What are some of the other hazards? We will develop them as we go on. The main one has to do with the seemingly limited ability of our logical system to take into account arguments that seem to be in some intuitive sense valid, and yet that do not fit the characterizations of validity in a standard logic. We have already characterized validity in terms of truth: a valid argument cannot have true premises and a false conclusion. The assumption here is that all the statements in question have a *truth-value*—that is, are either true or false. What, then, do we do with the following argument?

    1. Take all the boxes to the station.
    2. This is a box.
∴ 3. Take this to the station.

The problem is that the first premise and the conclusion are commands, and commands do not have a truth-value (think of saying "True!" to someone who utters the first premise). Yet any competent speaker of English would know what the conclusion of this "argument" is.

Other shortcomings concern the limited vocabulary of our logical language. Yet, as you will see, symbolic logic provides a tremendously powerful tool for the study of deduction. We will maintain the stance, for pragmatic reasons, that our logic system provides *translations* of some English sentences into symbols. This point needs some elaboration, here and elsewhere (Chapter Three).

It is crucial to understand that this chapter, which develops the idea of translation, is a necessary preliminary to a wider project. That project is the building of a clear model of validity for a certain set of arguments, *sentential* arguments (see Section 1, later for a definition of "sentential"). To do that we must see how to translate statements from English into a set of symbols, because after all, the premises and conclusions of arguments in ordinary language are statements. To build this model, we take what seem to be certain liberties with English. In particular, statements of conditionals—for example, "if it rains, then the sidewalks are wet"—may well seem richer in implication than our logic can capture. We hope, the reader can be patient; in Chapter Three, justifications of the procedures of this chapter are elaborated in detail. Think of what we are doing here as building a language by introducing its **syntax** and to a large extent, its **semantics.** The syntax of a language shows how to formulate correct statements using its vocabulary; the syntax is specified in what are called **formation rules.** A semantics, in the modern use of this term, shows the meaning of the symbols and under what conditions their combinations are true and false. That is the payoff this chapter anticipates.

1 *Atomic and Compound Sentences*

It is a familiar fact about the English language that longer sentences can be built up of shorter sentences. One way we do this is to use **sentence connectives** such as "and" and "or."

Examples

1. Reagan won in 1980, **and** he also won in 1984.
2. God's on our side, **or** He's on their side.
3. **If** we don't reduce the birth rate, **then** soon there won't be any room to sit down.

Sentences built from shorter sentences by means of sentence connectives such as "and" or "or" are called **compound sentences.** All others are said to be **atomic,** or simple. Thus, the two sentences "God's in his heaven" and "All's right with the world" are atomic, whereas "God's in his heaven and all's right with the world" is compound. (Note, however, that an atomic sentence may be quite long, as is the atomic sentence "On the 23rd of September, 1945, the jazz singer Maurice Klotzman filed a name-changing petition in Los Angeles Superior Court before Judge Bonny Robbins.")

Chapters Two through Six of this text are concerned with the part of logic that can be developed without considering the interior structure of atomic sentences, the part that's called **sentential logic.** (Sentential logic, along with the predicate logic to be discussed in Part Two of this text, forms what is often called **symbolic logic,** to distinguish it from the older, Aristotelian system discussed in Chapter Fourteen.)

2 *Truth-Functions*

The key to mastering sentential logic is to grasp the idea of a **truth-function.** To help you understand what a truth-function is, consider how functions work in mathematics. Mathematical functions operate like number-transforming machines. The 2× function, for example, might be pictured as a black box that automatically transforms any number dropped into it into a number that is twice as large. Drop in a 2, out pops a 4. Drop in 54, out pops 108, and so forth. No matter what number you input, the output is determined—it is a function of the number input.

For a familiar use of functions, consider a simple handheld calculator. The typical calculator has two kinds of keys: number keys and function keys. The function keys are used to perform various mathematical operations on numbers that are input by the number keys. Some function keys, such as the square root key, take one number as their input; others, such as the multiplication key, take two. But the point to keep in mind is that the output produced by pressing these keys is automatic and determined by the input.

Mathematical
Calculator

Now let's consider what a truth-functional calculator would be like. Here, things are much simpler. Instead of the infinitely many numerical inputs possible in mathematics, with truth-functions we have only two **truth-values**—either true or false. Likewise, the output of a truth-function can be only one of these two values. Sentential logic is sometimes called "the logic of truth-functions" in that every compound sentence in sentential logic has a definite truth-value (it is either true or false), and that truth-value is determined by—is a function of—the truth-values of the atomic sentences it contains.

We use symbols such as "+" and "÷" to represent common mathematical functions. These symbols are called "operators." Likewise, our system of logic has five **truth-functional operators**. One operator, "~" (not), takes only one input; the other four, "·" (and), "∨" (or), "⊃" (if . . . then), and "≡"; (if and only if) take two.

Truth-Functional
Calculator

As you will see, the logical form of sentences in ordinary English can be represented symbolically by means of the five truth-functional operators we are about to discuss.

3 *Conjunctions*

Compound sentences formed by use of the sentence connective "and" are called **conjunctions,** and the two sentences joined together by the "and" are called **conjuncts** of the conjunction.

Let's abbreviate the sentence "Art went to the show" by the capital letter *A,* the sentence "Betsy went to the show" by the capital letter *B,* and the connective "and" by the "·" **dot.** Then the sentence "Art went to the show and Betsy went to the show" can be symbolized as *A · B.* Now consider all the possible truth-values of the two conjuncts of this sentence. First, if *A* and *B* both are true (that is, if Art and Betsy both went to the show), then obviously the compound sentence *A · B* is true. Second, if *A* is true and *B* is false, then *A · B* is false. Third, if *A* is false and *B* is true, then *A · B* is false. And finally, if *A* and *B* both are false, then *A · B* is false. There are no other possible combinations of truth-values for the sentences *A* and *B.* We have thus characterized the truth-functional meaning of the "·" connective, because we've shown how the truth-values of the compound sentences formed by its use are uniquely determined by the truth-values of their two conjuncts. Anyone who is given the actual truth-values of *A* and *B* can "figure out" the truth-value of the compound sentence *A · B,* because (as was just illustrated) the truth-value of that compound sentence is determined by (is a function of) the truth-values of its component parts.

The information about the compound sentence *A · B* contained in the preceding paragraph can be put into the form of a table, called a **truth table,** as follows:

A	*B*	*A · B*
True (T)	True (T)	True (T)
True (T)	False(F)	False (F)
False (F)	True (T)	False (F)
False (F)	False (F)	False (F)

Line 1 of this truth table indicates that if *A* and *B* both are true, then *A · B* is true. Line 2 indicates that if *A* is true and *B* false, then *A · B* is false, and so on.

Let us be clear about some things that may be bothering you. Take "Art went to the show." That might be true today, if uttered by Betsy, but might have been false yesterday if she uttered it then. To be precise, the **sentence** "Art went to the show" can be used to make different **statements,** depending, say, on time and, in some cases, for example, "Art is happy here," on place. "He said she is happy" depends for making a statement, on who he is and who she is, as well as time and place. We will assume here that the sentences we discuss are used to make definite statements, and it is statements that have a truth-value. Furthermore, statements have a *fixed* truth-value, they are either true or they are false and not true at one time and possibly false at another or true in one place and possibly false in another. In the illustration just given, we treated *A* and *B* as abbreviations for—what? If statements, then they have a definite truth-value and it is somewhat misleading to say, as we did, that perhaps *A* could be true and *B* false, or both false, and so on. When we do that, we are doing one of two things. (1) We are treating *A* and *B* as statements whose truth-value *we do not know.* Of course, in life we often utter statements when we are ignorant of their truth-value. (2) We are treating *A* and *B* as *sentences that can be used to make statements* that have four different possible combinations of truth-values. For now, the ambiguity and the subsequent characterization of the preceding table as a truth table is harmless and, we hope, illustrative of the basic idea that *any two statements are such that either both are true, both are false, or one is true and the other false.* We make this more precise in Section 5; the student can safely read every use of "sentence" as "statement."

Not all uses of the word "and" are to be symbolized by the dot symbol. It would be wrong, for instance, to symbolize the sentence "Art and Betsy are lovers" as $A \cdot B$, for that would say that Art is a lover and Betsy is a lover, but not that they love each other. Similarly, it would be wrong to symbolize the sentence "Babe Ruth and Lou Gehrig were teammates" as $R \cdot G$, for that would say that Ruth was a teammate and Gehrig was a teammate, but not that they were teammates of each other.

However, some sentences that look like the two we have just considered are logically quite different. Consider "Art put on his parachute and jumped from the airplane," and contrast it with "Art went to the show and Betsy went to the show." The latter is surely *logically equivalent* to "Betsy went to the show and Art went to the show"; that is, $A \cdot B$ is true or false under exactly the same truth conditions that $B \cdot A$ is true or false. The dot is *commutative*. But clearly "Art jumped from the airplane and put on his parachute" is not logically equivalent to the first statement just given—if the last were true, the mortality rate would almost certainly be higher than if the first were! This is a temporal use of "and" in English and is not symbolized by our dot. Whether, as we progress, we might be able to capture this sense with other logical symbols is a subject in predicate logic. For another example, the sentence "Art and Betsy are intelligent" looks just like "Art and Betsy are lovers," and indeed it has the same grammatical structure. But it does not have the same logical structure. The sentence "Art and Betsy are intelligent" does say the same thing as "Art is intelligent and Betsy is intelligent," and thus can be correctly symbolized as $A \cdot B$.

It is essential to understand that the objection to translating a sentence such as "Art and Betsy are lovers" as $A \cdot B$ is *not* merely that this would leave out some information. As you will see, this is often the case. Rather, the problem is that the truth-value of this particular complex sentence *is not a function* of the truth-value of the sentences A, "Art is a lover" and B, "Betsy is a lover." If you know the truth-value of these two atomic sentences, you may still be in the dark about whether the sentence being symbolized is true. One can imagine possible circumstances where these two sentences are true and the longer sentence is clearly true, but one can also imagine circumstances where these two sentences are true and the longer sentence is clearly false (Art is a lover and Betsy is a lover, but Art and Betsy absolutely detest one another).

The fact that A and B could both be true even though the sentence "Art and Betsy are lovers" is false shows that it would not be accurate to symbolize this sentence as a conjunction using the dot truth-functional operator. But more fundamentally, the fact that one can imagine circumstances where A and B are both true and this sentence is clearly true, and other circumstances where A and B are both true and this sentence is clearly false shows that *no* truth-functional operator can be used correctly to symbolize this sentence as a compound of A and B. The truth-value of this sentence is simply not a function of the truth-values of A and B.

Our discussion has brought to light a useful way to test a proposed symbolization. Try to imagine circumstances where the two sentences—the English sentence and the symbolic sentence—clearly would have different truth-values. *If it is possible for your proposed symbolization to be true and the English sentence false, or the symbolization to be false and the English sentence true under the same circumstances, the proposed symbolization is not an adequate symbolization.*

Several other common English words often are used to connect sentences in the same truth-functional way as the word "and." Thus, the word "but" often means "and on the contrary" or "and on the other hand." For example, the word "but" in the compound sentence "Art is smart, but he's a poor athlete" informs the reader that the information to follow is significantly different from what came before. In this case, the information preceding the word "but" is favorable to Art; so this use of that word prepares us for contrasting information to follow. When the word "but" is symbolized by the dot, the part of its meaning that signals a switch of this kind is lost. However, only the truth-functional part of its meaning is important for sentential logic and that part is accurately captured by the dot symbol. Therefore, in this case, symbolization of the word "but" by the dot is acceptable for our purposes.

In addition to "and" and "but," the expressions "however," "yet," "on the other hand," "still," "although," "despite the fact that," and many others usually are correctly symbolized by the dot when they are used to join two sentences together to form a larger compound sentence.

Examples

All of the following sentences might be symbolized as the conjunction $B \cdot L$ (letting B = "many fought bravely," L = "some lost their lives").

1. Many fought bravely, **and** some lost their lives.
2. **Both** many fought bravely, **and** some lost their lives.
3. Many fought bravely, **but** some lost their lives.
4. Many fought bravely **in spite of the fact that** some lost their lives.
5. **Although** many fought bravely, some lost their lives.
6. **While** many fought bravely, some lost their lives.
7. Many fought bravely; **also** some lost their lives.

Exercise 2-1

Which of the following are truth-functional compound sentences that can correctly be symbolized by using the dot? Explain.

1. Paul McCartney went one way, and Ringo Starr went another way.

2. A large star is large, but a large flea is small.

3. Bonny and Eugene were classmates.

4. Beth is a top student, not to mention being a great athlete.

5. We'll always have death and taxes.

6. In the 1920s alcohol was prohibited, but now pot is.

7. Beethoven and Mozart were great composers.

8. Two and two are four.

9. Although she loved him, she left him.

10. Everything that's great fun is illegal, immoral, and fattening.

11. All sound arguments are valid, and they have true premises as well.

12. Both the right front fender and the passenger side door were damaged as a result of the accident.

4 *Non–Truth-Functional Connectives*

The connective "and" is a clear example of a truth-functional connective. Join two sentences with "and" and the truth-value of the resulting sentence will be a function of the truth-value of the two original sentences. Take any two true sentences and join them together with "and," and the result will be a true sentence. If either or both sentences are false, the conjunction of the two will be false.

A great many connectives in English are not truth-functional. Take, for example, the temporal connective "before." The sentence "Bill Clinton was president before George W. Bush was president" is true, and the sentence "Bill Clinton was president before Abraham Lincoln was president" is false. Yet for each of these two sentences the component sentences are both true. So the truth-value of a compound sentence formed by connecting two sentences with the word "before" is not a function of the truth-value of the component sentences.

This illustrates a way of showing that a connective is not truth-functional. If a connective is truth-functional, you will never be able to describe situations where in one case the sentence is true and in the other the sentence is false and yet the truth-value of the component sentence or sentences is the same in both cases.

Examples

1. "It is well known that" is not a truth-functional operator, because some true sentences are well known and others are not. The sentence "Tidman was once a contestant on *Wheel of Fortune*" is true (believe it or not), whereas "It is well known that Tidman once appeared on *Wheel of Fortune*" is not. However, adding "It is well known that" to "George Washington was the first president" results in a true sentence.

2. "Because" is not a truth-functional connective. "Art's computer crashed because his hard drive was defective" might be true, whereas "Art's computer crashed because Neptune is a planet" is not, even though the component sentences in both cases are both true.

5 *Variables and Constants*

Consider *C*, Charles is a logician, and *D*, Donna is a mathematician. We can symbolize this as $C \cdot D$. Because we are assuming that *C*, *D*, and $C \cdot D$ are definite statements, they have a definite truth-value. Let us assume that *C* is false and *D* is true. Clearly, it would be easy to find, among the vast array of English statements, two that are both true, or two that are both false, or two such that the first is true and the second false or two, like our *C* and *D,* where the first is false and the second true. As clear, any two statements will have one of the four possible combinations of truth and falsity. Consider *any* two statements *p* and *q*, and consider the following table:

p	*q*	*p · q*
T	T	T
T	F	F
F	T	F
F	F	F

This truth table indicates that, given any two sentences *p* and *q*,

1. If *p* and *q* both are true, then their conjunction, *p · q*, is true.
2. If *p* is true and *q* false, then their conjunction, *p · q*, is false.
3. If *p* is false and *q* true, then their conjunction, *p · q*, is false.
4. If *p* and *q* both are false, then their conjunction, *p · q*, is false.

Because this truth table specifies the truth-value of any conjunction, given the truth-values of its two conjuncts, it can be said to specify the meaning of the dot symbol. We can summarize the content of this table with a single sentence, as follows: *A conjunction is true if both conjuncts are true; otherwise it is false.* The truth tables are a semantic device; they summarize the conditions under which statements using our logical operators are true and conditions under which they are false. We say that the meaning of a logical operator is given by its truth conditions; for example, the meaning of the dot is given by the conditions under which *p · q* is true, and the conditions under which it is false.

It is important to understand that in the preceding truth table, the small letters *p* and *q* *are not abbreviations for specific sentences.* Rather they are **statement variables.** A statement variable has no truth-value; what *does* have a truth-value is a statement we *substitute* for it, and the truth-value *varies* according to what statement that happens to be. This notion of substitution is exactly analogous to that in algebra, when we say that $3 + 2 = 5$ is a substitution instance of $x + y = z$. Thus if we substitute *C* for *p* and *D* for *q*, and then we substitute *C · D* for *p · q*, what we obtain, given that *C* is false and *D* is true, is the third line of the truth table for the dot. Every substitution of statements for the variables must yield one of the four lines, because there are only four possible combinations of truth and falsity for every two statements. *Notice that a statement such as C · D does not have a truth table; a statement has a line in a truth table, depending on the truth-value of its component statements. Truth tables are not given for statements but only for statement forms,* such as *p · q*. A statement form such as *p · q* no more makes a statement than does $x + y = z$. We obtain statements from statement forms by substitution. As you will see, the notion of a statement form is extremely important to our study of logic.

We must note now one more item crucial to our logical language. In ordinary life, sane people usually don't mention things together that don't go together. "Art went to the movies, and Betsy stayed home" is a fine conjunction. But what about "Art went to the movies, and the moon is a long way from Earth"? As long as we have two statements, we can conjoin them, and the same is true for all the logical operators we introduce. If we translate two statements into our symbolism, then we may disjoin them, or conjoin them, and so on. Of course, given that our ultimate interest is in arguments, and arguments at least purport to connect premises and conclusion, we probably won't be faced very often with statements such as "Art went to the movies, and the moon is a long way from Earth." But we might be, and there is nothing wrong with them from a logical point of view.

In the remainder of our discussion of sentential logic we shall conform to the convention that the small letters *p, q, r,* and so on are to be used as sentence variables, and the capital letters *A, B, C,* and so on as sentence abbreviations, referred to as **sentence constants.**

6 *Negations*

The dot sentence connective is a kind of operator. It operates on two sentences, say, *A* and *B,* to produce a third—the compound sentence *A · B.* But some logical operators generate a new sentence out of just one starting sentence. For instance, the operator "It is well known that" operates on the sentence "Brad Pitt was a movie star" to produce the compound "It's well known that Brad Pitt was a movie star."

However, only one operator of this kind, **negation,** is used in standard sentential logic (practically all the others are non–truth-functional—as is the operator "It is well known that"). Negation is the easiest of the truth-functional operators to learn, because it operates only on individual sentences and it works just as you would expect. If you negate a true sentence, you get a false sentence, and if you negate a false sentence, you get a true one. We will use the **tilde** symbol, "~," to symbolize negations. Then we can symbolize, say, the statement "It's not the case that Jesse Jackson was a movie star" or, more colloquially, "Jesse Jackson was not a movie star," as ~ *J* (where *J* = "Jesse Jackson was a movie star"). For the sake of convenience we will follow the common practice of referring to "~" as a connective, although it does not literally connect two sentences.

Now let's consider the possible truth-values for compound sentences formed by adding a negation sign. Unlike the case for conjunctions, there are only two possibilities. Take the sentence "Art is smart," abbreviated as *A.* Either *A* is true, in which case ~ *A* is false, or *A* is false, in which case ~ *A* is true. Of course, we again can generalize because the truth table for any sentence and its negation will be just like the one for *A* and ~ *A.* We can express this general fact by constructing a truth table using the variable *p,* as follows:

p	$\sim p$
T	F
F	T

This truth table succinctly illustrates how the negation truth-function operates. Because this function operates on single sentences, there are only two possible cases, and the truth table shows the truth-value that results given any sentence *p*:

1. If the statement we substitute for *p* is true, then its negation is false.
2. If the statement we substitute for *p* is false, then its negation is true.

Again, we can summarize these results with a single sentence: *A negation is false if the sentence being negated is true, and true if the sentence being negated is false.*

Examples

Here are a few of the several ways of expressing a negation. All the following are correctly symbolized as ~ *T* (where *T* = "tomatoes are vegetables").

1. Tomatoes are *not* vegetables.
2. Tomatoes *aren't* vegetables.
3. It's *not true* that tomatoes are vegetables.
4. It's *not the case* that tomatoes are vegetables.
5. It is *false* to claim that tomatoes are vegetables.

7 *Parentheses and Brackets*

Consider the mathematical expression $6 \div 3 \times 2 = 1$. Is this expression true or false? If it states that 6 divided by the result of multiplying 3 times 2 (that is, 6 divided by 6) equals 1, then it is true. But if it states that 6 divided by 3 (which equals 2) multiplied by 2 equals 1, then it is false. As it stands, the expression is ambiguous (has more than one distinct meaning). In mathematics, ambiguity of this kind is removed by using parentheses and brackets. Thus $(6 \div 3) \times 2 = 4$, whereas $6 \div (3 \times 2) = 1$.

Similarly, parentheses, "(" and ")," brackets, "[" and "]," and braces, "{" and "}," are used to remove ambiguity in logic. Consider once again the sentences "Art went to the show," *A,* and "Betsy went to the show," *B.* To deny *A* and assert *B*, we can write ~ *A* · *B*. To deny *A* and deny *B*, we can write ~ *A* · ~ *B*. But to deny the combination (the conjunction) *A* · *B*, we need to use parentheses and write ~ (*A* · *B*), using the parentheses to indicate that it is the combination or conjunction of *A* and *B* that is being denied.

The sentence ~ *A* · *B* thus asserts that Art did not go to the show, but Betsy did. The sentence ~ *A* · ~ *B* asserts that Art did not go and Betsy didn't either (that is, neither Art nor Betsy went). And the sentence ~ (*A* · *B*) asserts that it is not the case that both Art and Betsy went. Notice that the sentences ~ *A* · ~ *B* and ~ (*A* · *B*) are not equivalent, as proved by the fact that if Art went to the show but Betsy didn't, then the sentence ~ *A* · ~ *B* is false whereas the sentence ~ (*A* · *B*) is true.

By using parentheses we can build up complex sentences out of shorter sentences. Thus the sentence ~ (*A* · *B*) can be combined with the sentence *C* ≡ *D* (recall from Section 2 that this says *C* if and only if *D*) using the connective "∨" (recall that "∨" is read *or*) to form the longer sentence ~ (*A* · *B*) ∨ (*C* ≡ *D*).

Let's call the shorter sentences that are combined to make longer sentences **component sentences.** Parentheses are used to indicate the **scope** of each logical operator in any well-formed sentence. The scope of an operator is the component sentence or sentences on which the operator operates. The negation operator "~" operates on a single component sentence. All the other operators operate on two component sentences.

An important concept to be introduced at this point is that of the main connective of a sentence. The **main connective** of a sentence is the truth-functional connective whose scope encompasses the entire remainder of the sentence. (Remember, we are calling the negation operator a connective even though it does not literally connect two sentences.) It is crucial that you develop the ability to pick out the main connective of any sentence. If you think of building up a sentence by starting with atomic sentences and forming larger and larger sentences, the main operator would be the last operator to be put into place. No sentence is legitimate, that is, **well-formed** unless it is clear which operator is the main operator for the sentence and for each component sentence contained within the sentence. The notion of being well-formed is a *grammatical* one. Our logical language has an exact, unambiguous grammar. For example, the sentence $A \vee B \supset C$ is not well-formed, because it is not clear whether "$\vee$" or "$\supset$" is the main connective. We can use parentheses to transform this string of symbols into a well-formed sentence. The main connective of the sentence $A \vee (B \supset C)$ is "$\vee$," and the main connective of the sentence $(A \vee B) \supset C$ is "$\supset$."

Two conventions help to eliminate unnecessary parentheses. First, it is not necessary to place an outermost pair of parentheses entirely surrounding a sentence (we can write $A \supset (B \vee C)$ instead of $[A \supset (B \vee C)]$). Second, the scope of the "$\sim$" operator is always the shortest complete sentence that follows it. We can write $\sim A \vee B$ instead of $(\sim A) \vee B$.

When symbolizing complicated compound sentences, more than a single pair of parentheses may be needed, as in the sentence $\sim ((A \cdot (B \cdot \sim C)) \vee D)$. We will alternate parentheses, brackets, and braces to make it visually easier to see how these grouping symbols are paired. For example, instead of $\sim ((A \cdot (B \cdot \sim C)) \vee D)$ we will write $\sim \{[A \cdot (B \cdot \sim C)] \vee D\}$. This is just a way to make our sentences a bit easier to read. There is no difference whatsoever in the logical function of the three varieties of parentheses.

8 *Use and Mention*

So far we have been rather careless about a distinction that is dear to the heart of both philosophers and logicians. This is a distinction between *using* a word, phrase, or statement, and *talking about* the word, phrase, or statement—that is, *mentioning* it. Consider the statement "Paris is a city in France." If one utters this statement, one is saying something about the city of Paris; one is using the words to make a statement about the city. Now consider the statement " 'Paris' has five letters." Here we are talking about the word "Paris," *not* the city. Logicians like precision. Thus, in the spirit of what has just been said, if one writes, "Paris has five letters," a rather ambiguous statement has been made. A knowledgeable speaker of English would almost certainly understand that it is the word and not the city that is being talked about. A speaker of English who had just read about ancient Greek history and the Trojan Wars might take the statement to be about the hero Paris, who had possibly received letters from Helen of Troy. Using a device such as quotation marks around a word or phrase or sentence to indicate we are talking about it rather than using it clears up the ambiguity. In this book we use such quotation marks when there is a possibility of ambiguity; otherwise, we allow context to tell you whether a word, phrase, or sentence is being used or mentioned.

As you will see, this distinction becomes very important as we become clearer about logical theory. For example, the symbolic language we are developing, sentential logic, has a grammar. When we state the rules for that grammar, the language in which we state the rules is English, and we *mention* symbols in the language of symbolic logic. For another example, the truth tables are not in the language of symbolic logic, but are in English. To see that more clearly, consider that the table is just a shorthand way of expressing the conditions under which statements are true (or false). Indeed, when we say that a statement is true, we are talking about the statement, and not the (alleged) fact that the statement presents. Facts are either there or not, statements are either true or false. Logicians call the language in which we speak about the logical language the **metalanguage,** and the language we are talking about, the **object language.** So English is our metalanguage, and sentential logic is our object language.

Examples

Sentence	Main Connective	Component Sentence(s)
$\sim B \supset C$	$\supset$	$\sim B$, C
$\sim [(A \vee B) \supset C]$	$\sim$	$(A \vee B) \supset C$
$(A \vee B) \cdot \sim (D \supset R)$	$\cdot$	$A \vee B$, $\sim (D \supset R)$
$\sim [(A \vee B) \equiv (\sim B \supset C)]$	$\sim$ (the first one)	$(A \vee B) \equiv (\sim B \supset C)$
$\sim (A \vee B) \equiv (\sim B \supset C)$	$\equiv$	$\sim (A \vee B)$, $\sim B \supset C$

Exercise 2-2

For each of the following sentences, identify the main connective.

1. $(A \vee B) \supset C$
2. $\sim (A \vee B) \supset C$
3. $\sim [(A \vee B) \supset C]$
4. $\sim [\sim (A \vee B) \supset C]$
5. $\sim \sim (A \vee B) \supset C$
6. $\sim [(A \vee B) \supset C] \supset D$
7. $\sim [(A \vee B) \vee (C \supset D)]$
8. $[\sim A \vee (B \supset C)] \equiv \sim D$
9. $\{[\sim (A \supset B) \vee C)] \equiv \sim D\} \vee L$
10. $[(\sim A \supset B) \vee C)] \equiv \sim (D \cdot R)$

9 *Disjunctions*

Another frequently used sentence connective is the English word "or" (and its variants, particularly "either . . . or"). Two sentences connected by the word "or" form a compound sentence called a **disjunction,** and the two sentences so connected are called **disjuncts** of the disjunction.

There are two different senses of the connective "or" in common use. One, the **exclusive** sense, is illustrated by the sentence "Art took the make-up exam on Tuesday or on Wednesday." Ordinarily, the implication of this sentence is that Art took the make-up exam on Tuesday or on Wednesday, but not on both Tuesday and Wednesday. The other sense of the term "or" is called its **inclusive** sense, or sometimes its nonexclusive sense. If a football coach exclaims, "We'll beat either Penn State or Army," his assertion is not false if the team wins both of these games. The coach means to say that either we'll beat Penn State, or we'll beat Army, or we'll beat both Penn State and Army.

The inclusive sense of the term "or" sometimes is expressed by the phrase "and/or"—especially in legal documents. Thus, a contract may state that "Repairs will be made by the landlord and/or the landlord's agent," meaning that repairs will be made by one or the other, or both.

The symbol "∨," called the **wedge,** is introduced to symbolize the inclusive sense of the word "or" and, like the dot, "∨" is a truth-functional connective. Abbreviating the sentence "We'll beat Penn State" by the capital letter P, and the sentence "We'll beat Army" by the capital letter A, we can symbolize the sentence "We'll beat Penn State or Army" as $P \vee A$.

The statement form $p \vee q$ has, quite obviously, many substitution instances—all we need do is pick a statement to substitute for p and a statement to substitute for q. Notice that when we see it that way, there is no reason why we could not substitute the same statement for both, and the same is true for $p \cdot q$! Yet all these myriad substitutions will be such that there are only four logical possibilities of their combined truth and falsity, as given in the following truth table:

p	q	$p \vee q$
T	T	T
T	F	T
F	T	T
F	F	F

This truth table indicates that, given any two sentences p and q, their disjunction $p \vee q$ is false only when both p and q are false; otherwise it is true.

In everyday English, disjunctions are usually signaled by means of the terms "or" or "either–or" (as in this very sentence). But not always. For example, the inclusive disjunction "Either Bush or Kerry spent over \$50 million on their presidential campaigns" can also be expressed by saying "At least one of the two candidates, Bush and Kerry, spent over \$50 million on his campaign," a statement not containing the word "or."

A sentence whose major connective is an exclusive "or" asserts more than it would if the "or" were inclusive. It says that (1) at least one of its disjuncts is true (which is all it would say if it were the inclusive "or"); and (2) at least one disjunct is false. Thus, there is a sense in which the whole meaning of the inclusive "or" is only part of the meaning of the exclusive "or." So if we symbolize an exclusive use of the word "or" by "∨," we lose part of its meaning. An example is the argument

    1. Art took the make-up exam on Tuesday or Wednesday ($T \vee W$).
    2. Art took the make-up exam on Tuesday (T).
∴ 3. Art did not take the make-up exam on Wednesday ($\sim W$).

If the inclusive "or" is used to symbolize the "or" in the first premise of this argument, then the resulting argument will be invalid, because it will state that

1. Art took the make-up exam on Tuesday, or Art took the make-up exam on Wednesday, or Art took the make-up exam on Tuesday and on Wednesday.
2. Art took the make-up exam on Tuesday.
∴ 3. Art did not take the make-up exam on Wednesday.

But the original argument is valid if the "or" in the first premise is understood in the exclusive sense. The additional claim made by the exclusive "or" cannot be omitted and the validity of the argument preserved. We must not only assert that Art took the make-up exam on at least one of the two days, stated in symbols as $T \vee W$, but also *deny* that he took the exam on both days, stated in symbols as $\sim (T \cdot W)$. So we should symbolize the whole of the first premise as $(T \vee W) \cdot \sim (T \cdot W)$.

What should you do, then, when you encounter a sentence such as, "Art took the make-up exam on Tuesday or Wednesday"? You need to ask whether the sentence clearly conveys an exclusive disjunction. One way to test whether this is the case is to ask whether the sentence would be false if both disjuncts were true. If Art took the make-up on both days, would the sentence be false? In ordinary contexts it would be reasonable to take the sentence as expressing just this, and so it is natural to symbolize this particular sentence as exclusive.

Unfortunately, taken in isolation many "or" sentences are just ambiguous. A father might say to his daughter, "We'll either play ball, or go fishing this weekend," and intend to communicate an exclusive disjunction. Don't be surprised if the daughter hears the sentence differently. In our example, Dad will probably clarify. But the sentence by itself could be legitimately interpreted either way. When faced with such ambiguity, seek clarification. If none is available, the rule to follow is, When in doubt, symbolize an "or" sentence as inclusive. So our practice will be to symbolize disjunctions as inclusive unless the exclusive interpretation is clearly intended.

Examples

Disjunctions are commonly expressed using "either . . . or" or just plain "or." Here are two sentences that might be properly symbolized as the disjunction $R \vee E$ (R = "we will reduce the deficit"; E = "the economy will collapse").

1. *Either* we will reduce the deficit *or* the economy will collapse.
2. We will reduce the deficit, *or* the economy will collapse.

Exercise 2-3

Symbolize the following so as to reveal as much structure as possible. (Specify the abbreviations you use.)

1. Either the deficit will be reduced soon or the income tax rate will be raised.
2. The greatest basketball player ever to play the game is either Michael Jordan or Kareem Abdul Jabbar.
3. Pete Rose bet on Reds games, or he didn't.
4. It's going to snow on Christmas Eve or on New Year's Eve.

5. They're going to play either Mozart's Piano Concerto No. 22 or Haydn's Symphony No. 94.

6. Either this sentence is true or it's false.

7. At least one of the two major political parties (the Democrats and the Republicans) supports an anti–flag-desecration amendment.

8. The A's are going to win the American League pennant this year; otherwise it'll be (at last) the Cleveland Indians!

9. Anita Hill or Clarence Thomas lied before the congressional committee.

10. Anita Hill either told the truth about Clarence Thomas, or the lie detector test is totally unreliable.

11. Abortion is either murder, or it's a harmless form of birth control.

12. The gunman must have been insane, or at the very least he was experiencing a severe emotional disturbance.

10 *"Not Both" and "Neither . . . Nor"*

Many English sentences contain more than one logical operator. For example, consider the sentence "Mary went to the movie, and she didn't like it." This sentence is a conjunction that contains a negation as one of its components—the claim that Mary did *not* like the movie. So it should be symbolized as $M \cdot \sim L$. Likewise, the sentence "Henry was either not driving very carefully or the officer was not in a very good mood that day" is a disjunction of two negations and could be symbolized $\sim C \vee \sim G$.

In symbolizing sentences with more than one operator, it is essential to pay attention to the scope of each operator. Compare the following two sentences:

1. It will not rain, and it will snow.
2. It will not both rain and snow.

The crucial difference is the scope of the negation operator "not." In the first sentence "not" negates the atomic claim that it will rain. The main connective of this sentence is the word "and." So this sentence might be symbolized $\sim R \cdot S$. In the second sentence what is negated is a conjunction—the claim that it will *both* rain *and* snow—and is correctly symbolized $\sim (R \cdot S)$. An equivalent, and equally acceptable, way of translating this sentence is $\sim R \vee \sim S$. The bottom line is that all that it takes to make a "not both" sentence true is for at least one of the two components to be false.

Now consider sentences built around the English connective "neither . . . nor," such as "It will neither rain nor snow tomorrow." It is tempting to think that these sentences should be symbolized as disjunctions, but this is a mistake. Someone who asserts that neither A nor B is true is not merely saying that either A or B is not true; rather, the claim is that *both* A and B are not true. For neither A nor B to be true, it must be the case that A is not true and it must be the case that B is not true. So for the sentence "It will neither rain nor snow tomorrow" to be true, it must *both* not rain *and* not snow tomorrow. Likewise, consider the sentence "Neither Bush nor Gore received a majority of the vote." If B = "Bush received a majority of the vote," and G = "Gore received a majority of the vote," then the correct symbolization of this sentence is $\sim B \cdot \sim G$. This sentence is correct only if Bush did not receive a majority *and* Gore did not receive a majority. It would also be correct to symbolize the sentence as $\sim (G \vee B)$. These sentences say the same thing in two different ways, namely, that Bush did not receive a majority and Gore did not receive a majority. However, it would not be correct to symbolize this sentence as $\sim G \vee \sim B$, because that sentence would be true even if only one of its two disjuncts were true, say if Gore didn't receive a majority of the vote but Bush did.

Examples

Not Both

1. Bush did not both end the war quickly and provide a quick exit strategy from Iraq. (Q = "Bush ended the war quickly"; E = "Bush provided a quick exit strategy from Iraq"):

   $\sim (Q \cdot E)$ or $\sim Q \vee \sim E$

Neither . . . Nor

2. Neither Saddam nor his generals displayed military genius. (S = "Saddam displayed military genius"; G = "Saddam's generals displayed military genius"):
   $\sim (S \vee G)$ or $\sim S \cdot \sim G$

Exercise 2-4

Symbolize the following sentences, using the indicated abbreviations.

1. Anthony will not both start at quarterback and miss practice this afternoon. (S = "Anthony will start at quarterback"; M = "Anthony misses practice this afternoon")

2. Anthony will neither start at quarterback nor attend practice. (A = "Anthony attends practice")

3. Although Anthony will not start at quarterback, he will attend practice.

4. Dennis neither completed his homework on time, nor did he participate in class. (H = "Dennis completed his homework on time"; P = "Dennis participated in class")

5. Samantha doesn't exercise or count calories. (E = "Samantha exercises"; C = "Samantha counts calories")

6. Although Samantha neither exercises nor counts calories, she still isn't overweight. (O = "Samantha is overweight")

7. Alex will either not be on time or he won't have all the equipment with him. (T = "Alex will be on time"; E = "Alex will have all the equipment with him")

8. We will go to either the movies or dinner tonight, but not both. (M = "we go to the movies tonight"; D = "we go to dinner tonight")

9. My client may have had a motive, but he had neither the means nor the opportunity to commit the crime. (C = "my client had a motive to commit the crime"; M = "my

client had the means to commit the crime"; O = "my client had the opportunity to commit the crime")

10. Neither Dennis nor Harry received an A on the final, but both actively participated in class. (D = "Dennis received an A on the final"; H = "Harry received an A on the final"; P = "Dennis actively participated in class"; C = "Harry actively participated in class")

11. Sally received an A, although she neither studied nor participated in class. (A = "Sally received an A"; S = "Sally studied"; P = "Sally participated in class")

12. Either unemployment and inflation both remain low or the stock market undergoes a major correction. (U = "unemployment remains low"; I = "inflation remains low"; C = "the stock market undergoes a major correction")

13. Neither stocks nor bonds provide an absolutely risk-free investment opportunity. (S = "stocks provide an absolutely risk-free investment opportunity"; B = "bonds provide an absolutely risk-free investment opportunity")

14. Dick invests in both stocks and bonds, although neither provide an absolutely risk-free investment opportunity. (D = "Dick invests in stocks"; I = "Dick invests in bonds")

15. Neither stocks nor bonds provide an absolutely risk-free investment opportunity, even though both inflation and unemployment remain low.

11 *Material Conditionals*

Consider the sentence "If Pablo puts an effort into his studies, Pablo gets straight A's." This compound sentence contains two atomic sentences, namely, "Pablo puts an effort into his studies" and "Pablo gets straight A's," joined together by the sentence connective "If . . . then." A compound sentence of this kind is called a **conditional**, or hypothetical. The sentence between the "if" and the "then" is called its **antecedent**, and the sentence after the "then" its **consequent**. Thus, the general form of a conditional sentence is "if (antecedent), then (consequent)."

In English, there are many other ways to assert a conditional sentence. For instance, the preceding conditional could be stated as "Assuming Pablo puts an effort into his studies, Pablo gets straight A's," or as "Pablo gets straight A's if Pablo puts an effort into his studies," "So long as Pablo puts an effort into his studies, Pablo gets straight A's," and so on.

Conditional sentences differ with respect to the kind of connection they express between antecedent and consequent. For example, the connection between antecedent and consequent in the sentence "If $2 + 2 = 4$ and $1 + 3 = 4$, then $2 + 2 = 1 + 3$" is logical (if the antecedent is true, the consequent must be); in the statement "If water is heated to 212° F under standard atmospheric conditions, then it boils" is causal (the conditions stated in the antecedent cause the conditions stated in the consequent). The connections expressed by the subjunctive "If that match had been struck, then it would have lit" is much harder to assess and is still being debated by philosophers.

If we are to introduce a logical operator for "if . . . then," we must present its truth table. But what sense of this operator in English should we capture? Students should be aware that this question has been hotly contested among philosophers and logicians since the great philosopher-logician Bertrand Russell and the mathematician A. N. Whitehead first presented symbolic logic in its present form in the early part of the 20th century (see bibliography at the end of the book). Everyone agrees on this: a conditional with a true antecedent and a false consequent is to be counted false, and if antecedent and consequent are both true, the conditional is true.

Take the conditional sentence "If Notre Dame beats Miami, then Notre Dame will win the national championship," partially symbolized as (1): "If M then C." Let's suppose Pat, an avid Notre Dame fan, loudly proclaims this sentence and places a bet that it is true. Clearly, if Notre Dame beats Miami and yet fails to win the national championship, so that M is true and C false, then Pat's assertion is false and she loses the bet. However, if Notre Dame does beat Miami and also wins the National Championship, Pat's proclamation was true and so she wins the bet. These results are represented by the first two lines of the standard truth table for the truth-functional connective "$\supset$," called the **horseshoe.**

p	q	$p \supset q$
T	T	T
T	F	F
F	T	
F	F	

But even here, because of the many meanings of "If . . . then" in English, one might well be dissatisfied. In our discussion of the dot, we made clear that any two statements can be conjoined, or disjoined in our language. What about a conditional such as "If Navy beats Army, then $2 + 2 = 4$"? Again, that no one would utter such a statement under ordinary conditions is irrelevant, if we stick to our decision, as we must, that any two statements can be legitimately put into conditional form.

Our malaise might well increase given the following. Suppose Notre Dame fails to beat Miami. Then it is not clear what to say about Pat's sentence. In a situation like this we can just call the bet off, but if our connective is to be fully truth-functional we need to specify an output truth-value for conditional sentences with false antecedents. We cannot simply leave the last two lines of our truth table blank. Many logic books construct artificial examples to get around this problem. Take "If the Phillies won the pennant in 2004, then I'm king of England." Both antecedent and consequent are false, yet the whole conditional is meant to assert a truth! So perhaps we can use this example and others like it to show that we must count a horseshoe statement true when its antecedent and consequent are false. But "If $2 + 2 = 5$, then $7 + 8 = 20$" might seem false to our intuitions when both antecedent and consequent are false.

What to do? It turns out that we can give a powerful justification for constructing the truth table for $\supset$ as is done at the end of Chapter Three. But we cannot present that justification until more of our logical machinery has been developed, which will be in the next chapter. For now, hopefully the student can take it on faith that this justification can be given! Also, exercises at the end of this chapter will allow you to discuss this whole complex issue further. For now, we can state the overall justification as follows: Unless the truth table for ⊃ (and the same goes for the other operators, as you will see) is as given, we will not be able to show why certain arguments in ordinary English are valid and others invalid. The ⊃, it turns out, functions in very surprising ways.

p q	$p \supset q$
T T	T
T F	F
F T	T
F F	T

As this truth table shows, a sentence joined by the horseshoe connective is true in every case except the line where the antecedent is true and the consequent is false. On every other line you find a **T.** A sentence whose main connective is the horseshoe is called a **material conditional,** and the truth-function represented by the horseshoe operator is called **material implication.** To memorize the defining truth table for this connective, just remember the following: *A material conditional is false if it has a true antecedent and a false consequent; otherwise it is true.*

When symbolizing conditional sentences of ordinary English, remember that most everyday conditionals are not merely truth-functional. In particular, when asserting a conditional it is ordinarily assumed that there is some *connection* between the antecedent and the consequent of a true conditional. A material conditional, in contrast, may be true even if the antecedent and consequent are entirely unrelated. All the following sentences are true if interpreted as material conditionals:

> If the Eiffel Tower is in Paris, then Saturn is a planet.
> If Osama is a space alien, then Florida is south of Georgia.
> If Osama is a space alien, then Florida is north of Georgia.

All that is asserted by a material conditional is that it is not the case that the antecedent is true and the consequent is false. So any material conditional with a false antecedent or a true consequent is true regardless of any relationship that may or may not exist between the antecedent and consequent. In a sense this is merely a result of the grammar rules we have adopted—to repeat, any two statements can be conjoined, or disjoined, or joined by ⊃. It is worth noting that more powerful systems of logic have been developed that purport to do a better job of capturing the ordinary meaning of conditionals, notably modal logic and relevance logic. These systems of logic are considerably more complex, however, and the student of logic interested in these systems should first master sentential logic.

In summary, don't write off truth-functional logic and its material conditional too quickly. In point of fact, people do not in real life offer serious arguments with entirely disconnected conditionals as in the preceding examples. Nor do they deliberately put forward conditionals with false antecedents. Sentential logic, despite the apparent shortcomings of the connective "⊃," does quite well at capturing the critical logical properties of the serious deductive arguments that are offered in everyday life, as you will see.

Examples

There are many different ways in which conditionals can be expressed. Here are some examples, all correctly symbolized as $M \supset R$ (letting M = "Barry Bonds breaks Mark McGwire's record" and R = "Barry Bonds breaks Babe Ruth's record").

1. If Barry Bonds breaks Mark McGwire's home run record, then he'll break Babe Ruth's record also.
2. If Bonds breaks McGwire's record, he'll break Ruth's record also.
3. Bonds will break Ruth's record, if he breaks McGwire's.
4. In case Bonds breaks McGwire's record, he'll have broken Ruth's also.
5. Bonds will break Ruth's record, should he break McGwire's.
6. Bonds's breaking McGwire's record means he'll also have broken Ruth's.

12 *Material Biconditionals*

Two sentences are said to be *materially equivalent* when they have the same truth-value. We introduce the symbol "≡," called the **tribar,** to stand for material equivalence. Thus, to assert that "Art went to the show" (A) is materially equivalent to "Betsy went to the show" (B), we can write "A is materially equivalent to B," or simply $A \equiv B$ (pronounced "A if and only if B"). Obviously, the sentence $A \equiv B$ is true if, and only if, A and B have the same truth-value; and in general, a sentence of the form $p \equiv q$ is true if and only if p and q have the same truth-value. Hence, the truth table for material equivalence must be

p	q	$p \equiv q$
T	T	T
T	F	F
F	T	F
F	F	T

We take this truth table to provide a definition or specification of meaning for the symbol "≡".

Compound statements formed by the symbol "≡" sometimes are called **material equivalences,** because they are true just in case they join together two smaller statements that have the same (equivalent) truth-values. But these compounds are more frequently referred to as **material biconditionals,** or simply **biconditionals,** because they are themselves equivalent to two-directional material conditionals. For instance, the material biconditional "Art went to the show if, and only if, Betsy went to the show," in symbols $A \equiv B$, is equivalent to the two-directional conditional "If Art went to the show, then Betsy went to the show, and if Betsy went to the show, then Art went to the show," in symbols $(A \supset B) \cdot (B \supset A)$.

The same problem concerning truth-functionality that arises for conditionals arises also for biconditionals. In general, the question as to when equivalences can be symbolized by "≡" is answered in the same way. Once again, the material biconditional captures only the minimal truth-functional content of English biconditionals. The material biconditional does not imply any connection between the two component sentences. It simply states that the two components have the same truth-value.

Examples

Unlike conditionals, equivalences are fairly uncommon in everyday English, and indeed there are only a few standard ways to express them (some quite stilted). The two most common are "just in case" and "if, and only if," illustrated by the following:

1. Bill Clinton kept warm at his inauguration if, and only if, he wore thermal underwear.
2. Bill Clinton kept warm at his inauguration just in case he wore thermal underwear.

We have now introduced each of our truth-functional connectives. The definitions of these connectives can each be precisely stated by means of their standard truth tables.

p	$\sim p$
T	F
F	T

p	q	$p \vee q$
T	T	T
T	F	T
F	T	T
F	F	F

p	q	$p \cdot q$
T	T	T
T	F	F
F	T	F
F	F	F

p	q	$p \supset q$
T	T	T
T	F	F
F	T	T
F	F	T

p	q	$p \equiv q$
T	T	T
T	F	F
F	T	F
F	F	T

Memorize these tables and be able to reproduce them on your own. *You cannot master sentential logic without mastering these tables.* It's just that simple. If the task of memorizing these tables seems daunting, here is a little help. The truth conditions for each connective can be summarized in a single sentence, so you can memorize the contents of the standard tables by memorizing the following five sentences:

1. *Negations* change *true* sentences to false and *false* sentences to true.
2. A *conjunction* is *true* if both conjuncts are true; otherwise it is false.
3. A *disjunction* is *false* if both disjuncts are false; otherwise it is true.

4. A *material conditional* is *false* if its antecedent is true and its consequent false; otherwise it is true.
5. A *material biconditional* is *true* if both component sentences have the same truth-value; otherwise it is false.

13 *"Only If" and "Unless"*

"Only if" sentences are like "if" sentences turned around. So, whereas the sentence "You will pass the course if you pay attention in class" might be symbolized $A \supset C$, the sentence "You will pass the course only if you pay attention in class" should be symbolized $C \supset A$. The two sentences say something quite different. If you pay attention, but don't pass, the first sentence is definitely false, but the second sentence may still be true. All the second sentence says is that paying attention is what philosophers call a *necessary condition* of passing the course, not a sufficient condition. That is, it might be true that to pass the course it is necessary to pay attention, but that alone may not be *sufficient* to guarantee passing—you may need to do some other things as well, such as performing well on your exams. Saying that you will pass the course only if you pay attention *doesn't* tell you that if you pay attention, you will pass, it *does* tell you this: If you do not pay attention, you will not pass. So another standard way of translating English sentences of the form "*p* only if *q*" is $\sim q \supset \sim p$.

Consider the sentence, "You will fail this course unless you study. One way to symbolize this sentence is to treat "unless" as synonymous to "if not" and so symbolize the sentence as $\sim S \supset F$. A slightly less intuitive, but even simpler way of translating these sentences is simply to treat "unless" sentences as "or" sentences, thus translating the sentence $F \vee S$.

As with "or," "only if" and "unless" may sometimes be interpreted more strongly than our standard symbolizations indicate. Consider the following two sentences:

> I will play golf with you tomorrow, only if it doesn't rain.
> I will play golf with you tomorrow, unless it rains.

According to the guidelines just given, we would standardly symbolize the first of these sentences as $G \supset \sim R$. But people might be intending to say more with this sentence. They might be saying not only that if they golf it won't be raining, but also that if it doesn't rain they will be golfing. If this is the meaning of the sentence, the correct symbolization would be $G \equiv \sim R$. Likewise, the second sentence could be symbolized according to the guidelines given earlier as $\sim R \supset G$ (or, equivalently, as $G \vee R$). The question to ask about the second sentence is, Would it be false if the person plays even if it rains? In some contexts perhaps so. If so, the sentence may be symbolized, once again, $G \equiv \sim R$ (or $\sim R \equiv G$, or $(G \vee R) \cdot \sim (G \cdot R)$—these are all logically equivalent). The situation here is precisely analogous to what we had with "or." "Unless," like "or," has both an inclusive and exclusive usage in English. (It is no coincidence that both can be symbolized with "$\vee$.")

Fortunately, clear-cut examples of these usages are even more rare than exclusive disjunctions. The guidelines are the same. Symbolize in the standard way unless the stronger meaning is clearly intended.

Examples

Only if

1. World peace will be gained only if third world countries gain economic stability. (*P* = "world peace will be gained in the Middle East"; *T* = "third world countries gain economic stability"):

   $P \supset T$

Unless

2. The war with Iraq was not a success unless the people of Iraq form a democratic government. (*I* = "the war with Iraq was a success"; *D* = "the people of Iraq form a democratic government"):

   $\sim D \supset \sim I$ or $\sim I \vee D$

Exercise 2-5

Symbolize the following sentences, which feature the connectives "unless" and "only if."

1. Harry will run (for class office) only if Janet runs also. (*H* = "Harry will run"; *J* = "Janet will run")
2. Harry won't run unless Janet runs.
3. Unless Harry runs, Janet won't.
4. Neither the Russians nor Americans will reduce their nuclear arsenals. (*R* = "The Russians will reduce their nuclear arsenal"; *A* = "The Americans will reduce their nuclear arsenal")
5. The Russians will not reduce their arsenals unless the Americans do the same.
6. The Russians will reduce their arsenals only if the Americans reduce theirs.
7. Only if the Russians will not reduce their arsenals will the Americans reduce theirs.
8. Anthony is not the starting quarterback unless he is at practice this afternoon. (*A* = "Anthony is the starting quarterback"; *P* = "Anthony is at practice this afternoon")
9. Anthony will start at quarterback only if he doesn't skip practice this afternoon.
10. Anthony is the starting quarterback, unless Chris recovers from his shoulder injury. (*C* = "Chris recovers from his shoulder injury.")

14 *Symbolizing Complex Sentences*

The grammatical structure of a sentence often mirrors its logical structure. So many sentences are correctly symbolized simply by following grammatical structure, replacing grammatical connectives such as "or" and "if–then" by their logical counterparts "∨" and "⊃."

Here is a list of sentences containing common English connectives and grouped according to the truth-functional connective that should typically be used to symbolize them.

Examples

Negations:

1. Susan is *not* at home.   ~ S
2. Money does*n't* grow on trees.   ~ M
3. It's *not true* that all Republicans are wealthy.   ~ R
4. It's *not the case* that water is lighter than oil.   ~ L
5. It is *false* to claim that happiness is the only intrinsic good.   ~ H

Conjunctions:

6. Woody Allen *and* Steve Martin were philosophy majors.   A · M
7. *Both* Bush *and* Kerry focused on the economy.   B · K
8. Kerry won the popular vote, *but* Bush won the electoral vote.   P · E
9. Bush won, *in spite of the fact that* the media was against him.   B · M
10. *Although* I liked Nader the best, I voted for Kerry.   N · K
11. *Although* Nader had some great ideas, he was too radical.   N · R

Disjunctions:

12. Rick *either* is a fast learner *or* he's very lucky.   F ∨ L
13. It will rain *or* snow tomorrow morning.   R ∨ S

Conditionals:

14. *If* anyone has a better plan, *then* I am all ears.   B ⊃ E
15. You will pass this course, *if* you pass the final.   F ⊃ C

Biconditionals:

16. The liquid is an acid *if, and only if,* the litmus paper is blue. A ≡ B
17. Today's lunch is nutritious *just in case* it is well balanced.   N ≡ W

In addition, we have discussed four very common, but less straightforward sentence patterns you should learn how to handle routinely. These include sentences with the following English connectives: "not both," "neither . . . nor," "only if," and "unless." Let's discuss each of these in turn.

"Not Both" Sentences

18. It will *not both* rain and snow.   ~ (R · S)

"Neither . . . Nor" Sentences

19. Candy bars are *neither* nutritious *nor* a good source for
    quick energy.   ~ (N ∨ E)
20. John isn't being considered for the position *nor* is he
    even interested.   ~ (C ∨ I)

"Only If" Sentences

21. The deficit goes down *only if* taxes go up.   D ⊃ T
22. *Only if* an eyewitness comes forward will the prosecution
    be able to prove its case.   P ⊃ E

> ### "Unless" Sentences
>
> 20. The stock market is due for a major correction, *unless* our
>   expert's predictions are based on faulty assumptions. $\sim A \supset C$
> 21. *Unless* you are accompanied by an adult, you are not
>   permitted to enter. $\sim A \supset \sim P$

The first step in symbolizing more complicated sentences is to identify the main connective of the sentence. Take sentence (1): "Either Art and Betsy will go to the show or else Art and Jane will go." Its correct symbolization is $(A \cdot B) \vee (A \cdot J)$, because its main connective is "or." Compare that with the case for sentence (2): "Either Art or Betsy will go to the show, but Jane is not going to go." Its correct symbolization is $(A \vee B) \cdot \sim J$, because its main connective is "but" (which is truth-functionally equivalent to "and").

Here are some tips for identifying the main connective of English sentences. Sometimes the first word of the sentence is a dead giveaway. If, for example, your sentence begins with the word "if," you likely should symbolize with "$\supset$" as the main connective. Similarly, if the sentence begins with "either," the main connective will usually be "$\vee$." So pay attention to the first word. However, transitional words or phrases at the beginning of a sentence such as "but," "however," "surely," "of course," and so on—usually have no truth-functional meaning and can simply be ignored when translating. (In contrast, remember that in the middle of a sentence, "but" and "however" are commonly truth-functionally equivalent to "and").

The second thing to look for is punctuation. Parentheses often mirror commas and semicolons. A single comma or semicolon often breaks a sentence into the same two parts you will place on each side of the main connective.

Once you have identified the main connective, you can then focus on translating each component sentence separately. Again, start by identifying the main connective of these component sentences. In this manner you can break down the task of translating a very complex compound sentence into manageable portions. Divide and conquer!

You now know how to deal routinely with sentences involving "Not both," "neither . . . nor," "only if," and "unless," as illustrated in the preceding examples. If the entire sentence, or any part of it, is of one of these types, symbolize accordingly. So the first step to symbolizing "Art and Betsy will go to the show only if Jane goes" is to recognize that it is an "only if" sentence. This gives you "Art and Betsy will go to the show" $\supset$ "Jane goes to the show." From here it's simple to complete the symbolization: $(A \cdot B) \supset J$.

In particular, *be careful to determine the correct scope of negations.* That is, make sure you pay attention to the question of how much of a sentence is negated by a negative term or expression. For instance, the scope of the negative expression in sentence (3), "Art will go, but it's not the case that Betsy will go" (colloquially, "Art will go but Betsy won't"), is just the atomic sentence "Betsy will go." So sentence (3) is correctly symbolized as $A \cdot \sim B$, where "$\sim$" negates just B. But the scope of the negative expression in sentence (4): "It won't happen both that Art will go and Betsy will go" (colloquially, "Art and Betsy won't both go") is the whole remainder of that compound sentence. So sentence (4) is correctly symbolized as $\sim (A \cdot B)$, where "$\sim$" negates all of $(A \cdot B)$.

We don't want to be too fussy translating everyday talk into symbols. We don't want to require that all the sentences symbolized by a single letter be exactly alike. We'll count

"Betsy won't go," "Betsy isn't going to go," and "She won't go" (when it's clear that the she referred to is Betsy) as enough alike to all be symbolized by the same letter. If we don't allow this shorthand, we're going to have to say that intuitively valid arguments such as "If Clinton won, then Bush lost. Clinton was the winner. So Bush lost" are invalid.

To avoid mistakes resulting from overly mechanical symbolization, pay close attention to the meanings particular English sentences convey in specific contexts, realizing that natural languages are quite flexible both in grammatical construction and in their use of grammatical connectives. The same expressions can mean quite different things in different contexts. So in each case, figure out what the sentence says and try to construct a symbolization that says the same (relevant) thing. And this takes a bit of practice. (Because we already know what these sentences mean, learning how to symbolize them correctly involves the odd-sounding but crucial knack of getting clear about *what* we understand when we understand the meaning of a particular sentence in a natural language.)

In this vein, it is always a good idea to double-check your answer. You can do this by forgetting about the original sentence for a moment and translating your proposed sentential logic sentence back into English. Compare the result with the original sentence. Do the two sentences say basically the same thing? *Do they have the same truth conditions?* If not, amend your symbolization so it can pass this test.

Examples

Here are a few relatively simple symbolizations (letting A = "Art watched *General Hospital*"; B = "Betsy watched *General Hospital*"; F = "Betsy flunked chemistry"; and M = "a miracle occurred").

1. Art watched *General Hospital,* but Betsy didn't. $A \cdot \sim B$
2. If Art watched *General Hospital,* then Betsy didn't. $A \supset \sim B$
3. If Betsy watched *General Hospital,* either she
    flunked her chemistry exam or a miracle occurred. $B \supset (F \vee M)$
4. If Betsy watched *General Hospital* and no miracle
    occurred, then she flunked her chemistry exam. $(B \cdot \sim M) \supset F$
5. Either Betsy watched *General Hospital* and a
    miracle occurred, or she flunked her chemistry exam. $(B \cdot M) \vee F$

Here are a few examples that are a bit more complicated:

6. If Melissa graduates with a strong academic record,
    she gets a good job and makes lots of money.
    (G = "Melissa graduates with a strong academic
    record"; J = "Melissa gets a good job";
    L = "Melissa makes lots of money") $G \supset (J \cdot L)$
7. If Melissa graduates with a strong academic record,
    she gets a good job and makes lots of money— $(G \cdot \sim O) \supset (J \cdot L)$
    if she doesn't pursue other goals.   or
    (O = "Melissa pursues other goals") $G \supset [\sim O \supset (J \cdot L)]$

8. If Melissa doesn't make lots of money, then either she doesn't graduate with a strong academic record, or she doesn't get a good job, or she pursues other goals. $\sim L \supset [(\sim G \lor \sim J) \lor O]$

9. Melissa doesn't make lots of money or pursue other goals, but she does graduate with a strong academic record and she gets a good job. $(\sim L \cdot \sim O) \cdot (G \cdot J)$

10. If we don't control the money supply and break the power of OPEC, we won't control inflation. (M = "we control the money supply"; O = "We break the power of OPEC"; I = "We control inflation") $\sim (M \lor O) \supset \sim I$

11. Either we control the money supply and break the power of OPEC, or we won't control inflation and the economy will collapse. (E = "the economy will collapse") $(M \cdot O) \lor (\sim I \cdot E)$

12. If the economy collapses, we'll know that we didn't break the power of OPEC, or perhaps didn't control the money supply—or maybe it'll be because of some international economic debacle. (D = "there is an international economic debacle") $E \supset [(\sim O \lor \sim M) \lor D]$

Exercise 2-6

Use this key to symbolize the following sentences:

A = Art attends class.
G = Art graduates.
H = Art completes his homework.
L = Art does well in logic.

M = Art does well in math.
P = Art does well in philosophy.
T = Art pays tuition.
W = Art does well in all his classes.

1. Art does not do well in either logic or math.
2. If Art completes his homework, he does well in both logic and math.
3. If Art does not complete his homework, he does well in neither logic nor math.
4. If Art does well in logic or math, he graduates.
5. Art graduates only if he does well in logic or math.
6. If Art neither pays tuition nor attends classes, he does not graduate.
7. Art does well in logic if he completes his homework and attends class.
8. Art does well in logic only if he either completes his homework or attends class.
9. If Art pays his tuition, he graduates, unless he doesn't attend class.
10. Art does well in all his classes if he does well in logic and philosophy.
11. Art does well in all his classes unless he doesn't do well in logic or philosophy.
12. Art does well in all his classes only if he does well in logic, philosophy, and math.

13. If Art does not do well in either logic or philosophy, he doesn't do well in all his classes, but he still graduates.

14. Art does well in neither math nor philosophy, but he still graduates if he pays tuition and attends class.

15. Art does well in all his classes, but he doesn't graduate unless he pays tuition and attends class.

Exercise 2-7

1. If nothing is perfect, then I can't be blamed for my mistakes. (N = "nothing is perfect"; B = "I can be blamed for my mistakes")

2. If it's not true that everything is perfect, then I can't be blamed for my mistakes. (E = "everything is perfect")

3. No, if nothing is perfect and I make mistakes, then I can be blamed for them. (M = "I make mistakes")

4. I can be blamed for my mistakes only if I make mistakes and someone discovers them. (S = "someone discovers my mistakes")

5. But if everything is perfect, I neither make mistakes nor can I be blamed for them.

6. So if I either make a mistake or am blamed for my mistakes, then it is not true that everything is perfect.

7. If a meteor caused the extinction of the dinosaurs, then a meteor could cause the extinction of the human species. (M = "a meteor caused the extinction of the dinosaurs"; H = "a meteor could cause the extinction of the human species")

8. If the extinction of the dinosaurs was not caused by a meteor, the spread of disease did it. (D = "the spread of disease caused the extinction of the dinosaurs")

9. Dinosaurs can be cloned only if scientists can fill in the missing gaps in dinosaur DNA. (D = "dinosaurs can be cloned"; G = "scientists can fill in the missing gaps in dinosaur DNA")

10. Dinosaurs cannot be cloned unless scientists can fill in the missing gaps in dinosaur DNA.

11. Dinosaurs cannot be cloned unless scientists can both obtain samples of dinosaur DNA and fill in the missing gaps. (S = "scientists can obtain samples of dinosaur DNA")

12. If dinosaurs were not cold-blooded, they were like birds, not big lizards. (B = "dinosaurs were like birds")

13. Dinosaurs were neither cold-blooded nor were they like big lizards. (C = dinosaurs were cold-blooded"; L = "dinosaurs were like big lizards")

14. You missed your appointment and the boss is not happy, but it is not my fault. (M = "you missed your appointment"; B = "the boss is happy"; F = "it is my fault")

15. You missed your appointment, but the boss is happy if you made the sale. (S = "you made the sale")

16. If you didn't miss your appointment and made the sale, the boss is still not happy.

17. If you made the sale, the boss is happy, unless she has a headache. (*H* = "the boss has a headache")

18. If you didn't miss your appointment and the boss is still not happy, then either you didn't make the sale or it's my fault.

19. If Art neither diets nor exercises, he will gain weight. (*D* = "Art diets"; *E* = "Art exercises"; *G* = "Art gains weight")

20. If Art doesn't gain weight, then he either diets or exercises.

21. Art neither diets nor exercises, but he still does not gain weight.

22. Bob will not win the election unless a miracle occurs, yet he is the best candidate. (*W* = "Bob will win the election"; *M* = "a miracle occurs"; *B* = "Bob is the best candidate")

23. Bob may be the best candidate, but he won't win the election unless he outspends his opponent on advertising. (*O* = "Bob outspends his opponent")

24. Bob will win the election if and only if he is the best candidate and outspends his opponent on advertising.

25. The deficit will be reduced only if we raise taxes and eliminate wasteful government spending. (*D* = "the deficit will be reduced"; *T* = " we raise taxes"; *S* = "we eliminate wasteful government spending")

26. Either we raise taxes and eliminate wasteful government spending, or the deficit will not be reduced.

27. If we raise taxes, the deficit will not be reduced unless we also eliminate wasteful government spending.

28. If we raise taxes and eliminate wasteful government spending, the deficit still will not be reduced if there is a natural catastrophe. (*N* = "there is a natural catastrophe")

29. If we raise taxes and eliminate wasteful government spending, then unless there is a natural catastrophe the deficit will be reduced.

30. Neither rain, nor snow, nor gloom of night will prevent your postal carrier from delivering the mail. (*R* = "rain will prevent your postal carrier from delivering the mail"; *S* = "snow will prevent your postal carrier from delivering the mail"; *G* = "gloom of night will prevent your postal carrier from delivering the mail")

Exercise 2-8

Translate the following into more or less colloquial English sentences (trying not to mask logical structure). Let *R* = "Sheila likes Russell Crowe"; *J* = "Sheila likes Johnny Depp"; *D* = "Sheila likes Ellen DeGeneres"; *K* = "Sheila likes Ted Kennedy"; *P* = "Sheila is a pacifist," T = "Sheila has a twisted sense of humor"; *B* = "Sheila is boring."

1. $R \cdot \sim J$

2. $\sim (J \vee D)$

3. $\sim (J \cdot D)$

4. $\sim J \cdot \sim D$

5. $\sim R \vee \sim K$

6. $R \supset \sim P$

7. $\sim D \supset B$

8. $(R \cdot K) \supset \sim P$

9. $(R \vee K) \supset \sim P$

10. $P \supset \sim (R \vee K)$

11. $[(\sim R \cdot \sim D) \cdot \sim K] \supset B$

12. $[(R \vee K) \cdot P] \supset T$

Now let B = "you should buy bonds"; R = "you should buy real estate"; S = "you should buy common stocks"; M = "you should invest in a mutual fund"; L = "interest rates are low"; D = "demand is high"; E = "the economy is in a recession"; K = "you are a knowledgeable investor"; and P = "you are a psychic."

13. $(D \cdot L) \supset \sim E$

14. $E \supset \sim (R \vee S)$

15. $\sim E \supset (R \cdot S)$

16. $(D \cdot L) \supset (\sim K \supset R)$

17. $S \equiv (K \cdot \sim E)$

18. $(S \vee B) \equiv [(K \vee P) \cdot \sim E]$

19. $\sim (K \vee P) \supset (E \supset \sim S)$

20. $\sim K \supset [\sim (S \vee B) \cdot M]$

21. $[(E \cdot L) \cdot \sim K] \supset M$

22. $\sim K \supset [\sim P \supset \sim (S \vee B)]$

23. $K \supset [(S \cdot B) \cdot R]$

24. $\{[(E \cdot L) \cdot \sim (K \vee P)]\} \supset R$

15 *Alternative Sentential Logic Symbols*

The symbols used in this chapter are widely used to represent the five truth-functional operators of sentential logic. However, a few textbooks use alternative sets of symbols. Here are some of the most common alternatives:

Negation	~	¬	—
Conjunction	·	∧	&
Disjunction	∨	(the wedge is almost always used for disjunction)	
Conditional	⊃	→	
Biconditional	≡	↔	

There are also some alternatives when it comes to how the scope of an operator is indicated. We use three different styles of parentheses—parentheses "( )," brackets "[ ]," and braces "{ }"—to make formulas such as $\sim \{[(A \equiv B) \equiv (B \equiv A)] \supset C\}$ a bit easier to read. Because the different styles of parentheses all perform exactly the same function, it's possible to make do with just one style of parentheses: $\sim (((A \equiv B) \equiv (B \equiv A)) \supset C)$.

More interestingly, you can use what is known as **Polish notation** to do without parentheses at all. The major difference is that instead of placing the operator between the sentences it operates on, the operator comes at the beginning of the sentence. You can use Polish notation in mathematics as well as logic. In Polish notation $2 + 3$ becomes $+2, 3$. "Reverse Polish notation," or "RPN," used in many calculators, puts the operator at the end. So to enter $2 + 3$ in RPN, you enter 2, 3, and then the addition operator.

Two other minor differences between Polish notation and the system introduced in this book is that Polish notation uses capital letters to represent the operators and lowercase letters to represent sentences. The five sentential logic operators are as follows:

Negation	N	(**N**egation)
Conjunction	K	(**K**onjunction)
Disjunction:	A	(**A**lternation)
Conditional	C	(**C**onditional)
Biconditional	E	(**E**quivalence)

Putting this together, $A \cdot B$ is represented in Polish notation as *Kab*, and $A \supset B$ is *Cab*, and so on. How does this let us do without parentheses? Well, in Polish notation the main operator is always at the *beginning* of the sentence, followed immediately by the sentences that the operator operates on. So $\sim A \supset B$ becomes *CNab* and $(A \supset B) \equiv (C \cdot B)$ becomes *ECabKcb*.

Examples

Standard Notation	Polish Notation
1. $\sim (A \cdot B)$	*NKab*
2. $A \vee (B \equiv C)$	*AaEbc*
3. $\sim A \supset \sim B$	*CNaNb*
4. $(A \vee B) \equiv \sim C$	*EAabNc*
5. $A \supset (B \supset C)$	*CaCbc*
6. $(A \supset B) \supset (A \supset C)$	*CCabCac*
7. $(A \vee \sim B) \cdot \sim (A \cdot \sim B)$	*KAaNbNKaNb*
8. $\sim \{[(A \equiv B) \equiv (B \equiv A)] \supset C\}$	*NCEEabEbac*

Exercise 2-9

Symbolize the following in Polish notation:

1. $\sim A \cdot \sim B$
2. $\sim (A \cdot B)$
3. $A \supset \sim B$
4. $\sim A \vee B$
5. $A \supset \sim (B \vee C)$
6. $(A \cdot B) \supset \sim C$
7. $\sim A \supset (B \cdot C)$
8. $A \equiv (B \cdot \sim C)$

9. $(A \cdot B) \supset (\sim C \supset D)$
10. $A \supset [(B \cdot C) \cdot C]$
11. $[(\sim A \cdot \sim B) \cdot \sim C] \supset D$
12. $[(A \vee B) \cdot C] \supset D$
13. $\sim (A \vee B) \supset (C \supset \sim D)$
14. $(A \vee B) \equiv [(C \vee D) \cdot \sim E]$
15. $\sim A \supset [\sim B \supset \sim (C \vee D)]$

Exercise 2-10

1. What's wrong with abbreviating the sentence "George Plimpton is not a public figure" by the letter *P*?

2. What are the two principal meanings of the term "or" when that term is used as a sentence connective? Include at least one original example of each.

3. Why isn't the expression "It is well known that . . ." truth-functional?

4. What common words, other than "and," are sometimes correctly symbolized by means of " · "? Use each of them in a sentence (original if possible).

5. Is the sentence "Archie Leach and Cary Grant are well-known public figures" atomic or compound?

6. What about the sentence "Archie Leach is not a well-known public figure"?

7. And how about "Archie Leach and Cary Grant have been lifelong best friends"?

8. Or, "George Burns is not now, never has been, and never will be God"?

Philosophical Discussions

1. In the introductory remarks to this chapter, an example was given of an argument that uses commands, which have no truth-values, as premises and conclusion. Can you think of any other kinds of arguments that one might consider legitimate that use premises and/or conclusions that have no truth-values? How about, for example, questions as premises or conclusions?

2. In the introductory remarks, you encountered the following:

    Some philosophers and logicians have argued that any language *necessarily* (that word again!) has the logical qualities that we will discuss here. How they know this when they have not studied all the thousands of natural languages in the world is a question left to the exercises in this chapter.

    Discuss.

3. Is it really correct to say that every statement is either true or false, that is, that it must be one or the other? How about "It is raining here now," when what we have is a mist or a very light drizzle? How about "I am in this room" when in fact I am in the doorway to it? Give your own examples, and discuss.

4. Why allow, in our logic, sentences that wouldn't ordinarily be uttered by a competent speaker? Sure, one sort of understands the statement "If Bob loves Mary, then Mars is the closest planet to Earth," but nobody would ever use such a statement in a real argument. Can't we rule them out somehow? But how?

5. Consider the following argument: Many, if not most or all, of the examples given in the text of English statements are highly artificial. Nobody ever says that "If Art went to the show, then Betsy stayed home," for example. So how can the study of logic, at least as done in this book, have the desired relation to English as it is spoken and written? Discuss.

Key Terms Introduced in Chapter Two

antecedent: The part that follows "if" in an "*if . . . then*" sentence. In sentential logic, the component sentence to the left of the "⊃" in a conditional sentence (or sentence form).

atomic sentence: A sentence that contains no sentence connectives.

biconditional: A compound sentence that expresses an "if and only if" relationship between two component sentences. In sentential logic, a sentence having "≡" as its main connective.

component sentence: The sentence or sentences operated on by a truth-functional operator.

compound sentence: A sentence containing at least one sentence connective. Example: "Art is handsome, and Betsy is smart".

conditional: A compound sentence that expresses an "If . . . then" relationship between its component sentences. In sentential logic a sentence having "⊃" as its main connective.

conjunct: One of the sentences joined together by "and", "·", and so on. Example: "Art is smart" is a conjunct of the compound "Art is smart, but he's lazy".

conjunction: A compound sentence whose main connective is "and", "but", or a similar term. In sentential logic a sentence (or sentence form) having "·" as its main connective.

consequent: The part that follows "then" in an "if . . . then" sentence. In sentential logic the component sentence to the right of the "⊃" in a conditional sentence (or sentence form).

disjunct: Either of the component sentences in a disjunction.

disjunction: A compound English sentence whose main connective is an "or". In sentential logic a compound sentence (or sentence form) whose main connective is "∨".

dot: The symbol " · ", read *and.*

exclusive disjunction: A compound English sentence whose main connective is an exclusive "or."

exclusive "or": The English word "or" used in this sense implies that one and only one of the two disjuncts is true, not both.

formation rules: Rules that specify how to form syntactically correct statements in a logical language. Syntactically correct statements are called *well-formed;* others are termed *ill-formed.*

horseshoe: The symbol "⊃", read "if . . . then."

inclusive disjunction: A compound sentence whose main connective is the inclusive "or." The sentential logic symbol "∨."

inclusive "or": The sense of the English word "or" correctly symbolized as "∨." "Or," used in its inclusive sense, implies only that at least one of the two disjuncts is true, but leaves open the possibility that both disjuncts are true.

main connective: The sentence connective that has the greatest scope.

material biconditional: (See *material equivalence.*)

material conditional: A compound statement whose main connective is "⊃." Synonym: *material implication.*

material equivalence: Statement whose main sentence connective is "≡." (See *tribar.*)

material implication: (See *material conditional.*)

metalanguage: The language in which we talk *about* another language, the object language. In this book, sentential logic is our object language, and English our metalanguage.

negation: A sentence whose main connective is "~," "not," "no," or a similar term. (Also see *tilde.*)

object language: The language we are studying, in this case sentential logic.

Polish notation: An alternative method of constructing a *wff* (see *well-formed*), which dispenses with parentheses in favor of the order of the signs.

scope: The scope of an operator is the component sentence or sentences that the operator operates on. The negation operator, "~," operates on a single component sentence. All the other operators operate on two component sentences.

semantics: A semantics for a logical language consists of (1) interpretations of all its symbols in terms of a natural language (the *metalanguage*), and (2) a way of determining the truth-values of all compound statements in the language, for example, as the truth tables do for the logical operators (this definition will be supplemented when we get to predicate logic).

sentence: A grammatically well-formed unit of English that can be used to make a statement, often different statements on different occasions. Thus "I am happy now" can be used by someone to make a true statement on a given day, and by another person to make a false statement on another day.

sentence connective: A term or phrase used to make a larger sentence from two smaller ones. Example: "It's raining and it's cold." Also, the term "not" and its variations, when used to negate a sentence. Example: the word "not" in "Fred will not win at poker tonight."

sentence constant: A capital letter abbreviating an English sentence, atomic or compound.

sentential logic: The logic that deals with relationships holding between sentences, atomic or compound, without dealing with the interior structure of atomic sentences. The logic of truth-functions. Synonyms: *logic of truth-functions, propositional logic.*

statement: The use of a sentence that has a definite, fixed truth-value. We deal with statements in our sentential logic.

statement variable: A lowercase letter *p* through *z* used as a placeholder in a sentence form (or other linguistic form) such that if all the sentence variables in a sentence form are replaced by capital letters (sentence constants), then the resulting expression is a sentence.

substitution: An operation performed by putting a statement in place of a variable.

symbolic logic: The modern logic that includes sentential logic as a part (as well as the predicate logic to be discussed later).

syntax: The permissible combinations of symbols as specified in formation rules.

tilde: The symbol "~," read "not."

tribar: The symbol "≡," read "if and only if."

truth-function: A function that takes one or more truth-values as its imput and returns a single truth-value as its output.

truth-functional operator: An operator is truth-functional if the truth-values of the sentences formed by its use are determined by the truth-values of the sentences it connects. Similarly, sentence forms constructed by means of truth-functional sentence connectives are such that the truth-values of their substitution instances are determined by the truth-values of their component sentences.

truth table: A table giving the truth-values of all possible substitution instances of a given sentence form, in terms of the possible truth-values of the component sentences of these substitution instances.

truth-value: There are two truth-values, namely true and false. Every sentence in sentential logic has a truth-value, and the truth-value of every compound sentence is a function of the truth-value of its component sentences.

variable: A letter that represents no statement and thus has no truth-value but for which statements can be substituted. The truth-value of the statement substituted for the variable will thus *vary* according to which statement is substituted.

wedge: The symbol "∨."

well-formed: A well-formed statement is one constructed according to the formation rules of a language. Sometimes such a statement is called a well-formed formula, abbreviation *wff.*

Chapter Three

Truth Tables

---

1 *Computing Truth-Values*

In Chapter Two truth tables were introduced for our five truth-functional sentence connectives. Here again are the standard truth tables for these connectives.

p	$\sim p$
T	F
F	T

p	q	$p \vee q$
T	T	T
T	F	T
F	T	T
F	F	F

p	q	$p \cdot q$
T	T	T
T	F	F
F	T	F
F	F	F

p	q	$p \supset q$
T	T	T
T	F	F
F	T	T
F	F	T

p	q	$p \equiv q$
T	T	T
T	F	F
F	T	F
F	F	T

With this information, we can determine the truth-value of any compound sentence containing one of these truth-functional connectives, when provided with the truth-values of the sentences they connect, simply by looking at the appropriate line in the truth tables and noting whether there is a **T** or an **F** at the appropriate spot.

Obviously, this method can also be used to determine the truth-values of more complicated sentences. Suppose Art and Betsy are running for class president, and consider the sentence "It's not the case either that Art and Betsy will run or that Betsy won't run," symbolized as $\sim [(A \cdot B) \vee \sim B]$. Assume we are told Art and Betsy both will run, so A and B both are true. Then we can "figure out" the truth-value of $\sim [(A \cdot B) \vee \sim B]$ as follows: Because A and B both are true, $A \cdot B$ must be true, by line 1 of the truth table for "$\cdot$". And because B is true, $\sim B$ must be false, by line 1 of the truth table for "$\sim$." Hence,

$[(A \cdot B) \vee \sim B]$ must be true, by line 2 of the truth table for "$\vee$." And finally, because $[(A \cdot B) \vee \sim B]$ is true, its negation $\sim [(A \cdot B) \vee \sim B]$ must be false, by line 1 of the truth table for "$\sim$."

The following diagram illustrates this process of truth table analysis as it was carried out on the sentence $\sim [(A \cdot B) \vee \sim B]$:

Notice that the process starts with the smallest units of the sentence and proceeds to larger and larger units, until the last loop determines the truth-value of the sentence as a whole.

This procedure, called **truth table analysis,** can be used to determine the truth-value of any compound sentence from the truth-values of its component sentences.

The *loop method* just introduced is very graphic, and so many students find it to be the best method to use when first learning to compute the truth-values of a sentence. But as soon as you've grasped the basic idea, you should move on to the more common, and more compact, way of computing truth-values that we will refer to as the *tabular method*. The tabular method is just the loop method without the loops. Instead, the truth-values are placed immediately beneath the main connectives of each component sentence. Thus, the truth-value of the sentence is the truth-value under the sentence's main connective. Here's what the preceding sentence looks like using the tabular method.

$$\downarrow$$
$$\sim [(A \cdot B) \vee \sim B]$$
$$\textbf{F T T T T F T}$$

Notice we have used an arrow to indicate the main connective.

🚶 Walk-Through: Computing Truth-Values

Having symbolized a compound sentence, the first step in determining its truth-value, when you know the truth-values of its atomic components, is to place the appropriate truth-value, **T** or **F**, directly beneath each atomic letter. Suppose our sentence is $(D \vee \sim B) \equiv \sim (C \cdot \sim D)$ and we are told that B and C are true and D is false. The first step will look like this on either the loop or tabular methods:

$$(D \vee \sim B) \equiv \sim (C \cdot \sim D)$$
$$\textbf{F} \qquad \textbf{T} \qquad \quad \textbf{T} \qquad \textbf{F}$$

The second step is to assign truth-values below any negation signs that negate just one atomic letter. In our example, because *B* is true, we place an **F** under the first negation sign, thus indicating that ~ *B* is false. Also, since *D* is false ~ *D* must be true—so we place a **T** under the third tilde.

$$(D \vee \sim B) \equiv \sim (C \cdot \sim D)$$
    F   FT   T   TF

$$(D \vee \sim B) \equiv \sim (C \cdot \sim D)$$
    F   T   T   F
        F   T

The third step is to look for connectives that have the next largest scopes and place the appropriate truth-values under them. In our example, we can at this stage place an **F** under the wedge in (*D* ∨ ~ *B*) since both disjuncts are false and a **T** under the " · " in the conjunction (*C* · ~ *D*), because both conjuncts are true.

$$(D \vee \sim B) \equiv \sim (C \cdot \sim D)$$
    F FFT   TTTF

$$(D \vee \sim B) \equiv \sim (C \cdot \sim D)$$
    F   T   T   F
        F   T
        F   T

By repeated applications of the procedure described in the third step—finding connectives that have the next larger scope and placing the appropriate truth-value beneath them—we can compute the truth-value of any sentential logic sentence, no matter how complicated. The truth-value for the entire sentence will be the last truth-value assigned, and will be placed below the main connective of the sentence. In our example, we first determine the truth-value of ~ (*C* · ~ *D*), which must be false because *C* · ~ *D* is true (justifying placing an **F** under the tilde), and finally that the whole statement must be true, since both components of the biconditional have the same truth-value (justifying placing a **T** under the tribar). So our completed analysis looks like this:

↓
$$(D \vee \sim B) \equiv \sim (C \cdot \sim D)$$
    F FFT TF TTTF

$$(D \vee \sim B) \equiv \sim (C \cdot \sim D)$$
    F   T   T   F
        F   T
        F   T
                        F
            T

Once again, we illustrate both methods in this section, but you should learn the tabular method since we will employ this method later in the chapter to construct more-complex truth tables.

Examples

(In these examples, assume *A*, *B*, and *C* are true, *D*, *E*, and *F* false.)

    Tabular Method   *Loop Method*

(Notice that the negation sign negates the whole compound sentence (*C* · *D*), and therefore is treated after the truth-value of (*C* · *D*) is determined.)

(Notice that the major connective in this sentence is "∨" and that therefore it would be possible to determine the truth-value of this sentence without knowing the truth-value of any of the sentences in the right-hand disjunct, because the left-hand disjunct— namely *A*—is true, and consequently the whole sentence is true.)

Exercise 3-1

If *A* and *B* are true, and *C*, *D*, and *E* are false, what are the truth-values of the following compound sentences?

1. $(A \lor D) \supset E$
2. $A \equiv (C \lor B)$
3. $B \supset (A \supset C)$
4. $\sim [C \lor (D \lor E)]$
5. $(A \equiv B) \equiv (D \equiv E)$
6. $\sim [(A \cdot \sim B) \supset (C \cdot \sim D)]$
7. $\sim (A \lor B) \lor \sim (\sim A \lor \sim B)$
8. $\sim (C \cdot D) \lor \sim (\sim C \cdot \sim D)$
9. $[(A \cdot B) \cdot C] \lor [(A \cdot C) \lor (A \cdot D)]$
10. $A \supset [(B \supset C) \supset (D \supset E)]$
11. $[(A \cdot B) \equiv (C \cdot D)] \supset E$
12. $[(A \supset \sim B) \lor (C \cdot \sim D)] \equiv [\sim (A \supset D) \lor (\sim C \lor E)]$
13. $[(\sim A \cdot \sim B) \supset C] \lor (A \supset B)$
14. $[A \supset (\sim A \lor A)] \cdot \sim [(A \cdot A) \supset (A \cdot A)]$
15. $[(E \lor \sim D) \cdot \sim A] \supset \{(\sim A \cdot \sim B) \cdot [(C \cdot D) \cdot E]\}$

Exercise 3-2

Knowing that *A* and *B* are true and *C* and *D* false, but not knowing the truth-values of *Q* and *R*, what can we tell, if anything, about the truth-values of the following compounds?

1. $Q \supset (C \supset D)$
2. $B \supset (Q \lor \sim C)$
3. $\sim C \supset (D \supset Q)$
4. $R \equiv \sim R$
5. $\sim [\sim R \equiv R]$
6. $\sim [R \supset (\sim A \supset D)]$

7. ~ [(~ *D* ∨ *Q*) ⊃ *R*]

8. [(*C* ⊃ *Q*) ⊃ ~ *R*] ⊃ *Q*

9. ~ (*A* ∨ *R*) ∨ ~ (~ *A* ∨ ~ *R*)

10. ~ (*C* · *R*) ∨ ~ (~ *C* · ~ *R*)

11. (*A* · *C*) ⊃ [(*D* · *Q*) ⊃ (~ *A* · *R*)]

12. [(*D* ⊃ *R*) ⊃ (*D* ⊃ *Q*)] ⊃ *C*

2 *Logical Form*

We have now seen how to compute the truth-value of a compound statement from the truth-values of its atomic constituents. We will henceforth call such an assignment a **valuation** (after Richmond Thomason—see bibliography). If we assign truth to a statement A, we write $V(A) = T$; if we assign B to be false, we write $V(B) = F$. With that valuation $V(A \vee B) = T$. The ability to calculate the truth-value of statements will be crucial in our analysis of sentential validity, because we know that in a valid argument, if the premises are true then the conclusion must be true.

The first major concept we now need in this analysis is that of the *logical form* of a statement.

Expressions such as $p \cdot q$, containing only sentence variables and sentence connectives, are called **sentence forms.** Of course, sentence forms are not sentences (and so are neither true nor false). But if we replace all the variables in a sentence form by expressions (atomic or compound) that are sentences, then the resulting expression is a sentence. For instance, if we replace the variables p and q in the sentence form $p \cdot q$ by the sentence constants A and B, respectively, then the resulting expression, $A \cdot B$, is a sentence. The sentence $A \cdot B$ is said to be a **substitution instance** of the sentence form $p \cdot q$. Of course, in replacing sentence variables with sentences, we must make sure that every occurrence of a given sentence variable is replaced by the same sentence. Thus, $A \cdot \sim (B \cdot A)$ and $\sim C \cdot \sim (B \cdot \sim C)$ are correct substitution instances of $p \cdot \sim (q \cdot p)$, but $A \cdot \sim (B \cdot C)$ and $\sim C \cdot \sim (B \cdot C)$ are not.

It is important to notice that compound sentences are substitution instances of more than one sentence form. For instance, the sentence $A \cdot B$, which is a substitution instance of the sentence form $p \cdot q$, also is a substitution instance of the sentence form p (because replacement of p, the one variable in the sentence form p, by the compound sentence $A \cdot B$ results in the sentence $A \cdot B$).

Because sentence forms are not sentences, they are neither true nor false. But all their substitution instances are sentences, and hence all their substitution instances are either true or false.

When we speak of all the substitution instances of $p \cdot q$ we must be absolutely clear on what we mean. $A \cdot B$, $C \cdot D$, $(A \equiv B) \cdot (C \cdot D)$, and $(A \supset B) \cdot D$ are all substitution instances of $p \cdot q$, *because each has the same logical form.* Each substitution instance will have a valuation, which is a function, ultimately, of the valuation of its atomic components. But of all the giant number of well-formed conjunctions we can construct, the truth table tells us there are only four logical possibilities: Either both conjuncts are true, or both are false, or one is true and the other false. Parallel arguments will hold for all our basic sentence forms.

Here is the important rule to keep in mind regarding sentence forms: *A sentence is a substitution instance of a form if and only if you can produce exactly that sentence by doing nothing other than replacing each variable in the form with a well-formed sentence.* So if there is any question about whether a sentence is a substitution instance of a form, take the form and show how one can get the sentence by plugging in a sentence for each variable in the form. For example, the sentence ~ (~ A ∨ B), is a substitution instance of the form ~ (p ∨ q) because one can produce this sentence by replacing p with the sentence ~ A, and q with the sentence B. This sentence is not a substitution instance of ~ p ∨ q, however, because there is no sentence one can substitute for the p and q in this form to get the original sentence. If we replace p with ~ A and q with B, we get a different sentence, namely, ~ ~ A ∨ B. The only way one could produce the original sentence from this form would be to replace one of the variables in the form with a sentence fragment (~ A). But that is just a sentence part, not itself a well-formed sentence. Any time the only way to produce the original sentence is to substitute sentence fragments (rather than complete sentences) for variables, the sentence is not a substitution instance of the form.

A common mistake you should be on guard against is confusing *logical form* with *logical equivalence.* For example, it is easy to see that the sentences A and ~ ~ A are **logically equivalent.** That is, they have exactly the same truth conditions. If one is true, so is the other. Yet despite being logically equivalent, these two sentences are not substitution instances of the same forms. A is only a substitution instance of the form p; whereas ~ ~ A is a substitution instance of three forms: p, ~ p, and ~ ~ p. A is not a substitution instance of ~ ~ p because there is no sentence that you can substitute for the variable p in this form that will yield the sentence A. No matter what sentence you replace p with, the result will not be an atomic sentence. It will be a double negation, that is a sentence governed by two negation signs. This example also illustrates an important rule of thumb regarding forms: A sentence may have more logical structure than a form of which it is a substitution instance, but it can never have less.

Understanding the difference between sentences and sentence forms and between variables and constants is the key to understanding the correct use of the rules of logic. As you will see, valid arguments depend on their logical form. The logical form of a valid argument is found by finding the forms of the premises and conclusion (because compound statements may have more than one form, finding the form that yields validity will take some explanation later). We can then decide whether there is any *possibility* that an argument with that form *could* have true premises and a false conclusion. This notion of possibility will be explained by the truth tables.

𝕜 **Walk-Through: Substitution Instances**

Complex sentences are substitution instances of many forms. Let's see how to go about determining all the forms for the sentence ~ (A ∨ B) ⊃ (C · D). If you can list all the forms for a sentence of this level of complexity, you should have no trouble with the following exercises.

1. First of all, every sentence is a substitution instance of what we can refer to as the "atomic form," namely the form p.

2. Second, if a sentence is not atomic, it will be a substitution instance of one of the five forms that have only one logical connective. We might call this the "basic form" of a sentence:

> ~ *p*
> *p* · *q*
> *p* ∨ *q*
> *p* ⊃ *q*
> *p* ≡ *q*

The basic form of a sentence is the form that consists only of the main connective of the sentence and variables. It provides the answer to the question "What kind of sentence is this?" Our sentence is a conditional and thus has the basic form *p* ⊃ *q*. Here is a very useful rule of thumb: *Other than the atomic form, every correct form should have the same main connective as the sentence's basic form.* So after we are done listing our forms, we can double-check. If any have some other main connective, they are wrong.

3. Another helpful guideline is that every sentence is a substitution instance of what we might refer to as its *expanded* form. The expanded form is the form you get when you systematically replace each atomic letter in the sentence with a variable. In our example the expanded form is ~ (*p* ∨ *q*) ⊃ (*r* · *s*). The expanded form shows all of a sentence's logical form. *No sentence is a substitution instance of a form that contains more logical structure, or a different kind of logical structure, than the sentence's expanded form.*

These guidelines allow you to automatically produce three forms for any complex sentence: the atomic form *p*, the basic form (*p* ⊃ *q* in our case), and the expanded form ~ (*p* ∨ *q*) ⊃ (*r* · *s*). If there are more forms than these three, they will have the same main connective as the basic form, they will be more complex than the basic form, and they will be less complex but otherwise have the same kind of form as the expanded form.

4. To produce the remaining forms systematically, you might begin by thinking about the sentences represented by the variables in the basic form. For each of these variables in turn ask, What kind of sentence does this variable represent? In our case *p* in the basic form *p* ⊃ *q* represents a negation, namely ~ (*A* ∨ *B*). This gives us the form ~ *p* ⊃ *q*. Likewise, *q* in the basic form represents a conjunction, (*C* · *D*), so we can represent this bit of logical structure with the form *p* ⊃ (*q* · *r*). Of course, we can show both these bits of structure at once with the form ~ *p* ⊃ (*q* · *r*).

If we had a really complicated sentence, we would just repeat this procedure for the new forms we've produced, revealing any structure represented by atomic letters in these new forms. In our case the only additional bit of structure we can reveal gives us the expanded form. So here are all the forms of which ~ (*A* ∨ *B*) ⊃ (*C* · *D*) is a substitution instance:

p (the "atomic" form)

$p \supset q$ (the "basic" form)

$\sim p \supset q$

$p \supset (q \cdot r)$

$\sim p \supset (q \cdot r)$

$\sim (p \vee q) \supset r$

$\sim (p \vee q) \supset (r \cdot s)$ (the "expanded" form)

Examples

Here are a few compound sentences with sentence forms of which they are substitution instances:

Sentences   *Forms:*

1. $\sim C$ p

    $\sim p$

2. $A \cdot C$ p

    $p \cdot q$

3. $\sim C \cdot R$ p

    $p \cdot q$

    $\sim p \cdot q$

4. $\sim M \equiv \sim N$ p

    $p \equiv q$

    $\sim p \equiv q$

    $p \equiv \sim q$

    $\sim p \equiv \sim q$

5. $C \cdot (D \cdot \sim S)$ p

    $p \cdot q$

    $p \cdot (q \cdot r)$

    $p \cdot (q \cdot \sim r)$

6. $\sim L \vee \sim (F \supset G)$ p

    $p \vee q$

    $\sim p \vee q$

    $p \vee \sim q$

    $\sim p \vee \sim q$

    $p \vee \sim (p \supset q)$

    $\sim p \vee \sim (p \supset q)$

7. $(A \supset B) \supset (C \supset D)$

p
$p \supset q$
$(p \supset q) \supset r$
$p \supset (q \supset r)$
$(p \supset q) \supset (r \supset s)$

8. $A \vee \sim [(B \cdot D) \vee F]$

p
$p \vee q$
$p \vee \sim q$
$p \vee \sim (q \vee r)$
$p \vee \sim [(q \cdot r) \vee s]$

Note that for each of the preceding forms it doesn't matter which variables are used. Instead of p we could have listed the form q, or r, etc. These are all just different ways of writing the very same form. Likewise, $p \cdot q, p \cdot r, r \cdot q, q \cdot r$, etc., are all ways to write the same form.

Exercise 3-3

1. Which of the following sentences **are not** substitution instances of the form $p \supset q$?
   A. $A \supset B$
   B. $\sim A \supset (B \supset C)$
   C. $A \vee (B \supset C)$
   D. $A \supset \sim B$
   E. $\sim A \supset \sim B$
   F. $(A \vee B) \supset C$

2. Which of the following sentences **are** substitution instances of the form $p \supset q$?
   A. $\sim (A \supset B)$
   B. $A \supset \sim B$
   C. A
   D. $A \vee B$
   E. $\sim A \vee \sim B$
   F. $(\sim A \vee \sim B) \supset C$

3. Which of the following sentences **are** substitution instances of the form $\sim p$?
   A. A
   B. $\sim A$
   C. $\sim \sim A$
   D. $\sim A \vee \sim B$
   E. $\sim A \supset B$
   F. $\sim (A \supset B)$

4. Which of the following sentences **are not** substitution instances of the form $\sim \sim p$?
   A. A
   B. $\sim (\sim A \supset B)$
   C. $\sim \sim (A \supset B)$
   D. $\sim \sim \sim A$
   E. $\sim \sim A \supset \sim B$
   F. $(A \vee B) \supset C$

5. $\sim A \supset (B \supset C)$ is a substitution instance of which of the following?
   A. p
   B. $\sim p$
   C. $p \supset q$
   D. $\sim p \supset q$
   E. $p \supset (q \supset r)$
   F. $(p \supset q) \supset r$

Exercise 3-4

For each sentence on the left, determine the sentence forms on the right of which it is a substitution instance. (Remember that a sentence may be a substitution instance of several different sentence forms.)

1. A
2. $A \supset B$
3. $(A \lor B) \supset C$
4. $A \lor (B \supset C)$
5. $(\sim A \lor B) \supset C$
6. $\sim (A \lor B) \supset C$
7. $\sim A \lor (B \supset C)$
8. $(A \lor B) \supset \sim C$
9. $\sim [A \lor (B \supset C)]$
10. $\sim (\sim A \lor B) \supset C$
11. $\sim [(A \lor B) \supset C$
12. $\sim (A \lor B) \supset \sim C$
13. $\sim [\sim (A \lor B) \supset C]$
14. $\sim [\sim (\sim A \lor B) \supset C]$
15. $\sim [(\sim A \lor B) \supset C]$

a. p
b. $\sim p$
c. $p \lor q$
d. $p \supset q$
e. $\sim p \lor q$
f. $\sim p \supset q$
g. $\sim p \supset \sim q$
h. $\sim (p \lor q)$
i. $\sim (p \supset q)$
j. $\sim (\sim p \supset q)$
k. $(p \lor q) \supset r$
l. $p \lor (q \supset r)$
m. $(\sim p \lor q) \supset r$
n. $\sim (p \lor q) \supset r$
o. $(p \lor q) \supset \sim r$
p. $\sim [p \lor (q \supset r)]$
q. $\sim [(p \lor q) \supset r]$

Exercise 3-5

Determine the sentence forms of which the following are substitution instances. *Example:*
The sentence $A \supset \sim B$ is a substitution instance of p, $p \supset q$, and $p \supset \sim q$.

1. $A \cdot \sim B$
2. $\sim D \supset \sim F$
3. $L \lor (M \cdot N)$
4. $\sim (H \lor K)$
5. $\sim (\sim R \supset S)$
6. $(A \cdot B) \equiv \sim B$

7. $\sim A \supset (B \supset A)$
8. $\sim (A \equiv B) \supset C$
9. $(\sim A \equiv B) \supset C$
10. $\sim [(A \equiv B) \supset C]$
11. $\sim (B \cdot D) \supset (R \lor D)$
12. $\sim [(B \cdot D) \supset (R \lor D)]$

3 *Tautologies, Contradictions, and Contingent Sentences*

So far we have seen how to determine the truth-value of a particular sentence when we know the truth-value of some or all of its atomic components. However, we can determine the truth-value of some sentences by logic alone, without needing such information. Consider the statement "Either Lincoln was president in 1862, or Lincoln was not president in 1862." It is true, of course, yet there is something obviously peculiar about it. Unlike "Lincoln was president in 1862," which is an alleged fact of history that we might wish to check on, the first statement gives us no factual information whatever that we can check on. Despite appearances to the contrary, such statements, called **tautologies,** are often uttered in everyday life as if they were profound. A secretary of state once said, to thunderous applause, "The future lies ahead." Where *else* might it lie? In other words, that which lies ahead lies ahead—a tautology if there ever was one.

How do we know that "Either Lincoln was president in 1862, or Lincoln was not president in 1862" is true without having to look at history books? Such statements are true in virtue of their logical form. In this case, the form in question is "$p \vee \sim p$." If we make a truth table for this statement form, we find there are only two possibilities: if we substitute a true statement for p the entire disjunction is true; if we substitute a false one for p, the disjunction is again true. Of all the statements we could substitute for p, then, there are only two logical possibilities—we substitute a true one or a false one and, on either condition, the disjunction is true. To put the point another way, although there are a gigantic number of possible substitution instances for p, there are only two *logical possibilities* for substitution. It is the idea of logical possibility that is crucial here. Our original statement about Lincoln is true not because of the facts, but because every other statement of the same logical form is also true, and what that means is shown by the truth table for the form:

$$\downarrow$$

p	p	$\vee$	$\sim$	p
T	**T**	**T**	**F**	**T**
F	**F**	**T**	**T**	**F**

Notice that each line of this truth table corresponds precisely to what you produced in the preceding unit by using the tabular method. The form $p \vee \sim p$ is a tautological form, and $A \vee \sim A$ is a tautology because of that form.

What if a sentence has two different atomic constituents, $A \supset (B \supset A)$, for example? Its form is $p \supset (q \supset p)$. Here there are four, and only four, logical possibilities: what we substitute for p and for q could be true, that is, $V(p) = \mathbf{T}$, and $V(q) = \mathbf{T}$; $V(p) = \mathbf{T}$ and $V(q) = \mathbf{F}$; $V(p) = \mathbf{F}$ and $V(q) = \mathbf{T}$; or finally, $V(p) = \mathbf{F}$ and $V(q) = \mathbf{F}$. Each of these possibilities is represented in a line of the following truth table:

$$\downarrow$$

p	q	p	$\supset$	$(q$	$\supset$	$p)$
T	**T**	**T**	**T**	**T**	**T**	**T**
T	**F**	**T**	**T**	**F**	**T**	**T**
F	**T**	**F**	**T**	**T**	**F**	**F**
F	**F**	**F**	**T**	**F**	**T**	**F**

Notice that every possible substitution of $p \supset (q \supset p)$ is a true sentence, no matter what the truth-values of its component sentences. So the sentence $A \supset (B \supset A)$ is a tautology. The form or structure of this sentence guarantees it is true, no matter what the truth-values of its component sentences.

That $A \supset (B \supset A)$ is a tautology might not strike you as obvious in the way that $A \vee \sim A$ did. Most tautologies are not at all obvious, as we will see as we go on; if they were, deciding which arguments are valid in sentential logic would be an easy task for, as you will see, there is an intimate connection between the validity of an argument and the notion of a tautology.

Contradictions are statements that cannot possibly be true, and their forms are contradictory forms. A simple example is "Lincoln was president in 1862 and Lincoln was not president in 1862." Its form is $p \cdot \sim p$. Look at the following table and notice that there are only two possibilities of substitution for p, $V(p) = \mathbf{T}$ and $V(p) = \mathbf{F}$. Each yields an F in the truth table; a contradictory form has all **F**'s in its truth table.

$$\downarrow$$

p	p	$\cdot$	$\sim$	p
T	T	F	F	T
F	F	F	T	F

Again, not every contradiction is easy to spot; if they were easy, both politics and mathematics might be the better for it. But what should be obvious, given that you know the truth table for the tilde, is that any tautology can be turned into a contradiction by simply putting a tilde in front of the entire statement. Because the tautology has all **T**'s in its truth table, the negation of it will have all **F**'s! Correlatively, we can turn contradictions into tautologies with the flick of a tilde. The notion of a contradictory form will play a crucial role in our logical and philosophical discussions; contradictions are of high theoretic interest. In sum: A statement is a contradiction in virtue of its form.

Finally, consider $(A \supset B) \supset B$. Its form is $(p \supset q) \supset q$.

$$\downarrow$$

p	q	$(p$	$\supset$	$q)$	$\supset$	q
T	T	T	T	T	T	T
T	F	T	F	F	T	F
F	T	F	T	T	T	T
F	F	F	T	F	F	F

Notice that there is at least one **T** and one **F** in the column below the main connective in this truth table. This means the sentence is *contingent*. A contingent statement is one whose form has at least one **T** and at least one **F** in its truth table. Every atomic statement is contingent, because its only form is p, and p has two possibilities for substitution, $V(p) = \mathbf{T}$ and $V(p) = \mathbf{F}$. We know from our discussions of logical form that every statement, even a tautological or a contradictory one, can be treated as a substitution instance of a single variable p. But this does not make every statement a contingent one. A statement is a tautology if it has at least one logical form which is a tautological form, a contradiction if it has at least one form which is a contradictory form. *However,* a statement is *not* a contingency if it has a contingent form, because every statement has one such form.

Here is how to determine if a statement is a contingent one. Replace each statement letter by a variable, making sure that the same letter is replaced by the same variable throughout. We can call this, for convenience, the *one–one logical form* of a statement. If the one–one logical form has at least one **T** and at least one **F** in its truth table, then the statement is a contingency. This notion prevents us from calling $A \lor \sim A$ a contingency. The statement *is* an instance of the logical form p, and the table for p has one **T** and one **F** in it, but p is not the one–one logical form of $A \lor \sim A$; rather $p \lor \sim p$ is. The same reasoning prevents us from calling $A \cdot \sim A$ a contingency. Notice that if a statement has a **tautologous form,** which is not its one-one form, it will also be a tautology under the one-one form. Thus the statement $\{[(A \cdot B) \supset (C \lor D)] \cdot (A \cdot B)\} \supset (C \lor D)$ is an instance of the form $[(p \supset q) \cdot p] \supset q$, which is *not* its one-one form but is a truth table tautology, and the one-one form of the statement is also a tautology. However, it should be clear that this rule doesn't go the other way. A statement that has a one-one form which is a tautology, may have no other tautologous forms. Thus the one-one form of $[(A \supset B) \cdot A] \supset B$ is a tautological one, namely $[(p \supset q) \cdot p] \supset q$, but this is its only such tautological form. The same reasoning goes for contradictions. Once you see how this works, you will see that if the one-one form of a statement is a contingency, then it cannot be a tautology under any other form. If it were, then its one-one form would also be a tautology.

☆   Walk-Through: How to Construct a Truth Table

1. The first step in constructing a truth table is to determine from the one-one form the total number of lines needed. This depends on how many different variables are contained in a sentence form. As we have seen, a sentence with only one atomic letter has a form with only two lines. A sentence with two letters has a form with twice as many lines, four. A sentence with three different letters needs twice as many again, namely eight; four atomic letters requires a form with a sixteen-line table, and so on. For the mathematically inclined, the number of lines needed to construct a truth table for a form for a sentence with n different atomic constituents is 2^n.

2. The second step is to systematically list each of the possible ways of assigning truth-values to the variables of the sentence form. The rightmost column below the variables always merely alternates truth-values every other line.

$$\downarrow$$

p	q	r	$(p$ · ~ $q)$ $\supset$ $[(p \lor r)$ $\lor$ ~ $r)]$
		T	
		F	
		T	
		F	
		T	
		F	
		T	
		F	

The next column to the left alternates truth-values every two lines, the next alternates every four, and so on. So an easy way to construct truth-values is to proceed from right to left in this manner until the table is complete.

$$\downarrow$$

p	q	r	$(p$ · ~ $q)$ $\supset$ $[(p \lor r)$ $\lor$ ~ $r)]$
T	T	T	
T	T	F	
T	F	T	
T	F	F	
F	T	T	
F	T	F	
F	F	T	
F	F	F	

3. Now we are ready to begin computing the truth table of the sentence form. Basically, we proceed in the same order used in computing single lines, only completing entire columns at a time. (We could proceed by rows instead of columns, but this would go much slower.) First, we place truth-values in columns directly below the variables. This amounts to merely repeating the relevant column already displayed on the left-hand portion of the line.

									↓						
p	q	r	(p	·	~	q)	⊃	[(p	∨	r)	∨	~	r]		
T	T	T	T			T		T		T			T		
T	T	F	T			T		T		F			F		
T	F	T	T			F		T		T			T		
T	F	F	T			F		T		F			F		
F	T	T	F			T		F		T			T		
F	T	F	F			T		F		F			F		
F	F	T	F			F		F		T			T		
F	F	F	F			F		F		F			F		

4. The next step is to begin computing the truth-value of the compound components of the sentence form. We begin with negated variables.

					↓								
p	q	r	(p	·	~	q)	⊃	[(p	∨	r)	∨	~	r]
T	T	T	T		F	T		T		T		F	T
T	T	F	T		F	T		T		F		T	F
T	F	T	T		T	F		T		T		F	T
T	F	F	T		T	F		T		F		T	F
F	T	T	F		F	T		F		T		F	T
F	T	F	F		F	T		F		F		T	F
F	F	T	F		T	F		F		T		F	T
F	F	F	F		T	F		F		F		T	F

We continue by computing the truth-values of connectives with greater and greater scope.

					↓								
p	q	r	(p	·	~	q)	⊃	[(p	∨	r)	∨	~	r]
T	T	T	T	F	F	T		T	T	T	T	F	T
T	T	F	T	F	F	T		T	T	F	T	T	F
T	F	T	T	T	T	F		T	T	T	T	F	T
T	F	F	T	T	T	F		T	T	F	T	T	F
F	T	T	F	F	F	T		F	T	T	T	F	T
F	T	F	F	F	F	T		F	F	F	T	T	F
F	F	T	F	F	T	F		F	T	T	T	F	T
F	F	F	F	F	T	F		F	F	F	T	T	F

5. The truth table is complete when we have completed the column below the main connective.

$$\downarrow$$

p	q	r	$(p$	$\cdot$	$\sim$	$q)$	$\supset$	$[(p$	$\vee$	$r)$	$\vee$	$\sim$	$r]$
T	T	T	T	F	F	T	T	T	T	T	T	F	T
T	T	F	T	F	F	T	T	T	T	F	T	T	F
T	F	T	T	T	T	F	T	T	T	T	T	F	T
T	F	F	T	T	T	F	T	T	T	F	T	T	F
F	T	T	F	F	F	T	T	T	F	T	T	F	T
F	T	F	F	F	F	T	T	T	F	F	F	T	T	F
F	F	T	F	F	T	F	T	F	T	T	T	T	F	T
F	F	F	F	F	T	F	T	F	F	F	F	T	T	F

In summary, the division of sentences into tautologies, contradictions, and contingent sentences is of fundamental importance. In the first place, there is an important relationship between tautologies and valid arguments. To every valid argument there corresponds a tautologous conditional sentence whose antecedent is the conjunction of the premises and whose consequent is the conclusion (see p. 73). And in the second place, the truth-values of all tautologies and contradictions can be determined by logic alone, without appeal to experience or to any kind of empirical test, although this is not the case for contingent sentences. Thus the division into tautologies, contradictions, and contingent sentences is pertinent to basic philosophical questions about the ways in which knowledge can be acquired.

Exercise 3-6

Determine which of the following sentences are tautologies, which are contradictions, and which are contingent. You must first find the logical form of the statement, then the truth table for that form.

1. $\sim (A \cdot \sim A)$ 4. $A \supset (A \vee B)$

2. $\sim (A \equiv \sim A)$ 5. $A \equiv (B \vee \sim B)$

3. $A \vee (A \supset B)$ 6. $A \equiv (B \vee A)$

7. $(A \cdot B) \supset (\sim A \supset \sim B)$

8. $(B \supset A) \supset (A \supset B)$

9. $(A \equiv B) \equiv (A \supset B)$

10. $(B \vee A) \supset (A \supset B)$

11. $(A \supset B) \supset (B \supset C)$

12. $A \supset [B \supset (A \supset C)]$

13. $[(A \cdot B) \cdot C] \vee [(A \cdot C) \vee (A \cdot B)]$

14. $\{A \supset [(B \vee C) \vee (D \vee \sim B)]\} \vee \sim A$

15. $\{(C \supset D) \supset [A \cdot (C \vee D)]\} \equiv [A \supset (D \supset C)]$

4 *Logical Equivalences*

In algebra, finding identities or equivalences amongst operations on numbers is a main goal. That the sum of 3 and 2 is equivalent to the sum of 2 and 3 is of interest to a mathematician; the equivalence is an instance of the fact that $x + y = y + x$ for any two numbers x and y; that is, the "+" sign is commutative. In logic too, there are important equivalences between statements that are a necessary result of how our operators function. When two statements are logically equivalent, the truth-value of one determines the truth-value of the other; more accurately, each has the same truth-value under the same truth conditions. It is easy to see that this could not be true of two atomic statements, because no atomic statement could by its truth determine the truth of another atomic statement. So if two statements are such that the truth conditions that determine the truth or falsity of one determine the same results in the other, at least one of the two must contain one or more of our logical operators. For example, consider any statement p and its double negation $\sim \sim p$. Any substitution of a statement for p that renders $V(p) = \mathbf{T}$ will, because of the truth table for $\sim$, yield the same truth-value for $\sim \sim p$. The same goes for $V(p) = \mathbf{F}$.

Examples

Consider $A \supset B$ and $\sim A \vee B$.

p	q	p	$\supset$	q	$\sim$	p	$\vee$	q
T	T	T	**T**	T	F	T	**T**	T
T	F	T	**F**	F	F	T	**F**	F
F	T	F	**T**	T	T	F	**T**	T
F	F	F	**T**	F	T	F	**T**	F

These two sentences are logically equivalent since there is no line of the table on which the two sentences forms have different truth-values. Note that if we connected these two sentence forms with "≡" the result would be a **logical equivalence.** Recall the truth table for the tribar. If $p \equiv q$ is a tautological form, then any substitution of a statement for p will be true or will be false under exactly the same conditions as a substitution for q.

p	q	$(p$	$\supset$	$q)$	$\equiv$	$(\sim$	p	$\vee$	$q)$
T	T	T	T	T	**T**	F	T	T	T
T	F	T	F	F	**T**	F	T	F	F
F	T	F	T	T	**T**	T	F	T	T
F	F	F	T	F	**T**	T	F	T	F

This is an important theoretical idea, and it will play a major role in later chapters when we turn to proving formulas from others deductively.

Exercise 3-7

Use a truth table to determine which of the following pairs of sentences are logically equivalent.

1. $A, A \cdot C$
2. $F \vee G, F$
3. $L, L \vee L$
4. $A, A \vee \sim A$
5. $F, \sim F \supset G$
6. $F \cdot \sim F, F \equiv \sim F$
7. $A \cdot \sim A, A \vee \sim A$
8. $A \vee \sim B, A \cdot \sim B$
9. $M \cdot \sim R, (M \vee L) \vee \sim L$
10. $L \supset \sim M, L \cdot M$
11. $\sim (M \supset \sim M), K \vee M$

12. $A \vee B, A \vee (B \supset B)$
13. $(M \vee \sim A) \cdot (M \vee A), M$
14. $(M \cdot \sim A) \supset (M \cdot A), M \cdot A$
15. $(M \cdot \sim A) \vee (M \vee A), M$
16. $A \supset (B \supset A), B \supset (A \supset B)$
17. $\sim (H \cdot \sim K), (\sim H \cdot K) \vee \sim K$
18. $\sim (H \cdot \sim K), (\sim H \cdot \sim K) \vee (H \vee K)$
19. $[(H \cdot K) \supset L] \cdot (K \supset \sim L), H \supset L$
20. $(H \cdot K) \vee (K \cdot L), (\sim H \cdot \sim K) \vee (\sim K \cdot \sim L)$

5   *Truth Table Test of Validity*

We can use truth tables to determine whether any argument in sentential logic is valid. Recall that an argument is valid if and only if it is not possible for its premises to all be true while its conclusion is false. Using the concept introduced earlier, we can say that a sentential logic argument is valid if and only if there is no possible substitution in the forms of the premises and form of the conclusion that will yield true premises and a false conclusion. Recall that by "substitution" we here mean *logical* substitution of truth-values: If the forms of premises and conclusion contain just two variables, there will be four possibilities of substitution of truth-values, if three variables, eight possibilities, and so on. What is being maintained is that if the argument in question is indeed valid, then there will be no line of the truth table for these forms in which all the premises are true and the conclusion false. *If the argument is valid, that is because its form is a valid form.* Look at the following argument and its corresponding forms:

	1. $A \supset B$	$p \supset q$
	2. $B \supset C$	$q \supset r$
	3. $\sim C$	$\sim r$
$\therefore$	4. $\sim A$	$\sim p$

Is this a valid argument? To find out, we test its form by seeing if there is any line in the truth tables that yields all true premises and a false conclusion.

| | | | ↓ | | | ↓ | | | ↓ | | | | |
p	q	r	p	⊃	q	q	⊃	r	~	r	/∴	~	p
T	T	T	T	T	T	T	T	T	F	T		F	T
T	T	F	T	T	T	T	F	F	T	F		F	T
T	F	T	T	F	F	F	T	T	F	T		F	T
T	F	F	T	F	F	F	T	F	T	F		F	T
F	T	T	F	T	T	T	T	T	F	T		T	F
F	T	F	F	T	T	T	F	F	T	F		T	F
F	F	T	F	T	F	F	T	T	F	T		T	F
F	F	F	F	T	F	F	T	F	T	F		T	F

The argument is valid because there is no line on which the premises are all true and the conclusion false. The only line where all the premises are true is line 8 and on that line the conclusion is true as well. Notice in the table that any line in which the truth-values of the premises are both true, the conclusion is made true by those same truth-values. Any argument that has the same form as this one will be valid, *independent of what the premises and conclusion mean or assert.* Validity and invalidity are in this sense independent of the content of what is being argued. Validity depends only on form; truth-values are as close to content as we get. To speak of a substitution instance, then, is to speak of a line (or lines) in a truth table, because any substitution instance has a definite truth-value. So, if in the argument just discussed, $V(A) = \mathbf{T}$, $V(B) = \mathbf{F}$, and $V(C) = \mathbf{T}$, we have an instance of the third line of the preceding table.

Think of it this way. Let $P_1, P_2 \ldots P_n$ be the premises of a sentential argument, and C its conclusion. If there is no possibility that the premises be true and the conclusion false then the statement $P_1 \cdot P_2 \ldots \cdot P_n \cdot \sim C$ *can't* be true. A statement that cannot be true is a contradiction. We know that the negation of a contradiction is a tautology. Thus the statement $\sim (P_1 \cdot P_2 \ldots \cdot P_n \cdot \sim C)$ must be a tautology. Now it turns out—and you can do this yourself as an exercise!—that this tautology is logically equivalent to the statement $(P_1 \cdot P_2 \ldots \cdot P_n) \supset C$! So that too is a tautology and we have found that we can test an argument for validity by conjoining the premises into the antecedent of a conditional, putting the conclusion C in the consequent, and testing its form to see if it is a tautological form. If it is, the argument in question is valid. But after all, this is precisely what to expect from the preceding truth table. In any line, if the premises are true, the conclusion is also, and so $(P_1 \cdot P_2 \ldots P_n) \supset C$ is true in that line. Any line in which one or more of the premises are false, their conjunction $P_1 \cdot P_2 \ldots \cdot P_n$ is false, and so again $(P_1 \cdot P_2 \ldots P_n) \supset C$ must be true, because that is how the ⊃ functions. This statement is called the **corresponding conditional,** or **test statement form, of an argument** and, if it is a tautology, the premises are said to **logically imply** *or entail* the conclusion of the argument, and the antecedent of the conditional is said to logically entail its consequent.

An argument is invalid if it is possible that the premises be true and the conclusion false. We can now give a clear meaning to this use of "possible." Let's take as a premise "John F. Kennedy was assassinated" and as a conclusion, "Lincoln was assassinated." Given the historical facts, there is no possibility that the premise is true and the conclusion false, *but this is not the sense of possibility at issue,* because the argument is nonetheless invalid. Why? Because it has an invalid *form.* The corresponding conditional form for this argument is simply $p \supset q$, and a four line truth table for it shows that if we substitute a true statement for p and a false one for q, we get $V(p \supset q) = \mathbf{F}$ in line 2. So the sense of "possibility" we want is again shown by the lines of the truth table. The truth table shows how to construct what is called a **counterexample:** It tells us what assignment of truth-values will yield true premises and a false conclusion. Coming up with actual statements that are true or are false and substituting them into the form of the argument is a time-honored way of showing invalidity. So if someone argues, for example, that (1) if Smith wins the election fair and square he will be a great chairperson, and (2) it is a fact he is a great chairperson, so it follows that (3) he won the election fair and square, we can give a counterexample. One might as well say that (1) if it is raining now, then the sidewalks are wet, and (2) the sidewalks are wet, therefore (3) it must have rained just now. We point out that the premises are, say in this case, true, yet the sidewalks got wet by using a garden hose. So, even if Smith did win fair and square, it doesn't follow logically from the truth of the premises that he did so. The form of the argument does not *guarantee* a true conclusion from true premises. It matters not that a particular invalid argument has true premises and a true conclusion. Given that it is invalid, its form guarantees *via* at least one line in its truth table, that we get true premises and a false conclusion. In Section 10, you will see more clearly exactly how this works. Let's look at a truth table analysis of the preceding argument about Smith being a great chairperson. The argument and its form look like this:

$$
\begin{array}{ll}
\text{1. } A \supset B & p \supset q \\
\text{2. } B & q \\
\therefore \text{ 3. } A & p
\end{array}
$$

Here is the truth table:

p	q	$(p \supset q)$	q	/ $\therefore p$
T	T	T T T	T	T
T	F	T F F	F	T
F	T	F T T	T	F
F	F	F F T	F	F

Invalidity is shown by the fact that in the third line of the table, if we let $V(p) = \mathbf{F}$ and $V(q) = \mathbf{T}$, then the premises are true and the conclusion false. This is our recipe for a counterexample, which we provided earlier.

Exercise 3-8

Use a truth table to determine which of the following arguments are valid.* Remember, you must first find the logical form of each statement.

(1) 1. $A \cdot B$
     2. $B \supset C$ /∴ C

(2) 1. $C \supset A$
     2. $A \supset (B \cdot C)$
     3. C /∴ B

*From now on we will write the conclusion of an argument to the right of the argument's last premise, preceded by a slash, "/," to keep the items separate.

(3)   1. $(A \cdot B) \supset C$
      2. $A \ / \therefore \ B \supset C$
(4)   1. $(H \cdot K) \supset L$
      2. $H \ / \therefore \ K \supset L$
(5)   1. $\sim D \vee \sim F$
      2. $G \supset (D \cdot F) \ / \therefore \ \sim G$
(6)   1. $A \supset B$
      2. $\sim (C \cdot B)$
      3. $C \ / \therefore \ \sim A$
(7)   1. $\sim (D \vee \sim K)$
      2. $H \supset D \ / \therefore \ H \supset K$
(8)   1. $L \vee N$
      2. $L \supset \sim R$
      3. $R \ / \therefore \ \sim N$
(9)   1. $A \equiv B \ / \therefore \ \sim B \vee A$
(10) 1. $(A \cdot B) \vee C$
      2. $\sim A \ / \therefore \ C$
(11) 1. $F \supset G$
      2. $(G \cdot H) \vee K \ / \therefore \ F$
(12) 1. $(A \cdot B) \vee C$
      2. $\sim (A \vee B) \ / \therefore \ C$

(13) 1. $M \supset N$
      2. $K \supset P$
      3. $N \vee K \ / \therefore \ M \vee P$
(14) 1. $A \vee (\sim B \cdot C)$
      2. $B \supset \sim A \ / \therefore \ \sim B$
(15) 1. $A \supset (A \supset A)$
      2. $B \supset (A \supset B)$
      3. $A \supset B \ / \therefore \ B$
(16) 1. $A \supset B$
      2. $C \supset D$
      3. $B \vee D \ / \therefore \ A \vee C$
(17) 1. $\sim (A \vee \sim B)$
      2. $C \supset A \ / \therefore \ C \supset D$
(18) 1. $A \supset B$
      2. $C \supset D$
      3. $B \vee C \ / \therefore \ A \vee D$
(19) 1. $L \supset M$
      2. $K \supset P$
      3. $(M \vee P) \supset Z$
      4. $\sim Z \ / \therefore \ \sim (L \vee K)$
(20) 1. $F \supset (G \supset H)$
      $/ \therefore \ (\sim H \cdot K) \supset (G \supset \sim F)$

6 *Truth Table Test of Consistency*

Just as we can use truth tables to check for validity, so also we can use truth tables to determine whether a set of sentences is consistent. In sentential logic a set of sentences is consistent if and only if there is at least one line in the truth table for the conjunction of all the sentence forms in which each substitution instance is true. To use a truth table to check for consistency, simply construct the table for the conjunction of the forms and look for a line on which all the substitutions are true. Since the truth table displays all the logically possible substitutions for the forms of the set being tested, the set is consistent if and only if there is such a line.

Examples

			↓			↓			↓	
p	*q*	*p*	$\supset$	*q*	*p*	$\vee$	*q*	$\sim$	*q*	
T	T	T	T	T	T	T	T	F	T	
T	F	T	F	F	T	T	F	T	F	
F	T	F	T	T	F	T	T	F	T	
F	F	F	T	F	F	F	F	T	F	

This truth table shows that the set of sentences

    1. $A \supset B$
    2. $A \vee B$
    3. $\sim B$

is inconsistent, because there is no line on which all of their forms are true.

However, the set

    1. $A \supset B$
    2. $A \vee \sim B$
    3. $\sim A$

is shown to be consistent by line 4 of the following truth table:

		↓			↓				↓	
p	*q*	*p*	⊃	*q*	*p*	∨	∼	*q*	∼	*p*
T	T	T	T	T	T	T	F	T	F	T
T	F	T	F	F	T	T	T	F	F	T
F	T	F	T	T	F	F	F	T	T	F
F	F	F	T	F	F	T	T	F	T	F

Exercise 3-9

Use a truth table to show whether each of the following sets of sentences is consistent.

    1. $A \equiv B, A \supset \sim B$
    2. $A \equiv B, A \equiv \sim B$
    3. $A \equiv B, B, \sim B \vee \sim A$
    4. $A \supset B, \sim B \vee \sim C, C \cdot \sim A$
    5. $R \supset S, T \supset R, \sim (T \supset S)$
    6. $(K \cdot L) \supset \sim M, K \supset M, L \supset M$
    7. $A \equiv B, C, C \supset \sim B$
    8. $A \equiv \sim B, A, B \vee C, \sim C$
    9. $\sim (A \equiv B), A \equiv \sim B, A \vee B$
  10. $(H \supset J) \vee (H \supset K), \sim (J \vee K), H$

7   *Validity and Consistency*

We are now ready to cash in a suggestion made in Section 6: Any test of consistency can be used as a test of validity. To see why this is so, let's introduce the notion of an argument's **counterexample set.** The counterexample set of an argument consists of the premises of the argument together with the denial of the conclusion. For example, the counterexample set for the following argument

1. $\sim A \supset \sim B$
2. $B \vee C$ $/\therefore$ $\sim A \supset C$

is the set consisting of the following three sentences:

1. $\sim A \supset \sim B$
2. $B \vee C$
3. $\sim [\sim A \supset C]$

We can now say that for an argument to be invalid is just the same as for its counterexample set to be consistent—that is, for the conjunction of the premises together with the negation of the conclusion to be consistent. Put in terms of validity, an argument is valid if and only if the conjunction of the premises together with the negation of the conclusion is inconsistent. Recall that a valid argument is defined as any argument such that it is not possible for its premises to be true and its conclusion false, which amounts to it not being possible for the premises of the argument and the denial of the conclusion all to be true.

We can now entertain a powerful and somewhat shocking result. Suppose we have an argument that has inconsistent—that is, contradictory—premises. What conclusion can we draw about the validity of the argument? The answer is that all arguments with inconsistent premises are valid. Obviously, if it is not possible for even all the premises to be true, it is not possible for all the premises to be true *and* the denial of the conclusion to be true as well. This surprising result will be borne out if you think of testing such arguments for validity using a truth table. Consider, for example, an argument that has A as one premise and $\sim A$ as the other premise. The truth table for this argument is guaranteed not to have a line on which all the premises are true and the conclusion false (no matter what its conclusion is), because there is not even a line where all the premises are true.

Likewise, any argument whose conclusion is a tautology is also valid no matter what its premises. Since it is not possible to make a tautology false, it is not possible for the premises of the argument to be true and the conclusion false.

This leaves us with three varieties of valid arguments—the normal sort and two special cases. These different kinds of valid argument correspond to three different ways the form of an argument can guarantee that it is not possible for the premises of the argument to be true and the conclusion to be false.

The normal case
1. It is possible for all the premises to be true. It is possible for the conclusion to be false as long as at least one premise is false. It is not possible for all the premises to be true and the conclusion to be false.

Two special cases
2. It is not possible for all the premises to be true (the premises are inconsistent); therefore it is not possible for all the premises to be true and the conclusion to be false. When you think of this for a moment more, the somewhat shocking result becomes apparent. The conclusion of such an argument could be any sentence whatever, and the argument would remain valid. Logicians summarize this by saying that from a contradiction anything follows. We will have much more to

say about this result when we get to the notion of indirect proof in succeeding chapters. For now we just make this comment: Some people like to say that a foolish consistency is the hobgoblin of little minds. Once we realize that if we hold inconsistent beliefs we can deductively prove anything whatever from them, consistency does not seem such a bad thing! One would have to have a very large mind to hold all the things one can prove from an inconsistency and, as is true in many areas, bigger is not always better!

3. It is not possible for the conclusion of the argument to be false (the conclusion is a tautology); therefore, it is not possible for the premises to all be true and the conclusion to be false.

As a shorthand way of summarizing these last two cases, remember that *anything follows from an inconsistency,* and *a tautology follows from anything.*

8 *The Short Truth Table Test for Invalidity*

We have seen how to use a truth table to demonstrate the *invalidity* of an argument. We can, however, employ a shortcut that enables us to demonstrate invalidity without having to go through the tedium of producing an entire truth table. All it takes to show that an argument is invalid is a single counterexample—a single line of a truth table on which the premises are all true and the conclusion false. It is often possible to produce such a counterexample in short order simply by reversing the process we used to construct truth tables. Instead of starting with the truth-values of the atomic constituents and working outward until we determine the truth-value of the entire sentence, we will start by assigning a truth-value to entire sentences and then work inward to find an appropriate assignment of truth-values to the atomic constituents.

It is easiest to see how this method works by working through a specific example. Suppose we wanted to prove that the following argument is invalid:

1. $A \supset B$
2. B $/\therefore A$

We begin by finding the logical form of the argument, and then *assigning* an **F** to the entire conclusion and a **T** to each premise. Remember, we are *assuming* here that the argument in question is invalid. That means there will be at least one line in the truth table where our assignment reveals itself. Let's go through this in stages, first by assigning a **T** to each of the premises and an **F** to the conclusion.

1. $p \supset q$
      T

2. q $/\therefore p$
     T   **F**

We have to be consistent in our assignments of truth-values, so once a truth-value is assigned to a variable in one line, we must assign the same truth-value to that letter on every other line on which it occurs. So we must make q in the first premise true (since we made q true in the second premise), and p in the first premise must be false (because we made p false in the conclusion).

1. $p \supset q$
     F T T
2. q $/\therefore\ p$
    T   **F**

We have thus, in very short order, produced a counterexample of the argument, where $V(p) = \mathbf{F}$ and $V(q) = \mathbf{T}$.

Let's take a more complicated argument.

1. $A \supset (B \supset D)$
2. $\sim C$
3. $(B \vee C) \supset D /\therefore A \supset B$

Again, we begin by finding the logical form and assigning the desired truth-values:

1. $p \supset (q \supset r)$
       T
2. $\sim s$
    T
3. $(q \vee s) \supset r$ $/\therefore p \supset q$
       T   **F**

When using the shortcut method, always be on the lookout for lines where you are forced to make a particular truth-value assignment. Obviously, anytime you have an atomic sentence form, immediately assign that sentence form the desired truth-value. Likewise, whenever you have a negated atomic sentence form (such as our second premise), you can immediately assign the appropriate truth-value to the atomic sentence form (in this case an **F**). Again, once we've determined the truth-value for a letter, we fill in that truth-value for that letter wherever else it occurs in the proof.

1. $p \supset (q \supset r)$
       T
2. $\sim s$
    T F
3. $(q \vee s) \supset r$ $/\therefore p \supset q$
     F   **T**   **F**

After you have assigned truth-values to any atomic sentence forms and negated atomic sentence forms that occur, you should look for other sentence forms that force your hand. In our example it is unclear at this point how to deal with the first and third premises, but there is only one way to arrive at the desired truth-value for the conclusion. To make a conditional false, one must make the antecedent true and the consequent false. So we must assign $\mathbf{V}(p) = \mathbf{T}$ and $\mathbf{V}(q) = \mathbf{F}$.

1. $p \supset (q \supset r)$
    T T F
2. $\sim \quad s$
    T F
3. $(q \vee s) \supset r$ $/\therefore \ p \supset q$
    F F F T   **T F F**

It turns out not to matter which truth-value is assigned to *r* in this case. There are two counterexamples to this particular argument—$V(p) = $ **T**, $V(q) = $ **F**, $V(r) = $ **T**, $V(s) = $ **F** and $V(p) = $ **T**, $V(q) = $ **F**, $V(r) = $ **F**, $V(s) = $ **F**. All that it takes to show that the argument is invalid is a single counterexample, so let's just, say, make *r* true and produce our counterexample as follows:

1. $p \supset (q \supset r)$
    T T F T T
2. $\sim \quad s$
    T F
3. $(q \vee s) \supset r$ $/\therefore \ p \supset q$
    F F F T T   **T F F**

It is interesting to notice what happens when we try to prove a *valid* argument invalid by this method. Consider the valid argument and corresponding form

1. $[(A \cdot B) \supset \sim C]$ $[(p \cdot q) \supset \sim r]$
2. A p
3. $C /\therefore \sim B$ $r \ /\therefore \sim q$

In this example, we must assign $V(q) = $ **T** to falsify the conclusion, and $V(p) = $ **T**, as well as $V(r) = $ **T**, to render the second and third premises true. But notice that if we do so, then we falsify the first premise, as the following indicates:

1. $[(p \cdot q) \supset \sim r]$
    T T T F F T
2. p
    T
3. r $/\therefore \sim q$
    T   **F T**

Because the argument is valid, there is no way to falsify the conclusion and at the same time render all the premises true.

The argument we just examined is a simple case, because only one assignment of truth-values make the conclusion false and the second and third premises true, and on that assignment we cannot get the first premise true. But in more complex arguments there may be more than one assignment that yields a false conclusion, for example, if the conclusion had the form $p \cdot q$, then either $V(p) = $ **F** or $V(q) = $ **F** yields a false conclusion, and we would then have to see whether these assignments and the assignments to the other variables would yield at least one false premise. It follows that *if we don't know* whether the argument we are testing is valid or invalid, the assignment of a false conclusion may not help us much. What to do? The truth tables are our resource here. Suppose, for example, you have made a 16-line table, reflecting that you are making assignments to four variables. You don't need to work every line. Find the lines in which the conclusion is false, given the assignments to the variables, and then see whether, in those lines, the premises are true. If there is one line in which the premises are true and the conclusion false, the argument is invalid; otherwise, it is valid.

Later, we will examine an ingenious method for showing validity and invalidity called truth trees. But they too are based on assignments of truth-values, so the concept of the truth table is basic to our work in sentential logic.

Exercise 3-10

Use the short truth table method to show that the following arguments are invalid. Give the truth-value assignments that show the invalidity. For the purposes of this exercise, you may treat the sentence letters *as if* they were variables.

(1)   1. $H \supset K$
     2. $\sim H$ /∴ $\sim K$

(2)   1. $A \supset B$
     2. B /∴ A

(3)   1. $(H \cdot K) \supset L$ /∴ $L \supset (K \cdot H)$

(4)   1. $R \vee N$
     2. $L \supset N$
     3. R /∴ $\sim N$

(5)   1. $(\sim R \vee M) \supset N$
     2. $\sim N$ /∴ $\sim R$

(6)   1. $A \supset B$
     2. $(C \cdot B) \vee D$ /∴ A

(7)   1. $A \supset \sim B$
     2. $(B \cdot C) \vee A$ /∴ $\sim B$

(8)   1. $[A \supset (\sim A \supset A)] \supset \sim A$ /∴ A

(9)   1. $H \equiv (K \vee L)$
     2. $K \equiv (L \vee H)$
     3. $L \equiv (H \vee K)$
     4. $\sim H$ /∴ $H \vee (K \vee L)$

(10)   1. $[(A \supset B) \supset C] \supset D$
      2. $D \supset [C \supset (B \supset A)]$ /∴ $A \equiv D$

(11)   1. $P \supset Q$
      2. $R \supset S$
      3. $R \vee Q$ /∴ $P \vee S$

(12)   1. $(A \cdot B) \supset (C \vee D)$
      2. $C \supset A$
      3. $\sim C \vee \sim D$
      4. B /∴ $A \supset D$

(13)   1. $A \supset (B \supset C)$
      2. $C \supset (D \supset E)$
      3. $A \supset B$
      4. $E \supset A$ /∴ $D \supset E$

(14)   1. $A \supset B$
      2. $\sim (B \vee C)$
      3. $D \supset (C \vee A)$
      4. $E \supset (D \vee F)$ /∴ $\sim E$

(15)   1. $(A \vee B) \supset C$
      2. $D \supset (\sim E \supset B)$
      3. $(E \supset A) \supset \sim F$
      4. $\sim C \vee (B \vee F)$ /∴ $B \equiv C$

(16)   1. $\sim [(R \cdot \sim L) \cdot (L \cdot \sim R)]$
      2. $\sim [(D \cdot \sim R) \cdot (R \vee \sim D)]$
      3. $\sim [(D \cdot \sim L) \vee (L \cdot \sim D)]$ /∴ L

(17)   1. $(R \vee S) \supset T$
      2. $T \supset [(S \cdot L) \vee V]$
      3. $(L \cdot \sim S) \vee (R \vee \sim S)$
      4. $\sim R \supset (V \vee \sim T)$
         /∴ $R \supset (L \supset \sim S)$

(18)   1. $A \supset (B \cdot C)$
      2. $\sim D \vee \sim E$
      3. $D \supset (A \vee F)$
      4. $F \supset (C \supset E)$ /∴ $F \vee \sim D$

(19)   1. $(H \vee \sim R) \cdot (K \supset L)$
      2. $S \supset (M \supset T)$
      3. $R \supset (T \supset N)$
      4. $K \vee R$
      5. $(H \vee L) \supset (M \cdot S)$ /∴ R

(20)   1. $Q \supset W$
      2. $\sim P \supset \sim W$
      3. $\sim N$
      4. $W \supset (P \vee Q)$
      5. $R \supset (S \vee T)$
      6. $S \supset (Q \vee N)$
         /∴ $R \supset (\sim Q \supset W)$

9 The Short Truth Table Test for Consistency

All that it takes to show that a set of sentences is consistent is to produce a single line in a truth table that makes them all true. We can use the short truth table method introduced in the previous section to do just this. Suppose, for example, we want to show that the premises of an argument are consistent. Here, instead of attempting to make premises true and conclusions false, we need only to find a way to make the premises true.

For example, suppose we want to show that the argument

1. $A \supset B$
2. $A \supset \sim B$ /∴ ~ A

has consistent premises. We begin by assigning a **T** to both sentence forms and work backward, as before, until we come up with a complete line of a truth table. The current example may take a little trial and error, but it is possible to produce such an interpretation so long as we make p false. So, for example, by producing the following truth-values we show that these sentences are consistent:

1. $p \supset q$
    F T T

2. $p \supset \sim q$ /∴ ~ p
    F T F T

(We could just as well have made q false.)

Exercise 3-11

Use the short truth table method to show that the following sets of premises are consistent. Again, you may treat the sentence letters *as if* they were variables for purposes of this exercise.

(1) 1. $B \supset A$
     2. $C \supset B$
     3. $\sim C \cdot A$ /∴ $A \supset C$

(2) 1. $\sim (F \equiv G)$
     2. $\sim (F \supset H)$ /∴ F

(3) 1. $(D \supset E) \vee (D \supset C)$
     2. A
     3. $A \supset (C \supset D)$ /∴ $A \cdot D$

(4) 1. $F \equiv \sim G$
     2. $\sim (F \vee H)$
     3. $F \vee G$ /∴ G

(5) 1. $A \cdot \sim B$
     2. $B \vee \sim C$
     3. $\sim (\sim C \cdot B)$ /∴ $\sim B \cdot C$

(6) 1. $(A \vee B) \supset C$
     2. $C \supset A$
     3. $\sim (D \supset C)$ /∴ $\sim A$

(7) 1. $\sim [(A \vee B) \supset (C \vee D)]$
     2. $C \supset \sim A$
     3. $D \supset E$ /∴ $\sim (A \supset C)$

(8) 1. $A \supset (B \cdot \sim C)$
     2. $D \supset E$
     3. $\sim (\sim D \vee F)$
     4. $D \supset (A \vee C)$
     5. $C \supset (\sim F \supset \sim C)$ /∴ $B \cdot \sim F$

10 *A Method of Justification for the Truth Tables*

One reason for building truth tables is to explain what is meant by saying that in a valid argument, if the premises are true the conclusion must be true (that is, cannot possibly be false). A happy consequence of building the tables is that they also provide a mechanical decision procedure for determining the truth-value of every statement in sentential logic and, therefore, for the validity of every sentential argument.

However, the connection between the truth tables for a logical connective of our symbolic language and the corresponding connective in ordinary language needs to be clarified. As you know, words such as "or" and "and" and "if . . . then" have many uses in English; we need to see more clearly which uses are codified by the truth tables and, in the case of "if . . . then," whether any are accurately codified at all. In the case of the horseshoe, there has been skepticism among philosophers and logicians because of the third and fourth lines of its truth table: It somehow seems wrong, even counterintuitive, to count a conditional as true when its antecedent is false. It has thus been argued that the horseshoe doesn't represent any English use of "if . . . then." Many textbooks in the past have given very weak justifications for the horseshoe table, using English examples, for example, "If Hitler was a good guy, then I'm a monkey's uncle." Because both the antecedent and consequent are false, yet the speaker allegedly intends the whole to be true, this is supposed to be an example of the fourth line of the truth table for the horseshoe. However, critics point out that the statement in question is really a badly expressed version of a statement in the subjunctive mood, and subjunctives are not truth-functional. Fortunately, we can do much better than appeal to such statements in justifying the truth table for the horseshoe and, for that matter, any connective in our sentential language.

We can build the truth table for *any* connective given the following information: (1) A set of intuitively valid and invalid arguments (there are certain restrictions on this set; see Exercise 3-12, number 4). (2) In a valid argument, if the premises are true the conclusion must be. (3) In an invalid argument, there must be the logical possibility that the premises are true and the conclusion false; if that logical possibility does not exist, then the argument is valid, not invalid.

Sentential arguments are just those whose validity or invalidity depend on connections between statements. For example, consider the following argument:

> Premiums will be waived in the event of sickness or unemployment.
> It is not the case that premiums will be waived in the event of sickness.
> Therefore, premiums will be waived in the event of unemployment.

This argument depends for its validity on the connection between statements, which connections are a function of the logical connectives *not* and *or* (in this case, clearly the inclusive *or*). Suppose now that we want to translate this argument into our symbolism; pretend for the sake of the example that this symbolism *does not yet contain the wedge* but does contain the tilde. Let's now introduce the wedge as a symbol and propose the following translation of the argument's logical form into sentential logic:

$$p \lor q$$
$$\sim p$$
$$\therefore \quad q$$

We know that the original argument in English is valid, so we assume it has at least one valid form. Let A and B be two statements, where A is substituted for p and B for q. Let $V(B) = \mathbf{F}$, and let $V(A) = \mathbf{F}$, so that ~ A is true. The argument thus has a false conclusion and its second premise true. Under these conditions, how shall we count $p \lor q$? If we count it as true, then the argument will have true premises and false conclusion; yet by hypothesis it is valid. Thus we must count $V(p \lor q)$ as false under the conditions that $V(p) = \mathbf{F}$ and $V(q) = \mathbf{F}$. If we did not do this, then our truth table for the wedge would not capture the fact that the original argument in English is valid, and our proposed translation would have failed.

It thus becomes clear that we are building the truth tables the way they are to *preserve* the validity of arguments that are intuitively valid, and the invalidity of arguments that are intuitively invalid. The argument in question has enabled us to determine one line of the truth table for the wedge.

But what of the other lines? After all, there are four, and the argument in question doesn't seem to determine any but the last. To get the others, we must look to other arguments in English using *or*, and to use a procedure similar to the one we just performed. For example, consider any intuitively invalid argument in English whose translated form is

$$p \lor q$$
$$p$$
$$\therefore \quad q$$

If this form were valid, there would be no way to substitute for the variables to get true premises and a false conclusion. But since it is invalid, there must be such a way. That is, under the conditions that its conclusion is false and its second premise true, we must count $V(p \lor q)$ as true; thus the second line of the truth table for the wedge. If we did not do this, there would be no way to get the premises true and the conclusion false, and the argument would be valid—but we know it is invalid. That fact *forces* us to assign $V(p \lor q) = \mathbf{T}$, when $V(p) = \mathbf{T}$ and $V(q) = \mathbf{F}$. To get more lines of the truth table, we would need more arguments, which are intuitively valid or intuitively invalid.

To see the point (about forcing an assignment) more clearly, consider the following. There are only four ways to substitute for p and q in the given argument form. Either both are true, or both false, or one is true and the other false. Let us represent these ways by writing, instead of statement letters, their truth-values:

(1) $\mathbf{T} \lor \mathbf{T}$	(2) $\mathbf{T} \lor \mathbf{F}$	(3) $\mathbf{F} \lor \mathbf{T}$	(4) $\mathbf{F} \lor \mathbf{F}$
$\mathbf{T}$	$\mathbf{T}$	$\mathbf{F}$	$\mathbf{F}$
$\mathbf{T}$	$\mathbf{F}$	$\mathbf{T}$	$\mathbf{F}$

Do any of these show that the argument form in question is invalid? (2) would, *if* we counted the compound $\mathbf{T} \lor \mathbf{F}$ as $\mathbf{T}$. *But suppose we don't, and count it (mistakenly) as false.* Then (2) is compatible with the argument form being valid. And so are (1), (3), and (4); in none of them is it possible to get true premises and a false conclusion. Thus *no assignment of truth-values* would make the premises true and the conclusion false, and the argument form would turn out to be valid. Because we know it is invalid, we assign $V(\mathbf{T} \lor \mathbf{F}) = \mathbf{T}$ in (2).

The preceding shows you how to proceed in justifying truth tables: Find valid and invalid argument forms, using the connective in question, that force the lines of the truth table. To force a line of a table for a connective, find a valid form using the connective. Assign the conclusion as false, then try to deduce the truth-value assignment for the compound using the connective. For example, given the valid argument form

$$p \supset q$$
$$p$$
$$\therefore \quad q$$

start by assigning $V(q) = \mathbf{F}$. Now if we assign $V(p) = \mathbf{T}$, then since the argument is valid, we know $V(p \supset q) = \mathbf{F}$; it couldn't be $\mathbf{T}$ or we would have true premises and a false conclusion, which no valid form can have as a substitution instance.

It is now easy to show why the four lines of the truth table for the horseshoe are the way they are. Consider the following four arguments, only the first of which is valid; their logical forms in our notation are also given:

(A) If Bob loves Sally, then Sally loves Bob. $p \supset q$
     Bob loves Sally. p
     Therefore Sally loves Bob. $\therefore q$

(B) If Bob loves Sally, then Sally loves Bob. $p \supset q$
     Bob doesn't love Sally. $\sim p$
     Therefore, Sally does not love Bob. $\therefore \sim q$

(C) If Bob loves Sally, then Sally loves Bob. $p \supset q$
     Sally does not love Bob. $\sim q$
     Therefore, Bob loves Sally. $\therefore p$

(D) If Bob loves Sally, then Sally loves Bob. $p \supset q$
     Bob loves Sally. p
     Therefore, Sally does not love Bob. $\therefore \sim q$

Now, if you work through each of these four you will find that each determines one and only one line of the truth table for the horseshoe. Most important, line 3 is determined by (B) and line 4 by (C). So the reason why we count a horseshoe statement true when its antecedent is false is that if we did not do so arguments (B) and (C) would end up valid according to our logical system. This would be a most unhappy result, because we know both are intuitively invalid.

Here is a set of exercises to help test your abilities on justification of truth tables. Note that the first four exercises here reverse the procedure we have been following. Earlier, we began with argument forms and constructed lines of truth tables "forced" by these lines. Here, to test your knowledge of what is happening, we go backwards; we start with lines of truth tables and work backward to argument forms that "force" those lines.

Exercise 3-12

1. Construct an argument form, which forces us to say that a conjunction (in our sense, that is, the dot) is false when both its conjuncts are. Briefly explain your construction.

2. Find four argument forms, each one of which justifies a different line of the truth table for the tribar. Briefly explain your constructions.

3. Given the "unknown" connective "$p ! q$," such that it is true in the first line of its truth table and false in its third (given the conventional way we build truth tables), find argument forms that determine these lines. Briefly explain your work.

4. *Given* that the following argument form is *valid*, is there any way to determine a line of the truth table for "$p \# q$"? Why or why not? Is there a lesson here for our justificatory procedure?

$$p$$
$$q$$
$$\therefore \quad p \# q$$

5. Now for a do-it-yourself *mystery* connective. Give a truth table for a mystery connective (that is, it shouldn't be one of the standard operators we know and love), then make up argument forms, which justify each line. Briefly explain your work.

6. (*Note:* This one is very tricky. Think of it as a graduation exercise!) Determine a line of the truth table for the mystery connective "$*$," given that the following is an invalid argument form. You may assume you know the tables for the wedge and tilde. Explain your work.

$$p * \sim q$$
$$p \vee q$$
$$\therefore \quad q$$

Exercise 3-13—Exercises over Chapter Three

1. What is a valuation? Is it possible for a given statement A that occurs in the compound premises and conclusion of an argument, to have more than one valuation in that argument?

2. Can a sentence be a substitution instance of more than one sentence form? Explain, including an original example.

3. Some substitution instances of contingent sentence forms are not themselves contingent sentences. Do any substitution instances of tautologous sentence forms exist that are not themselves tautologous sentences?

4. Suppose the conclusion of an argument is a tautology. What do we know about the validity or invalidity of the argument?

5. If a sentence form contains four variables, how many lines must its complete truth table analysis have?

6. Suppose you know only that one of the premises of an argument is a contradiction. What, if anything, can you conclude about the argument's validity? Explain.

7. If the premises of a valid argument are consistent, is its conclusion necessarily true? (Give an example.)

8. Suppose you know that a particular argument is deductively valid and has a false conclusion. What, if anything, can you tell from this about its premises?

Key Terms Introduced in Chapter Three

contingent sentence: A sentence whose one–one form has at least one **T** and at least one **F** in the truth table.

contingent sentence form: A sentence form that has at least one true and one false substitution instance. A statement may have a contingent form yet not be a contingency.

contradiction: A sentence whose logical form guarantees that it is false. Every contradiction is a substitution instance of a contradictory sentence form.

contradictory sentence form: A sentence form that has all **Fs** in its truth table. Synonym: *contradiction*.

corresponding conditional of an argument: The conditional whose antecedent is the conjunction of the argument's premises (adding parentheses where appropriate) and whose consequent is the argument's conclusion. An argument is valid if and only if its corresponding conditional is a tautology.

counterexample of an argument: A substitution instance that makes the premises true and the conclusion false. A sentential logic argument is valid if and only if it has no counterexample.

counterexample set: The set consisting of the premises of an argument together with the denial of the argument's conclusion. An argument is valid if and only if its counterexample set is inconsistent.

logical equivalence: A tautology whose main connective is "$\equiv$." A tautological equivalence whose truth can be determined by means of logic alone.

logically equivalent: A sentence p is logically equivalent to a sentence q if and only if $p \equiv q$ is a tautology. Thus p and q have the same truth-values in every line of the truth-table.

logical implication: A tautology whose main connective is "$\supset$."

logically implies: A sentence p logically implies a sentence q if and only if it is not possible for p to be true and q false.

sentence form: An expression containing sentence variables, such that if all its sentence variables are replaced by sentence constants, the resulting expression is a sentence.

substitution instance: A sentence obtained from a sentence form by replacing all the sentence variables in the sentence form by sentences, making sure that every occurrence of a given sentence variable is replaced by the same sentence.

tautologous sentence form: A sentence form all of whose substitution instances are true. Synonym: *tautology*.

tautology: A sentence whose logical form guarantees that it is true. Every tautology is a substitution instance of a tautologous form.

test statement form: (See *corresponding conditional of an argument*.)

truth table analysis: A method for determining the truth-value of a sentence from knowledge of the truth-values of its component sentences. Similarly, a method for determining whether a sentence form is tautologous, contradictory, or contingent by considering the truth-values of all possible substitution instances, and for determining the validity of arguments in sentential logic.

valuation: An assignment of truth-values to atomic statements from which the truth-value of compound statements in which they occur can be calculated using truth tables. A substitution instance of a compound sentence form can be considered, after a valuation of its atomic components is made, to be a line in a truth table. Thus a compound statement form, which contains two variables, has only four substitution instances, as shown by its four-line truth table.

Chapter Four

Proofs

---

1 *Argument Forms*

As stated in Chapter One, an *argument* consists of a list of sentences, one of which (the conclusion) is claimed to be supported by the others (the premises). An **argument form** is a group of *sentence forms* such that all its substitution instances are arguments. For example, all substitution instances of the form

    1. $p \supset q$
    2. $p / \therefore q$

are arguments, and hence that form is an argument form. (Of course, in substituting into an argument form, every occurrence of a given sentence variable must be replaced by the same sentence wherever that variable occurs in the argument form.) The order of the premises in an argument is irrelevant. Thus,

    1. $A \supset B$ and   1. A
    2. $A / \therefore B$ 2. $A \supset B / \therefore B$

both can be thought of as substitution instances of the preceding form.

Examples

The following arguments are substitution instances of the argument form

    1. $p \supset q$
    2. $p / \therefore q$

(1) 1. $A \supset B$ (3) 1. $(A \vee B)$
     2. $A / \therefore B$ 2. $(A \vee B) / \therefore C$

(2) 1. $H \supset \sim K$ (4) 1. $\sim (A \cdot B) \supset (C \vee D)$
     2. $H / \therefore \sim K$ 2. $\sim (A \cdot B) / \therefore (C \vee D)$

If an argument form has no substitution instances that are invalid, it is said to be a **valid argument form.** Every valid argument is a substitution instance of at least one valid form. Of course, no substitution instances of a valid argument form could have all its premises true and its conclusion false, or, to put this another way, an invalid argument cannot be a substitution instance of a valid argument form. An argument form that has even one invalid argument as a substitution instance is called an **invalid argument form.** Remember, though, that when we speak of substitution instances in connection with the truth tables, we are in effect speaking of the logical possibilities of substitution: If the argument form contains three variables, there are really just eight substitution instances, one for each line of the eight-line truth table for the argument form.

We can use truth table analysis to demonstrate the validity of any argument form. Take the argument form just mentioned:

1. $p \supset q$
2. $p / \therefore q$

The truth table analysis for this argument form is as follows:

p	q	p	p	$\supset$	q	$/\therefore q$
T	T	T	T	T	T	T
T	F	T	T	F	F	F
F	T	F	F	T	T	T
F	F	F	F	T	F	F

Notice there is a **T** for both premises only on line 1 of this truth table, and there also is a **T** for the conclusion on that line. Hence, there is no substitution instance of this argument form having all its premises true and its conclusion false. Therefore, this argument form is a valid argument form.

An example of a valid argument in English having this form is

1. If it's fall, then winter can't be far away.
2. It's fall.
/∴ 3. Winter can't be far away.

Or, in symbols,

1. $F \supset \sim W$
2. F
/∴ 3. $\sim W$

Now consider the invalid argument form

1. $p \supset q$
2. $\sim p / \therefore \sim q$

Its truth table analysis is as follows:

p q	$\sim p$	$p \supset q$	$/\therefore \sim q$
T T	**F T**	**T T T**	**F T**
T F	**F T**	**T F F**	**T F**
F T	**T F**	**F T T**	**F T**
F F	**T F**	**F T F**	**T F**

Both premises yield a **T** on lines 3 and 4 of this truth table. But although the conclusion yields a **T** on the fourth line, it yields an **F** on the third. Thus line 3 of this truth table indicates it is possible for a substitution instance of this argument form to have true premises and a false conclusion, and therefore proves the argument form is not deductively valid.

Here is an example of an invalid argument in English that has this form (with its symbolization on the right):

    1. If it rained last night, then the streets are wet.   1. $R \supset W$

    2. It did not rain last night.   2. $\sim R$

/∴ 3. The streets are not wet.   /∴ 3. $\sim W$

Clearly, this argument is invalid. (If the street cleaner just came along, the streets may be wet even though both premises are true, so it is possible for this argument to have true premises and a false conclusion.)

2   *The Method of Proof: Modus Ponens and Modus Tollens*

Truth tables are the crucial *semantic* device (see the key terms list at the end of Chapter Two) used in sentential logic. They give us a **decision procedure** for any sentential argument; that is, a procedure that you, or a suitably constructed machine can follow that—when you follow it correctly—will always yield the right answer to the question over the validity of the argument. As you will see later, another infallible method, called truth trees, yields the same result.

However, we do not always have decision-making computers available, and making truth tables can be tedious—even a 16-line table is taxing on the eye and the patience. There is another method available to demonstrate validity (but *not invalidity*) of sentential arguments: the *method of proof*, sometimes called *natural deduction*. If we know that certain argument forms are truth table valid, we can use them to show that arguments that are instances of them are valid. A **proof of an argument** is a series of steps that start with premises; each step beyond the premises is derived from a valid argument form by being a substitution instance of it; the last step is the conclusion (we will have occasion to modify this definition a bit later in the book). Let's take an example.

The argument form just proved valid, namely,

    $p \supset q$
    $p /\therefore q$

is called **Modus Ponens** (abbreviated **MP**).

This form tells us that any time you have two lines of a proof, one of which has the form $p \supset q$ and the other of which has the form p, you can validly infer q. (Again, the order in which these lines occur is irrelevant.) For example, here is a proof that uses this argument form twice:*

1. $A \supset (B \vee C)$ p (premise)
2. $(B \vee C) \supset D$ p
3. A p $/\therefore D$
4. $B \vee C$ 1,3 **MP**
5. D 2,4 **MP**

Each line of a proof must be justified in virtue of being a substitution instance of a valid argument form. Take line 4: Here we have substituted A for p (we will henceforth write A / p) and $B \vee C$ for q ($B \vee C / q$). In line 5 we have $B \vee C / p$ and D / q in order to derive the conclusion D. You can think of each new line of a proof as the conclusion of a short argument whose premises are the lines cited to the right of the new line.

Now, clearly there are lots and lots of valid argument forms, **MP** being only one. So which other valid argument forms are we allowed to use? Most logic texts, and this one is no exception, provide a convenient list—see the inside front cover of the book. What determines the list is (1) convenience to the student and (2) the **completeness** of the list. We must be able to demonstrate that the list can prove valid any sentential argument *that is truth table valid.* It turns out that our list is demonstrably complete but that a different, shorter list is also demonstrably complete—there are, indeed, many complete lists. A shorter list (mathematicians would term such a list more *elegant* than ours) makes proofs more difficult.

The method of proof is a *syntactic* method for proving validity, it depends only on the geometric shapes of the signs in the argument forms and the arguments that are substitution instances of them. Natural deduction is a game based on geometric design. In the 1960s, a logic game called Wff'n Proof—well-formed formulas and proof—was introduced by some Yale University students (the name of the game is a play on words of the title of a famous Yale song). Although the game used a different notation from what we use—so-called Polish notation, discussed in Chapter Two, Section 15—its basic idea was to produce natural deduction proofs, and very young children learned quite successfully to play the game without knowing anything about the theory of logic! All they did was follow rules for manipulating shapes. But the rules themselves would have no force unless we could justify them by some other method, in this case, the method of truth tables. Otherwise, any form could be proposed as a rule and followed faithfully by a machine or by us. Thus, using the method of rules, one is ultimately relying on the reasonableness of the truth tables.

The recognition of sentence forms is crucial. You must be able to look, say, at the first premise just given and see that it is a substitution instance of the form $p \supset q$, where for p we substitute A and for q we substitute $B \vee C$. In using the valid argument forms, we may substitute any sentences, no matter how complex, provided we substitute consistently—that is, provided that whatever we substitute for one occurrence of a particular variable also is substituted for every occurrence of that variable in the given use of that argument form.

---

*We use the letter p (not italicized) to indicate an argument's premises.

Because we already have the sentence substituted for p (namely, A) elsewhere in the proof (line 3), we can use **MP** to add the substitution instance of q (in this case, $B \lor C$) as our new line 4. We can then use **MP** with lines 2 and 4 to produce our conclusion as line 5. This time $B \lor C$ is substituted for p and D for q.

Another of the our valid argument forms is **Modus Tollens (MT):**

$$p \supset q$$
$$\sim q \, / \therefore \sim p$$

Here is an example of a valid argument having this form (with its symbolization on the right):

	1. If it's spring, then the birds are chirping.	1. $S \supset B$	p
	2. The birds aren't chirping.	2. $\sim B$	p
$\therefore$	3. It isn't spring.	$\therefore$ 3. $\sim S$	1,2 **MT**

Modus Ponens and Modus Tollens are rules that you will use over and over again in natural deduction proofs. Any time both a conditional and its antecedent are true, the consequent must also be true. If both a conditional and the negation of its consequent are true, it follows that the negation of the antecedent is true.

Do not confuse these forms with two invalid forms that resemble them. These invalid forms are so notorious that they too have traditional names:

Affirming the Consequent (*invalid*)

$$p \supset q$$
$$q \, / \therefore p$$

Denying the Antecedent (*invalid*)

$$p \supset q$$
$$\sim p \, / \therefore \sim q$$

We used a truth table to demonstrate the invalidity of Denying the Antecedent in the immediately preceding section. We could do the same for Affirming the Consequent. Here's a quicker way to make the point. If for p we substitute a false sentence and for q we substitute a sentence that is true, the result would be a substitution instance of Denying the Antecedent that has true premises and a false conclusion.

Examples

Here are two more examples of proofs using the valid argument forms **MP** and **MT**.

(1)   1. $M \supset \sim N$ p
       2. M p
       3. $H \supset N$ p $/ \therefore \sim H$
       4. $\sim N$ 1,2 **MP**
       5. $\sim H$ 3,4 **MT**

(2) 1. $(R \vee S) \supset (T \supset K)$ p
      2. $\sim K$ p
      3. $R \vee S$ p /∴ $\sim T$
      4. $T \supset K$ 1,3 **MP**
      5. $\sim T$ 2,4 **MT**

(Notice that in using **MP** to obtain line 4, the compound sentence $R \vee S$ was substituted for p, and the compound sentence $T \supset K$ was substituted for q.)

3   *Disjunctive Syllogism and Hypothetical Syllogism*

Another of the valid argument forms is **Disjunctive Syllogism (DS),** which has two forms:

$$p \vee q$$
$$\sim p /\therefore q$$

and

$$p \vee q$$
$$\sim q /\therefore p$$

The validity of these forms is obvious. Given that at least one of two sentences is true and that one of the sentences is definitely false, it follows that the other sentence must be true.

Now let's look at the valid argument form **Hypothetical Syllogism (HS):**

$$p \supset q$$
$$q \supset r /\therefore p \supset r$$

This form tells us that material implication is transitive, as is "greater than" in mathematics. If one statement materially implies a second statement, and the second statement materially implies a third, it follows that the first statement materially implies the third.

Examples

Here is a proof using both Hypothetical Syllogism and Disjunctive Syllogism (as well as Modus Tollens):

      1. $A \vee B$ p
      2. $C \supset D$ p
      3. $A \supset C$ p
      4. $\sim D$ p   /∴ B
      5. $A \supset D$ 2,3 **HS**
      6. $\sim A$ 4,5 **MT**
      7. B 1,6 **DS**

Exercise 4-1

For each line (other than premises) in the following proofs, state the line or lines from which it follows and the valid argument form (**MP, MT, DS,** or **HS**) used to obtain it. (The sample proof illustrates this procedure.)

Sample Proof

    1. $A \supset \sim B$ p
    2. $\sim \sim B$ p
    3. $\sim A$ 1,2 **MT** (correct justification for line 3)

(1) 1. $A \supset B$ p
     2. $A \vee C$ p
     3. $\sim B$ p
     4. $\sim A$
     5. C

(2) 1. $A \supset B$ p
     2. $B \supset C$ p
     3. $\sim C$ p
     4. $A \supset C$
     5. $\sim A$

(3) 1. $A \vee (H \cdot K)$ p
     2. $A \supset (B \vee C)$ p
     3. $\sim (B \vee C)$ p
     4. $\sim A$
     5. $H \cdot K$

(4) 1. $(H \vee K) \supset L$ p
     2. $M \supset \sim L$ p
     3. M p
     4. $\sim L$
     5. $\sim (H \vee K)$

(5) 1. $D \vee E$ p
     2. $D \supset \sim A$ p
     3. $\sim E$ p
     4. $A \vee B$ p
     5. D
     6. $\sim A$
     7. B

(6) 1. $\sim R$ p
     2. $\sim S \supset T$ p
     3. $(A \supset B) \supset \sim S$ p
     4. $\sim R \supset (A \supset B)$ p
     5. $\sim R \supset \sim S$
     6. $\sim R \supset T$
     7. T

(7) 1. $A \supset (B \supset C)$ p
     2. $H \supset A$ p
     3. $H \vee (A \vee B)$ p
     4. $\sim (B \supset C)$ p
     5. $\sim A$
     6. $\sim H$
     7. $A \vee B$
     8. B

(8) 1. $A \supset (B \supset C)$ p
     2. $\sim \sim F$ p
     3. $\sim D \supset A$ p
     4. $\sim C \vee \sim F$ p
     5. $\sim D$ p
     6. $\sim D \supset (B \supset C)$
     7. $B \supset C$
     8. $\sim C$
     9. $\sim B$

(9) 1. $(H \vee K) \supset R$ p
     2. $A \supset (\sim M \supset \sim R)$ p
     3. $\sim M$ p
     4. $A \vee M$ p
     5. A
     6. $\sim M \supset \sim R$
     7. $\sim R$
     8. $\sim (H \vee K)$

(10) 1. $F \supset (G \supset H)$ p
     2. G p
     3. $B \supset F$ p
     4. $R \supset B$ p
     5. R p
     6. $R \supset F$
     7. F
     8. $G \supset H$
     9. H

Exercise 4-2

Use **MP, MT, DS,** and **HS** to prove that the following arguments are valid.

(1) 1. $\sim R$
     2. $S \supset R / \therefore \sim S$

(2) 1. $A \cdot S$
     2. $(A \cdot S) \supset R / \therefore R$

(3) 1. $\sim (H \cdot K)$
     2. $R \vee (H \cdot K) / \therefore R$

(4) 1. $(P \vee Q) \supset (R \cdot W)$
     2. $L \supset (P \vee Q) / \therefore L \supset (R \cdot W)$

(5) 1. $R \supset S$
     2. $T \supset R$
     3. $\sim S / \therefore \sim T$

(6) 1. $\sim M$
     2. $N \supset G$
     3. $N \vee M / \therefore G$

(7) 1. $\sim D \supset E$
     2. $D \supset F$
     3. $\sim F / \therefore E$

(8) 1. $G \vee H$
     2. $\sim H \vee I$
     3. $\sim I / \therefore G$

(9) 1. $\sim G \supset (A \vee B)$
     2. $\sim B$
     3. $A \supset D$
     4. $\sim G / \therefore D$

(10) 1. $(A \supset B) \supset C$
      2. $\sim D \vee A$
      3. $\sim D \supset (A \supset B)$
      4. $\sim A / \therefore C$

(11) 1. $A \supset (B \supset C)$
      2. $\sim C$
      3. $\sim D \supset A$
      4. $C \vee \sim D / \therefore \sim B$

(12) 1. $\sim (D \cdot F)$
      2. $(L \vee M) \vee R$
      3. $\sim T \supset \sim (L \vee M)$
      4. $(D \cdot F) \vee \sim T / \therefore R$

(13) 1. $(A \vee B) \supset (B \vee C)$
      2. $(B \supset C) \vee A$
      3. $(B \supset C) \supset (A \vee B)$
      4. $\sim A / \therefore B \vee C$

(14) 1. $(P \cdot Q) \supset [R \vee (T \cdot S)]$
      2. $(T \vee R) \supset (P \cdot Q)$
      3. $\sim (T \cdot S)$
      4. $T \vee R / \therefore R$

4 *Simplification and Conjunction*

Another of the valid argument forms is **Simplification (Simp)**, which, like **DS,** has two forms:

$$p \cdot q / \therefore p \qquad \text{and} \qquad p \cdot q / \therefore q$$

You should have no problem with this rule. Obviously, from the fact that two sentences are both true you can infer that one of the sentences is true. So anytime you have a line of a proof that is a conjunction, you can use simplification to derive one of the conjuncts.

Now let's look at the valid argument form **Conjunction (Conj):**

$$p$$
$$q / \therefore p \cdot q$$

This rule allows you to take any two lines of a proof and put them together to make a conjunction. You can think of Simplification as the rule you use to take apart conjunctions and of Conjunction as the rule you use to put them together.

Examples

Here is a proof that uses both **Simp** and **Conj**:

(1) 1. $A \cdot B$ p
    2. $B \supset C$ p /∴ $A \cdot C$
    3. B 1 **Simp**
    4. C 2,3 **MP**
    5. A 1 **Simp**
    6. $A \cdot C$ 4,5 **Conj**

5   *Addition and Constructive Dilemma*

Another of the valid argument forms is **Addition (Add):**

p /∴ $p \lor q$

Remember that all it takes to make a disjunction true is for *at least one* of the disjuncts to be true. So once you've proven a sentence true, it follows that *any* disjunction that contains this sentence as one of its disjuncts is also true.

Addition allows us to infer the sentence $A \lor B$ from the sentence A; it also lets us infer $A \lor \sim B$. Indeed, from A we can use addition to infer the sentence $A \lor \{\sim [Z \equiv \sim (X \lor Y)] \supset R\}$. In short, you can add *any* sentence you like as the second disjunct, because you have already established that the first disjunct is true. This makes Addition very useful. In particular, if the conclusion of your proof contains atomic constituents not found in any of your premises, you can use Addition to introduce them to the proof. This is illustrated in the following proof:

    1. $A \cdot C$ p /∴ $(A \lor E) \cdot (C \lor D)$
    2. A 1 **Simp**
    3. C 1 **Simp**
    4. $A \lor E$ 2 **Add**
    5. $C \lor D$ 3 **Add**
    6. $(A \lor E) \cdot (C \lor D)$ 4,5 **Conj**

The sentence E contained in the conclusion is not in the premise. Nor is the sentence D. Addition allows us to introduce E into the proof at line 4, and D at line 5.

Now let's look at the valid argument form **Constructive Dilemma (CD):**

$p \lor q$
$p \supset r$
$q \supset s$ /∴ $r \lor s$

Constructive Dilemma is the only argument form in our system that requires you to cite *three* lines. To use Constructive Dilemma, you need a disjunction and two conditionals, where the antecedents of the two conditionals are the two disjuncts of the disjunction. Here is an example of an argument in English that has the form **CD:**

 1. If a Democrat is elected, then taxes will go up.
 2. But if a Republican is elected, then unemployment will go up.
 3. A Democrat or a Republican will be elected.
∴ 4. Either taxes will go up, or unemployment will go up.

In symbols, this reads

 1. $D \supset T$ p
 2. $R \supset U$ p
 3. $D \vee R$ p
 4. $T \vee U$ 1,2,3 **CD**

Here are two very important restrictions on the use of the eight valid argument forms we have just introduced.

 1. These forms work in *one direction* only. They permit inference, for example, from $A \cdot B$ to A, by Simplification, but surely not from A to $A \cdot B$. One-directional argument forms are said to be **implicational argument forms.**

 2. You can apply these forms to *entire lines* only, never to parts of a line. For example, you are not allowed to apply Simplification to $(A \cdot B) \supset C$ to get $A \supset C$. (These two restrictions are the chief differences between the eight valid argument forms just presented and the ten to be discussed next.)

What justifies these restrictions is this: If we did not allow them, we would be able to derive false conclusions from true premises. The reader can satisfy herself that this is the case by using truth tables on the examples just given. The basic issue is, as we hope you recognize at this point, the validity and invalidity of certain argument *forms*.

Here is the complete list of eight valid implicational argument forms to be used as rules of inference in our system:

Valid Implicational Argument Forms (rules of inference)

1. **Modus Ponens (MP):**

$p \supset q$
$p / \therefore q$

2. **Modus Tollens (MT):**

$p \supset q$
$\sim q / \therefore \sim p$

3. **Disjunctive Syllogism (DS):**

$p \vee q$ $p \vee q$
$\sim p / \therefore q$ $\sim q / \therefore p$

4. **Hypothetical Syllogism (HS):**

$p \supset q$
$q \supset r / \therefore p \supset r$

5. **Simplification (Simp):**

$p \cdot q / \therefore p$

$p \cdot q / \therefore q$

6. **Conjunction (Conj):**

p

$q \quad / \therefore p \cdot q$

7. **Addition (Add):**

$p / \therefore p \vee r$

8. **Constructive Dilemma (CD):**

$p \vee q$

$p \supset r$

$q \supset s / \therefore r \vee s$

Exercise 4-3

For each line (other than premises) in the following proofs, state the line or lines from which it follows and the valid implicational argument form on the preceding list used to obtain that line.

(1) 1. $D \cdot R$ p
     2. $(D \cdot R) \vee [A \vee (B \cdot D)]$

(2) 1. $[L \supset (B \supset A)] \cdot (L \vee M)$ p
     2. $L \supset (B \supset A)$

(3) 1. $C \vee D$ p
     2. $A \supset (B \supset \sim C)$ p
     3. $[A \supset (B \supset \sim C)] \cdot (C \vee D)$

(4) 1. $(A \cdot B) \supset S$ p
     2. $(D \cdot C) \vee (A \cdot B)$ p
     3. $(D \cdot C) \supset L$ p
     4. $L \vee S$

(5) 1. $A \supset D$ p
     2. $(B \cdot C) \supset H$ p
     3. $D \supset (B \cdot C)$ p
     4. $A \supset (B \cdot C)$
     5. $A \supset H$

(6) 1. $A \supset (B \supset D)$ p
     2. $\sim D$ p
     3. $D \vee A$ p
     4. A
     5. $B \supset D$
     6. $\sim B$

(7) 1. $A \supset \sim B$ p
     2. $A \vee C$ p
     3. $\sim \sim B \cdot D$ p
     4. $\sim \sim B$
     5. $\sim A$
     6. C

(8) 1. $A \supset B$ p
     2. $A \cdot \sim D$ p
     3. $B \supset C$ p
     4. A
     5. $A \supset C$
     6. C
     7. $\sim D$
     8. $C \cdot \sim D$

(9) 1. C p
     2. $A \supset B$ p
     3. $C \supset D$ p
     4. $D \supset E$ p
     5. $C \supset E$
     6. $C \vee A$
     7. $E \vee B$

(10) 1. $(A \vee M) \supset R$ p
     2. $(L \supset R) \cdot \sim R$ p
     3. $\sim (C \cdot D) \vee (A \vee M)$ p
     4. $\sim R$
     5. $\sim (A \vee M)$
     6. $\sim (C \cdot D)$

(11) 1. $(H \cdot K) \supset L$ p
     2. $\sim R \cdot K$ p
     3. $K \supset (H \vee R)$ p
     4. K
     5. $H \vee R$
     6. $\sim R$
     7. H
     8. $H \cdot K$
     9. L

(12) 1. $(R \cdot S) \supset \sim (Q \vee T)$ p
    2. $\sim B$ p
    3. $(Q \vee T) \vee \sim (\sim B \cdot \sim A)$ p
    4. $(\sim B \vee A) \supset (R \cdot S)$ p
    5. $(\sim B \vee A) \supset \sim (Q \vee T)$
    6. $\sim B \vee A$
    7. $\sim (Q \vee T)$
    8. $\sim (\sim B \cdot \sim A)$
    9. $\sim (\sim B \cdot \sim A) \cdot \sim B$

(13) 1. $(D \vee \sim H) \supset [R \cdot (S \vee T)]$ p
    2. L p
    3. $(L \vee M) \supset (D \cdot E)$ p
    4. $L \vee M$
    5. $D \cdot E$

    6. D
    7. $D \vee \sim H$
    8. $R \cdot (S \vee T)$
    9. $S \vee T$
   10. $D \cdot (S \vee T)$

(14) 1. $C \supset B$ p
    2. $\sim D \cdot \sim B$ p
    3. $[A \supset (B \supset C)] \vee D$ p
    4. $A \vee C$ p
    5. $\sim D$
    6. $\sim B$
    7. $A \supset (B \supset C)$
    8. $(B \supset C) \vee B$
    9. $B \supset C$

6   *Principles of Strategy*

Books on chess and checkers often start out with a brief summary of the rules of the game, a list of rules indicating which kinds of moves are permitted. But the major part of a book of this kind discusses not permissive rules, but what might be called *principles of strategy*. The permissive rules usually allow more than one move (for instance, there are twenty permitted opening moves in a game of chess). However, only a very few of these are likely to lead to winning positions. A good chess book helps the chess student to get the "feel" of good play and to become familiar with principles of good strategy, principles that in general lead to strong positions. (For example, in chess, other things being equal, it is good strategy to develop a piece into the center of the board rather than to one side.) Of course, as every chess tyro soon learns, strict adherence to conventional strategy sometimes leads to disaster.

The analogy between the game of chess and the "game" of logic problem solving is very close. The valid argument forms introduced so far plus the rules soon to be added correspond to the rules of chess. They determine which steps (moves) are permitted in an argument or proof. Generally they permit many steps at any given point in a proof, only a very few of which are likely to lead to "winning the game"—that is, to deriving the conclusion of the argument. A good logic player is one who develops a feel for good play, perhaps by becoming familiar with good strategy principles. We give you a few general suggestions here that you can use in the next exercise. Later in the chapter, after we introduce the remaining argument forms, we add some more strategy hints. Of course, principles useful to one person may not be useful to another, for psychological reasons. The few hints given next have proved useful to many students.

Remember, however, that just as chess strategy principles are not part of the rules of chess, so logic strategy principles are not part of the rules of logic. In fact, logic strategy rules belong not to the context of justification, but rather to the context of discovery, because they do not justify moves in proofs, but rather help us to discover winning moves.

The justification for the assertion of a line in a proof must always be a valid argument form or rule of inference.

Perhaps the most important strategy rule is to *look for forms that correspond to valid rules of inference.* Consider the following argument:

1. $[A \lor (\sim B \supset C)] \supset [\sim D \lor (C \cdot E)]$
2. $\sim [\sim D \lor (C \cdot E)] / \therefore \sim [A \lor (\sim B \supset C)]$

Beginners are likely to be overwhelmed by the large number of letters in this argument, or by the complexity of its premises, and thus be unable to discover a proof for it. But if they try to "see" the premises and conclusion in terms of their major forms, they discover the proof is quite simple. Notice that the major connective of the premise on line 1 is an implication, and that premise has the form $p \supset q$. Now notice that the major connective of line 2 is negation, and that line 2 has the form $\sim q$, because what is negated on line 2 is the consequent (q) of line 1. (So the first two lines of the proof have the forms $p \supset q$ and $\sim q$.) Clearly, here is an opportunity to use the argument form Modus Tollens, to obtain $\sim p$, which in this case is $\sim [A \lor (\sim B \supset C)]$, the desired conclusion. So we have "figured out" a simple proof:

1. $[A \lor (\sim B \supset C)] \supset [\sim D \lor (C \cdot E)]$ p
2. $\sim [\sim D \lor (C \cdot E)]$ p / $\therefore \sim [A \lor (\sim B \supset C)]$
3. $\sim [A \lor (\sim B \supset C)]$ 1,2 **MT**

A simple proof indeed, once attention is paid to the general forms of the sentences that make up the proof.

This proof illustrates another general rule of thumb: whenever the same sentence occurs on two different lines, look for ways to apply **MP, MT, DS,** or **HS** using those two lines. These four rules are particularly useful. Pay attention to the main connective of your premises with these four rules in mind. If you have a premise that is a conditional, see if you have (or can easily get) another line that allows you to employ **MP, MT,** or **HS.** If you have a premise that is a disjunction, look for ways to apply **DS.** If you have a line that is a negation, see if you can use **MT** or **DS.**

Now for some more specific strategy hints. Keep in mind that *small sentences (especially atomic sentences or negated atomic sentences) are your friends.* If you have them, use them. If you can get them, do so. Consider the following argument:

1. $B \supset A$
2. $\sim D \lor B$
3. $\sim A$ / $\therefore \sim D$

The place to start to work on this proof is with the third premise. We can use this premise to apply **MT** to the first premise to get $\sim B$, which we can then use to apply **DS** to the second premise to derive the conclusion.

4. $\sim B$ 1,3 **MT**
5. $\sim D$ 2,4 **DS**

Real proficiency in natural deduction requires more than merely memorizing the rules. You need to learn how to use them to get what you want. Keep the conclusion in mind. Once you've mastered the rules, *you will find completing many proofs much easier by working backward from the conclusion.* To do this, begin by examining the logical structure of the conclusion and asking whether there is some line that, together with premises, could be used to derive the conclusion. Ask yourself, "Given my premises, what would it take to get my conclusion?" Consider, for example, the following proof:

1. $C \supset A$ p
2. $M \supset B$ p
3. $B \supset C$ p
4. M p /∴ A

Eventually, you should get to the place where you can work a proof like this one backward in your head (for longer proofs you may want to use a piece of scrap paper). You should be able to see that you could get the conclusion, A, from the first premise using **MP** if somehow you could derive C.

1. $C \supset A$ p
2. $M \supset B$ p
3. $B \supset C$ p
4. M p /∴ A

   .
   .
   .

   C
   A 1, _ **MP**

But then, in the same manner, it should be obvious that you can get C if you can get B (using the third premise). So all it takes to complete the proof is to see that you can, in fact, derive B by using **MP** on the second and fourth premises. Filling in the line numbers, the completed proof is as follows:

1. $C \supset A$ p
2. $M \supset B$ p
3. $B \supset C$ p
4. M p /∴ A
5. B 2,4 **MP**
6. C 3,5 **MP**
7. A 1,6 **MP**

Notice also that the letter A, which occurs in the conclusion, is connected to the letter C in one of the premises, and C to B, and B to M. Short of working the entire proof backward, it is often useful to *trace the connections between the letters occurring in an argument, starting with the letter (or letters) occurring in the conclusion.* And then, having done so, it is often good strategy to *begin the proof with the letter (or letters) most distant from those in the conclusion,* which in this case means beginning with the letter M.

This proof also illustrates that usually it is not fruitful to use the same line in a proof over and over again. "Fresh information" (an untapped line in a proof) tends to be most useful. Thus, after line 6 has been written down, every premise has been used in the proof except premise 1. At this point, the information in premise 1 is untapped, unused, and the information on line 6 is fresh, in the sense that it is psychologically new information. This is a strong clue that it is time to use line 6 in conjunction with premise 1, as in fact it is used to obtain line 7.

Beginning logic students are often reluctant to use Addition. Don't be. Some proofs cannot be completed without using this rule. (In the next chapter, however, we will learn some new rules that will make this no longer true.) In particular, if the conclusion contains an atomic component that does not occur in any premise, you must use Addition to introduce this information into the proof. For example, notice that the letter D in the conclusion of the following proof

$$
\begin{array}{lll}
1. & B \supset C & \text{p} \\
2. & \sim C & \text{p} \\
3. & \sim B \supset R & /\therefore (R \vee D) \cdot \sim B
\end{array}
$$

does not occur in any of the premises. This tips us off that we must at some point use Addition to complete the proof. We start to work on this proof with the handy short second premise. This gives us half of our conclusion, $\sim B$, by using **MT** on the first premise. We can then use **MP** on the third premise to get R.

$$
\begin{array}{lll}
4. & \sim B & \text{1,2 MT} \\
5. & R & \text{3,4 MP}
\end{array}
$$

This is where some students get stuck. What do we do now? Simple—add the D. We can then finish the proof as follows:

$$
\begin{array}{lll}
6. & R \vee D & \text{5, Add} \\
7. & (R \vee D) \cdot \sim B & \text{4,6 Conj}
\end{array}
$$

Notice that you won't know what to add, and probably won't even think of adding in the first place, if you are looking only at the premises and not the conclusion. *Pay attention to where you are going.*

One final point. If you get stuck, don't be afraid to produce a line you end up not using. If there is some rule you can legitimately apply, do it—even though you can't see how it helps. That's much better than just not finishing the proof. There's nothing wrong with trial and error. When completely stuck, try something—anything—you haven't tried yet. Of course, we mean anything that is valid.

That's enough strategy for now. Let's summarize some of the main hints offered in this section:

- Look for sentence portions that are repeated, with a view toward applying **DS, HS, MP,** or **MT**.
- Small sentences are extremely useful.
- Work backward from the conclusion.
- Tap into fresh information. Use unused premises.
- When the conclusion contains atomic sentences not found in any premise, use **Add** to introduce this information.
- If stuck, try anything valid.

🚶 Walk-Through: Basic Proofs

Here is a proof as difficult as any you will find in the following exercise:

1. $(\sim A \vee B) \supset L$
2. $\sim B$
3. $A \supset B$
4. $L \supset (\sim R \vee D)$
5. $\sim D \cdot (R \vee F) / \therefore (L \vee G) \cdot \sim R$

One of the first things to notice is the small sentence on line 2. We can use this right away, as follows:

6. $\sim A$ 2,3 **MT**

We can also go ahead and simplify line 5.

7. $\sim D$ 5 **Simp**
8. $R \vee F$ 5 **Simp**

Lines 1 and 4 invite us to use **HS.**

9. $(\sim A \vee B) \supset (\sim R \vee D)$ 1,4 **HS**

It's not very clear how to proceed. When this happens, we check to see if we need to use **Add.** In this case, using **Add** will let us apply **MP** to line 9.

10. $\sim A \vee B$ 6 **Add**
11. $\sim R \vee D$ 9,10 **MP**

Next, notice that the conclusion is a conjunction. Working backward, we can solve the proof using Conjunction if we can get $L \vee \sim G$ on one line and $\sim R$ on another. Looking more carefully, we see that $\sim G$ is not in any premise. This tips us off that we will need to use **Add** again.

$\sim R$ is already at our fingertips:

12. $\sim R$ 7,11 **DS**

As is L.

13. L 1,10 **MP**

This leaves us only the **Add** and **Conj** steps to complete the proof.

14. $L \vee G$ 13 **Add**
15. $(L \vee G) \cdot \sim R$ 12, 14 **Conj**

As usual, there is more than one way of completing this particular proof. Indeed, it is possible to complete this proof using only thirteen lines. Can you do it?

The best way for you to pick up strategy is to complete proofs on your own. We supply lots of basic exercises you can use to hone your skills. We have some more strategy hints for you at the end of the chapter.

Exercise 4-4

Supply the premises and lines that are missing from the following proofs.

(1)   1. $Q \supset R$ p
      2.   p
      3. Q 1,2 **MP**

(2)   1. $A \equiv B$ p
      2.   p
      3. B 1,2 **MP**

(3)   1. $\sim (A \equiv B)$ p
      2.   p
      3. $\sim B$ 1,2 **MT**

(4)   1. $(\sim A \vee B) \vee C$ p
      2.   p
      3.   p
      4. $\sim A \vee B$ 1,2 **DS**
      5. $\sim A$ 3,4 **DS**

(5)   1. $A \supset (\sim B \supset C)$ p
      2. $D \supset (R \vee \sim W)$ p
      3.   p
      4.   p
      5. $(R \vee \sim W) \vee$
          $(\sim B \supset C)$ 1,2,3 **CD**
      6. $\sim B \supset C$ 4,5 **DS**

(6)   1. $A \supset B$ p
      2.   p
      3. $\sim D$ p
      4.   2,3 **DS**
      5. B 1,4 **MP**

(7)   1. $A \supset B$ p
      2. $D \supset E$ p
      3.   p
      4.   p
      5. $\sim D$ 2,3 **MT**
      6.   4,5 **DS**
      7. $A \supset C$ 1,6 **HS**

(8)   1.   p
      2.   p
      3. $G \supset L$ p
      4. $(T \cdot S) \vee U$ 1 **Add**
      5. $\sim L$ 2,4 **MP**
      6.   3,5 **MT**
      7.   1 **Simp**
      8. $T \cdot \sim G$ 6,7 **Conj**

Exercise 4-5

Use the eight implicational argument forms to prove that the following arguments are valid.

(1)   1. $(B \cdot M) \supset R$
      2. $L \supset (B \cdot M) / \therefore L \supset R$

(2)   1. $R \vee S$
      2. $(A \supset L) \cdot [(R \vee S) \supset T]$
          $/ \therefore T \vee L$

(3)   1. $R \cdot S$
      2. $T / \therefore (T \vee L) \cdot (R \cdot S)$

(4)   1. $A \cdot B$
      2. $B \supset C / \therefore C$

(5)   1. $A \supset (A \cdot B)$
      2. $C \supset A$
          $/ \therefore [C \supset (A \cdot B)] \cdot (C \supset A)$

(6)   1. $A \supset B$
      2. $C \cdot A / \therefore B \vee D$

(7)   1. $C \supset A$
      2. $A \supset (B \cdot D)$
      3. $C / \therefore B$

(8)   1. $A \supset (\sim B \cdot C)$
      2. $C \supset D$
      3. $E \vee B$
      4. $A / \therefore D \cdot E$

(9)   1. $(F \supset G) \vee H$
      2. $\sim G$
      3. $\sim H / \therefore \sim F$

(10) 1. L
      2. $T \vee \sim R$
      3. $(L \vee R) \supset \sim T$
         $/ \therefore \sim R \vee B$

(11) 1. $R \lor \sim W$
    2. $\sim W \supset L$
    3. $R \supset T / \therefore T \lor L$

(12) 1. $(R \cdot A) \lor E$
    2. $(R \cdot A) \supset D$
    3. $\sim D / \therefore E \cdot \sim D$

(13) 1. $(A \cdot D) \supset \sim C$
    2. $(R \lor S) \supset (A \cdot D)$
    3. $\sim C \supset \sim (A \cdot D)$
      $/ \therefore (R \lor S) \supset \sim (A \cdot D)$

(14) 1. A
    2. $(A \lor \sim D) \supset (R \cdot S)$
      $/ \therefore (R \cdot S) \lor B$

(15) 1. $\sim A$
    2. $(C \lor A) \supset L$
    3. $A \lor D$
    4. $(D \lor U) \supset C / \therefore L$

(16) 1. $R \supset (\sim P \lor \sim M)$
    2. $\sim R \supset (\sim M \cdot \sim N)$
    3. $\sim (\sim P \lor \sim M)$
    4. $Z \lor R / \therefore (\sim M \cdot \sim N) \cdot Z$

(17) 1. A
    2. $(B \lor C) \supset D$
    3. $(A \lor E) \supset (B \cdot C) / \therefore D$

(18) 1. $A \lor B$
    2. $C \supset A$
    3. $(B \cdot \sim C) \supset (D \cdot \sim C)$
    4. $\sim A / \therefore D$

(19) 1. $(\sim A \cdot \sim B) \supset (C \supset B)$
    2. $B \supset A$
    3. $\sim A / \therefore \sim C$

(20) 1. $[\sim A \cdot \sim (D \cdot E)] \supset (B \supset \sim D)$
    2. $\sim (D \cdot E) \cdot \sim R$
    3. $E \supset F$
    4. $\sim A \lor (D \cdot E)$
    5. $\sim (D \cdot E) \supset (B \lor E)$
      $/ \therefore \sim D \lor F$

7   *Double Negation and DeMorgan's Theorem*

We noted earlier that implicational argument forms are one-directional, and permit, for instance, inference from $A \cdot B$ to A, but not the reverse inference from A to $A \cdot B$. The sentence $A \cdot B$ *implies* the sentence A, but is *not equivalent* to it. (So the argument $A / \therefore A \cdot B$ is invalid.)

Now consider the valid inference from A to $\sim \sim A$. In this case, we can reverse the process, that is, we can validly infer from $\sim \sim A$ to A. This reversibility is due to the fact that the sentence A not only implies the sentence $\sim \sim A$ but also is equivalent (indeed logically equivalent) to it, and equivalent sentences imply each other. It follows, then, that both of the following argument forms are valid:

    1. $p / \therefore \sim \sim p$
    2. $\sim \sim p / \therefore p$

Because these two argument forms are just the reverse of each other, we can simplify matters by combining them into one "two-directional" argument form. Let's introduce the symbol "::" and use it to indicate that an argument form is two-directional. Then we can combine the preceding 2 one-directional (implicational) forms into 1 two-directional (equivalence) form as follows:

    $p :: \sim \sim p$

This equivalence argument form is called **Double Negation (DN)**. It permits inferences from any substitution instance of p to the analogous substitution instance of $\sim \sim p$, and from any substitution instance of $\sim \sim p$ to the analogous substitution instance of p. Thus, it permits all the inferences permitted by the two implicational argument forms $p / \therefore \sim \sim p$ and $\sim \sim p / \therefore p$.

Argument forms, such as Double Negation, that permit inferences in both directions are called **equivalence argument forms** (because they permit inferences from given statements to statements with which they are logically equivalent).

Now let's consider the pair of valid equivalence argument forms called **DeMorgan's Theorem (DeM)**:

$$\sim (p \cdot q) :: \sim p \vee \sim q$$
$$\sim (p \vee q) :: \sim p \cdot \sim q$$

The first of these forms permits inferences from any substitution instance of $\sim (p \cdot q)$ to the analogous substitution instance of $\sim p \vee \sim q$, and from $\sim p \vee \sim q$ to the analogous substitution instance of $\sim (p \cdot q)$; the second permits similar substitutions in both directions.

DeMorgan's Theorem is intuitively valid. For instance, it permits the intuitively valid inferences from

  1. It's not true that Candice Bergen and Jennifer Flowers both were invited to the Inaugural Ball.

in symbols, $\sim (C \cdot M)$, to

  2. Either Candice Bergen or Jennifer Flowers wasn't invited to the Inaugural Ball.

in symbols, $\sim C \vee \sim M$, and from

  3. Alexander the Great wasn't so great, and neither was Bonaparte.

in symbols, $\sim A \cdot \sim B$, to

  4. It's not the case that either Alexander the Great or Bonaparte was great.

in symbols, $\sim (A \vee B)$.

The intuitive validity of DeMorgan's Theorem is reflected in the standard ways we used to translate English sentences of the forms "Not both . . ." and "Neither . . . nor . . .". Recall that in Chapter Two we said that a sentence such as "It will not both rain and snow tomorrow," can be translated as $\sim (R \cdot S)$, or it can equally well be translated as $\sim R \vee \sim S$. Likewise, we learned that "It will neither rain nor snow tomorrow" can be translated by either $\sim (R \vee S)$ or $\sim R \cdot \sim S$. DeMorgan's is the natural deduction rule that certifies that these alternative translations are equivalent.

When we use an equivalence argument form, we move from a given expression to one that is logically equivalent to it. In Chapter Three we showed how to use truth tables to demonstrate that sentences or sentence forms are equivalent. Two sentences (or sentence forms) are equivalent if and only if there is no line of the truth table on which the forms have different truth-values. So two sentences that are logically equivalent have exactly the same truth conditions—they say exactly the same thing. Hence, we can use equivalence argument forms on *parts of lines* without fear of changing truth-values, and thus without fear of inferring from true premises to a false conclusion. Thus, we can use Double Negation to infer validly from $A \vee B$ to $\sim \sim A \vee B$, because A is equivalent to $\sim \sim A$ and hence $A \vee B$ is equivalent to $\sim \sim A \vee B$. This is a very important difference between equivalence and implicational argument forms: *Implicational argument forms must be used on whole lines only; equivalence forms may be used on parts of lines.*

We are in effect adopting a *rule*, the *Rule of Replacement*, which says that any sentence *p* can be replaced by one logically equivalent to it anywhere *p* occurs. Note that replacement *need not be uniform*: if we have a statement, say $\sim \sim A \supset (B \vee \sim \sim A)$, we can obtain $A \supset (B \vee \sim \sim A)$ using the Rule of Replacement, but we could also obtain $A \supset (B \vee A)$ by applying the rule to both occurrences of $\sim \sim A$. It is important not to confuse *replacement* with *substitution*; they are very different ideas. Substitution must be uniform throughout. To take an analogy from algebra, if we have the equation $x + y + x = 7$, and we are given that $x = 2$, we obtain $2 + y + 2 = 7$ by substituting 2 for *x*; we must substitute 2 for *x* at every occurrence. Substitution does not, in algebra, give us a logically equivalent statement. The original equation is an algebraic form that contains two variables *x* and *y*. After substitution, we can now solve the equation and determine the value of *y*. In logic $A \supset (B \supset A)$ is a substitution instance of $p \supset (q \supset p)$, with A / p and B / q. It would be illegitimate to obtain $A \supset (B \supset p)$ when we perform a substitution, for this would leave open another assignment to *p*, say *C*, and then we would have changed the logical form of the statement from $p \supset (q \supset p)$ to $p \supset (q \supset r)$. Note finally that $A \supset (B \supset A)$ is not logically equivalent to $p \supset (q \supset p)$. The latter statement form contains two variables, and it has no truth-value. The former contains statement constants and has a definite truth-value.

Exercise 4-6

Complete the following proofs, which emphasize the rules **DN** and **DeM**:

(1) 1. $A \supset \sim B$
     2. $B / \therefore \sim A$

(2) 1. $\sim A \supset \sim B$
     2. $B / \therefore A$

(3) 1. $\sim T \vee S$
     2. $T / \therefore S$

(4) 1. $\sim (J \vee K) / \therefore \sim K$

(5) 1. $\sim (F \cdot G)$
     2. $F / \therefore \sim G$

(6) 1. $H \vee (J \cdot K)$
     2. $\sim J \vee \sim K$
     3. $\sim H \vee \sim A / \therefore \sim A$

(7) 1. $\sim (A \cdot B) \vee C$

    2. $\sim C$
    3. $B / \therefore \sim A$

(8) 1. $\sim W \supset \sim X$
     2. X
     3. $\sim (W \cdot \sim Z) / \therefore Z$

(9) 1. $(P \cdot Q) \supset R$
     2. $\sim R$
     3. $Q / \therefore \sim P$

(10) 1. $\sim B \supset \sim C$
     2. $\sim (\sim A \vee B)$
     3. $C \vee D / \therefore D$

(11) 1. $\sim (\sim A \cdot \sim B)$
     2. $B \supset C$
     3. $\sim A$
     4. $\sim (C \cdot \sim D) / \therefore D$

(12) 1. ~ $(A \cdot \sim B)$
     2. $(B \cdot C) \supset D$
     3. ~ $(\sim A \vee \sim C) / \therefore D$

8 *Commutation, Association, and Distribution*

Intuitively, the statement "Art will go, or Betsy will go" $(A \vee B)$ is equivalent to the statement "Betsy will go, or Art will go" $(B \vee A)$, and the statement "Art will go, and Betsy will go" $(A \cdot B)$ is equivalent to the statement "Betsy will go, and Art will go" $(B \cdot A)$. These intuitions are captured by the two equivalence forms called **Commutation (Comm):**

$$p \vee q :: q \vee p$$
$$p \cdot q :: q \cdot p$$

The import of these two Commutation principles is that reversing the order of statements connected by "·" or "∨" does not change the truth-values of the compound sentences they form. (Once again, the reader may prove by truth table analysis that both forms of Commutation are valid.)

Notice that Commutation does not hold for sentences connected by "⊃." For instance, the sentence "If you overcooked the potatoes, you spoiled the meal" $(O \supset S)$ is certainly not equivalent to the analogous statement "If you spoiled the meal, then you overcooked the potatoes" $(S \supset O)$, given all the other ways there are to spoil a meal.

Now consider the valid equivalence argument forms called **Association (Assoc):**

$$p \vee (q \vee r) :: (p \vee q) \vee r$$
$$p \cdot (q \cdot r) :: (p \cdot q) \cdot r$$

The point of these two argument forms is that the movement of parentheses in either of the ways specified does not change the truth-values of compound sentences in which they occur.

Notice that Association holds only for compounds formed by two occurrences of "∨" or two occurrences of "·". Thus, an inference from, say, $A \vee (B \cdot C)$ to $(A \vee B) \cdot C$ is *invalid.* Similarly, Association does not hold for compounds formed by two occurrences of "⊃". For instance, the inference from $A \supset (B \supset C)$ to $(A \supset B) \supset C$ is *invalid.* (You can use a truth table to prove that this is true.)

Next, let's look at the two valid equivalence argument forms called **Distribution (Dist):**

$$p \cdot (q \vee r) :: (p \cdot q) \vee (p \cdot r)$$
$$p \vee (q \cdot r) :: (p \vee q) \cdot (p \vee r)$$

Distribution is an extremely powerful rule. To apply Distribution, look for a conjunct that is a disjunction or a disjunct that is a conjunction. Notice that if you apply distribution to a conjunction, the result should be a disjunction, and if you apply Distribution to a disjunction, the result should be a conjunction. This gives you a handy way of double-checking to see that you've applied Distribution correctly. Make sure you have replaced a conjunction with a disjunction, or a disjunction with a conjunction.

9 *Contraposition, Implication, and Exportation*

The valid equivalence form **Contraposition (Contra)**

$$p \supset q :: \sim q \supset \sim p$$

is useful when dealing with conditional sentences, in particular in some uses of the rule of conditional proof (to be introduced in Chapter Five).

The valid equivalence form **Implication (Impl)**

$$p \supset q :: \sim p \vee q$$

also is useful, in this case when we need to replace a conditional sentence by its disjunctive equivalent, or a disjunction by its conditional equivalent.

Equivalences such as Implication and DeMorgan's show us that we need not have introduced all the logical operators that we have. We could define the horseshoe in terms of $\sim p \vee q$ and we could then define the wedge as $\sim (\sim p \cdot \sim q)$. As we shall soon see, $p \equiv q$ is logically equivalent to $(p \supset q) \cdot (q \supset p)$ and so, since we can define the horseshoe, it turns out we can express all our current operators in terms of the dot and the tilde! Mathematicians are fond of such elegance, but students (and most professors) are not, because it would make the sentences of logic long and cumbersome. But from the mathematical, theoretical point of view, this is irrelevant. What is important is whether our operators will allow us to construct a statement form for every possible truth table. If the answer is yes, sentential logic is said to be **expressively complete.** For more on this idea, see the exercises at the end of this chapter.

Next, let's look at the valid equivalence argument form called **Exportation (Exp):**

$$(p \cdot q) \supset r :: p \supset (q \supset r)$$

This rule captures the intuitive idea that if the conjunction of two sentences, $(p \cdot q)$, implies a third, then the first (p) implies that the second (q) implies the third (and vice versa). For instance, if it is true that if Fran is intelligent and works hard, then she'll get an A in her philosophy class (in symbols, $(I \cdot H) \supset A$), then it follows that if she is intelligent, then if she works hard, she'll get an A—in symbols, $I \supset (H \supset A)$.

10 *Tautology and Equivalence*

The two valid equivalence forms called **Tautology (Taut)**

$$p :: p \cdot p$$
$$p :: p \vee p$$

are used chiefly to get rid of redundant letters, as in the following proof:

1. $A \supset \sim A$ p /∴ $\sim A$
2. $\sim A \vee \sim A$ 1 **Impl**
3. $\sim A$ 2 **Taut**

The two valid equivalence forms called **Equivalence (Equiv)**

$$p \equiv q :: (p \supset q) \cdot (q \supset p)$$
$$p \equiv q :: (p \cdot q) \vee (\sim p \cdot \sim q)$$

(the last of the eighteen valid forms to be introduced into our system), are needed to manipulate statements in which the symbol "$\equiv$" occurs, as in the following proof:

1. $A \equiv B$ p
2. B p /$\therefore$ A
3. $(A \supset B) \cdot (B \supset A)$ 1 **Equiv**
4. $B \supset A$ 3 **Simp**
5. A 2,4 **MP**

Here is a list of the ten valid equivalence argument forms to be used along with the eight valid implicational forms listed on pages 97–98 as rules of inference in our system (for handy reference all eighteen rules are also printed inside the front cover):

Valid Equivalence Argument Forms (rules of inference)

9. Double Negation (DN):

$$p :: \sim \sim p$$

10. DeMorgan's Theorem (DeM):

$$\sim (p \cdot q) :: \sim p \vee \sim q$$
$$\sim (p \vee q) :: \sim p \cdot \sim q$$

11. Commutation (Comm):

$$p \vee q :: q \vee p$$
$$p \cdot q :: q \cdot p$$

12. Association (Assoc):

$$p \vee (q \vee r) :: (p \vee q) \vee r$$
$$p \cdot (q \cdot r) :: (p \cdot q) \cdot r$$

13. Distribution (Dist):

$$p \cdot (q \vee r) :: (p \cdot q) \vee (p \cdot r)$$
$$p \vee (q \cdot r) :: (p \vee q) \cdot (p \vee r)$$

14. Contraposition (Contra):

$$p \supset q :: \sim q \supset \sim p$$

15. Implication (Impl):

$$p \supset q :: \sim p \vee q$$

16. Exportation (Exp):

$$(p \cdot q) \supset r :: p \supset (q \supset r)$$

17. Tautology (Taut):

$$p :: p \cdot p$$
$$p :: p \vee p$$

18. Equivalence (Equiv):

$$p \equiv q :: (p \supset q) \cdot (q \supset p)$$
$$p \equiv q :: (p \cdot q) \vee (\sim p \cdot \sim q)$$

Our list is quite similar to those of many standard texts. In Section 2 we discussed briefly the *completeness* of a set of rules. The eighteen we have introduced so far do not yet comprise a complete list; to complete it we must, in the next chapter, present a powerful procedure called Conditional Proof. Then every valid sentential argument that can be shown so by the truth tables is also provable by the forms we have introduced. More than convenience is attached to some of these valid forms. Some provide food for philosophical thought; for example, Exportation helps us understand Conditional Proof; others, such as Implication as we have discussed it earlier, show how we could define some of our operators in terms of others.

In the following Exercise 4-7 you are asked to justify steps in proofs that are given to you; in Exercise 4-8, you must do your own proofs. One question that naturally arises here is whether it is permissible to combine steps in proofs. You will see, in Exercise 4-7, some examples of this. For example, in number (8) of Exercise 4-7, step 6, strictly speaking we get $\sim \sim G \supset \sim \sim H$ by Contraposition and then $G \supset H$ by two applications of Double Negation, thus combining three steps into one. Steps 6 and 7 of number (7) do similar things, as do steps 6, 8, and 9 of number (10). Generally, it is *not* a good idea to combine steps this way, however. It is too easy to make errors, for one thing. For another, combining steps makes it harder to check the proof. Many instructors do not allow such combinations; others allow one **DN** with any *step other than* **DN,** and two **DN**s in one step provided no other valid argument form is involved in that step. We generally follow that policy in the proofs you will see: If two steps are combined into one, at least one step of those must be a **DN.**

Exercise 4-7

For each line (other than premises) in the following proofs, state the line or lines from which it follows and the valid argument form used to obtain it.

(1) 1. $(B \cdot C) \vee D$ p
     2. $\sim C$ p
     3. $D \vee (B \cdot C)$
     4. $(D \vee B) \cdot (D \vee C)$
     5. $D \vee C$
     6. D

(2) 1. R p
     2. $(\sim C \vee \sim D) \vee S$ p
     3. $\sim (D \cdot C) \supset \sim R$ p
     4. $\sim \sim R$
     5. $\sim (C \cdot D) \supset \sim R$
     6. $\sim \sim (C \cdot D)$
     7. $\sim (C \cdot D) \vee S$
     8. S

(3) 1. $(A \cdot B) \vee C$ p
     2. $\sim (A \vee \sim D)$ p
     3. $C \vee (A \cdot B)$
     4. $(C \vee A) \cdot (C \vee B)$
     5. $C \vee A$
     6. $\sim A \cdot \sim \sim D$
     7. $\sim A$
     8. C

(4) 1. $(A \vee B) \vee \sim C$ p
     2. $(\sim A \cdot \sim C) \vee (\sim A \cdot D)$ p
     3. $A \vee (B \vee \sim C)$
     4. $\sim A \cdot (\sim C \vee D)$
     5. $\sim A$
     6. $\sim C \vee D$
     7. $B \vee \sim C$
     8. $\sim C \vee B$
     9. $(\sim C \vee B) \cdot (\sim C \vee D)$
     10. $\sim C \vee (B \cdot D)$

(5) 1. $\sim R \vee S$ p
     2. $(A \vee B) \supset (R \cdot \sim S)$ p
     3. $\sim R \vee \sim \sim S$
     4. $\sim (R \cdot \sim S)$
     5. $\sim (A \vee B)$
     6. $\sim A \cdot \sim B$
     7. $\sim A$
     8. $\sim A \vee (\sim B \vee D)$
     9. $(\sim A \vee \sim B) \vee D$
     10. $D \vee (\sim A \vee \sim B)$
     11. $D \vee \sim (A \cdot B)$

(6) 1. $E \equiv F$ p
     2. $\sim E \vee \sim F$ p
     3. $(E \cdot F) \vee (\sim E \cdot \sim F)$
     4. $\sim (E \cdot F)$
     5. $\sim (E \cdot F) \vee E$
     6. $(E \cdot F) \supset E$

7. $E \supset \sim F$
8. $(E \cdot F) \supset \sim F$
9. $E \supset (F \supset \sim F)$
10. $E \supset (\sim F \vee \sim F)$
11. $E \supset \sim F$

(7) 1. $A \supset (\sim B \supset C)$ p
    2. $\sim B$ p
    3. $\sim C$ p
    4. $\sim C \cdot \sim B$
    5. $\sim (C \vee B)$
    6. $A \supset (\sim B \supset \sim \sim C)$
    7. $A \supset (\sim C \supset B)$
    8. $A \supset (\sim \sim C \vee B)$
    9. $A \supset (C \vee B)$
   10. $\sim A$

(8) 1. $\sim H \supset \sim G$ p
    2. $(R \vee \sim H) \vee K$ p
    3. $(\sim H \vee R) \vee K$
    4. $\sim H \vee (R \vee K)$
    5. $H \supset (R \vee K)$
    6. $G \supset H$
    7. $G \supset (R \vee K)$
    8. $\sim G \vee (R \vee K)$
    9. $(\sim G \vee R) \vee K$
   10. $K \vee (\sim G \vee R)$
   11. $\sim \sim K \vee (\sim G \vee R)$
   12. $\sim K \supset (\sim G \vee R)$
   13. $\sim K \supset (G \supset R)$

(9) 1. $G \equiv (H \cdot K)$ p
    2. $\sim G \supset H$ p
    3. $K \vee G$ p

    4. $[G \cdot (H \cdot K)] \vee [\sim G \cdot \sim (H \cdot K)]$
    5. $\sim \sim G \vee H$
    6. $G \vee H$
    7. $G \vee K$
    8. $(G \vee H) \cdot (G \vee K)$
    9. $G \vee (H \cdot K)$
   10. $\sim \sim G \vee (H \cdot K)$
   11. $\sim \sim G \vee \sim \sim (H \cdot K)$
   12. $\sim [\sim G \cdot \sim (H \cdot K)]$
   13. $G \cdot (H \cdot K)$
   14. G

(10) 1. $(R \equiv \sim S) \supset \sim R$ p
    2. $\sim R \vee \sim S$ p
    3. $[(R \supset \sim S) \cdot (\sim S \supset R)] \supset \sim R$
    4. $\sim [(R \supset \sim S) \cdot (\sim S \supset R)] \vee \sim R$
    5. $[\sim (R \supset \sim S) \vee$
       $\sim (\sim S \supset R)] \vee \sim R$
    6. $[\sim (\sim R \vee \sim S) \vee$
       $\sim (\sim \sim S \vee R)] \vee \sim R$
    7. $[\sim (\sim R \vee \sim S) \vee$
       $\sim (S \vee R)] \vee \sim R$
    8. $[(\sim \sim R \cdot \sim \sim S) \vee$
       $(\sim S \cdot \sim R)] \vee \sim R$
    9. $[(R \cdot S) \vee (\sim S \cdot \sim R)] \vee \sim R$
   10. $(R \cdot S) \vee [(\sim S \cdot \sim R) \vee \sim R]$
   11. $\sim (R \cdot S)$
   12. $(\sim S \cdot \sim R) \vee \sim R$
   13. $\sim R \vee (\sim S \cdot \sim R)$
   14. $(\sim R \vee \sim S) \cdot (\sim R \vee \sim R)$
   15. $\sim R \vee \sim R$
   16. $\sim R$

Exercise 4-8

Using the eighteen valid argument forms, prove that the following arguments are valid. (These proofs are very basic. None requires more than six additional lines to complete).

(1) 1. $(A \cdot B) \supset C$
    2. $A /\therefore B \supset C$

(2) 1. $\sim R \vee \sim S$
    2. $A \supset (R \cdot S) /\therefore \sim A$

(3) 1. $\sim M \vee N$
    2. $\sim R \supset \sim N /\therefore M \supset R$

(4) 1. $A \supset B$
    2. $\sim (B \cdot \sim C) /\therefore A \supset C$

(5) 1. $\sim A \supset (B \cdot C)$
    2. $\sim C /\therefore A$

(6) 1. $F \supset G$
    2. $\sim (H \cdot G)$
    3. $H /\therefore \sim F$

(7) 1. $\sim (H \vee \sim K)$
    2. $L \supset H / \therefore L \supset M$

(8) 1. $M \equiv N / \therefore \sim N \vee M$

(9) 1. $A \supset \sim A$
    2. $(\sim A \vee \sim B) \supset C / \therefore \sim A \cdot C$

(10) 1. $R \supset S$
    2. $R \supset T / \therefore R \supset (S \cdot T)$

(11) 1. $H \supset K$
    2. $C \equiv D$
    3. $\sim C \supset \sim K / \therefore H \supset D$

(12) 1. $A \cdot (B \supset C)$
    2. $\sim (C \cdot A) / \therefore \sim B$

(13) 1. $(A \cdot B) \vee (C \cdot D)$
    2. $\sim A / \therefore C$

(14) 1. $D \vee \sim A$
    2. $\sim (A \cdot \sim B) \supset \sim C$
    3. $\sim D / \therefore \sim C$

(15) 1. $(A \cdot B) \supset C$
    2. $A \cdot \sim C / \therefore \sim B$

11   *More Principles of Strategy*

We conclude this chapter with some additional strategy hints involving equivalence forms. Recall that we have already emphasized the usefulness of short sentences, especially atomic or negated atomic sentences. You can use equivalence forms to break sentences down. DeMorgan's Theorem is particularly useful in this respect. Anytime you have a negated complex sentence, you can use DeMorgan's to produce a simpler sentence, that will almost always be easier to work with. Consider the following argument:

1. $(B \supset C) \supset A$
2. $\sim (D \vee A)$ $/ \therefore B$

The place to start to work on this proof is with the second premise. When you see a sentence like this, you should automatically be thinking of using DeMorgan's Theorem. Applying DeMorgan's to this sentence will give us a conjunction, on which we can then use Simplification to get $\sim A$. Of course, this little sentence is very useful because we can use it to apply **MT** to the first premise.

3. $\sim D \cdot \sim A$ 2 **DeM**
4. $\sim A$ 3 **Simp**
5. $\sim (B \supset C)$ 1,4 **MT**

With line 5 we have once again a negated complex sentence. This sentence should still make you think of DeMorgan's; it just takes an extra step to get into position to use this rule. Once you do this, the rest of the proof is obvious.

6. $\sim (\sim B \vee C)$ 5 **Impl**
7. $\sim \sim B \cdot \sim C$ 6 **DeM**
8. $\sim \sim B$ 7 **Simp**
9. B 8 **DN**

This proof illustrates another useful strategy. Notice that the letter D does not occur in the conclusion and that it occurs in the premises only once. Obviously, the information its presence adds to premise 2 is not necessary in deriving the conclusion. *A letter that occurs only once in the premises of an argument and not at all in the conclusion usually is excess baggage, to be gotten rid of or (if possible) ignored.* In this case, we used DeMorgan's and then Simplification to get rid of the superfluous letter D by separating the information it contains (which is not needed to derive the conclusion) from the other information contained in premise 2 (which is needed to derive the conclusion).

It should be obvious that DeMorgan's Theorem is a very useful rule. Whenever you have a complex sentence governed by a negation, that sentence can be transformed so that DeMorgan's can be applied to it. Unless the sentence governed by the negation sign is repeated in another premise, using DeMorgan's to remove the negation sign will almost always give you a sentence that is easier to work with.

Here are some other moves you should make almost automatically when you are not sure how to proceed. Break apart any nonrepeated conjunctions, using Simplification. Break down nonrepeated biconditionals, using Equivalence (the form that gives you a conjunction of two conditionals).

If you have some premises that are disjunctions and some that are conditionals, it will usually help either to change the conditionals into disjunctions, or the disjunctions into conditionals, using Implication. Consider, for example, the following argument:

1. $A \vee B$
2. $C \supset \sim A$ $/\therefore C \supset B$

Here you should change the disjunction into a conditional by using **DN** and then **Imp** (a very useful trick). You can then apply **HS** to complete the proof.

3. $\sim \sim A \vee B$ 1 **DN**
4. $\sim A \supset B$ 3 **Imp**
5. $C \supset B$ 2,4 **HS**

The solution to other proofs may hinge on your changing the conditional to a disjunction, as the following proof illustrates:

1. $A \supset B$
2. $\sim A \vee C$ $/\therefore A \supset (B \cdot C)$

In this case, changing the second premise into a conditional is of no use. There is no obvious way to use the resulting conditional, $A \supset C$, in combination with the other premise. However, if we change the conditional into a disjunction, we can apply Distribution after we conjoin the two disjunctions.

3. $\sim A \vee B$ 1 **Impl**
4. $(\sim A \vee B) \cdot (\sim A \vee C)$ 2, 3 **Conj**
5. $\sim A \vee (B \cdot C)$ 4 **Dist**
6. $A \supset (B \cdot C)$ 5 **Impl**

This proof illustrates a very common pattern. When all else fails, break down all the conditionals (and biconditionals) so that you have lines equivalent to the premises, but now containing just the connectives "·", "∨", or "~". Then look for ways to rearrange this information so that you can get a line that contains just the same sentences as the conclusion. Once you get to that point, usually the proof can be completed in short order.

Now consider the following proof:

   1. $A \supset (B \cdot C)$ $/\therefore A \supset C$

Obviously, to solve this proof we need to dispense with the *B* in the premise, another case of excess baggage. We've already seen how to use DeMorgan's to dispense with unneeded information. The solution to this proof illustrates how Distribution can also be used for the same purpose.

   2. $\sim A \vee (B \cdot C)$ 1 **Impl**
   3. $(\sim A \vee B) \cdot (\sim A \vee C)$ 2 **Dist**
   4. $\sim A \vee C$ 3 **Simp**
   5. $A \supset C$ 4 **Impl**

In our earlier section on strategy we stressed the usefulness of *working backward from the conclusion* as well as forward from the premises. If we work backward from the conclusion and find a sentence that appears derivable from the premises, then we have discovered an intermediate target to aim at and have divided a relatively difficult task into two easier ones. Equivalence argument forms provide us with many more ways to work backward. We can use them to produce lines equivalent to the conclusion we want to reach.

Consider the argument

   1. $A \supset B$ p
   2. $C \supset B$ p $/\therefore (A \vee C) \supset B$

We can work backward from the conclusion, as follows:

   1. $A \supset B$ p
   2. $C \supset B$ p $/\therefore (A \vee C) \supset B$

       .
       .
       .

   $(B \vee \sim A) \cdot (B \vee \sim C)$
   $B \vee (\sim A \cdot \sim C)$ **Dist**
   $(\sim A \cdot \sim C) \vee B$ **Comm**
   $\sim (A \vee C) \vee B$ **DeM**
   $(A \vee C) \supset B$ **Impl**

At this point, we have learned that the conclusion $(A \vee C) \supset B$ is equivalent to $(B \vee \sim A) \cdot (B \vee \sim C)$. So by working backward from the conclusion, we have learned that the problem can be solved by working forward from the premises toward the intermediate sentence $(B \vee \sim A) \cdot (B \vee \sim C)$. This turns out to be fairly easy, as the following illustrates:

   1. $A \supset B$ p
   2. $C \supset B$ p $/\therefore (A \vee C) \supset B$
   3. $\sim A \vee B$ 1 **Impl**
   4. $B \vee \sim A$ 3 **Comm**
   5. $\sim C \vee B$ 2 **Impl**
   6. $B \vee \sim C$ 5 **Comm**
   7. $(B \vee \sim A) \cdot (B \vee \sim C)$ 4,6 **Conj**

We are now ready to add on the final portion of the proof we have already worked out. This time we can supply the line numbers.

8. $B \vee (\sim A \cdot \sim C)$ 7 **Dist**
9. $(\sim A \cdot \sim C) \vee B$ 8 **Comm**
10. $\sim (A \vee C) \vee B$ 9 **DeM**
11. $(A \vee C) \supset B$ 10 **Impl**

So by working backward from the conclusion as well as forward from the premises, we were able to construct a proof that might otherwise have eluded us.

Let's summarize some of the most important of these strategy hints:

- Break down complex sentences with **DeM, Simp,** and **Equiv.**
- Use **DeM** and **Dist** to isolate "excess baggage."
- Use **Imp** when you have a mix of conditionals and disjunctions.
- Again, work backward from the conclusion.

Exercise 4-9

All the following proofs have only one premise and can be completed in a very few steps. (We've indicated for each proof the minimum number of additional steps it takes to complete each proof.) Although short, many of these proofs are fairly difficult. Each proof embodies a very useful pattern of inference. You will find longer proofs much easier if you have these basic moves at your fingertips.

(1)   1. $\sim A \supset B$ /∴ $A \vee B$ (2 steps)
(2)   1. $A \vee B$ /∴ $\sim A \supset B$ (2 steps)
(3)   1. $\sim A$ /∴ $A \supset B$ (2 steps)
(4)   1. $\sim A$ /∴ $\sim (A \cdot B)$ (2 steps)
(5)   1. $A \supset \sim B$ /∴ $\sim (A \cdot B)$ (2 steps)
(6)   1. $\sim (A \cdot B)$ /∴ $A \supset \sim B$ (2 steps)
(7)   1. $\sim (A \vee B)$ /∴ $\sim B$ (2 steps)
(8)   1. $\sim (A \supset B)$ /∴ $\sim B$ (3 steps)
(9)   1. $\sim (A \supset B)$ /∴ A (4 steps)
(10) 1. A /∴ $\sim \{\sim [L \vee (\sim M \equiv R)]\} \vee A$ (2 steps)
(11) 1. A /∴ $\sim [L \vee (\sim M \equiv R)] \supset A$ (3 steps)
(12) 1. $A \supset \sim B$ /∴ $B \supset \sim A$ (2 steps)
(13) 1. $\sim A \supset B$ /∴ $\sim B \supset A$ (2 steps)
(14) 1. $A \supset (B \supset C)$ /∴ $B \supset (A \supset C)$ (3 steps)
(15) 1. $(A \cdot B) \vee (C \cdot D)$ /∴ $(A \cdot B) \vee D$ (2 steps)
(16) 1. $(A \cdot B) \vee (A \cdot C)$ /∴ $B \vee C$ (2 steps)
(17) 1. $A \vee (B \cdot C)$ /∴ $A \vee C$ (2 steps)
(18) 1. $(A \cdot B) \vee C$ /∴ $C \vee A$ (3 steps)
(19) 1. $\sim (A \equiv B)$ /∴ $\sim (A \cdot B)$ (3 steps)
(20) 1. $A \supset \sim A$ /∴ $\sim A$ (2 steps)

12 *Common Errors in Problem Solving*

Beginners are likely to make several kinds of mistakes in deriving proofs for arguments.

Using Implicational Forms on Parts of Lines

The valid implicational forms (numbers 1 through 8) can be used on *complete lines only.* For instance, we cannot go from

$$(A \cdot B) \supset C$$

to

$$(A \supset C)$$

dropping the letter *B* by Simplification. The reason is that the form of this process, namely, $(p \cdot q) \supset r /\therefore (p \supset r)$, is *not* the form of Simplification, and, in fact, is an invalid argument form. (An example of an invalid argument that has this form is the following: If George drives an automobile 70 miles per hour and smashes into a reinforced concrete structure, then he will be killed. Therefore, if George drives an automobile 70 miles per hour, then he will be killed.)

Examples

Here is a *correct* use of the implicational argument form Simplification:

1. $(A \vee \sim B) \cdot (C \vee \sim A)$ p /∴ $A \vee \sim B$
2. $A \vee \sim B$ 1 **Simp**

In this case, the "·" in line 1 is the major connective. Thus, the whole of line 1 has the form $(p \cdot q)$ required for the use of the valid argument form Simplification.
Here is another example of the correct use of implicational forms:

1. $A \supset (B \cdot C)$ p
2. $(B \cdot C) \supset D$ p
3. $A \supset D$ 1,2 **HS**

This is a correct use of the implicational form Hypothetical Syllogism (**HS**), because **HS** requires that one whole line in a proof have the form $(p \supset q)$, and another whole line have the form $(q \supset r)$, and this proof does have two such lines, namely line 1, which has the form $(p \supset q)$, and line 2, which has the form $(q \supset r)$. Therefore, **HS** permits the assertion of line 3, since that whole line has the required form $(p \supset r)$.

Remember that although the ten equivalence argument forms may be used on whole lines, just as the implicational forms, they also may be used on parts of lines, as in the following example:

1. $\sim (A \cdot B) \supset C$ p /∴ $(\sim A \vee \sim B) \supset C$
2. $(\sim A \vee \sim B) \supset C$ 1 **DeM**

The use of equivalence argument forms on parts of lines is justified because their use always leads from a given sentence to an equivalent sentence.

Reluctance to Use Addition

Even after proving that Addition is a valid argument form, some students are reluctant to use it because they believe that somehow it is "cheating" to be able to "add" letters to a line simply at will. But a little thought about the matter should convince the hesitant that no cheating is involved in the use of Addition. Consider this example:

Art committed the crime. Therefore, either Art committed the crime, or Barbara did.

symbolized as

1. A $p / \therefore A \vee B$
2. $A \vee B$ 1 **Add**

Although $A \vee B$ is a longer and more complicated formula than A alone, do not be tempted into concluding that it therefore makes a stronger claim. The addition of B to A, to get $A \vee B$, doesn't strengthen or extend the claim made by A alone; it weakens, waters down, that claim. Notice, for instance, how much more useful it is to know that Art is the guilty one rather than just that either Art or Barbara committed the crime.

The following extreme case nicely illustrates the weakening effect of the use of Addition:

1. A $p / \therefore (A \vee \sim A)$
2. $A \vee \sim A$ 1 **Add**

In this extreme case, the use of Addition leads to the weakest possible kind of assertion, namely a tautology, which has no factual content whatever.

Exercise 4-10

Prove that the following arguments are valid. These proofs especially emphasize **Add.**

(1) 1. $\sim A \supset \sim B$
    2. $\sim A / \therefore \sim B \vee C$

(2) 1. $A \supset B$
    2. $\sim B / \therefore \sim A \vee \sim B$

(3) 1. $(A \vee B) \supset C$
    2. $A / \therefore C$

(4) 1. $(A \vee B) \supset C$
    2. $(C \vee E) \supset F$
    3. $A / \therefore F$

(5) 1. A
    2. $A \supset B$
    3. $C \supset D / \therefore B \vee D$

(6) 1. A
    2. $[(A \vee B) \vee C] \supset D / \therefore D$

(7) 1. A
    2. $\sim A / \therefore B$

(8) 1. $(A \vee B) \supset C$
    2. $(C \vee B) \supset (D \vee F)$
    3. A
    4. $\sim F / \therefore D$

(9) 1. $\sim A$
    2. $(\sim A \vee B) \supset \sim C$
    3. $(\sim C \vee \sim D) \supset (A \vee B) / \therefore B$

(10) 1. $(A \vee \sim B) \supset C$
     2. $A / \therefore \sim B \vee C$

(11) 1. $A \cdot C$
     2. $(A \vee B) \supset D / \therefore D$

(12) 1. ~ A

    2. $B \supset A$

3. C

4. $[(\sim B \cdot C) \vee D] \supset E$ / ∴ E

Reluctance to Use Distribution

In this case, the reluctance generally stems not from doubts as to its validity, but rather from inability to spot places where its application will be useful. The following proof contains a typical useful application of Distribution:

1. $(A \vee B) \supset C$ / ∴ $A \supset C$
2. $\sim (A \vee B) \vee C$ 1 **Impl**
3. $(\sim A \cdot \sim B) \vee C$ 2 **DeM**
4. $C \vee (\sim A \cdot \sim B)$ 3 **Comm**
5. $(C \vee \sim A) \cdot (C \vee \sim B)$ 4 **Dist** (the crucial use of **Dist**)
6. $C \vee \sim A$ 5 **Simp**
7. $\sim A \vee C$ 6 **Comm**
8. $A \supset C$ 7 **Impl**

Notice that the use of Distribution is crucial in getting rid of the unwanted letter *B*, which occurs in the premise but not in the conclusion. Notice also that the second of the two distributive equivalence forms was used, and that it was used from left to right (that is, the move was from line 4, whose form $[p \vee (q \cdot r)]$ is that of the left side of the second distributive equivalence form, to line 5, whose form $[(p \vee q) \cdot (p \vee r)]$, is that of the right side). This is the most common use of Distribution, because the line obtained in this way always has a "·" as its major connective, and thus has the form $(p \cdot q)$ necessary for the use of Simplification.

Trying to Prove What Cannot Be Proved

The number of mistakes of this kind is much too large to catalog. We consider two such mistakes, committed perhaps because they are very similar to two valid procedures.

Consider the following four argument forms:

1. $(p \vee q) \supset r$ / ∴ $p \supset r$
2. $(p \cdot q) \supset r$ / ∴ $p \supset r$
3. $p \supset (q \vee r)$ / ∴ $p \supset r$
4. $p \supset (q \cdot r)$ / ∴ $p \supset r$

The first and fourth of these argument forms are valid. The second and third are *invalid*, as we can prove by truth table analysis.

The important point is not to waste time and effort trying to prove substitution instances of invalid forms. For example, in trying to prove the validity of the argument

1. $(A \cdot B) \supset C$
2. $\sim (\sim B \vee D)$
3. $(C \cdot \sim D) \supset E$ / ∴ $A \supset E$

it is useless to try to derive the sentence $A \supset C$ from line 1 alone because the form of such an inference, namely the form $(p \cdot q) \supset r$ / ∴ $p \supset r$, is invalid. The sentence $A \supset C$ can be derived in this proof, but not from line 1 alone.

Similarly, it is useless to try to derive the sentence $A \supset B$ from the sentence $A \supset (B \vee C)$, since the form of such an inference, namely the form $p \supset (q \vee r) / \therefore p \supset q$, is invalid.

Failure to Notice the Scope of a Negation Sign

A mistake of this kind is usually merely an oversight; however, it is quite common. In particular, negation signs that negate a whole sentence, or a large unit in a sentence, are misconstrued as negating only one letter. Thus, in a sentence such as $\sim (A \vee B)$ the negation sign sometimes is misconstrued as negating merely the letter A, instead of the whole unit $(A \vee B)$. The remedy for this kind of error is care, plus the realization that a negation sign before a unit set off by parentheses (or brackets) negates that entire unit.

🕴 Walk-Through: More Challenging Proofs

Here is a fairly difficult proof:

   1. $(A \supset \sim B) \cdot \sim C$
   2. $B \supset (\sim A \supset C)$ $/ \therefore \sim B$

Obviously, we can simplify the first line.

   3. $A \supset \sim B$ 1 **Simp**
   4. $\sim C$ 1 **Simp**

Looking for a way to use $\sim C$, we see we can perform Exportation on the second line.

   5. $(B \cdot \sim A) \supset C$ 2 **Exp**

This lets us use **MT.** We can then use **DeM** and **DN** to simplify the result.

   6. $\sim (B \cdot \sim A)$ 4,5 **MT**
   7. $\sim B \vee \sim \sim A$ 6 **DeM**
   8 $\sim B \vee A$ 7 **DN**

Here the proof grows more difficult. We want to get $\sim B$. It would be great if somehow we could get $\sim A$, but we can't. It's tempting to use **Impl** on line 3 to change $A \supset \sim B$ to $\sim A \vee B$. We could then conjoin this with line 8 and Distribute. But this gets us only $\sim B \vee (A \cdot \sim A)$. Unfortunately, although this sort of distribution move often works, it doesn't help us here. A more obscure strategy is this: We can get $\sim B$ if we can get $B \supset \sim B$. To get this formula, we use **Impl** in the other direction, changing the disjunction to a conditional. We then use **HS** on the two conditionals.

   9. $B \supset A$ 8 **Impl**
  10. $B \supset \sim B$ 3, 9 **HS**

To get $\sim B$, we use **Impl** again, and then **Taut**, completing the proof.

  11. $\sim B \vee \sim B$ 10 **Impl**
  12. $\sim B$ 11 **Taut**

Exercise 4-11

Prove that the following arguments are valid. These proofs especially emphasize **Dist,** **Comm,** and **Assoc.** This exercise is fairly challenging. Remember that **Dist,** like all our equivalence rules, works in *both directions.*

(1) 1. $A \vee (B \cdot C)$
   2. $\sim C / \therefore A$

(2) 1. $(A \vee B) \vee C$
   2. $\sim (B \vee C) / \therefore A$

(3) 1. $(A \vee B) \cdot C$
   2. $\sim (B \cdot C) / \therefore C \cdot A$

(4) 1. $(A \cdot B) \vee (C \cdot D)$
   2. $\sim C / \therefore A$

(5) 1. $(A \cdot B) \vee (C \cdot D)$
   $/ \therefore (A \cdot B) \vee D$

(6) 1. $(A \cdot B) \vee (C \cdot D) / \therefore D \vee A$

(7) 1. $(A \cdot B) \vee (C \cdot D)$
   $/ \therefore (C \cdot D) \vee A$

(8) 1. $(A \vee B) \cdot C$
   2. $\sim A \vee \sim C / \therefore C \cdot B$

(9) 1. $[(A \cdot B) \cdot D] \vee (C \cdot A) / \therefore A$

(10) 1. $(\sim R \cdot A) \vee \sim (Q \vee R) / \therefore \sim R$

(11) 1. $[(A \vee B) \cdot (D \cdot F)] \vee$
   $[(A \vee B) \cdot C] / \therefore C \vee F$

(12) 1. $[(A \cdot B) \vee (D \cdot F)] \vee (B \cdot C)$
   2. $\sim (D \cdot F) / \therefore B$

Exercise 4-12

Prove valid using the eighteen valid argument forms. (These proofs are moderately difficult. They will require between six and fifteen additional lines to complete.)

(1) 1. $(A \cdot B) \supset R$
   2. A
   3. $C \supset \sim R / \therefore \sim (C \cdot B)$

(2) 1. $\sim A$
   2. $(A \vee B) \equiv C$
   3. $\sim B / \therefore \sim (C \cdot D)$

(3) 1. $(A \cdot H) \supset (M \cdot N)$
   $/ \therefore (A \cdot H) \supset N$

(4) 1. $S \vee (\sim R \cdot T)$
   2. $R \supset \sim S / \therefore \sim R$

(5) 1. $H \supset K$
   2. $(K \cdot L) \supset M / \therefore L \supset (H \supset M)$

(6) 1. $A \supset B$
   2. $C \supset D$
   3. $(B \vee D) \supset E$
   4. $\sim E / \therefore \sim (A \vee C)$

(7) 1. $\sim H$
   2. $H \vee K$
   3. $L \supset H$
   4. $\sim (K \cdot \sim L) \vee (\sim L \cdot M) / \therefore M$

(8) 1. $(A \cdot B) \equiv C$
   2. $\sim (C \vee \sim A) / \therefore \sim B$

(9) 1. $(H \vee K) \supset (A \supset B)$
   2. $(H \vee M) \supset (C \supset D)$
   3. $(H \vee N) \supset (A \vee C)$
   4. $L \cdot H / \therefore B \vee D$

(10) 1. $W \equiv Y$
   2. $\sim W \vee \sim Y$
   3. $X \supset (Y \cdot Z) / \therefore \sim X$

(11) 1. $A \vee B$
   2. C
   3. $(A \cdot C) \supset D$
   4. $\sim (\sim F \cdot B) / \therefore D \vee F$

(12) 1. $P \supset R$
    2. $\sim P \supset (\sim R \supset S) /\therefore R \vee S$

(13) 1. $\sim (D \vee C)$
    2. $\sim C \supset (A \supset \sim B)$
    3. $A \equiv B /\therefore \sim A$

(14) 1. $\sim (C \vee A)$
    2. $B \supset (\sim A \supset C) /\therefore \sim B$

(15) 1. $\sim (A \cdot B) \equiv \sim C$
    2. $(D \vee E) \supset C /\therefore E \supset A$

Exercise 4-13

Prove valid using the eighteen valid argument forms. (These proofs are difficult, and require between ten and twenty additional lines to complete.)

(1) 1. $R \supset (\sim A \cdot T)$
   2. $B \vee \sim S$
   3. $R \vee S /\therefore A \supset B$

(2) 1. $S \vee (\sim R \cdot T)$
   2. $R \supset \sim S /\therefore \sim R$

(3) 1. $A \vee B$
   2. C
   3. $(A \cdot C) \supset D /\therefore D \vee B$

(4) 1. $C \vee D$
   2. $C \supset B$
   3. $\sim C \supset \sim D /\therefore B$

(5) 1. $P \supset [(Q \cdot R) \vee S]$
   2. $(Q \cdot R) \supset \sim P$
   3. $T \supset \sim S /\therefore P \supset \sim T$

(6) 1. $D \supset B$
   2. $D \supset (B \supset W)$
   3. $B \supset (W \supset S) /\therefore D \supset S$

(7) 1. $A \supset B$
   2. $A \vee (B \cdot C) /\therefore B$

(8) 1. $K \supset [(L \vee M) \supset R]$
   2. $(R \vee S) \supset T /\therefore K \supset (M \supset T)$

(9) 1. $(P \vee R) \cdot (P \vee Q)$
   2. $(Q \cdot R) \supset (V \supset W)$
   3. $\sim [(P \supset S) \supset \sim (S \supset W)]$
   4. $\sim W /\therefore V \supset S$

(10) 1. $A \supset B$
    2. $A \vee C$
    3. $D \supset B$
    4. $D \vee \sim C /\therefore B$

(11) 1. $(M \vee N) \supset (M \supset \sim N)$
    2. $\sim (N \supset P) \supset \sim (M \supset \sim N)$
    3. $M \vee N /\therefore M \vee P$

(12) 1. $(A \supset A) \supset (\sim A \supset \sim A)$
    $/\therefore A \vee \sim A$

(13) 1. $A \equiv B$
    2. $\sim (A \cdot \sim R) \supset (A \cdot S)$
    $/\therefore \sim (B \cdot S) \supset \sim (A \cdot R)$

(14) 1. $A \supset B$
    2. $C \supset D /\therefore (A \vee C) \supset (B \vee D)$

(15) 1. $\sim [D \cdot \sim (E \vee B)]$
    2. $\sim (E \vee F)$
    3. $C \supset (E \vee A)$
    $/\therefore \sim (\sim A \cdot \sim B) \vee \sim (C \vee D)$

Summary

We will soon have a complete list of rules—so that any sentential argument that can be shown valid by the truth tables can be proved valid using the rules. Now, we know that the truth tables provide a mechanical decision procedure to determine if an argument is valid; we could program a machine to do the work. Can we program a machine—or can you program yourself—to do proofs? With the rules we have introduced, the answer is no. Proofs here are a matter of ingenuity. That is, it can be shown, because the rules are complete, that there is a proof for each valid sentential argument, but given the rules in this textbook there is no mechanical procedure for producing that proof. As you will see later, there is a method of proof that *can* be mechanized—unfortunately, it is long, complicated, and tedious.

You may wonder what the point of doing complex proofs is. After all, you might say, nobody reasons in such complex ways. If one looks at the exercises, and tries to find English equivalents of the statements involved that would "make sense," they would be few and far between. Here logic is closer to mathematics. Mathematicians often do problems and have theories that do not seem practical. Some allegedly impractical results, however, sometimes do become practical. For example, mathematicians discovered in the nineteenth century that they could construct systems of geometry, called non-Euclidean geometries, that went against the assumptions made by the familiar Euclidean geometry. No one thought such geometries could be of use in our world—until Einstein showed that one could consider our universe as non-Euclidean in character! The point is this: What is merely theoretical today can become useful tomorrow and, as important, what is useful today is a part of a general theory that also yields results like our exercises. The deductive sentential arguments that are used, in science and in mathematics and in everyday life, are part of the general theory of sentential logic we are studying.

Exercise 4-14

1. Why can't implicational argument forms be used on parts of lines in a proof? (Give an example.)

2. Why *can* equivalence argument forms be so used? (Give an example.)

3. Why are all substitution instances of a valid argument form valid arguments?

4. We said that all substitution instances of a valid argument form are thereby valid arguments. Why can't we say that all substitution instances of an invalid argument form are invalid arguments? (Give an example.)

5. Assume for the sake of this exercise that we have all test statement forms that are tautological by the truth tables. Why *not* add each argument form that such test statement forms express as a rule of natural deduction?

6. Consider that we need *not* do what is suggested in problem 5 in order to have a complete list of rules. What does this show about the forms that we do *not* need to add to the list?

7. Show how all our operators can be expressed in terms of the tilde and the wedge.

8. Can the tilde be expressed in terms of the other operators? If so, show how. If *not,* what does this show about the concept of negation?

9. Given a *wff* that contains just two variables, how many possible truth tables are there for such expressions? (*Hint:* One such table will have a **T** in its first line, and **F**'s in the rest). Show that sentential logic is expressively complete by constructing a sentential expression for each possible truth table.

10. Consider Exercise 4-10, problem 7. If you did it correctly, you used *DS* to prove *B.* Could we have proved anything *other* than *B?* What does this show about arguments that contain contradictory premises?

Key Terms Introduced in Chapter Four

For the argument forms introduced in this chapter see the charts on pages 97–98 and 110. All of the forms are also listed on the inside front cover.

argument form: A group of sentence forms, all of whose substitution instances are arguments.

completeness: The natural deduction rules for sentential logic are said to be complete if every argument valid by the truth tables can be proved by the rules.

decision procedure: A procedure that you, or a suitably constructed machine, can follow that—when you follow it correctly—will always yield the right answer to the question over the validity of the argument.

equivalence argument form: A two-directional argument form. For example, Double Negation is a valid equivalence argument form.

expressive completeness: Sentential logic has this feature because every possible truth table for a *wff* containing two variables can be expressed using our operators.

implicational argument form: A one-directional argument form. For example, Modus Ponens is a valid implicational argument form.

invalid argument form: An argument form that has at least one invalid substitution instance.

proof of an argument: A series of sentences such that each member of the series is either a premise or else follows from a previous member of the series by a valid argument form, the last line being the argument's conclusion.

valid argument form: An argument form all of whose substitution instances are valid arguments.

Chapter Five

Conditional and Indirect Proofs

---

1 *Conditional Proofs*

Here is a very simple valid argument that so far cannot be proved valid in our system:

$$A \supset B \ / \therefore \ A \supset (A \cdot B)$$

To prove it valid, we can reason as follows: What would be the case *if A* were true? (We don't *know* that it is. It isn't given to us as a premise. But what *if* it were true?) If *A* were true, then clearly *B* also would be true, since by Modus Ponens we could move from $A \supset B$ (the given premise) and *A* (the assumed premise) to *B*. So if *A* were true, *B* also would be true, and thus $A \cdot B$ would be true (by Conjunction). We therefore have shown that *if A,* then $(A \cdot B)$, or in symbols, $A \supset (A \cdot B)$, which is the conclusion of the argument in question. Thus we have proved that the argument just displayed is valid.

A proof of this kind is called a *conditional proof,* and the rule permitting the crucial step is therefore called the rule of Conditional Proof. Once we add this rule, our natural deduction procedure for sentential logic is complete, meaning that now every argument in sentential logic that can be shown valid by truth tables can be shown to be valid by means of a proof.*

Now let's put this proof into symbols:

1.	$A \supset B$	p $/\therefore A \supset (A \cdot B)$
2.	A	**Assumed Premise** (or simply **AP**)
3.	B	1,2 **MP**
4.	$A \cdot B$	2,3 **Conj**

---

*There remain, however, valid arguments whose validity cannot be demonstrated by means of sentential logic. For these arguments, we need more powerful systems of logic, such as predicate logic, to be introduced in Chapter Seven.

What we have proved so far is that *if A then* (*A* · *B*). Replacing the expression
"if . . . then . . ." by "⊃," we get

     5. *A* ⊃ (*A* · *B*)   2–4, **Conditional Proof** (or **CP**)

The important point to notice is that the conclusion, line 5, depends only on the *original premise,* and not on the assumed premise stated on line 2. If premise 1 is true, then
line 5 must be true, whether *A* (the assumed premise) is true or false. Line 5 does not assert
that (*A* · *B*) is the case, but only that (*A* · *B*) is the case *on the condition* that *A* is the case.
The notation to the right of line 5 indicates that the technique used is that of conditional
proof (**CP**) using an **assumed premise** (an assumption—something not stated as a premise in the original problem); it lists the line of the assumed premise as well as the last line
that depends on the assumed premise.

To keep track of assumed premises, what we wish to prove from them, and the lines
that depend on them, let's use arrows and lines so that the proof we have been discussing
will look like this:

    1. *A* ⊃ *B*   p /∴ *A* ⊃ (*A* · *B*)
→2. *A*   **Assumed Premise** (or simply **AP**) /∴ *A* · *B*
    3. *B*   1,2 **MP**
    4. *A* · *B*   2,3 **Conj**
    5. *A* ⊃ (*A* · *B*)   2–4 **CP**

The arrow pointing at line 2 indicates that line 2 is an assumed premise not given as
part of the original problem. The line drawn down from line 2 to below line 4 indicates
that lines 3 and 4 *depend on* line 2 (in addition perhaps to the original premise). Such lines
are said to be within the *scope of the assumed premise.* The horizontal line drawn between
lines 4 and 5 indicates that the lines to follow do not depend on line 2; that is, it indicates
the scope of this assumed premise ends with line 4. From this point onward the assumption is said to have been **discharged.**

Using the arrow and line notation just introduced, we can express the structure of the
rule of conditional proof (or argument form) as follows:

   → *p*   **AP** /∴ *q*
      ·
      ·
      ·
    q
    p ⊃ *q*   **CP**

This indicates a premise is assumed, other lines are derived from it, and then the assumed
premise is discharged as a premise, being retained as the antecedent of the line *p* ⊃ *q*.

Example

Every correct application of **CP** incorporates the following elements:

1. The sentence justified by **CP** must be a conditional.
2. The antecedent of that conditional must be the assumed premise.
3. The consequent of that conditional must be the sentence from the preceding line.
4. Lines are drawn indicating the scope of the assumed premise.

1.	~ A	p
2.	C ∨ B	p /∴ (A ∨ ~ B) ⊃ (D ∨ C)
3.	A ∨ ~ B	AP /∴ D ∨ ~ C
4.	~ B	1,3 DS
5.	C	2,4 DS
6.	C ∨ D	5 Add
7.	D ∨ C	6 Comm
8.	(A ∨ ~ B) ⊃ (D ∨ C)	3–7 CP

Another way to consider conditional proofs is this. In a sense, *every* valid argument is conditional, since the truth of the conclusion is conditional on the truth of the premises on which the conclusion depends. What is different about a so-called conditional proof is simply that some lines in a conditional proof depend on a line (the assumed premise) on which the conclusion does not depend, a line that was not given as a premise in the original problem. It is as though a line were introduced as a premise, a conclusion were drawn from it (in conjunction with the other premises), and then that premise were discharged as premise (or "taken back" as a premise), being retained rather as a *condition on* the acceptance of the conclusion, that is, retained as the antecedent of a new conditional's conclusion.

It is important to note that once an assumed premise is discharged, we no longer can use it, or any line that depends on it, to derive additional lines. For instance, in the previous example, we cannot assert as line 6 the sentence ~ ~ (A · B), following from line 4 by **DN**, since we have already discharged line 2 as a premise. It may help you to think of the horizontal line as boxing off all the lines between the arrow (the assumed premise) and the line just above the horizontal line. *In effect, all you gain from a conditional proof is one line, a conditional, which will be the line just below the horizontal line.* Of course, that conditional may very well be the key to solving the proof, if not the conclusion itself.

One reason for introducing rule **CP** is to render our system complete, as we remarked earlier. But this goal of completeness could have been reached just as easily by introducing any one of several other rules. The one most frequently chosen, as a matter of fact, is **Absorption:** $p \supset q / \therefore p \supset (p \cdot q)$ (a generalization of the argument $A \supset B / \therefore A \supset (A \cdot B)$) discussed earlier. One reason to choose **CP** over Absorption is its tremendous power to shorten the proofs of many valid arguments and, in particular, to make proofs of a great many arguments a good deal easier to discover.

But the most important reason for introducing a rule such as **CP** is that we want our system of rules to be a natural deduction system; that is, we want our rules to capture the sort of argumentation that goes on in, say, mathematics, or indeed, in everyday life. "Natural" arguments such as these commonly employ assumptions. A geometer may ask you to assume the existence of a given triangle, to prove a general truth about all triangles. A lawyer may quite reasonably ask the jury to assume, for the moment, that her client is guilty, to show what would follow from this assumption. "So you see, ladies and gentlemen, if my client is guilty as the prosecution says, their own star witness is not telling the truth about what happened that night." **CP** is designed to capture this natural way of deducing a conditional.

Rule **CP** turns out to be useful in almost any kind of case, but it tends to be most useful when we're dealing with arguments that have conditional conclusions, or conclusions that can be translated into conditional form. Here is a classic example, with **CP** proof attached:

$$
\begin{array}{lll}
1. & A \supset B & \text{p} \\
2. & C \supset D & \text{p} /\therefore (A \vee C) \supset (B \vee D) \\
\to 3. & A \vee C & \textbf{AP} /\therefore B \vee D \\
 4. & B \vee D & 1, 2, 3 \textbf{ CD} \\
5. & (A \vee C) \supset (B \vee D) & 3\text{--}4 \textbf{ CP}
\end{array}
$$

Short and easily discovered, this **CP** proof contrasts starkly with proofs of the argument that do not use **CP**. Anyone who doubts that is invited to prove the argument valid using only the eighteen valid argument forms (toss in Absorption if you feel like it).

Notice that we chose the antecedent of the conditional conclusion as our assumed premise. When *using CP, always assume the antecedent of the conditional you hope to justify via CP.*

In the preceding example, only one assumed premise was used. But *any number* of assumptions can be introduced into a proof, provided every one is eventually discharged, so the conclusion of the argument depends only on the given premises. Proofs of equivalences commonly involve two separate subproofs, as the following proof illustrates:

$$
\begin{array}{lll}
1. & A \supset {\sim} C & \text{p} \\
2. & {\sim} B \supset C & \text{p} \\
3. & A \vee {\sim} B & \text{p} /\therefore A \equiv B \\
\to 4. & A & \textbf{AP} /\therefore B \\
 5. & {\sim} C & 1,4 \textbf{ MP} \\
 6. & {\sim}{\sim} B & 2,5 \textbf{ MT} \\
 7. & B & 6 \textbf{ DN} \\
8. & A \supset B & 4\text{--}7 \textbf{ CP} \\
\to 9. & B & \textbf{AP} /\therefore A \\
 10. & {\sim}{\sim} B & 9 \textbf{ DN} \\
 11. & A & 3,10 \textbf{ DS} \\
12. & B \supset A & 9\text{--}11 \textbf{ CP}
\end{array}
$$

13. $(A \supset B) \cdot (B \supset A)$ 8, 12 **Conj**
14. $A \equiv B$ 13 **Equiv**

Here is a different kind of case involving multiple assumptions:

1. $C \supset D$ $p / \therefore A \supset [B \supset (C \supset D)]$
2. A **AP** $/ \therefore B \supset (C \supset D)$
3. B **AP** $/ \therefore C \supset D$
4. C **AP** $/ \therefore D$
5. D 1,4 **MP**
6. $C \supset D$ 4–5 **CP**
7. $B \supset (C \supset D)$ 3–6 **CP**
8. $A \supset [B \supset (C \supset D)]$ 2–7 **CP**

In this example, there are *three* assumed premises, *A, B,* and *C*. But the proof itself is really quite simple. Every step of this proof is automatic with the exception of line 5, an obvious **MP** step. There is no need to agonize over which rule to use. As a general rule of thumb when you need to derive a line that is a conditional, assume the antecedent and try to derive the consequent, thereby allowing you to derive the entire conditional by **CP**. In this case, since we need to derive $A \supset [B \supset (C \supset D)]$ we assume *A* and try to get $B \supset (C \supset D)$. Once again, we find ourselves needing to derive a conditional, so we assume *B* and work toward $C \supset D$. Of course, this is another conditional, so we assume *C* and try to derive *D*—leaving us needing only the obvious **MP** step to complete the proof.

A great deal of freedom comes with **CP.** You can assume *anything,* provided that each assumption is eventually discharged properly. Our notation is designed to ensure that every assumption has been properly discharged. Every assumption should be marked by an arrow, each arrow must terminate in a horizontal line, and no two lines should intersect.

You can assume anything, but not all assumptions are profitable. Here is a very important rule of thumb: *In deciding what to assume, be guided by the conclusion or intermediate step you hope to reach, not by the premises.* For example, consider the following proof:

1. $A \supset B$ p
2. $(A \supset C) \supset D$ $p / \therefore (B \supset C) \supset D$

Looking at the premises, you may be tempted to assume *A*, or $A \supset C$ (so you can apply **MP**). You can make these assumptions if you like, but whatever assumption you make must be discharged. So if you assume *A,* all you eventually gain, after you discharge the assumption with **CP,** is a conditional that has *A* as its antecedent. Likewise, assuming $A \supset C$ will eventually leave you with a conditional that has $A \supset C$ as its antecedent. Neither assumption gets you any closer to completing the proof.

What you *should* assume in this particular proof is the antecedent of the conclusion, as follows:

1. $A \supset B$	p
2. $(A \supset C) \supset D$	p /∴ $(B \supset C) \supset D$
→3. $B \supset C$	AP /∴ D
4. $A \supset C$	1,3 **HS**
5. D	2,4 **MP**
6. $(B \supset C) \supset D$	3–5 **CP**

Sometimes you can make a proof much shorter by working backward from the conclusion a bit before deciding what to assume, as the following example illustrates:

1. $(E \cdot C) \supset B$	p
2. $C \supset (D \cdot E)$	p /∴ $\sim B \supset \sim C$
→3. C	AP /∴ B
4. $D \cdot E$	2,3 **MP**
5. E	4 **Simp**
6. $E \cdot C$	3,5 **Conj**
7. B	1,6 **MP**
8. $C \supset B$	3–7 **CP**
9. $\sim B \supset \sim C$	8 **Contra**

What is assumed in this proof isn't the antecedent of the conclusion. Rather, it is the antecedent of the contrapositive (obtained by Contraposition) of the conclusion. You can complete this proof by assuming $\sim B$, but it is a much more difficult proof. So keep in mind that it sometimes is useful to assume the antecedent of the contrapositive of a conditional rather than the antecedent of the conditional itself. (This strategy will be especially useful in completing predicate logic proofs as we explain in Chapter Seven.)

An assumption that falls within the scope of another assumption is called a *nested assumption*. We had an example earlier of a proof with two nested assumptions. The thing to remember with nested assumptions is that you must discharge the nested assumption before you can discharge the original assumption. The lines that indicate the scope of your assumptions must never intersect.

You can avoid nesting assumptions, and make your proof a bit shorter, by working backward from your conclusion, using Exportation. So here is a shorter proof of the argument on page 129:

1. $C \supset D$	p /∴ $A \supset [B \supset (C \supset D)]$
→2. $(A \cdot B) \cdot C$	AP /∴ D
3. C	2 **Simp**
4. D	1,3 **MP**
5. $[(A \cdot B) \cdot C] \supset D$	2–5 **CP**
6. $(A \cdot B) \supset (C \supset D)$	5 **Exp**
7. $A \supset [B \supset (C \supset D)]$	6 **Exp**

Even if your conclusion is not a conditional, you may be able to use **CP**. If the conclusion is a disjunction, you can work backward using implication to find a conditional that is equivalent to the conclusion, and then use **CP** to obtain that conditional. If your conclusion is a biconditional, work backward using **Equiv** to change the biconditional into a conjunction of two conditionals. You can use **CP** to separately prove each conditional. These two strategies are illustrated among the examples that follow.

🚶 Walk-Through: Using CP

Here's a proof that would be impossible without **CP**:

1. $A \supset B$ p
2. $C \vee \sim B$ p /∴ $A \supset (A \cdot C)$

Looking at the conclusion, we assume the antecedent and work to derive the consequent:

→3. A AP /∴ $A \cdot C$

    .
    .
    .

_. $A \cdot C$ _
. $A \supset (A \cdot C)$ 3– **CP**

Completing the rest of the proof is quite straightforward.

→3. A AP /∴ $A \cdot C$
 4. B 1,3 **MP**
 5. $\sim \sim B$ 4 **DN**
 6. C 2,5 **DS**
 7. $A \cdot C$ 3,6 **Conj**

 8. $A \supset (A \cdot C)$ 3–7 **CP**

Once you get used to it, **CP** is really quite simple. When to use it is obvious. Use it routinely whenever you need to derive a conditional. Here is a slightly more complicated proof:

1. $(M \vee N) \supset P$ p /∴ $[(P \vee Q) \supset R] \supset (M \supset R)$

Right away we assume our antecedent, and pencil in the consequent as our next-to-last step.

1. $(M \vee N) \supset P$ p /∴ $[(P \vee Q) \supset R] \supset (M \supset R)$
→2. $(P \vee Q) \supset R$ AP /∴ $M \supset R$

    .
    .
    .

_. $M \supset R$ _
. $[(P \vee Q) \supset R] \supset (M \supset R)$ 2– **CP**

We still need to derive a conditional, so let's use another assumption:

1. $(M \vee N) \supset P$ p /∴ $[(P \vee Q) \supset R] \supset (M \supset R)$
→2. $(P \vee Q) \supset R$ AP /∴ $M \supset R$
→3. M AP /∴ R

      .
      .
      .

_. R _
. $M \supset R$ 3– **CP**
. $[(P \vee Q) \supset R] \supset (M \supset R)$ 2– **CP**

Note that by using **CP** we have, in effect, taken a difficult one-premise proof and transformed it into a much simpler three-premise proof. Completing the proof now is simply a matter of making liberal use of Addition.

1. $(M \vee N) \supset P$ p /∴ $[(P \vee Q) \supset R] \supset (M \supset R)$
→2. $(P \vee Q) \supset R$ AP /∴ $M \supset R$
→3. M AP /∴ R
4. $M \vee N$ 3 **Add**
5. P 1,4 **MP**
6. $P \vee Q$ 5 **Add**
7. R 2,6 **MP**
8. $M \supset R$ 3–7 **CP**
9. $[(P \vee Q) \supset R] \supset (M \supset R)$ 2–8 **CP**

Examples

The following proofs contain correct uses of the rule of conditional proof:

(1)   1. $(A \vee B) \supset (C \cdot D)$ p
      2. $(D \vee E) \supset F$ p /∴ $\sim A \vee F$
→3. A AP /∴ F
      4. $A \vee B$ 3 **Add**
      5. $C \cdot D$ 1,4 **MP**
      6. D 5 **Simp**
      7. $D \vee E$ 6 **Add**
      8. F 2,7 **MP**
      9. $A \supset F$ 3–8 **CP**
    10. $\sim A \vee F$ 9 **Imp**

(2) 1. $(Z \supset Y) \supset X$ p
    2. $T \lor S$ p
    3. $\sim (Z \cdot T)$ p
    4. $\sim Y \supset \sim S$ p /∴ X
  →5. Z AP /∴ Y
    6. $\sim Z \lor \sim T$ 3 DeM
    7. $\sim \sim Z$ 5 DN
    8. $\sim T$ 6,7 DS
    9. S 2,8 DS
  10. $S \supset Y$ 4 Contra
  11. Y 9,10 MP
  12. $Z \supset Y$ 5–11 CP
  13. X 1,12 MP

(3) 1. $A \supset C$ p
    2. $B \supset D$ p
    3. $(C \lor D) \supset A$ p /∴ $(A \lor B) \equiv (C \lor D)$
  →4. $A \lor B$ AP /∴ $C \lor D$
    5. $C \lor D$ 1,2,4 CD
    6. $(A \lor B) \supset (C \lor D)$ 4–5 CP
  →7. $C \lor D$ AP /∴ $A \lor B$
    8. A 3,7 MP
    9. $A \lor B$ 8 Add
  10. $(C \lor D) \supset (A \lor B)$ 7–9 CP
  11. $[(A \lor B) \supset (C \lor D)] \cdot$
      $[(C \lor D) \supset (A \lor B)]$ 6,10 Conj
  12. $(A \lor B) \equiv (C \lor D)$ 11 Equiv

Exercise 5-1

Prove valid using **CP** (and the eighteen valid argument forms).

(1) 1. B /∴ $A \supset (A \cdot B)$

(2) 1. $A \supset (B \cdot C)$ /∴ $A \supset C$

(3) 1. $B \supset C$
        /∴ $(A \supset B) \supset (A \supset C)$

(4) 1. $A \supset (B \supset C)$
    2. $\sim C$ /∴ $A \supset \sim B$

(5) (Hint: This one is tricky but
    can be done!)
    1. C /∴ $A \supset (B \supset C)$

(6) 1. $A \supset (B \supset C)$
    2. $A \supset B$ /∴ $A \supset C$

(7) 1. $A \supset B$
    2. $A \supset C$ /∴ $A \supset (B \cdot C)$

(8) 1. $(A \cdot B) \supset C$
    2. $(B \cdot C) \supset D$ /∴ $(A \cdot B) \supset D$

(9) 1. $R \supset (L \cdot S)$
    2. $(L \lor M) \supset P$ /∴ $\sim P \supset \sim R$

(10) 1. $A \supset (B \supset C)$
     2. $C \supset D / \therefore A \supset (B \supset D)$

(11) 1. $A \lor \sim (B \cdot C) / \therefore B \supset (C \supset A)$

(12) 1. $A \supset (B \cdot C)$
     2. $D \supset (E \cdot F)$
     3. $D \lor A / \therefore B \lor F$

(13) 1. $\sim H \lor \sim F$
     2. $\sim M \supset F$
     3. $(\sim H \lor M) \supset \sim F$
         $/ \therefore (H \supset M) \cdot \sim F$

(14) 1. $D \supset G / \therefore (D \cdot G) \equiv D$

(15) 1. $N \equiv P / \therefore (N \supset R) \equiv (P \supset R)$

Exercise 5-2

Use **CP** to prove arguments (5), (6), (8) (9), (13), (14), and (15) in Exercise 4-13. Compare the length and difficulty of your answers with your answers to Exercise 4-13.

2   *Indirect Proofs*

A **contradiction**, or *contradictory sentence,* is any sentence that is inconsistent—any sentence that cannot possibly be true. Some contradictions are more obvious than others. An **explicit contradiction** is a sentence of the form $p \cdot \sim p$. Obviously, such sentences cannot possibly be true; they are necessarily false. Logic alone guarantees the falsity of contradictions. Given the definition of a valid argument, a false sentence cannot be validly inferred from true premises. So if we infer validly to a contradiction, we have shown, without question, that at least one of our premises must be false.

Now consider, say, a four-premise argument, and assume we know three of its four premises are true. If we derive a contradiction from that set of four premises, we have proved the fourth premise in the set is false (since at least one member of the set is false, and we assume the other three are true). So we also have proved the negation of the fourth premise is true (since the negation of a false sentence is true). We have here the main ideas behind the rule of **indirect proof (IP).** (Indirect proofs also are known as **reductio ad absurdum proofs,** because in an indirect proof an assumption is "reduced to absurdity" by showing that it implies a contradiction.)

Take the following argument:

    1. $A \supset B$ p
    2. $B \supset C$ p
    3. A p $/ \therefore C$

First, let's add the negation of the conclusion, namely $\sim C$, to this set of premises, to obtain the following set:

1. $A \supset B$ p
2. $B \supset C$ p
3. A p

→ 4. ~ C **AP** /∴ C

Then we can obtain a contradiction as follows:

5. ~ B 2,4 **MT**
6. ~ A 1,5 **MT**
7. $A \cdot {\sim} A$ 3,6 **Conj**

Obviously, if premises 1, 2, and 3 are true, then the added premise 4, ~ C, is false. And if ~ C is false, then C must be true. Using our new rule, **IP,** we can now discharge ~ C, having shown that that assumption implies a contradiction, and place the desired conclusion, C, on a new line.

8. C 4–7 **IP**

To sum up, by assuming ~ C and then deriving a contradiction we have shown that the argument

1. $A \supset B$ p
2. $B \supset C$ p
3. A p /∴ C

is valid, because we have shown that if its premises are true, then its conclusion, C, must be true (because ~ C must be false).

The general method employed in an indirect proof, then, is to add the negation of the conclusion of an argument to its set of premises and derive a contradiction. If the conclusion is already a negation, you can just assume the conclusion minus the initial negation sign, instead of assuming a double negation. The following diagram illustrates these two versions of the rule.

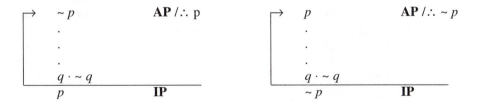

The derivation of the contradiction proves that if the original premises are true, then the *negation* of the added premise must be *true*. Since the negation of the added premise is the conclusion of the argument in question, the conclusion must be true, and hence proves that the argument is valid.

Example

Every correct application of **IP** incorporates the following elements:

1. The sentence justified by **IP** must be the denial of the assumed premise.
2. The preceding line must be a substitution instance of the form p · ~ p.
3. Lines are drawn indicating the scope of the assumed premise.

$$
\begin{array}{lll}
1. & \sim A & \text{p} \\
2. & C \vee B & \text{p} \\
3. & C \supset (A \vee B) & \text{p} /\therefore B \\
4. & \sim B & \textbf{AP} /\therefore B \\
5. & C & 2,4\ \textbf{DS} \\
6. & A \vee B & 3,5\ \textbf{MP} \\
7. & A & 4\text{–}6\ \textbf{DS} \\
8. & A \cdot \sim A & 1\text{–}7\ \textbf{Conj} \\
9. & B & 4\text{–}8\ \textbf{IP}
\end{array}
$$

Here is another example of an indirect proof (using arrows and lines as in conditional proofs to keep track of assumed premises and the lines that depend on them):

$$
\begin{array}{lll}
1. & A \supset X & \text{p} \\
2. & (C \vee \sim X) \supset A & \text{p} /\therefore X \\
3. & \sim X & \textbf{AP (the negation of the conclusion)} /\therefore X \\
4. & \sim A & 1,3\ \textbf{MT} \\
5. & \sim (C \vee \sim X) & 2,4\ \textbf{MT} \\
6. & \sim C \cdot \sim \sim X & 5\ \textbf{DeM} \\
7. & \sim C \cdot X & 6\ \textbf{DN} \\
8. & X & 7\ \textbf{Simp} \\
9. & X \cdot \sim X & 3,8\ \textbf{Conj} \\
10. & X & 3\text{–}9\ \textbf{IP}
\end{array}
$$

Notice that the contradiction obtained is simply the conjunction of the assumed premise and the conclusion. This is perfectly permissible: The derivation of any explicit contradiction is all that is required. Notice also that the proof does not stop with line 8. As with conditional proof, the assumption must be discharged. We could discharge the assumption with conditional proof, but that would prove only ~ X ⊃ X. But once the explicit contradiction is obtained, the rule of indirect proof permits the assertion of the conclusion independently of the assumed premise.

Given what we have said in Chapter Three about the test statement form for the validity of sentential arguments, our results here should be easy to understand. If an argument is valid, then the conjunction of its premises with the negation of its conclusion must be a contradiction. When we add as an assumed premise the negation of the conclusion of a valid argument, we have in effect *conjoined the original premises of the argument with a statement that, together with those premises, must be a contradiction.* When we use the method of indirect proof, we make the contradiction explicit by deriving if from that conjunction.

Another way to see that the rule of indirect proof is valid is to recognize that anything that can be proved by indirect proof can be proved by a slightly longer conditional proof. Consider the following skeleton of a typical indirect proof:

```
1.  ?              p
2.  ?              p /∴ A
3.  ~ A            AP /∴ A
4.  ?
5.  ?
6.  B · ~ B        ?,? Conj
```

Every indirect proof begins by assuming the negation of the desired conclusion (here we've arbitrarily chosen *A* as our conclusion, but the point we are making will work with any conclusion) and deriving a contradiction. (Again, we've just arbitrarily supplied a contradiction—any contradiction would do.) Once a contradiction is derived, the rule of indirect proof permits the assertion of the conclusion, in this case *A:*

```
7.  A              3–6 IP
```

Line 7 is permitted in an indirect proof because the premise assumed (in line 3) is the negation of the conclusion, *A;* and use of that assumed premise (plus the original premises) led to a contradiction.

But line 7, or any line derived by **IP,** can be derived by **CP.** This is because any sentence can be derived from a proof that contains a contradiction. This is illustrated by the following argument:

```
1.  B · ~ B        p /∴ X
2.  B              1 Simp
3.  B ∨ X          2 Add
4.  ~ B            1 Simp
5.  X              3,4 DS
```

Obviously, the conclusion *X* might have been *any* sentence whatever. Therefore, from the contradiction *B · ~ B,* indeed from any contradiction, it is clear that *any* sentence whatever can be obtained.

Returning to our skeleton of an indirect proof, one sentence in particular that can be derived is the negation of our assumed premise, as follows:

```
1.  ?              p
2.  ?              p /∴ A
3.  ~ A            AP /∴ A
4.  ?
5.  ?
6.  B · ~ B        ?,? Conj
7.  B              6 Simp
8.  B ∨ A          7 Add
9.  ~ B            6 Simp
10. A              8,9 DS
```

The proof is not complete at this point because we have not discharged the assumption. If we now discharge the assumption with **CP,** we get the following odd conditional:

11. ~ *A* ⊃ *A*   3–10 **CP**

But from this point it is a simple matter to obtain *A*:

12. ~ ~ *A* ∨ *A*   11 **Impl**
13. *A* ∨ *A*   12 **DN**
14. *A*   13 **Taut**

This example illustrates that whenever the negation of the conclusion of an argument is taken as an assumed premise in a conditional proof and a contradiction is derived, then it must be possible to obtain the conclusion of the argument by the procedure just illustrated (so that the conclusion depends on the original premises, but not on the assumed premise). But since this always can be done, there is little point in actually doing so in every case. Instead, we permit the use of the rule of indirect proof, which we now see is simply a shorter way of proving what could have been proved by conditional proof.

Exercise 5-3

Prove the following arguments valid, using **IP.**

(1) 1. *A* ∨ *B*
     2. *A* ∨ ~ *B* /∴ *A*

(2) 1. ~ *A* ⊃ *B*
     2. ~ (~ *A* · *B*) /∴ *A*

(3) 1. *A* ⊃ (*B* · *C*)
     2. ~ *B* /∴ ~ *A*

(4) 1. *A* ∨ (~ *B* · *C*)
     2. *B* ⊃ ~ *A* /∴ ~ *B*

(5) 1. *A* ⊃ ~ *B*
     2. *B* ∨ *C*
     3. *A* ∨ *C* /∴ *C*

(6) 1. (*A* · *B*) ⊃ *C*
     2. ~ *A* ⊃ *C*
     3. *B* /∴ *C*

(7) 1. *A* ⊃ *B*
     2. *C* ⊃ *D*
     3. (*B* ∨ *D*) ⊃ *E*
     4. ~ *E* /∴ ~ (*A* ∨ *C*)

(8) 1. *A* ⊃ (*B* ⊃ *C*)
     2. *A* ⊃ *B*
     3. ~ *C* ⊃ (*A* ∨ *D*) /∴ *C* ∨ *D*

(9) 1. ~ *A*
     2. (*A* ∨ *B*) ≡ *C*
     3. ~ *B* /∴ ~ (*C* · *D*)

(10) 1. *C* ⊃ [*D* ∨ ~ (*A* ∨ *B*)]
     2. ~ *A* ⊃ *B* /∴ ~ *D* ⊃ ~ *C*

Exercise 5-4

Prove valid, first without using **IP** or **CP,** and then using **IP,** and compare the lengths and difficulty of the corresponding proofs. Warning! Some of these are very difficult when worked without **IP** or **CP!**

(1) 1. *A* ⊃ *B*
     2. *C* ⊃ *A*
     3. *C* ∨ (*B* · *D*) /∴ *B*

(2) 1. *H* ⊃ (*A* ⊃ *B*)
     2. ~ *C* ⊃ (*H* ∨ *B*)
     3. *H* ⊃ *A* /∴ *C* ∨ *B*

(3)   1. $P \vee Q$
       2. $Q \supset (R \cdot S)$
       3. $(R \vee P) \supset T /\therefore T$

(4)   1. $(R \supset M) \supset L$
       2. $(N \vee S) \supset (M \cdot T)$
       3. $(P \supset R) \supset L$
       4. $(T \vee K) \supset \sim N /\therefore L$

(5)   1. $H \supset (A \cdot B)$
       2. $B \supset (M \vee \sim A)$
       3. $M \supset (\sim H \vee \sim B) /\therefore \sim H$

3   *Strategy Hints for Using CP and IP*

The main point of strategy is that by prudent use of **CP** or **IP** you can often make a difficult proof much easier to solve. Use **CP** routinely if your conclusion is a conditional. Even if it is not a conditional, if it is equivalent to a conditional, use **CP** to derive *that* formula. Also, remember to check to see if it would be even more useful to assume the negation of the target conditional's consequent, derive the negation of the antecedent, use **CP**, and apply contraposition to the result.*

    Every proof can be solved using **IP.** So if all else fails, try using **IP.** (Note, however, that it isn't necessarily a good idea to routinely try **IP** first; sometimes solving with **IP** makes the proof more difficult.) When you use **IP,** you should try to break down complex formulas into simpler units. This is often the quickest way to find a contradiction. **IP** is particularly useful when the conclusion is either atomic or a negated atomic sentence. In this case, **IP** is not just a last recourse—it's the preferred method. More often than not short premises make for easier proofs and short conclusions make for harder ones. Using **IP** on a proof that has a short conclusion gives you an additional useful short premise to work with, and you are no longer forced to derive the difficult short conclusion directly— any contradiction will do.

Exercise 5-5

Prove valid using **IP** or **CP:**

(1)   1. $\sim (P \cdot \sim Q)$
       2. $\sim Q \vee M$
       3. $R \supset \sim M /\therefore P \supset \sim (R \vee \sim M)$

(2)   1. $F \vee G$
       2. $H \cdot (I \supset F)$
       3. $H \supset \sim F /\therefore G \cdot \sim I$

(3)   1. $(A \cdot B) \vee C$
       2. $(A \cdot B) \supset (E \supset A)$
       3. $C \supset D /\therefore (E \supset A) \vee D$

(4)   1. $S \vee (T \supset R)$
       2. $S \supset T$
       3. $\sim (T \supset R) /\therefore T$

(5)   1. $\sim (T \vee U)$
       2. S
       3. $R \equiv \sim S /\therefore \sim (U \vee R)$

(6)   1. $\sim A \supset (D \cdot C)$
       2. $\sim (B \cdot A) /\therefore \sim C \supset \sim B$

---

*For an example, see the discussion on page 130.

(7) 1. $A \supset (\sim D \supset C)$
     2. $\sim D \supset (C \supset B)$
     3. $\sim (D \cdot A) /\therefore A \supset B$

(8) 1. $A \vee (\sim B \vee \sim C)$
     2. $A \supset (D \supset E)$
     3. $\sim (\sim B \vee \sim D) /\therefore C \supset E$

(9) 1. $I \supset F$
     2. $G \supset (H \supset I)$
     3. $\sim (\sim H \vee F) /\therefore \sim G$

(10) 1. $S \vee (T \cdot R)$
     2. $S \supset T /\therefore T$

(11) 1. $(D \vee E) \supset C$
     2. $(A \vee B) \supset \sim C /\therefore D \supset \sim B$

(12) 1. $(H \vee K) \supset (L \vee K)$
     2. $M \supset [H \supset (N \cdot \sim L)]$
           $/\therefore (M \cdot H) \supset (N \cdot K)$

(13) 1. $C \equiv D$
     2. $B \supset (D \cdot E)$
     3. $\sim C \vee \sim D /\therefore \sim B$

(14) 1. $D \supset (E \supset F)$
     2. $H \supset (E \vee G)$
     3. $D \supset (G \supset \sim H)$
           $/\therefore \sim (\sim F \supset \sim H) \supset \sim D$

(15) 1. $N \supset (P \supset R)$
     2. $\sim (R \supset S) \supset \sim T$
     3. $(M \vee \sim T) \vee \sim (P \supset S)$
           $/\therefore \sim M \supset \sim (N \cdot T)$

4 *Zero-Premise Deductions*

Every truth table tautology can be proved in our natural deduction system by what is called a **zero-premise deduction.** This is a result of the fact that our system of rules is complete (see Section 7 for a full discussion) and that a tautology follows from any set of premises validly, because there is no way, when we have a tautology as a conclusion, to have true premises and a false conclusion. Tautologies are thus sometimes termed **theorems** of logic. But how can we prove that a tautology follows from any premises whatever? Since the negation of a tautology is a contradiction, if we use **IP** by assuming the negation of a tautology, we should be able to derive a contradiction independently of any other premises; the tautology is only derived from our assumption. Hence we describe the process as a *zero-premise deduction.*

Indeed, **CP** often works as well; we note again that every test statement of a valid argument is a conditional and is a tautology. Assuming the antecedent of this conditional is equivalent to assuming the premises of the valid argument. So we can then derive its consequent just as we would if the argument we had been given to prove had the corresponding premises and conclusion. Discharging the assumptions then gives us the test statement form in question.

Since you are not provided with premises in proofs of theorems, you must use either **CP** or **IP** and begin the proof with an assumed premise. Suppose, for example, you want to prove the theorem $A \vee \sim A$. You can prove this theorem using **IP** as follows:

```
→1. ~(A ∨ ~A)        AP /∴ A ∨ ~A
  2. ~A · ~~A         1 DeM
  3. A ∨ ~A           1–2 IP
```

Here is an example of a theorem that is proved with **CP**:

```
→1.  ~A                     AP /∴ A ⊃ B
  2.  ~A ∨ B                1 Add
  3.  A ⊃ B                 2 Impl
  4.  ~A ⊃ (A ⊃ B)          1–3 CP
```

Exercise 5-6

Prove that the following sentences are theorems.

(1) $A \supset (A \lor B)$

(2) $(A \cdot B) \supset A$

(3) $A \supset (\sim A \supset B)$

(4) $[A \supset (B \supset C)] \supset$
     $[(A \supset B) \supset (A \supset C)]$

(5) $(A \lor B) \supset [C \supset (A \lor B)]$

(6) $(A \lor B) \supset \{[(A \supset C) \cdot$
     $(B \supset C)] \supset C\}$

(7) $(A \lor B) \supset [(A \supset B) \lor (B \supset A)]$

(8) $(A \equiv B) \equiv (\sim A \equiv \sim B)$

5 *Proving Premises Inconsistent*

In general, logic alone cannot determine the truth values of premises. But if the premises of an argument (taken as a unit) are inconsistent, then at least one of them must be false, and this fact can be proved by logic alone. Of course, we can use truth tables to show that a set of premises is inconsistent, but we can also show this by means of natural deduction. To prove that an argument has inconsistent premises, use the eighteen valid argument forms to derive a contradiction from the premises. (And, of course, to prove *any* set of statements inconsistent, use the same method.)

For example, consider an argument with the following premises:

```
1.  A ⊃ B          p
2.  A ⊃ ~B         p
3.  A              p
```

From these premises we can derive a contradiction, as follows:

```
4.  B              1,3 MP
5.  ~B             2,3 MP
6.  B · ~B         4,5 Conj
```

Since line 6 is an explicit contradiction, it must be false. And if it is false, then at least one premise must be false, since line 6 follows from the premises. Thus, taken together, the premises form a false conjunction. But that conjunction is not contingently false, since its falsehood is proved by logic alone. so it must be false because it is *contradictory*, that is, inconsistent.

In Chapter Three we used truth tables to explain why all arguments with inconsistent premises are valid. Now we are in position to see how this same result is borne out in natural deduction. If you can derive a contradiction from the premises alone, obviously you can prove any conclusion you like by means of the rule of Indirect Proof. Simply assume the negation of the desired conclusion and derive a contradiction. For example, consider the following proof:

$$
\begin{array}{lll}
1. & A & \text{p} \\
2. & \sim A & \text{p}\ /\therefore\ X \\
\rightarrow 3. & \sim X & \textbf{AP}\ /\therefore\ X \\
4. & A \cdot \sim A & 1,2\ \textbf{Conj} \\
5. & X & 3\text{--}4\ \textbf{IP}
\end{array}
$$

Obviously, we could prove *any* conclusion from these two premises, or from any other inconsistent premises.

Exercise 5-7

A. Prove that the following arguments all have inconsistent premises.

(1) 1. $B \supset (\sim C \cdot \sim D)$
    2. $C \lor D$
    3. $B\ /\therefore\ \sim D \supset C$

(2) 1. $\sim A \lor B$
    2. $\sim B \lor \sim A$
    3. $A\ /\therefore\ B$

(3) 1. $A \cdot \sim B$
    2. $B \supset A$
    3. $A \supset B\ /\therefore\ B$

(4) 1. $\sim R \cdot \sim S$
    2. $S \lor (\sim S \cdot T)$
    3. $\sim (R \lor S) \supset \sim (S \lor T)\ /\therefore\ R$

(5) 1. $A \supset (B \lor C)$
    2. $\sim (\sim A \lor C)$
    3. $\sim B\ /\therefore\ C$

(6) 1. $(H \lor \sim H) \supset (L \lor K)$
    2. $(L \lor K) \supset (H \lor \sim H)$
    3. $(H \cdot \sim H) \supset (L \lor K)$
    4. $(L \lor K) \supset (H \cdot \sim H)$
        $/\therefore\ (K \cdot \sim L) \supset H$

(7) 1. $K \supset (L \supset M)$
    2. $N \lor K$
    3. $\sim (\sim L \lor M)$
    4. $\sim N\ /\therefore\ K \supset (\sim M \lor L)$

(8) 1. $A \supset (C \supset B)$
    2. $(B \cdot C) \lor A$
    3. $C \lor (B \cdot A)$
    4. $B \supset \sim C$
    5. $D \lor B$
    6. $B \cdot \sim A\ /\therefore\ B \lor (A \supset D)$

(9) 1. $A \supset (C \supset D)$
    2. $\sim A \supset (D \supset C)$
    3. $(A \lor \sim A) \supset \sim D$
    4. $(A \cdot D) \lor (\sim A \cdot \sim D)$
    5. $(C \cdot D) \lor (\sim C \cdot \sim D)$
    6. $A\ /\therefore\ D$

(10) 1. $A \supset (B \supset C)$
    2. $\sim [\sim C \lor (A \lor \sim D)]$
    3. $\sim \{\sim A \lor [C \supset (B \cdot D)]\}$
        $/\therefore\ (A \lor C) \supset D$

B. You can know that all these arguments are valid without proving any of them. Why? How?

6 *Adding Valid Argument Forms*

Once we have become familiar with the eighteen valid argument forms, once we have become *practiced* in their use, once all systematic errors in their use have been eliminated, it becomes convenient to simplify proofs by combining two or more rules into one step. Logical candidates are rules that are frequently used together—for example, **DeM** and **DN, DN** and **Impl,** and two uses of **DN.**

Here is a proof using the first two of these shortcuts:

1. $A \vee B$ p
2. $\sim (B \cdot \sim C)$ p /∴ $\sim A \supset C$
3. $\sim A \supset B$ 1 **DN, Impl**
4. $\sim B \vee C$ 2 **DeM, DN**
5. $B \supset C$ 4 **Impl**
6. $\sim A \supset C$ 3,5 **HS**

And here is one using Double Negation twice on one line:

1. $(F \cdot G) \supset H$ p
2. $\sim (\sim F \vee \sim G)$ p /∴ H
3. $\sim \sim F \cdot \sim \sim G$ 2 **DeM**
4. $F \cdot G$ 3 **DN** (twice)
5. H 1,4 **MP**

We could, of course, accomplish the same proof simplification by introducing new rules analogous to these rule combinations. For example, we could introduce a new rule allowing inferences of the form $p \vee q /∴ \sim p \supset q$, and use it in going from line 1 to line 3 in the first proof above.

In fact, there is no reason why we could not add any reasonable number of valid rules to our list of eighteen (plus **CP** and **IP**), *provided* that any new rule added is proved to be valid, say by truth table analysis. Here are a few candidates that may be useful in shortening proofs:

$p \equiv q$ $p \supset q /∴ p \supset (p \cdot q)$
$p /∴ q$

$\sim (p \cdot \sim q) :: (p \supset q)$

$p \equiv q$
$\sim p /∴ \sim q$ $\sim (p \supset q) :: (p \cdot \sim q)$

Exercise 5-8

Determine which of the following can, and which cannot, be added to our set of valid argument forms.

1. $p \vee (q \vee r) :: r \vee (q \vee p)$ 4. $p \vee \sim q /∴ p \supset \sim q$
2. $p \cdot (q \cdot r) :: r \cdot (p \cdot q)$ 5. $p \supset q /∴ \sim (\sim q \supset p)$
3. $p \supset (q \supset r) :: r \supset (q \supset p)$ 6. $p \supset q, p \supset \sim q /∴ \sim p$

7 *The Completeness and Soundness of Sentential Logic*

Notice that we have produced two different conceptions of "logical truths"—tautologies and theorems. Tautologies have been defined in terms of truth tables, theorems in terms of proofs. Corresponding to this difference is a distinction drawn by logicians between the syntax and the semantics of a system of logic. The **semantics** of a formal system includes those aspects of the system having to do with meaning or truth. For example, the core of the semantics for sentential logic consists of specifying truth tables for each of the connectives.

The **syntax** of a system of logic, on the contrary, comprises those elements of the system having to do with matters of form or structure, which are independent of issues of meaning or truth. Questions about whether a sentence is well-formed, or whether a sentence is a substitution instance of a particular form—these are syntactic questions. In principle we can address these questions without any notion whatsoever of what the symbols of our system actually mean. Likewise, even the question of whether something qualifies as a valid proof is a syntactic question because our rules are purposely stated solely by means of argument forms. Again, we could determine whether a proof is valid without knowing anything about the meaning of the connectives, since all this requires is that we determine whether each step of the proof is a substitution instance of one of a given set of argument forms.

Thus, we characterize logical truths in sentential logic semantically as tautologies, syntactically as theorems. Correspondingly, we have also explored validity both semantically in Chapter Three and syntactically in Chapters Four and Five. Semantically speaking, an argument is valid if and only if there is no interpretation of its form on which the premises are true and the conclusion false. Syntactically, an argument is valid just in case it is possible to construct a proof of the conclusion from the premises.

Examples

Syntactic Concepts:

A sentence is a **tautology** if and only if it its form yields truth on every interpretation.

An argument is **valid** if and only if there is *no* interpretation of its form on which the premises are all true and the conclusion false.

A group of sentences is **consistent** if and only if there is an interpretation on which all of the sentences are true.

Semantic Concepts:

A sentence is a **theorem** if and only if it can be proven without any premises.

An argument is **valid** if and only if it is possible to construct a proof of the conclusion from the premises.

A group of sentences is **consistent** if and only if it is *not* possible to prove a contradiction from them.

It is, of course, no coincidence that the same sentences are both tautologies and theorems and that arguments that are semantically valid are also syntactically valid. Our system of rules would be incomplete if there were arguments that could be shown to be valid with a truth table but that could not be proven. At the beginning of this chapter we explained that our system of sentential logic without **CP** or **IP** is incomplete in this sense. We can say that a system of logic is **complete** if every argument that is semantically valid is syntactically valid. Sentential logic is complete in this sense. The reason for this was given in our discussion of zero-premise deductions in Section 4. Because all valid sentential arguments have corresponding conditionals that are tautologies and all sentential tautologies are provable in our natural deduction system, sentential logic is complete.

Our system of sentential logic is not only complete, it is sound as well. A system of logic is **sound** if every argument that is syntactically valid is semantically valid. Sentential logic is sound. Again as we saw in Section 4, among the theorems provable in our natural deduction system are those in the form of a conditional; for each argument provable in the system, there is such a conditional whose antecedent is the conjoined premises and the consequent, the argument's conclusion. All such theorems are *provably* truth table tautologies, of which more in a moment. Our system of rules would be unsound if there were proofs for arguments that could be shown to be invalid with a truth table. Suppose, for example, we modified the rule Simplification so that it applied to disjunctions as well as conjunctions, allowing argument of the form $p \vee q$ /∴ p. We could go on constructing "proofs" with such a system, but such proofs would be worthless, since they would permit us to deduce falsehoods from truths.

It can be rigorously proven that our system of sentential logic is both sound and complete. Such proofs are part of what is known as **metalogic** or metatheory, because they are proofs *about* a logical system rather than proofs *within* a logical system. These proofs are complex and lie outside the scope of this book. We will, however, describe some of the more important metatheoretical results for each of the systems of logic we introduce.

8 Introduction and Elimination Rules

Practically all introductory logic texts take one of two approaches to the rules of sentential logic. The approach employed here begins with implicational argument forms such as Modus Ponens and Disjunctive Syllogism, adds equivalence rules such as DeMorgan's and Implication, and finally moves on to add two rules, Conditional Proof and Indirect Proof, that make use of assumptions.

The alternative approach is built around a system of ten rules, consisting of an introduction rule and an elimination rule for each of the five sentential logic operators, plus one additional rule called Reiteration. What is particularly interesting about these rules is that they constitute a set of rules for doing proofs that is both complete and sound. Although these "Int-Elim" rules have different names from the rules you've learned they should seem quite familiar.

Int-Elim Rules

1. Conjunction Introduction (• I):

p
q $/\therefore p \cdot q$

2. Conjunction Elimination (• E):

$p \cdot q /\therefore p$
$p \cdot q /\therefore q$

3. Disjunction Introduction (∨ I):

$p /\therefore p \vee q$
$p /\therefore q \vee p$

4. Disjunction Elimination (∨ E):

$p \vee q$ $p \vee q$
$\sim p /\therefore q$ $\sim q /\therefore p$

5. Conditional Introduction (⊃ I):

$\rightarrow \quad p$ $AP /\therefore q$
      .
      .
      .
   q
   $\overline{p \supset q}$ ⊃ I

6. Conditional Elimination (⊃ E):

$p \supset q$
$p /\therefore q$

7. Negation Introduction (~I):

$\rightarrow \quad p$ $AP /\therefore \sim p$
      .
      .
      .
   $q \cdot \sim q$
   $\overline{\sim p}$ ~ I

8. Negation Elimination (~E):

$\sim \sim p /\therefore p$

9. Equivalence Introduction (≡I):

$p \supset q$
$q \supset p /\therefore p \equiv q$

10. Equivalence Elimination (≡E):

$p \equiv q /\therefore p \supset q$
$p \equiv q /\therefore q \supset p$

11. Reiteration (R):

$p /\therefore p$

The only difference between many of these rules and the ones we have employed is the name. ⊃ **E** is just **MP**, ⊃ **I** is **CP**, • **I** is **Conj**, • **E** is **Simp**, ∨ **I** is just **Add**, and ∨ **E** is just **DS**. But note that while ~ **I** is just **IP**, there is an important difference between ~ **E** and **DN**. **DN** is an equivalence rule, whereas ~ **E** (like all the Int-Elim rules) is an implicational rule. It allows only the inference from a sentence of the form ~ ~ p to p, and not vice versa, and it cannot be used on part of a line.

The Reiteration rule, **R**, lets you repeat a line at any time (so long as the original line is not within the scope of an undischarged assumption). We need this rule for proofs such as this one:

1. B $/\therefore A \supset B$
→2. A **AP** $/\therefore B$
   3. B 1**R**
4. $A \supset B$ 2–3 ⊃ **I**

We used an equivalence rule like **DN** twice to deal with such situations, but because we have no equivalence rules in our Int-Elim system, we need **R** for the system to be complete.

Examples

Here are some sample proofs using the Int-Elim rules just introduced:

1.	$B \supset \sim A$	$p /\therefore A \supset \sim B$
2.	A	$\mathbf{AP} /\therefore \sim B$
3.	B	$\mathbf{AP} /\therefore \sim B$
4.	$\sim A$	$1,3 \supset \mathbf{E}$
5.	$A \cdot \sim A$	$2,4 \cdot \mathbf{I}$
6.	$\sim B$	$3\text{--}5 \sim \mathbf{I}$
7.	$A \supset \sim B$	$2,6 \supset \mathbf{I}$

1.	$A \vee B$	p
2.	$\sim (A \cdot B)$	$p /\therefore A \equiv \sim B$
3.	A	$\mathbf{AP} /\therefore \sim B$
4.	B	$\mathbf{AP} /\therefore \sim B$
5.	$A \cdot B$	$3,4 \cdot \mathbf{I}$
6.	$(A \cdot B) \cdot \sim (A \cdot B)$	$2,5 \cdot \mathbf{I}$
7.	$\sim B$	$4\text{--}6 \sim \mathbf{I}$
8.	$A \supset \sim B$	$3,7 \supset \mathbf{I}$
9.	$\sim B$	$\mathbf{AP} /\therefore A$
10.	A	$1,9 \vee \mathbf{E}$
11.	$\sim B \supset A$	$9,10 \supset \mathbf{I}$
12.	$A \equiv \sim B$	$8,11 \equiv \mathbf{I}$

The strength of Int-Elim systems such as this one is that we have here a very minimal set of rules that is both sound and complete. This is a system built with soundness and completeness proofs in mind. Thus, a key virtue of such a system is that it lends itself to metatheory. Its weakness, in our view, is pedagogical. Rules employing assumptions, such as $\supset \mathbf{I}$ and $\sim \mathbf{I}$, must be mastered early. Very intuitive inferences such as **MT** or **DeM** are added much later (as "derived" rules). Until these rules are added, proofs that are intuitively quite elementary can be rather tricky. Consider, for example, the following simple proof:

1. $B \supset A$
2. $\sim D \vee B$
3. $\sim A /\therefore \sim D$

Without **MT** another way to solve this is to derive the conclusion by $\sim \mathbf{I}$. You might be tempted to go about this as follows:

1. $B \supset A$
2. $\sim D \vee B$
3. $\sim A$ $/\therefore \sim D$
4. D $\mathbf{AP} /\therefore \sim D$
   .
   .
   .
_. $\sim D$ $4 \_ \sim \mathbf{I}$

The problem is that to perform ∨**E** on line 2, we need ~ ~ *D*. Without **DN** there is no way to derive ~ ~ *D* from *D*. The solution is to assume ~ ~ ~ *D* and perform ~ **E** on the last step of the proof, as follows:

```
1.  B ⊃ A
2.  ~ D ∨ B
3.  ~ A              /∴ ~ D
4.  ~ ~ D            AP /∴ ~ ~ ~ D
  5.  B              2,4 ∨ E
  6.  A              1,5 ⊃ E
  7.  A · ~ A        3,6 • I
8.  ~ ~ ~ D          4–7 ~ I
9.  ~ D              8 ~ E
```

Derived Rules

The set of Int-Elim rules just given is complete. Therefore, for any valid argument, you can construct a proof using just these rules. However, the scarcity of rules makes many of these proofs quite complex. As the preceding proof illustrates, what could be done in a single step with the help of a rule such as Modus Tollens can take many (nonobvious) steps to accomplish.

On the Int-Elim system we have described, Modus Tollens is an example of what is known as a derived rule. Any inference that can be made with a derived rule can be accomplished just using the original rules. Because the original rules are not, in this way, dispensable, they are called "primitive" rules.

For any derived rule we should be able to explain how to do without it. Consider, for example, a typical use of Modus Tollens:

```
1.  A ⊃ B
2.  ~ B
3.  ~ A              1,2 MT
```

To derive ~ *A* without **MT**, one can simply use ~ **Int** as follows:

```
1.  A ⊃ B
2.  ~ B
3.  A                AP /∴ ~ A
4.  B                1,3 ⊃
5.  B · ~ B          2,4 • Int
6.  ~ A              3–5 ~ Int
```

Obviously, the strategy employed here will work, not just for *A* ⊃ *B* and ~ *B*, but for any sentences that are substitution instances of **MT**. In the following exercise we leave it to you to show how the conclusions of other familiar argument forms can be justified by using just the primitive rules.

Exercise 5-9

(1) 1. *A* ⊃ *B*
    2. *B* ⊃ *C*   /∴ *A* ⊃ *C*

(2) 1. $\sim (A \vee B)$	$/\therefore \sim A \cdot \sim B$
(3) 1. $\sim A \cdot \sim B$	$/\therefore \sim (A \vee B)$
(4) 1. $\sim (A \cdot B)$	$/\therefore \sim A \vee \sim B$
(5) 1. $\sim A \vee \sim B$	$/\therefore \sim (A \cdot B)$
(6) 1. $A \supset B$	$/\therefore \sim B \supset \sim A$
(7) 1. $\sim A \supset \sim B$	$/\therefore B \supset A$
(8) 1. $A \vee A$	$/\therefore A$
(9) 1. $A \vee B$	$/\therefore B \vee A$
(10) 1. $A \cdot B$	$/\therefore B \cdot A$
(11) 1. $(A \cdot B) \supset C$	$/\therefore A \supset (B \supset C)$
(12) 1. $A \supset (B \supset C)$	$/\therefore (A \cdot B) \supset C$
(13) 1. A	$/\therefore \sim \sim A$
(14) 1. $A \supset B$	
2. $C \supset D$	
3. $A \vee C$	$/\therefore B \vee D$
(15) 1. $A \equiv B$	$/\therefore (A \cdot B) \vee (\sim A \cdot \sim B)$

Key Terms Introduced in Chapter Five

absorption: The valid implicational argument form $p \supset q /\therefore p \supset (p \cdot q)$

assumed premise: An assumption added to the given premises in an argument.

complete: A system of logic is complete if every argument that is semantically valid (can be shown valid by means of a truth table) is syntactically valid (can be shown valid by means of a proof). Sentential logic is complete.

contradiction: A single sentence that is inconsistent. Examples: $A \cdot \sim A$, $\sim (A \vee \sim A)$, $\sim (B \supset C) \cdot \sim B$.

discharged premise: A premise has been discharged in the course of a proof once its truth is no longer being assumed. Every assumed premise must be discharged before a proof is complete.

explicit contradiction: A sentence that is a substitution instance of the form $p \cdot \sim p$. Examples: $A \cdot \sim A$, $[C \equiv \sim (B \vee \sim D)] \cdot \sim [C \equiv \sim (B \vee \sim D)]$

indirect proof (IP): (See *reductio ad absurdem proof.*)

metalogic: The study of the formal properties of logical systems. The proofs of metalogic are proofs about a logical system rather than proofs within a system.

Examples of such proofs include proofs of the completeness or soundness of a system of logic.

reductio ad absurdum proof: The traditional name for an indirect proof. In an indirect proof the assumed premise is reduced to absurdity by showing that an explicit contradiction can be validly inferred from it.

semantics: The semantics of a formal system includes those aspects of the system having to do with meaning or truth of its elements.

sound: A system of logic is sound if every argument that is syntactically valid is semantically valid. Sentential logic is complete.

syntax: The syntax of a system of logic comprises those aspects of the system having to do with the form or structure of its elements.

theorem: A theorem is a tautology derived by a **zero-premise deduction.**

zero-premise deduction: Tautologies can be proved in our natural deduction system using assumed premises, CP and IP. Such deductions have no premises except assumed ones.

Chapter Six

Sentential Logic Truth Trees

---

1 The Sentential Logic Truth Tree Method

The final method we shall study for determining validity and invalidity of sentential arguments is that of truth trees. This method introduces no new concepts, but rather a new way of combining ones you already know. In fact, it is an interesting cross between truth tables and proofs. Like the truth tables and unlike the method of proofs, the **truth trees method** provides a mechanical decision procedure for the validity *and invalidity* of any sentential argument. However, like proofs and unlike truth tables, this procedure is "purely" syntactical; it does not explicitly rely on semantics. Truth trees provide a kind of *picture* or *representation* of semantics, that is, of truth conditions. They pictorially represent lines of truth tables in a very efficient and perspicuous way.*

The basic principle behind the tree method is that of *reductio* proof, so let's review that for a moment. If an argument with premises $P_1 \ldots P_n$ and conclusion C *is valid*, then the statement "$P_1 \ldots P_n \cdot \sim C$" is a contradiction. There is no possibility that the premises and the negation of the conclusion are all true. In *reductio* proof, we show that the assumption of the negation of the conclusion together with the premises yields a contradiction and thus that the original conclusion follows validly from the premises. Or, to put it in terms of truth tables: if we find the logical form of the argument in question, then there will be no line in the table we build for the premise statement forms and the conclusion statement form that yields true premises and a false conclusion. That is, there is no line in which the premises and the negation of the conclusion all turn out true; the conjunction of the premises and the negation of the conclusion has all **F**'s in its truth table. However, as just mentioned, trees also yield a decision about invalidity: assuming the negation of the conclusion and finding that we *do not* get a contradiction shows the argument invalid, because in effect we will have demonstrated that it is possible to have $V(P_1 \ldots P_n \cdot \sim C) = \mathbf{T.}$

---

*The first major text to discuss trees was Richard Jeffrey's *Formal Logic: Its Scope and Limits* (New York: McGraw Hill, 1967). The discussion here is often, but not always, indebted to Jeffrey. Jeffrey, in turn, derived the tree method from the work of E. W. Beth (who called the method "semantic tableaux") and J. Hintikka (who pioneered a method using what are called model sets). Consult Jeffrey's work for further details and bibliography.

Let's look at a summary of what we will now do. When we build a tree to test an argument, we will *represent* the premises and the *negation of the conclusion* by means of their truth conditions. We then determine if there is any way in which the truth conditions for all the represented statements are consistent—that is, could be true together. If they can be, then we know there is at least one way to get the premises true and the conclusion false, so the argument in question must be invalid. Otherwise, it is valid.

2 *The Truth Tree Rules*

Now, you should know from having worked with truth tables that, strictly speaking, the only lines we need to look at when testing for validity of an argument form are those in which the conclusion is false; in those lines, we look to see if we have all the premises true. If so, the argument form is invalid and, if not, valid. Trees give us a new method for doing exactly the same thing; they enable us to depict the crucial lines of truth tables. Consider the invalid argument form "$p \supset q$," $\sim p$ /∴ $\sim q$." Notice its truth table analysis, with the crucial lines filled in as far as one needs to.

		C	P_2	P_1
p	q	$\sim q$	$\sim p$	$p \supset q$
T	T	F	F	
T	F			
F	T	F	T	T
F	F			

The table "presents" the truth conditions. A tree *pictures* truth conditions. How does it picture? Consider any statement, such as P. The picture of $V(P) = \mathbf{T}$ is just P itself. The picture of $V(P) = \mathbf{F}$ is $\sim P$. *The tree rule for a logical connective is the picture of the truth table for it.* It does not picture every line but rather only the lines in which the connective yields truth. Given any binary (that is, two-place) logical operator $R(p, q)$, a tree rule answers the question: what must be true for $R(p, q)$ to be true? Thus, consider the conditional $p \supset q$. Its tree rule is

The branch represents the wedge. Hence the tree tells us that the conditional is true when either $V(\sim p) = \mathbf{T}$, or $V(q) = \mathbf{T}$. That is a very economical way of summarizing the conditions under which a conditional is true; it summarizes the essentials of three lines of the truth table. *A tree rule for a formula $R(p, q)$ has a branch when there is more than one line of the truth table in which the formula is true.* The tree rule for a conjunction thus does *not* produce a branch; it is

Notice there is no branching here, but the truth conditions are listed in a straight vertical line. Such a line represents the notion that the conjunction is true when both its conjuncts are true, which occurs in only one line of the truth table for a conjunction. These are the basic conventions with respect to how trees picture. Now you can easily see that the picture of a disjunction will be

and, as a graduation exercise so far:

Notice that this last tree tells us that a biconditional is true when either $V(p) = \mathbf{T}$ and $V(q) = \mathbf{T}$, or when $V(\sim p) = \mathbf{T}$ and $V(\sim q) = \mathbf{T}$—the first and last lines of the truth table for the tribar.

So far we have four tree rules. But we must also know how to depict the negations of all statements using our connectives. For example, we must have a rule for breaking down $\sim (p \supset q)$. Here we can either appeal to our knowledge of the logical equivalences we have used for proofs, or simply appeal to the truth table for a negated conditional. When is it true? Obviously, when the conditional itself is false its negation will be true. But the only conditions under which a conditional is false is when $V(p) = \mathbf{T}$ and $V(q) = \mathbf{F}$; that is, $V(\sim q) = \mathbf{T}$. Hence

$$\sim (p \supset q)$$
$$p$$
$$\sim q$$

You could have come to the same conclusion by thinking of transforming $p \supset q$ by Implication, and then using DeMorgan's Theorem on the result: You get $p \cdot \sim q$. Consider then the negation of a conjunction. Thinking of it in terms of DeMorgan's Theorem, we get $\sim p \lor \sim q$, which we depict, as we already know from our depiction of the wedge, as follows:

Again as a graduation exercise, think of the negation of the biconditional. A biconditional is false when *p* and *q* have opposite truth values. Hence the negation of a biconditional will be true when either $V(p) = \mathbf{T}$ and $V(\sim q) = \mathbf{T}$, or when $V(\sim p) = \mathbf{T}$ and $V(q) = \mathbf{T}$. Thus

You can now easily figure out the tree rule for the negation of the wedge. Using DeMorgan's on $\sim (p \vee q)$, we get

Here is the complete list of rules (they also are printed in the very back of the book):

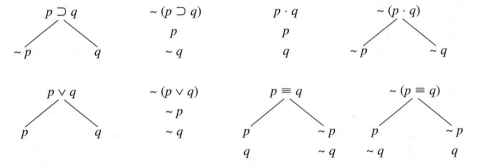

Our final rule simply tells us *we can always cross off double negations whenever and wherever they occur.*

3 *Details of Tree Construction*

Now that we have our tree rules, you can begin to see how to build a tree. To start a tree, we list the forms of the premises of the argument we want to test, and the negation of the conclusion.* Then we break down all the lines that contain connectives according to our rules; the breakdown goes until we have listed the truth conditions for all relevant formulas. We will refine this procedure as we go on. The premises and negated conclusion are the trunk of the tree. We then have to examine all branches (if any). Each completed branch will

---

*Note that trees are customarily constructed with sentential constants, which is not accurate theoretically; they should be done with variables, just as truth tables are done. Strictly speaking we are making trees for the forms of premises and conclusions, not for actual statements that have definite truth-values. That is what we do in this book.

picture truth conditions for the *wff*s in question, and so picture a row in a truth table. You will notice that, by using check marks and numbering lines and indicating which line a line is derived from, we are performing a kind of bookkeeping. When you actually construct trees, which you will be doing by hand and not with the neat straight lines we have in a printed text, the bookkeeping will very much help you keep your bearings in the tree. In the case of the argument whose table we made earlier, the procedure is simple.

✔1.　　$p \supset q$　　　p
　2.　　　$\sim p$　　　　p /∴ ~ q
　3.　　　~~q　　　　(negation of conclusion)
　4.

　　　~ p　　　　q　　　from line 1

Here, the only one of our original statements that needs to be broken down is line 1; the rest are either broken down as far as they can go or will be if we do double negation, as we can with 3; you will note the double negative is crossed out. Line 4 comes from line 1 by one of our rules, for the conditional. When we break down a line, we check it off, so it is clear we are done with it. Justification for each line not a premise is provided as illustrated in the tree in line 4.

We end in this particular case with two branches. We scan each branch all the way back up the trunk, to see if it contains any contradictions—that is, both a letter and its negation. If so, we put an "x" under that branch, to show that there is no way in that branch to get all the statements true; that is called *closing a path or branch*. A **closed branch** would tell us that the conditions that make some of the premises or the negation of the conclusion true make some other of them false; that is, they cannot all be true together. **Open branches** represent sets of truth conditions that will make all the premises and the negation of the conclusion true. In this case, if we scan the left branch, which is open, we find it tells us that when $V(\sim p) = T$, thus $V(p) = F$, and $V(q) = T$, the premises and the negation of the conclusion are all true. That is enough to show the argument invalid because, if it were valid, there would be no way to get all those statements true. Note this result corresponds exactly with what the third line of the truth table analysis of the argument tells us. The right branch tells us the same thing: The trees sometimes give redundant results. In effect, all we need is *one open path* and that shows there is at least one line of the truth table in which we can get all the premises true and the conclusion false; it even gives you a recipe, by telling you what truth-values to assign to the atomic parts to get the desired results. If all branches had closed off, this would have shown that the assumption of the negation of the conclusion, together with the premises, is a contradiction, and the argument is valid. So let's consider a valid argument form:

1. $p \supset \sim q$　　　p
2. $\sim r \supset p$　　　p /∴ $q \supset r$

The first thing we do is list the negation of the conclusion.

3. $\sim (q \supset r)$　　　(negation of conclusion)

Now we need a strategy. We have more than one statement on which to apply the tree rules. *Logically speaking it makes no difference which statement we start with but strategically it matters: we want the smallest tree possible, since that is the least amount of work.* If you start with a statement that produces a branch, *then breakdowns of other statements must now go under each branch.* That means the tree can get unwieldy fast. Therefore it is best to save breakdowns that produce branching until the end, with the hope we can cross off lines before we have to branch. Starting with line 3 we do not get a branching, so

4. q
    $\sim r$ From line 3

We check off line 3 (see the completed tree, later) because we are done with it for the entire tree; we have listed its truth conditions. Lines 3 and 4 can be seen to be illustrating the logical equivalence between $\sim (q \supset r)$ and $(q \cdot \sim r)$. Now, since both lines 1 and 2 are conditionals, both will produce branching, so which shall we choose? Choosing line 1 to work with first, we can see that in its right-hand branch we will get $\sim q$, and since that will contradict q in line 4, we will be able to close off that branch immediately, thus keep the tree from growing on the right. So

5. $\sim p$ $\sim q$ From line 1
         x

In general a branch is produced when a formula is true under more than one set of conditions. Line 1 is true when either $V(\sim p) = \mathbf{T}$ or $V(\sim q) = \mathbf{T}$. As we read up the right-hand branch we find a contradiction between $\sim q$ and q, so we x out that branch. Think of the right-hand branch as making a selection from among the *lines* of a truth table in which the conditions clash that make line 3 true and the conditions that make line 1 true. That is, the branch tells us that—thinking in truth table terms—in lines where $V(\sim q) = \mathbf{T}$ is sufficient for the truth of line 1, it is also sufficient for the falsehood of line 3. In some lines when $V(q) = \mathbf{T}$ is sufficient for the truth of line 3 we need $V(\sim q) = \mathbf{T}$ for the truth of line 1. So what we are doing is eliminating lines of truth tables when we x out a branch. The open path on the left indicates a set of truth conditions under which lines 1 and 3 will both be true, namely $V(q) = \mathbf{T}$, $V(r) = \mathbf{F}$, $V(p) = \mathbf{F}$. In effect, we are overlapping the truth conditions for lines 1 and 3 to see if there is a common set that makes both true; this is what we are doing in general in the trees—overlapping truth conditions to find a common set if we can. You can verify all this by building the truth tables for lines 1 and 3; you will find there is one line in the table in which both are true (the sixth line in a standard table, to be exact).

We still have to break down line 2. We do this under the left-hand branch, because it is the only one open; had both branches been open, we would have done our breakdown under both branches.

6. $\not\sim\not\sim r$ p From line 2
      x   x

Notice that we cross the double negation, and that both branches are closed off. In the left one, we have found a contradiction as we go back up the tree toward the trunk, between r in line 6 and $\sim r$ in 4. The right-hand branch contains a contradiction between p in 6 and $\sim p$ in 5. Thus there is no way to get the premises true and the negation of the conclusion true—that is, the conclusion false. So the argument is valid. Had the argument been invalid, at least one open path would have remained at the end, and the truth-values that make the premises true and the conclusion false could be read off the branch. Here is the entire tree:

✔ 1. $p \supset \sim q$ p
✔ 2. $\sim r \supset p$ p /∴ $q \supset r$
✔ 3. $\sim (q \supset r)$ Negation of conclusion
   4. q

        $\sim r$ From line 3

5. $\sim p$ $\sim q$ From line 1
                   x

6. $\not r$ p From line 2
    x   x

All paths closed; argument is valid.

Notice that the final step is to state whether the argument is valid or not. If invalid, you should list one set of truth-values, read off from one branch in the tree, that make the premises true and the conclusion false.

Some things to remember:
1. The breakdown of a *wff* may produce the necessity for further breakdowns. Thus suppose we want to break down line (*n*):

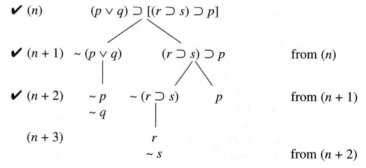

✔ (*n*) $(p \lor q) \supset [(r \supset s) \supset p]$

✔ (*n* + 1) $\sim (p \lor q)$ $(r \supset s) \supset p$ from (*n*)

✔ (*n* + 2) $\sim p$ $\sim (r \supset s)$ p from (*n* + 1)
                  $\sim q$

(*n* + 3) r from (*n* + 2)
                                  $\sim s$ from (*n* + 2)

Notice that line (*n*), when fully broken down, produces three branches. The left branch tells us that the *wff* on (*n*) is true when $V(p) = \mathbf{F}$ and $V(q) = \mathbf{F}$—that is, that is sufficient for its truth, because those values make the antecedent false. The center branch tells us that the *wff* on (*n*) is true when $V(r) = \mathbf{T}$ and $V(s) = \mathbf{F}$. Finally the right-hand branch tells us that $V(p) = \mathbf{T}$ is sufficient to make the whole formula on line (*n*) true. You could now literally calculate the number of lines in the sixteen-line truth table in which (*n*) is true.
2. Consider the *wffs* and their breakdowns in the following:

(*n*) $p \equiv q$
(*n* + 1) $r \lor s$

(*n* + 2) p $\sim p$
                 q $\sim q$ from (*n*)

(*n* + 3) r s r s from (*n* + 1)

So we have four branches here. The thing to notice is that we had to break down $(n + 1)$ under each open path. Why? Because $(n + 2)$ tells us the conditions under which (n) is true, and there is more than one set of such conditions. We now try to see if $(n + 1)$ can be true under each of those sets.

3. Trees give us an easy way to test to see if a statement is a tautology. Just negate it and build its tree. If all paths close, this negation is a contradiction and the original *wff* is a tautology. Because statements of logical equivalence are tautologies, trees can enable us to test for logical equivalence. As a special case, remember that every valid argument can be expressed in a test statement form that is a tautology. Be careful here, though. It does not follow that a tautology's tree (as opposed to its negation) will have all open branches. Obviously, $p \vee q$ has no closed branches, but is not a tautology.

4. Clearly, trees can enable us to test for contradictions. If a statement form has all branches closed in its tree, then no set of truth conditions can make it true.

5. A contingent statement form is one that has at least one **T** and at least one **F** in its truth table. Trees enable us to test for contingency as well. For any *wff* p, make the tree for p. If it has an open branch, we know there is a set of conditions where $V(p) = \mathbf{T}$. Now make the tree for $\sim p$. If we have an open branch, that means there are conditions under which $V(\sim p) = \mathbf{T}$, and thus $V(p) = \mathbf{F}$.

6. Trees enable us to test sets of statements for consistency. If there is at least one open path in the tree for the statement forms, then there is one way to get them all true and they are consistent.

🏃 Walk-Through: Truth Trees

Let's walk through the strategy steps in building the following tree. Like a natural deduction proof, each line after the negation of the conclusion follows from a previous line* and is justified by at least one of the tree rules; we are permitted to combine double negations with another tree rule in any step.

✔ 1. $\sim p \equiv (\sim q \cdot r)$	p
✔ 2. $\sim r \cdot \sim s$	p
✔ 3. $\sim [(p \vee q) \supset r]$	p $/\therefore \sim s \supset \sim p$
✔ 4. $\sim (\sim s \supset \sim p)$	Negation of conclusion
5. $\sim s$	From line 4
 ~~$\sim p$~~	
6. $\sim r$	From line 2
 $\sim s$	

---

*In proofs, however, we often use more than one previous line to justify a line we have derived, whereas in trees each numbered line beyond the premises and negation of the conclusion is the breakdown of a single previous line.

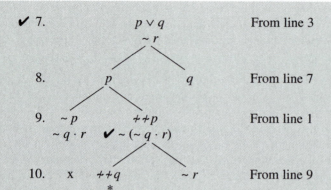

7.	$p \lor q$		From line 3
	$\sim r$		
8.	p	q	From line 7
9.	$\sim p$	$\not{+}\not{+}p$	From line 1
	$\sim q \cdot r$	$\sim (\sim q \cdot r)$	
10.	x	$\not{+}\not{+}q$	$\sim r$	From line 9

Invalid open branches. In the branch marked with *, let

$$V(q) = \mathbf{T}$$
$$V(p) = \mathbf{T}$$
$$V(r) = \mathbf{F}$$
$$V(s) = \mathbf{F}$$

So line 4 is the negation of the conclusion. Now the strategy is to break down formulas, if we can, to produce straight lines as far as we can do this; to do otherwise is to risk production of a very unwieldy tree. Furthermore, if we can see possible contradictions in breaking down lines, do these lines first, since we might then be saved a lot of work breaking down other formulas. In this case nothing like that presents itself, but given our tree rules, lines 4 and 2 both will give us straight branches, so that is where we start. On line 5 we have broken down line 4, and done a double negation; we indicate this to the right, and we check off line 4—we are through with it. In line 6 we break down line 2, justifying it with a reference to line 2 on line 6's right, and then checking off line 2. Now line 3 also gives us a straight line in line 7, but notice that one of the formulas in that line is a disjunction that will branch, and that is why we saved it to do until after the breaking down of lines 4 and 2; we check off line 3. Line 8 represents using the rule for a disjunction on line 7, which gives us our first branch. We dutifully check line 7, and we are now ready for our most difficult step. We must break down line 1 under each branch. But wait: Given this is our last formula, if we *provisionally* break it down *simply under line 8's left-hand branch*, as we do in line 9, something interesting occurs. We can see that now our left-hand branch contains a contradiction between lines 8 and 9: p in 8 and $\sim p$ in 9. So that closes that branch. Meanwhile in the right-hand branch in line 9, after we double-negate p, we have a breakdown to perform that in line 10 produces a branch.

The fact that there is more than one formula in line 9 that could have been subject to our rules—the contradiction in the left branch allows us to skip using the rule for conjunction on $\sim q \cdot r$—produces a refinement of our checkoff strategy. We place a check mark by the formula, rather than by the number of the line, if there is more than one formula on a line that could be broken down by the rules (if you check off the *line* when you do, say, the first one of the breakdowns, you may forget to do the others!).

As we look up the tree, we see no contradictions and so we know the argument is invalid. We know this without having to break down line 1 under the right-hand branch in line 8, and so this gives us a new strategy. When breaking down formula *f* under branch *n*, say, if you can see that *n* will remain open when all breakdowns of all *wffs* are completed, you need not break down *f* under any other branch. This is equivalent to finding a line in a truth table that has true premises and a false conclusion. We need not test *all* lines when we see *that line*.

Exercise 6-1

Use the truth tree method to determine the validity or invalidity of the arguments in Exercise 3-8. Be sure to find the logical form of the argument before you make the tree.

Exercise 6-2

Use the truth tree method on the problems in Exercise 3-9. Be sure to find the logical form of the statements being tested for consistency before you construct the tree.

 Normal Forms and Trees

Consider the statement form $p \vee q$. It is true in the first three lines of its truth table. We can represent each line as a conjunction; for example, line 1 is true when both p and q are true, which we represent by $p \cdot q$. Line 2 is true when p is true and q is false, that is, $p \cdot \sim q$, line 3, when p is false and q is true, that is, $\sim p \cdot q$. If we disjoin these three statements we get $(p \cdot q) \vee (p \cdot \sim q) \vee (\sim p \cdot q)$. This statement is logically equivalent to $p \vee q$. Every statement form except a contradictory form (which has no lines in its truth table that yield a truth) can be given such an equivalent expression, called its **disjunctive normal form (DNF)**. A DNF is a syntactic picture of the truth conditions given by the semantic truth tables. If a formula contains two variables and has four disjuncts in its DNF, we know it is a tautology; a three-variable statement that has eight disjuncts will also be a tautology, and so on.

DNFs can be constructed mechanically (we won't get into the rules here) *and can be used to construct natural deduction proofs mechanically*. Again, without going into detail here, because our interest in DNFs is elsewhere, this is an interesting, but not very useful feature. Students don't get your hopes up! The rules for constructing proofs mechanically using DNFs would be long and tedious and not something you would want to do.

But DNFs show us that, at least in sentential logic, syntax mirrors semantics—the truth trees are really just a very efficient version of DNFs. For example, instead of saying a conditional is true when its normal form has the disjuncts that mirror the first, third, and fourth lines of its truth table, we say a conditional is true when its antecedent is false or its consequent is true.

5 Constructing Tree Rules for Any Function

Given any truth table, you should be able to construct the tree rule for the function that goes on top of it, even if you don't know specifically what the function is. Suppose, for example, you have the following table, and represent the function by $R(p, q)$.

p	q	$R(p, q)$
T	T	F
T	F	F
F	T	F
F	F	T

Now a study of the truth table reveals that $V(p) = \mathbf{F}$ and $V(q) = \mathbf{F}$ are both necessary for the truth of $R(p, q)$. So its tree rule must be

$$R(p, q)$$

$$\sim p$$
$$\sim q$$

Now the rule for $\sim R(p, q)$ should be easy; we think of a DeMorgan's on $\sim (\sim p \cdot \sim q)$. Hence the tree is

$$\sim R(p, q)$$

$$p \qquad q$$

Here, finally, is an exercise that combines many of the concepts we have learned so far in the course.

Suppose that the following is a valid argument form:

1. $p\,?\,q$ p
2. q $p / \therefore\ p$

Now let us find the tree rules for $p\,?\,q$ and its negation, and test the following argument form for validity using trees.

1. $p \equiv (q \vee \sim p)$ p
2. $(\sim p \supset q)\,?\,(\sim q \cdot \sim p)$ $p / \therefore\ \sim q\,?\,\sim (p \cdot q)$

How shall we proceed? Given the valid argument form, we know that if $V(p) = \mathbf{F}$, then the conclusion is false. If $V(p) = \mathbf{F}$ and $V(q) = \mathbf{T}$, then $V(2) = \mathbf{T}$. Since a valid argument cannot have true premises and a false conclusion, this means we must count $V(p\,?\,q) = \mathbf{F}$ when $V(p) = \mathbf{F}$ and $V(q) = \mathbf{T}$, the third line of its truth table. Let us assume, for the sake of the example, that other valid and invalid argument forms using our "?" function shows us that $V(p\,?\,q) = \mathbf{T}$ in all other lines. So our table looks like this:

p	q	(p ? q)
T	T	T
T	F	T
F	T	F
F	F	T

So our tree rules look like this:

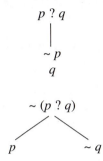

$$p \; ? \; q$$

$$\sim p$$
$$q$$

$$\sim (p \; ? \; q)$$

$$p \qquad \sim q$$

Now for the tree:

✔ 1. $p \equiv (q \vee \sim p)$ p

✔ 2. $(\sim p \supset q) \; ? \; (\sim q \cdot \sim p)$ $p \; / \therefore \; \sim q \; ? \sim (p \cdot q)$

✔ 3. $\sim [\sim q \; ? \sim (p \cdot q)]$ Negation of conclusion

4.   ✔ $\sim (\sim p \supset q)$ From line 2
        ✔ $\sim q \cdot \sim p$

5. $\sim p$ From line 4
        $\sim q$

6. $\sim q$ From line 4
        $\sim p$

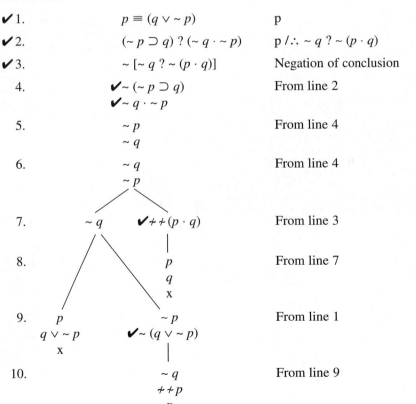

7. $\sim q$ ✔ $\not{\sim} \not{\sim} (p \cdot q)$ From line 3

8. p From line 7
        q
        x

9. p $\sim p$ From line 1
    $q \vee \sim p$ ✔ $\sim (q \vee \sim p)$
     x

10. $\sim q$ From line 9
        $\not{\sim} \not{\sim} p$
        x

Since all paths have closed, the argument form is a valid form.

Exercise 6-3 (answers given in back of book)

(1)   Find one line of the truth table for the mystery connective p ? q, given the following *invalid* argument form. Show your work—that is, how you reason this out:

     1. $p \supset q$ p

     2. p ? q p /∴ q

(2)   Next, find the tree rules for both p ? q and ~ (p ? q), assuming that every other line in the truth table for p ? q, besides the one you found, is **F**.

(3)   Finally, test the following argument form for validity, using trees.

     1. $p \supset (q \supset r)$ p

     2. $r \equiv [\sim (\sim p\ ?\ \sim r)]$ p

     3. $\sim (\sim p \vee \sim q)$ p /∴ $\sim [\sim p\ ?\ (\sim q \vee \sim r)]$

Key Terms Introduced in Chapter Six

closed branch: A path, or branch, of a truth tree that contains an explicit contradiction and that we have therefore marked with an x. (See also *open branch*.)

disjunctive normal form (DNF): A disjunctive normal form is a *syntactic* picture of the truth conditions given by the semantic truth tables. Every *wff* except a contradiction has such a form, which consists of a disjunction of the truth conditions expressed in each line of the truth table for the *wff* in which it is true. Trees are efficient ways of doing the same thing such normal forms do. That we can syntactically picture semantics in this way is of theoretical importance to logicians.

open branch: A branch of a truth tree that does not contain an explicit contradiction. (See also *closed branch*.)

truth tree method: A method for diagramming arguments to determine whether they are valid or invalid (also used to determine the consistency or inconsistency of argument premises).

Part Two

Predicate Logic

Chapter Seven

Predicate Logic Symbolization

The sentential or propositional logic presented in the preceding chapters deals with the internal structure of compound sentences, but not with the internal structure of atomic sentences. Let's now examine what is called **predicate logic,** or quantifier logic, a logic concerned with the interior structure of both atomic and compound sentences.

Predicate logic gives us a way to prove the validity of many valid arguments that are invalid when symbolized in the notation of sentential logic. For example, the standard and ancient syllogism

1. All humans are mortal.
2. All Greeks are human.
    /∴ All Greeks are mortal.

must be symbolized in sentential logic in a way that makes it invalid, for instance as

1. *A*
2. *B* /∴ *C*

Yet surely this syllogism is valid. Once we have introduced the machinery of predicate logic, we'll be able to prove its validity quite easily.

1   *Individuals and Properties*

Consider the sentence "Art is happy." This sentence asserts that some particular object or entity, Art, has a certain property—namely, the property of being happy. If we let the capital letter *H* denote the property of being happy, and the lowercase letter *a* name the individual, Art, we can symbolize this sentence as *Ha.* Similarly, the sentence "Betsy is happy" can be symbolized as *Hb,* the sentence "Art is friendly" as *Fa,* and the sentence "Betsy is friendly" as *Fb.* The sentences *Fa, Fb, Ha,* and *Hb* are alike in that they have the same general structure. In each of these sentences a *property* is ascribed to some *individual entity.* This is one of the basic patterns of atomic sentences.

Examples

Here are a few more examples of this fundamental sentence structure, with symbolizations attached.

1. Elvis Presley was a rock star.   *Rp*
2. Alpha Centauri is a star.   *Sa*
3. Mike Tyson is headstrong.   *Ht*
4. Al Gore is environmentally correct.   *Cg*
5. Jeremiah was a bullfrog.   *Bj*

Another basic pattern is illustrated by the sentence "Art is taller than Betsy." This sentence asserts that there is a particular property (_____ being taller than _____) that holds *between* the two individual objects Art and Betsy. If we let *a* denote Art, *b* Betsy, and *T* the property of one thing being taller than another, we can symbolize the sentence "Art is taller than Betsy" as *Tab*. Similarly, we can symbolize the sentence "Betsy is taller than Art" as *Tba*. And if we let *F* denote the property of one thing being a friend of another (_____ is a friend of _____), then we can symbolize the sentence "Art is a friend of Betsy" as *Fab,* and so on.

Properties such as *is taller than* and *is a friend of*, which hold between two or more entities, are called **relational properties.** The particular properties in question are *two-place* relational properties, since they hold between two entities. But we can also have three- or four- (or more) place properties. For instance the property of being between two other objects (_____ is between _____ and . . . .) is a three-place relational property. Properties such as "is happy" or "is wise," which are ascribed to only one individual, are called *monadic properties.*

In some respects, the preceding analysis of the structure of atomic sentences is very much like those given in traditional grammar texts. For instance, a traditional grammar text would analyze the sentence "Art is human" as containing a subject, "Art," and a predicate, "is human." (Indeed, the term "predicate" is often used by logicians instead of the term "property." Hence the name "predicate logic.") However, traditional grammars generally analyze all atomic sentences into this subject–predicate form. For instance, they construe the sentence "Art is taller than Betsy" as ascribing a predicate, being taller than Betsy, to a subject, Art. This is quite different from our analysis, because our analysis construes the sentence "Art is taller than Betsy" as concerning two subjects (or individual objects or entities), namely Art and Betsy, and construes this sentence as stating that a relational property holds between them. Of course, we also can construe the sentence "Art is taller than Betsy" as ascribing the nonrelational property of being-taller-than-Betsy to Art, in which case that sentence will be symbolized as *Ta*, but to do so is to mask part of the structure of that sentence. If we mask that structure, as you will see in our discussion of relational logic in Chapter Ten, we will not be able to show that many of the most important valid arguments in mathematics and everyday life are valid in our system of logic.

To simplify matters, the next few chapters deal entirely with predicate logic sentences that contain only monadic properties. In Chapter Ten we then broaden our coverage of predicate logic to include relational predicates.

Let's now be more specific about the two notational conventions just introduced. First, *capital letters* are used to denote properties, whether relational or nonrelational. And second, *lowercase letters* (up to and including the letter *t*) are used to denote individual objects, things, and entities—that is, any things that can have properties ascribed to them about which we wish to speak. Capital letters used to denote properties are called **property constants,** and small letters (up to and including *t*) used to denote things, objects, and individual entities are called **individual constants.** Individual constants should never be used to designate groups of individuals, nor will we use these letters to designate properties. Systems that permit ascription of properties to properties encounter serious technical difficulties. (See, for instance, Chapter Thirteen, Section 4.)

In addition, the small letters *u* through *z* are used as **individual variables,** replaceable by individual constants. We will use individual variables when defining property constants. For example, instead of saying, "Let *M* denote the property of being a material object," we will say, "$Mx = x$ is a material object." (The use of individual variables is further explained later.)

These notational conventions are to be used in addition to those previously introduced. We still allow the use of capital letters as sentence abbreviations, and the use of the small letters from *p* through *z* as sentence variables, just as in propositional logic.

Examples

Let $Px = x$ is president, $Cx = x$ is charismatic, b = Bush, c = Clinton, and g = Gore. Then the expressions on the right symbolize the sentences on the left into the notation of predicate logic:

1. Bush is president.	1. Pb
2. Gore is not president.	2. $\sim Pg$
3. Clinton is president, or Bush is president.	3. $Pc \lor Pb$
4. Either Clinton or Bush is charismatic.	4. $Cc \lor Cb$
5. Bush is president but is not charismatic.	5. $Pb \cdot \sim Cb$
6. If Bush is president, then neither Clinton nor Gore is president.	6. $Pb \supset (\sim Pc \cdot \sim Pg)$
7. It's not the case that Bush is both president and charismatic.	7. $\sim (Pb \cdot Cb)$
8. If Bush is president and Gore isn't, then although Clinton is not president he is not terribly disappointed.	8. $(Pb \cdot \sim Pg) \supset (\sim Pc \cdot \sim Tc)$

Exercise 7-1

Symbolize the following sentences, using the indicated letters.

1. Bo knows football. (b = "Bo," Fx = "*x* knows football")

2. Bo knows baseball. (Bx = "*x* knows baseball")

3. Bo knows football and Bo knows baseball, but Bo doesn't know field hockey. (Hx = "*x* knows field hockey")

4. Neither Phil Jackson nor Pat Riley is a mild-mannered coach. (*Mx* = "*x* is an ill-mannered coach"; *j* = "Phil Jackson"; *r* = "Pat Riley")

5. Jackson and Riley both demand perfection. (*Dx* = "*x* demands perfection")

6. Not only is Riley a great basketball coach, he's a pretty good fly fisherman as well. (*Gx* = "*x* is a great basketball coach"; *Px* = "*x* is a pretty good fly fisherman")

7. Eminem is not the lead singer of Nirvana. (*Nx* = "*x* is the lead singer of Nirvana"; *e* = "Eminem")

8. If Tom Cruise is not married, then neither is Nicole Kidman. (*Mx* = "*x* is married"; *c* = "Tom Cruise"; *k* = "Nicole Kidman")

In developing a predicate logic, we do not abandon sentential logic. Instead we include it within predicate logic. So mixed sentences are possible. An example is the sentence "Adam was foolish and Methuselah long-lived" symbolized as *A* · *Lm*. Of course, we also can symbolize that sentence as *Fa* · *Lm* (so as to reveal the structure of the two atomic sentences "Adam was foolish" and "Methuselah was long-lived"). And we also can symbolize it as *Fa* · *B*. (Of these three symbolizations, the second is preferred because it reveals more logical structure).

These uses of the capital letters *A* and *B* call attention to the fact that capital letters may serve more than one function. For instance, the letter *A* in this example serves in one place as a sentence constant and in another as a property constant. This ambiguity is harmless because it is clear in every case which function a letter serves. A property constant always occurs with a small letter next to it, while a sentence constant never does.

The expression formed by combining a property constant and an individual constant is a sentence. The sentence *Pc* just referred to is an example. It has a truth value, namely, the value **T** if Clinton is indeed president, and **F** if he is not. But what about an expression formed by combining a property constant with an *individual variable,* say the form *Hx*? First, this form is not a sentence, because *x* is a variable. (Writing *Hx* is like writing *H* _____, where the solid line serves as a placeholder, to be filled in by an individual constant.) So the form *Hx* is neither true nor false. And second, since we can obtain a sentence from *Hx* by **substituting** a small letter denoting some object or entity for the variable *x*, *Hx* is a *sentence form.* For instance, we can obtain the sentence *Ha* from *Hx* by substituting the small letter *a* for the variable *x*.

Examples

The following are examples of sentence forms and some of their substitution instances that are sentences.

	Sentence Form		*Substitution Instances*
1.	*Hy*	1.	*Ha, Hb, Hc,* . . .
2.	*Bx* ⊃ *Hy*	2.	*Bb* ⊃ *Ha, Bb* ⊃ *Hb,*
			Ba ⊃ *Hb, Ba* ⊃ *Ha,* . . .
3.	(*Hx* · *Bx*) ⊃ *Hy*	3.	(*Hb* · *Bb*) ⊃ *Ha,* (*Ha* · *Ba*) ⊃ *Hc,* . . .

2 *Quantifiers and Free Variables*

In sentential logic, to obtain a sentence from a sentence form we have to substitute sentence constants for all the sentence variables. Thus, from the sentence form $p \supset q$ we obtain the sentence $A \supset B$, as well as many others. In predicate logic this also can be done, as was explained earlier. Thus, from the sentence form Hx we obtain the sentences Ha, Hb, and so on. However, it is a fact of fundamental importance that in predicate logic a sentence can be obtained from a sentence form without replacing its individual variables by individual constants. For example, we can obtain a sentence from the sentence form Hx without specifying some particular entity that has the property H, by specifying instead how many entities have that property. This idea is familiar from its use in everyday English. For instance, in English we can form a sentence by ascribing the property of honesty to a particular man. The sentence "Art is honest" is an example. But we can also form a sentence by saying how many men are honest. The sentences "All men are honest" and "Some men are honest" are examples.

In predicate logic two symbols, called **quantifiers,** are used to state how many. The first is the **universal quantifier,** used to assert that *all* entities have some property or properties. The symbols (x), (y), and so on—that is, individual variables placed between parentheses—are used for this purpose. Thus, to symbolize the sentence "Everything moves" or "All things move," start with the sentence form Mx and prefix the universal quantifier (x) to obtain the sentence $(x)(Mx)$, which is read as "For all x, Mx," or "Given any x, Mx."

The **existential quantifier** is used to assert that *some* individual or individuals have one or more properties. Here we use a symbol that looks like a backward letter E along with an individual variable, placing both symbols within parentheses, as in $(\exists x)$, $(\exists y)$, and so on. Thus, to symbolize "Some things move," we again start with the sentence form Mx but this time we prefix the existential quantifier $(\exists x)$ to obtain the sentence $(\exists x)$ (Mx), which is read as "there is an x, Mx" or "For some x, Mx."

In sentential logic, parentheses are used to remove ambiguity. For instance, the parentheses in the sentence $\sim (A \cdot B)$ indicate that the negation sign negates the whole compound sentence $A \cdot B$, not just the atomic sentence A. The parentheses indicate the scope of the negation sign, that is, how much of the sentence the negation sign negates.

In predicate logic, parentheses serve a similar function. They indicate the **scope of a quantifier.** Take the sentence "Everything has mass and is extended." It is correctly symbolized as $(x)(Mx \cdot Ex)$ (where $Mx =$ "x has mass" and $Ex =$ "x is extended"), and is read "For all x, x has mass and x is extended" or "Given any x, that x has mass and is extended." The parentheses around the expression $(Mx \cdot Ex)$ indicate that the scope of the (x) quantifier is the entire remaining part of the sentence, namely $(Mx \cdot Ex)$, which is said to be within the scope of the (x) quantifier. Similarly, the brackets in $(x)[(Mx \cdot Ex) \supset Cx]$ indicate that the scope of this (x) quantifier is the entire remainder of that sentence.

However, when the scope of a quantifier extends just over the next minimal unit, parentheses may be omitted for the sake of simplicity. Thus, we may symbolize the sentence "Everything is heavy" either as $(x)(Hx)$ or as $(x)Hx$ (omitting parentheses of scope).

The expression $(x)(Mx \cdot Ex)$ is a sentence, but $(Mx \cdot Ex)$ is a sentence form, not a sentence. Is the expression $(x)(Mx) \cdot Ex$ a sentence? The answer is no, because it contains an individual variable that is not quantified, namely the x in Ex. Unquantified variables are called **free variables.** Quantified variables, such as the middle x in $(x)(Mx) \cdot Ex$, are said to be **bound variables.** An expression that contains one or more free variables is a sentence form, not a sentence.

Finally, note that merely being within the scope of a quantifier is not sufficient to make a variable a bound variable. To be bound, a variable must be within the scope of a quantifier using the same letter. Thus, the y in $(x)(Fy \supset Gx)$ is within the scope of the (x) quantifier but is not bound by it, whereas the x in $(x)(Fy \supset Gx)$ is both within the scope of the (x) quantifier and bound by it.

Exercise 7-2

For each of the following expressions indicate (1) which variables are free and which bound; (2) which letters serve as individual constants and which as property constants; (3) which free variables are within the scope of some quantifier or other and which individual constants are not within the scope of any quantifier.

1. $(x)(Fx \supset Ga)$
2. $(\exists x)\,(Fa \cdot Gx)$
3. $(x)[Fx \supset (Gy \lor Hx)]$
4. $(x)Fx \supset (\exists y)(Gy \lor Dx)$
5. $Fa \lor (x)[(Ga \lor Dx) \supset (\sim Ky \cdot Hb)]$
6. $(x)(Fa \supset Dx) \supset (y)[Fy \supset (\sim Gx \lor Fx)]$

3 *Universal Quantifiers*

When we use the universal quantifier, (x), we are saying something about all the individuals represented by the variable x in the quantifier. Just how many x's constitute *all* depends on how many things we want our language to be able to deal with. For instance, in some systems for arithmetic, we want the individual constants to denote numbers, so in such a system the number of x's will be infinite. The **domain of discourse** (or **universe of discourse**) for a system for arithmetic is (so to speak) the "world of numbers." Or, more specifically, it might be just, say, all the positive integers. Usually, the domain of discourse is not explicitly specified but assumed to be "everything." Everything, obviously, includes quite a lot. It specifically includes all concrete (as opposed to abstract) things, such as people and trees, and logic books, but it also includes all the numbers, as well as individual times and places. So to say, for example, $(x)Mx$ (with an unrestricted domain), is to say that the property designated by M applies to everything, including say, Hillary Rodham Clinton, the book you are presently reading, the number 5, and the city of Los Angeles. Obviously, few sentences will be correctly symbolized as $(x)Mx$ (with an unrestricted domain).

Now consider the sentence "All humans are mortal." It is correctly symbolized as $(x)(Hx \supset Mx)$ (where Hx = "x is human" and Mx = "x is mortal") and is read "For all x, if x is human, then x is mortal" or "Given any x, if x is human, then x is mortal," which is roughly what the sentence "All humans are mortal" asserts.

Notice that "All humans are mortal" is not symbolized as $(x)(Hx \cdot Mx)$, because that says that given any x, it is both human *and* mortal, or, what amounts to the same thing, that all things are both human and mortal, and this is not what the sentence "All humans are mortal" means. (Note that "All humans are mortal" is true (alas!), whereas "All things are both human and mortal" is false.)

Remember, all material implications with false antecedents are true. So, given the truth conditions of "$\supset$," it *is* true of everything that *if* it is a human, then it is mortal. This is true of humans, but it is also automatically true of all nonhumans as well. For example, it is true of one's desktop computer that if it is a human, then it is mortal, because the antecedent of this material conditional is false—the computer is not a human. This conditional is true of the computer, it's true of any individual oak tree that exists, and it's true of any number you care to pick out. So if we plug in, say, the individual constant c in place of the variable x in the formula $Hx \supset Mx$, where c designates a particular computer (or any other nonhuman), the resulting conditional, $Hc \supset Mc$, will be true because its antecedent, Hc, is false.

As was the case for some of our translations into sentential logic, we have quickly reached a controversial one here. It follows immediately from what was said in the last paragraph that "All persons are mortal" is true if there are no persons and, in general, any universally quantified conditional is true if there are no instances of the kinds of entities described in its antecedent. Many will, and have, considered this an anomaly. Aristotle's logic does not allow for this, and in ordinary language it is indeed considered odd if we knowingly assert a universally quantified conditional when there are no instances of the antecedent. So if you say, to shush a crowd at a party at your house, "All my children are upstairs asleep" and you have no children, you have violated the conventions of utterance: The audience has every right to assume that you would not have said what you said unless you had at least one child. The assumption in question is called that of *Existential Import*, and clearly modern logic makes no such assumption if it insists—as it does—on the translation in question. We discuss this issue—a very old and intense one in philosophy of logic—in Chapter Fourteen. But for now, let's reassure ourselves that we have not done anything silly. There are many times when asserting a universally quantified conditional with no instances of the antecedent being true is useful to say the least. Consider "All bodies in motion remain in motion in a straight line at uniform speed forever unless impeded by an external force." There are no bodies that remain in motion "forever," let alone unimpeded, but the law of inertia has proved very useful.* Often in science we need to test hypotheses for logical consequences without assuming there are any instances of the conditional's antecedent. For a more mundane example, consider "Everyone who does not study will fail the logic exam." This may well be true—even if everyone studies and there are no instances of the antecedent!

---

*Certainly one might object that, nevertheless, the absence of such bodies makes the law of inertia automatically true, at least according to modern logic, hardly a result we want in physics! However, the equivalent formulation—to the effect that all bodies impeded by an external force do not move at a uniform speed or in a straight line—is quite testable.

We noted earlier that ordinarily few true sentences would be correctly symbolized by the simple quantified formula $(x)Mx$, with an unrestricted domain. Mx would have to be a property that literally everything possesses. Few properties can be ascribed to everything. One way to provisionally work around this is to specify a more limited domain. For example, here are two equally accurate ways of symbolizing the sentence "All humans are mortal":

Domain: All humans	*Domain:* Unrestricted
Symbolization: $(x)Mx$	*Symbolization:* $(x)(Hx \supset Mx)$

There are some important advantages to symbolizations with unrestricted domains, such as the one on the right. Sometimes our ability to prove, say, that a particular argument is valid hinges on displaying the logical structure that using an unrestricted domain makes possible. For example, to use a predicate logic proof (introduced in Chapter Nine) to demonstrate the validity of the following obviously valid argument:

    1. All humans are mortal.
    2. Not everything is mortal.
∴ 3. Not everything is human.

it is necessary to symbolize the first premise by using an unrestricted quantifier.

So instead of restricting the domain and then producing a symbolization, we, in effect, place the restrictions within the sentence itself, as the antecedent of a conditional bound by a universal quantifier. This pattern is so common that if you produce a symbolization that is a universally quantified sentence, and the main connective of the sentence is *not* "$\supset$," you should suspect something may be wrong with your symbolization. There are exceptions, as some of the following examples illustrate, but the rule of thumb is that in symbolizing, the universal quantifier usually binds a sentence that has the horseshoe as its main connective.

Examples

Here are some English sentences and their correct symbolizations in predicate logic notation (using obvious abbreviations).

English Sentence	*Symbolization*
1. Everything is movable.	1. $(x)Mx$
2. Not everything is movable.	2. $\sim(x)Mx$
3. Nothing is movable.	3. $(x)\sim Mx$
4. Everything is immovable.	4. $(x)\sim Mx$

(Notice that 3 and 4 are equivalent.)

5. It's not true that everything is immovable.	5. $\sim(x)\sim Mx$
6. Sugar tastes sweet.	6. $(x)(Sx \supset Tx)$

(In English, the quantifiers "all" and "some" often are omitted when context makes it clear what is intended.)

7. If something is a piece of sugar, then it tastes sweet.	7. $(x)(Sx \supset Tx)$

(Notice that 6 and 7 are equivalent.)

8. Everything is either sweet or bitter.	8. $(x)(Sx \lor Bx)$
9. Either everything is sweet, or else everything is bitter.	9. $(x)Sx \lor (x)Bx$

(Notice that 8 and 9 are not equivalent.)

10. Each person fears death.	10. $(x)(Px \supset Fx)$
11. Everyone fears death.	11. $(x)(Px \supset Fx)$

(Notice that 10 and 11 are equivalent.)

12. No one fears death.	12. $(x)(Px \supset {\sim} Fx)$
13. Not everyone fears death.	13. ${\sim}(x)(Px \supset Fx)$
14. All honest people fear death.	14. $(x)[(Px \cdot Hx) \supset Fx]$
15. Everyone who is honest fears death.	15. $(x)[(Px \cdot Hx) \supset Fx]$
16. Not all honest people fear death.	16. ${\sim}(x)[(Px \cdot Hx) \supset Fx]$
17. Anyone who doesn't fear death isn't honest.	17. $(x)[(Px \cdot {\sim} Fx) \supset {\sim} Hx)]$
18. Although all honest people fear death, Shirley MacLaine doesn't.	18. $(x)[(Px \cdot Hx) \supset Fx] \cdot {\sim} Fm$
19. Everyone either is honest or fears death.	19. $(x)[Px \supset (Hx \lor Fx)]$
20. It's not the case that no dishonest people fear death.	20. ${\sim}(x)[(Px \cdot {\sim} Hx) \supset {\sim} Fx]$
21. Either all human beings are mortal or none are.	21. $(x)(Hx \supset Mx) \lor (x)(Hx \supset {\sim} Mx)$
22. If all human beings are mortal, then not to fear death indicates not being human.	22. $(x)(Hx \supset Mx) \supset (x)({\sim} Fx \supset {\sim} Hx)$

Of course, there is nothing sacred about the variable *x*. For instance, the sentence "Sugar tastes sweet" can be symbolized as $(y)(Sy \supset Ty)$ or $(z)(Sz \supset Tz)$, just as well as $(x)(Sx \supset Tx)$. All three of these sentences say the same thing. In math we can write $(y + z) = (z + y)$ just as well as $(x + y) = (y + x)$; both of these formulas say the same thing.

Exercise 7-3

Symbolize the following sentences, using the indicated letters.

1. All events have causes. (Ex = "*x* is an event"; Cx = "*x* has a cause")
2. Every event has a cause.

3. Not all events have causes.
4. No events have causes.
5. All natural events have causes. (Nx = "x is natural")
6. All events that have causes are natural.
7. No unnatural events have causes.
8. Anything that is caused is a natural event.
9. No natural events are uncaused.
10. Events are either natural or uncaused.
11. All miracles are unnatural events. (Mx = "x is a miracle")
12. Miracles have causes, but they aren't natural.
13. There are no uncaused events, but there are events that are miracles.
14. If there are no unnatural events, then there are no miracles.

Exercise 7-4

Symbolize the following sentences, letting Px = "x is (was) U.S. president"; Ix = "x is (was) well informed"; r = "Ronald Reagan"; and b = "George H. W. Bush."

1. All U.S. presidents have been well informed.
2. No U.S. presidents have been well informed.
3. Not all U.S. presidents have been well informed.
4. If Ronald Reagan wasn't well informed, then not all U.S. presidents have been well informed.
5. But not all U.S. presidents have been ill informed (not well informed) if George H. W. Bush was well informed.
6. Provided either Bush was well informed or Reagan was not well informed, U.S. presidents have been neither all well informed nor all ill informed.

Now let Sx = "x is a logic student"; Lx = "x is logical"; Px = "x is popular"; and a = "Art."

7. Logic students are logical.
8. No. Logic students definitely are not logical.
9. Well, not all logic students are logical.
10. Anyway, it's true that those who are logical are not popular.
11. So if all logic students are logical, none of them is popular.
12. But if not all of them are logical, then not all of them are unpopular.
13. Nor is it true that those who are unpopular all are illogical.
14. Now if those who are popular haven't studied logic, then if Art is illogical, he must have studied logic.
15. And if Art is illogical, it's false that logic students universally are logical or that the unpopular universally are logical.
16. Supposing Art is both unpopular and illogical, then logic students are neither all popular nor all logical.

4 *Existential Quantifiers*

The existential quantifier (∃x) is used to assert that some entities (at least one) have a given property. Thus, to symbolize the sentence "Something is heavy" or the sentence "At least one thing is heavy," start with the sentence form *Hx* and prefix an existential quantifier to it. The result is the sentence (∃x)*Hx*, read "For some *x*, *x* is heavy," or "There is an *x* such that *x* is heavy," or just "Some *x* is heavy."

The sentence (∃x)*Hx* is as simple as an existentially quantified sentence can be. Other equally simple sentences are "Something is expensive," (∃x)*Ex*, "Something is important," (∃x)*Ix*, and so on. Adding negation increases complexity. For example, the expression (∃x) ~ *Hx* symbolizes the sentence "Something is not heavy," and the expression ~ (∃x)*Hx* the sentence "It's not the case that something is heavy." (Note that these two are not equivalent!)

More complicated symbolizations are obtained in other ways. Thus, to symbolize the sentence "Something is both heavy and expensive," conjoin *Hx* (for "*x* is heavy") with *Ex* (for "*x* is expensive") to get (*Hx* · *Ex*), and then add an existential quantifier to get (∃x)(*Hx* · *Ex*). Similarly, to symbolize "Something is both sweet and fattening," conjoin *Sx* (for "*x* is sweet") with *Fx* (for "*x* is fattening") to get (*Sx* · *Fx*), and then add an existential quantifier to get (∃x)(*Sx* · *Fx*).

Examples

Here are some other English sentences and their symbolizations using existential quantifiers (letting *Px* = "*x* is a person" and using other obvious abbreviations).

English Sentence	*Symbolization*
1. Some people are honest.	1. (∃x)(*Px* · *Hx*)
2. Some people are not honest.	2. (∃x)(*Px* · ~ *Hx*)
3. Some honest people are mistreated.	3. (∃x)[(*Px* · *Hx*) · *Mx*]
4. Some people are liars and thieves.	4. (∃x)[*Px* · (*Lx* · *Tx*)]
5. It's not true that some people are honest.	5. ~ (∃x)(*Px* · *Hx*)
6. Some people are neither honest nor truthful.	6. (∃x)[*Px* · ~ (*Hx* ∨ *Tx*)], or (∃x)[*Px* · (~ *Hx* · ~ *Tx*)]
7. Some things are neither expensive nor worthwhile.	7. (∃x)~ (*Ex* ∨ *Wx*), or (∃x)(~ *Ex* · ~ *Wx*]
8. Some people are liars, and some are thieves. (Compare with example 4 and note the difference!)	8. (∃x)(*Px* · *Lx*) · (∃x)(*Px* · *Tx*)
9. Some thieving liars are caught, and some aren't.	9. (∃x)[(*Tx* · *Lx*) · *Cx*] · (∃x)[(*Tx* · *Lx*) · ~ *Cx*]

Exercise 7-5

Symbolize the following sentences, using the indicated symbols as abbreviations.

1. Some athletes are overpaid. (*Ax* = "*x* is an athlete," *Ox* = "*x* is overpaid")

2. Some athletes aren't overpaid.

3. It's not true that there are overpaid athletes.

4. Some elected officials are overpaid. (*Ex* = "*x* is an elected official")

5. But somewhere there is at least one who is not overpaid.

6. There are PTA members who are parents and others who are teachers. (*Ax* = "*x* is a PTA member," *Px* = "*x* is a parent," and *Tx* = "*x* is a teacher")

7. And some members are parents and teachers.

8. But teachers aren't all parents, by any means.

9. So the PTA has members who aren't parents and members who aren't teachers.

10. There are some French restaurants that actually serve french fries. (*Rx* = "*x* is a French restaurant," *Sx* = "*x* serves french fries")

11. Some of them serve Dijon mustard along with the fries. (*Dx* = "*x* serves Dijon mustard with the fries")

12. But there are some French restaurants that serve French's mustard with their fries. (*Fx* = "*x* serves French's mustard with fries")

13. And, of course, French restaurants that serve Dijon don't serve French's.

14. From which it follows that the ones serving French's don't serve Dijon.

15. So, there're some French restaurants where you can get french fries and Dijon mustard, but not French's; some that serve French's mustard with their fries, but no Dijon; and some that don't serve french fries at all.

5 *Basic Predicate Logic Symbolizations*

In sentential logic you learned to symbolize by learning how to deal with common patterns that frequently occur in English. For example, you learned that English sentences with the form "Neither A nor B" can be symbolized as ~ *A* · ~ *B,* and sentences of the form "A, unless B" can be symbolized ~ *B* ⊃ *A.* You should approach predicate logic symbolization in the same way. Let's begin with four basic patterns we have already seen in previous sections.

All A's are B's.

These sentences are ones where every individual of a certain kind is said to have some property or other. Such sentences commonly begin with words such as *all, every,* or *any.* Such sentences can be straightforwardly symbolized using the universal quantifier. Here are some more examples:

English Sentence	**Symbolization**
1. All dogs have fleas.	$(x)(Dx \supset Fx)$
2. Every dog has fleas.	$(x)(Dx \supset Fx)$
3. Dogs have fleas.	$(x)(Dx \supset Fx)$

Some A's are B's.

The sentences that follow are easily symbolized using the existential quantifier. These are sentences that ascribe a property to some but not necessarily to all members of a group.

4. Some dogs have fleas.	$(\exists x)(Dx \cdot Fx)$
5. There are dogs that have fleas.	$(\exists x)(Dx \cdot Fx)$

No A's are B's (or equivalently, All A's are not B's).

Sentences that say that no individual of a certain kind has a property are equivalent to those that say all individuals of that kind lack the property. So both of these kinds of sentences can be symbolized either as negations of existentially quantified sentences or as universally quantified sentences with a negation sign before the consequent of the bound conditional. We provide both kinds of symbolizations for our examples.

6. No dogs have fleas.	$\sim(\exists x)(Dx \cdot Fx)$ or
	$(x)(Dx \supset \sim Fx)$
7. There aren't any dogs that have fleas.	$\sim (\exists x)(Dx \cdot Fx)$ or
	$(x)(Dx \supset \sim Fx)$
8. Dogs do not have fleas.	$\sim (\exists x)(Dx \cdot Fx)$ or
	$(x)(Dx \supset \sim Fx)$

Not all A's are B's (some A's are not B's).

Sentences having the pattern *Not all A's are B's* (for example, "Not all leopards have stripes") are logically equivalent to sentences having the pattern *Some A's are not B's* ("Some leopards do not have stripes"). You will probably find it most natural to symbolize the first of these sentences using a universal quantifier and the second using an existential. Either way of symbolizing is perfectly acceptable, so again we illustrate both.

9. Not all dogs have fleas.	$\sim (x)(Dx \supset Fx)$ or
	$(\exists x)(Dx \cdot \sim Fx)$
10. Not every dog has fleas.	$\sim (x)(Dx \supset Fx)$ or
	$(\exists x)(Dx \cdot \sim Fx)$
11. Some dogs don't have fleas.	$\sim (x)(Dx \supset Fx)$ or
	$(\exists x)(Dx \cdot \sim Fx)$

Most of the sentences you will be asked to symbolize in this chapter are simply elaborations of these four basic sentence patterns. Complex sentences commonly just build on these patterns. So to symbolize "Wealthy people should pay more taxes and receive fewer Social Security benefits," the first step is to realize that this sentence is just a complex all A's are B's kind of sentence. This gives you the basic form $(x)(\underline{\quad\quad} \supset \underline{\quad\quad})$, and you simply fill in the blanks with the subject and the predicate. In this case both the subject and the predicate are compound, so we can fill in the blanks as follows: $(x)[(Wx \cdot Px) \supset (Tx \cdot Sx)]$.

6   *The Square of Opposition*

It is worth noting that any sentence that can be symbolized with a universal quantifier can be symbolized with an existential quantifier, and vice versa. For example, you can symbolize "All dogs have fleas" using the existential quantifier as ~ $(\exists x)(Dx \cdot \sim Fx)$, and "Some dogs have fleas" can be symbolized with the universal quantifier as ~ $(x)(Dx \supset \sim Fx)$. This means our symbols are redundant—we could dispense with one of the two quantifiers and still be able to symbolize just as accurately (though not as easily).

A traditional way of illustrating the relationship between the quantifiers is known as the **square of opposition:**

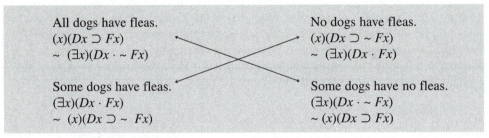

All dogs have fleas.	No dogs have fleas.
$(x)(Dx \supset Fx)$	$(x)(Dx \supset \sim Fx)$
~ $(\exists x)(Dx \cdot \sim Fx)$	~ $(\exists x)(Dx \cdot Fx)$
Some dogs have fleas.	Some dogs have no fleas.
$(\exists x)(Dx \cdot Fx)$	$(\exists x)(Dx \cdot \sim Fx)$
~ $(x)(Dx \supset \sim Fx)$	~ $(x)(Dx \supset Fx)$

Each of the four basic sentence patterns reviewed in the previous section is represented in the square. For each sentence two equivalent symbolizations are provided, one with a universal quantifier and one with an existential quantifier. The sentences connected by the arrows contradict one another. (Notice that the second symbolization is simply the denial of the first symbolization at the other end of the arrow.)

A good way to gain additional practice at symbolizing is to use the other quantifier to produce a second, equivalent symbolization. (See the extended discussion of these points in Chapter Fourteen.)

7   *Common Pitfalls in Symbolizing with Quantifiers*

Some English expressions that *look* like compound subjects or predicates should not be symbolized that way. "Some professional athletes excel in both football and baseball" can be symbolized (using the obvious abbreviations) as $(\exists x)[Px \cdot (Fx \cdot Bx)]$. Do not symbolize the "professional athletes" portion of this sentence as $Px \cdot Ax$ (where Px = "x is professional" and Ax = "x is an athlete"), because one can be professional and an athlete without being a professional athlete.

Also be careful with sentences that contain the words "a" or "any." These particles sometimes operate logically just like the particle "all," but often they do not, as the following sentences illustrate:

12. A barking dog never bites. $(x)[(Dx \cdot Bx) \supset \sim Ix]$
13. A barking dog is in the road. $(\exists x)[(Dx \cdot Bx) \cdot Rx]$

14. Anyone is welcome to enroll. $(x)(Px \supset Wx)$
15. There is not anyone here. $\sim (\exists x)(Px \cdot Hx)$

So there is no general rule of thumb for how to symbolize these sentences.

Most other frequently occurring sentence patterns are fairly easy to symbolize. But a few are tricky. For instance, the sentence "Women and children are exempt from the draft" is correctly symbolized as $(x)[(Wx \lor Cx) \supset Ex]$, *not* as $(x)[(Wx \cdot Cx) \supset Ex]$. The latter asserts all things that are *both* women *and* children are exempt, whereas the original sentence states all things that are *either* women *or* children are exempt.

In this case the "and" in the antecedent of the sentence misleads us into using the symbol " $\cdot$ " instead of " $\lor$ ". However, there is a fairly straightforward symbolization of the sentence that contains the symbol " $\cdot$ "—namely, $(x)(Wx \supset Ex) \cdot (x)(Cx \supset Ex)$. To say all women are exempt from the draft and all children are exempt from the draft is to say exactly that all women and children are exempt from the draft. And, indeed, $(x)(Wx \supset Ex) \cdot (x)(Cx \supset Ex)$ and $(x)[(Wx \lor Cx) \supset Ex]$ are logically equivalent.

Finally, consider the superficially similar sentence "Some dogs and cats do not make good house pets." Again, do not let the word "and" mislead you into a symbolization such as $(\exists x)[(Dx \cdot Cx) \cdot \sim Gx]$, because this symbolization says that there is something that is both a dog and a cat and (not surprisingly) not a good house pet as well. But in this case, you should *not* symbolize this sentence as $(\exists x)[(Dx \lor Cx) \cdot \sim Gx]$ because on this symbolization the sentence would be true if, say, some dogs but no cats failed to be good house pets. So you should symbolize the sentence as the conjunction of two existentially quantified sentences, as follows: $(\exists x)(Dx \cdot \sim Gx) \cdot (\exists x)(Cx \cdot \sim Gx)$.

⃗ Walk-Through: Predicate Logic Symbolizations

A great many sentences simply predicate some property (simple or complex) of some or all individuals of a certain sort. A good way to symbolize these sentences is to first decide on the subject (who is the sentence about?), then supply the appropriate quantifier (is the sentence saying something about some or all of these individuals?), and finally fill in the predicate (what does it say about them?). For example, take the sentence "Some shifty-eyed lawyers are actually hard-working and honest." Obviously, this sentence is about lawyers who have shifty eyes. This gives us

   $Lx \cdot Sx$

We then supply the quantifier (and the connective that characteristically accompanies that quantifier).

   $(\exists x)\ (Lx \cdot Sx) \cdot$

We complete our symbolization by filling in the predicate half of our sentence.

   $(\exists x)\ [(Lx \cdot Sx) \cdot (Hx \cdot Wx)]$

Suppose our sentence is "Not all infomercials are about hair loss or psychic predictions." Who is this sentence about?

   Ix

Some or all?

   ~ (x) *Ix* ⊃

What does it say about them?

   ~ (x)[*Ix* ⊃ (*Hx* ∨ *Px*)]

Examples

1. All students who attend college   (x)[(*Sx* · *Cx*) ⊃ *Ex*] or
   are well educated.   ~ (∃x)[(*Sx* · *Cx*) · ~ *Ex*]
2. All men and women are adults.   (x)[(*Mx* ∨ *Wx*) ⊃ *Ax*] or
                                             ~ (∃x)[(*Mx* ∨ *Wx*) · ~ *Ax*]
3. All lawyers are intelligent and shifty.   (x)[*Lx* ⊃ (*Ix* · *Sx*)] or
                                             ~ (∃x)[*Lx* · ~ (*Ix* · *Sx*)]
4. All doctors are intelligent or high-priced. (x)[*Dx* ⊃ (*Ix* ∨ *Hx*)] or
                                             ~ (∃x)[*Dx* · ~ (*Ix* ∨ *Hx*)]
5. Not all doctors are moneygrubbers.   ~ (x)(*Dx* ⊃ *Mx*), or
                                             (∃x)(*Dx* · ~ *Mx*)
6. No doctors are moneygrubbers.   (x)(*Dx* ⊃ ~ *Mx*), or
                                             ~ (∃x)(*Dx* · *Mx*)
7. No one who attends college is ignorant.   (x)[(*Px* · *Ax*) ⊃ ~ *Ix*], or
                                             ~ (∃x)[(*Px* · *Ax*) · *Ix*]
8. There are no ignorant people who have   (x)[(*Ix* · *Px*) ⊃ ~ *Ax*] or
   attended college.   ~ (∃x)[(*Ix* · *Px*) · *Ax*]

Exercise 7-6

Symbolize the following so as to reveal as much logical structure as possible. Indicate the meanings of your abbreviations.

1. All marsupials have pouches.
2. Any animal that has a pouch is a marsupial.
3. Actually, not all marsupials have pouches.
4. Any animal without a pouch is no marsupial.
5. Kangaroos and opossums are both marsupials.
6. Wombats and bandicoots are marsupials that are not well known.
7. Koala bears are not really bears at all.
8. If all marsupials are cute and furry, then opossums are cute and furry.
9. Marsupials can be found in their natural habitats in both Australia and North America.
10. Neither aardvarks nor armadillos are marsupials.
11. Female marsupials have pouches, but males don't.
12. Armadillos are neither marsupials nor reptiles.

13. Any physician who is patient has plenty of patients.
14. There are physicians who are competent but lack tact.
15. Everyone who cheats feels guilty, or should feel guilty.
16. Not every soldier who fought in Iraq is a hero.
17. All Girl Scouts and Boy Scouts are to be congratulated by President Bush.
18. Some Girl Scouts and Boy Scouts are to be congratulated by President Bush.
19. President Bush will meet with dignitaries from China and Japan.
20. Neither all of the Democrats, nor all of the Republicans, supported President Bush's tax plan.

Exercise 7-7

Translate the following into English, being as colloquial as possible. Let Tx = "x is a TV newscaster," Px = "x has a pleasant personality," Ex = "x is a political expert," b = "Barbara Walters," r = "Dan Rather," and m = "John Madden."

1. $(\exists x)(Tx \cdot Px)$
2. $(\exists x)(Tx \cdot \sim Ex)$
3. $\sim (\exists x)(Tx \cdot Ex)$
4. $(x)(Tx \supset \sim Ex)$
5. $\sim (x)(Tx \supset Ex)$
6. $(x)[(Ex \cdot \sim Px) \supset \sim Tx]$

7. $(\exists x)[Tx \cdot \sim (Px \cdot Ex)]$
8. $(\exists x)[Tx \cdot (Px \vee Ex)]$
9. $(x)(Tx \supset Ex) \supset \sim Tb$
10. $Tr \supset \sim (y)[(Ty \cdot Py) \supset Ey]$
11. $(Pm \cdot \sim Em) \supset \sim Tm$
12. $(x)[Tx \supset (Px \cdot Ex)] \supset \sim (Tr \vee Tb)$

8 *Expansions*

So far we have been doing translations rather intuitively, appealing to common usage. But standing behind these intuitions is a more reliable guide: comparing the truth conditions of the ordinary language sentence with those of its translation. To accomplish this, we must first find truth conditions for our quantified statements. As you will see, we sometimes might reject a translation once we realize that its truth conditions fail to capture what we want for our English statement.

Imagine a limited universe containing, say, only four individual entities. What would quantified sentences assert in such a universe? For instance, what would the sentence $(x)Fx$ assert? The answer is that it would assert at least that Fa and Fb and Fc and Fd. But universally quantified sentences also assert that the items listed are all of the items there are in the universe of discourse, and merely listing the items, even though all in fact are listed, does not say that all are listed. In other words, it would assert that $(Fa \cdot Fb) \cdot (Fc \cdot Fd)$. Thus, in this limited universe, $(x)Fx$ would be true if the expression $(Fa \cdot Fb) \cdot (Fc \cdot Fd)$, called the **expansion** of $(x)Fx$ with respect to that limited universe, is true.

Of course our logic is applicable to the real universe, which contains many more than four individual entities. Can we construe quantified sentences in a universally applicable logic as a shorthand way of writing very long conjunctions? The answer is that we *could* construe them in this way if (1) there were only a finite number of entities in the real universe, and (2) we had a name in our language for every entity. But unfortunately we do not have a name for every entity in the real universe of discourse, and the number of entities we want to talk about frequently is not finite. For instance, in arithmetic we want to be able to assert the sentence "Every even number is divisible by 2"—that is, assert that 2 is divisible by 2, *and* 4 is divisible by 2, *and* 6 is divisible by 2, *and so on.* But since the number of numbers is infinite, we can't actually write down a conjunction listing each number that is equivalent to the sentence "Every even number is divisible by 2." Instead we can use a universal quantifier to symbolize that sentence. For instance, using obvious abbreviations, we can symbolize it as $(x)[(Nx \cdot Ex) \supset Dx]$. So the answer to the question posed in the second sentence of the last paragraph is as follows. Because there are universes of discourse with an infinite number of entities in them, such as the natural numbers, we cannot construe universally quantified formulas as logically equivalent to conjunctions. In the finite case—a universe of discourse with only a finite number of members—that we do not have the names of everything is a mere practical inconvenience, not a theoretical one. Nevertheless, the objection that even in the finite case a universally quantified statement says more than a conjunction, is sufficient for our purposes to deny their logical equivalence. But we can certainly think of the minimal truth conditions for universally quantified statements to be conjunctions, and that is what we will do henceforth.* In the following chapters on natural deduction, it will be clear that no conjunction of the kind in question, even if it is exhaustive, logically implies a universally quantified statement.

Now consider a sentence containing an *existential* quantifier, say, the sentence $(\exists x)Fx$. In a limited universe containing only three objects, this sentence asserts not that *Fa* and *Fb* and *Fc,* because that is what is asserted by $(x)Fx$, but rather that *Fa* or *Fb* or *Fc.* So its expansion in this limited universe is $[(Fa \vee Fb) \vee Fc]$. Once again, we must resist the temptation to conclude there is a logical equivalence between the disjunction and the existentially quantified statement. Since no list says about itself that it is complete, we could not simply replace the existentially quantified statement by a disjunction, because it would be logically possible that each of the listed disjuncts is *not* true, and one *we have not listed is* true. Of course, if any of the disjuncts is true it will logically entail the existentially quantified statement; if $V(Fa) = $ **T,** then $V((\exists x) Fx) = $ **T.** All this said, the disjunction will be useful to us. If we are given the information that we have a complete list of names, then the truth conditions of the disjunction will be the truth conditions of the existentially quantified statement.

Examples

The following are expansions for a universe containing three individuals—*a, b,* and *c.*

1. *Symbolization:* $(\exists x) \sim Fx$
   Expansion: $\sim Fa \vee (\sim Fb \vee \sim Fc)$

---

*To add to the conjunction the statement "and that is all the entities there are," we would need another universally quantified statement! The considerable philosophical controversy about this issue goes back to Bertrand Russell's discussions of it in his "Lectures on Logical Atomism" (see the Bibliography). The correct semantics for quantified statements is still a debate among philosophers of logic. Fortunately, for our purposes we need not take a side.

2. *Symbolization:* ~ (∃x)Fx
   Expansion: ~ [Fa ∨ (Fb ∨ Fc)]

3. *Symbolization:* (x)(Fx ⊃ Gx)
   Expansion: (Fa ⊃ Ga) · [(Fb ⊃ Gb) · (Fc ⊃ Gc)]

4. *Symbolization:* (∃x) ~ (Fx · Gx)
   Expansion: ~ (Fa · Ga) ∨ [~ (Fb · Gb) ∨ ~ (Fc · Gc)]

5. *Symbolization:* (x)[(Fx · Gx) ⊃ Hx]
   Expansion: [(Fa · Ga) ⊃ Ha] · {[(Fb · Gb) ⊃ Hb] · [(Fc · Gc) ⊃ Hc]}

6. *Symbolization:* (∃x)[(Fx · Gx) ∨ Hx]
   Expansion: [(Fa · Ga) ∨ Ha] ∨ {[(Fb · Gb) ∨ Hb] ∨ [(Fc · Gc) ∨ Hc]}

Exercise 7-8

Construct expansions in a two-individual universe of discourse for the following sentences.

1. (x)(Fx · Gx)
2. (∃x)(Fx ∨ Gx)
3. (x)[Fx ⊃ (Gx ∨ Hx)]
4. (∃x)[Fx · (Gx ∨ Hx)]
5. (x) ~ (Fx ⊃ Gx)
6. (∃x) ~ (Fx ∨ Gx)
7. ~ (x)(Fx ⊃ Gx)

8. ~ (∃x)(Fx ∨ Gx)
9. (x)[Fx ⊃ (Gx ⊃ Hx)]
10. (x)[Fx ⊃ ~ (Gx · Hx)]
11. (∃x)[(Fx · Gx) ∨ (Hx · Kx)]
12. (x)[(Fx · Gx) ⊃ (Hx · Kx)]
13. (∃x) ~ [(Fx ⊃ Gx) ∨ (Fx ⊃ Hx)]
14. ~ (x) ~ [(Fx · Gx) · ~ (Hx · Kx)]

We can now refine our claim that truth conditions can help us with translations. Let us introduce the idea of a **model universe,** a domain of a small number of individuals about which we shall construe our quantified statements. It should be intuitively clear that if we assert all dogs are mammals, it makes no difference if there are 3 or 103 entities to check, as far as the logic of the situation is concerned. There will be exceptions, as we shall see in later chapters, when we consider translating such statements as "There are exactly five cats." But for now, for convenience, we will think of our model universe as consisting of three entities, *a*, *b*, and *c*. To see the use of the model universe idea, consider the following.

Sentences of the form "Some _____ are _____," such as the sentence "Some humans are mortal," are often symbolized incorrectly by beginners. The correct symbolization is (∃x)(Hx · Mx), because this sentence asserts that there is something, *x*, which is both human and mortal. The temptation is to symbolize it as (∃x)(Hx ⊃ Mx), by analogy with the symbolization of the sentence "All humans are mortal," which *is* correctly symbolized as (x)(Hx ⊃ Mx). But in this case the similar grammatical structure of the two English sentences is misleading.

To see the difference between the sentence (∃x)(Hx · Mx) and the sentence (∃x)(Hx ⊃ Mx), examine their expansions, namely [(Ha · Ma) ∨ (Hb · Mb)] ∨ (Hc · Mc) and [(Ha ⊃ Ma) ∨ (Hb ⊃ Mb)] ∨ (Hc ⊃ Mc). The expansion [(Ha · Ma) ∨ (Hb · Mb)] ∨ (Hc · Mc) is true if there are some things that are both human and mortal, but the expansion [(Ha ⊃ Ma) ∨ (Hb ⊃ Mb)] ∨ (Hc ⊃ Mc) would be true even if there were no humans at all, mortal or immortal. The reason it would be true is this: Suppose *a* denotes some item that is not human. Then the disjunct *Ha* ⊃ *Ma* is true, because its antecedent *Ha* is false. Therefore, because one of its disjuncts is true the whole disjunction [(*Ha* ⊃ *Ma*) ∨ (*Hb* ⊃ *Mb*)] ∨ (*Hc* ⊃ *Mc*) is true. Its truth has nothing to do with human mortality; it would be true even if there were no human beings. The reason why symbolizations having the same form as (∃x)(*Hx* ⊃ *Mx*) are almost always incorrect is that such sentences will be trivially true so long as the property in the antecedent (*Hx* in this case) is not possessed by everything. But the expansion [(*Ha* · *Ma*) ∨ (*Hb* · *Mb*)] ∨ (*Hc* · *Mc*) would not be true if there were no human beings, because if that were the case, then all of its disjuncts would be false. If there were no human beings in the universe, then (*Ha* · *Ma*) would be false, (*Hb* · *Mb*) would be false, and (*Hc* · *Mc*) would be false. So the correct symbolization for "Some humans are mortal" is (∃x)(*Hx* · *Mx*) and not (∃x)(*Hx* ⊃ *Mx*).

9 *Symbolizing "Only," "None but," and "Unless"*

A good deal of care is needed in symbolizing sentences containing words or phrases such as "only," "none but," and "unless."

Consider a statement a professor might make in the classroom: (1) "Only those who study will pass the test." Restricting the universe of discourse to the professor's students, this sentence is correctly symbolized as (x)(*Px* ⊃ *Sx*). It is tempting to symbolize it incorrectly as (x)(*Sx* ⊃ *Px*), thus interpreting it to mean that all who study will pass. But to say that *only* those who study will pass does not (unfortunately) guarantee that *all* of those who do study will pass. Suppose it is a very difficult test and that some students who study pass and some do not, but no one passes who does not study. Then the sentence "All who study will pass the test" is false (since some who study do not pass), whereas the professor's sentence, "Only those who study will pass the test" turns out to be true. Hence, the symbolization (x)(*Sx* ⊃ *Px*) cannot be the correct symbolization of the professor's statement.

Another way to look at the problem is as follows. To say that only those who study will pass is to say that anyone who does not study will not pass. Because the sentence "All who do not study will not pass the test" is correctly symbolized as (x)(~ *Sx* ⊃ ~ *Px*), the equivalent sentence (1) "Only those who study will pass the test" also is correctly symbolized in this way. And since (x)(~ *Sx* ⊃ ~ *Px*), is equivalent to (x)(*Px* ⊃ *Sx*) as will be proved in later chapters, it follows that (1) is correctly symbolized as (x)(*Px* ⊃ *Sx*).

Sentences containing the phrase "none but" are handled in a similar fashion. Thus, the sentences "Only the good die young" and "None but the good die young" are equivalent and can each be symbolized (x)(*Yx* ⊃ *Gx*).

The phrase "none but" in a sentence of this kind means roughly the same thing as the phrase "none except." For instance, the sentence "None but the ignorant are happy" means the same thing as the sentence "None, except the ignorant, are happy." Therefore, both of these sentences are symbolized as (x)(*Hx* ⊃ *Ix*).

English usage allows us to use the word "unless" to produce sentences that are equivalent to the ones we've just been discussing. For instance, instead of saying "Only those who study will pass" or "None but those who study will pass," we can say, "No one will pass unless they study." (We use "they" here to avoid the masculine pronoun "he." Some object to this usage as ungrammatical. An alternative is "No one will pass unless he or she studies.") "Without" sometimes performs a similar function in English, as in, "No one will pass without studying." All these sentences say roughly the same thing, and hence for our purposes can be symbolized in the same way, namely, $(x)(Px \supset Sx)$.

Remember that "unless" also often functions as a truth-functional connective, as explained in Chapter Two. So a sentence such as "No one will get dessert unless everyone quiets down" should be symbolized $\sim (x)(Px \supset Qx) \supset \sim (\exists x)(Px \cdot Dx)$. The word "if" has a similar dual usage. It can function as a truth-functional connective as in "If everyone in the class studies, no one in the class will fail" symbolized $(x)(Cx \supset Sx) \supset \sim (\exists x)(Cx \cdot Fx)$—and can also be used to make generalizations, as in "If H_2O freezes, it expands"—symbolized $(x)[(Hx \cdot Fx) \supset Ex)]$.

Examples

1. Only celebrities can be elected president.
   $(x)(Ex \supset Cx)$ or $\sim (\exists x)(Ex \cdot \sim Cx)$

2. No one can be elected president unless he or she is a celebrity.
   $(x)(Ex \supset Cx)$ or $\sim (\exists x)(Ex \cdot \sim Cx)$

3. None but celebrities can be elected president.
   $(x)(Ex \supset Cx)$ or $\sim (\exists x)(Ex \cdot \sim Cx)$

4. Only glib politicians can be elected president.
   $(x)[Ex \supset (Gx \cdot Px)]$ or $\sim (\exists x)[Ex \cdot \sim (Gx \cdot Px)]$

5. None but glib politicians can be elected president.
   $(x)[Ex \supset (Gx \cdot Px)]$ or $\sim (\exists x)[Ex \cdot \sim (Gx \cdot Px)]$

6. No one can be elected president unless that person is a glib politician.
   $(x)[(Ex \supset (Gx \cdot Px)]$

7. No one can be elected president unless someone is nominated.
   $\sim (\exists x)(Px \cdot Nx) \supset (x)(Px \supset \sim Ex)$

Exercise 7-9

Symbolize the following, and indicate your use of abbreviations.

1. Only those students who don't study regularly will flunk logic.
2. There won't be any students who flunk logic, except those who don't study regularly.
3. The gates of heaven shall open only to the poor.
4. None but the poor shall enter heaven.
5. No one will die of lung cancer unless they smoke tobacco.
6. Only those who smoke tobacco will die of lung cancer.
7. Unfortunately, it is not true that only those who smoke tobacco will die of lung cancer.
8. Unless John quits smoking, his entire family is at risk for lung cancer.

9. Unless all elephants are protected, all elephants are doomed.
10. If all elephants are not protected, all elephants are doomed. (See Exercise 7-11, problem 1.)
11. If a rhinoceros feels threatened, it may charge.
12. A rhinoceros is a peaceful animal, unless threatened.

Exercise 7-10

Symbolize the following sayings so as to reveal as much of their structure as possible and indicate the meanings of the abbreviations you use:

1. There is no such thing as a free lunch.—Milton Friedman
2. All sin is a form of lying.—St. Augustine
3. If a thing is worth doing, it is worth doing badly.—G. K. Chesterton
4. All that glitters is not gold. (*Lx* = "*x* glitters," *Gx* = "*x* is gold")
5. And all that is gold does not glitter.
6. Sometimes a cigar is just a cigar.—Sigmund Freud
7. He who can, does. He who cannot, teaches.—George Bernard Shaw (among others)
8. The only completely consistent people are the dead.—Aldous Huxley
9. You have to be over 30 to enjoy Proust.—Gore Vidal
10. No one but a blockhead writes except for money.—Samuel Johnson

Now symbolize the following sentences, letting *Px* = "*x* is a person," *Bx* = "*x* is brilliant," *Sx* = "*x* is a complete scoundrel," *Cx* = "*x* is charismatic," and *Lx* = "*x* succeeds in life":

11. There are some brilliant people who are complete scoundrels.
12. And some of these brilliant scoundrels are quite charismatic.
13. Fortunately, most brilliant scoundrels aren't very charismatic.
14. And some of the charismatic ones aren't at all brilliant.
15. Scoundrels who aren't either brilliant or charismatic always are failures (don't succeed) in life.
16. If some scoundrels are failures, then at least a few people who aren't brilliant are scoundrels.
17. But in fact, no brilliant people are scoundrels, or failures in life for that matter.
18. Having every single scoundrel be brilliant would result in failed lives for the rest of us.
19. And having everyone be a scoundrel would result in life being "nasty, brutish, and short" (a complete failure) for everyone.
20. Of course, even if there were no scoundrels whatsoever, there would be people whose lives would be complete failures—along with those who would lead successful lives.

Exercise 7-11

The following are thought questions, meant to have you think carefully about the relationship between logic and ordinary language. There is no answer to (2) in the back of the book!

1. Consider Exercise 7-9, problem 10. We are given an antecedent of a conditional that appears to say "All elephants are not protected," which is the same as "No elephants are protected," which translates into the symbolism as (x) $(Ex \supset \sim Px)$. But the answer to the question in the back of the book has a different, nonequivalent translation. Decide which is right, and give reasons.

2. Consider the discussion in Section 3 of the translation of "All humans are mortal" into modern predicate logic. In that light, think about "All unicorns are one-horned beasts." What should we say intuitively about its truth or falsity? How does that compare with the example given in the text "All my children are upstairs asleep"? To make matters more difficult, translate the unicorn example into our logic notation, then try the same with "All unicorns are not one-horned beasts," and discuss the truth (or falsity) of both translations.

3. In the discussion in Section 3 of unrestricted domains, it was stated that "everything" includes "all concrete (as opposed to abstract) things . . . but it also includes all the numbers." Surely, one might well argue, numbers are about as abstract as a thing can get, and if we include numbers in an unrestricted domain that contains, say, horses, we are going to get *wffs* such as "3 is a horse," which is absurd. Discuss this problem. What might be lost by excluding numbers from the unrestricted domain? Can you think of any other restrictions that might be justifiable?

Key Terms Introduced in Chapter Seven

bound variable: A variable within the scope of a relevant quantifier. For example, in the expression $(x)Fx \cdot Gy$ the variable x, but not the variable y, is bound by the (x) quantifier.

domain of discourse: The items we want our statements to deal with. For instance, in arithmetic the domain of discourse is the "world of numbers." In daily life the domain of discourse could be apples, or persons, or even everything.

existential quantifier: The symbols $(\exists x)$, $(\exists y)$, and so on, as used in sentences such as $(\exists x)(Fx \cdot Gx)$ and $(\exists y)(Fy \lor Gy)$. $(\exists x)$ can be read as "for some x" or "there is at least one x such that. . . ."

expansion (of a quantified sentence): A quantified sentence "spelled out" for a particular domain of individuals; for example, the expansion of the sentence $(x)(Fx \lor Gx)$ for a domain of two individuals, a and b, is $(Fa \lor Ga) \cdot (Fb \lor Gb)$, and the expansion of the sentence $(\exists x)(Fx \cdot Gx)$ for the same domain is $(Fa \cdot Ga) \lor (Fb \cdot Gb)$.

free variable: An unbound variable. A variable not within the scope of a relevant quantifier. For example, in the expression $(x)Fx \supset (Gx \lor Dy)$ the second x variable and the y variable are free.

individual constants: The small letters a through t used to denote particular individuals, as opposed to properties; for example, a may be used to designate the person Art.

individual variables: The small letters u through z used as variables for which individual constants are substituted.

model universe: A domain of a small number of individuals about which we construe our quantified statements. Unless context tells us otherwise, we can use just three individuals for our expansions of quantified statements.

predicate logic: The logic that deals with the interior structure of atomic as well as compound sentences. Synonym: *quantifier logic*.

property constants: Capital letters used to denote particular properties, as opposed to individuals; for example, the F in $(x)Fx$ used to denote the property, say, of being friendly.

quantifier: A symbol used to state how many items (all or some) in the universe of discourse are being referred to. See also *universal quantifier* and *existential quantifier.*

relational property: A property that holds between two (or more) individual entities, for example, the property "_____ is next to _____," which can be symbolized as Nxy. (Relational properties are covered more extensively in Chapter Ten.)

scope of a quantifier: The extent of an expression bound by a quantifier. For example, the scope of the (x) quantifier in $\sim (x) \sim (Fx \supset Gx)$ is $\sim (Fx \supset Gx)$.

square of opposition: A diagram used to illustrate several of the inferential relationships (such as contradictoriness and contrariety) holding between some quantified propositions. (The square of opposition is covered more extensively in Chapter Fourteen.)

substitution: An operation performed by writing an individual constant in place of a free variable. Substitution is distinguished in later chapters from *replacement,* which takes place between logically equivalent statements or statement forms.

universal quantifier: The expressions (x), (y), and so on, as used in sentences such as $(x)(Hx \supset Mx)$ and $(y)Fy$. (x) can be read as "for all x," or "for every x."

universe of discourse: Another name for the domain of discourse.

Chapter Eight

Predicate Logic Semantics

---

1 *Interpretations in Predicate Logic*

We used the idea of a valuation to explain each fundamental concept as we explored the semantics of sentential logic. The good news is that all these basic definitions remain the same in predicate logic. An argument is **valid** in predicate logic if and only if there is no valuation on which the premises are true and the conclusion is false, sentences are **consistent** just in case there is some valuation on which they are all true, two sentences are **logically equivalent** if and only if there is no valuation on which they differ in truth-value, and so on.

What is different is that more is involved in specifying a valuation in predicate logic. In sentential logic we could typically list every one of a sentence form's valuations in short order. We did this by finding the logical form of any given sentence, written in terms of sentential variables, and building a truth table for this *form*. To understand what is being done in predicate logic we must first realize that although we have individual variables and quantification using such variables, *we have no predicate variables*. To introduce them, and quantification over them, would add an enormous complication to our logic. Predicate logic is in part characterized by the fact that we only have individual and not predicate variables at our disposal. Wwellhen we introduce predicate constants into a specific context, however, we must, to have a useful semantics, treat them as if they have other **interpretions** besides the one we are giving for the context in question. To speak of different interpretations of a predicate letter, such as *H,* is to treat it as if it were a variable for which we are substituting another predicate: We assign it to different domains in different contexts. Let's see in more detail how this works.

A complete interpretation consists of four steps.

First, we must specify a domain. Second, for each individual constant we must specify which individual in the domain it designates. Third, we must specify the meaning of each predicate constant so it is clear which individuals in the domain have that property and which do not. Fourth, we give a valuation of any sentential logic statement letters in the *wff*. In other words, an interpretation provides all the information needed to determine a sentence's truth-value—that is, its valuation.

A few words more are necessary about the interpretation of predicates. In modern semantics it is customary to give what is called the *extensional* interpretation of predicates, namely treating a predicate as if it is a class of its members. So we would assign a class of individuals to the predicate. For our purposes at this point we treat predicates **intensionally,** relying on commonsense meanings of them. Later in this chapter, when we use the method of expansion, we in effect stipulate extensions for the predicates. This sounds complicated, but a few examples should help make the idea clear. Here are a number of different interpretations of the simple sentence $(x)(Ax \supset Bx)$.

> *Domain:* unrestricted
> *Ax:* x is an elephant
> *Bx:* x has a trunk

In this interpretation the sentence says that every elephant has a trunk. Here is a completely different interpretation, again using an unrestricted domain:

> *Domain:* unrestricted
> *Ax:* x is a professor
> *Bx:* x is an astronaut

Here is another, this time with the domain restricted to the set of natural numbers.

> *Domain:* natural numbers
> *Ax:* x is an even number
> *Bx:* x is divisible by 2

All our examples so far have had infinitely large domains. But in other interpretations the domain can be much smaller, such as the following:

> *Domain:* citrus fruits
> *Ax:* x is orange
> *Bx:* x contains vitamin C

Is this sentence true or false? Although in an unrestricted domain it is false that all orange things contain vitamin C, the sentence is true in this interpretation because it is true that all orange citrus fruits contain vitamin C.

Finally, the domain can be very small indeed, as the following illustrates:

> *Domain:* one yellow pencil, one green textbook
> *Ax:* x is a pencil
> *Bx:* x is yellow

Note that in this interpretation the sentence is true because it correctly states that all pencils (in this domain) are yellow.

Exercise 8-1

Provide two completely different interpretations for each of the following sentences. Construct your interpretations so that in one interpretation the sentence is clearly true and in the other the sentence is false. For each interpretation, specify the domain and the meaning of each predicate constant. Write out in English what each sentence says in each of your interpretations.

1. $(\exists x)(Ax \cdot Bx)$
2. $(\exists x)(Ax \cdot \sim Bx)$
3. $(x)(Ax \supset \sim Bx)$
4. $\sim (x)(Ax \supset Bx)$

5. $(x)[(Ax \vee Bx) \supset Cx]$
6. $(\exists x)[(Ax \cdot Bx) \cdot \sim Cx]$
7. $(\exists x)Gx \supset \sim (x)(Bx \supset Gx)$
8. $(x)(Ax \supset Bx) \supset (\exists x)(Bx \cdot Cx)$

2 *Proving Invalidity*

As we pointed out when discussing sentential logic, failure to find a valid proof for an argument does not justify concluding that the argument is invalid (because we may lack sufficient ingenuity or simply have overlooked the proof). Nor can we prove an argument is not valid by deriving the negation of its conclusion from its premises (because if its premises are *inconsistent,* then we can validly infer both the conclusion and its negation). Instead, to show an argument is invalid, we need only show that it is possible for the premises all to be true and the conclusion false. To do so, we produce a counterexample, an *interpretation* that makes the premises all true and the conclusion false. Producing such an interpretation shows the argument is invalid no matter what the actual truth-value of the premises or conclusion may be. It is the *possible* truth-values of the premises and conclusion that are important here, not the *actual* truth-values of these claims. These possibilities are a function of interpretations into the same or other domains, but with different assignments of meanings to the individual and predicate "constants"—we are, to repeat, acting as if these constants were variables for which different constants could be substituted.

In sentential logic finding a counterexample was relatively straightforward. For example, to show that

1. $(A \supset B) \supset C$
2. $\sim (B \cdot C) /\therefore \sim A$

is invalid, all that we need to do is to produce the truth table for the form that shows at least one line in which the premises are true and the conclusion is false. In predicate logic we show that an argument is invalid by producing a counterexample, but it is not always so easy to produce one. We have already seen examples of the different kinds of interpretations possible for individual sentences. Now we need an interpretation for an entire argument, one that makes the premises all true and the conclusion false.

Often one can find counterexamples that leave the domain of discourse unrestricted. Take the argument

1. $(x)(Ax \supset Bx)$
2. $(x)(Cx \supset Bx) /\therefore (x)(Ax \supset Cx)$

We can prove this argument is invalid by producing an interpretation with an unrestricted domain where $Ax = $ "x is human," and $Bx = $ "x is mortal," and $Cx = $ "x is a dog." This interpretation demonstrated that the argument is invalid (since we know all humans are mortal and all dogs are mortal but all humans are *not* dogs).

We can also use a more limited domain. For example, restrict the domain of discourse to human beings and consider the argument

1. $(\exists x)(Ax \cdot Bx)$
2. $(\exists x)(Ax \cdot Cx)$ /∴ $(\exists x)(Bx \cdot Cx)$

We can prove this argument invalid with the interpretation on which $Ax = $ "x is an NFL football player," $Bx = $ "x is a world-class sprinter," and $Cx = $ "x weighs more than 350 pounds." There are football players who are world-class sprinters, and football players who weigh over 350 pounds, but no one who weighs more than 350 pounds is a world-class sprinter.

Restricting the universe of discourse to mammals, we can prove that the argument

1. $(x)(Fx \supset Gx)$
2. $(x)(Hx \supset Gx)$ /∴ $(x)(Fx \supset Hx)$

is invalid with the following interpretation:

> *Domain:* mammals
> $Fx = $ "x is a fox"
> $Gx = $ "x is a mammal"
> $Hx = $ "x is a horse"

On this interpretation the argument has true premises and a false conclusion. We can be sure both premises of this argument are true because we know all foxes are mammals and all horses are mammals. We can be sure the conclusion of this argument is false because it is false that all foxes are horses.

Remember, *any* interpretation will do so long as it makes the premises all true and the conclusion false.

🚶 Walk-Through: Invalidity in Predicate Logic

Admittedly, it is often not easy to come up with a counterexample in predicate logic. There are so many possible interpretations to choose from. Unless another interpretation suggests itself right away, it may help to use a mathematical interpretation. For example, if we restrict the domain to the positive integers, this gives us a ready supply of different sorts of predicates. If we need a predicate true of no individual in the domain, we can use "x is < 0," or "x is >1 and <2," and so on. If we need a predicate true of every individual, we can use "$x > 0$" or even "x is an integer." Finally, for predicates true of some individuals and false of others we have such predicates as "$x < 2$," "x is even," "x is odd," "x is divisible by 4," "x is prime," and so on.

Suppose our argument is

1. $(\exists x)(Fx \cdot Gx)$
2. $(x)(Fx \supset Hx)$ /∴ $\sim (\exists x)(Gx \cdot \sim Hx)$

Restricting the domain to the positive integers, we attempt to make the premises all true and the conclusion false. It is often useful to start with the conclusion. In this case we need to define Gx and Hx so that there is some individual that has the first property and lacks the second. Let's let $Gx = x > 1$ and $Hx = x > 2$. Moving to the first premise, we need Fx to be a property possessed by an integer greater than 1, and to make the second premise true, every integer that has this property must also be greater than 2. Lots of predicates will do the trick. For example, we can let Fx = "x is a multiple of 4." Here then is our completed interpretation:

> *Domain:* The positive integers
> $Fx = x$ is a multiple of 4
> $Gx = x > 1$
> $Hx = x > 2$

Clearly, premise 1 is true (4 is a positive integer that is a multiple of 4 and is greater than 1), and premise 2 is true (every multiple of 4 is greater than 2), while the conclusion is not true (There *is* an integer that is greater than 1 and not greater than 2, namely, the number 2 itself.)

(While acknowledging the usefulness of using the domain of numbers and the predicates that we introduce, let us be clear that strictly speaking many of these predicates are *relational*—for example, $x > 1$—and so have a different logical form than one-place predicates as we render them here. No harm is done, but we will see more clearly in Chapter Ten how to translate relational statements.)

Exercise 8-2

Prove that the following arguments are invalid:

(1) 1. $(\exists x)(Ax \cdot Bx)$
    2. $(\exists x)(Bx \cdot Cx)$
    $/\therefore (\exists x)(Ax \cdot Cx)$

(2) 1. $(x)(Ax \supset Bx)$
    2. $(\exists x) \sim Ax /\therefore (\exists x) \sim Bx$

(3) 1. $(\exists x)(Ax \cdot \sim Bx)$
    2. $(\exists x)(Ax \cdot \sim Cx)$
    3. $(\exists x)(\sim Bx \cdot Dx)$
    $/\therefore (\exists x)[Ax \cdot (\sim Bx \cdot Dx)]$

(4) 1. $(x)(Fx \supset Gx)$
    2. $(x)(\sim Fx \supset Ex)$
    $/\therefore (x)(\sim Gx \supset \sim Ex)$

(5) 1. $(\exists x)(Px \cdot \sim Qx)$
    2. $(x)(Rx \supset Px)$
    $/\therefore (\exists x)(Rx \cdot \sim Qx)$

(6) 1. $(x)[(Px \cdot Qx) \supset Rx]$
    2. $(\exists x)(Qx \cdot \sim Rx)$
    3. $(\exists x)(Px \cdot \sim Rx)$
    $/\therefore (\exists x)(\sim Px \cdot \sim Qx)$

(7) 1. $(x)(Px \supset Qx)$
    2. $(x)(Qx \supset Rx)$
    $/\therefore (x)(Px \cdot Rx)$

(8) 1. $(x)[Mx \supset (Nx \supset Px)]$
    2. $(x)(Qx \supset \sim Px)$
    $/\therefore (x)[Qx \supset (Mx \cdot Nx)]$

(9) 1. $(\exists x)(Ax \cdot Bx)$
    2. $(x)(\sim Bx \vee \sim Cx)$
    $/\therefore (x)(\sim Ax \vee \sim Cx)$

(10) 1. $(\exists x)(Ax \vee \sim Bx)$
    2. $(x)[(Ax \cdot \sim Bx) \supset Cx]$
    $/\therefore (\exists x)Cx$

3 *Using Expansions to Prove Invalidity*

So far we have shown arguments to be invalid using interpretations with quite large domains (the universal domain, the domain of humans, the domain of numbers). But one of the easiest ways to prove invalidity is to use an interpretation with a very small domain. For example, consider the following argument:

1. $\sim (\exists x)(\sim Ax \cdot Bx)$
2. $(\exists x)(Ax \cdot Cx) \, / \therefore \sim (x)(Cx \supset \sim Bx)$

To show that this argument is invalid, we need only postulate a domain that contains just two individuals; let's call them John and Mary. In providing an interpretation we need only stipulate whether the properties Ax, Bx, and Cx apply to John and/or Mary so that it is possible to determine the truth-values of the premises and conclusion. To show that the argument is invalid, we need only do this in a way that makes the premises true and the conclusion false.

But it actually doesn't matter which particular properties we choose so long as we have individuals and properties assigned in such a way as to make the premises all true and the conclusion false. We can simply stipulate whether it is true that a particular individual has a particular property. And the really nice thing is that we can find out how to assign these truth values mechanically by using expansions. First, construct the expansion of the premises and conclusion for a two-individual domain:

1. $\sim [(\sim Aa \cdot Ba) \vee (\sim Ab \cdot Bb)]$
2. $(Aa \cdot Ca) \vee (Ab \cdot Cb) \quad / \therefore \sim [(Ca \supset \sim Ba) \cdot (Cb \supset \sim Bb)]$

Next, we show this argument is invalid by using the shortcut technique we used in sentential logic. Remember, we can assign truth values any way we like, provided only that we do so *consistently*. All it takes to show that the argument is invalid is some interpretation, *any* interpretation, that makes the premises true and the conclusion false. Here is one such interpretation:

$$\downarrow$$
$$\text{1.} \quad \sim \ [(\sim Aa \ \cdot \ Ba) \vee \ (\sim Ab \ \cdot \ Bb)]$$
$$\quad\quad \textbf{T} \ \ \textbf{F} \ \textbf{T} \ \ \textbf{F} \ \ \textbf{F} \ \ \textbf{F} \ \ \ \textbf{F} \ \textbf{T} \ \ \textbf{F} \ \ \ \textbf{F}$$
$$\quad\quad\quad\quad\quad \downarrow \quad\quad\quad\quad\quad\quad\quad \downarrow$$
$$\text{2.} \ (Aa \ \cdot \ Ca) \vee (Ab \ \cdot \ Cb) \, / \therefore \sim [(Ca \supset \ \sim Ba) \ \cdot \ (Cb \supset \ \sim Bb)]$$
$$\quad\quad \textbf{T} \ \textbf{T} \ \textbf{T} \ \ \textbf{T} \ \textbf{T} \ \textbf{T} \ \ \ \textbf{F} \ \ \textbf{T} \ \textbf{T} \ \textbf{T} \ \textbf{F} \ \textbf{T} \ \ \textbf{T} \ \textbf{T} \ \textbf{T} \ \textbf{F}$$

This proves that in a domain that contains exactly two individuals, a and b, the premises, $\sim (\exists x)(\sim Ax \cdot Bx)$ and $(\exists x)(Ax \cdot Cx)$, both could be true while the conclusion, $\sim (x)(Cx \supset \sim Bx)$, is false. Our expansion shows this would be the case in an interpretation where both individuals have the properties designated by A and C, but neither individual has property B.

This makes it much easier to find a counterexample. Simply produce an expansion and assign truth values in a manner that makes the premises all true and the conclusion false. Unfortunately, not all invalid arguments can be shown to be invalid using a two-individual domain. Some may require expansions of three or even more individuals. However, as a practical rule of thumb two-individual expansions will usually do the trick for most invalid arguments you are likely to encounter.

Examples

Argument:

1. $(x)[(Ax \cdot Bx) \supset Cx] / \therefore (x)[(Ax \lor Bx) \supset Cx]$

Counterexample: Let the domain contain two individuals, *a* and *b*. In this domain the argument in question is equivalent to the expansion

1. $[(Aa \cdot Ba) \supset Ca] \cdot [(Ab \cdot Bb) \supset Cb]$
   $/ \therefore [(Aa \lor Ba) \supset Ca] \cdot [(Ab \lor Bb) \supset Cb]$

and is proved invalid by assigning truth-values as follows:

1. $[(Aa \cdot Ba) \supset Ca] \cdot [(Ab \cdot Bb) \supset Cb]$
      T F F   T F T   T T T T T

$/ \therefore [(Aa \lor Ba) \supset Ca] \cdot [(Ab \lor Bb) \supset Cb]$
   T T F   F F F T T T T T

Exercise 8-3

Use the expansion method to prove that the arguments in Exercise 8-2 are invalid.

4   *Consistency in Predicate Logic*

Just as in sentential logic, so also in predicate logic, the whole method for proving the consistency of the premises of an argument is basically part of the method used for proving invalidity. To show that an argument is invalid, we produce an interpretation in which the premises are true and the conclusion is false. To show that the premises are consistent, one needs only an interpretation on which all the premises are true. Note that whenever one proves an argument invalid, one also proves the premises are consistent, since, of course, any interpretation in which the premises are all true and the conclusion is false is an interpretation in which the premises are consistent.

Examples

We can prove that the argument

1. $(x)(Fx \supset Gx)$
2. $(x)(Gx \supset Hx)$
3. $(\exists x)Fx$ /∴ $(\exists x)Hx$

has consistent premises by finding an interpretation that makes these premises all true. (The truth-value of the conclusion is irrelevant to the consistency of the premises.) For instance, if the universe of discourse is restricted to numbers, and the predicate Fx = "x is greater than 10," Gx = "x is greater than 5," and Hx = "x is greater than 0," then the argument's premises are all true (Every number greater than 10 is greater than 5, every number greater than 5 is greater than 0, there is some number greater than 10), hence these premises are consistent.

Exercise 8-4

Show that the following arguments have consistent premises.

(1) 1. $(x)[Ax \supset (Bx \cdot Cx)]$
     2. $(\exists x)(Bx \cdot \sim Cx)$
        /∴ $(\exists x)(Ax \cdot \sim Bx)$

(2) 1. $(\exists x)(Rx \vee Mx)$
     2. $(x)(Mx \supset \sim Rx)$ /∴ $(\exists x)Mx$

(3) 1. $(x)[(Lx \cdot \sim Mx) \supset Nx]$
     2. $(x)[(Lx \cdot Mx) \supset \sim Nx]$
     3. $(\exists x)Mx$
     4. $(\exists x) \sim Mx$ /∴ $(\exists x)(Lx \cdot \sim Nx)$

(4) 1. $(\exists x)Bx$
     2. $\sim (\exists x)Kx$
     3. $(x)(Kx \supset \sim Bx)$ /∴ $(x)Kx$

(5) 1. $(x)[Rx \supset \sim (Tx \cdot Sx)]$
     2. $(\exists x)(Rx \cdot Tx)$
     3. $(\exists x)(Rx \cdot Sx)$ /∴ $(\exists x)(Tx \cdot Sx)$

(6) 1. $\sim (x)[Dx \supset (\sim Fx \vee Gx)]$
     2. $(\exists x)[Fx \cdot (Dx \vee \sim Gx)]$
        /∴ $(\exists x)(Dx \cdot Fx)$

(7) 1. $(\exists x)Fx$
     2. $(x)[(Fx \vee Gx) \supset Dx]$
     3. $(x) \sim Gx$ /∴ $(\exists x)Dx$

(8) 1. $(x)(Fx \supset Gx)$
     2. $\sim (x)(Gx \supset Fx)$
     3. $(\exists x)(Fx \cdot Gx)$ /∴ $(\exists x) \sim Fx$

5 *Validity and Inconsistency in Predicate Logic*

So far we have shown how to show that an argument is invalid or that a set of sentences is consistent. But what about demonstrating validity and inconsistency? An argument is valid just in case among all of the argument's many interpretations there is not a single one where the premises are true and the conclusion false. A set of sentences is inconsistent if and only if there is not a single interpretation in which all the sentences are true. Unfortunately, we cannot do here as we did in sentential logic and survey all of an argument's interpretations. Hence to demonstrate validity or inconsistency in predicate logic, we must either use a proof (as explained in the next chapter) or a truth tree (as explained in Chapter Twelve).

Key Terms Introduced in Chapter Eight

consistent: A sentence or group of sentences is consistent in predicate logic if and only if there is an interpretation in which the sentences are all true.

intensional interpretation of a predicate: The commonsense meaning of the predicate, rather than a list of the things that have it. We know, for example, what "is an elephant" means even if we do not have a list of the things that are elephants.

interpretation: To provide an interpretation for a sentence or group of sentences in predicate logic, we must specify
- A domain
- An assignment for each individual constant
- The extension of each predicate constant (a list of the individuals in the domain that have the property in question).

We must also specify a truth-value for any atomic sentential logic sentences if any are present. In other words, an interpretation provides all the information needed to determine the sentences' truth-value.

logically equivalent: Two predicate logic sentences are logically equivalent if and only if there is no interpretation in which they have different truth-values.

valid: A predicate logic argument is valid if and only if there is no interpretation in which the premises are all true and the conclusion false.

Chapter Nine

Predicate Logic Proofs

___

1   *Proving Validity*

The eighteen valid argument forms plus **CP** and **IP** that constitute the proof machinery of sentential logic are incorporated intact into predicate logic. Here is a proof that illustrates their use in predicate logic:

$$
\begin{array}{lll}
 & p \quad\ q & \\
1. & Fa \supset Ga & p \\
 & p & \\
2. & Fa & p \,/\therefore\, Ga \\
 & q & \\
3. & Ga & 1,2\ \textbf{MP}
\end{array}
$$

Notice that in this use of Modus Ponens the expressions *Fa* and *Ga* are treated as units, just as we treated the capital letters *A, B,* and so on, in propositional logic. Thus, the expression on line 1 is taken to be a substitution instance of the sentence form $p \supset q$, where the unit *Fa* is substituted for p and the unit *Ga* is substituted for q.

But, somewhat surprisingly, that's about as far as we can go in proving arguments in predicate logic without new rules. Here is why it is surprising. Consider the following attempt at a proof:

$$
\begin{array}{lll}
 & p \quad\ q & \\
1. & (x) \sim (\, Fx \cdot Gx \,) & p \,/\therefore\, (x)(\sim Fx \vee \sim Gx) \\
 & p \qquad\ q & \\
2. & (x)\,(\sim Fx \vee \sim Gx) & 1\ \textbf{DeM}
\end{array}
$$

In this case the application of DeMorgan's Theorem to line 1 does not involve the whole of line 1. This seems permissible because, as stated in Chapter Four, the ten equivalence forms among the eighteen valid argument forms can be used on parts as well as wholes of sentences and sentence forms.

But, in what sense is $\sim (Fx \cdot Gx)$ a *part* of the entire formula in, say, the first premise? That premise is not truth-functional, and $\sim (Fx \cdot Gx)$ is not a truth-functional component of it, for two reasons. First, $\sim (Fx \cdot Gx)$ contains free variables and has no truth-value and second, its relationship to the quantifier is a totally different one from, say, an atomic statement to a molecular one. The rules for sentential logic were formulated for truth-functional statements. We cannot simply transfer, without further ado, the sentential equivalence rules to statements that are not truth-functional.

Here is another attempt at a proof:

1. $(x)(Fx \supset Gx)$ p
2. $(x)Fx$ p /∴ $(x)Gx$
3. $(x)Gx$ 1,2 **MP**

This "proof" is invalid because the argument does not have the form of **Modus Ponens.** Because of the quantifier, we do not have, in the first premise, a *wff* of the form $p \supset q$.

Both of the arguments we have attempted to prove are in fact valid. To deal with them and the rest of proofs in predicate logic, we must introduce four new rules of implication, and a fifth, which is an equivalence rule. The rules of implication tell us when taking off quantifiers is justified and when putting them back on is justified. Thus, mastery of predicate logic largely comes down to learning when you can, and when you can't, take off or add a quantifier.

The equivalence rule, **QN,** it turns out, is reasonably easy to understand and use, as we shall see. (It is introduced in the last section of this chapter.) But it has to be admitted that the four rules for adding and deleting quantifiers are a bit complicated and even, in some odd details, somewhat nonintuitive (although never counterintuitive!). Most students quickly grasp the fundamental idea on which these four rules are based but need more time (and effort) to fully comprehend some of the theoretically important (and, some of us think, fascinating) details. So let's make the task of mastering the four quantifier rules easier by breaking our discussion of this topic into three parts. In the first part we informally describe the way in which the four quantifier rules function, omitting complicated details; next we discuss the five primary restrictions that govern the use of these rules; and finally we will then introduce a precisely stated version of the four rules, with all the restrictions and provisos carefully spelled out.

2 *The Four Quantifier Rules*

We now introduce four quantifier rules used to add quantifiers to formulas or to delete them.

Universal Instantiation (UI)

Consider the argument

1. $(x)(Fx \supset Gx)$
2. Fa /∴ Ga

Suppose Fx = "x is friendly" and Gx = "x is generous." Then line 1 asserts that for all x, if x is friendly, then x is generous, or that everything that is friendly is generous. Surely it follows from this that if a particular person, say Anna, is friendly, then she's also generous, because whatever is true of *everything* must be true of any *particular* thing. Hence it is legit-imate to write as the next line in the proof

> 3. *Fa* ⊃ *Ga*   1 **UI** (Universal Instantiation)

Then we can assert the conclusion

> 4. *Ga*   2,3 **MP**

We call the rule of inference that permits the leap from line 1 to line 3 Universal Instantiation, because it yields an *instance*, (*Fa* ⊃ *Ga*), of the *universal* generalization (*x*)(*Fx* ⊃ *Gx*).

It is important to note that a universal quantifier must quantify a *whole line* in a proof to be dropped by **UI**. Thus, **UI** cannot be applied to the line

> 1. (*x*)*Fx* ⊃ (∃*x*)*Gy*

to obtain

> 2. *Fa* ⊃ (∃*x*)*Gy*

because the (*x*) quantifier in line 1 does not quantify the whole of that line.

Similarly, **UI** cannot be applied to the line

> 1. ~ (*x*)(*Fx* ⊃ *Gx*)

to obtain

> 2. ~ (*Fa* ⊃ *Ga*)

because the (*x*) quantifier in line 1 does not quantify the negation sign, and thus does not quantify the entire line. The restriction on using **UI** only on a whole line that is univer-sally quantified is, as we shall see later, easily justified. To permit otherwise would allow us to conclude false conclusions from true premises.

Perhaps a better intuitive understanding of the nature and general validity of **UI** can be obtained by again thinking of symbolizations containing quantifiers as a kind of shorthand for expanded expressions. Take the quantified expression (*x*)(*Fx* ⊃ *Gx*). Its expansion is a conjunction of conditionals. If we take this expansion as a premise, rather than the expres-sion itself, then we can infer *Fa* ⊃ *Ga* by Simplification without appealing to a new inference rule at all. Using rule **UI** to move from (*x*)(*Fx* ⊃ *Gx*) to *Fa* ⊃ *Ga* is like using Simplification to move from the conjunction of conditionals to *Fa* ⊃ *Ga*.

In our example we use Universal Instantiation to replace the variables freed by drop-ping the universal quantifier with *constants*. But, as you will see, it is useful to permit their replacement by what appear to be individual variables also. For instance, we permit infer-ences by **UI** from (*x*)(*Fx* ⊃ *Gx*) to *Fx* ⊃ *Gx* and *Fy* ⊃ *Gy*, as well as to *Fa* ⊃ *Ga* and *Fb* ⊃ *Gb*.

Doing a **UI** to *x*, however, should raise a red flag in the student's mind. After all, *Fx* ⊃ *Gx* is a propositional function, and has no truth-value, whereas the premise from which it is derived does have a truth-value. How can we justify the move from a true prem-ise to one that is neither true nor false, since this defies the whole idea of validity we have so far developed in this book? That idea, we recall, is that a valid argument goes from true premises to a *true* conclusion. The answer is that we treat our instantiations to *x*'s and *y*'s as mathematicians do when they say, for example, "Let *n* be any arbitrarily selected prime number between 1 and 1000." So, to apply this to our case: If all persons are mortal, then any arbitrarily selected individual is such that, if that individual is a person, then she is mortal. That statement is true given the truth of the universally quantified statement. Thus when we do a **UI** from $(x)(Fx \supset Gx)$ to $Fx \supset Gx$ we are inferring, from the fact that all *F* are *G*, that any arbitrarily selected individual that is an *F* is a *G*. In such a formulation, *x* is *not a free variable in the sense that we have discussed in which a propositional function contains a free variable*, but rather is what we will call a **quasivariable.** You will see the usefulness of this idea as we proceed. Sometimes, however, as we formulate our rules of inference, we will use the term "free variable" for convenience; context will tell us when this use is synonymous with that of "quasivariable."

Examples

The following are examples of correct uses of **UI.**

(1)	1. $(x)[(Fx \cdot Gx) \supset Hx)]$	p
	2. $(Fy \cdot Gy) \supset Hy$	1 **UI**
	3. $(Fa \cdot Ga) \supset Ha$	1 **UI**
	4. $(Fx \cdot Gx) \supset Hx$	1 **UI** (replacing each freed variable with itself)
(2)	1. $(x)[Fx \supset (Gx \supset Ha)]$	p
	2. $Fx \supset (Gx \supset Ha]$	1 **UI**
	3. $Fy \supset (Gy \supset Ha)$	1 **UI**
	4. $Fa \supset (Ga \supset Ha)$	1 **UI**
	5. $Fb \supset (Gb \supset Ha)$	1 **UI**

Universal Generalization (UG)

Now consider the proof

1.	$(x)(Hx \supset Mx)$	p
2.	$(x)(Gx \supset Hx)$	p /∴ $(x)(Gx \supset Mx)$
3.	$Hy \supset My$	1 **UI**
4.	$Gy \supset Hy$	2 **UI**
5.	$Gy \supset My$	3,4 **HS**

Note, once again, that to use **HS** to derive line 5 we *must* first use **UI** to remove the quantifiers. This illustrates a crucially important function of our four quantifier rules: making it possible to use the eight implicational argument forms of sentential logic in predicate logic proofs. If we were not allowed to drop or add quantifiers, the eight implicational forms could not be used on quantified sentences, because these rules must be used on *wffs* that have a certain *form.*

Now, having dropped the quantifiers and derived line 5, we need to add a quantifier to obtain the conclusion:

6.	$(x)(Gx \supset Mx)$	5 **UG** (Universal Generalization)

We introduce the rule called Universal Generalization (**UG**) to permit valid steps such as the one from line 5 to line 6. Subject to certain important restrictions to be discussed later, rule **UG** permits the addition of universal quantifiers *that quantify whole sentences.*

Note, by the way, that if we let Hx = "x is human"; Mx = "x is mortal"; and Gx = "x is Greek," then we have just proved the quintessential syllogism that we used as our example (on page 165) of a valid argument not yet provable in our system of logic. Now, we can prove arguments of this kind valid (if they are, of course).

The use of **UG** should be familiar to students of geometry. In geometry a proof that a given triangle has a particular property is considered proof that all triangles have that property, provided the proof does not depend on something peculiar to the given triangle, that is, provided the given triangle is arbitrarily selected. Similarly, **UG** is a valid step (with the exceptions to be noted in the next chapter) provided that it is applied in cases where the actual letters employed (in the preceding example, the letter y) are arbitrarily selected, and any other letters could have been selected just as well.

Examples

Here are two typical proofs using rules **UI** and **UG**:

(1) 1. $(x)[(Fx \supset Gx) \cdot (Hx \supset Kx)]$ p /∴ $(x)(Fx \supset Gx)$
     2. $(Fx \supset Gx) \cdot (Hx \supset Kx)$ 1 **UI**
     3. $Fx \supset Gx$ 2 **Simp**
     4. $(x)(Fx \supset Gx)$ 3 **UG**

(2) 1. $(x)(Fx \supset Gx) \supset (x)(Hx \supset Fx)$ p
     2. $(x) \sim Fx$ p /∴ $(x) \sim Hx$
     3. $\sim Fy$ 2 **UI**
     4. $\sim Fy \vee Gy$ 3 **Add**
     5. $Fy \supset Gy$ 4 **Impl**
     6. $(x)(Fx \supset Gx)$ 5 **UG**
     7. $(x)(Hx \supset Fx)$ 1,6 **MP**
     8. $Hy \supset Fy$ 7 **UI**
     9. $\sim Hy$ 3,8 **MT**
    10. $(x) \sim Hx$ 9 **UG**

Existential Instantiation (EI)

Next, consider the proof

    1. $(x)(Hx \supset Kx)$ p
    2. $(\exists x)Hx$ p /∴ $(\exists x)Kx$
    3. Hy 2 **EI** (Existential Instantiation)

In this proof, line 3 follows from line 2 by the inference rule called Existential Instantiation (**EI**).

Technically, it appears we should not permit this step from line 2 to line 3, because once again it appears we are going from a premise that has truth-value to one that does not. Again, we take a cue from mathematics. We construe *"y"* in our **EI** step not as a variable but as an *unknown;* it is not a free variable in the sense in which a propositional function contains a free variable, but another example of a kind of quasivariable. The difference between a variable and an unknown is illustrated by an example from algebra. In the algebraic theorem

$$(a + b) = (b + a)$$

a and *b* function as variables, because the theorem is true of all numbers. But in the algebraic problem

1. $x + 1 = 3$
2. $x = 2$

the *x* on line 1 functions not as a variable but as an unknown value, to be discovered, as it is on line 2, where it turns out to be the number 2. So also, in the step from

2. $(\exists x)Hx$

to

3. Hy

the letter *y* serves not as a variable but as an unknown, in the sense that if $(\exists x)Hx$ is true, then there is some value of *x* (exactly which value is unknown) that has the property *H*. In line 3 we call that unknown value *y*.

It is important to note that although the result of a **UI** or **EI** step may look just the same, there is a significant difference. The *x* produced by **UI** we might call a universal name. It designates an *arbitrarily* selected individual. That is, it could designate *anything* in the domain. The *x* in an **EI** line is different. It is not a universal name, but rather a name we make up to designate a particular individual. This individual is not arbitrarily selected. For all we know, what an **EI** line says of this individual may be true of that individual only and no other.

Compare the difference between the made-up names "John Doe" and "Jack the Ripper." "John Doe" is commonly used to stand for just anyone. (This is sexist, of course. Perhaps we should take a page from *Saturday Night Live* and change the name to "Pat Doe.") "Jack the Ripper," in contrast, designates a particular historical individual who committed a series of grisly murders in London in the 1800s. "Jack" isn't this person's real name. Someone (Jack, in fact) just made this name up for the sake of convenience. We essentially do the same thing in an **EI** step. Since an existentially quantified sentence assures us that at least one individual of a certain kind exists, we introduce a name for one such individual, whoever she is.

Existential Generalization (EG)

So far, the proof we have been constructing reads as follows:

1. $(x)(Hx \supset Kx)$ p
2. $(\exists x)Hx$ p /∴ $(\exists x)Kx$
3. Hy 2 **EI**

Continuing,

4.	$Hy \supset Ky$	1 **UI**
5.	Ky	3,4 **MP**
6.	$(\exists x)Kx$	5 **EG** (Existential Generalization)

The step from line 5 to line 6 is justified by the inference rule Existential Generalization (**EG**). This use of **EG** obviously is valid, because if the unknown individual designated by the free variable y has the property K, then there is something that has that property.

Examples

The following proofs contain examples of correct uses of **EI** and **EG**.

(1)	1.	$(\exists x)(Fx \cdot Gx)$	p
	2.	$(Fx \cdot Gx)$	1 **EI**
	3.	$(Fy \cdot Gy)$	1 **EI**
	4.	$(\exists x)(Fx \cdot Gx)$	2 **EG** (or 3 **EG**)
	5.	$(\exists z)(Fz \cdot Gz)$	2 **EG** (or 3 **EG**)

(2)	1.	$(\exists x)[Fx \cdot (y)Gy]$	p
	2.	$Fx \cdot (y)Gy$	1 **EI**
	3.	$Fz \cdot (y)Gy$	1 **EI**
	4.	$(y)Gy$	2 **Simp**
	5.	Gz	4 **UI**
	6.	$(\exists y)Gy$	5 **EG**
	7.	$(\exists x)Gx$	5 **EG**
	8.	$(\exists z)Gz$	5 **EG**
	9.	Fz	3 **Simp**
	10.	$Fz \cdot Gz$	5,9 **Conj**
	11.	$(\exists x)Fx$	9 **EG**
	12.	$(\exists x)[Fx \cdot (y)Gy]$	3 **EG**
	13.	$(\exists x)Fx \cdot (\exists x)Gx$	7,11 **Conj**
	14.	$(\exists x)(Fx \cdot Gx)$	10 **EG**

To summarize, we have introduced two instantiation rules for removing quantifiers, **UI** and **EI,** and two generalization rules for putting them back on, **UG** and **EG.** As noted earlier, we cannot just add and remove quantifiers haphazardly. In particular, there are important restrictions on the use of **EI** and **UG** that will be explained in the next section. However, you already have enough information to complete the following exercise, which involves only **UI** and **EG.** Remember, for **UI** you remove the quantifier and replace the variable that had been bound by that quantifier with a quasivariable or constant. For **EG** you reverse the process, taking either a quasivariable or a constant and replacing it by a variable that is bound by an existential quantifier that is added to the front of the line. Remember also that these rules are implicational rules, and thus cannot be used on parts of lines. *You can remove or add a quantifier only if its scope includes the entire sentence.*

Exercise 9-1

Complete the following proofs using the rules for adding and removing quantifiers where appropriate.

(1) 1. $(x)Fx \lor (x) \sim Gx$ p
     2. $\sim (x)Fx$ p
     3. $(x)(Dx \supset Gx)$ p
                                               $/\therefore \; (\exists x(\sim Dx \lor Gx)$

(2) 1. $(x)[Ax \lor (Bx \cdot \sim Cx)]$ p
     2. $(x)Cx$ $p /\therefore \; (\exists x)(Dx \supset Ax)$

(3) 1. $(x)[\sim Ax \lor (Bx \cdot Cx)]$ p
     2. $(x)[(Ax \supset Cx) \supset Dx]$ p
     3. $(x)(Dx \supset \sim Cx)$ $p /\therefore \; (\exists x) \sim Ax$
(4) 1. $Ab \supset Bc$ p
     2. $(x)(Ax \supset Bx)$ p
     3. $(x)[(Ax \supset Bx) \supset Ax]$ $p /\therefore \; Bc$

(5) 1. $Ab \lor Bc$ p
     2. $(x) \sim Bx$ $p /\therefore \; (\exists x)Ax$

(6) 1. $(y)(Ry \supset \sim Gy)$ p
     2. $(z)(Bz \lor Gz)$ p
     3. $(y)Ry$ $p /\therefore \; (y)By$

(7) 1. $(z)[Az \supset (\sim Bz \supset Cz)]$ p
     2. $\sim Ba$ $p /\therefore \; Aa \supset Ca$

(8) 1. $(x)[(Rx \cdot Ax) \supset Tx]$ p
     2. Ab p
     3. $(x)Rx$ $p /\therefore \; Tb \cdot Rb$

3 *The Five Main Restrictions*

In the next section we will provide a precise version of the four quantifier rules. But let's anticipate a bit and discuss five of the simpler cases in which these rules must be restricted. *Understanding these five restrictions is the key to mastery of predicate logic proofs.*

The first two restrictions apply to uses of **EI**. Here, for instance, is an example of the first kind of case:

(1) 1. $(\exists x)Hx$ p
     2. Ha 1 **EI** (invalid)

Because some item or other has the property *H,* say of being honest, it doesn't follow that a particular item *a,* say Adolf Hitler, ever was associated with that quality. The precise version of the quantifier rules blocks this kind of invalid inference by requiring that when an existential quantifier is dropped by **EI,** the variables thus freed must be replaced by quasi-variables, never constants. Remember, constants are always names of specific individuals. *An EI must be done to a quasivariable.*

Here is an example of another kind of case concerning **EI:**

(2)   1. $(\exists x)Fx$ p
     2. $(\exists x)Gx$ p
     3. Fx 1 **EI**
     4. Gx 2 **EI** (invalid)

And this is what can happen when steps like 4 are permitted:

     5. $Fx \cdot Gx$ 3,4 **Conj**
     6. $(\exists x)(Fx \cdot Gx)$ 5 **EG**

Letting Fx = "x is a fox," and Gx = "x is a goose," this invalid inference moves from the true facts that there are foxes and there are geese to the silly conclusion that there exist items that are both foxes and geese. (It would have been all right to move from "$(\exists x)Gx$" to, say, Gy, or to Gz, but not to Gx.) We're going to block this kind of invalid move in the next section by requiring that *a quasivariable introduced into a proof by rule EI must not have occurred as a quasivariable previously in the proof.*

The remaining three restrictions have to do with the rule **UG.** Here is an inference that is obviously invalid:

(3)   1. Fa p
     2. $(x)Fx$ 1 **UG** (invalid)

Believing, say, that Adam was a fool (anyone who manages to get himself evicted from the Garden of Eden can't be too smart) doesn't justify believing that everyone is a fool. So the argument clearly is invalid. To block moves of this kind, we're going to restrict rule **UG** so that it forbids Universal Generalization on a constant.

Next consider this example:

(4)   1. $(\exists x)Fx$ p
     2. Fx 1 **EI**
     3. $(x)Fx$ 2 **UG** (invalid)

Clearly, although there are plenty of foxes, not everything is a fox. So the argument is invalid. To block moves of this kind, we're going to restrict rule **UG** so that it forbids generalization on a quasivariable in a line that is justified by **EI.** The point of using **UG** is to generalize on arbitrarily selected letters. In the case at hand, we generalized on the quasivariable x that was introduced into the argument by rule **EI** and hence was not arbitrarily selected.

So before using **UG** we must check every previous line that is justified by **EI.** *If the variable is free in an EI line, we cannot use UG to bind that variable.* Think of **EI** as poisoning, for the purposes of **UG,** every quasivariable in an **EI** line.

The last restriction also applies to proofs that have assumed premises. In making an assumption with a quasivariable, the variable does not name an arbitrary individual. Rather, it names an individual assumed to have a particular property. So *we cannot bind that variable with UG so long as we are relying on that assumption.*

1. $\sim (x)Fx$ p
→ 2. Fx **AP** /∴ $\sim Fx$
3. $(x)Fx$ 2 **UG** (invalid)
4. $(x)Fx \cdot \sim (x)Fx$ 1,3 **Conj**
5. $\sim Fx$ 2–4 **IP**
6. $(x) \sim Fx$ 5 **UG**

We can't, for example, infer that everyone is not fat from the fact that not everyone is fat. Remember, we can bind a variable using **UG** only provided that the variable functions as a universal name for an arbitrarily selected individual.

However, once the assumption is discharged we are free to use **UG** to bind that variable, since we no longer are depending on an assumption about the individual designated by the variable. Unlike **EI,** an assumed premise poisons the variable only temporarily. This move may strike you as somewhat facile, so let's explore its logic in a bit more detail. In the case in question, the assumption in line 2 is equivalent to assuming that there is something that is *F.* When we prove—invalidly in this case, but let's ignore that for the moment—that this assumption leads to a contradiction, we may conclude that it is not the case that there is something that is *F*—that is, that everything is not *F.* We are, in effect, taking line 5 as if there were a quantifier in front of $\sim Fx$. You may well ask why we don't just assume an existentially quantified statement to begin with since, after all, we are allowed to assume anything we wish. This would work here, but as you will see in the next chapter, there are proofs that would be difficult to do unless we make assumptions without quantifiers on them (such as proving that $(x)(Fx \supset P)$ follows logically from $(\exists x) Fx \supset P$.

So the following use of **UG** is legitimate:

1. $(x) \sim Fx$ p
→ 2. Gx **AP** /∴ $\sim Fx$
3. $\sim Fx$ 1 **UI**
4. $Gx \supset \sim Fx$ 2–3 **CP**
5. $(x)(Gx \supset \sim Fx)$ 4 **UG** (valid)

Here we may think of step 4 as follows: The antecedent and the consequent are both implicitly quantified, and so 4 has the implicit logical form $(\exists x)Gx \supset (x) \sim Fx$. Or, to put it another way, if we assumed $(\exists x)Gx$ in line 2, we could then conclude, using line 1 unchanged on line 3., the conditional $(\exists x)Gx \supset (x) \sim Fx$ on line 4. It can be shown that this conditional logically implies line 5. We can thus look at the introduction of quasi-variables in assumptions as a very convenient mathematical "trick."

To summarize: The first two of our restrictions have to do with **EI,** the last three with **UG.** The two restrictions on **EI** both require that the quasivariable introduced by **EI** be a new letter. You cannot use a constant and you cannot use a variable that already occurs free earlier in the proof—those letters are already taken. The three restrictions on **UG** discussed so far are designed to ensure that when we add a universal quantifier, we bind only a symbol that functions as a universal name designating an arbitrarily chosen individual. Obviously, this is not true of a constant—but it is also not true of variables that are free in an **EI** line and quasivariables in an undischarged assumed premise.

However, we have not yet given a clear reason behind *all* the restrictions we are going to present in Section 4, where a precise rendition of the quantifier rules is given. There is, for example, a fourth restriction on **UG** that cannot be fully understood until the introduction of *relational* predicate logic in Chapter Ten. All the restrictions in the precise rendition of the rules are illustrated in greater detail in Chapter Eleven.

Examples

The following contain examples of both valid and invalid uses of the four quantifier rules.

(1) 1. $(Aa \cdot Bb) \supset Cc$ p
     2. $(x)(Ax \cdot Bx)$ p
     3. $Aa \cdot Bb$ 2 **UI** (invalid, can't change a variable into two *different* constants with **UI**)
     4. Cc 1,3 **MP**
     5. $(x)Cx$ 4 **UG** (invalid, can't use **UG** with a constant)

(2) 1. $(x)(\sim Gx \supset \sim Fx)$ p
     2. $\sim Gc \supset \sim Fc$ 1 **UI**
     3. $Fc \supset Gc$ 2 **Contra**
     4. $(x)(Fx \supset Gx)$ 3 **UG** (invalid, can't bind a constant with **UG**)
     5. $\sim Gx \supset \sim Fx$ 1 **UI**
     6. $Fx \supset Gx$ 5 **Contra**
     7. $(x)(Fx \supset Gx)$ 6 **UG**

(3) 1. $(x)(Fx \supset Gx)$ p
     2. $(\exists y)(Fy \cdot Hy)$ p
     3. $Fx \supset Gx$ 1 **UI** (valid)
     4. $Fx \cdot Hx$ 2 **EI** (invalid, x already occurs free)
     5. Fx 4 **Simp**
     6. Gx 3,5 **MP**
     7. $(x)Gx$ 6 **UG** (invalid, x is free in an **EI** line)

(4) 1. $Sb \cdot Cb$ p
     2. $(x)(Sx \cdot Cx) \supset \sim (\exists y)Fy$ p
     3. $(Sb \cdot Cb) \supset \sim (\exists y)Fy$ 2 **UI** (invalid, can't use **UI** on part of a line)
     4. $\sim (\exists y)Fy$ 1,3 **MP**
     5. $\sim Fz$ 4 **EI** (invalid, this time **EI** on part of a line)
     6. $(\exists x) \sim Fx$ 5 **EG**

(5) 1. $(x)[Fx \supset (\exists y)Gy]$ p
     2. $(\exists x)Fx$ p
     3. Fz 2 **EI**
     4. $Fz \supset (\exists y)Gy$ 1 **UI**
     5. $(\exists y)Gy$ 3,4 **MP**
     6. Gz 5 **EI** (invalid, z already occurs free)

7. $Fz \cdot Gz$ 3,6 **Conj**

8. $(x)(Fx \cdot Gx)$ 7 **UG** (invalid, z is free in line 3—an **EI** line)

(6) 1. $(x)(Fx \supset Gx)$ p

   → 2. Fx **AP**

     3. $Fx \supset Gx$ **UI** (valid)

     4. Gx 2,3 **MP**

     5. $(x)Gx$ **UG** (invalid, x is free in an undischarged assumption)

     6. $Fx \supset (x)Gx$ 2-5 **IP**

     7. $(x)Fx \supset (x)Gx$ 6 **UG** (invalid, **UG** on part of a line)

Exercise 9-2

Which lines in the following are not valid? Explain why in each case.

(1) 1. $(x)[(Hx \cdot Kx) \supset Mx]$ p

     2. $(\exists x)(Hx \cdot Kx)$ p

     3. $Hx \cdot Kx$ 2 **EI**

     4. Mx 1,3 **MP**

     5. $(\exists x)Mx$ 4 **EG**

(2) 1. $(x)(Mx \supset Gx) \supset Fa$ p

     2. $(x)(\sim Gx \supset \sim Mx)$ p

     3. $\sim Gy \supset \sim My$ 2 **UI**

     4. $(x)(\sim Gx \supset \sim Mx) \supset Fa$ 1 **Contra**

     5. $(\sim Gx \supset \sim Mx) \supset Fa$ 4 **UI**

     6. Fa 3,5 **MP**

     7. $(x)Fx$ 6 **UG**

(3) 1. $(\exists x)(Fx \cdot \sim Mx)$ p

     2. $(x)[(Gx \vee Hx) \supset Mx]$ p

     3. $(Gy \vee Hy) \supset My$ 2 **UI**

     4. $Fy \cdot \sim My$ 1 **EI**

     5. $\sim My$ 4 **Simp**

     6. $\sim (Gy \vee Hy)$ 3,5 **MT**

     7. $(\exists x) \sim (Gx \vee Hx)$ 6 **EG**

(4) 1. $(\exists x)(Px \cdot Qx)$ p

     2. $Py \cdot Qy$ 1 **EI**

     3. Qy 2 **Simp**

     4. $Qy \vee \sim Ry$ 3 **Add**

     5. $(x)(Qx \vee \sim Rx)$ 4 **UG**

(5) 1. $(\exists x)[(Px \cdot Qx) \vee Rx]$ p

     2. $(x) \sim Rx$ p

     3. $(\exists x)(Px \vee Rx)$ 1 **Simp**

     4. $Px \vee Rx$ 3 **EI**

     5. $\sim Px$ 2,4 **DS**

     6. $(x) \sim Px$ 5 **UG**

     7. $\sim Py$ 6 **UI**

     8. $(z) \sim Pz$ 7 **UG**

(6) 1. ~ (x)Fx   p
     2. (∃x)Lx   p
     3. (x) ~ Fx   p
     4. ~ Fx   1 **UI**
     5. La   2 **EI**
     6. Lx   2 **EI**
     7. Lx · ~ Fx   4,6 **Conj**
     8. (∃x)(Lx · ~ Fx)   7 **EG**
     9. (x)Lx   5 **UG**

4 *Precise Formulation of the Four Quantifier Rules*

To state the quantifier rules precisely and economically, we need a way to refer to a great many expressions at once. For example, we want our precise statement of rule **UI** somehow to refer to, and permit, all of the following inferences:

(1)   1. (x)Fx   p
       2. Fy   1 **UI**

(2)   1. (x)Fx   p
       2. Fx   1 **UI**

(3)   1. (x)Fx   p
       2. Fa   1 **UI**

(4)   1. (z)(Fz ⊃ Gz)   p
       2. Fy ⊃ Gy   1 **UI**

(5)   4. (x)(Fx ⊃ Gx)   p
       2. Fx ⊃ Gx   1 **UI**

(6)   1. (x)[Fx ⊃ (∃y)Gy]   p
       2. Fz ⊃ (∃y)Gy   1 **UI**

In each of these examples, the universal quantifier is dropped and the variables thus freed are replaced by some variable or constant. Thus, in the first example, we dropped the (x) quantifier and replaced the one x variable thus freed by a free y variable, to get the conclusion Fy. In the fifth we dropped the (x) quantifier and replaced the x variables thus freed by themselves (it's perfectly all right to do this), to arrive at the conclusion Fx ⊃ Gx. And in the third, we dropped the (x) quantifier and replaced the x thus freed by the constant a, to arrive at the conclusion Fa.

Suppose that we use the letter u to refer to the variables that become free as a result of dropping a quantifier, and to the quantifier itself as (u). Then we can think of each of the premises in the preceding six arguments as having the form (u)(. . . u . . .). For instance, the premise (x)(Fx ⊃ Gx) of the fifth argument is clearly a substitution instance of this form, obtained from it by substituting (x) for (u) and (Fx ⊃ Gx) for (. . . u . . .). In fact, we can use the form (u)(. . . u . . .) to represent the logical structure of any expression in which the initial universal quantifier, whether (x), (y), (z), or whatever, quantifies the whole remainder of the expression. And similarly, we can use, say, the expression $(\ldots w \ldots)$ to represent the structure of the expression that results when we drop a quantifier and replace the variables thus freed either with themselves or with some other letter.

Using this notation, we can say that each use of rule **UI** involves moving from an expression of the form

$(u)(\ldots u \ldots)$

to an expression of the form

$(\ldots w \ldots)$

where the expression $(\ldots w \ldots)$ resulted from replacing all occurrences of u free in $(\ldots u \ldots)$ by occurrences of w free in $(\ldots w \ldots)$.

All six examples introduced at the beginning of this section satisfy this form. They move from premise to conclusion by first dropping the quantifier that binds the remainder of the premise and then replacing the variables that become free in this process by instances of some variable or constant or other. Typical is number 4, in which the universal quantifier (z) is dropped, freeing two z variables that are then replaced by two free y variables. Of course, if we replace one of the z variables by a free y variable, we must replace the other z by a y. Such replacement must be uniform.

The schematic notation just introduced also is to be used in the formulation of rules **EI, UG, EG**. For instance, we will characterize **UG** as a process in which we move from an expression $(\ldots u \ldots)$ to an expression $(w)(\ldots w \ldots)$, by replacing all free occurrences of u in $(\ldots u \ldots)$ by occurrences of w free in $(\ldots w \ldots)$. Of course, such occurrences of w will then be bound in the whole expression $(w)(\ldots w \ldots)$. The point is that they should not be bound by a w quantifier occurring within $(\ldots w \ldots)$. This restriction will become clearer in Chapter Eleven.

We now are ready to state our precise version of the quantifier rules.

Rule UI: $(u)(\ldots u \ldots) / \therefore (\ldots w \ldots)$ *Provided:*
1. $(\ldots w \ldots)$ results from replacing each occurrence of u free in $(\ldots u \ldots)$ with a w that is either a constant or a variable free in $(\ldots w \ldots)$ (making no other changes).

Rule EI: $(\exists u)(\ldots u \ldots) / \therefore (\ldots w \ldots)$ *Provided:*
1. w is not a constant.
2. w does not occur free previously in the proof.
3. $(\ldots w \ldots)$ results from replacing each occurrence of u free in $(\ldots u \ldots)$ with a w that is free in $(\ldots w \ldots)$ (making no other changes).

Rule UG: $(\ldots u \ldots) /\therefore (w)(\ldots w \ldots)$ *Provided:*

1. u is not a constant.
2. u does not occur free previously in a line obtained by **EI.**
3. u does not occur free previously in an assumed premise that has not yet been discharged.
4. $(\ldots w \ldots)$ results from replacing each occurrence of u free in $(\ldots u \ldots)$ with a w that is free in $(\ldots w \ldots)$ (making no other changes) and there are no additional occurrences of w already contained in $(\ldots w \ldots)$.

Rule EG: $(\ldots u \ldots) /\therefore (\exists w)(\ldots w \ldots)$ *Provided:*

1. $(\ldots w \ldots)$ results from replacing *at least one* occurrence of u, where u is a constant or a variable free in $(\ldots u \ldots)$ with a w that is free in $(\ldots w \ldots)$ (making no other changes) and there are no additional occurrences of w already contained in $(\ldots w \ldots)$.

---

5   *Mastering the Four Quantifier Rules*

The task of mastering the four quantifier rules can be lightened a bit by concentration on the rules beginners are most tempted to violate. Most problems are associated with the five restrictions we have already discussed. But let's look briefly at the other restrictions contained in our rules. These restrictions rule out such peculiar inferences as

1. $(x)(Fx \supset Gx)$	p	
2 $Fa \cdot Gb$	p	
3. $Fy \supset Gz$	1 **UI** (invalid)	
4. $Fx \supset Gz$	1 **UI** (invalid)	
5. $(\exists x)(Fx \cdot Gx)$	2 **EG** (invalid)	
6. $(x)(Fx \supset Gx)$	4 **UG** (invalid)	

Steps 3 and 4 of this proof amount to attempting to do two different things with the x variables that are bound in line 1. In line 3 the attempt is made to change these variables into a free y and a free z, and in line 4 they are changed into a free x and a free z. Likewise, lines 5 and 6 amount to attempting to bind two different variables at once. Don't concern yourself too much with these restrictions at this stage. For the proofs you will encounter in this chapter, problems with these rules rarely arise. We discuss them in greater detail in our coverage of relational predicate logic in Chapter Ten, and Chapter Eleven consists of an exhaustive list of every type of bad inference these rules are designed to prevent. Just remember not to try to do two things at once, such as change bound x's to free x's and y's, bind both an x and a y in one swoop, etc.

Returning to our five major restrictions, even beginners are not likely to violate the two restrictions having to do with constants. Consider rule **EI**. Few will be tempted to infer, say, from $(\exists x)Hx$ to Ha. For that would be like arguing (invalidly) that since something or other has the property of being an ax murderer, a particular entity, say Kofi Annan, has that property. The same holds for the similar restriction on **UG**. In actual applications of **UG**, even beginners are not likely to attempt to infer from Fa to $(x)Fx$. That would be like arguing (invalidly) that since the Hope diamond is valuable, everything is valuable.

So beginners should concentrate on the remaining three of the five major restrictions. These restrictions require that we check previous lines whenever we justify a line with **EI** or **UG**. When we use **EI**, we must check to be sure the variable we are introducing does not occur free on any earlier line. When we use **UG**, we must be sure that the variable we are binding is not free in an **EI** line or an undischarged assumed premise.

In particular, beginners should be on the lookout for invalid inferences such as the one from 5 to 6 in the proof

1.	$(\exists x)Fx$	p
2.	$(y)Gy$	p
3.	Fx	1 **EI**
4.	Gx	2 **UI**
5.	$Fx \cdot Gx$	3,4 **Conj**
6.	$(x)(Fx \cdot Gx)$	3 **UG** (invalid)

for this inference violates the second restriction on **UG**. Similarly, they should look out for invalid inferences such as the one from 1 to 2 in the proof

→ 1.	$Fy \supset (x)Gx$	**AP**
2.	$(z)[Fz \supset (x)Gx]$	1 **UG** (invalid)

for this inference violates the third restriction on **UG**.

Violations of the second restriction on **EI** are very common for beginners, but many are easily avoided. Remember: *If you must use **EI**, do so as soon as possible.* The following argument illustrates the point:

1.	$(x)(Ax \supset Bx)$	p
2.	$(\exists x)Ax$	p /∴ $(\exists x)Bx$

If we remove the universal quantifier first, there will be no quick way to complete the proof without violating the second restriction on **EI**.

3.	$Ax \supset Bx$	1 **UI**
4.	Ax	2 **EI** (invalid)
5.	Bx	3,4 **MP**
6.	$(\exists x)Bx$	5 **EG**

Instead, when faced with such a choice, always use **EI** first.

3.	Ax	2 **EI**
4.	$Ax \supset Bx$	1 **UI**

5. *Bx*   3,4 **MP**
6. (∃*x*)*Bx*   5 **EG**

If you follow this simple rule of thumb, you will minimize your chance of running afoul of this particular restriction.

There *is* a way to save a proof if you begin by making the mistake of doing a **UI** first, as just done, without starting over, as it were. Discard line 4, and replace it with a correct use of **EI,** say to *Aw.* Now do another **UI** from line 1 to *w*, to obtain *Aw* ⊃ *Bw.* You can now complete the proof easily. What this illustrates is that in a proof from a given universally quantified statement you are permitted to do as many **UI**s as you wish.

To sum up, in using the four quantifier rules, students should pay special attention to the second and third restrictions on **UG,** and the second restriction on **EI.** Most problems with the second restriction on **EI** will be avoided by using **EI** as soon as possible.

One last word: It must be remembered that these rules are to be applied to *whole lines of proofs only.* Inferences such as the one from 1 to 2 in the proof

1. ~ (*x*)*Fx*   p
2. ~ *Fx*   1 **UI** (invalid)

are never valid. If they were valid, then in this case we could move to

3. (*x*) ~ *Fx*   2 **UG**

thus inferring from, say, "It's not true that everything is friendly" to "Everything is not friendly," a clearly invalid inference.

🚶 Walk-Through: Basic Predicate Logic Proofs

Here is a typical argument is predicate logic:

1. (*y*)(*By* ⊃ *Ny*)   p
2. (*z*)(~ *Bz* ⊃ ~ *Az*)   p
3. (∃*x*)*Ax*   p /∴ (∃*x*)(*Ax* · *Nx*)

We remove the existential quantifier first, to avoid violating the second restriction on **EI.**

4. *Ax*   3 **EI**

Now we remove the remaining quantifiers. As we remove the quantifiers, we change the bound variables so they are all free variables of the same kind.

5. *Bx* ⊃ *Nx*   1 **UI**
6. ~ *Bx* ⊃ ~ *Ax*   2 **UI**

We complete the proof by using sentential logic and then binding the result with **EG.**

7. *Ax* ⊃ *Bx*   6 **Contra**
8. *Ax* ⊃ *Nx*   5,7 **HS**

9.	Nx	4,8 **MP**
10.	$Ax \cdot Nx$	4,9 **Conj**
11.	$(\exists x)(Ax \cdot Nx)$	10 **EG**

Examples

Here are two more examples:

(1)
1.	$(x)(Ax \supset Bx)$	p
2.	$(x)[Bx \supset (Ax \supset \sim Fx)]$	p
3.	$(x)[(\sim Cx \cdot Dx) \supset Fx]$	p /∴ $(x)[Ax \supset (Cx \vee \sim Dx)]$
→ 4.	Ax	**AP**
5.	$Ax \supset Bx$	1 **UI**
6.	$Bx \supset (Ax \supset \sim Fx)$	2 **UI**
7.	$(\sim Cx \cdot Dx) \supset Fx$	3 **UI**
8.	Bx	4,5 **MP**
9.	$(Bx \cdot Ax) \supset \sim Fx$	6 **Exp**
10.	$Bx \cdot Ax$	4,8 **Conj**
11.	$\sim Fx$	9,10 **MP**
12.	$\sim (\sim Cx \cdot Dx)$	7,11 **MT**
13.	$\sim \sim Cx \vee \sim Dx$	12 **DeM**
14.	$Cx \vee \sim Dx$	13 **DN**
15.	$Ax \supset (Cx \vee \sim Dx)$	4–14 **CP**
16.	$(x)[Ax \supset (Cx \vee \sim Dx)]$	15 **UG**

Note the use of **CP** in this proof. This is a very useful way to solve proofs that have universally quantified conclusions.

(2)
1.	$(\exists x) Fx \supset (x)(Gx \supset Fx)$	p
2.	$(\exists x) Hx \supset (x)(Fx \supset Hx)$	p
3.	$(\exists x) (Fx \cdot Hx)$	p /∴ $(x)(Gx \supset Hx)$
4.	$Fx \cdot Hx$	3 **EI**
5.	Fx	4 **Simp**
6.	Hx	4 **Simp**
7.	$(\exists x)Fx$	5 **EG**
8.	$(\exists x)Hx$	6 **EG**
9.	$(x)(Gx \supset Fx)$	1,7 **MP**
10.	$(x)(Fx \supset Hx)$	2,8 **MP**
11.	$Gy \supset Fy$	9 **UI**
12.	$Fy \supset Hy$	10 **UI**
13.	$Gy \supset Hy$	11,12 **HS**
14.	$(x)(Gx \supset Hx)$	13 **UG**

Two things are notable about this example. First, we could not use **EI** on the first two premises. Second, in the last half of the proof we were forced to use some other free variable than x, because x was poisoned by **EI** in line 4.

Exercise 9-3

Prove valid:

(1) 1. $(x)(Rx \supset Bx)$ p
     2. $(\exists x) \sim Bx$ p /∴ $(\exists x) \sim Rx$

(2) 1. $(x)(Fx \supset Gx)$ p
     2. $(y)(Gy \supset Hy)$ p /∴ $(z)(\sim Hz \supset \sim Fz)$

(3) 1. Ka p
     2. $(x)[Kx \supset (y)Hy]$ p /∴ $(x)Hx$

(4) 1. $(x)(Fx \supset Gx)$ p
     2. $(x)(Ax \supset Fx)$ p
     3. $(\exists x) \sim Gx$ p /∴ $(\exists x) \sim Ax$

(5) 1. $(x)(Mx \supset Sx)$ p
     2. $(x)(\sim Bx \vee Mx)$ p /∴ $(x)(\sim Sx \supset \sim Bx)$

(6) 1. $(x)(Rx \supset Ox)$ p
     2. $(\exists y) \sim Oy$ p
     3. $(z)(\sim Rz \supset Pz)$ p /∴ $(\exists z)Pz$

(7) 1. $(\exists x)(Ax \cdot Bx)$ p
     2. $(y)(Ay \supset Cy)$ p /∴ $(\exists x)(Bx \cdot Cx)$

(8) 1. $(\exists x)Rx$ p
     2. $(x)(\sim Gx \supset \sim Rx)$ p
     3. $(x)Mx$ p /∴ $(\exists x)Gx \cdot (\exists x)Mx$

(9) 1. $(x)[(Fx \vee Rx) \supset \sim Gx]$ p
     2. $(\exists x) \sim (\sim Fx \cdot \sim Rx)$ p /∴ $(\exists y) \sim Gy$

(10) 1. $(x)(Kx \supset \sim Lx)$ p
     2. $(\exists x)(Mx \cdot Lx)$ p /∴ $(\exists x)(Mx \cdot \sim Kx)$

(11) 1. $(x)(Fx \supset Gx)$ p
     2. $(y)(Ey \supset Fy)$ p
     3. $(z) \sim (Dz \cdot \sim Ez)$ p /∴ $(x)(Dx \supset Gx)$

(12) 1. $(x)(Lx \supset \sim Kx)$ p
     2. $(\exists z)(Rz \cdot Kz)$ p
     3. $(y)[(\sim Ly \cdot Ry) \supset By]$ p /∴ $(\exists x)Bx$

6 *Quantifier Negation (QN)*

The four other inference rules to be introduced into our predicate logic proof procedure all are referred to by the name *Quantifier Negation* (**QN**). Our proof system is complete without the addition of these four rules, but it is customary to include them because they are so useful in reducing the length and difficulty of a great many proofs.

To see how rule **QN** works, consider the following two statements:

1. $(x)(Wx)$ Everything has weight.
2. $\sim (\exists x) \sim (Wx)$ There isn't anything that doesn't have weight.

Clearly, if everything has weight, then there isn't anything that doesn't have weight, and if there isn't anything that doesn't have weight, then everything must have weight. So statements 1 and 2 are logically equivalent statements. They say the same thing, only in different words. And so we ought to be able to substitute one for the other in any context, which is what the first of the four **QN** rules allows.

Of course, that rule does not concern just this one pair of sentences. Any two sentences related in the way that these two are fall under this rule. Here are several other examples:

1. From $\sim (\exists y) \sim (Fy \cdot Gy)$ we can derive $(y)(Fy \cdot Gy)$, and, vice versa, from $(y)(Fy \cdot Gy)$ we can derive $\sim (\exists y) \sim (Fy \cdot Gy)$.
2. From $\sim (\exists z) \sim (\sim Rz \lor Lz)$ we can derive $(z)(\sim Rz \lor Lz)$, and vice versa.
3. From $(x)[Fx \supset \sim (Mx \supset \sim Nx)]$ we can derive $\sim (\exists x) \sim [Fx \supset \sim (Mx \supset \sim Nx)]$, and vice versa.

The point is that adding (x) to an expression does the same job as adding $\sim (\exists x) \sim$ to that expression, and similarly, adding $\sim (\exists x) \sim$ to an expression does the same job as adding (x) to it. And the first version of rule **QN** permits us to make inferences from one of these sorts of expressions to the other.

Now consider two proofs that illustrate the usefulness of this first version of rule **QN.** Here is the first proof:

1. $(y)(Wy) \supset (\exists x)(Hx)$ p
2. $\sim (\exists y) \sim (Wy)$ p /∴ $(\exists x)(Hx)$

In this case rule **QN** permits us to move from premise 2 to

3. $(y)Wy$ 2 **QN**

And then we can complete the proof quite easily:

4. $(\exists x)Hx$ 1,3 **MP**

In this case rule **QN** permitted us to replace the argument's second premise with an equivalent premise that permitted us then to use another rule of inference (**MP**) and successfully derive the argument's conclusion.

Now consider a second argument:

1. $\sim (\exists z) \sim (Wz \supset Hz)$ p
2. Wa p /∴ Ha

To construct this proof, we need to drop the $(\exists z)$ quantifier from the first premise, but we can't use rule **EI** to do so, because the quantifier $(\exists z)$ does not quantify the whole of the first line. Using rule **QN,** however, we can replace the first premise of this argument with the equivalent statement $(z)(Wz \supset Hz)$, obtained by replacing the expression $\sim (\exists z) \sim$ with (z):

3. $(z)(Wz \supset Hz)$ 1 **QN**

And then we can use rules **UI** and **MP** to obtain the argument's conclusion:

> 4. *Wa* ⊃ *Ha*   3 **UI**
> 5. *Ha*   2,4 **MP**

What the first version of rule **QN** tells us is that if we have a statement quantified by a universal quantifier, we can replace that quantifier by an existential quantifier provided we place negation signs both to the right and the left of the existential quantifier. And, of course, the first version of **QN** also permits the reverse process, replacing an existential quantifier that has negation signs both right and left with a universal quantifier that has negation signs neither to the right nor to the left.

Examples

Here are several examples of correct uses of this first version of rule **QN:**

(1)   1. (*x*)(*Fx* ⊃ *Gx*)   p
      2. ~ (∃*x*) ~ (*Fx* ⊃ *Gx*)   1 **QN**

(2)   1. ~ (∃*x*) ~ (*Fx* ⊃ *Gx*)   p
      2. (*x*)(*Fx* ⊃ *Gx*)   1 **QN**

(3)   1. (*y*)[*Fy* ⊃ (*Ry* ∨ *Hya*)]   p
      2. ~ (∃*y*) ~ [*Fy* ⊃ (*Ry* ∨ *Hya*)]   1 **QN**

(4)   1. ~ (∃*z*) ~ [~ *Sz* ∨ ~ (~ *Tz* ∨ ~ *Pz*)]   p
      2. (*z*)[~ *Sz* ∨ ~ (~ *Tz* ∨ ~ *Pz*)]   1 **QN**

The other three varieties of rule **QN** are quite similar to the first one. Here is what all four of the **QN** rules say with respect to one set of substitution instances:

> 1. (*x*)*Wx* :: ~ (∃*x*) ~ *Wx*
> 2. (∃*x*)*Wx* :: ~ (*x*) ~ *Wx*
> 3. (*x*) ~ *Wx* :: ~ (∃*x*)*Wx*
> 4. (∃*x*) ~ *Wx* :: ~ (*x*)*Wx*

The first of these formulas tells us that we can move from "Everything has weight" to "There isn't anything that does not have weight," the second from "Something has weight" to "It's not the case that nothing has weight," the third from "Everything is such that it does-n't have weight" to "It's not the case that something has weight," and the fourth from "There is something that doesn't have any weight" to "It's not the case that everything has weight."

Examples

The **QN** rules permit indefinitely many moves like the ones just given. For instance, it permits all the following inferences:

> 1. (∃*y*)(~ *Fy* ∨ *Gy*)
> /∴ 2. ~ (*y*) ~ (~ *Fy* ∨ *Gy*)

1. $\sim (\exists x)[\sim Rx \supset (\exists y)(Cy \vee \sim Dy)]$
/∴ 2. $(x) \sim [\sim Rx \supset (\exists y)(Cy \vee \sim Dy)]$

1. $(z) \sim (Fz \supset Gz)$
/∴ 2. $\sim (\exists z)(Fz \supset Gz)$

1. $\sim (x) \sim [Pxa \vee (Gx \supset \sim Fx)]$
/∴ 2. $(\exists x)[Pxa \vee (Gx \supset \sim Fx)]$

The key to successful use of the four quantifier negation rules is to notice that they all require us to do exactly the same three things: (1) change the quantifier in question from an existential to a universal quantifier, or vice versa; (2) remove any negation signs there may be either to the left or to the right of that quantifier; and (3) put negation signs in whichever of these two places there may not have originally been one. Thus, in one of the preceding examples, we moved from $(x)(Fx)$ to $\sim (\exists x) \sim (Fx)$ by changing the quantifier from (x) to $(\exists x)$ and by adding negation signs both to the right and to the left of the quantifier (where there had been none before). And in moving from, say, $\sim (\exists y)(Fy \cdot \sim Gy)$ to $(y) \sim (Fy \cdot \sim Gy)$, we would change the existential quantifier to a universal, remove the negation sign from in front of the quantifier, and add a negation sign right after the quantifier.

The notation introduced to state the four quantifier rules in a precise manner also can be used to do the same for the four versions of the Quantifier Negation (**QN**) rule:

1. $(u)(. . . u . . .) :: \sim(\exists u) \sim (. . . u . . .)$
2. $(\exists u)(. . . u . . .) :: \sim (u) \sim (. . . u . . .)$
3. $(u) \sim (. . . u . . .) :: \sim (\exists u)(. . . u . . .)$
4. $(\exists u) \sim (. . . u . . .) :: \sim (u)(. . . u . . .)$

where the expression $(. . . u . . .)$ is some sentence form containing at least one occurrence of u free in $(. . . u . . .)$.

The **QN** rules are rules of *replacement:* Logically equivalent formulas may replace one another wherever they occur. Replacement, recall from our previous discussions in sentential logic, need not be uniform.

The **QN** rules have interesting relationships to one another: given any one of them, others may be proved, using only the techniques of sentential logic. Let's see how this would go. Consider the logical equivalence $(p \equiv \sim q) \equiv (\sim p \equiv q)$; this was not one of the equivalences we introduced in sentential logic, but you can easily satisfy yourself that it is one by using truth tables. Now consider our first **QN** formula: It has the form $p \equiv \sim q$, where our q is $(\exists u) \sim (. . . u . . .)$. Our sentential equivalence tells us that the first **QN** rule is thus logically equivalent to $\sim p \equiv q$, that is, $\sim (u)(. . . u . . .) \equiv (\exists u) \sim (. . . u . . .)$, which is in effect our fourth **QN** rule. The second and third **QN** rules are likewise interderivable.

Finally, the **QN** rules have a very interesting theoretical consequence. They show— and mathematicians, logicians, and philosophers all love this kind of thing!—that we could introduce, say, the universal quantifier by definition: **QN** rule (1) shows us that we could define it in terms of the existential quantifier and negation. Or, given our second **QN** rule, we could do it the other way around: introduce the existential quantifier defined by the universal quantifier and negation. So the concepts of "all" and "some" are, for logical purposes, intimately connected.

Exercise 9-4

Which of the following are not correct uses of rule **QN?** For each incorrect use, provide an alternative sentence that can be correctly derived using this rule.

(1) 1. $(x) \sim Fx$ p   (6) 1. $(z)(Fz \supset Gz)$ p
  $/\therefore$ 2. $\sim (\exists x) \sim Fx$ $/\therefore$ 2. $\sim (\exists z) \sim (Fz \supset Gz)$

(2) 1. $\sim (\exists x)Fx$ p   (7) 1. $\sim (z) \sim [(Fz \supset Gz) \supset \sim Gz]$ p
  $/\therefore$ 2. $(x) \sim Fx$ $/\therefore$ 2. $(\exists z)[(Fz \supset Gz) \supset \sim Gz]$

(3) 1. $(x) \sim (\sim Fx \vee Gx)$ p   (8) 1. $(y) \sim [Fx] \supset (\exists z)(Gz \cdot Hz)]$ p
  $/\therefore$ 2. $\sim (\exists x)(Fx \vee Gx)$ $/\therefore$ 2. $\sim (\exists y)[Fx \supset (\exists z)(Gz \cdot Hz)]$

(4) 1. $\sim (\exists y) \sim (Ry \cdot \sim Ky)$ p   (9) 1. $(y) \sim Fx \supset (\exists z)(Gz \cdot Hz)$ p
  $/\therefore$ 2. $(y) \sim (Ry \cdot \sim Ky)$ $/\therefore$ 2. $\sim (\exists y) \sim Fx \supset (\exists z)(Gz \cdot Hz)$

(5) 1. $\sim (\exists y)(\sim Ry \cdot \sim Ky)$ p   (10) 1. $(x) \sim (Fx \supset Gx)$ p
  $/\therefore$ 2. $(y)(Ry \cdot \sim Ky)$ $/\therefore$ 2. $\sim (\exists x) \sim (Fx \supset Gx)$

🚶 Walk-Through: Predicate Logic Proofs with QN

Rule **QN** makes it possible to solve many proofs efficiently using **IP**. Let's work through an example.

  1. $\sim (\exists x) \sim (\sim Ax \vee Bx)$
  2. $\sim (x) Bx$ $/\therefore \sim (x)Ax$

We need to use **QN** on our premises to get them in shape for removing quantifiers.

  3. $(x)(\sim Ax \vee Bx)$ 1 **QN**
  4. $(\exists x) \sim Bx$ 2 **QN**

Now we can remove the quantifiers, remembering to use **EI** first. Then we can use **DS.**

  5. $\sim Bx$ 4 **EI**
  6. $\sim Ax \vee Bx$ 3 **UI**
  7. $\sim Ax$ 5,6 **DS**

To solve the proof, we need to recognize that the conclusion is equivalent to $(\exists x) \sim Ax$ (by **QN**). So we can complete the proof by adding on the *existential* quantifier and then applying **QN** to the result.

  8. $(\exists x) \sim Ax$ 7 **EI**
  9. $\sim (x)Ax$ 8 **QN**

Exercise 9-5

Prove valid:

(1)   1. $(\exists x)Fx \lor (\exists x)Gx$ p
      2. $(x) \sim Fx$ p
                    $/\therefore (\exists x)Gx$

(2)   1. $(x)(Hx \supset \sim Kx)$ p
              $/\therefore \sim (\exists y)(Hy \cdot Ky)$

(3)   1. $\sim (x)Ax$ p
               $/\therefore (\exists x)(Ax \supset Bx)$

(4)   1. $\sim (\exists x)Fx$ p
               $/\therefore Fa \supset Ga$

(5)   1. $(\exists x)Fx \supset (x) \sim Gx$ p
      2. $(\exists x)Ex \supset \sim (x) \sim Fx$ p
            $/\therefore (\exists x)Ex \supset \sim (\exists x)Gx$

(6)   1. $(\exists x)(Ax \cdot Bx) \supset (y)Cy$ p
      2. $\sim Ca$ p
            $/\therefore (x)(Ax \supset \sim Bx)$

(7)   1. $(x)[(Fx \lor Hx) \supset (Gx \cdot Ax)]$ p
      2. $\sim (x)(Ax \cdot Gx)$ p
            $/\therefore (\exists x) \sim Hx$

(8)   1. $\sim (x)(Hx \lor Kx)$ p
      2. $(y)[(\sim Ky \lor Ly) \supset My]$ p
            $/\therefore (\exists z)Mz$

(9)   1. $(x)[(Fx \lor Gx) \supset Hx]$ p
      2. $(x)[(Hx \lor Kx) \supset Lx]$ p
            $/\therefore (x)(Fx \supset Lx)$

(10) 1. $(\exists x)Rx \supset (\exists x)Sx$ p
      2. $(x)(Tx \supset Rx)$ p
            $/\therefore (\exists x)Tx \supset (\exists x)Sx$

(11) 1. $(x)[(Ax \lor Bx) \supset Cx]$ p
      2. $\sim (\exists y)(Cy \lor Dy)$ p
            $/\therefore \sim (\exists x)Ax$

(12) 1. $(x)(Gx \supset Hx)$ p
      2. $(\exists x)(Ix \cdot \sim Hx)$ p
      3. $(x)(\sim Fx \lor Gx)$ p
            $/\therefore (\exists x)(Ix \cdot \sim Fx)$

(13) 1. $(x)[(Ax \cdot Bx) \supset Cx]$ p
      2. $\sim Cb$ p
            $/\therefore \sim (Ab \cdot Bb)$

(14) 1. $\sim (x)(Fx \supset Gx)$ p
      2. $\sim (\exists x)(\sim Gx \cdot Hx)$ p
            $/\therefore (\exists x) \sim Hx$

(15) 1. $(x)(Hx \supset Kx)$ p
      2. $(\exists x)Hx \lor (\exists x)Kx$ p
            $/\therefore (\exists x)Kx$

(16) 1. $(\exists x)Fx \supset (\exists x)(Gx \cdot Hx)$ p
      2. $(\exists x)(Hx \lor Kx) \supset (x)Lx$ p
            $/\therefore (x)(Fx \supset Lx)$

(17) 1. $(x)[(Bx \cdot Ax) \supset Dx]$ p
      2. $(\exists x)(Qx \cdot Ax)$ p
      3. $(x)(\sim Bx \supset \sim Qx)$ p
            $/\therefore (\exists x)(Dx \cdot Qx)$

(18) 1. $(x)[Px \supset (Ax \lor Bx)]$ p
      2. $(x)[(Bx \lor Cx) \supset Qx]$ p
            $/\therefore (x)[(Px \cdot \sim Ax) \supset Qx]$

(19) 1. $(x)[Px \supset (Qx \lor Rx)]$ p
      2. $(x)[(Sx \cdot Px) \supset \sim Qx]$ p
       $/\therefore (x)(Sx \supset Px) \supset (x)(Sx \supset Rx)$

(20) 1. $(x)[(Ax \lor Bx) \supset (Cx \cdot Dx)]$ p
       $/\therefore (\exists x)(Ax \lor Cx) \supset (\exists x)Cx$

Key Term Introduced in Chapter Nine

The natural deduction rules introduced in this chapter can be found on pages 211 and 212. For convenient reference they are also printed inside the front cover.

quasivariable: A letter introduced by **UI** or **EI** that stands for any arbitrarily selected individual or some individual or other, respectively. The latter is a kind of John Doe name; we instantiate not to the entity's "real" name, but to a made-up one that stands for the individual. Quasivariables are not genuine free variables; if they were, **UI** and **EI** would lead us from true premises to conclusions that have no truth-value.

Chapter Ten

Relational Predicate Logic

---

1 Relational Predicates

We now broaden our coverage of predicate logic to include relational predicates. This allows us to symbolize sentences such as "Kareem is taller than Mugsy" as *Tkm*. With relational predicates the order in which letters occur is significant. If we reverse the individual constants in the sentence just mentioned, giving us *Tmk*, the sentence now asserts that Mugsy is taller than Kareem.

The addition of relations to predicate logic is a major theoretic advance. It allows us to capture the validity of crucial inferences from both mathematics; for example,

> 5 is less than 7.
> 3 is less than 5.
> ∴ 3 is less than 7.

and everyday life, such as

> Somebody loves everybody.
> ∴ There is at least one person who loves somebody.

Relational predicate logic tremendously increases the power of our logical system. For further discussion, see Chapter Fourteen, Section 14.

Examples

Let *Dxy* denote the relational property of *x* having defeated *y*, *j* denote Joe Louis, *m* Max Schmeling, *r* Rocky Marciano, and *b* Billy Conn:

1. Joe Louis defeated Max Schmeling.	*Djm*
2. Schmeling also defeated Louis.	*Dmj*
3. Louis didn't defeat Rocky Marciano.	*~ Djr*

4. But he did beat Billy Conn.   *Djb*
5. So Louis defeated Conn and Schmeling.   *Djb · Djm*
6. And he lost to Marciano and Schmeling.   *Drj · Dmj*

Here are several utterances translated using obvious abbreviations:

7. Mt. Everest is taller than Mt. Godwin Austen (K-2).   *Teg*
8. Lake Huron is larger than Lake Erie.   *Lhe*
9. But it's smaller than Lake Superior.   *Lsh*
10. Hillary was sitting between Barbara and Nancy.   *Bhbn*

Simple sentences with relational predicates, such as those just given, are not particularly difficult to symbolize. Neither are sentences where a relational predicate is accompanied by a single quantifier. The three-step strategy we employed in Chapter Seven works well here also. For example, if our sentence is "Everyone likes Henry," we first ask who or what the sentence is about. In this case our subject is people—*Px*. Our sentence says something about all people; this gives us $(x)(Px \supset$ _____ $)$. And, finally, what it says about all people is that they like Henry, which we can symbolize using a relational predicate: $(x)(Px \supset Lxh)$.

Note that the subject we should use for symbolizations involving relational predicates is not always the grammatical subject of the sentence. For example, we can rephrase the sentence "Henry likes everyone" as "Everyone is liked by Henry," which can then be translated $(x)(Px \supset Lhx)$. Rephrasing in this way gives us a subject that is coupled with a quantifier, so that the sentence as reformulated is predicating something of some or all individuals of a certain kind. Sentences often need to be reworked this way before it becomes obvious how they should be symbolized.

Examples

Let $Axy = x$ is afraid of y, b = Biff, and p = Percy. For the sake of simplicity, we will restrict our domain of discourse to humans.

1. Biff is afraid of no one. $\sim (\exists x)Abx$
2. Biff is afraid of everyone. $(x)Abx$
3. Everyone is afraid of Biff. $(x)Axb$
4. No one is afraid of Biff. $\sim (\exists x)Axb$
5. No one is afraid of Biff or Percy. $\sim (\exists x)(Axb \lor Axp)$
6. Everyone who is afraid of Biff is also afraid of Percy. $(x)(Axb \supset Axp)$
7. Biff is afraid of everyone who is not afraid of Percy. $(x)(\sim Axp \supset Abx)$
8. Biff is not afraid of anyone who is afraid of Percy. $(x)(Axp \supset \sim Abx)$

Exercise 10-1

Symbolize the following sentences, using the indicated letters.

1. Cybill Shepherd isn't married to Bruce Willis. (*Mxy* = "*x* is married to *y*"; *c* = "Cybill Shepherd"; *b* = "Bruce Willis")

2. So, obviously, Willis isn't married to Shepherd.

3. But if Willis is married, it isn't to Jane Fonda. (*Mx* = "*x* is married"; *j* = "Jane Fonda")

4. In fact, Bruce Willis is not married to anyone. (*Px* = "*x* is a person")

5. Bruce Willis and Kevin Bacon are not in the same movie. (*k* = "Kevin Bacon"; *Sxy* = "*x* is in the same movie as *y*")

6. So, if Willis appeared in *The Sixth Sense*, then Bacon was in *Stir of Echos*. (*Axy* = "*x* appeared in *y*"; *s* = *The Sixth Sense; e = Stir of Echos*)

7. David Letterman is not interested in anyone who breaks into his house. (*d* = "David Letterman"; *Ixy* = "*x* is interested in *y*"; *Bxy* = "*x* breaks into *y*'s house")

8. There is some woman who keeps breaking into Dave's house, but he is not interested in her. (*Wx* = "*x* is a woman")

9. If Beth can't pass the final, no one can. (*b* = "Beth"; *f* = "the final"; *Pxy* = "*x* can pass *y*"; *Px* = "*x* is a person")

10. If someone didn't pass the final, it was Jeff or Kate. (*j* = "Jeff"; *k* = "Kate")

11. If someone is sitting between Julia and Harry, then there must not be anyone between Alice and Bob. (*j* = "Julia"; *h* = "Harry"; *a* = "Alice"; b = "Bob"; *Sxyz* = "*x* is sitting between *y* and *z*")

12. If there is an empty chair, then no one is sitting between Elmer and Gertrude. (*Cx* = "*x* is a chair"; *Ex* = "*x* is empty"; *e* = "Elmer"; *g* = "Gertrude")

13. Harriet has read all of Shakespeare's works. (*h* = "Harriet"; *Rxy* = "*x* has read *y*"; *Wxy* = "*x* is a work of *y*")

14. Laura doesn't like any of Woody Allen's movies (*l* = "Laura"; *Lxy* = "*x* likes *y*"; *Mxy* = "*x* is a movie directed by *y*"; *a* = "Woody Allen")

15. Melissa likes some of Woody's movies, but not others. (*m* = "Melissa")

16. If Paul likes *Manhattan*, then he likes at least one of Woody Allen's movies. (*m* = "Manhattan"; *p* = "Paul")

17. Some people think Clarence Thomas harassed Anita Hill, and some do not. (*c* = "Clarence Thomas"; *a* = "Anita Hill"; *Txyz* = "*x* thinks *y* harassed *z*")

18. If Thomas harassed Hill, then at least one Supreme Court judge is not qualified. (*Hxy* = "*x* harassed *y*"; *Sx* = "*x* is a Supreme Court judge"; *Qx* = "*x* is qualified")

19. If Thomas did not harass Hill, then some of the things said by Hill at the hearing are not true. (*h* = "the hearing"; *Sxyz* = "*x* is said by *y* at *z*"; *Tx* = "*x* is true")

20. If everything Hill said about Thomas at the hearing is true, then Thomas did harass her. (*Swxyz* = "*w* is said by *y* about *x* at *z*")

2 *Symbolizations Containing Overlapping Quantifiers*

Symbolizations may contain quantifiers having overlapping scopes. An example is the sentence "Everything is different from everything," which in symbols becomes $(x)(y)Dxy$. This sentence is false, of course, because nothing can be different from itself. But it is meaningful, and so we want to have a way to symbolize it. (Notice that the false sentence "Everything is different from everything" is not the same as the true sentence "Everything is different from everything *else*." To symbolize the latter, we need a symbol for identity, which is introduced in Chapter Thirteen.)

Examples

Here are some examples of multiply quantified sentences with overlapping quantifier scopes, along with their correct symbolizations (letting Lxy = "x loves y," and to simplify matters, restricting the domain of discourse to human beings).

Sentence	*Symbolization*
1. Everyone loves everyone.	1. $(x)(y)Lxy$
2. Someone loves someone.	2. $(\exists x)(\exists y)Lxy$
3. Not everyone loves everyone.	3. $\sim (x)(y)Lxy$
4. No one loves anyone.	4. $(x)(y) \sim Lxy$ or $\sim (\exists x)(\exists y)Lxy$

The examples just considered all contain overlapping quantifiers of the same type. For instance, in sentence 1, both quantifiers are universal quantifiers; in sentence 2 both are existential quantifiers. In such cases, the order in which the quantifiers occur is not relevant to the meanings of the sentences. Thus $(x)(y)Lxy$ says the same thing as $(y)(x)Lxy$.*

But when an existential and a universal quantifier are involved, order becomes crucial. Compare, for instance, the order of quantifiers in the two expressions $(x)(\exists y)Lxy$ and $(\exists y)(x)Lxy$. (In the former, the existential quantifier is within the scope of the universal quantifier, while in the latter it is the other way around.) If we let Lxy = "x loves y" and restrict the domain of discourse to human beings, then $(x)(\exists y)Lxy$ says that every x (every person) loves some person or other, whereas $(\exists y)(x)Lxy$ says that some y (some person) is such that everyone loves that person. In other words, $(x)(\exists y)Lxy$ says that everyone loves someone or other, while $(\exists y)(x)Lxy$ says that there is someone who is loved by everyone, and these clearly are different.

3 *Expansions and Overlapping Quantifiers*

One way to better understand sentences of this kind is to become familiar with the *expansions* of various multiply quantified sentences. Take the sentence "Everyone loves

---

*Of course, in more complex sentences order can be important even if the quantifiers are of the same type. For example, we can't reverse the positions of the universal quantifiers in $(x)[Fx \supset (y)Gxy]$ to get $(y)[Fx \supset (x)Gxy]$ because these two symbolizations clearly have different meanings (the second is not even a sentence, because the first x in it is a free variable).

everyone," in symbols (x)(y)Lxy, and consider its expansion in a universe containing just two individuals, *a* and *b*. To say that everyone loves everyone is to say that every *x* loves every *y*. Since there are exactly two *x*'s in this universe, this says that the first *x*, namely *a*, loves every *y* (in symbols (y)Lay), and the second *x*, namely *b*, loves every *y* (in symbols (y)Lby). So a partial expansion of (x)(y)Lxy is just the conjunction of (y)Lay *and* (y)Lby, or (y)Lay · (y)Lby. To obtain the complete expansion of (x)(y)Lxy, we also have to expand for the (y) quantifier. First, the left conjunct, (y)Lay, says that *a* loves every *y*, which in *this* two-individual universe means that *Laa · Lab*. And second, the right conjunct, (y)Lby, says that *b* loves every *y*, which in this two-individual universe means that *Lba · Lbb*. So the complete expansion of (x)(y)Lxy is the conjunction (*Laa · Lab*) · (*Lba · Lbb*).

Now consider the sentence "Someone loves someone (or other)," in symbols (∃x)(∃y)Lxy. To say that someone loves someone is to say that there is some *x* that loves some *y*. Since there are exactly two individuals in the universe in question, this is to say that either *a* loves some *y* [in symbols (∃y)Lay] *or* *b* loves some *y* [in symbols (∃y)Lby], in other words that (∃y)Lay ∨ (∃y)Lby. The left disjunct, (∃y)Lay, says that *a* loves either *a or b*, or in symbols that *Laa ∨ Lab*. And the right disjunct, (∃y)Lby, says that *b* loves either *a or b*, or in symbols that *Lba ∨ Lbb*. So the complete expansion for (∃x)(∃y)Lxy is the disjunction (*Laa ∨ Lab*) ∨ (*Lba ∨ Lbb*). (Compare this with the expansion for (x)(y)Lxy.)

Examples

Here are more examples of multiply quantified sentences (including a few with mixed quantifiers), their correct symbolizations, and their expansions in a two-individual universe of discourse.

1. *Sentence:* No one loves anyone.
   Symbolization: (x)(y) ~ Lxy
   Expansion: (~ Laa · ~ Lab) · (~ Lba · ~ Lbb)

2. *Sentence:* It's not the case that someone loves some person (or other).
   Symbolization: ~ (∃x)(∃y)Lxy
   Expansion: ~ [(Laa ∨ Lab) ∨ (Lba ∨ Lbb)]

Notice that this is just the expansion of the sentence "Someone loves someone (or other)" *negated*. (Notice also that the expansions of sentences 1 and 2 are logically equivalent.)

3. *Sentence:* There is somebody who doesn't love someone (or other).
   Symbolization: (∃x)(∃y) ~ Lxy
   Expansion: (~ Laa ∨ ~ Lab) ∨ (~ Lba ∨ ~ Lbb)

4. *Sentence:* Not everyone loves everyone.
   Symbolization: ~ (x)(y)Lxy
   Expansion: ~ [(Laa · Lab) · (Lba · Lbb)]

Notice that number 4 is just the expansion of the sentence "Everyone loves everyone" negated. (Notice also that the expansions of sentences 3 and 4 are logically equivalent by DeMorgan's Theorem.)

5. *Sentence:* Everyone loves someone (or other).
   Symbolization: $(x)(\exists y)Lxy$
   Expansion: $(Laa \lor Lab) \cdot (Lba \lor Lbb)$

We arrive at this expansion by expanding first with respect to the universal quantifier to obtain the semiexpansion $(\exists y)Lay \cdot (\exists y)Lby$, then expanding the left conjunct to obtain $(Laa \lor Lab) \cdot (\exists y)Lby$, and finally the right conjunct to obtain $(Laa \lor Lab) \cdot (Lba \lor Lbb)$.

6. *Sentence:* Someone is such that everyone loves that person. (Or, more collo-
             quially, someone is loved by everyone.)
   Symbolization: $(\exists y)(x)Lxy$
   Expansion: $(Laa \cdot Lba) \lor (Lab \cdot Lbb)$

To arrive at this expansion, we can expand first with respect to the existential quanti-fier, to obtain the semiexpansion $(x)Lxa \lor (x)Lxb$, then expanding the left disjunct to obtain $(Laa \cdot Lba) \lor (x)Lxb$, and finally the right disjunct to obtain $(Laa \cdot Lba) \lor (Lab \cdot Lbb)$. (Sentences 5 and 6 are important because their expansions show that the order of mixed quantifiers *does* make a difference.)

7. *Sentence:* There is someone whom no one loves.
   Symbolization: $(\exists x)(y) \sim Lyx$
   Expansion: $(\sim Laa \cdot \sim Lba) \lor (\sim Lab \cdot \sim Lbb)$

8. *Sentence:* Everyone is such that someone (or other) does not love that person.
             (Or, more colloquially, everyone is unloved by someone (or other).)
   Symbolization: $(x)(\exists y) \sim Lyx$
   Expansion: $(\sim Laa \lor \sim Lba) \cdot (\sim Lab \lor \sim Lbb)$

Exercise 10-2

Symbolize the following sentences (letting Sxy = "x is smaller than y"), and construct their expansions in a two-individual universe of discourse.

1. Everything is smaller than everything.
2. Something is smaller than something (or other).
3. There is something that is smaller than everything.
4. Everything is smaller than something (or other).
5. Not all things are smaller than something (or other).
6. There isn't anything that is smaller than everything.
7. Nothing is smaller than anything.

8. There is something such that everything is smaller than that thing.
9. It's not the case that nothing is smaller than anything.
10. It's not the case that everything is smaller than something (or other).
11. Nothing is smaller than itself.
12. Anything that is smaller than everything is smaller than itself.

🚶 Walk-Through: Symbolizations with Multiple Quantifiers

To symbolize with multiple quantifiers, we employ a slightly modified version of our standard three-step strategy. The first two steps are usually the same. We begin by determining the subject (not necessarily the grammatical subject) and the quantifier that goes with that subject. If our sentence is "Cheaters never prosper," we can construe this as making a claim about all cheaters. This gives us the first half of our symbolization— $(x)(Cx \supset$ _____). The third step is just a bit trickier. What does this sentence say about all cheaters? It says there is no time at which they prosper. To complete our symbolization, we, in effect, translate as though our variable x were a constant. To see how this is so, consider how we would symbolize the sentence "Larry never prospers." We could symbolize the sentence this way: $\sim (\exists y)(Ty \cdot Ply)$. The second half of our more complex symbolization looks just like this, except instead of the constant l we have our variable x: $\sim (\exists y)(Ty \cdot Pxy)$. Here then is our complete symbolization: $(x)[Cx \supset \sim (\exists y)(Ty \cdot Pxy)]$.

Here's another example.

Sentence: "The only good test is one that some students will fail."
Subject: Good tests.

$$Gx$$

Some or all? All.

$$(x)(Gx \supset$$

What does it say about them? At least one student fails the test.

$$(x) [Gx \supset (\exists y)(Sy \cdot Fyx)]$$

Here is a sentence where the second quantifier is added in the first step:

Sentence: "Any test that everyone fails is a bad test."
Subject: Tests that are failed by everyone (who takes them).

$$Tx \cdot (y)(Dyx \supset Fyx)$$

Some or all? All.

$$(x)[Tx \cdot (y)(Dyx \supset Fyx)] \supset$$

What does it say about them? They are bad tests.

$$(x)\{[Tx \cdot (y)(Dyx \supset Fyx)] \supset Bx\}$$

Exercise 10-3

Bx = "x is boring"	Hxy = "x is more difficult than y"
Cx = "x is a course"	Ixy = "x is more interesting than y"
Dx = "x is demanding"	Kxy = "x knows y"
Ex = "x is an exam"	Pxy = "x passes y"
Gx = "x is good"	Txy = "x takes y"
Px = "x is a person"	
Qx = "x is a quiz"	j = "John"
Sx = "x is a student"	m = "Mary"

Symbolize the following sentences, using the predicate and individual constants just given.

1. There are students who don't know anything.
2. No student knows everything.
3. Some students pass every quiz they take.
4. No student passes every exam she takes.
5. Good students pass every course they take.
6. Every good student takes at least one demanding course.
7. Mary is a good student, but she doesn't pass every exam she takes.
8. There are students and courses that are not boring.
9. John takes every course that Mary passes.
10. Every student takes some of the courses that John takes.
11. No courses are taken by everyone.
12. Quizzes and exams are demanding.
13. Quizzes are more interesting than exams.
14. Boring courses are more difficult than demanding ones.
15. No one is more interesting than John.
16. Good students won't take boring courses.
17. Some students don't take any courses that are more interesting than the courses John takes.
18. The exams Mary doesn't pass are more difficult than any of the exams John takes.
19. No one passes all the exams John takes.
20. There are demanding courses that are more interesting than any boring course.
21. Some students will take any course that isn't demanding.
22. Mary knows everything and everyone that John knows.
23. Only good students take demanding courses.
24. Mary doesn't take a course unless it is a good one.
25. Mary takes courses only if they are more difficult than the courses John takes.
26. John passes all of the exams he takes unless they are demanding.
27. Only good students pass every course they take.

28. Good students won't take courses unless the courses are demanding.
29. John won't take any course unless Mary does too.
30. Mary won't take a course unless it is both more difficult and more interesting than any of the courses John has passed.

 Places and Times

Mastering multiply quantified symbolizations generally just requires a bit of practice to get the hang of it. But the symbolizations of statements concerning places or times are particularly interesting and sometimes cause trouble.

Consider the statement "Somewhere the streets are all paved with gold." This sentence asserts that there is someplace where all things that are streets are paved with gold. So it can be symbolized as $(\exists x)[(Px \cdot (y)(Syx \supset Gy)]$, where Px = "x is a place"; Sxy = "x is a street in y"; and Gx = "x is paved with gold."

Similarly, the sentence "The sun never sets on the U.S. empire" can be symbolized as $\sim (\exists x)(Tx \cdot Ssbx)$, where Tx = "x is a time"; b = "the U.S. empire"; s = "the sun"; and $Sxyz$ = "x sets on y at time z." This symbolization makes clear the idea that it is not the case that there is a time when the sun sets on the U.S. empire. (This is what is called a "dated" example in the trade.)

And then there is the famous line "The poor will always be with us," which we can symbolize as $(x)[Tx \supset (\exists y)(Py \cdot Wyx)]$, where Tx = "x is a time"; Px = "x is poor"; and Wxy = "x is with us at y." This symbolization expresses the idea that, given any time whatsoever, there is some poor person or other who is alive at that time. (This, unfortunately, is not a dated example.)

Finally, here is one that is somewhat more complicated: "If all industrial nations don't stop polluting the atmosphere, then every place on earth will be contaminated." Letting Ix = "x is an industrial nation"; Sx = "x stops polluting the atmosphere"; Pxy = "x is a place on y"; e = "earth"; and Cx = "x is contaminated," we can symbolize this sentence as $\sim (x)(Ix \supset Sx) \supset (y)(Pye \supset Cy)$. Note that no quantifier quantifies the whole of this symbolization and that the major logical connective is the horseshoe.

Exercise 10-4

Symbolize the following, revealing as much structure as you can and indicating the meanings of the abbreviations that you use. Some of these you may find ambiguous. If so, discuss the possibilities before you give an interpretation. What do you want to be true if the given sentence is true?

1. There are cheaters in some places.
2. But there aren't cheaters in every place.
3. Cheaters are everywhere.
4. There is no place more beautiful than Hawaii.
5. A person's work is never done.

6. There comes a time in every person's life when that person must face reality.
7. You can fool all of the people some of the time.
8. You can fool some of the people all of the time.
9. You can't fool all of the people all of the time.
10. It's never too late to reform.
11. A barking dog never bites.
12. Hillary Rodham Clinton always wears designer dresses.
13. There never was a time or place without sin.
14. But there also never was a time or place without honesty.
15. A sucker is born every minute.—David Hannum (A competitor of P. T. Barnum)

5   *Symbolizing "Someone," "Somewhere," "Sometime," and So On*

Finally, we need to consider a few somewhat different symbolizations. Take the sentence "If someone is too noisy, then everyone in the room will be annoyed." Restricting the universe of discourse to human beings, we can partially symbolize this sentence as

If $(\exists x)$ Nx, then $(y)(Ry \supset Ay)$

and then complete the symbolization as

$(\exists x)Nx \supset (y)(Ry \supset Ay)$

But the grammatically similar sentence "If someone is too noisy, then everyone in the room will be annoyed *with that person*" must be symbolized somewhat differently. We cannot partially symbolize it as

If $(\exists x)$ Nx, then $(y)(Ry \supset Ayx)$

and then complete the symbolization as

$(\exists x)Nx \supset (y)(Ry \supset Ayx)$

because the last x variable in this expression is a *free variable,* so this expression is not a sentence.

And we cannot rectify this error simply by extending the scope of the existential quantifier; that is, we cannot correctly symbolize the sentence as

$(\exists x)[Nx \supset (y)(Ry \supset Ayx)]$

Although this is a sentence, it is not equivalent to the one we are trying to translate. This new sentence asserts that there is at least one person such that if that person is too noisy, then everyone in the room will be annoyed with that person. This would be true even if everyone became annoyed when one person, say Smith, was too noisy, but not when some other person, say Jones, was too noisy. But the implication of our original sentence is that if *anyone* is too noisy, then everyone will be annoyed with that person. So the symbolization just suggested will not do.

Instead, we can symbolize our sentence as

$$(x)[Nx \supset (y)(Ry \supset Ayx)]$$

using a *universal* quantifier.

In this case it is the word "someone" that is misleading. It sometimes functions as an existential quantifier and sometimes as a universal quantifier. The words "something," "somewhere," "sometime," and so on, can be misleading in the same way. Hence it is wise to pay close attention to the precise meaning of a sentence in which any of these terms occurs before deciding whether its correct symbolization requires an existential or a universal quantifier.

Even so, it still may seem strange that "If someone is too noisy, then everyone in the room will be annoyed" is correctly symbolized as $(\exists x)(Nx) \supset (y)(Ry \supset Ay)$, using an existential quantifier whose scope is restricted to the antecedent of the symbolization, whereas "If someone is too noisy, then everyone in the room will be annoyed with that person" is correctly symbolized as $(x)[Nx \supset (y)(Ry \supset Ayx)]$, using a universal quantifier whose scope is the entire symbolization. But perhaps this strangeness can be dispelled to some extent by pointing out that $(\exists x)(Nx) \supset (y)(Ry \supset Ay)$ *is equivalent to* $(x)[Nx \supset y)(Ry \supset Ay)]$. In other words, there is a sense in which the term "something" functions as a universal quantifier in both sentences.

We may best approach the issue of translation through truth conditions. What do we want to be true for the given statement to be true? How can I best express those conditions? Take this example: Let B = the bridge will fall, $Mx = x$ moves, and assume our universe of discourse is persons. How shall we express "If anyone moves, the bridge will fall" in our symbolism, capturing what we want to be the truth conditions? Suppose we try this: $(\exists x)(Mx \supset B)$. One might be tempted to read this as "if someone moves, the bridge will fall," but it does not say that. In a three-member universe our expansion of the given translation would be $(Ma \supset B) \vee (Mb \supset B) \vee (Mc \supset B)$, and this would be true if a moved and the bridge fell, even if b and c moved and the bridge did not fall. What we want is that if a moves, the bridge falls, and if b does, the bridge falls, and if c does, the bridge falls. Either of the following expresses this:

(a) $(\exists x)Mx \supset B$
(b) $(x)(Mx \supset B)$

(a) says that if a moves or b moves or c moves, the bridge will fall. Any one of the three disjuncts being true means the bridge will fall, or the original statement is not true. (b) says that if a moves, the bridge falls, and if b moves, the bridge falls, and if c moves, the bridge falls. (a) and (b) can be shown to be logically equivalent, simply using the rules of sentential logic. Those are the conditions we want true for the original statement to be true.

Now consider the sentence "If someone is too noisy, then if everyone in the room is annoyed, someone will complain." Restricting the universe of discourse to human beings, we can partially symbolize this sentence as

If $(\exists x)Nx$, then [if $(y)(Ry \supset Ay)$, then $(\exists z)(Cz)$]

and complete the symbolization as

$$(\exists x)Nx \supset [(y)(Ry \supset Ay) \supset (\exists z)(Cz)]$$

But the grammatically similar sentence "If someone is too noisy, then if all of the people in the room are annoyed, they all will dislike *that person*" must be symbolized somewhat differently. We cannot partially symbolize *it* as

If $(\exists x)Nx$, then [if $(y)(Ry \supset Ay)$, then Dyx]

and complete the symbolization as

$(\exists x)Nx \supset [(y)(Ry \supset Ay) \supset (Dyx]$

because the last variables in this symbolization are *free,* so that this expression is not a sentence. Instead, the correct symbolization of our sentence is

$(x)[Nx \supset (y)[(Ry \supset Ay) \supset (Ry \supset Dyx)]]$

Examples

1. Everyone knows somebody (or other).
   $(x)[Px \supset (\exists y)(Py \cdot Kxy)]$

2. Everyone knows everyone.
   $(x)[(Px \supset (y)(Py \supset Kxy)]$ *or* $\sim (\exists x)[Px \cdot (\exists y)(Py \cdot \sim Kxy)]$

3. Someone knows everyone.
   $(\exists x)[Px \cdot (y)(Py \supset Kxy)]$ *or* $(\exists x)[Px \cdot \sim (\exists y)(Py \cdot \sim Kxy)]$

4. Someone knows somebody (or other).
   $(\exists x)[Px \cdot (\exists y)(Py \cdot Kxy)]$

5. No one knows everybody.
   $(x)[Px \supset (\exists y)(Py \cdot \sim Kxy)]$ *or* $\sim (\exists x)[Px \cdot (y)(Py \supset Kxy)]$

6. No one knows anybody.
   $(x)[Px \supset \sim (\exists y)(Py \cdot Kxy)]$ *or* $\sim (\exists x)[Px \cdot (\exists y)(Py \cdot Kxy)]$

7. Some people don't know everybody.
   $(\exists x)[Px \cdot (\exists y)(Py \cdot \sim Kxy)]$

8. Some people don't know anybody.
   $(\exists x)[Px \cdot (y)(Py \supset \sim Kxy)]$

9. Honest candidates always get defeated by dishonest ones.
   $(x)\{(Cx \cdot Hx) \supset (\exists y)[(Cy \cdot \sim Hy) \cdot Dyx]\}$

10. Some honest candidates get defeated by dishonest ones.
    $(\exists x)\{(Cx \cdot Hx) \cdot (\exists y)[(Cy \cdot \sim Hy) \cdot Dyx]\}$

11. No honest candidates get defeated by dishonest ones.
    $\sim (\exists x)\{(Cx \cdot Hx) \cdot (\exists y)[(Cy \cdot \sim Hy) \cdot Dyx]\}$

12. All candidates who get defeated by honest candidates are themselves dishonest.
    $(x)\{\{Cx \cdot (\exists y)[(Cy \cdot Hy) \cdot Dyx]\} \supset \sim Hx\}$

13. All barbers who don't shave themselves don't shave any barbers.
    $(x)[(Bx \cdot \sim Sxx) \supset \sim (\exists y)(By \cdot Sxy)]$

14. Barbers who don't shave themselves are shaved by someone who is a barber.

$(x)[(Bx \cdot \sim Sxx) \supset (\exists y)(By \cdot Syx)]$

15. Barbers shave all and only those who are barbers.

$(x)[Bx \supset (y)(Sxy \equiv By)]$

16. If someone is a barber who does not shave himself, then someone does not get shaved by any barber.

$(\exists x)(Bx \cdot \sim Sxx) \supset (\exists y)[Py \cdot (z)(Bz \supset \sim Szy)]$

17. If there is anyone who does not shave himself, then if no one is shaved by any barber, he (who does not shave himself) will not be shaved by any barber.

$(x)\{(Px \cdot \sim Sxx) \supset \{(y)[Py \supset \sim (\exists z)(Bz \cdot Szy)] \supset \sim (\exists v)(Bv \cdot Svx)\}\}$

18. If there is someone who does not shave himself, then if no barber shaves anyone, there is someone who is not shaved by anyone.

$(\exists x)(Px \cdot \sim Sxx) \supset \{(y)[By \supset (z)(Pz \supset \sim Syz)] \supset (\exists u)[Pu \cdot (w)(Pw \supset \sim Swu)]\}$

Exercise 10-5

Symbolize the following sayings, revealing as much of their internal structure as possible and indicating the intended meanings of your abbreviations.

1. A drama critic is a man who leaves no turn unstoned.—George Bernard Shaw

2. The one who laughs last laughs best.

3. What is a cynic? A man who knows the price of everything and the value of nothing. —Oscar Wilde

4. A cult is a religion with no political power.—Tom Wolfe

5. Where there's smoke, there's fire.

6. All governments are run by liars.—I. F. Stone

7. Let the one who is without sin cast the first stone.—Jesus Christ

8. Uneasy lies the head that wears the crown.—William Shakespeare

9. He jests at scars that has never felt a wound.—William Shakespeare

10. A good professional can outperform any amateur.

11. Anyone who consults a psychiatrist ought to have his head examined.

12. God only helps those who help themselves.

13. God helps those who help themselves.

14. No one learns anything unless he teaches it to himself.

15. Every major horror of history was committed in the name of an altruistic motive.—Ayn Rand (among others)

16. Virtue has never been as respectable as money.—Mark Twain

17. A lawyer who pleads his own case has a fool for a client.
18. No one ever went broke underestimating the intelligence of the American public.— H. L. Mencken
19. Whosoever sheddeth man's blood, by man shall his blood be shed.—Genesis 9:6
20. The good that I want to do, I do not; but the evil I don't want to do, I do.—Romans 7:19

Exercise 10-6

Follow the instructions for Exercise 10-5. (Some of these are difficult.)

1. If a company goes bankrupt, then it deserves to go out of business.
2. Any candidate who doesn't cater to all potential voters is going to lose.
3. If any frontrunners don't cater to all potential voters, then some longshots are going to win.
4. If any politicians engage in demagoguery, then all politicians have to.
5. Everyone who believes in God obeys all of His commandments.
6. Everyone who believes in God always obeys all of His commandments.
7. Everyone who has benefited from a scientific discovery owes money to some scientist or other.
8. There isn't a single person in the whole world who has not benefited at one time or another from some scientific discovery or other.
9. If everyone has benefited from some scientific discovery or other, then some people haven't paid all of their bills.
10. If everyone has benefited from the scientific discoveries of Isaac Newton, then lots of us owe a debt of gratitude to him.
11. There is no psychiatrist who can help anyone who acts on astrological advice.
12. If everybody owes some amount of money or other to somebody or other, then no one is debt-free.
13. If some of us owe money to Isaac Newton, then there will come a time when we should pay him what we owe.
14. Everyone who has not paid any money to some scientist or other looks down on anyone who has.

Exercise 10-7

Translate the following into English, giving the predicate letters and individual constants their indicated meanings, making sure your translations are as close to colloquial English as you can make them.

a = "Art"
g = "God"
Dx = "x is disenfranchised"
Px = "x is a person"
Rx = "x is a redeeming feature"

Vx = "x votes"
Bxy = "x believes in y"
Hxy = "x has y"
Mxy = "x is the master of y"

1. $(x)(Px \supset Bxg)$
2. $(\exists x)(Px \cdot Bxg)$
3. $(\exists x)(Px \cdot \sim Bxg)$
4. $\sim (x)(Px \supset Bxg)$
5. $\sim (\exists x)(Px \cdot Bxg)$
6. $(x)[(Px \cdot \sim Vx) \supset Dx]$
7. $(x)[(Px \cdot Dx) \supset \sim Mxx]$
8. $\sim (x)[(Px \cdot \sim Vx) \supset Dx]$
9. $(x)[Px \supset (\exists y)(Ry \cdot Hxy)]$
10. $(\exists x)[Px \cdot (y)(Ry \supset \sim Hxy)]$
11. $(\exists x)[Rx \cdot (y)(Py \supset Hyx)]$
12. $(x)[Rx \supset (\exists y)(Py \cdot \sim Hyx)]$
13. $\sim (\exists x)(\exists y)[(Px \cdot Ry) \cdot Hxy]$
14. $(x)[Px \supset (y)(Ry \supset \sim Hxy)]$
15. $(x)\{Px \supset [(y)(Ry \supset Hxy) \supset Bxg]\}$
16. $\sim Va \supset \{(x)[(Px \cdot \sim Vx) \supset Dx] \supset Da\}$
17. $(x)\{(Px \cdot Vx) \supset (y)[(Py \cdot \sim Vy) \supset Mxy]\}$
18. $(x)\{(Px \cdot Vx) \supset (\exists y)[(Py \cdot \sim Vy) \cdot Mxy]\}$

6   Invalidity and Consistency in Relational Predicate Logic

We demonstrate invalidity and consistency in relational predicate logic using the same techniques we employed for monadic predicate logic. For invalidity we produce an interpretation that makes the premises all true and the conclusion false. For consistency we need only an interpretation that makes all the sentences true. As in monadic predicate logic we can provide a complete interpretation, or we can use the more mechanical method where we replace the quantified sentences with their expansions. Consider, for example, the following invalid argument:

1. $(x)(\exists y)$ Fxy p $/\therefore$ $(\exists x)(y)$ Fxy

We can show this argument to be invalid by providing an interpretation such as the following:

Domain: the integers
Fxy: x is greater than y

In this interpretation the premise says that every integer is greater than some integer, which is true, whereas the conclusion makes the obviously false assertion that some integer is greater than all integers.

We can also show this argument to be invalid by producing an expansion of the premise and conclusion, assigning truth values so as to make the premise true and the conclusion false, as follows (with a different interpretation of *Fxy*):

$$\begin{array}{l}
1. \quad (Faa \lor Fab) \cdot (Fba \lor Fbb) \\
\quad\quad \mathbf{F\ T\ T\ T\ \ F\ T\ T} \\
/\therefore \quad (Faa \cdot Fab) \lor (Fba \cdot Fbb) \\
\quad\quad \mathbf{F\ F\ T\ F\ \ F\ F\ T}
\end{array}$$

Exercise 10-8

Show that the following arguments are invalid.

(1) 1. $(\exists x)(y)Fxy$ p /∴ $(x)(y)Fyx$

(2) 1. $(x)(\exists y)(Fxy)$ p /∴ $(\exists x)(y)(Fxy)$

(3) 1. $(\exists x)(\exists y)Fxy$ p
      2. $(\exists x)(\exists y)Gxy$ p /∴ $(\exists x)(\exists y)(Fxy \cdot Gxy)$

(4) 1. $(x)(\exists y)(Fx \supset Gxy)$ p /∴ $(\exists x)(y)(Fx \supset Gxy)$

(5) 1. $(\exists x)(y)\ Fxy$ p /∴ Faa

(6) 1. $(x)(\exists y)(Fxy \supset Gxy)$ p
      2. $(x)(\exists y)(Gxy \supset Hxy)$ p /∴ $(x)(\exists y)(Fxy \supset Hxy)$

(7) 1. $(x)(y)(\exists z)Fxyz$ p /∴ $(\exists x)(y)(z)Fxyz$

(8) 1. $(\exists x)(y)(z)Fxyz$ p /∴ $(x)(y)(\exists z)Fxyz$

7   *Relational Predicate Logic Proofs*

The rules for predicate logic proofs introduced in Chapter Nine were devised to handle the complexities of relational predicate logic as well. If you have a premise that has multiple quantifiers, simply take them off one at a time left to right. Remember, you can use **UI** or **EI** only if the sentence begins with a quantifier that governs the entire sentence. If you need to deduce a conclusion that begins with multiple quantifiers, put them back on in reverse order. Again, when you add a quantifier with **EG** or **UG,** the scope of that quantifier must include the entire sentence. The following proof illustrates the process:

1. $(x)(y)Lxy$ p
2. $(\exists x)(y)(Lxy \supset Gxy)$ p /∴ $(\exists x)(y)Gxy$
3. $(y)(Lxy \supset Gxy)$ 2 **EI** (Notice we use **EI** first)

4. $(y)Lxy$	1 **UI**
5. $Lxy \supset Gxy$	3 **UI**
6. Lxy	4 **UI**
7. Gxy	5,6 **MP**
8. $(y)Gxy$	7 **UG** (OK because y is not free in line 3)
9. $(\exists x)(y)Gxy$	8 **EG**

In Chapter Nine we applied **UI** or **EI** to lines that had only one quantifier and only one type of variable—for example,

1. $(x)(Fx \supset Gx)$	p
2. $Fx \supset Gx$	1 **UI**

Relational predicate logic is more complex, because here we encounter lines with more than one quantifier and more than one type of variable.

Examples

Here are some valid applications of **UI** and **EI**.

1. $(\exists x)(y)(Fx \cdot Fxy)$	p
2. $(y)(Fx \cdot Fxy)$	1 **EI**
3. $(Fx \cdot Fxy)$	2 **UI**
.	
.	
.	

1. $(x)(\exists y)[(Fx \cdot Gy) \supset Hxy]$	p
2. $(\exists y)[(Fw \cdot Gy) \supset Hwy]$	1 **UI**
3. $(Fw \cdot Gz) \supset Hwz$	2 **EI**
.	
.	
.	

The presence of more than one quantifier and more than one type of variable in the same line presents some new dangers. For example, consider the following proof:

1. $(\exists x)(\exists y)Hxy$	p
2. $(\exists y)Hyy$	1 **EI** (Invalid)

The problem with this proof is that no free (*quasi*) variable is introduced in the **EI** step. Remember, when we use **EI** we drop an existential quantifier and replace the variables that were bound by that quantifier with *free* variables. In the invalid **EI** step just noted, there are no free variables—instead the new variable is still bound by the remaining quantifier. To avoid invalid proofs we must not allow such steps. (That the preceding proof is invalid can be seen if we let $Hxy = x$ is heavier than y, because "Something is heavier than something" is true and "Something is heavier than itself" is false.)

The only rule for **UI** and the third rule for **EI** forbid such inferences. Here is **UI**:

Rule UI: $(u) (\ldots u \ldots) / \therefore (\ldots w \ldots)$ *Provided:*

                                                               1. $(\ldots w \ldots)$ results from replacing each occurrence of u free in $(\ldots u \ldots)$ with a w that is free in $(\ldots w \ldots)$ (making no other changes).

And here is the third restriction on **EI:**

Rule EI: $(\exists u) (\ldots u \ldots) / \therefore (\ldots w \ldots)$ *Provided:*

                                                               3. $(\ldots w \ldots)$ results from replacing each occurrence of u free in $(\ldots w \ldots)$ with a w that is free in $(\ldots w \ldots)$ (making no other changes).

In less formal terms, when you remove a quantifier you must replace *all* the variables that were bound by that quantifier with only one kind of *free* variable (or, in the case of **UI,** you may also replace the variables with constants).

It may help to picture the process of removing a quantifier like this: We begin with the original bound formula—for example,

     1. $(x)(\exists y)[(Fx \cdot Gy) \supset Lxy]$ p

We then remove the leftmost quantifier and all the variables that were bound by that quantifier.

         $(\exists y)[(F\_\_ \cdot Gy) \supset L\_\_y]$ (The blanks indicate the spots that were occupied by the variables.)

Finally, we fill in the blanks with a free variable (or with **UI** we can use a constant):

     2. $(\exists y)[(Fw \cdot Gy) \supset Lwy]$ 1 UI
     3. $(\exists y)[(Fa \cdot Gy) \supset Lay]$ 1 UI

We can use any kind of free variable we like. So all the following can be validly derived from our original sentence:

     3. $(\exists y)[(Fu \cdot Gy) \supset Luy]$ 1 UI
     4. $(\exists y)[(Fx \cdot Gy) \supset Lxy]$ 1 UI
     5. $(\exists y)[(Fz \cdot Gy) \supset Lzy]$ 1 UI

We cannot fill in the blanks with two *different* kinds of variables, as in

     6. $(\exists y)[(Fw \cdot Gy) \supset Lxy]$ 1 UI (Invalid)

And the new variables must all be *free*—so in this case we cannot fill in the blanks with the variable y, as in

     7. $(\exists y)[(Fy \cdot Gy) \supset Lyy]$ 1 UI (Invalid)

Similar problems can arise when adding on quantifiers. For example, we cannot permit the following inference

.
.
.

4. $(x)Fxy$

5. $(\exists x)(x)Fxx$ 4 **EG** (Invalid)

.
.
.

because here we would be replacing a free variable (y) with a variable (the second x) that is bound *twice*.

Our rules for adding quantifiers have restrictions that are carefully designed to prevent such inferences. The fourth restriction on **UG** reads as follows:

> **Rule UG:** $(\ldots u \ldots) / \therefore (\,w\,)(\ldots w \ldots)$ *Provided:*
>
> 4. $(\ldots w \ldots)$ results from replacing each occurrence of u free in $(\ldots u \ldots)$ with a w that is free in $(\ldots w \ldots)$ (making no other changes) and there are no additional occurrences of w already contained in $(\ldots w \ldots)$.

Less formally, we use **UG** to replace all the occurrences of a particular kind of free variable with variables that are bound by the newly introduced universal quantifier.

Again, it may help to visualize this process graphically. We begin with a line that contains one or more free variables, such as

1. $(\exists y)[(Fw \cdot Gy) \supset Lwy]$ p

We then erase all of the free variables

$(\exists y)[(F\_\_ \cdot Gy) \supset L\_\_y]$

and we fill in these blanks with a new variable that is bound only by the universal quantifier we add to the front of the line

2. $(x)(\exists y)[(Fx \cdot Gy) \supset Lxy]$ 1 **UG**

We cannot bind just *some* occurrences of the original free variable—so, in this case, we cannot infer

3. $(x)(\exists y)[(Fw \cdot Gy) \supset Lxy]$ 1 **UG** (Invalid)

We cannot fill in the blanks with two *different* kinds of variables, as in

4. $(w)(\exists y)[(Fw \cdot Gy) \supset Lxy]$ 1 **UG** (Invalid)

And the variable we use to fill in the blanks must not occur *elsewhere* in the line. So in our case we cannot fill in the blanks using the variable y, as follows:

5. $(y)(\exists y)[(Fy \cdot Gy) \supset Lyy]$ 1 **UG** (Invalid)

This inference is doubly problematic. First, the new variable is bound twice—by the new universal quantifier and the old existential quantifier. Second, not only is our new variable bound by the old quantifier, but the variable that was formally bound by this quantifier gets bound again by the new quantifier. The quantifier we add must not bind any other variables besides those we've used to fill in the blanks. Remember, when filling in the blanks, you must use some other variable than those that remain in the proof. If our line is

1. $(Fz \cdot Gy) \supset (y)(Lyx \supset Rwz)$ p

and we want replace the free z with a bound variable, we cannot use y, x, *or* w because these variables are used elsewhere in the line. So from this line we can derive

2. $(z)[(Fz \cdot Gy) \supset (y)(Lyx \supset Rwz)]$ 1 **UG**

and

3. $(u)[(Fu \cdot Gy) \supset (y)Lyx \supset Rwu]$ 1 **UG**

but *not*

4. $(y)[(Fy \cdot Gy) \supset (y)Lyx \supset Rwy]$ 1 **UG** (Invalid)

or

5. $(x)[(Fx \cdot Gy) \supset (y)Lyx \supset Rwx]$ 1 **UG** (Invalid)

or

6. $(w)[(Fw \cdot Gy) \supset (y)Lyx \supset Rww]$ 1 **UG** (Invalid)

Now let's look at the only restriction on **EG**:

> **Rule EG:** $(\ldots u \ldots) / \therefore (\exists w)(\ldots w \ldots)$ *Provided:*
>
> 1. $(\ldots w \ldots)$ results from replacing **at least one** occurrence of u free in $(\ldots u \ldots)$ with a w that is free in $(\ldots w \ldots)$ (making no other changes) and there are no additional occurrences of w already contained in $(\ldots w \ldots)$.

The boldface type indicates the crucial difference between **EG** and **UG**. With **EG** you are permitted to replace *some but not all* variables or constants of a particular kind with a bound variable.

To illustrate, suppose we wish to apply **EG** to the following line:

1. *Lhh*   p

Not only can we infer

2. $(\exists x)Lxx$ 1 **EG**

but we can also infer

3. $(\exists x)Lxh$ 1 **EG**

or

4. $(\exists x)Lhx$ 1 **EG**

The reason for this exception is to permit obviously valid inferences to existentially quantified sentences. From "Henry loves himself" we can infer "Someone loves Henry" and "Henry loves someone" in addition to "Someone loves someone."

Other than this exception, applying **EG** is like applying **UG.** We take one or more occurrences of a free variable or constant, erase it, and fill in the blanks with a bound variable. We fill in the blanks with only one kind of variable, and that variable must not occur elsewhere in the line.

Examples

The following proofs contain examples of both valid and invalid uses of the four quantifier rules.

(1) 1. $(\exists x)(\exists y)(Fx \supset Gy)$ p

  2. $(\exists y)(Fx \supset Gy)$ 1 **EI**

  3. $Fx \supset Gy$ 2 **EI**

  4. $Fx \supset Gx$ 2 **EI** (Invalid, because x occurs free previously in the proof, namely on line 2)

  5. $(\exists x)Fx \supset Gy$ 3 **EG** (Invalid, because $(\exists x)$ does not quantify the whole of line 3)

  6. $(\exists x)(Fx \supset Gy)$ 3 **EG**

  7. $(z)(\exists x)(Fx \supset Gz)$ 6 **UG** (Invalid, because y is free in a line obtained by **EI**)

(2) 1. $(\exists x)(y)[Fxy \supset (\exists z)(Gxz \supset Hy)]$ p

  2. $(y)[Fxy \supset (\exists z)(Gxz \supset Hy)]$ 1 **EI**

  3. $(y)[Fzy \supset (\exists z)(Gzz \supset Hy)]$ 1 **EI** (Invalid, because every x free in $(y)[Fxy \supset (\exists z)(Gxz \supset Hy)]$ is not replaced by a z not already bound.)

  4. $Fxx \supset (\exists z)(Gxz \supset Hx)$ 2 **UI**

  5. $Fxx \supset (Gxz \supset Hx)$ 4 **EI** (Invalid, because $(\exists z)$ does not quantify the whole of line 4)

  → 6. Fxx **AP** /∴ $(\exists z)(\exists y)(Gyz \supset Hy)$

  7. $(\exists z)(Gxz \supset Hx)$ 4,6 **MP**

  8. $Gxu \supset Hx$ 7 **EI**

  9. $(\exists y)(Gyu \supset Hx)$ 8 **EG** (Valid)

  10. $(\exists z)(\exists y)(Gyz \supset Hz)$ 9 **EG** (Invalid, because to each z free in $(\exists y)(Gyz \supset Hz)$ there does not correspond an x free in $(\exists y)(Gyu \supset Hx)$)

  11. $(\exists y)(Gyu \supset Hy)$ 8 **EG**

  12. $(\exists z)(\exists y)(Gyz \supset Hy)$ 11 **EG**

  13. $Fxx \supset (\exists z)(\exists y)(Gyz \supset Hy)$ 6–12 **CP**

  14. $(x)[Fxx \supset (\exists z)(\exists y)(Gyz \supset Hy)]$ 13 **UG** (Invalid, because x was introduced into the proof free by **EI**)

  15. $(\exists x)[Fxx \supset (\exists z)(\exists y)(Gyz \supset Hy)]$ 13 **EG**

Exercise 10-9

Indicate which (if any) of the inferences in the following proofs are invalid, and state why they are invalid.

(1) 1. $(\exists x)(y)Fxy$ p
    2. $(y)Fxy$ 1 EI
    3. Fxx 2 UI
    4. $(\exists y)Fyy$ 3 EG
    5. $(x)(\exists y)Fyx$ 4 UG

(2) 1. $(\exists x)Fx$ p
    2. $(\exists x)Gx$ p
    3. Fy 1 EI
    4. Gy 2 EI
    5. $Fy \cdot Gy$ 3,4 Conj
    6. $(\exists y)(Fy \cdot Gx)$ 5 EG
    7. $(\exists z)(\exists y)(Fy \cdot Gz)$ 6 EG

(3) 1. $(x)(\exists y)(Fx \supset Gy)$ p
    2. $(\exists y)(Fx \supset Gy)$ 1 UI
    3. $Fx \supset Gy$ 2 EI
    4. $(x)(Fx \supset Gy)$ 3 UG
    5. $(\exists y)(x)(Fx \supset Gy)$ 4 EG

(4) 1. $(x)(\exists y)(Fx \supset Gy)$ p
  → 2. Fx AP /∴ $(\exists w)[(Fw \supset Gw) \cdot Gy]$
    3. $(\exists y)(Fy \supset Gy)$ 1 UI
    4. $Fy \supset Gy$ 3 EI
    5. Gy 2,4 MP
    6. $(\exists w)(Fw \supset Gy)$ 4 EG
    7. $Fw \supset Gy$ 6 EI
    8. $(\exists w)(Fw \supset Gw)$ 7 EG
    9. $(\exists w)[(Fw \supset Gw) \cdot Gy]$ 5,8 Conj
   10. $Fx \supset (\exists w)[(Fw \supset Gw) \cdot Gy]$ 2–9 CP
   11. $(x)\{Fx \supset (\exists w)[(Fw \supset Gw) \cdot Gy]\}$ 10 UG

(5) 1. $(x)(y)[(z)Fzx \cdot (Gy \cdot Hd)]$ p
    2. $(y)[(z)Fza \supset (Gy \cdot Hd)]$ 1 UI
    3. $(z)Fza \supset (Ga \cdot Hd)$ 2 UI
    4. $Fba \supset (Ga \cdot Hd)$ 3 UI
    5. $(\exists y)[Fby \supset (Gy \cdot Hd)]$ 4 EG
  → 6. Fby AP /∴ $(x)Gx$
    7. $Gy \cdot Hd$ 5,6 MP
    8. Hd 7 Simp
    9. $(\exists x)Hx$ 8 EG
   10. Gy 7 Simp
   11. $(x)Gx$ 10 UG
   12. $Fby \supset (x)Gx$ 6–11 CP
   13. $(y)Fby \supset (x)Gx$ 12 UG

(6)   1. $(x)[(y)Fxy \supset Gx]$ p
      2. $(y)Fay \supset Ga$ 1 UI
      3. $Fay \supset Ga$ 2 UI
   → 4. $\sim Ga$ AP $/\therefore (x) \sim Fax$
      5. $\sim Fay$ 3,4 MT
      6. $(x) \sim Fax$ 5 UG
      7. $\sim Ga \supset (x) \sim Fax$ 4–6 CP
      8. $(\exists y) \sim Gy \supset (x) \sim Fyx$ 7 EG

8   *Strategy for Relational Predicate Logic Proofs*

If a premise contains more than one quantifier, you may have no choice but to use **EI** after you have already used **UI**. Still, you should usually remove the existential quantifier as soon as possible, as illustrated in the following proof:

1. $(x)(y)(Fx \supset Gxy)$ p
2. $(x)(\exists y) \sim Gxy$ p
3. $(\exists y) \sim Gxy$ 2 UI
4. $\sim Gxy$ 3 **EI** (Valid, because in an earlier line, y is not free)
5. $(y)(Fx \supset Gxy)$ 1 UI
6. $Fx \supset Gxy$ 5 UI
7. $\sim Fx$ 4,6 **MT**
8. $(\exists x) \sim Fx$ 7 **EG**

Sometimes it helps when removing quantifiers to introduce entirely new variables, as in the following proof:

1. $(\exists x)(y)Fxy$ p
2. $(y)(x)(Fyx \supset Gxy)$ p
3. $(y)Fwy$ 1 **EI**
4. Fwz 3 UI
5. $(x)(Fwx \supset Gxw)$ 2 UI
6. $Fwz \supset Gzw$ 5 UI
7. Gzw 4,6 **MT**
8. $(\exists x)Gzx$ 7 **EG**
9. $(y)(\exists x)Gyx$ 8 UG

Suppose we had used x and y when we removed the quantifiers from line 1, as follows:

1. $(\exists x)(y)Fxy$ p
2. $(y)(x)(Fyx \supset Gxy)$ p
3. $(y)Fxy$ 1 **EI**
4. Fxy 3 UI

The problem is that now we cannot drop the first universal quantifier from line 2 and substitute an x.

5. $(x)(Fxx \supset Gxx)$ 2 UI (Invalid, the new variable, x, is not free)

Introducing new variables avoids this problem entirely.

The last point of strategy is very important. There are some proofs that can be solved only by using **IP.** Consider the following:

1. $(x)(\exists y)(Fx \cdot Gy)$ p $/\therefore$ $(x)Fx$

If we proceed directly, we will have a problem at the end of the proof when we want to add the universal quantifier on using **UG.**

2. $(\exists y)(Fx \cdot Gy)$ 1 **UI**
3. $Fx \cdot Gy$ 2 **EI**
4. Fx 3 **Simp**
5. $(x)Fx$ 4 **UG** (Invalid, x is free in an **EI** line)

Note that our rules do not permit line 5—even though x was not made free by the **EI** step. If x if free in an **EI** line, no matter how it became free, we cannot use **UG** to replace the x with a bound variable. The way around this difficulty is to use **IP.**

1. $(x)(\exists y)(Fx \cdot Gy)$ p $/\therefore$ $(x)Fx$
→ 2. $\sim (x)Fx$ **AP** $/\therefore$ $(x)Fx$
3. $(\exists x) \sim Fx$ 2 **QN**
4. $\sim Fx$ 3 **EI**
5. $(\exists y)(Fx \cdot Gy)$ 1 **UI**
6. $Fx \cdot Gy$ 5 **EI**
7. Fx 6 **Simp**
8. $Fx \cdot \sim Fx$ 4,7 **Conj**
9. $(x)Fx$ 2-8 **IP**

Using this strategy lets us dispense with having to use **UG.** Thus, the free x in the **EI** line presents no difficulty.

Exercise 10-10

Prove the following arguments valid.

(1) 1. $\sim Oa$ p
     2. $(x)(y)[(Mx \vee Py) \supset (Oa \vee Ob)]$ p $/\therefore$ $Ma \supset Ob$

(2) 1. $(x)(y)(Fxy \cdot Fya)$ p $/\therefore$ Faa

(3) 1. $(x)[(Ax \cdot Bx) \supset (\exists y) Cy]$ p
     2. $(\exists y)(Ay \cdot By)$ p $/\therefore$ $(\exists x)Cx$

(4) 1. $(x)[Fx \vee (\exists y) Gy]$ p
     2. $(\exists x) \sim Fx$ p $/\therefore$ $(\exists x)Gx$

(5) 1. $(x)(y)(Mxa \supset Oay)$ p $/\therefore$ $(y)(Mya \supset Oay)$

(6) 1. $(\exists x)(y)(Fxy \supset Gyx)$ p $/\therefore$ $(x)(\exists y)(Fyx \supset Gxy)$

(7) 1. $(\exists x)(y)(z) Azyx$ p $/\therefore$ $(x)(y)(\exists z)Axyz$

(8) 1. $(\exists x)(y) \sim Fxy$ p $/\therefore$ $\sim (x)Fxa$

(9) 1. $\sim (y)(\exists x) \sim (Bxy \cdot Byx)$ p $/\therefore$ $(\exists x)Bxx$

(10) 1. $(\exists x)(y)(\sim Axy \supset Ayx)$ p $/\therefore \sim (x)(y) \sim Axy$

(11) 1. $(x)(y) \sim Gxy$ p
    2. $(\exists y)(x)(Fx \supset Gyx)$ p $/\therefore \sim (x)Fx$

(12) 1. $(\exists x)(y)(Cx \supset \sim Byx)$ p
    2. $\sim (\exists y)(\exists x) \sim Bxy$ p $/\therefore \sim (y)Cy$

(13) 1. $(\exists x)(y) Axy$ p
    2. $(x)(\exists y)(Axy \supset \sim Bxx)$ p $/\therefore \sim (y)Byy$

Exercise 10-11

Prove valid (some of these are rather difficult).

(1) 1. $(\exists x)[Ax \cdot (y)(Qy \supset Lxy)]$ p
    2. $(x)[Ax \supset (y)(Ey \supset \sim Lxy)]$ p $/\therefore (x)(Qx \supset \sim Ex)$

(2) 1. $(\exists x)[Fx \cdot (y)(Gy \supset Hxy)]$ p $/\therefore (\exists x)[Fx \cdot (Ga \supset Hxa)]$

(3) 1. $(x)(\exists y)(\sim Fx \vee Gy)$ p $/\therefore (x)Fx \supset (\exists y)Gy$

(4) 1. $(x)(Ax \supset Hx)$ p
    2. $(\exists x)Ax \supset \sim (\exists y)Gy$ p $/\therefore (x)[(\exists y)Ay \supset \sim Gx]$

(5) 1. $(\exists x)Hx \supset (\exists y)Ky$ p
    2. $(\exists x)[Hx \cdot (y)(Ky \supset Lxy)]$ p $/\therefore (\exists x)(\exists y)Lxy$

(6) 1. $(x)(\exists y)Fxy \supset (x)(\exists y)Gxy$ p
    2. $(\exists x)(y) \sim Gxy$ p $/\therefore (\exists x)(y) \sim Fxy$

(7) 1. $(x)[(Fx \vee Gx) \supset (Hx \cdot Kx)]$ p
    2. $(x)\{(Hx \vee Lx) \supset [(Hx \cdot Nx) \supset Px]\}$ p $/\therefore (x)[Fx \supset (Nx \supset Px)]$

(8) 1. $(x)[Ax \supset (\exists y)(Ay \cdot Bxy)]$ p
    2. $(\exists x)\{Ax \cdot (y)[(Ay \cdot Bxy) \supset Cxy]\}$ p $/\therefore (\exists x)(\exists y)[(Ax \cdot Ay) \supset Cxy]$

(9) 1. $\sim (\exists x)(Axa \cdot \sim Bxb)$ p
    2. $\sim (\exists x)(Cxc \cdot Cbx)$ p
    3. $(x)(Bex \supset Cxf)$ p $/\therefore \sim (Aea \cdot Cfc)$

(10) 1. $(x)[Ax \supset (Bx \supset \sim Cx)]$ p
    2. $\sim (\exists x)(Cx \cdot Dx) \supset (x)(Dx \supset Ex)$ p $/\therefore \sim (\exists x)[Dx \cdot (\sim Ax \vee \sim Bx)] \supset$
                                                    $(x)(Dx \supset Ex)$

(11) 1. $(x)(Ex \vee Gx)$ p
    2. $(x)(y)[(\sim Lx \vee Mx) \supset Nyx]$ p $/\therefore (x)[\sim (\exists y)(Gy \vee Lx) \supset$
                                                   $(\exists z)(Ez \cdot Nzx)]$

(12) 1. $(x)[(\exists y)(Ay \cdot Bxy) \supset Cx]$ p
    2. $(\exists y)\{Dy \cdot (\exists x)[(Ex \cdot Fx) \cdot Byx]\}$ p
    3. $(x)(Fx \supset Ax)$ p $/\therefore (\exists x)(Cx \cdot Dx)$

(13) 1. $(x)(Ax \supset Bx)$ p /∴ $(x)[(\exists y)(Ay \cdot Cxy) \supset$
                                    $(\exists z)(Bz \cdot Cxz)]$

(14) 1. $(\exists x)(\exists y)(Axy \lor Bxy) \supset (\exists z)Cz$ p
     2. $(x)(y)(Cx \supset \sim Cy)$ p /∴ $(x)(y) \sim Axy$

(15) 1. $(\exists x)Fx \supset (x)[Px \supset (\exists y)Qxy]$ p
     2. $(x)(y)(Qxy \supset Gx)$ p /∴ $(x)[(Fx \cdot Px) \supset (\exists y)Gy]$

9 *Theorems and Inconsistency in Predicate Logic*

As explained in Chapter Five, the conclusion of a valid deduction in which there are no given premises is said to be a **theorem of logic.** All the tautologies of sentential logic are theorems of logic because they can be proved without using premises.

But the tautologies of sentential logic also can be proved by truth table analysis. In this respect, they differ from most theorems of predicate logic, for we can prove by truth table analysis only those theorems of predicate logic that are substitution instances of tautologous sentence forms of sentential logic. The sentence $(x)Fx \lor \sim (x)Fx$ is an example, because it is a substitution instance of the tautology $p \lor \sim p$ and a theorem of predicate logic provable by truth table analysis. But most theorems of predicate logic must be proved by the standard predicate logic proof method. Theorems are sometimes referred to as **logical truths,** or **truths of logic,** because they are truths provable without the aid of contingent information. They are, so to speak, truths knowable by the use of logic alone.

Examples

As in sentential logic, since there are no premises to prove that an expression is a theorem, we must use either **CP** or **IP.** Here is a fairly simple but otherwise typical proof of a theorem of predicate logic using **CP:**

To prove: $(x)Fx \supset (\exists x)Fx$

→ 1. $(x)Fx$	**AP** /∴ $(\exists x)Fx$
2. Fx	1 UI
3. $(\exists x)Fx$	2 EG
4. $(x)Fx \supset (\exists x)Fx$	1–3 **CP**

In this proof the assumed premise is the antecedent of the theorem to be proved (the conclusion of the proof). However, sometimes it is easier to assume the negation of the consequent of the desired conclusion, derive the negation of the antecedent, and then obtain the conclusion by Contraposition. This strategy is illustrated by the following proof:

To prove: $[(\exists x)Fx \lor (\exists x)Gx] \supset (\exists x)(Fx \lor Gx)$

→1.	~ $(\exists x)(Fx \lor Gx)$	**AP** /∴ ~ $[(\exists x)Fx \lor (\exists x)Gx]$
2.	$(x) \sim (Fx \lor Gx)$	1 **QN**
3.	~ $(Fx \lor Gx)$	2 **UI**
4.	~ $Fx \cdot \sim Gx$	3 **DeM**
5.	~ Fx	4 **Simp**
6.	$(x) \sim Fx$	5 **UG**
7.	~ Gx	4 **Simp**
8.	$(x) \sim Gx$	7 **UG**
9.	~ $(\exists x)Fx$	6 **QN**
10.	~ $(\exists x)Gx$	8 **QN**
11.	~ $(\exists x)Fx \cdot \sim (\exists x)Gx$	9,10 **Conj**
12.	~ $[(\exists x)Fx \lor (\exists x)Gx]$	11 **DeM**
13.	~ $(\exists x)(Fx \lor Gx) \supset \sim [(\exists x)Fx \lor (\exists x)Gx]$	1–12 **CP**
14.	$[(\exists x)Fx \lor (\exists x)Gx] \supset (\exists x)(Fx \lor Gx)$	13 **Contra**

Many theorems of logic are equivalences. In general, the easiest way to prove a theorem of logic that is an equivalence is to prove the two conditionals that together imply the equivalence, and then join them together by Conjunction.

To prove: $(\exists x)(P \supset Fx) \equiv [P \supset (\exists x)Fx]$

We assume that P is any *wff* that does not contain free variables or any bound occurrences of x.

→1.	$(\exists x)(P \supset Fx)$	**AP** /∴ $[P \supset (\exists x)Fx]$
→2.	P	**AP** /∴ $(\exists x)Fx)$
3.	$P \supset Fx$	1 **EI**
4.	Fx	2,3 **MP**
5.	$(\exists x)Fx$	4 **EG**
6.	$[P \supset (\exists x)Fx]$	2–5 **CP**
7.	$(\exists x)(P \supset Fx) \supset [P \supset (\exists x)Fx]$	1,6 **CP**
→8.	$P \supset (\exists x)Fx$	**AP** /∴ $(\exists x)(P \supset Fx)$
→9.	P	**AP** /∴ Fx
10.	$(\exists x)Fx$	8,9 **MP**
11.	Fx	10 **EI**
12.	$P \supset Fx$	9–11 **CP**
13.	$(\exists x)(P \supset Fx)$	12 **EG**
14.	$[P \supset (\exists x)Fx] \supset (\exists x)(P \supset Fx)$	8,12–13 **CP**
15.	$7 \cdot 14$	7,14 **Conj**
16.	$(\exists x)(P \supset Fx) \equiv [P \supset (\exists x)Fx]$	15 **Equiv**

It is also possible to use a predicate logic proof to show that the premises of an argument are inconsistent. Just as we did in sentential logic, we simply deduce a contradiction from the premises. A **logical contradiction,** or **logical falsehood,** is a single statement that can be proved false without the aid of contingent information, that is, proved false by logic alone. As in sentential logic, to show that a statement is a logical falsehood, we deduce a contradiction from it. (Note that the negation of a logical falsehood is a logical truth, and vice versa.)

Example

The following argument is shown to have inconsistent premises:

1. $\sim (\exists x)Fx$ p
2. $\sim (x)(Fx \supset Gx)$ p
3. $(x) \sim Fx$ 1 QN
4. $(\exists x) \sim (Fx \supset Gx)$ 2 QN
5. $\sim (Fx \supset Gx)$ 4 EI
6. $\sim Fx$ 3 UI
7. $\sim (\sim Fx \vee Gx)$ 5 Imp
8. $\sim \sim Fx \cdot \sim Gx$ 7 DeM
9. $\sim \sim Fx$ 8 Simp
10. $\sim Fx \cdot \sim \sim Fx$ 6,9 **Conj**

Exercise 10-12

Prove that the following are theorems of logic.*

1. $(x)(y)Fxy \equiv (y)(x)Fxy$
2. $(x)(Gx \equiv Gx)$
3. $(\exists x)Gx \equiv (\exists y)Gy$
4. $(\exists x)(y)Fxy \supset (y)(\exists x)Fxy$ (but *not* vice versa)
5. $(x)(Fx \cdot Gx) \supset [(x)Fx \cdot (x)Gx]$
6. $[(x)Fx \vee (x)Gx] \supset (x)(Fx \vee Gx)$ (but *not* vice versa)
7. $(x)(Fx \supset Gx) \supset [(\exists x)Fx \supset (\exists x)Gx]$ (but *not* vice versa)
8. $(\exists x)(Fx \cdot Gx) \supset [(\exists x)Fx \cdot (\exists x)Gx]$ (but *not* vice versa)
9. $(\exists x)(Fx \vee Gx) \supset [(\exists x)Fx \vee (\exists x)Gx]$

In the following theorems, the letter P denotes any sentence that does not contain a free occurrence of the variable x. Thus, in number 10, P might be Fa, Fy, $(y)(Fy \supset Gy)$, and so on.

10. $[(x)Fx \cdot P] \equiv (x)(Fx \cdot P)$
11. $(x)(Fx \vee P) \equiv [(x)Fx \vee P]$

---

*These theorems are extremely important. First, each one is a substitution instance of what might be called a *theorem schema*, and the proofs of the theorem schemas exactly parallel the proofs of their substitution instances. For example, the first theorem, $(x)(y)Fxy \equiv (y)(x)Fxy$, is a substitution instance of the general schema $(u)(w)(\ldots u \ldots w \ldots) \equiv (w)(u)(\ldots u \ldots w \ldots)$, and the proof of the schema exactly parallels the proof of its substitution instance. And second, these theorem schemas are very important in deriving what are known as *normal forms of formulas* (not discussed in this text, but useful when doing higher-level work in logic). In addition, it's useful to notice which of these are only one-way, or implicational, theorems so that we don't waste time trying to prove substitution instances of their reversals.

12. $(x)(P \supset Fx) \equiv [P \supset (x)Fx]$
13. $(x)(Fx \supset P) \equiv [(\exists x)Fx \supset P]$
14. $(\exists x)(P \cdot Fx) \equiv [P \cdot (\exists x)Fx]$
15. $(\exists x)(P \lor Fx) \equiv [P \lor (\exists x)Fx]$
16. $(\exists x)(Fx \supset P) \equiv [(x)Fx \supset P]$

10 *Predicate Logic Metatheory*

You will recall that, toward the end of our discussion of sentential logic proofs, we introduced some of the basic concepts of metatheory. The key idea here is the match between arguments that are semantically valid (that is, no interpretation on which the premises are true and the conclusion false) and those that are syntactically valid (that is, can be shown to be valid by means of a proof). There are two ways a system of proof rules could be deficient—if there are valid arguments that cannot be proven, the rules would be incomplete; if there are invalid arguments that can be proven, the rules would be unsound.

Obviously, it is crucial that our system of rules for predicate logic be both sound and complete. But that is not all we want. In addition, we want our rules to mirror ordinary inferences as much as possible. We want them, that is, to be a natural deduction system. Finally, an issue particularly important, given the complexities inherent in predicate logic: we want the rules to be as intuitive and as easy to learn as possible.

Although the formal metatheoretical proofs of completeness and soundness are beyond the scope of this book, we will explore this issue by looking at some alternatives and discussing the rationale behind constructing the rules as we have. First, we conclude this chapter with a look at a way of simplifying our present system of rules. Chapter Eleven then systematically reviews the kinds of cases any system of predicate logic rules must address, and then briefly reviews an alternative approach to predicate logic rules.

11 *A Simpler Set of Quantifier Rules*

The quantifier rules **UI, EI, UG, EG,** and **QN** (together with the eighteen valid argument forms plus **CP** and **IP**) form a complete set of rules for quantifier logic. Sets of this kind have become standard because they allow inferences that fairly closely resemble a great many of those made in everyday life and, in particular, in certain technical fields (such as mathematics), and also because they permit relatively short proofs.

But there are simpler sets of quantifier rules. We now present a very simple set indeed, almost as simple as any set can be and still be complete. However, we pay a price for this simplicity of rules, namely, complexity of proofs—as well as an inability to parallel certain standard ways of reasoning.

First, let's adopt two of the four **QN** rules. Where *u* is any individual variable,

1. $(u) \sim (\ldots u \ldots) :: \sim (\exists u)(\ldots u \ldots)$
2. $(\exists u) \sim (\ldots u \ldots) :: \sim (u)(\ldots u \ldots)$

And now, let's restate and adopt rules **UI** and **EI:**

Rule UI: $(u) (\ldots u \ldots) / \therefore (\ldots w \ldots)$ *Provided:*

1. $\ldots w \ldots$ results from replacing each occurrence of *u* free in $\ldots u \ldots$ with a *w* that is free in $\ldots w \ldots$ (making no other changes).

Rule EI: $(\exists u) (\ldots u \ldots) / \therefore (\ldots w \ldots)$ *Provided:*

1. *w* is not a constant.
2. *w* does not occur free previously in the proof.
3. $\ldots w \ldots$ results from replacing each occurrence of *u* free in $\ldots u \ldots$ with a *w* that is free in $\ldots w \ldots$ (making no other changes).

It should be obvious from this formulation that every inference permitted by the simpler rules also is permitted by the standard rules, although the reverse is not true. So the alternative rules permit a subset of the inferences permitted by the standard rules. It follows that the standard rules contain features that are logically superfluous, although they are certainly not superfluous in other ways (chiefly in permitting proofs that more faithfully mirror everyday reasoning and the informal reasoning encountered in mathematics and logic).

The key to use of the simpler quantifier rules is that in most cases we must use **IP.*** Here is a simple example:

1. $(x)(Fx \supset Gx)$	p
2. $(\exists x)Fx$	p $/ \therefore (\exists x)Gx$
$\rightarrow$3. $\sim (\exists x)Gx$	**AP** $/ \therefore (\exists x)Gx$
4. $(x) \sim Gx$	3 **QN**
5. Fx	2 **EI**
6. $Fx \supset Gx$	1 **UI**
7. Gx	5,6 **MP**
8. $\sim Gx$	4 **UI**
9. $Gx \cdot \sim Gx$	7,8 **Conj**
10. $(\exists x)Gx$	3–9 **IP**

---

*The reason is that we have no **UG** or **EG** at our disposal, and hence no way of deriving a conclusion that is either a Universal or an Existential Generalization.

And here is a more complicated example:

1.	(∃y)(x)(Fx ⊃ Gy)	p /∴ (∃x)Fx ⊃ (∃x)Gx
→2.	~ [(∃x)Fx ⊃ (∃x)Gx]	AP /∴ (∃x)Fx ⊃ (∃x)Gx
3.	(x)(Fx ⊃ Gy)	1 EI
4.	~ [~ (∃x)Fx ∨ (∃x)Gx]	2 Impl
5.	~ ~ (∃x)Fx · ~ (∃x)Gx	4 DeM
6.	~ ~ (∃x)Fx	5 Simp
7.	(∃x)Fx	6 DN
8.	Fx	7 EI
9.	Fx ⊃ Gy	3 UI
10.	Gy	8,9 MP
11.	~ (∃x)Gx	5 Simp
12.	(x)~ Gx	11 QN
13.	~ Gy	12 UI
14.	Gy · ~ Gy	10,13 **Conj**
15.	(∃x)Fx ⊃ (∃x)Gx	2–14 **IP**

Exercise 10-13

Using the simpler set of quantifier rules, prove that each of the following is valid.

(1) 1. (∃x)(Fx · Gx) /∴ (∃x)Fx

(2) 1. ~ (∃x)Fx /∴ Fa ⊃ Ga

(3) 1. (x)(Hx ⊃ ~ Kx) /∴ (∃y) ~ (Hy · Ky)

(4) 1. (y)[Fy ∨ (∃x)Gx]
      2. (x) ~ Fx /∴ (∃x)Gx

(5) 1. (x)[(Rx · Ax) ⊃ Tx]
      2. Ab
      3. (x)Rx /∴ Tb · Rb

(6) 1. Ka
      2. (x)[Kx ⊃ (y)Hy] /∴ (x)Hx

(7) 1. (x)(Fx ⊃ Gx)
      2. (∃x) ~ Gx /∴ (∃x) ~ Fx

(8) 1. ~ (∃x)Ax /∴ (∃x)(Ax ⊃ Gx)

(9) 1. (x)(Mx ⊃ Sx)
      2. (x)(~ Bx ∨ Mx) /∴ (x)(~ Sx ⊃ ~ Bx)

(10) 1. (∃x)Rx
       2. (x)(~ Gx ⊃ ~ Rx)
       3. (∃x)Mx /∴ (∃x)Gx · (∃x)Mx

Exercise 10-14

Using the simpler set of quantifier rules, prove that each of the following is valid (the last two are rather difficult).

(1) 1. $(x)(y)(Fxy \supset Gx)$ p
     2. $(\exists x)(\exists y)Fxy$ p /∴ $(\exists x)Gx$

(2) 1. $(\exists y)(x)Fxy$ p /∴ $(x)(\exists y)Fxy$

(3) 1. $(\exists x)[Fx \cdot (y)Hxy]$ p /∴ $(\exists x)(Fx \cdot Hxa)$

(4) 1. $(x)[Fx \supset (\exists y)Gxy]$ p
     2. $(\exists x)Fx$ p /∴ $(\exists x)(\exists y)Gxy$

(5) 1. $(\exists x)[Ax \cdot (y)(By \supset Cxy)]$ p /∴ $(y)[By \supset (\exists x)(Ax \cdot Cxy)]$

(6) 1. $(\exists x)Ax \supset \sim (\exists y)Gy$ p /∴ $(x)[(\exists y)Ay \supset \sim Gx]$

(7) 1. $(\exists x)Fx \supset (\exists x)Gx$ p /∴ $(\exists y)(x)(Fx \supset Gy)$

Chapter Eleven

Rationale Behind the Precise Formulation of the Four Quantifier Rules

Although the general idea behind the rules for dropping and adding quantifiers is fairly simple (and intuitive), the reason why these rules are so complicated is, as should be expected, rather complicated. There are 18 kinds of cases that the four quantifier rules must handle correctly.

1 Cases Involving the Five Major Restrictions

The first case concerns uses of rule **EI** such as this one:

(1) 1. $(\exists x)Hx$ p
   2. *Ha*   1 **EI** (Invalid)

Although it follows from line 1 that some entity or other has the property *H*, it doesn't follow that whatever is named by the individual constant *a* is that entity. Knowing that somebody or other is happy doesn't justify belief that Abe Lincoln was happy. The moral of this example is that when **EI** is used to drop an existential quantifier, the variables thus freed cannot validly be replaced by individual constants. Instead, they must be replaced by individual quasivariables. This case is handled by restriction 1 on **EI.**

Now consider the proof

(2) 1. $(\exists x)Fx$ p
   2. $(\exists x)Gx$ p /∴ $(\exists x)(Fx \cdot Gx)$
   3. *Fx*   1 **EI**
   4. *Gx*   2 **EI** (Invalid)
   5. $Fx \cdot Gx$ 3,4 **Conj**
   6. $(\exists x)(Fx \cdot Gx)$ 5 **EG**

The trouble with line 4 is the use of the same free variable, *x*, that already had been used free (on line 3). This makes it possible to derive the unfortunate conclusion that there is some object that is *both,* say, red and square from the fact that something or other is red and the fact that something or other is square. The moral this time is that a variable intro-duced free into a proof by **EI** must not occur free previously in the proof. (Of course, we could have used some variable other than x on 4. For instance, we could have used the variable y to obtain Gy on that line, because y does not occur free previously in the proof.) This case is handled by restriction 2 on **EI**.

Now consider the use of **UG** in the following proof:

(3) 1. *Fa*   p
     2. *(x)Fx*   1 UG (Invalid)

That a particular item, say Adam, had a certain property, say of being foolhardy, hardly proves the universality of foolhardiness. The moral this time is that we cannot use **UG** on a constant. This is handled by restriction 1 on **UG**.

Next consider another invalid use of **UG**:

(4) 1. *(∃x)Fx*   p /∴ *(x)Fx*
     2. *Fy*   1 EI
     3. *(x)Fx*   2 UG (Invalid)

That there are foxes can't by itself justify the conclusion that everything is a fox (and a good thing it is too, for all of us nonfoxes). To eliminate this bad kind of passage from "some" to "all," *we must forbid use of* **UG** *on a variable introduced free into a proof by* **EI**. This is taken care of by restriction 2 on **UG**.

Now we have to consider a more difficult example:

(5) 1. *(x)(∃y)Lyx*   p /∴ *(∃y)(x)Lyx*
     2. *(∃y)Lyx*   1 UI
     3. *Lyx*   2 EI
     4. *(x)Lyx*   3 UG (Invalid)
     5. *(∃y)(x)Lyx*   4 EG

Suppose Lyx = "y loves x," and the universe of discourse has been restricted to persons only. Then premise 1 asserts that everybody is loved by somebody. But its conclusion, line 5, asserts that there is some person y who loves everybody. Clearly, even if line 1 is true, there may not be a universal lover! Line 1 is true if each person loves herself. Line 5 is not true under those conditions. Notice, by the way, that if there is only *one* person, if the premise is true, the con-clusion is also—but this is not necessarily so if there are two or more persons!

It is rather difficult to see what went wrong in this proof, and in particular what is wrong with the inference from line 3 to line 4. After all, the x free on 3, to which **UG** was applied, does not result from an application of **EI**, as in the previous invalid proof. Rather it results from an application of **UI** to line 1, so that we seem to be simply dropping and then adding the same universal quantifier. This seems as harmless as the similar process in the following proof:

     1. *(x)Fx*   p
     2. *Fx*   1 UI
     3. *(x)Fx*   2 UG

But the use of **UG** in proof (5) is not harmless by any means. The mere fact that x is free on line 3 of that proof, a line obtained by **EI**, is sufficient to make the application of **UG** to x invalid. It is as though (to use a metaphor) the "taint" of **EI** placed on the y variable in line 3 "rubbed off" the y variable onto the other variable, x, free on that line. The moral is that we cannot use **UG** on a variable free in a line obtained by **EI** (restriction 2) whether that variable became free by using **EI** or not. (Notice that by forbidding such applications of **UG** we eliminate not only the invalid use of **UG** in proof (5), but also the invalid use of **UG** in proof (4).)

This restriction on **UG** introduces a nonintuitive element into our discussion for the very first time, for taken in isolation it is neither intuitive nor counterintuitive. Its justification is that without it, or some similar restriction, we would be able to go from true premises to false conclusions, whereas with it we cannot do so. However, you might well wonder if this—or any other of our restrictions—*blocks* inferences that we wish to be able to make. This is a very difficult issue (although the simple answer is no) that we will discuss again later.

Next, consider the following proof:

(6)
1. Fy **AP** /∴ $(z)[Fz \supset (x)Fx]$
2. $(x)Fx$ 1 **UG** (Invalid)
3. $Fy \supset (x)Fx$ 1–2 **CP**
4. $(z)[Fz \supset (x)Fx]$ 3 **UG**

Suppose Fy = "y is friendly." Then the conclusion, which depends on no premises whatever, asserts that if anything is friendly, then everything is friendly, an obviously false statement. The moral is that within the scope of an assumed premise we cannot use **UG** on a variable free in that assumed premise. Restriction 3 on **UG** takes care of this case. This restriction rules out the use of **UG** on line 2 of the preceding proof, because it occurs within the scope of the assumed premise 1. But it does not rule out the valid use of **UG** that yields line 4, because 4 is outside the scope of that assumed premise.

To some extent, this restriction on **UG** may seem nonintuitive, just like the previous one. However, as explained in Chapter Nine, the point of this restriction on **UG** is to make sure that the variable bound in a **UG** step names an arbitrary individual. As our discussion of a premise such as Fy indicated, think of the free variable as in effect the result of **EI**. The bottom line is that without this restriction we could go from true premises to false conclusions.

Notice, however, that this restriction does not rule out all uses of **UG** within the scope of an assumed premise. It forbids only those uses where the Universal Generalization takes place on a variable free in the assumed premise itself. Thus the restriction does not rule out the use of **UG** in the following proof:

1. $(x)(Fx \supset Gx)$ p /∴ $(x)Fx \supset (x)Gx$
2. $(x)Fx$ **AP** /∴ $(x)Gx$
3. Fx 2 **UI**
4. $Fx \supset Gx$ 1 **UI**
5. Gx 3, 4 **MP**
6. $(x)Gx$ 5 **UG** (Valid)
7. $(x)Fx \supset (x)Gx$ 2–6 **CP**

2 *One-to-One Correspondence Matters*

One might naively characterize a particular application of **EI** or **UI** as a process in which a quantifier is dropped and all the variables thus freed are replaced by a particular variable.* Thus, in the following use of **EI**,

1. $(\exists x)(Fx \cdot Gx)$ p
2. $(Fy \cdot Gy)$ 1 **EI**

the quantifier $(\exists x)$ is dropped, and each x thus freed is replaced by a free y. (Of course we could just as well have replaced each x by itself.) The important point is that there is a *one-to-one correspondence* between the x's freed by dropping the $(\exists x)$ quantifier and the free y's that replaced them; that is, to each x freed by dropping the $(\exists x)$ quantifier in line 1, there corresponds a y free in line 2; and to each y free in line 2, there corresponds an x in line 1 that is freed by dropping the $(\exists x)$ quantifier.

The question naturally arises as to whether all valid uses of **UI, EI, UG,** and **EG** require one-to-one correspondences of this kind. Surprisingly, it turns out that there are two cases in which this one-to-one correspondence cannot be required, if our logic is to be complete.

The first case concerns **UI.** Consider the argument

(7)   1. $(\exists y)(x)Lyx$ p /∴ $(\exists x)Lxx$
     2. $(x)Lyx$ 1 **EI**
     3. Lyy 2 **UI** (Valid)
     4. $(\exists x)Lxx$ 3 **EG**

Suppose the domain of discourse is limited to human beings only, and suppose $Lyx = $ "y loves x." Then the premise of this argument asserts that there is someone who loves everyone, while its conclusion asserts that there is someone who loves himself. Now this premise may be true or it may be false. But if it is true, then surely the conclusion is true also, for if it is true that someone loves everyone, then it follows that that person loves himself. So we must have a way to infer from the premise of this argument to its conclusion, and the most intuitive way is to permit inferences such as the one on line 3. Notice that there is not a one-to-one correspondence between free y variables on line 3 and bound x variables on line 2. Since we must allow the step from line 2 to line 3, it follows that *we cannot require a one-to-one correspondence between* x *and* y *variables in the application of* **UI.**

The other case in which we cannot require a one-to-one correspondence concerns **EG.** Consider the argument:

(8)   1. $(x)Fxx$ p /∴ $(x)(\exists y)Fxy$
     2. Fxx 1 **UI**
     3. $(\exists y)Fxy$ 2 **EG** (Valid)
     4. $(x)(\exists y)Fxy$ 3 **UG**

---

*We sometimes refer to the variables thus freed as x variables and their replacements in the resulting formulas as y variables. An analogous x and y notiation is used in discussing **UG** and **EG**. Remember, these are all quasivariables.

Suppose Fxx = "x is identical with x." Then the premise of this argument asserts that everything is identical with itself, which is true, and its conclusion that, given any x, there is something (y) identical with x, is true also, since the y in question for any particular x is that x itself. Clearly, if 1 is true, and it is, then 4 must be true also. We must permit a step such as the one from 2 to 3 to enable us to draw the conclusion on line 4. So in general, *we cannot require a one-to-one correspondence between* x *and* y *variables in the application of* **EG**.

The eight possibilities we have just considered comprise a catalog of cases that might puzzle students, or concerning which they might incline toward error. Before going on to the more technical cases, let's summarize what the eight examples were designed to prove:

1. When **EI** is used to drop an existential quantifier, the variables thus freed cannot validly be replaced by individual constants.
2. A variable introduced free into a proof by **EI** must not occur free previously in the proof.
3. We cannot use **UG** on a constant.
4. We cannot use **UG** on a variable introduced free into a proof by **EI.**
5. We cannot use **UG** on a variable free in a line obtained by **EI.**
6. Within the scope of an assumed premise we cannot use **UG** on a variable free in that assumed premise.
7. We cannot require a one-to-one correspondence between x and y variables in the application of **UI.**
8. We cannot require a one-to-one correspondence between x and y variables in the application of **EG.** A close look at the way our rules are formulated shows they handle all these cases.

Now let's look at a few cases that are a bit more obscure but still related to this issue of one-to-one correspondence. When we add an existential quantifier, we want to quantify (bind) occurrences of one variable only, not two. Thus we don't want to allow the use of **EG** in the following proof:

(9) 1. $(\exists y)(\exists x)Fxy$ p
     2. $(\exists x)Fxy$ 1 **EI**
     3. Fxy 2 **EI**
     4. $(\exists y)Fyy$ 3 **EG** (Invalid)

This time, let Fxy = "x is the father of y" and restrict the domain of discourse to human beings. Then line 1 asserts (truly) that someone is the father of someone (or other), while line 4 asserts (falsely) that someone is the father of himself. The trouble is that the added existential quantifier on line 4 binds not only the y that replaces the free x on line 3, but also an extra y that just happens to be free on line 3. This case is handled by the last clause in restriction 1 on **EG.**

Similarly, when we add a universal quantifier, we want to quantify occurrences of one variable only, and not two. The unhappy consequence of capturing occurrences of two different variables is illustrated by the following example:

(10) 1. $(\exists y)(x)Lyx$ p
      2. $(x)Lyx$ 1 **EI**

3. *Lyx*   2 **UI**
4. *(y)Lyy*   3 **UG** (Invalid)

Suppose this time that *Lyx* = "*y* loves *x*," and the domain of discourse is restricted to persons. Then 1 asserts that someone loves every person, while 4 asserts that every person loves himself. Since 1 could be true when 4 is false, the proof is not valid. The trouble is that in generalizing on the *x* variable in 3, we also quantified the *y* variable that is free on that line. The moral of this and the previous example is that *in using **EG** or **UG**, the replacements for the occurrences of only one variable in the original formula are to be bound in the resulting formula by the newly introduced quantifier*. The last clause in restriction 4 on **UG** eliminates such invalid moves.

We stated previously that when applying **UI** we cannot require a one-to-one correspondence between bound *x* variables in the original formula and free *y* variables in the resulting formula, because this would block perfectly valid inferences, such as the one in example (7) from *(x)Lyx* to *Lyy*. In that proof, one *x* variable was freed when we dropped the universal quantifier, and yet we ended up with two free *y* variables. So we ended up with more variables free than were bound in the original formula.

But what about the reverse process? What about dropping a quantifier by **UI** and replacing, say, only one of two variables thus freed by some other variable? The answer is that such a use of **UI** is invalid, as the following example illustrates:

(11) 1. *(x)(Ox ∨ Ex)*   p
     2. *Ox ∨ Ey*   1 **UI** (Invalid)
     3. *(y)(Ox ∨ Ey)*   2 **UG**
     4. *(x)(y)(Ox ∨ Ey)*   3 **UG**

Suppose *Ox* = "*x* is odd" and *Ex* = "*x* is even," and the domain of discourse is restricted to positive whole numbers. Then 1 asserts (truly) that every number *x* is either odd or even, while 4 asserts (falsely) that given any two numbers, *x* and *y*, either *x* is odd or *y* is even. (That 4 is false can be seen by considering the substitution instance of 4 obtained by replacing *x* by 2 and *y* by 1, because this substitution instance asserts the falsehood that either 2 is odd or 1 is even.)

The moral this time is that *if one occurrence of some variable* x *is freed by **UI** and replaced by a free* y *variable, then all* x *variables freed by this application of **UI** must be replaced by free* y *variables*.

*Whether a similar restriction must also be placed on **EI** depends on how the restric*-tions on **UG** have been worded. Consider the following example:

(12) 1. *(∃x)Ixx*   p
     2. *Iyx*   1 **EI** (?)

Should we allow the step from 1 to 2 by **EI**, even though only one of the *x* variables freed by dropping the existential quantifier from line 1 is replaced by a *y* variable? The answer is that it depends on how we have restricted **UG.** The essential thing is to forbid passage from 1 to

3. *(x)Iyx*   2 **UG**

and then to

    4. $(\exists y)(x)Iyx$ 3 EG

Let Iyx = "y is identical with x," and it becomes obvious that we must block the inference from 1 to 4, because 1 then asserts that something is identical with itself, while 4 says that something is identical with everything.

It turns out that we can block this inference either by putting a restriction on **UG,** forbidding the inference from 2 to 3, or on **EI,** forbidding the inference from 1 to 2. Most sets of quantifier rules place the restriction on **EI.** However, it happens that the set of rules presented in Chapter Nine places appropriate restrictions on both **EI** and **UG** (because to do otherwise would make the statement of the rules slightly more complicated). These are restrictions 3 and 2, respectively.

We said earlier that we must permit uses of **UI** such as the one from $(x)Lyx$ to Lyy. But what about similar uses of **EI,** such as the one inferring from $(\exists x)Fxy$ to Fyy? Should we allow these also? The answer is no; all such uses of **EI** are invalid. But it turns out that all cases in which such inferences might arise are forbidden by the restriction (already mentioned) that a free variable introduced into a proof by **EI** must not occur free previously in the proof. The following argument contains an example:

(13) 1. $(\exists y)(\exists x)Txy$ p
       2. $(\exists x)Txy$ 1 **EI**
       3. Tyy 2 **EI** (Invalid)
       4. $(\exists x)Txx$ 3 EG

Suppose Txy = "x is taller than y" and the domain of discourse is restricted to persons. Then the premise of this argument, line 1, asserts that someone is taller than someone, which clearly is true, while its conclusion, line 4, asserts that someone is taller than himself, which obviously is false.

We also said earlier that we must permit uses of **EG** such as the one from Fxx to $(\exists y)Fxy$. But what about similar uses of **UG,** such as the one from Fxx to $(y)Fxy$? The answer is that such inferences are invalid, as the following example illustrates:

(14) 1. $(x)Ixx$ p
       2. Ixx 1 **UI**
       3. $(y)Ixy$ 2 **UG** (Invalid)
       4. $(x)(y)Ixy$ 3 **UG**

Suppose Ixy = "x is identical with y." Then line 1 states the truth that everything is identical with itself, while line 4 states the falsehood that everything is identical with everything.

So our last moral on the issue of one-to-one correspondence is that *in the use of* **UG,** *if a free x in the original formula is replaced by a y that becomes bound in the resulting formula, then all free occurrences of* x *in the original formula must be replaced by bound* y *variables in the resulting formula.* Our wording of restriction 1 on **UI** takes care of this.

3 *Accidentally Bound Variables and Miscellaneous Cases*

Now let's consider four remaining possibilities. These cases all involve the accidental binding of a free variable by an extraneous quantifier.

The primary aim in the use of **UI** and **EI** is to drop a quantifier and free the variables that it bound. Consequently, we must forbid uses of **UI** and **EI** in which the variable that is supposed to be freed ends up bound. The following is an example involving **UI**:

(15) 1. $(x)(\exists y)Lyx$ p
       2. $(\exists y)Lyy$ 1 UI (Invalid)

Suppose $Lyx =$ "y is larger than x," and x and y range over numbers only. Then the premise of this argument asserts the true statement that, given any number x, there is some number larger than x, while its conclusion asserts the falsehood that there is some number larger than itself. The trouble is that the x variable in line 1, which the application of **UI** is supposed to free, is replaced in line 2 by a bound y variable.

Similarly, the use of **EI** in the following proof is invalid:

(16) 1. $(\exists x)(y) \sim Dxy$ p
       2. $(y) \sim Dyy$ 1 EI (Invalid)

Suppose $Dxy =$ "x dislikes y," and the domain of discourse is restricted to human beings. Then the premise of this argument asserts that there is someone who doesn't dislike anyone, which is true (surely there is a newborn baby somewhere who doesn't dislike anyone), while its conclusion asserts that no one dislikes himself, which (unfortunately) is false.

The moral of all this is that *when a quantifier is dropped by UI or EI, all the variables thus freed must be uniformly replaced by free variables (or, in the case of UI, by free variables or constants)*. Our formulation of the rule **UI** and the third restriction on rule **EI** take care of these cases.

Now let's consider a slightly different case concerning **UG** and **EG.** When we use **UG** or **EG,** we want the occurrences of the appropriate y variables to be bound by the newly introduced quantifier. We definitely do not want any of the occurrences of that variable to be bound by some other quantifier that just happens to occur in the resulting formula. For instance, we don't want to allow the following use of **UG**:

(17) 1. $(x)(\exists y)Lyx$ p
       2. $(\exists y)Lyx$ 1 UI
       3. $(y)(\exists y)Lyy$ 2 UG (Invalid)

Suppose again that $Lyx =$ "y is larger than x," and the domain of discourse is restricted to numbers. Then line 1 asserts the truth that given any number x, there is some number larger than x, while line 3 asserts the falsehood that some number is larger than itself. The universal quantifier on line 3 is said to be a *vacuous* quantifier, because the *closer* existential quantifier binds the y variables that follow it.

The case is just the same for **EG,** as this example illustrates:

(18) 1. $(\exists x)(y)Dxy$ p
    2. $(y)Dxy$ 1 **EI**
    3. $(\exists y)(y)Dyy$ 2 **EG** (Invalid)

This time, let Dxy = "x dislikes y," with the domain of discourse restricted to humans. Then line 1 asserts that someone dislikes everyone, which even if true, does not entail that everyone dislikes everyone (again, the initial quantifier is vacuous).

The moral is that *in using* **UG** *or* **EG,** *the variables to be quantified by the newly introduced quantifier must not be bound by some other quantifier* (restrictions 4 and 1).

The preceding constitutes a catalog of the kinds of inferences we must forbid (as well as two kinds we must permit). The four quantifier rules (**EI, UI, EG, UG**) were carefully spelled out (in Chapter Nine) so as to forbid all the kinds of inferences that we've just seen must be forbidden, while permitting the two kinds we've found must be permitted. Let's review quickly. Here is a list of the eighteen kinds of cases we have described in this chapter. The line numbers refer to the examples in the text given previously.

Cases involving the five main restrictions

(1) 1. $(\exists x)Hx$
    2. Ha 1 **EI** (Invalid—when **EI** is used to drop an existential quantifier, the variables thus freed cannot validly be replaced by individual constants)

(2) 3. Fx
    4. Gx 2 **EI** (Invalid—a variable introduced free into a proof by **EI** must not occur free previously in the proof)

(3) 1. Fa
    2. $(x)Fx$ 1 **UG** (Invalid—we cannot use **UG** on a constant)

(4) 2. Fy 1 **EI**
    3. $(x)Fx$ 2 **UG** (Invalid—we cannot use **UG** on a variable introduced free into a proof by **EI**)

(5) 1. $(x)(\exists y)Lyx$
    2. $(\exists y)Lyx$ 1 **UI**
    3. Lyx 2 **EI**
    4. $(x)Lyx$ 3 **UG** (Invalid—we cannot use **UG** on a variable free in a line obtained by **EI**, even if **EI** is not used to introduce the variable)

(6) 1. Fy **AP**
    2. $(x)Fx$ 1 **UG** (Invalid—within the scope of an assumed premise we cannot use **UG** on a variable free in that assumed premise)

The first kind of inference is forbidden by the first restriction on **EI;** the second by the second restriction on **EI;** the third by the first restriction on **UG;** the fourth and fifth by the second restriction on **UG;** and the sixth by the third restriction on **UG.**

One-to-one correspondence cases

(7) 2. $(x)Lyx$
   3. Lyy 2 **UI** (Valid—we are *permitted* to drop a quantifier with **UI** and replace the variable that was bound with one that already occurs free elsewhere in the formula)

(8) 2. Fxx
   3. $(\exists y)Fxy$ 2 **EG** (Valid—when we add a quantifier with **EG** we are *permitted* to choose not to bind all the free variables of a certain sort)

(9) 3. Fxy
   4. $(\exists y)Fyy$ 3 **EG** (Invalid—we may not use **EG** to bind two different free variables at once)

(10) 3. Lyx
   4. $(y)Lyy$ 3 **UG** (Invalid—we may not use **UG** to bind two different kinds of free variables at once)

(11) 1. $(x)(Ox \vee Ex)$
   2. $Ox \vee Ey$ 1 **UI** (Invalid—we may not use **UI** to replace one kind of bound variable with two different free variables)

(12) 1. $(\exists x)Ixx$
   2. Iyx 1 **EI** (Invalid—we may not use **EI** to replace one kind of bound variable with two different free variables)

(13) 2. $(\exists x)Txy$
   3. Tyy 2 **EI** (Invalid—unlike **UI,** we may *not* drop a quantifier with **EI** and replace the variable that was bound with one that already occurs free elsewhere in the formula)

(14) 2. Ixx
   3. $(y)Ixy$ 2 **UG** (Invalid—unlike **EG** [see case (8)], when we add a quantifier with **UG,** we may *not* bind only some of the free variables of a certain sort)

Cases such as (9), (10), (11), and (12) are forbidden by the precise wording used (respectively) in the only restriction on **EG,** the fourth restriction on **UG,** the only restriction on **UI,** and the third restriction on **EI.** Note, in particular, the phrase that is repeated in each of these very similar restrictions: ". . . making no other changes."

The way that cases such as (7) are permitted, but cases such as (13) are prohibited, is the second restriction on **EI,** for which no analog exists in the case of **UI.**

The way that cases such as (8) are permitted, but cases such as (14) are prohibited, is that, whereas the fourth restriction on **UG** begins with "provided that . . . w . . . results from replacing *each* occurrence of u free in . . . u . . . ," the only restriction for **EG** begins with "provided that . . . w . . . results from replacing *at least one* occurrence of u free in . . . u . . . ."

Cases involving accidentally bound variables

(15) 1. $(x)(\exists y)Lyx$
    2. $(\exists y)Lyy$ 1 **UI** (Invalid—when we use **UI** to introduce a free variable, we must be sure that variable is not accidentally bound by another quantifier)

(16) 1. $(\exists x)(y) \sim Dxy$
    2. $(y) \sim Dyy$ 1 **EI** (Invalid—when we use **EI** to introduce a free variable, we must be sure that variable is not accidentally bound by another quantifier)

(17) 2. $(\exists y)Lyx$
    3. $(y)(\exists y)Lyy$ 2 **UG** (Invalid—when we use **UG** to bind a free variable, we must be sure that the variable that results from the generalization is not already bound in some of its new occurrences by a quantifier in the line on which the generalization is performed.

(18) 2. $(y)Dxy$
    3. $(\exists y)(y)Dyy$ 2 **EG** (Invalid—when we use **EG** to bind a free variable, we must be sure that the variable that results from the generalization is not already bound in some of its new occurrences by a quantifier in the line on which the generalization is performed.

The only restriction on **UI** and the third restriction on **EI** prevent cases such as (15) and (16), with the phrase "with a *w* that is *free* in . . . *w* . . . ." The fourth restriction on **UG** and the only restriction on **EG** use this same phrase to prohibit cases such as (17) and (18).

There are, of course, many other ways to write the quantifier rules so that they correctly handle all eighteen of these cases. The formulation in this book was chosen for simplicity and relative ease of comprehension. For example, strictly speaking the last clause in restriction 4 on **UG** and the corresponding clause in restriction 1 on **EG** are redundant, because the requirement that the variable *w* resulting in the generalization must be free in (. . . *w* . . .) accomplishes the same thing.

Exercise 11-1

(Some of these questions are rather difficult. Don't get discouraged.)

1. Why can't we use **UG** on a variable introduced free into a proof by **EI**?

2. State which step in the following proof is invalid, and explain how the quantifier rules are designed to block steps of this kind:

    1. $(\exists x)[(Px \cdot (y)(Py \supset Lxy)]$ p
    2. $Px \cdot (y)(Py \supset Lxy)$ 1 **EI**
    3. $(y)(Py \supset Lxy)$ 2 **Simp**
    4. $Py \supset Lxy$ 3 **UI**
    5. $(x)(Px \supset Lxx)$ 4 **UG**

3. Why can't we require a one-to-one correspondence between variables freed when using **UI** and resulting free variables? That is, why shouldn't we say that the use of **UI** in the following proof is invalid on grounds that there is not such a one-to-one correspondence?

1. $(\exists x)(y)(Fx \cdot Gxy)$	p
2. $(y)(Fx \cdot Gxy)$	1 **EI**
3. $Fx \cdot Gxx$	2 **UI**
4. Gxx	3 **Simp**
5. $(\exists x)Gxx$	4 **EG**

4. When we drop a quantifier, it seems intuitively right that the variables thus freed not be captured by some other quantifier. Prove that our intuition on this is correct by violating it and deriving a false sentence from a true one. (Try to find an original example.)

5. Is the following use of **UG** valid or invalid? Explain why in either case, supporting what you say with an example.

1. $(y)[Py \supset (\exists x)Rxy]$	p
2. $Py \supset (\exists x)Rxy$	1 **UI**
3. $(x)[Px \supset (\exists x)Rxx]$	2 **UG**

6. Explain why, to quote the text, "if one occurrence of some variable x is freed by **UI** and replaced by a free y variable, then all x variables freed by this application of **UI** must be replaced by free y variables." Support your answer with an example, original if possible.

7. Carefully explain the need for the fourth restriction on rule **UG,** the restriction that states, "(. . . w . . .) results from replacing each occurrence of u free in (. . . u . . .) with a w that is free in (. . . w . . .) (making no other changes) and there are no additional occurrences of w already contained in (. . . w . . .)." Support your answer with an example, original if possible.

8. Carefully explain the need for this similar restriction on rule **EG.** Support your answer with an example, original if possible.

4 *Predicate Logic Proofs with Flagged Constants*

We conclude this chapter with a look at an alternative system of predicate logic proof rules. This system is both sound and complete, and therefore deals with all the problem cases we have just outlined. There is much in common with the system you have already learned. The rule **QN** is the same. Likewise, there are still two rules, **UI** and **EI,** for taking off quantifiers, and **UG** and **EG** are used for putting them back on—although these rules will be stated a bit differently. The typical sequence is still the same—use **UI** or **EI** to remove quantifiers, use sentential logic, and finish by using **UG** or **EG** to put the needed quantifiers back into place.

The difference is that this method uses flagged constants instead of freed variables in the intermediate steps of the proof. To simplify our discussion, we will call the system you have already learned "the standard system," and the new system we are about to introduce "the flagging system."

In the flagging system, a typical **EI** step might be as follows:

1. $(\exists x)(Fx \cdot Gx)$
2. $Fa \cdot Ga$ 1 **EI,** *flag a*

When we flag a constant, we "raise a red flag" to note that there is something special about the constant. Flagged constants are subject to three important restrictions. The first and most obvious restriction is that a flagged constant may not appear in the conclusion of the proof. Otherwise we could use **EI** to justify the invalid inference from "Someone is smart" to "Art is smart." So a flagged constant is a temporary name of an unknown individual, introduced when the quantifier is removed. We used quasivariables for this purpose, but in the flagging system you are not permitted to use quasivariables in this way.

The second restriction on flagged constants is that they must be new to the proof—that is, they cannot occur on any previous line. This is very much like the two restrictions on **EI** in the standard system. The purpose of those restrictions, as explained in Chapter Nine, is to make sure that the variable introduced by **EI** is always a new name. In the flagging system we accomplish this by saying that when we use **EI**, we must flag a constant and restrict flagging so that flagging requires us to introduce a new constant.

Of course we can have constants in a proof that are not flagged. Unflagged constants may occur in one or more premises, or may be introduced when we remove a universal quantifier with **UI,** as in the following proof:

1. $(x)Fx$
2. Fa 1 **UI**

We used **UI** to do this before. The difference is that with the flagging method we always use **UI** this way. Likewise, as before we can use **EG** to replace a constant with a variable, as in the following:

1. Fa
2. $(\exists x)Fx$ 1 **EG**

Basically, unflagged constants work the same in both systems.

The rule **UG** is where the flagging method differs most from the standard system. In the flagging system **UG** involves a subproof, similar to **CP** or **IP.** However, the first step of the subproof consists, not in an assumption, but in what is known as a flagging step. A flagging step simply amounts to a declaration that a particular constant is being flagged for the purposes of **UG.** The subproof ends when a formula containing the flagged constant is replaced by a universally quantified formula with a bound variable in place of the constant. Here is an example:

1. $(x)(Fx \supset Gx)$
2. $(x)(Gx \supset Hx)$
→ 3. flag *a*
     4. $Fa \supset Ga$ 1 **UI**
     5. $Ga \supset Ha$ 2 **UI**
     6. $Fa \supset Ha$ 4,5 **HS**
     7. $(x)(Fx \supset Hx)$ 2–6 **UG**

The subproof ensures that the constant that is replaced by a bound variable in the **UG** step is what in Chapter Nine we referred to as a "universal name." It represents an arbitrarily chosen individual.

The third restriction is that any constant introduced within a subproof can be used only within that subproof. This restriction is needed to block the invalid inference from $(x)(\exists y)Lyx$ to $(\exists y)(x)Lyx$ discussed in case (5) earlier. Let's look at how this works. Since we will need to use **UG** to get the conclusion, we might begin by setting up a **UG** subproof as follows:

(5) 1. $(x)(\exists y)Lyx$ p /∴ $(\exists y)(x)Lyx$
   → 2. flag a
    3. $(\exists y)Lya$ 1 **UI**
    4. Lba 3 **EI**, *flag b*
    5. $(x)Lbx$ 3 **UG** (Invalid, b cannot occur outside the subproof in which it is introduced)

We now are ready to state our flagging version of the quantifier rules more precisely.

Rule UI: $(u)(\ldots u \ldots) / \therefore (\ldots a \ldots)$ *Provided:*
    1. $(\ldots a \ldots)$ results from replacing each occurrence of u free in $(\ldots u \ldots)$ with a constant in $(\ldots a \ldots)$ (making no other changes)

Rule EI: $(\exists u)(\ldots u \ldots) / \therefore (\ldots a \ldots)$ *Provided:*
    1. $(\ldots a \ldots)$ results from replacing each occurrence of u free in $(\ldots u \ldots)$ with a constant a in $(\ldots a \ldots)$ (making no other changes)
    2. We *flag a*

Rule UG: → *flag a*
    .
    .
    .
    $(\ldots a \ldots)$
    $(w)(\ldots w \ldots)$ **UG**   *Provided:*
    1. $(\ldots w \ldots)$ results from replacing each occurrence of a constant in $(\ldots a \ldots)$ with a w that is free in $(\ldots w \ldots)$ (making no other changes)

Rule EG: $(\ldots a \ldots) / \therefore (\exists w)(\ldots w \ldots)$ *Provided:*
    1. $(\ldots w \ldots)$ results from replacing at least one occurrence of a constant in $(\ldots a \ldots)$ with a w that is free in $(\ldots w \ldots)$ (making no other changes)

Flagging restrictions

1. A flagged constant may not appear in the conclusion of the proof.
2. A newly flagged constant cannot occur on any previous line.
3. A flagged constant introduced within a subproof can be used only within that subproof.

The flagging system has much to recommend it. Because it uses flagged constants rather than free variables, problems involving "accidentally bound" variables are avoided. The downside is that in addition to the quantifier rules, one must also learn about flagged constants and their accompanying restrictions. Students must also "work backward" to construct **UG** subproofs, declaring a flagged constant for **UG** well in advance. Both systems are complete and sound, but we find students have an easier introduction to the quantifier rules in a system without flagging.

Exercise 11-2

Use the flagging system to complete the proofs in Exercise 10-14.

Chapter Twelve

Predicate Logic Truth Trees

1 *Introductory Remarks*

The tree method for predicate logic is an extension of that already presented for sentential logic.* However, there are some important differences. The trees for sentential logic give us the feature of *decidability*—there is a mechanical decision procedure that a machine could follow to give us a correct answer to the question of validity or invalidity of each argument in sentential logic. But the tree method for predicate logic does *not* yield such a procedure. This is because it has been proved (by the American mathematician Alonzo Church) that *there can be no such decision procedure for predicate logic*—**Church's undecidability result.** What can be proved is this: If an argument in predicate logic is valid, a machine will be able to decide it is valid in a finite number of steps (although that number may be fantastically large). But if an argument is invalid, the machine may *not* be able to *show* it invalid in a finite number of steps.

These facts show up in the trees in the following way. Given a tree in predicate logic, the following three things may occur: (1) All paths will close, in which case the argument is valid. (2) There will be at least one open path, and there will be no way to apply the tree rules to any line in that path, in which case the argument is invalid. (3) The tree may *seem* to grow infinitely, in which case we cannot give a definite answer as to whether the argument is invalid. The point is that if we could predict when a tree will grow infinitely (the **infinitely growing tree**), we would know by the tree method that the argument is invalid; but some trees that seem as if they will grow infinitely may, at some point, stop growing, and there is no way that can be given to decide whether or not this will happen. This is analogous to the case of repeating decimals. There are some cases where we simply cannot show whether or not a process of, say, division, will produce a repeating decimal.

So one is in a funny position with respect to the trees as a mechanical procedure. The tree method will tell us, for any valid argument in predicate logic, that it is valid. But for some arguments that we know intuitively to be invalid—we give examples later—the trees do not yield a definite answer.

---

*The original inspiration for this chapter on predicate trees comes from Richard C. Jeffrey's pioneering work on this subject in his *Formal Logic: Its Scope and Limits* (1967). See the footnote in Section 1 of Chapter Six of our textbook.

2 *General Features of the Method*

Like the method for sentential trees, we use a form of indirect proof. We always begin testing an argument by listing its premises and the *negation* of the conclusion. The rules for sentential trees are in effect. But of course we have new operators in predicate logic, for which we must have tree rules. The only new rules we actually need are two of the four **QN** rules, and **UI** and **EI**. Like the sentential tree method, the predicate tree method combines features of several different procedures with which you are already familiar. It uses the method of expansion into model universes, and means in effect that we will always do **UI** and **EI** to *constants*. That, in turn, calls for some special procedures for both **UI** and **EI**, as you will see shortly.

Note that if we incorporate the identity sign, "="—for example,"$a = b$"—into our symbolism, as we do in Chapter Thirteen, trees become much more difficult to construct. So we will not do this (although of course it can be done). No argument we will work with will contain the "=" sign.

In Chapter Six, we noted that sentential trees are customarily constructed with sentential constants, which is not accurate theoretically; they should be done with variables, just as truth tables are. Strictly speaking, we are making trees for the forms of premises and conclusions, not for actual statements that have definite truth-values. We will not continue that practice here. For one thing, we do not have predicate variables in our logic with which to completely "formalize" our sentences. Our trees in predicate logic are much more akin to predicate logic proofs. We can be thought, when showing an argument valid, to be showing the validity of any other argument with the same form. The same goes for invalidity.

3 *Specific Examples of the Method*

As you might expect, predicate trees differ from sentential trees as a function of the way predicate logic differs from sentential logic. Predicate logic is a richer language in that it contains sentential logic and quantified statements, and we know from even our limited contact with expansions into model universes that the truth conditions for such statements are more complex that those for sentential formulas. We also know from doing proofs in predicate logic that the order in which we choose to do **EI**s and **UI**s, and to what letters we do instantiations, makes a difference for what we can prove. These differences are reflected in predicate trees in the following ways:

1. We have new rules for predicate trees that supplement the rules for sentential trees (that is, the latter are still in force, just as in doing proofs in predicate logic, our sentential rules are still in force). There are rules for negation of quantified statements that correspond to the **QN** rules. There are also rules for taking off the quantifiers. These rules are given on the next page.
2. A strict procedure must be followed in constructing predicate trees. A prescribed order must be adhered to. These procedures are summarized in a **flow chart for predicate trees,** which appears on page 272. Thus, unlike sentential trees, where

Denial	Erase "~ ~" wherever it appears in unchecked sentences in open paths. (**QN** rules) Check sentences of forms "~ (x) . . . x . . ." and "~ (∃x) . . . x . . ." in open paths and rewrite them as "(∃x) ~ . . . x . . ." and "(x) ~ . . . x . . ." at the bottoms of those paths.

Universal Quantifier (UI)	Given an open path in which a sentence of form (x) . . . x . . . occurs, for *each* name *n** that appears anywhere in the path, write the sentence . . . n . . . at the bottom of the path unless that sentence already occurs in the path. (If no name appears in the path, choose some *n* and write . . . n . . . at the bottom of the path.) When you are done, *do not* check the sentence (x) . . . x . . . .
Existential Quantifier (EI)	Given an unchecked sentence of form (∃x) . . . x . . . that occurs in an open path: Choose a name *n* that is not used anywhere in the path, and write the sentence . . . n . . . at the bottom of the path. When this has been done for every open path on which the given sentence of form (∃x) . . . x . . . occurs, check that sentence.

*Remember, our names are "a," "b," "c," "d," etc.

Rules of inference

See Jeffrey, 1st ed., p. 113. Reprinted with symbolic alterations by permission of McGraw-Hill.

---

strategy is called for, but not necessary, since the same result (although not the same-looking tree) would be reached whether we used that strategy or not, here one must do the breakdowns of formulas in the order prescribed by the flow chart. More accurately, there is a step in the flow chart where sentential rules apply, and in that step we may use strategy to shorten trees. But the sentential step is part of a larger picture, in the sense that we must proceed step by step to construct a tree, and we cannot deviate from these steps. Even simple steps such as **DN** can only be done when the flow chart calls for it.

Now, let's examine the following tree (on page 273), line by line, using the flow chart and the rules for trees.

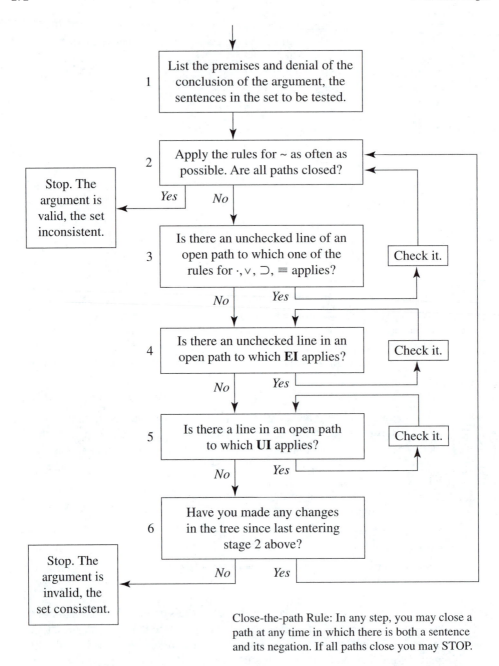

Close-the-path Rule: In any step, you may close a path at any time in which there is both a sentence and its negation. If all paths close you may STOP.

Flowchart for rules of inference
Close-the-path rule: In any step, you may close a path at any time in which there is both a sentence and its negation. If all paths close, you may STOP.

See Jeffrey, 3rd ed. (1991), p. 45. Reprinted with symbol changes by permission of McGraw-Hill.

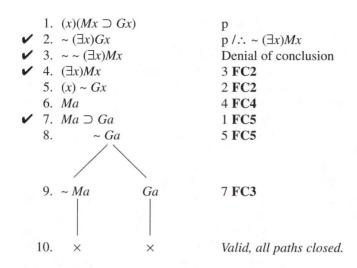

1. $(x)(Mx \supset Gx)$ p
2. $\sim (\exists x)Gx$ p /∴ $\sim (\exists x)Mx$
3. $\sim \sim (\exists x)Mx$ Denial of conclusion
4. $(\exists x)Mx$ 3 **FC2**
5. $(x) \sim Gx$ 2 **FC2**
6. Ma 4 **FC4**
7. $Ma \supset Ga$ 1 **FC5**
8. $\sim Ga$ 5 **FC5**

9. $\sim Ma$ Ga 7 **FC3**

10.   ×   ×   *Valid, all paths closed.*

The flow chart was followed rigorously in constructing the tree. The justifications for each line are the line from which the given line is derived and the number of the step in the flow chart used to derive it—**FC2**, for example. Starting with **FC1**, we list the premises and the denial of the conclusion in 1–3. We are then directed by the arrow to **FC2**, which tells us to apply the rule of denial to all relevant sentences. We thus apply the rule of denial to 3 to get 4, and to 2 to get line 5; we check off both lines because we are done with them, no more operations can be or need be performed on them. **FC2** now enjoins us to see whether all paths are closed. The answer is no in this case, so the chart takes us to **FC3**, which asks us to apply the sentential rules for connectives, if there are any sentences to which they can be applied. There are not, since 1, 4, and 5 are all quantified statements. Because we cannot apply the sentential rules, we are directed to **FC4**. The answer to the question in **FC4** is yes; the yes arrow in **FC4** then tells us to apply the rule for **EI**—see the tree rules for how to do this. Notice that in applying **EI**, we must choose a name, that is, a constant, not appearing anywhere in the tree so far. The chosen constant is "*a*." Thus line 6 represents, in effect, an **EI** from "*x*" to "*a*." We check off line 4; we cannot do any more **EI**s from that *wff*.

Some theoretical comments are in order before we proceed. You may recall that when we introduced **EI** for proofs, we were specifically enjoined not to do **EI** to a constant but to a letter that in effect represented some individual in our domain, a "John Doe" name, as it were. If we had five individuals in our domain, we would only know that one of them was John Doe, but not which one. In selecting "*a*," we are saying which one. Notice that if we had had a premise using the constant *a*, our **EI** would have to have been to another letter, say *b*. How do we know whether *a* and *b* are identical or not? We don't! Our logic leaves open the possibility that the two are identical, and so assumes that we can have more than one name for a given individual. This of course shows that the need for an identity sign is indeed important, but as we mentioned in Section 2, we will not use it in our discussion of trees, because our main points about trees can be made without it.

To return to the tree: Now the yes arrow directs us to **FC4** once again; that is, we must do an **EI** again if there is some other existentially quantified statement in the path. But there is not, and the answer "no" now directs us to **FC5**. The answer to the question in

FC5 is yes; in fact, we have two sentences to choose from on which to perform **UI,** either 1 or 5. The order won't matter, because **FC5** directs us back to itself each time a **UI** is performed, until there are no more universally quantified formulas left to instantiate. Let us start with 1 and, following the rule, instantiate it to every constant already in the path. We do the **UI** to *a* in line 7. Notice we do not check off 1, since we may have to do more **UI**s from it later, depending on what happens as we follow the flow chart. This corresponds in proofs to the fact that we can do a **UI** as often as we wish to as many letters as we wish.

Now we have done the **UI** to 7, **FC5** directs us back to itself, and we perform **UI** on 5, again to *a*, which gives us line 8. We are directed back to **FC5** for a third try, but there are no further formulas on which to perform **UI,** so the answer "no" guides us to **FC6.** Here we get a yes answer, so the chart directs us all the way back to **FC2.**

At this point the tree looks exactly like a proof. In fact, no step has been done any differently from would have been done in a *reductio* proof except for the **EI** to a constant. But don't be misled. The divergence between trees and proofs has not shown up yet; this tree was chosen primarily to illustrate the flow chart. We will now get a divergence. **FC2** tells us to apply our rules for denial if we can. Since there are no formulas on which to do denial, we are directed to **FC3.** **FC3** tells us to apply the rules for connectives if we can, and indeed we can apply them to 7, resulting in 9. Using the close-the-path rule, we heed the command to close all paths that contain a sentence and its denial. We do this at 10, and all paths close. The rule directs us to **STOP.** The inference is valid.

That is how we would program a computer to construct trees. How do we know that it works every time to give us what we want? We will discuss this later in the chapter.

Let's do another one. Notice that the premises already contain constants.

	1. $(x)(Mx \supset Ma)$	p
	2. $\sim Ma$	p /∴ $\sim (\exists x)Mx$
✔	3. $\sim \sim (\exists x)Mx$	Denial of conclusion
✔	4. $(\exists x)Mx$	3 **FC2**
	5. Mb	4 **FC4**
	6. $Ma \supset Ma$	1 **FC5**
✔	7. $Mb \supset Ma$	1 **FC5**
	8. $\sim Mb$ Ma	7 **FC3**
	9. × ×	Valid, all paths closed.

Once again, we consult the flow chart. **FC1** tells us to list the premises and the negation of the conclusion, which we do from 1–3. **FC2** tells us to apply the rules of denial to all relevant sentences, which we do in line 4. Since all paths are not closed, we are moved to **FC3,** and an answer no moves us to **FC4.** Now we do an **EI** to *b* in 5. Why? Because our tree rule for **EI** tells us that we must choose a name not already in the path, and so we cannot choose *a* since it is in both 1 and 2. Notice that, although *b* was chosen, we could have used *any* constant not already in the path. Now we check off 4 as the rule enjoins us to. We move to **FC5,** since there are no more **EI**s to perform, and the answer to the question there is yes. The next move is important to understand. We are going to apply the **UI** rule to 1, and according to the rule we must do a **UI** to every constant already in the path. Since *a* and *b* are already in the path, we must do two **UIs** from 1, which result in 6 and 7. There are no other **UIs** to perform, so we go to **FC6,** which directs us back to **FC2,** because changes have been made in the tree. An answer no to **FC2** leads us to **FC3,** and now strategy is called for, since there are two sentences, 6 and 7, to which **FC3** applies. We choose 7 because it will, when broken down, close all paths. Now 7 is broken down on 8, 7 is checked off, and since we now have a *yes* answer to the question in **FC3,** we are led back to **FC3.** But, before we have to do the breakdown of 6, we may close each path that contains a sentence and its denial. We do this on line 9 by our close-the-path rule, and we are directed to **STOP.** The argument is valid.

4 *Some Advantages of the Trees*

So far, it may look as if the trees are as much work as proofs. Actually, for "simple" natural deduction proofs, trees are probably more trouble than they are worth. For longer natural deduction proofs, though, trees will usually give fewer steps. The same, of course, was true for sentential trees.

One big advantage that trees give us over proofs is that we can break down sentences such as the following much more easily than we can in proofs:

(*n*) $(x)(Fx \supset Hx) \supset (\exists y)Gy$

Now in a proof we cannot apply our quantifier rules to (*n*), either to the antecedent or to the consequent, and we might have to work very hard to derive either the antecedent or the consequent so as to be in a position to apply the quantifier rules. But when we do trees, we can break down (*n*) by the ordinary rules for the horseshoe, because that is the main connective. The same is true for such formulas as

$$(x)Fx \lor (\exists x)(Gx \cdot Hx), (x)(y)Rxy \equiv (\exists z)(u)Gzu$$

and any *wff* whose main connective is sentential, and so to which **FC3** applies.

It is important to note that, using trees, we can test a statement for being either a logical truth or a contradiction. The tree for a contradiction will have all paths close; the demonstration that a formula is a logical truth is done by negating it, thus getting a contradiction. Most important, we can also get the result, which we cannot get using natural deduction, that an argument is *invalid.* Let us see.

5 *Example of an Invalid Argument with at Least One Open Path*

The following example is very important from a theoretical viewpoint. In it, we apply the tree rules until we can no longer apply them, and we end with at least one open path. This shows that we have an invalid argument. We can then read off the truth-values of the atomic sentences and actually construct a counterexample to the argument.

1. $(x)(Fx \vee Gx)$ p $/\therefore$ $(x)Fx \vee (x)Gx$

✔ 2. $\sim [(x)Fx \vee (x)Gx]$ Denial of conclusion

3. ✔ $\sim (x)Fx$ 2 **FC3**
      ✔ $\sim (x)Gx$

4. ✔ $(\exists x) \sim Fx$ 3 **FC2**
      ✔ $(\exists x) \sim Gx$

5. $\sim Fa$ 4 **FC4**
      $\sim Gb$

6. ✔ $Fa \vee Ga$ 1 **FC5**
      ✔ $Fb \vee Gb$

7. Fa Ga 6 **FC3**

8. $\times$

9. Fb Gb 6 **FC3**

10. $\times$ Invalid. Open path.

Once again, to the flow chart. We will be brief now, since (we hope) everyone is catching on to the routine. Line 3 comes from our first application of **FC3,** to 2. We are then returned to **FC2,** and we do our denials on 4. We now do **FC4** twice, once for each **EI,** and of course each **EI** is to a different constant. Now we go to **FC5,** and we must do two **UIs** from 1, one for each constant already in the path. The chart takes us through **FC6,** back through **FC2,** to **FC3.** Line 7 is a result of **FC3,** and we close off the path as we do in 8. We note again that we are allowed to close off a path at any time that we see a contradiction. Then we go to **FC3** again, get 9, then use our close-the-path rule to obtain 10. Notice that **FC3** has us do sentential breakdowns *one at a time,* such that we must go back through **FC2** before we do another sentential breakdown. This allows us to do **QNs** before we get to **FC4** and **FC5.**

Now what happens? We have line 10, and an open path at line 9. We have completed **FC3,** and if we follow the chart closely, we will now be directed a step at a time to **FC7,** where we are told to **STOP.** The argument is invalid.

6 *Metatheoretic Results*

Given the way the rules are stated, after line (10) of the tree just completed, there is no further way to apply the rules. You may think that because line (1) is not checked off—a universally quantified formula never is checked off—we could now go on and do more **UIs** to different constants. But the **UI** rule says that we do **UIs** to all constants already in the path or, if there are none, to a new constant. We have done **UI**s to all constants in the path, hence we need do no more. This is how a machine would be programmed to construct trees.

Now we can read off the truth-values of the atomic sentences in the open path and construct a counterexample to the argument in a domain of two individuals, *a* and *b*. The expansion is

$(Fa \lor Ga) \cdot (Fb \lor Gb)$ (premise expansion)
$(Fa \cdot Fb) \lor (Ga \cdot Gb)$ (conclusion expansion)

Now look at the open paths. We get the following: $V(Fa) = $ **F,** $V(Gb) = $ **F,** $V(Ga) = $ **T,** $V(Fb) = $ **T.** If we plug those truth-values back into the expansion, we obtain a true premise and a false conclusion. Hence, in a domain of two members, we have shown that we get true premises and a false conclusion.

Imagine now, as could well be the case—although we wouldn't want to make a tree this large, we are making a theoretical point—that our tree yielded an open path with atomic formulas that involve us in a domain of, say, 20 individuals. That is, 20 different constants are in the open path. Had we tried the method of expansion to try to find a counterexample, *we would not have found one in a universe of 1, or of 2 or of 3* . . . and we might have given up after 4 or 5, thinking the argument was valid. But wait! How do we know this? The tree gives us at least 20 atomic formulas with different constants, but maybe the method of expansion *would have* shown us invalidity after just 2! The answer to this question, which can be proved (but which we will not prove) is that the tree method gives us the smallest domain in which we can find a counterexample!

Technically, logicians first introduce the idea of **invalidity in a domain.** An argument is invalid in a domain if we can find a counterexample in it. A domain with *n* members is said to be of cardinality *n*. It can then be proved that if an **argument is invalid** in a domain with **cardinality** *n*, then it is invalid in all domains of higher cardinality. An argument is invalid if it has a counterexample in any domain greater than zero cardinality.

To see these points, we hope, a bit more clearly, consider the following argument:

$(\exists x)Fx \;/\therefore\; (x)Fx$

If we do an expansion into a domain of cardinality 1, this argument may look valid, because there is no way to get the premise true and the conclusion false. But if we do an expansion into a two-member domain, then it is possible to get the premise true and the conclusion false. This shows that using the method of expansion, we cannot demonstrate validity, in the following sense: No matter how large a domain we pick in which to expand our premises and conclusion, it is possible a larger domain will yield invalidity. If an argument is such that we cannot get true premises and a false conclusion in a domain of cardinality *n*, we would not be able to get true premises and a false conclusion in a domain with a lower cardinality, but it would still be possible we could obtain such a result in a domain of higher cardinality.

This is in effect what Church has proved. It is worth noting, although we shall not go into details here, that this result is a function of relational predicate logic. Without relations there is a formula for testing for invalidity: Take the number of monadic predicates in the argument, say *n;* then we only need test domains up through cardinality 2^n; if the argument is not found invalid in any of those domains, then it is valid. Thus *monadic* predicate logic does have a decision procedure!

Now look at the second tree we constructed in Section 3. It may *appear* that we have expanded the argument, via the tree, into a domain of two members. We get the result that the argument is valid from this tree—this means in all domains of cardinality greater than zero. *So it sounds as if this contradicts what we learned in the last paragraph.* If we have expanded into a domain of two members, and we do not get a counterexample, why should that tell us anything about cardinalities of higher domains? Our result earlier says it does not tell us anything about those domains!

The problem is only apparent. First, recall again that a tree will always consider enough domains—that is, domains of just the size that, if the tree rules no longer can be applied and there is an open path, the argument is invalid. Thus, although the method of expansion may fail us because we inadvertently choose a domain that is not large enough to show invalidity, the tree method will never do that. Either the tree will stop, and we can no longer apply the rules, and there is at least one open path, in which case we know it is invalid, or the tree may *seem* to grow forever, in which case we must withhold judgment as to the argument's invalidity. A machine programmed with the tree rules would never give us a *wrong answer* to the question of whether or not an argument is invalid.

Now back to our question about the apparent inconsistency of our theoretic argument. Is it the case that the tree in question has expanded into a domain of two members, as the method of expansion would do? If so, how do we know that a larger domain won't show invalidity?

Notice first that when we construct a tree, we use the *negation* of the conclusion. That is the key to our answer. The tree in question shows us that in a domain of cardinality 2, there is no way to get the premises and the *negation* of the conclusion both true. That is, the statement consisting of the conjunction of the premises and the negation of the conclusion cannot be true in that domain. There is a metatheoretic result, which again we will not prove here, that *if a tree closes,* then we have shown that the premises and the negation of the conclusion cannot be true in a domain of cardinality n, and thus in all domains with a cardinality greater than zero. In other words, the conjunction of the premises and the negation of the conclusion is a contradiction and thus its negation, the test statement of the argument, is a logical truth. There is no way to get the premises true and the conclusion false in any domain of cardinality greater than zero. The tree rules guarantee that we will consider domains of just the right size to show this. Putting the point another way, when the tree stops with no open paths, what in effect we are seeing *is that no more cases—that is, domains of a different cardinality—need be considered; all other cases would be like this one.*

But the method of expansion cannot establish this claim, because it does not prescribe what size domain to use for expansions. The method of expansion is such that when we take the premises of the argument and the negation of the conclusion and interpret them into a domain of cardinality n, we may find that we cannot get the premises and the negation of the conclusion all true, which appears to affirm validity. But if we expand into a larger domain, we may find that we can get them simultaneously true, and so the argument would be invalid. This is what happens with our tree earlier that has an open path: An expansion into a one-member domain would yield an inconsistency between the premises and the negation of the conclusion, but the two-member universe shows we can get them all true together. When all paths close in a tree, the tree method run by a perfect machine will always have considered the right size domain so that no further cases need be considered.

Let us summarize our rather complex results:

1. The tree method will mechanically yield a correct decision on every argument on which it yields any decision at all, and it will yield a correct decision on all valid arguments.
2. We *should* be able to figure out a method such that with the method of expansion we could know that if we choose a domain of a certain size, a valid argument will show up valid for that domain and thus for all domains of cardinality greater than zero. We leave this for advanced logic class!
3. If the argument we are testing by trees is invalid, the method may fail, and the method of expansion equally fails. Even for some argument we *know* to be invalid, the tree method will not yield a decision.

Points 1–3 are in effect Church's undecidability results, mentioned in the introduction to this chapter. To see these results in action, as it were, consider the following invalid argument:

$(x)(\exists y)Lxy$ /∴ *Laa*

How do we know this is invalid? Suppose that "*Lxy*" stands for "*x* loves *y*." The premise says that everybody loves somebody, the conclusion, that *a* loves *a*. But it could easily be true that every person loves some person *not* themselves, while the conclusion is false if *a* does not love herself. Now if we make a tree, this is what we get:

	1.	$(x)(\exists y)Lxy$	p /∴ *Laa*
	2.	~ *Laa*	Negation of conclusion
✔	3.	$(\exists y)Lay$	1 **FC5**
	4.	*Lab*	3 **FC4**
✔	5.	$(\exists y)Lby$	1 **FC5**
	6.	*Lbc*	5 **FC4**
✔	7.	$(\exists y)Lcy$	1 **FC5**
	8.	*Lcd*	7 **FC4**

.
.
.

This tree looks as if it would grow forever. Thus a machine would not give us a decision, it would—if an ideal machine—never stop doing instantiations. Why? Our rule for UI tells us we must do a **UI** to every constant in an open path. When we do an **EI** from 3 to 4, we must of course do it to some other constant than *a*, because *a* appears already in the tree. But this means that 4 now contains a constant *b*, to which, when we recycle back by the flow chart, we must now do a **UI** in line 5. Now we have another **EI** to do, and the whole process starts over. If we could construct a machine to predict when a tree will grow indefinitely, we would know the argument invalid. But Church's results tell us this is precisely what a machine cannot do. If it could, we would have a decision procedure, and Church has proved there *cannot be* such a procedure.

Since *we* know that the argument is invalid, and Church has shown that this knowledge cannot be gotten by a mechanical procedure, does this show we are not machines? Fortunately (or unfortunately, because this is a highly interesting subject), this is a question for other philosophy classes!

7 *Strategy and Accounting*

It is important to note that when predicate trees branch, *the rules apply serially to each open path.* Given the preceding formulas, we may well get, say, a universally quantified formula in one branch and an existentially quantified one in another. We apply the rules down each branch, as it were treating each one as if it were a separate tree. Thus the rules may call for doing **FC5** in a left-hand branch, while on the same line but across from it we must perform, say, **FC4** or some other step on some other *wff* in another branch. As in sentential trees, strategy is thus called for at this point. If we can forsee that a branch will not close after we perform all tasks in it, then we can work with that branch and let the others go, as it were.

However, our accounting system, using checkoffs, becomes much more difficult in predicate trees if we proceed serially down each branch. Such a procedure means that if we check off a formula, say, on the trunk of the tree because we have performed an operation on it in a given branch, we may yet have to use that formula again when performing an operation on it in another branch. Consider the following, for example:

✔ (n) $(y)Gy \supset (\exists u)Gu$
    $(n + 1)$ $(\exists x)Fx$

If we now use **FC3** on (n), we will get a branch under $(n + 1)$:

$(n + 2)$ $\sim (y)Gy$ $(\exists u)Gu$ (n) **FC3**

Suppose we now proceed down the left hand-branch, use **FC2** on $\sim (y)Gy$, and then use **FC4,** as (say) we must do next, on $(n + 1)$. We are tempted to check off line $(n + 1)$, yet we are not done with it because we still must use it in the right-hand branch! There is no set procedure for indicating this—you may want to think of your own accounting system here. One obvious possibility is not to check off line $(n + 1)$, but instead, put a mark like a check mark to the *right* of the line number, thereby indicating that the formula has been used, but may be used again. We did something similar in sentential trees when we had more than one formula on a given line, and used one in a branch while not yet using the other in another branch. But this situation is a bit less obvious because we are dealing with one formula that could be used twice or more. Another obvious possibility is to use a different symbol than a check mark on line $(n + 1)$, thereby distinguishing a line that is checked off from one that has been used but could be used again (such a situation, we must recall, differs significantly from the use of universally quantified statements, where those are *never* checked off). In Exercise 12-1, you will encounter this situation, and can experiment for yourself. The point, after all, of the accounting system is not just to indicate a justification, but to keep track of where you are.

It is important to follow out the flow chart *to its completion* on each branch on which you work. For example, suppose you are looking at a branch that contains $(\exists y)Gy$, and you have done at least one or more cycles through the rules, although you have not used **FC4** on the formula in question. You may look up and down a branch and see no formula that contradicts it and thus think that you now have an open path and can stop. But a closer inspection may well reveal that if you perform **FC4** to a constant, you may have to do a new **UI** using **FC5,** and that you will then get a branch or branches that totally changes the tree. For an example of all these problems and procedures, look carefully at (6) in Exercise 12-1.

Exercise 12-1

Use the truth tree method to determine which of the following arguments are valid and which invalid (noting the one argument whose tree is inconclusive). If invalid, use the constants in an open path to expand the premises and conclusion and assign truth-values to show the invalidity.

(1) 1. $(x)(Fx \supset Gx)$
     2. $(\exists x) \sim Gx$ /∴ $(\exists x) \sim Fx$

(2) 1. $(x)[Fx \supset (y)Gy]$
     2. Fa /∴ $(x)Gx$

(3) 1. $(x)(Ax \supset Bx)$
     2. $(x)(\sim Ax \supset Cx)$
        /∴ $(x)(\sim Bx \supset \sim Cx)$

(4) 1. $(\exists x)Fx$
     2. $(x)(\sim Gx \supset \sim Fx)$
     3. $(x)Mx$ /∴ $(\exists x)Gx \cdot (\exists x)Mx$

(5) 1. $(\exists x)[Fx \cdot (y)(Gy \supset Lxy)]$
     2. $(x)[Fx \supset (y)(My \supset \sim Lxy)]$
        /∴ $(x)(Gx \supset \sim Mx)$

(6) 1. $(x)(Ax \supset Fx)$
     2. $(\exists x)Fx \supset \sim (\exists y)Gy$
        /∴ $(x)[(\exists y)Ay \supset \sim Gx]$

(7) 1. $(\exists x)(Ax \cdot \sim Bx)$
     2. $(\exists x)(Ax \cdot \sim Cx)$
     3. $(\exists x)(\sim Bx \cdot Dx)$
        /∴ $(\exists x)[Ax \cdot (\sim Bx \cdot Dx)]$

(8) 1. $(x) \sim Fxx$
     2. $\sim (x)Gx \supset (\exists y)Fya$
        /∴ $(\exists z)(Gz \cdot Fzz)$

(9) 1. $(\exists x)(Ax \vee \sim Bx)$
     2. $(x)[(Ax \cdot \sim Bx) \supset Cx]$
        /∴ $(\exists x)Cx$

(10) 1. $(x)(\exists y)(Fx \cdot Gxy)$
        /∴ $(\exists y)(x)(Fx \cdot Gxy)$

Exercise 12-2

Go back to any of the exercises in Chapters Nine and Ten that ask for proofs of validity or showing invalidity by the method of expansion (10-8 is especially interesting), and construct trees instead. Remember, some that can be shown invalid by a judicious use of the method of expansion may not be capable of being proved invalid by trees.

Exercise 12-3

Here is a philosophical problem for discussion. We have been told by Church that if an argument in predicate logic is valid, a suitably programmed machine will show it is valid using trees in a finite number of steps. But suppose we are watching a machine perform and it has not yet reached the end of a tree, and *we do not know* if the argument being tested is valid or invalid. Can we know the difference between a machine appearing to be on an endless cycle, and a machine that just has not yet done enough steps to prove the argument valid? Invalid?

Key Terms Introduced in Chapter Twelve

cardinality of a domain: The number of objects that are in the domain. A domain may have an infinite cardinality.

Church's undecidability result: The proof by Alonzo Church that there is no mechanical decision procedure for predicate logic that will enable us to decide whether any given argument is valid or invalid.

flow chart for predicate trees: A mechanical procedure for testing arguments in predicate logic. If an argument in predicate logic is valid, the procedure will show it is in a finite number of steps. But it can only yield a correct answer in the case of some invalid arguments—see **Church's undecidability result.**

infinitely growing tree: A predicate tree in which the rules apply an infinite number of times. There is no mechanical procedure for deciding whether a given tree will grow infinitely, thus no decision on the invalidity of the argument being tested.

invalid argument: An argument is invalid if it is invalid in any domain with cardinality greater than zero.

invalidity in a domain: An argument is invalid in a domain if we can find a counterexample in it.

Chapter Thirteen

Identity and Philosophical Problems of Symbolic Logic

1   *Identity*

The verb "to be," in all its variations ("is," "was," and so on), is ambiguous. Take the following sentences:

> John is tall.
> Mark Twain is Samuel Clemens.

In the first sentence, the word "is" indicates that the property of being tall is a property of John. This is sometimes called the predicating function of the word "is." But in the second sentence, no property is predicated of Mark Twain. Instead, the word "is" indicates an identity between the person who is Mark Twain and the person who is Samuel Clemens. It would be correct to symbolize the first sentence as *Tj*, but incorrect to symbolize the second sentence as *Ct* (where *t* = "Mark Twain" and *C* = "Samuel Clemens").

We introduce a new symbol, the identity symbol " = ," so that we can correctly translate statements of identity into our logical notation. Using this new symbol, we can symbolize the sentence "Mark Twain is Samuel Clemens" as $t = c$. Similarly, we can symbolize the sentence "United Brands is United Fruit" as $b = f$, the sentence "Archie Leach is Cary Grant" as $l = g$, and so on.

Now let's look at the following argument, in which the identity sign is used:

1. *Wtf* (Mark Twain wrote *Huckleberry Finn*.)
2. $t = c$ (Mark Twain is Samuel Clemens.)
 /∴ *Wcf* (Samuel Clemens wrote *Huckleberry Finn*.)

Clearly, this argument is valid. But so far, our system provides no justification for the conclusion. Let's now introduce such a justification, namely the *rule of identity* (**ID**), which states, in effect, that we may substitute identicals for identicals. The rule can be schematized as follows:

   1. $(\ldots u \ldots)$
   2. $u = w \;/\therefore\; (\ldots w \ldots)$

where u and w are any individual constants or individual variables, and where $(\ldots w \ldots)$ results from replacing one or more occurrences of u free in $(\ldots u \ldots)$ by occurrences of w free in $(\ldots w \ldots)$.

Further, since if $u = w$, then $w = u$, we allow the following variation on the rule of identity:

   1. $(\ldots u \ldots)$
   2. $w = u \;/\therefore\; (\ldots w \ldots)$

Examples

The following examples illustrate the use of the identity sign and also the rule of identity (**ID**) in proofs.

(1) 1. $Fa \supset Ga$ p
     2. $\sim Ga$ p
     3. $a = b$ p $/\therefore \sim Fb$
     4. $\sim Fa$ 1,2 **MT**
     5. $\sim Fb$ 3,4 **ID** (rule of identity)

(2) 1. $(x)[(x = b) \supset Fx]$ p
     2. $a = b$ p
     3. $a = c$ p $/\therefore Fc$
     4. $(a = b) \supset Fa$ 1 **UI**
     5. Fa 2,4 **MP**
     6. Fc 3,5 **ID**

(3) 1. $Fa \supset Ga$ p
     2. $\sim (Fb \supset Gb)$ p $/\therefore \sim (a = b)$
  → 3. $\sim\sim (a = b)$ **AP** $\sim (a = b)$
     4. $a = b$ 3 **DN**
     5. $Fb \supset Gb$ 1,4 **ID**
     6. $(Fb \supset Gb) \cdot \sim (Fb \supset Gb)$ 2,4 **Conj**
     7. $\sim (a = b)$ 3,6 **IP**

Expressions such as $\sim (a = b)$ also can be written as $a \neq b$. Here is a proof using this notation:

(4) 1. $(x)[(x \neq b) \supset Fx]$ p
     2. $a \neq b$ p $/\therefore Fa$
     3. $(a \neq b) \supset Fa$ 1 **UI**
     4. Fa 2,3 **MP**

To make our system complete, we introduce a rule—let's call it *Identity Reflexivity,* or **IR**—allowing introduction of the formula $(x)(x = x)$ into a proof at any time.* Most valid arguments containing uses of the identity symbol can be proved without resorting to **IR,** but a few cannot. Here is an example:

1. $(x)[(x = a) \supset Fx]$ $/\therefore Fa$
2. $(a = a) \supset Fa$ 1 **UI**
3. $(x)(x = x)$ **IR**
4. $a = a$ 3 **UI**
5. Fa 2,4 **MP**

Exercise 13-1

Prove valid:

(1) 1. $Fa \cdot (x)[Fx \supset (x = a)]$ p
    2. $(\exists x)(Fx \cdot Gx)$ p $/\therefore Ga$

(2) 1. $(x)(Px \supset Qx)$ p
    2. $(x)(Qx \supset Rx)$ p
    3. $Pa \cdot \sim Rb$ p $/\therefore \sim (a = b)$

(3) 1. $Hc \supset Kc$ p
    2. $Md \supset Nd$ p
    3. $Hc \cdot Md$ p
    4. $c = d$ p $/\therefore Kd \cdot Nc$

(4) 1. $(x)[Fx \supset (\exists y)Gyx]$ p
    2. Fa p
    3. $(y) \sim Gyb$ p $/\therefore \sim (a = b)$

(5) 1. $(\exists x)\{\{Px \cdot (y)[Py \supset (y = x)]\} \cdot Qx\}$ p
    2. $\sim Qa$ p $/\therefore \sim Pa$

(6) 1. $(\exists x)(y)\{[\sim Fxy \supset (x = y)] \cdot Gx\}$ p
    $/\therefore (x)\{\sim Gx \supset (\exists y)[\sim (y = x) \cdot Fyx]\}$

(7) 1. $(\exists x)\{Px \cdot \{(y)[Py \supset (y = x)] \cdot Qx\}\}$ p
    2. $(\exists x) \sim (\sim Px \vee \sim Ex)$ p $/\therefore (\exists x)(Ex \cdot Qx)$

(8) 1. $(x)[Fx \supset (x = a)]$ p
    2. $(x)[Mx \supset (x = b)]$ p
    3. $(\exists x)(Fx \cdot Mx)$ p $/\therefore a = b$

(9) 1. $(x)(Gx \supset Fx)$ p
    2. $(x)(y)[(Fx \vee Fy) \supset (x = y)]$ p
    3. Gb p $/\therefore a = c$

---

*In the history of logic, the idea that any given thing is identical with itself, called the law of identity (one of the basic principles believed in times past to be the fundamental laws of thought), has usually been expressed as "*a* is *a*." But the meaning of this formula is better expressed in our notation by $(x)(x = x)$. Why we have named this principle Identity Reflexivity will become apparent from the discussion of the property of reflexivity later in this chapter.

(10)   1. $\sim (x) \sim (Ax \cdot Bx)$ p
        2. $(y)[\sim (y = a) \supset \sim Ay]$ p
        3. $(z) \sim [(z \neq b) \cdot Bz]$ $p \; / \therefore \; a = b$

Once the identity sign is added to predicate logic, we can symbolize sentences stating quantities other than all, some, and none.

At least

We already know how to symbolize sentences containing the expression "at least one," namely by means of the existential quantifier. Thus, the sentence "There is at least one student" can be symbolized as $(\exists x)Sx$.

But we cannot symbolize the sentence "There are at least two students" as $(\exists x)(\exists y)$ $(Sx \cdot Sy)$, because the x and y referred to might be the same entity. However, using the identity sign, we can correctly symbolize it as

$$(\exists x)(\exists y)[(Sx \cdot Sy) \cdot (x \neq y)]$$

This expression says that there is an x that is a student, and a y that is a student, and x is not identical with y, which is what the sentence "There are at least two students" states.

Similarly, we can symbolize the sentence "There are at least three students" as

$$(\exists x)(\exists y)(\exists z)\{[(Sx \cdot Sy) \cdot Sz] \cdot \{[(x \neq y) \cdot (x \neq z)] \cdot (y \neq z) \}\}$$

And in the same way, we can handle the phrases "at least four," "at least five," and so on

At most

Next, take the sentence "There is at most one student." It is correctly symbolized as

$$(x)\{Sx \supset (y)[Sy \supset (x = y)]\}$$

The reason for the universal quantifier is that this sentence asserts not that there are any students, but rather that there is not more than one student. It would be true if there were no students at all, as well as if there were exactly one.

Similarly, we can symbolize the sentence "There are at most two students" as

$$(x)(y)\{[(Sx \cdot Sy) \cdot (x \neq y)] \supset (z)\{Sz \supset [(z = x) \vee (z = y)]\}\}$$

And in the same way we can handle sentences containing the phrases "at most three," "at most four," and so on.

Exactly

Now consider the sentence "There is exactly one student." First, if there is exactly one student, then there is at least one. So part of the meaning of "exactly one" is captured by the phrase "at least one," and hence part of the meaning of the sentence "There is exactly one student" can be symbolized as $(\exists x)Sx$. Second, if there is exactly one student, then there is at most one student. So the rest of the meaning of "exactly one" is captured by the phrase "at most one." Thus "There is exactly one student" is correctly symbolized as

$$(\exists x)\{Sx \cdot (y)[Sy \supset (x = y)]\}$$

This asserts there is at least one student, x, and given any allegedly other student, y, y is identical with x. That is, it asserts there is at least one student and at most one student, which is what is said by "There is exactly one student."

Similarly, we can symbolize the sentence "There are exactly two students" as

$$(\exists x)(\exists y)\{[(Sx \cdot Sy) \cdot (x \neq y)] \cdot (z)\{Sz \supset [(z = x) \vee (z = y)]\}\}$$

And obviously, the same method can be applied in symbolizing the phrases "exactly three," "exactly four," and so on.

Addition of the identity sign to our vocabulary also enables us to symbolize several other kinds of statements we couldn't handle before, including the following two.

Only

Take the statement "Only George didn't pass the exam." We can't symbolize that statement simply as $\sim Pg$, because that says just that George didn't pass the exam, but not that only George didn't pass. Instead, we can symbolize it as

$$\sim Pg \cdot (x)\{[Sx \cdot (x \neq g)] \supset Px\}$$

This statement says that George didn't pass the exam but that all the other students did, which is what the original statement asserts.

Everyone but

Now consider the statement "Every student in this class but George passed the exam." Another way to say the same thing is to say that George didn't pass the exam, but every student in the class not identical with George passed, easily symbolized using identity (and obvious abbreviations) as

$$\sim Pg \cdot (x)\{[Sx \cdot (x \neq g)] \supset Px\}$$

Similarly, all sorts of other expressions can be captured once the identity sign is introduced. Perhaps the most important of these expressions are the definite descriptions discussed in the next section.

Examples

Here are a few more examples of symbolizations using the identity sign (restricting the universe of discourse to human beings).

1. Everyone loves exactly one person.
   $(x)(\exists y)\{Lxy \cdot (z)[Lxz \supset (z = y)]\}$

2. Everyone loves exactly one other person.
   $(x)(\exists y)\{[(x \neq y) \cdot Lxy] \cdot (z)[Lxz \supset (z = y)]\}$

3. We all love only ourselves (interpreted to mean that we all love ourselves and no one else).
   $(x)\{Lxx \cdot (y)[(y \neq x) \supset \sim Lxy]\}$

4. At most, we all love only ourselves.
   $(x)(y)[Lxy \supset (x = y)]$

5. Someone loves someone.
   $(\exists x)(\exists y)Lxy$

6. Someone loves someone else.
   $(\exists x)(\exists y)[Lxy \cdot (x \neq y)]$

7. Some people love only other people.
   $(\exists x)(y)[Lxy \supset (x \neq y)]$

8. Some people love no one else.
   $(\exists x)(y)[(x \neq y) \supset \sim Lxy]$

9. Only Art loves Betsy (interpreted to imply that Art does love Betsy).
   $Lab \cdot (x)[Lxb \supset (x = a)]$

10. Every planet except Earth is uninhabitable.
    $(x)\{[Px \cdot (x \neq e)] \supset \sim Ix\} \cdot Ie$

Exercise 13-2

Symbolize the following, using the indicated letters.

1. Only George Washington was the first president of the United States. (g = "George Washington"; Fx = "x is the first U.S. president")

2. Only Ronald Reagan was president of the Screen Actors' Guild and also U.S. president. (r = "Ronald Reagan"; Px = "x is president of the United States"; Sx = "x is president of the Screen Actors' Guild")

3. At least one famous Hollywood actor was elected governor of California. (Fx = "x is a famous Hollywood actor"; Gx = "x was elected governor of California")

4. At most, two famous Hollywood actors ran for governor of California. (Rx = "x ran for governor of California")

5. Exactly three famous Hollywood actors have been president of the Screen Actors' Guild.

6. No president of the United States has also been president of the Screen Actors' Guild, except for Ronald Reagan.

7. Adolf Hitler hated every human being—except for himself, of course. (h = "Adolf Hitler"; Px = "x is a person"; Hxy = "x hated y")

8. Abe Lincoln was more compassionate than any other U.S. president. (a = "Abe Lincoln"; Cxy = "x is more compassionate than y")

9. All the other U.S. presidents have been less compassionate than Abraham Lincoln.

10. Daryl Zanuck knew every celebrity in Hollywood, not counting himself. (z = "Daryl Zanuck"; Cx = "x is a Hollywood celebrity"; Kxy = "x knew y")

2 *Definite Descriptions*

We can refer to a person or entity by name, for example, "Samuel Clemens," "Mt. Everest," or by description, for example, "the author of *Huckleberry Finn*," "the tallest mountain in the world." A description of this kind is called a **definite description,** because it picks out or describes one definite entity. The identity sign is needed to symbolize sentences containing definite definitions.

Take the sentence "The president of the United States is religious." A person who utters this sentence asserts (in part) that there is one and only one person who is president of the United States, because it would be inappropriate to talk about the president of the United States if there were more than one such person. Therefore, this sentence can be symbolized by first symbolizing "There is exactly one president of the United States" and then adding that he is religious. So the sentence "The president of the United States is religious" is symbolized as

$$(\exists x)\{\{Px \cdot (y)[Py \supset (x = y)]\} \cdot Rx\}$$

The first conjunct asserts that some (at least one) entity is president of the United States, the second that at most one is, and the third that that entity is religious.*

Examples

Here are a few more sentences containing definite descriptions and their correct symbolizations (again restricting the universe of discourse to human beings).

1. Everyone admires the most intelligent person in the world.
   $(\exists x)(y)[Ixy \cdot (x \neq y) \cdot (z)(Izy \supset z = x) \cdot (u)Aux]$
   (Ixy = "x is more intelligent than y"; Axy = "x admires y")

2. The most intelligent person in the world is also the most admired.
   $(\exists x)(y)\{Ixy \cdot Axy \cdot (x \neq y) \cdot (z)[(Izy \cdot Axy) \supset z = x]\}$
   (Axy = "x is more admired than y")

3. The most intelligent person in the world admires only intelligent people.
   $(\exists x)(y)\{Ixy \cdot (x \neq y) \cdot (z)(Izy \supset z = x) \cdot (u)(Axu \supset Ix)\}$
   (Ix = "x is intelligent")

4. The person most admired by Art is also admired by Betsy.
   $(\exists x)(y)[Aaxy \cdot (z)(Aazy \supset z = x) \cdot Abx]$
   ($Axyz$ = "x admires y more than z"; Axy = "x admires y"; a = "Art"; b = "Betsy")

5. Art's father admires him.
   $(\exists x)\{\{Fxa \cdot (y)[Fya \supset (x = y)]\} \cdot Axa\}$
   (Fxy = "x is a father of y")

---

*This analysis was first proposed by Bertrand Russell. See his "On Denoting," *Mind*, n.s., vol. 14 (1: 05), reprinted in Robert C. Marsh, ed., *Logic and Knowledge* (New York: Macmillan, 1956). This analysis has been enormously important to subsequent philosophy. See the Marsh volume.

6. Art's father admires the most intelligent person in the world.
    $(\exists x)(y)\{Ixy \cdot (x \neq y) \cdot (z)(Izy \supset z = x) \cdot (\exists u)[Fua \cdot (w)(Fwa \supset w = u) \cdot Aux\}$

7. Everyone admires the most generous person.
    $(\exists x)(y)[Gxy \cdot (x \neq y) \cdot (z)(Gzy \supset z = x) \cdot (u)Aux]$
    (Gxy = "x is more generous than y")

The same caution is necessary in symbolizing sentences containing phrases such as "the Chairman" and "the tallest person in the world" as is necessary in symbolizing other complicated sentences. In particular, sentences of this kind frequently are ambiguous; before symbolizing them we must get clear as to which meaning we intend our symbolization to capture.

Take the sentence "It is not the case that the present king of France is bald," which can mean either that there is one and only one present king of France and he is not bald, or that it is not the case that there is one (and only one) bald present king of France. If the former is intended, then the sentence in question is correctly symbolized as

$$(\exists x)\{\{Px \cdot (y)[Py \supset (x = y)]\} \cdot \sim Bx\}$$

(where Px = "x is, at present, king of France" and Bx = "x is bald"). If the latter is intended, then it is correctly symbolized as

$$\sim (\exists x)\{\{Px \cdot (y)[Py \supset (x = y)]\} \cdot Bx\}$$

Caution also is necessary because phrases that usually function as definite descriptions occasionally do not. An example is the sentence "The next person who moves will get shot," snarled by a gunman during a holdup. Clearly, the gunman does not intend to assert that there is one and only one person who will get shot if he moves. Instead, he intends to say that *anyone* who moves will get shot. So his threat is correctly symbolized as

$$(x)[(Px \cdot Mx) \supset Sx]$$

Another example is the chauvinistic saying "The female of the species is vain," which means something like "All females are vain" or "Most females are vain," but surely does not say anything about the one and only female.

However, some uses of the phrase "the so and so" that may appear not to function as definite descriptions, really do. For instance, when the presiding officer of the U.S. Senate recognizes "the senator from California," it may appear that that phrase cannot be functioning as a definite description, because there are two California senators. In this context, however, the phrase "the senator from California" means the one who has requested the floor. But if, say, both California senators request the floor at the same time (and they're standing right next to each other), the presiding officer would use a phrase such as "the junior senator from California" or "the senior senator from California," thus unambiguously selecting one definite person to have the floor.

Exercise 13-3

Symbolize the following sentences, and indicate the meanings of the abbreviations you use.

1. Every student is more intelligent than some student (or other).
2. Bonny is more intelligent than any other student.
3. The hardest thing to put up with is a good example.
4. There are no rules, other than this one, that have no exceptions.
5. Bobby Fisher is the best chess player who ever lived.
6. Gary Kasparov is the current chess champion of the world.
7. Any current chess player who is better at the game than Anatoli Karpov must be one and the same as Gary Kasparov.
8. The two Maine senators like each other.
9. The two presidential candidates dislike each other.
10. If Carl Lewis isn't the best sprinter, then there is just one who is better than he is.

3 *Properties of Relations*

There are several interesting properties that relational properties themselves may possess. The reason they are interesting is that these properties (and other properties of relations that are less commonly used than the ones we will discuss) are used in mathematics and the sciences to generate *orders* between things—for example, orders of numbers, orders of the colors on a color wheel, orders of points on a straight line. For example, if *a, b,* and *c* are points on a straight line, and *a* is next to *b,* and *b* is next to *c,* we can define a relation of between-ness, such that *b* is between *a* and *c,* based on the fact that "next to" is *intransitive, symmetrical,* and *irreflexive* (see later). That is, if two things are next to the same thing, then that third thing must be between them. In arithmetic, from the fact that 2 is the next number after 1 (the successor of 1), and 3 is the next number after 2, we can see that the relation of between-ness holds between these numbers. Because every number can have only one successor and cannot succeed itself, it follows that if a number *x* succeeds *y* and is succeeded by *z,* that *x* is between *y* and *z*—that is, we can define what it means for a number to be between two others by using the relation of "successor of." Along these same lines, we might think of the fact that if *x* is between *y* and *z,* and succeeds *y,* that *x* is larger than *y* but smaller than *z.* The properties of relations thus show us many interesting things about domains of objects, such as numbers, and how some relations among numbers can be seen to depend logically on others.

Symmetry

All two-place relations (relations of the general form *Fxy*) are either *symmetrical, asymmetrical,* or *nonsymmetrical.* A relation is **symmetrical** if and only if, when one thing

bears that relation to a second, the second must* bear it to the first. So a relation designated by *Fxy* is a symmetrical relation if and only if it must be the case that

$$(x)(y)(Fxy \supset Fyx)$$

The relation "_____ is married to _____" is an example of a sym-
metrical relation. For given any *x* and *y*, if *x* is married to *y*, then *y* must be married to *x*.

An **asymmetrical** relation is just the opposite of a symmetrical relation. Thus, a relation is asymmetrical if and only if when one thing bears that relation to a second, the second thing cannot bear it to the first. So a relation designated by *Fxy* is asymmetrical if and
only if it must be the case that

$$(x)(y)(Fxy \supset \sim Fyx)$$

The relation "_____ is the father of _____" is an example of an
asymmetrical relation. For given any *x* and *y*, if *x* is the father of *y*, then it must be false
that *y* is the father of *x*.

All relations that are neither symmetrical nor asymmetrical are **nonsymmetrical.**
For example, the relation "_____ loves _____" is nonsymmetrical,
because loving someone entails neither being loved by that person nor not being loved by
that person.

Transitivity

All two-place relations are either *transitive, intransitive,* or *nontransitive*. A relation is
transitive if and only if when one thing bears that relation to a second, and the second to
a third, then the first must bear it to the third. Thus, a relation designated by *Fxy* is transitive if and only if it must be the case that

$$(x)(y)(z)[(Fxy \cdot Fyz) \supset Fxz]$$

The relation "_____ is taller than _____" is an example. For if a
given person is taller than a second, and the second is taller than a third, then the first must
be taller than the third.

It is interesting to note that the statement of a property of a relation often is required in
order to present a valid proof for an otherwise invalid argument. For instance, the argument

1. *Tab* (Art is taller than Betsy.)
2. *Tbc* (Betsy is taller than Charles.)
   /∴ *Tac* (Art is taller than Charles.)

is invalid as it stands (using the machinery of predicate logic), but can be made valid by the
introduction of a premise concerning the transitivity of the relation "taller than," as follows:

---

*The sense of "must" involved here, indeed even the use of that term in characterizing relations of this kind, is in dispute. The
same is true of the related term "cannot" used as a synonym for "it is not possible that."

1. *Tab*	p
2. *Tbc*	p
3. $(x)(y)(z)[(Txy \cdot Tyz) \supset Txz]$	p /∴ *Tac*
4. $(y)(z)[(Tay \cdot Tyz) \supset Taz]$	3 **UI**
5. $(z)[(Tab \cdot Tbz) \supset Taz]$	4 **UI**
6. $(Tab \cdot Tbc) \supset Tac$	5 **UI**
7. $(Tab \cdot Tbc)$	1,2 **Conj**
8. *Tac*	6,7 **MP**

A relation is **intransitive** if and only if, when one thing bears that relation to a second, and the second to a third, then the first cannot bear it to the third. Thus a relation designated by *Fxy* is intransitive if and only if it must be the case that

$$(x)(y)(z)[(Fxy \cdot Fyz) \supset \sim Fxz]$$

The relation "_____ is the father of _____" is an example. For if one person is the father of a second, and the second of a third, then the first cannot be the father of the third.

All relations that are neither transitive nor intransitive are **nontransitive.** For example, the relation "_____ loves _____" is nontransitive, since if one person loves a second, and the second loves a third, it follows neither that the first person loves the third nor that the first person doesn't love the third.

Reflexivity

The situation with respect to reflexivity is more complex.

A relation is **totally reflexive** if and only if everything must bear that relation to itself. So a relation designated by *Fxy* is totally reflexive if and only if it must be the case that

$$(x)Fxx$$

The relation "_____ is identical with _____" is an example. For everything must be identical with itself.

Almost all interesting relations are *not* totally reflexive. There is no name in common use for relations that are not totally reflexive, but we can say that a relation designated by *Fxy* is *not totally reflexive* if and only if it is not necessarily the case that

$$(x)Fxx$$

The relation "_____ loves _____" (restricting the domain of discourse to human beings) is an example. It is not necessarily true that all human beings love themselves.

A relation is said to be **reflexive** if and only if everything that bears that relation to anything must bear it to itself. That is, a relation designated by *Fxy* is reflexive if and only if it must be the case that

$$(x)(y)[Fxy \supset (Fxx \cdot Fyy)]$$

An example is the relation "_____ belongs to the same political party as _____," because if a given entity, say Art, belongs to the same political party as anyone else, say Betsy, then Art must belong to the same political party as himself, and so must Betsy.

Notice that "_____ belongs to the same political party as ...." is not totally reflexive, because not everything belongs to the same political party as itself. For example, a piece of chalk doesn't belong to any political party at all. So some reflexive relations are not totally reflexive. But all totally reflexive relations are reflexive.

A relation is **irreflexive** if and only if nothing can bear that relation to itself. Thus, a relation designated by *Fxy* is irreflexive if and only if it must be the case that

$$(x) \sim Fxx$$

The relation "_____ is taller than ...." is an example. For nothing can be taller than itself.

Finally, all relations that are neither reflexive nor irreflexive are **nonreflexive.** For example, the relation "_____ loves ...." is nonreflexive because (1) it is not reflexive (a person can love someone else, but not love himself), and (2) it is not irreflexive (a person can love someone else and also love himself).

Exercise 13-4

A. Determine the status of the following relations with respect to symmetry, transitivity, and reflexivity:

1. _____ is ashamed of.................... .
2. _____ is the mother of ....
3. _____ is ≥ .... (concerning numbers only)
4. _____ is north of ....
5. _____ is at least one year younger than ....
6. _____ is identical with ....
7. _____ is the sister of ....
8. _____ sees ....

B. Prove that all asymmetrical relations are irreflexive.

4 *Higher-Order Logics*

The predicate logic discussed so far expressly forbids sentences that ascribe properties to properties themselves and restricts quantification to individual variables. A predicate logic restricted in this way is said to be a **first-order predicate logic.** We now consider the bare bones of a higher-order predicate logic.

Quantifying over property variables

Just as we can have individual variables, so we can have **property variables.** Let's use the capital letters *F*, *G*, *H*, and *K* as property variables, for the time being forbidding their use as property constants. The expression *Fa* will then be a sentence form, and not a sentence. But we obviously can obtain a sentence from this expression by replacing the property variable *F* by a property constant. Thus we can obtain the sentence *Sa* (where *Sx* = "x is smart") from the sentence form *Fa*. (Hence *Sa* is a substitution instance of *Fa*.)

But we also can obtain a sentence from the sentence form *Fa* by quantifying the property variable *F*. Thus we can obtain the sentences (*F*)(*Fa*), read "Art has every property," or "Given any property, *F*, Art has *F*," and (∃*F*)(*Fa*), read "Art has some property (or other)," or "There is some property *F* such that Art has *F*."

We also can have sentences that quantify both property variables and individual variables. An example would be the sentence "Everything has some property (or other)," symbolized as (*x*)(∃*F*) *Fx*.

Examples

Some other examples of symbolizations containing quantified property variables are

1. (*x*)(*F*)*Fx*	Everything has every property.
2. (∃*x*)(*F*)*Fx*	Something has every property.
3. (∃*x*)(∃*F*)*Fx*	Something has some property (or other).
4. (*F*)(∃*x*)*Fx*	Every property belongs to something (or other).
5. (∃*F*)(*x*)*Fx*	Some property belongs to everything.
6. ~ (∃*x*)(*F*)*Fx*	Nothing has all properties.
7. (*F*){*Fa* ⊃ ~ (∃*x*)[(*Fx*) · (*x* ≠ *a*)]}	No one else has any property that Art has.
8. (∃*F*){*Fa* · (*y*){[(*y* ≠ *a*)] · ~ *Fy*}}	Art has some property no one else has.

Now that we have introduced property variables and the quantification of property variables, we can give a more precise definition of the identity symbol, for we can say that the expression *x* = *y* means that necessarily (*F*)(*Fx* ≡ *Fy*). It follows then that (*x*)(*y*)[(*x* = *y*) ≡ (*F*)(*Fx* ≡ *Fy*)],* from which we can prove that the identity relation is transitive, symmetrical, and reflexive. (Recall that we labeled one of the identity rules of inference Identity Reflexivity.)

Higher-order properties

So far, we have considered only properties of individuals. But properties themselves can have properties. For instance, honesty is a rare property, while (unfortunately) dishonesty is quite common. Similarly, courage is an honorable property, cowardice dishonorable.

---

*A variation on Leibniz's law.

Let's use the symbols A_1, B_1, C_1, and so forth, to refer to properties of properties. Then we can symbolize the sentence "Honesty is a rare property" as R_1H, and the sentence "Courage is a useful property" as U_1C. Similarly, we can symbolize the sentence "We all have useful properties" as $(x)(\exists F)(Fx \cdot U_1F)$, and so on.

Examples

Some other examples of symbolizations containing properties of properties are

1. $(F)U_1F$	All properties are useful.
2. $(\exists F)(U_1F \cdot R_1F)$	Some useful properties are rare.
3. $(\exists F)(G_1F \cdot Fa)$	Art has some good properties (qualities).
4. $(\exists F)[(G_1F \cdot Fa) \cdot Fb]$	Art and Betsy share some good qualities.
5. $(F)[(Fb \cdot G_1F) \supset Fa]$	Art has all of Betsy's good qualities.
6. $(x)\{(\exists F)\{Fx \cdot (G)[Gx \supset (F = G)]\}$ $\supset \sim (\exists H)(Hx \cdot G_1H)\}$	Nothing that has only one property has any good properties.

Unfortunately, higher-order logics involving properties of properties have encountered important difficulties, which have as yet not been satisfactorily worked out. In contrast to first-order predicate logic, there is no system of inference rules for second-order logic that is both sound and complete.

5 *Limitations of Predicate Logic*

At the beginning of the discussion of predicate logic, we pointed out that certain kinds of valid arguments are invalid when symbolized in the notation of sentential logic. We then proceeded to develop predicate logic, which provides a method for symbolizing these arguments and for proving them valid.

The question naturally arises whether there are other arguments that, although invalid using the notation and proof technique of predicate logic, are valid in some wider (perhaps ideal) deductive system. The answer is that there seem to be such arguments.

Consider the argument

1. Art believes that he'll go either to the show or to the concert (but not to both).
2. Art believes he won't go to the show.
   /∴ Art believes he'll go to the concert.

Clearly, this argument is valid in some sense or other. But there is no way to symbolize it in the standard predicate logic notation so that we can prove it is valid. We might try to introduce a two-place relational predicate, which instead of having two terms in the usual way (both individuals), describes a relation between an individual and what is expressed by a statement.

1. $Ba\ [(P \lor Q) \cdot \sim (P \cdot Q)]$
2. $Ba \sim P$
   $/\therefore BaQ$

where "*Bxp*" is read "*x* believes that *p.*" The problem here is that none of these statements is truth-functional, because the truth of *x* believes that *p* is independent of the truth-value of *p*! After all, one can have false beliefs. Given that our statements are not truth-functional and are not quantified statements either, we have no rules that would justify the deduction.

This is an example of an argument involving what are sometimes called **indirect or intensional contexts.** In this case the clue that we are dealing with an indirect context is the phrase "believes that." Contexts that use terms that refer to what we normally think of as states of the mind, such as, remembering, doubting, and believing, where what is remembered, doubted, or believed is expressed by a statement, are sometimes called **intentional contexts.** So intentional contexts are a species of intensional or indirect contexts. Some other phrases that usually indicate indirect contexts are "is looking for," "prays to," and "is necessary that."

Special problems are raised by statements such as "Bob saw that the train was in the station." Some philosophers argue that if the train was not in the station, Bob could not have seen that it was, which is unlike the case of belief. Bob might believe the train is in the station even if it isn't, but he cannot *see* that it is in the station if it is not. So sensory states give special problems for translation.

So far, the logic of indirect contexts, or intensional contexts, has not been worked out, at least not to the satisfaction of most philosophers. The whole area is one of extreme disagreement, and the predicate logic presented in this and other textbooks is not able to deal adequately with it.

There are other cases where it is claimed that the predicate logic presented here is inadequate. We present two that are the centers of interesting disputes.

The first is illustrated by the following argument:

1. Art sang the Hamilton school song beautifully.
   $/\therefore$ Art sang the Hamilton school song.

Again, the argument is valid, and again it is claimed we cannot prove that it is valid using the notation-and-proof technique of predicate logic.

Several solutions have been proposed for this problem. One is simply that there is a "missing premise." According to this solution, the argument in question is invalid as it stands, but can be made valid by supplying an obvious "missing premise," namely the premise that if someone sang a particular song beautifully, then he sang that song. Once we add this missing premise, the argument can be proved quite easily in predicate logic. Arguments with missing premises are called *enthymematic.*

Another dispute involves what we might call "semantically valid arguments." Suppose for the moment that the term "bachelor" means exactly the same thing as "unmarried adult male." Then it is clear that the argument

1. All bachelors are handsome.
   $/\therefore$ All unmarried adult males are handsome.

is valid in some sense or other. But again, it appears to be invalid in the predicate logic system developed in this text.

Several ways have been proposed to handle so-called semantically valid arguments. One is to introduce a rule permitting the substitution of terms *synonymous* with any terms occurring in an argument as stated.

Another way is to claim that these arguments are enthymematic. In the example in question, the missing premise is that all bachelors are unmarried adult males.

And a third way is to deny that the argument in question is valid, on the grounds that truly synonymous expressions do not exist, at least not in natural languages.

Finally, note that predicate logic has trouble dealing with statements about *dispositional properties* and with *subjunctive statements*, in particular *counterfactual conditionals*.

Dispositional properties are powers, potentials, or dispositions of objects. An example is the dispositional property of being flammable. Although dispositional properties cannot be experienced through the five senses, in some cases their observable "mates" can be. For instance, we can't see that a piece of dry wood is flammable (dispositional term), but when it is lighted, we can see it burn (observational property). Since dispositional properties can't be experienced directly, we must infer their existence.

Obviously, dispositional properties such as being flammable or flexible are closely connected to their observational mates. Being flexible, for instance, is connected to the observational property of bending, for to say that something is flexible is to say that it has the power, potential, or disposition to bend, under certain conditions. Similarly, to say that something is flammable is to say that it has the power, disposition, or potential to burn. And so on for other dispositional properties.

The problem for logic has to do with the correct symbolization of statements about dispositional properties. What does it mean to say, for instance, that sugar is soluble (dispositional property) in water? What is a disposition, power, or potential?

The problem is easy to overlook in everyday life because an easy answer seems readily available. It seems natural to suppose, for instance, that when we say a particular lump of sugar has the dispositional property of being soluble in water, we mean simply that if we place the lump into water (under suitable conditions of temperature, water saturation, and so on), then it will dissolve. Similarly, if we say that a plastic tube is flexible, we mean that if suitable pressure is applied to it, then it will bend. And so on.

Therefore, it seems initially plausible to say that, given a sentence containing a dispositional term, we can replace it by an "If _____ then _____" sentence containing not the dispositional term but rather its observational mate. For instance, we seem able to replace the dispositional sentence "Lump of sugar *s* is soluble" by the statement "If *s* is placed into water under suitable conditions, then *s* will dissolve," and replace the dispositional sentence "Piece of wood *w* is flammable" by the sentence "If oxygen and heat are applied to *w* under suitable conditions, then *w* will burn."

All this seems reasonable until we try to put these sentences into the symbolic notation of predicate logic or into some other equally precise notation. Take the dispositional sentence "Lump of sugar *s* is soluble." It seems plausible to translate that sentence into the nondispositional sentence "If *s* is placed into water, then it will dissolve," symbolized as $Ws \supset Ds$ (omitting the qualification about suitable conditions for the moment). But does the sentence $Ws \supset Ds$ really mean the same thing as the dispositional sentence "Lump of sugar *s* is soluble"? Unfortunately, it does not.

To see that it does not, consider the false dispositional sentence "Piece of copper *c* is soluble" and its analogous translation to "If *c* is placed into water, then *c* will dissolve," symbolized as $Wc \supset Dc$. Suppose we never place c into water, so that the antecedent Wc is false. If so, then the whole sentence $Wc \supset Dc$ will be true, because all conditional statements with false antecedents are true. But if the sentence $Wc \supset Dc$ is true, it cannot possibly be a correct translation of the false sentence "Piece of copper c is soluble," since a sentence and its correct translation cannot have different truth values.

Analogously, the translation of the sentence "Lump of sugar s is soluble" into $Ws \supset Ds$ also must be incorrect, even though in this case, luckily, both the sentence translated and the sentence it is translated into have the same truth value. That this is a matter of luck becomes obvious when we realize that the analogous translation of the sentence "Lump of sugar s is not soluble" into "If s is placed into water, then it will not dissolve" also is true if s is never placed into water. But surely the two statements "s is soluble" and "s is not soluble" cannot both be true.

To put the difficulty another way, if we translate all dispositional sentences into nondispositional conditional sentences in the way just outlined, then all these conditionals with false antecedents will have to be judged true, even though many of the dispositional sentences they are intended to translate (for example, "Piece of copper c is soluble," "Lump of sugar s is not soluble") are false.

The conclusion we must draw is that dispositional sentences cannot be replaced by nondispositional material conditional sentences, or at least not in this simple way. The so-called problem of dispositionals is to find a satisfactory way to translate sentences of this type.

It has been suggested that the correct analysis of dispositional sentences is not into indicative conditionals but rather into **subjunctive** or **contrary-to-fact conditionals.** For instance, according to this view, the correct translation of "s is soluble" is not into the indicative conditional "If s is placed into water, then it will dissolve" but rather into the subjunctive conditional "If s were placed into water, then it would dissolve" or into the contrary-to-fact conditional "If s had been placed into water, then it would have dissolved."

The trouble with this analysis of dispositional sentences into subjunctive or contrary-to-fact (counterfactual) conditionals is that subjunctive and counterfactual sentences present a translation problem just as baffling as the one presented by dispositional sentences.

Take the counterfactual "If s had been placed into water, then it would have dissolved." Suppose we try to translate that sentence into the truth-functional notation of propositional or predicate logic.

The obvious starting point in such a translation procedure is to replace the "If _____ then --------------------" of the counterfactual by the " $\supset$ " of truth-functional logic. If we do so, then the counterfactual in question translates into "(s had been placed into water) $\supset$ (s would have dissolved)." The trouble with this translation is that its antecedent and consequent are not sentences, and so the whole conditional is not a sentence. To make it a sentence, we must replace the subjunctive antecedent and consequent with their corresponding "mates" in the indicative mood. For instance, we must replace the antecedent "s had been placed into water" by the indicative sentence "s is placed into water" (or by "s was placed into water") and replace the consequent "s would have dissolved" by the indicative sentence "s dissolves" (or by "s dissolved"). The result is the translation of the counterfactual "If s had been placed into water, then s would have dissolved" into the indicative conditional "If s is placed into water, then s will dissolve" (or "If *s* was placed into water, then *s* dissolved"), which in symbols is *Ps* ⊃ *Ds*. In a similar way, we can translate all other counterfactuals.

But once we actually translate in this way, it becomes obvious that such translations are unsatisfactory, because the end product of this translation procedure for counterfactual sentences is exactly the same, and just as inadequate, as the end product of the translation procedure for dispositional sentences discussed in the preceding section. So the suggested method of translating counterfactual sentences cannot be correct. Similar remarks apply to other kinds of subjunctive conditionals. The so-called problem of counterfactuals, really a problem concerning all kinds of subjunctive conditionals, is to find a way to symbolize subjunctives so that they can be handled by some sort of appropriate logical machinery. Until it is solved, the formal logic we have developed so far will not be able to handle all arguments about dispositions or arguments in the subjunctive mood (e.g., contrary-to-fact conditionals).

6 *Philosophical Problems*

In addition to the problems discussed in the previous section, there are serious philosophical problems underlying the whole of sentential and predicate logic. Let's now briefly discuss a few of these problems.

Propositions versus Sentences

One basic issue is whether logic deals with sentences or propositions. For instance, in using the argument form

> If *p* then *q*
> If *q* then *r*
> ∴ If *p* then *r*

the English equivalent of Hypothetical Syllogism, whatever is substituted for one *p* must be substituted for the other, and similarly for *q* and *r*. We must substitute *the very same thing* for both occurrences of *p*. But what is this same thing we must substitute? Some philosophers say we must substitute the same *sentence,* whereas others say we must substitute sentences that express the same *proposition.*

We can think of a *sentence* as a series of ink marks on paper (or sounds in the air). Thus, as you read the sentence that precedes this one, you look at particular ink marks on a particular sheet of paper, and those ink marks may be said to *be* a particular sentence. But we would ordinarily say that someone else reading another copy of this book might read the *same* sentence. Thus the everyday meaning of the word "sentence" is ambiguous. So let's resolve the ambiguity by saying that both of you looked at different **sentence tokens** of the same **sentence type.** Here is another sentence token of that sentence type:

We can think of a sentence as a series of ink marks on paper (or sounds in the air).

During the rest of this discussion, when we use the word "sentence," let's mean sentence type, because no one would argue that the same sentence token has to be substituted in two different places in an argument form (because that is impossible). Thus no one would argue that the principal unit dealt with in logic is sentence tokens.

As for *propositions*, recall our earlier example. The expressions "Snow is white" and "Der Schnee ist weiss" are tokens of two different sentence types, and thus of two different sentences. But they seem to have something in common, they seem to "express the same idea," or "say the same thing," or "have the same meaning." Whatever they have in common, whether meaning or something else like it, we will call a proposition. Then we can say that these two expressions, although different sentences, express the same proposition.

Of course, two sentences don't have to be in different languages to express the same proposition. For instance, the two different sentences "John loves Mary" and "Mary is loved by John" express the same proposition.

Now the principal objection to saying that logic deals with propositions rather than sentences is simply that the very existence of propositions can be doubted. Sentences, or at least sentence tokens, can be *looked at* or *heard*; they are perceivable. But you can't perceive a proposition. (Nor is it exactly clear what a proposition is supposed to be.)

Well, if propositions are such doubtful entities, can we make sense of logic without them? There seem to be good reasons to answer no to that question.

In the first place, if logic deals with sentences and not propositions, then the rules of logic are at best much more restricted than is normally supposed. Take Simplification. We ordinarily suppose that the following argument is valid because it is an instance of Simplification:

(1)　1.　Art will get elected, and he'll serve well.
　　　 /∴ He's going to get elected.

But if logic deals with sentences, this argument is not a valid instance of Simplification (or any other standard rule of inference). Simplification has the form

　　　 p and *q*
　　　 /∴ *p*

and if we substitute the sentence "Art will get elected" for the first *p*, we must substitute the same sentence for the second *p*. We can't substitute the sentence "He's going to get elected" for the second *p*, because that is a different *sentence* from "Art will get elected" (although it expresses the same proposition).

The obvious thought is that in this case "Art will get elected" and "He's going to get elected" are *synonymous* (have the same meaning), and that all we have to do is allow synonymous sentences to replace one another whenever it is convenient to do so. The trouble is that those who reject propositions cannot appeal to sameness of meaning, for in the last analysis that amounts to a tacit appeal to propositions (or at least to abstract entities just as mysterious to those who reject propositions as propositions themselves).

In addition, when propositions are rejected, problems arise because terms and sentences in natural languages tend to be *ambiguous*. For ambiguity also leads to trouble when substituting sentences into valid argument forms. Take the following argument:

1.	Whales are fish.	p
2.	If whales are fish, then whales are cold-blooded.	p
/∴ 3.	Whales are cold-blooded.	1,2 **MP**

Premise 1 of this argument is true if we construe the word "fish" in its everyday sense, and premise 2 is true if we construe that word in its scientific sense. And yet the conclusion clearly is false. So it seems that **MP** has let us down.

The usual explanation, of course, is that the trouble arises because the word "fish" is being used ambiguously. If the word "fish" is used unambiguously throughout the proof, then the argument is valid, but one or the other of its premises is false (depending on what sense of that word we use). But if we use the word "fish" *equivocally*, meaning one thing in one premise and another thing in the other, then the argument is *invalid*. In either case, we have not validly proceeded from true premises to a false conclusion.

But this explanation is not open to those who claim that logic deals with sentences and not propositions. For them, the form of **MP** is satisfied whenever the letters *p* and *q* are replaced, respectively, in each of their occurrences by the same *sentences*. And in the example given, each use of *p* is replaced by the same sentence, namely, "Whales are fish." Of course, that sentence is used ambiguously, but that is another matter.

Another way to put the problem facing those who advocate sentences over propositions is just that those who reject propositions have a hard time separating uses of a sentence that have one meaning from those that have another. (For instance, they won't be able to say that in the argument the sentence "Whales are fish" expresses one proposition when said truly and another proposition when said falsely.) Their problem, in other words, is to find some way to distinguish ambiguous uses of terms and sentences without appealing to propositions, a problem some of their opponents (including most definitely your authors) feel confident they cannot solve.

A third truth-value?

Sentential logic is a two-valued truth-functional logic. But do most natural language sentences have two values? It has been argued that they do not.

Recall our discussion of definite descriptions (in Section 2), and consider the sentence "The present king of France is bald." According to the analysis in Section 2, asserting this sentence amounts to saying (1) there is a present king of France; (2) there is only one present king of France; and (3) that person is bald.

But it has been argued that this analysis is incorrect, because it confuses *referring* to something with asserting that it exists. In saying that the present king of France is bald, according to this view, a speaker does not assert that a present king of France exists. Instead, *he presupposes* that the thing referred to, the present king of France, exists. But to presuppose that there is a present king of France is not to *assert* that there is a present king of France (nor—according to this view—does that presupposition *logically imply* the existence of a present king of France).

Now as a matter of fact there is no present king of France. So a person uttering the sentence "The present king of France is bald" will fail in his attempt to refer. Hence, it is claimed, that sentence, although meaningful, is neither true nor false, and thus literally has no truth value. It follows then that it is incorrect to say that all sentences are either true or false.*

---

*This is roughly the view argued by P. F. Strawson. (More precisely, he argues that assertion of the sentence "The present king of France is bald" fails to make a true or false statement. But what it is to utter a statement other than asserting a proposition is not clear.) See Strawson's "On Referring," *Mind*, n.s., vol. 59 (1950), and Bertrand Russell's reply, "Mr. Strawson on Referring", in Russell, *My Philosophical Development* (London: Allen & Unwin, 1959), pp. 238–245.

If correct, this is a very serious matter for logic. A crucial element of our explication of validity is that it is characterized in terms of truth and falsity. The question at issue here is what sort of inferences using such locutions as "The present king of France is bald" we wish to license if the possibility exists that the statement has no truth-value. As you saw in the introductory remarks of Chapter Two, there are other kinds of arguments that present (roughly) similar problems, and we encounter a related class of difficulties in Chapter Fourteen.

But the presupposition theory is not the only argument in favor of giving up two-valued logic. Another takes its cue from paradox-generating sentences such as "This very sentence is false."* Someone uttering this sentence intends to refer to that very sentence; and because the sentence does exist, there is no failure of reference. Nevertheless, it has been argued that, though meaningful, this sentence has no truth-value. For if it is true, then it is false, and if it is false, then it is true. Hence we must regard it as neither true nor false, even though meaningful, and therefore we must give up two-valued logic.[†]

The status of sentence connectives in predicate logic

In sentential logic we explained the meaning of the logical connectives "~," "·," "∨," "⊃," and "≡," by means of truth tables, thus making them truth-functional connectives. But now consider their occurrences in quantified sentences, for instance in the sentence $(x)(Fx \supset Gx)$. The expressions Fx and Gx are sentence forms and hence cannot have truth-values. Thus there is no truth-value for the expression $Fx \supset Gx$, and so the use of the horseshoe symbol "⊃" in $(x)(Fx \supset Gx)$ does not appear to be truth-functional. But if it isn't truth-functional, how is it defined?

This problem is frequently overlooked, perhaps because an easy solution seems readily at hand. Recall that when we first discussed quantifiers, we said (in Chapter Seven, Section 8) that it was convenient to regard quantified sentences as conjunctions (in the case of universally quantified sentences) or disjunctions (in the case of existentially quantified sentences). For instance, in a two-individual universe of discourse $(x)(Fx \supset Gx)$ amounts to the expansion $(Fa \supset Ga) \cdot (Fb \supset Gb)$, and $(\exists x)(Fx \supset Gx)$ amounts to the expansion $(Fa \supset Ga) \vee (Fb \supset Gb)$. Now clearly, the horseshoe symbols occurring in these expansions are truth-functional. Hence we can regard those occurring in the related quantified sentences as truth-functional.

The trouble with this, alluded to earlier, is that in some cases the domain of discourse is infinitely large (an example is the domain of positive integers), or even nondenumerably large (an example is the domain of real numbers). When dealing with domains of this size, we cannot replace quantified sentences with their expansions.

Nevertheless, some philosophers[‡] regard quantified sentences as very long conjunctions or disjunctions, even though they cannot actually be written down, and thus feel justified in believing that the connectives occurring in quantified sentences are truth-functional. Perhaps, then, the issue is whether it makes a difference that we cannot actually write down an infinitely long conjunction or disjunction. If so, this dispute may

---

*Discussed further in the last section of this chapter.

†This is essentially the argument proposed in Frederick B. Fitch, *Symbolic Logic* (New York: The Ronald Press, 1952), p. 8.

‡See, for instance, Richard L. Purtill, *Logic for Philosophers* (New York: Harper & Row, 1971), pp. 226–227.

be related to the dispute about propositions and sentences. There are no infinitely long sentences, but assuming there are any propositions at all, there may be propositions that could be expressed by infinitely long conjunctions or disjunctions, if only we were able to write them down.

Whatever the solution to the preceding may be, there is another objection to the view that quantified sentences are shorthand for very long conjunctions or disjunctions. When we say, for instance, that $(x)Fx$, we seem to say more than that $(Fa \cdot Fb) \cdot \ldots$. The sentence $(x)Fx$ seems to do more than merely list all the items, $a, b, c, \ldots$ and say they have the property F. It also says that the items $a, b, c, \ldots$ in the expansion of $(x)Fx$ are in fact all the items there are (or all the items in the domain of discourse). The expansion doesn't say this, whereas the quantified sentence does. Hence, it can be argued that a quantified sentence and its expansion are not equivalent. If this argument is a good one, then the question of how to interpret the occurrences of connectives in quantified sentences remains unsolved.

Difficulties with truth-functional translations

When we introduced the sentence connective " $\supset$," we pointed out that it is a truth-functional connective and is to be used in translating everyday "If _____, then --------------------." sentences, even though most such sentences are not truth-functional. We justified this on several grounds, one of which was that such translations render valid arguments into valid arguments and invalid arguments into invalid arguments.

We saw in the previous section how this translation procedure failed when applied to subjunctive sentences. But some philosophers claim that it fails also for indicative sentences. Consider the following argument.*

(1) If this is gold, then it is not soluble in water.
    /∴. It's not the case that if this is gold, then it is soluble in water.

If we mechanically translate this argument as

(2) $G \supset {\sim} S$
    /∴. ${\sim} (G \supset S)$

we get into trouble, because (2) is invalid, whereas (1) is valid. And yet (2) seems to be the straightforward truth-functional translation of (1).

One way to solve this problem is to deny that the conclusion of (1) is correctly symbolized as ${\sim} (G \supset S)$. It might be claimed, for instance, that the placement of the negating expression in the conclusion deceives us into thinking that the whole remainder of the sentence is being negated, whereas only the consequent is being negated.

We already have precedent for the assumption that the placement of a negating expression doesn't always reflect its logical scope. Recall our discussion of the sentence "It is not the case that the present king of France is bald," which in some contexts may mean a denial of the entire statement, either because one believes that there is no present king of France, there is more than one, or he is not bald—or simply a denial that he is bald, in which case what is meant is that the present king of France is not bald. In examples of this

---

*Taken from Charles L. Stevenson, "If-iculties," *Philosophy of Science,* vol. 41 (1970), pp. 27–49.

kind, the negating term, although toward the end of the sentence, actually negates all the rest of the sentence. So in the gold example, the negating term, although at the beginning of the sentence, may negate just the second half of the sentence.

However, it isn't at all clear that this proposed solution to the problem is adequate.* And if it isn't, then we are faced with an extremely serious translation problem, standing in the way of the acceptance of any truth-functional logic as a device useful in dealing with real-life arguments.

The use of a truth-functional conditional also has been objected to on grounds that it generates so-called **paradoxes of material implication.** Thus it is sometimes held to be paradoxical that a false sentence materially implies any sentence whatever (that is, paradoxical that if p is false, then $p \supset q$ is true, no matter what q happens to be) and paradoxical that a true sentence is materially implied by any sentence whatever (that is, paradoxical that if q is true, then $p \supset q$ is true, no matter what p happens to be).

But these alleged paradoxes are not truly paradoxical. They stem from a misunderstanding of the nature of material implication. Most important, from the fact that a false statement p materially implies any statement q it does not follow that the argument consisting of p as a premise and q as a conclusion is valid. That would only be the case if p *logically* implied q, as is the case when p is the conjunction of the premises and q the conclusion of a valid argument.

Second, as we discussed in Section 10 of Chapter Three, the truth table for the $\supset$ preserves the validity and invalidity of arguments that we intuitively accept as valid or invalid.

Finally, recall that material implication was introduced in earlier chapters to capture the part of their meaning that all implications share, namely the claim that it won't happen that their antecedents are true and their consequents false. We said that a statement of the form $p \supset q$ is defined to be equivalent to the analogous statement of the form $\sim (p \cdot \sim q)$. And clearly, for any statement of this form, if p is false, or if q is true, then $\sim (p \cdot \sim q)$ has to be true, as is easily proved by truth table analysis. So the alleged paradoxes of material implication aren't really paradoxical.

No doubt some of those who say that they are paradoxical simply mean to assert their objection to the translation of everyday non–truth-functional implications by means of a truth-function sentence connective such as "$\supset$." That is, they mean to say that the truth-functional implication of sentential logic cannot successfully translate everyday implications. And this is a point we've already encountered.

What is a deductively valid argument?

In Chapter One, we stated that the fundamental property of a deductively valid argument is that, roughly speaking, if all its premises are true, then its conclusion *must* be true also, so that it is *impossible* for all its premises to be true and yet its conclusion be false. This characterization of deductive validity has been objected to on several grounds.

One objection stems from the ambiguity of the terms "must" and "impossible." What we mean by these terms can be specified more closely by the concept of *necessity*. If all

---

*Most objections to it tend to be quite complicated, but one is fairly simple: In the gold example, if we symbolize as suggested, the argument becomes totally trivial, namely, $G \supset \sim S / \therefore \ G \supset \sim S$; yet the original argument seems to have more to it than that.

premises of a deductively valid argument are true, then its conclusion *necessarily* will be true. The trouble is that the concept of necessity also is ambiguous, as the discussion presented in Chapter Eighteen will make clearer. We can, of course, remove the ambiguity by specifying that we have in mind here the idea of logical necessity, and indeed this is what is done in Chapter Eighteen. But what is logical necessity, as opposed, say, to the physical necessity that is involved in the laws of nature? One way to answer this question is to say that logical necessity is, in the case of sentential logic, for example, explicated by appeal to the truth tables. The truth tables give us a clear sense of logical possibility: Each line of the truth table of a *wff* shows us one possibility for its truth-value given the truth-values of its component sentences, and the table exhausts all such possibilities. The sense of "possibility" involved here seems straightforwardly commonsensical. The test statement form of a valid argument shows there is no possibility, in the sense explicated, that the conjunction of the premises be true and the conclusion false. The sense of "possibility" involved in the semantics of predicate logic is obviously more difficult, but we glimpsed it when we spoke of expanding our quantified formulas into universes of two members, three members, and so on.

Another way to answer the question is to appeal to the "spelling out" view of logical necessity that we used in explaining deductive validity in Chapter One. In this view, it is necessary that the conclusion of a deductively valid argument be true if all its premises are true because, as we said in Chapter One, the conclusion of a valid deduction already is contained in its premises, although usually only implicitly, not explicitly. If the deductive process is one of drawing out all or part of what the premises of an argument assert, then this accounts for and explains the kind of necessity we have in mind when we speak of logical necessity.

But this just brings us to a second objection to our conception of deductive validity, because there are two important kinds of cases where it seems that logical necessity cannot be explained in this way. The first concerns certain arguments whose conclusions are theorems of logic or logical truths. Consider the following example:

(1)   1. Sugar tastes sweet.
     /∴ 2. All cats are cats.

This argument is without doubt deductively valid, at least it is according to the criterion of deductive validity we have provided in this text. But the spelling-out view of deductive validity does not seem to account for its validity. After all, the premise of this argument is about sugar; it says absolutely nothing about cats. In what sense, then, does the conclusion of this argument spell out anything whatever that is in its premise?

The example shows the limitations of the spelling-out view. We might try to claim that because tautologies and logical truths give no factual information, because they are true no matter what, they are somehow contained in any set of premises. We can explicate that by pointing out that a tautology or logical truth can be added to the premises of any argument without affecting its validity or invalidity (you can try this as an exercise!). Indeed, it can be shown that a rule that would allow us to add a tautology or logical truth as a premise to any argument would in effect be a substitute for conditional proof!

Another way to look at this situation, when we have a tautology or logical truth as a conclusion, is to see that by Contraposition the test statement form of such an argument will have a contradiction as its antecedent, and we know already that from a contradiction we can prove anything whatever. This is a desirable consequence. Without it, the whole notion of *reductio*/indirect proof, so important in mathematics for example, would flounder. Given that anything can be proved from a contradictory set of premises, every conclusion is in that sense, contained in the premises.

This brings us to another objection to our view of the nature of deductively valid argument. This objection is that the everyday use or sense of language is violated in calling argument (1) a deductively valid *argument*. (A similar objection can be made against our calling argument (1) a *sound* argument, and our saying that we have *proved* the conclusion of argument (1).) And to this objection we have to plead guilty. Even though the concepts in question are both vague and ambiguous in everyday speech, our use of these terms does stretch matters beyond what would sound right in everyday conversation. Or rather it would do so without an explanation of how we are using these terms. But we have provided such an explanation, and we have a very good reason for using these terms in the way we have specified, for all the cases we have called deductively valid arguments share an important characteristic: If their premises are true, then their conclusions must be true.

7 *Logical Paradoxes*

In addition to the problems just discussed that trouble first-order predicate logic, higher-order logics are plagued by the so-called **logical paradoxes,** some of which date back to the time of the early Greeks.

Syntactic paradoxes

In a first-order predicate logic there is no straightforward way to express the predication of properties to other properties. The usual way to express such predications is via the symbolism of a *second-order* (or higher) predicate logic. In Section 4 of this chapter we very briefly discussed higher-order logics and in particular the predication of properties to other properties. (An example is the property of *honesty*, which seems itself to have the property of being *rare*—in that its extension is rather small.) But if we allow the predication of properties to properties, then certain alleged paradoxes called **syntactic paradoxes** can be generated.

If we can predicate properties of other properties, it seems reasonable to suppose that we can predicate properties of *themselves*. For example, it seems reasonable to suppose that the property of being *comprehensible* itself is comprehensible (in contrast to the property of being *incomprehensible*, which itself is not incomprehensible), and reasonable to suppose that the property of being *common* (as opposed to rare) is itself common. But sometimes the predication of a property to itself yields trouble. The most famous example is the so-called **impredicable paradox.**

Let's call any property that can be truly predicated of itself a *predicable property*, and any property that cannot be truly predicated of itself an *impredicable property*. Using this notation we can say that the property of being common is a predicable property, because being *common* is a common property, and that the property of being *rare* is an *im*predicable property, since being rare is *not* a rare property (because there are many kinds of rare things).

But what about the property of being *impredicable?* Can this property be truly predicated of itself? The unfortunate answer seems to be that if the property of being impredicable is predicated of itself, then it *is not* predicated of itself, and if it *is not* predicated of itself, then it is predicated of itself. Hence the paradox.

To make this clear, let's symbolize the property of being predicable as P, and the property of being impredicable as $\overline{P}$. Thus, to say a given property F is P is to say that FF, and to say that a given property F is $\overline{P}$ is to say that $\sim FF$.

To start with, either $\overline{P}$ is itself $\overline{P}$ or else $\overline{P}$ is P. Suppose $\overline{P}$ is $\overline{P}$. If $\overline{P}$ is $\overline{P}$, then $\overline{P}$ is predicated of itself, and hence $\overline{P}$ is P. So if $\overline{P}$ is $\overline{P}$, then $\overline{P}$ is P.

Now suppose $\overline{P}$ is P. If $\overline{P}$ is P, then $\overline{P}$ is not predicated of itself, and hence $\overline{P}$ is $\overline{P}$. So if $\overline{P}$ is P, then $\overline{P}$ is $\overline{P}$.

It follows that if $\overline{P}$ is $\overline{P}$, then it is P, and if $\overline{P}$ is P, then it is $\overline{P}$. Translating this back into plain English, what we have shown is that if the property of being impredicable is impredicable, then it is predicated of itself, and hence is predicable. And if the property of being impredicable is predicable, then it is not predicated of itself (impredicable would have to be impredicable to be predicated of itself), and hence is impredicable.

This contradictory result can be made even more explicit by writing down the definition of $\overline{P}$ and then constructing a simple argument, as follows:

1. $\overline{P}F = df \sim FF$

That is, to say that a property, F, is impredicable is to say that it is not the case that F is F. From which it follows that given any property F, F is $\overline{P}$ if and only if it is not the case that F is F. In other words,

2. $(F)(\overline{P}F \equiv \sim FF)$

Hence, substituting $\overline{P}$ for F, we get (by **UI**)

3. $\overline{P}\,\overline{P} \equiv \sim \overline{P}\,\overline{P}$

from which an explicit contradiction can be derived.

Several solutions to paradoxes of this kind have been proposed. One of them is the **simple theory of types.*** According to this theory, all entities divide into a hierarchy of types, starting with individual entities, moving to properties of individual entities, then to properties of properties of individual entities, and so on. For instance, Art is an individual entity; the property of being honest is a property Art may possess (hence honesty is a property of individuals); and the property of being rare is a property possessed by the property of being honest (hence rarity is a property of properties).

Having arranged entities in this way, the simple theory of types requires that the type of a property be higher than any property of which it can be predicated. For instance, if being old is predicated of Art, then it cannot be predicated either of itself or of any other property.

---

*Proposed by Bertrand Russell. See *Principles of Mathematics* (Cambridge, UK: Cambridge University Press, 1903), Appendix B.

It is customary to mark the distinction between properties of individuals and properties of properties by some notational device, such as the use of standard type to denote properties of individuals and boldface type to denote properties of properties of individuals.

Using a notation of this kind, a sentence such as "Art is not old" will be symbolized as ~ *Oa,* and a sentence such as "Honesty is rare" will be symbolized as **R**H.

Notice that the sentence "Honesty is rare" is correctly symbolized as **R**H, and *not* as *RH,* for according to the theory of types, the property of being rare, which is predicable of properties, is of a type one level higher than properties that are predicable of individuals.

To summarize, the simple theory of types requires, first, that we arrange entities into a hierarchy of categories or types, starting with individuals, moving to properties of individuals, and then to properties of properties, properties of properties of properties, and so on; and second, that the type of a property be one type higher than any property or entity of which it can be predicated.

An obvious consequence of the simple theory of types is that no property can be predicated of itself. And it is this consequence that solves the impredicable paradox, for if no property can be predicated of itself, then it becomes senseless to ask if the property of being impredicable is itself impredicable.

The simple theory of types has been objected to as both *ad hoc* and *counterintuitive.* For example, according to the simple theory of types, the rareness we can predicate of, say, a postage stamp is different from the rareness we can predicate of the property of being honest. But it seems intuitively clear that it is the very same property of rareness that is predicable of postage stamps and of honesty. We could simply try a translation of "Honesty is rare" as "Every honest person is a rare person," making it in line with the predication of rarity to some postage stamps. Whether this would work for all such cases is not obvious.

The counterintuitive nature of the simple theory of types is further illustrated by the fact that it forbids assertion of sentences such as "Some members of every type (in the hierarchy of types) are rare," a sentence that seems not only *meaningful,* but also *true.*

Indeed, it has been argued that the very statement of the simple theory of types presupposes a violation of the theory itself. For instance, the simple theory of types presupposes that all individuals, properties of individuals, properties of properties, and so on, have the property of being *type classifiable* (that is, have the property of belonging to exactly one category in the hierarchy of types). But the property of being type classifiable is not permitted by the simple theory of types. Hence the theory presupposes what it will not permit. One answer to this problem is to claim that there are distinctions between kinds of predicates (and the properties they represent), which makes certain predicates inadmissible into *any* type. Such relational predicates as "is identical to," as we have seen, are part of the logical machinery of our logical language, and not included in its names or predicates that we use with names to form *wffs.* "Type classifiable" is such a predicate. Sometimes such logical predicates are, in a perfectly intelligible sense, seen in the very choice of vocabulary that we make. Thus, when we represent individuals by lowercase signs, predicates of them by uppercase signs, predicates of those predicates by uppercase boldface signs, and so on, each kind of shape and color of the sign represents a species of type classifiability. Many logicians and philosophers accept this distinction between what is sometimes called the logical and the descriptive use of predicates.

Semantic paradoxes

Although adoption of the simple theory of types has its difficulties, it does solve syntactic paradoxes such as the impredicable paradox. But unfortunately, it fails to solve the
paradoxes usually referred to as **semantic paradoxes.**

The most famous semantic paradox is the so-called paradox of the liar, which was first
posed by the ancient Greeks. Put into more modern dress, the paradox is this: It seems reasonable to suppose that every declarative sentence is either *true* or *false*. But consider the
sentence

(1)   Sentence (1) is false.

Is sentence (1) true, or is it false? The unfortunate answer seems to be that if sentence (1)
is true, then it is false, and if it is false, then it is true.

Take the first possibility, namely that sentence (1) is true. If (1) is true, and (1) asserts
that (1) is false, then it follows that (1) is false. So if (1) is true, then (1) is false.

Now suppose (1) is false. If (1) is false, and (1) asserts that (1) is false, then it follows
that it is false that (1) is false, and therefore follows that (1) is true. So if (1) is false, then
(1) is true. Either way, we have a contradiction, and hence a paradox.

An obvious thought is to solve the liar paradox by ruling out (as meaningless) any sentence that refers to itself. (Indeed, the liar paradox often is conceived of—erroneously—
as a paradox of self-reference.) But unfortunately, the liar paradox can be generated without self-reference. For example, consider the following two sentences:

(2)   Sentence (3) is false.
(3)   Sentence (2) is true.

Sentence (2) refers to sentence (3), and sentence (3) refers to sentence (2), but neither (2)
nor (3) refers to itself. So both of these sentences satisfy the requirement that sentences
not be self-referential, and they seem to have the form required of legitimate declarative
sentences.

But is sentence (2) true, or is it false? Again, the unfortunate answer seems to be that
if it is true, then it is false, and if it is false, then it is true.

Take the first possibility, namely that sentence (2) is true. If (2) is true, and (2) asserts
that (3) is false, it follows that (3) is false. But if (3) is false, and (3) asserts that (2) is true,
it follows that it is false that (2) is true, and hence that (2) is false. So if (2) is true, then
(2) is false.

Now suppose sentence (2) is false. If (2) is false, and (2) asserts that (3) is false, it follows that it is false that (3) is false, and hence that (3) is true. But if (3) is true, and (3)
asserts that (2) is true, it follows that (2) is true. So if (2) is false, then (2) is true. Again
we have a contradiction, and hence again we have a paradox.

One way to solve the semantic paradoxes is to distinguish between **levels of language,**
that is, between languages that are used to talk about nonlinguistic things and those used
to talk about other languages. A language used to talk about some other language is considered to be on a higher level than the language talked about,* so that sentences asserting the truth or falsity of a given sentence must be placed into a language at least one level

---

*This division into higher and lower language levels is discussed in greater detail in Chapter Seventeen, Section 4.

higher than the given sentence. We have discussed this distinction between object and metalanguage in Section 8 of Chapter Two. For instance, the sentence "The sentence 'Art is tall' is true" must be placed into a language one level higher than the language in which the sentence "Art is tall" occurs.*

It is clear that adoption of the preceding machinery solves the liar paradox. In the first place, all self-referential sentences, such as sentence (1), will be rejected as meaningless. And in the second place, at least one of every pair of sentences such as sentences (2) and (3) will be rejected as meaningless. (For instance, if (2) occurs in a given language, and (3) in a language one level higher, then (2) will be rejected as meaningless—whatever the fate of (3)—because no sentence can be permitted to assert the truth or falsity of a sentence in the same or a higher-level language.)

But not all philosophers accept the levels-of-language solution.† Perhaps the main reason is that it seems much too strong, eliminating as meaningless not only the troublesome sentence (1), but also many apparently meaningful sentences. For instance, it eliminates the sentence "Every language (including this one) permits the expression of at least one true sentence," which may be false but does seem to be meaningful.

Exercise 13-5

Here are versions of several well-known logical paradoxes. Show how in each case a solution offered for one of the paradoxes in this chapter might plausibly be said to solve these puzzles.

1. **Bonny:** My teacher said in class today that all generalities are false. Do you think that's true?

   Charlie: Who knows? Maybe yes, maybe no.

   Bonny: I know. It's false. Look. Suppose it were true. Then the statement (A) "All generalities are false" would be true. But (A) itself is a generality. So if (A) is true, it's true that all generalities are false, so (A) must be false. So if (A) is true, then it's false. Well then, (A) must be false. Right?

   Charlie: Wrong! But I don't know why.

2. **Charlie:** What we need is a bibliography listing all bibliographies.

   Bonny: That would be nice. But how about a bibliography that lists all and only those bibliographies that do not list themselves?

   Charlie: Not terribly useful. But why not?

   Bonny: Here's why not. Such a bibliography either lists itself or it doesn't. Right? If it does list itself, then it violates the condition that it list only those bibliographies that don't list themselves. So it can't list itself. But if it doesn't list itself, then it violates the condition that it list all those bibliographies that do not list themselves. So

---

*This solution was first proposed by Bertrand Russell in his "Introduction" to Ludwig Wittgenstein's *Tractatus Logico-Philosophicus* (New York: Harcourt Brace, 1922), p. 23. See also Alfred Tarski, "Semantic Conception of Truth," Philosophy and Phenomenological Research, vol. 4 (1944), pp. 241–275.

†For example, see Frederick B. Fitch, *Symbolic Logic* (New York: The Ronald Press, 1952), p. 111.

either way the conditions of such a bibliography are violated. So there cannot be such a bibliography.

Charlie: That's what's wrong with you philosophy majors—you think too much for your own good.

3. **Bonny:** Ready for another one?

   Charlie: No. But you'll go ahead anyway.

   Bonny: OK. Let's call a number interesting if we can say something special about that number that we can't say about any other number (not counting things such as being identical with themselves, or one greater than the next number, and things like that). Every low number clearly is interesting: 1 is the lowest number, 2 is the lowest even number; 3 is the number of logic books on my shelf; 4 is the number of offensive backs in football, and so on. But when we get to extremely large numbers, the situation would seem to be different; for instance, there seems to be nothing interesting about $(10^{61} + 33)$. So some numbers are not interesting. Right?

   Charlie: Right, . . . on your definition of interestingness.

   Bonny: Wrong! I'm going to prove to you that there are no uninteresting numbers. Imagine two huge bags, A and B, A containing all the interesting numbers, B the uninteresting ones. If there are no uninteresting numbers, bag B will be empty. So you think B will not be empty, because you think some numbers are uninteresting. But if there are any numbers in bag B, there must be a lowest one, right?

   Charlie: Right.

   Bonny: Well, if that's true, then we can say something about that number that we can't say about any other number, namely that it is the lowest uninteresting number. Right?

   Charlie: Right.

   Bonny: Well, isn't that interesting!

   Charlie: What?!?

   Bonny: So there can't be a lowest uninteresting number, because that would be interesting. But if there is no lowest uninteresting number, then there aren't any. Q.E.D.

4. **Bonny:** Now I'm going to show you that your intuitions about classes are all wet. For instance, you believe that any items can form a class, don't you, and also that there is a universal class that contains everything?

   Charlie: Sure, why not?

   Bonny: Well, here's why not. If any items can form a class, then classes themselves can be items that form a class. So we can construct a class containing other classes as members (for example, the class of all classes containing exactly 10 members), and even construct a class containing itself as a member (for example, the class consisting of itself and the class of states in the Union).

   Charlie: That last is a weird class, but why not?

   Bonny: Here's why not. Consider a class whose members are themselves classes. We might, for example, think of the class of vertebrates, which would include the class of persons, of tigers, and so forth. Now consider a class whose members are all the classes that do not contain themselves as members. The question is whether that class contains itself as a member. The answer is troubling. Suppose it doesn't contain itself as a member. Then it is one of those classes that do not contain themselves as members, and so does contain itself as a member after all. Suppose it does contain itself as a member. Then it is one of those classes that does not contain itself as a member, and so does not contain itself as a member after all! So, if it is a member of itself, it isn't a member of itself, and if it isn't, it is. Clearly, there is no class containing just those classes that are not members of themselves. Hence, every bunch of items does not form a class, and, incidentally, it therefore can't be true that there is a universal class containing everything.

Charlie: Very clever, but I'll figure out what's wrong . . . later.

Exercise 13-6

1. Which of the following require an identity sign if we are to symbolize them so as to reveal the most possible internal structure?

    (1) The horse is an intelligent animal.

    (2) The horse that wins the derby wins a lot of money.

    (3) W. A. Mozart is the greatest composer in history.

    (4) Mozart is a better composer than anyone else.

    (5) No one had a higher grade point average than Susan.

    (6) The graceful winner also is a graceful loser.

    (7) Susan had the highest grade point average.

2. Explain the difference between the properties of being *symmetrical, asymmetrical,* and *nonsymmetrical.* (Include at least one original example of each.)

3. In Part One we defined "⊃" *truth functionally.* What objection is there to the use of this truth-functional definition of "⊃" in predicate logic when dealing with indicative sentences?

4. When using, say, Modus Ponens, $p \supset q, p /\therefore q$, whatever is substituted for the first p must be substituted for the second. What is it that we must substitute? Is it sentence tokens, sentence types, propositions, or what? (Defend your answer.) If you don't know, explain what's troubling about each of the three alternatives mentioned.

5. True or false? Defend your answers.

    (1) To say that food has the disposition or power to nourish is to say that if we eat food, then we'll be nourished.

    (2) We can't solve the problem of dispositionals just by translating them into related counterfactuals, because the problems in symbolizing counterfactuals are pretty much the same as those encountered in symbolizing dispositionals.

    (3) The subjunctive conditional "If we were to make cigarettes illegal, then more people would smoke" is correctly symbolized as $C \supset S$, where C = "we make cigarettes illegal" and S = "more people will smoke."

6. Which of the following underlined words are used as dispositionals, and which are not? Explain.

    (1) The sugar was <u>observed</u> to dissolve.

    (2) But no one has ever observed the <u>solubility</u> of sugar.

    (3) Since I was wearing sunglasses, I assumed the leaves were not as <u>green</u> as they looked.

    (4) None of her teachers teach Betsy, but she is <u>teachable</u>.

    (5) Tobacco is a more <u>dangerous</u> drug than marijuana.

    (6) Bonny is a very <u>dependable</u> person.

    (7) In fact, she has a sterling <u>character</u>.

Key Terms Introduced in Chapter Thirteen

asymmetrical relation: A relation *Fxy* such that it must be the case that $(x)(y)(Fxy \supset \sim Fyx)$. The relation "_____ is the mother of _____" is asymmetrical.

contrary-to-fact conditional (counterfactual): A subjunctive conditional whose antecedent is contrary to fact. The sentence "If Art had studied hard, then he would have become a great logician" is a contrary-to-fact conditional.

definite description: A descriptive phrase used to select or refer to a particular individual entity; for example, "The tallest man in the world is over eight feet tall", "Mark Twain is the author of *Huckleberry Finn*," and "The chairman of the club is late tonight."

dispositional property: An unobservable power or potential of an item. *Example:* the power of being soluble.

enthymeme: An argument with at least one missing premise which, when supplied, will make the argument valid. In such arguments, the missing premises are usually understood from context. Thus in "3 < 5 and 5 < 7, so 3 < 7" the missing premise is the statement that the relation $x < y$ is *transitive.* Also see Chapter Fourteen, Section 12.

first-order predicate logic: The predicate logic that forbids sentences ascribing properties to properties themselves, and restricts quantification to individual variables. The logic presented in Part Two, prior to Section 4 of this chapter, is a first-order predicate logic.

impredicable paradox: The paradox concerning the predicate impredicable, namely, that if impredicable is itself impredicable, then it is predicable, and if impredicable is not impredicable, then it is impredicable.

indirect context: A context involving believing, knowing, seeking, necessity, or possibility, and so on. Sentences containing indirect contexts generally contain phrases such as "believes that", "is looking for", or "it is necessary that", which introduce the indirect context. (Some typical sentences containing indirect contexts are "Art is looking for Betsy", "Art believes that Betsy is tall", "It is possible that it will rain tomorrow.")

intensional context: A synonym for **indirect context.**

intentional context: A context in which a mental state is ascribed to someone. Thus "He believed that Sally loved him" and "He remembered that Sally loved him," count as intentional states, which are a species of intensional states. Such statements, like indirect contexts in general, are not truth-functional, so their transcription into our logic is problematic.

intransitive relation: A relation *Fxy* such that it must be the case that when one thing bears that relation to a second, and the second to a third, then the first cannot bear it to the third. The relation "_____ is the mother of _____" is an example.

irreflexive relation: A relation *Fxy* such that it must be the case that $(x) \sim Fxx$. The rela-

tion "_____ is lighter than
--------------------" is an example.

levels-of-language theory: The theory that certain parts of the semantic apparatus of a language, in particular the truth conditions of a language, must be contained not in the language itself but in the meta-language, to get around the difficulties illustrated by paradoxes such as the liar paradox.

logical paradoxes: Paradoxes generated or clarified by the use of logic, for example, the syntactic and semantic paradoxes.

nonreflexive relation: A relation that is neither reflexive nor irreflexive. The relation "_____ understands --------------------" is an example.

nonsymmetrical relation: A relation that is neither symmetrical nor asymmetrical. The relation "_____ loves --------------------" is nonsymmetrical.

nontransitive relation: A relation that is neither transitive nor intransitive. The relation "_____ loves --------------------" is an example.

paradoxes of material implication: The allegedly paradoxical results that a sentence of the form $p \supset q$ is true if p is false or q is true, no matter what p and q happen to be.

property variable: A variable ranging over properties. (Property variables are admissible only in higher-order logics.) An example is the property F in the statement "Art has some property, F, or other."

reflexive relation: A relation Fxy such that it must be the case that $(x)(y)[Fxy \supset (Fxx \cdot Fyy)]$. The relation "_____ belongs to the same church as --------------------" is a reflexive relation.

semantic paradox: A paradox such that most philosophers would accept only a semantic solution to it. For example, the liar paradox is a semantic paradox. Most philosophers accept a semantic theory,

the so-called levels-of-language theory, as a solution to this paradox.

sentence token: A series of marks on paper, or sounds in the air, used to make a sentence.

sentence type: The class of sentence tokens of the same sentence; for example, the two sentence tokens "Snow is white" and "Snow is white" are tokens of the same sentence type.

simple theory of types: The syntactic theory according to which all properties are categorized in a hierarchy of categories, starting with properties of things, properties of properties, properties of properties of properties, and so on. The theory was proposed as a solution to syntactic paradoxes such as the impredicable paradox.

subjunctive conditional: A conditional sentence in the subjunctive mood. The sentence "If Art were to study hard, then he would be a great logician" is a subjunctive conditional.

symmetrical relation: A relation Fxy such that it must be the case that $(x)(y)(Fxy \supset Fyx)$. The relation "_____ is divorced from --------------------" is an example.

syntactic paradox: A paradox such that most philosophers would accept only a syntactic solution to it. For instance, the impredicable paradox is a syntactic paradox.

totally reflexive relation: A relation Fxy such that it must be the case that $(x)Fxx$. (Hardly any interesting relations are totally reflexive.) The relation "_____ is identical with --------------------" is totally reflexive.

transitive relation: A relation Fxy such that it must be the case that $(x)(y)(z)[(Fxy \cdot Fyz) \supset Fxz]$. The relation "_____ is shorter than --------------------" is an example.

Chapter Fourteen

Syllogistic Logic

The logic discussed in Parts One and Two was first developed in the late nineteenth and early twentieth centuries. But it did not arise in a vacuum. The discipline of logic has existed for over two thousand years, since the first system was developed by Aristotle. It has become customary to apply the term "symbolic" to systems like sentential and predicate logic, and the terms **traditional, Aristotelian,** and **syllogistic** to the earlier systems. Predicate logic is much more powerful than syllogistic logic. However, the relationship between the two is, as you will see, rather complex. Nevertheless, within its limits, syllogistic logic constitutes a useful and (for many) fascinating logical tool.

1 *Categorical Propositions*

Syllogistic logic is primarily concerned with *categorical propositions*. **Categorical propositions** assert or deny relationships between terms or classes. For instance, the sentence "All humans are mortal" is a categorical proposition, and asserts (roughly) that all members of the class of humans are members of the class of mortals.

The term "humans," which designates the class of human beings, is said to be the **subject,** or **subject term,** and the term "mortal," which designates the class of mortals, is said to be the **predicate,** or **predicate term,** of the categorical proposition "All humans are mortal." Similarly, all categorical propositions contain a subject and a predicate, as well as some form of the verb "to be" ("is," "are," and so on) relating the subject and predicate.

There are four kinds of categorical propositions: (1) **universal affirmative,** having the general form "All *S* are *P*" (where *S* denotes some subject class and *P* some predicate class); (2) **universal negative,** having the general form "No *S* are *P*"; (3) **particular affirmative,** having the general form "Some *S* are *P*"; and (4) **particular negative,** having the general form "Some *S* are not *P*."

It is customary to use the capital letter *A* in symbolizing universal affirmative propositions. Similarly, it is customary to use *E* for universal negatives, *I* for particular affirmatives, and *O* for particular negatives. It also is customary to refer to universal affirmative propositions as *A* **propositions,** universal negative propositions as *E* **propositions,** and so on. According to tradition, these letters come from the Latin "AffIrmo" (*affirmo*, I affirm) and "nEgO" (*nego*, I deny).

Notice that **A, E, I,** and **O propositions** differ with respect to two kinds of properties; namely, **quality** (being either affirmative or negative) and **quantity** (being either universal or particular). Thus, all **I propositions** are both *affirmative* (quality) and *particular* (quantity). For example, the **I** proposition "Some humans are mortal" is affirmative (quality), because it affirms that some humans are mortal, and particular (quantity), because it affirms that some (not necessarily all) humans are mortal. In contrast, all **E** propositions are both *negative* (quality) and *universal* (quantity). For example, the **E** proposition "No humans are mortal" is negative (quality), because it denies that humans are mortal, and universal (quantity), because it denies of all humans that they are mortal.

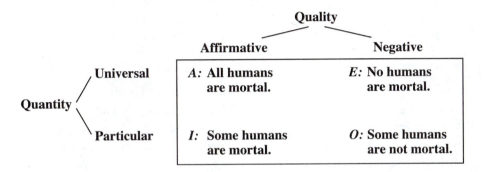

The English language, like all natural languages, permits a great deal of variety in the expression of propositions. Take St. Augustine's interesting thesis that all sin is a kind of lying, which can be put into **A** form as "All sins are lies." We can also express this thesis in English as "Sins are lies," "The one who sins, lies," "Sinning is lying," "To sin is to lie," "Anyone who sins, lies," "Whoever sins, lies," and so on. All these therefore translate into **A** propositions.

Examples

Here are a few more sentences that translate into **A** propositions.

Men are naturally selfish.	(All men are naturally selfish.)
Copper conducts electricity.	(All copper things are electrical conductors.)
Sugar tastes sweet.	(All things composed of sugar are sweet tasting.)
Vanity is a universal condition.	(All humans are vain.)
Those who live by the pen are called liars.	(All professional writers are liars.)
Whoever uses crack is foolish.	(All crack users are foolish.)
The gods have mercy.	(All gods are merciful.)
Show me an officer and I'll show you a dandy.	(All officers are dandies.)

And here are a few sentences that translate into **E** propositions.

Men are not selfish by nature.   (No men are naturally selfish.)
Copper doesn't conduct electricity.   (No copper things are electrical
                                                  conductors.)
Sugar doesn't taste sweet.   (No things made from sugar are sweet
                                                  tasting.)
Vanity is unheard of among humans.   (No humans are vain.)
There has never been a professional
    writer who lies.   (No professional writers are liars.)
The gods have no mercy.   (No gods are merciful.)
No one who is an officer also is a dandy.   (No officers are dandies.)

Here are some sentences that translate into **I** propositions.

There are honest men.   (Some men are honest.)
There exist some elements that are inert.   (Some elements are inert.)
There are active paraplegics.   (Some paraplegics are active.)
Lots of rivers have wide mouths.   (Some rivers are wide-mouthed.)
Musicians occasionally have tin ears.   (Some musicians are tin-eared.)
Killers frequently are paranoid.   (Some killers are paranoid.)
A few senators are against big business.   (Some senators are against big business.)
An occasional *Playboy* interview is   (Some *Playboy* interviews are inter-
    with a presidential candidate.   views with presidential candidates.)
Policemen have been known who will   (Some policemen are bribable.)
    take bribes.

And here are some sentences that translate into **O** propositions.

There are dishonest men.   (Some men are not honest.)
There are women who aren't maternal.   (Some women are not maternal.)
Most elements are not inert.   (Some elements are not inert.)
There are inactive paraplegics.   (Some paraplegics are not active.)
Many rivers don't have wide mouths.   (Some rivers are not wide-mouthed.)
Most musicians don't have a tin ear.   (Some musicians are not tin-eared.)
A few killers are not paranoid.   (Some killers are not paranoid.)
The majority of senators are not against   (Some senators are not against big
    big business.   business.)
Most *Newsweek* interviews are not   (Some *Newsweek* interviews are not
    with presidential candidates.   with presidential candidates.)
Policemen have been known who will   (Some policemen are not bribable.)
    not take bribes.

Exercise 14-1

Translate the following sentences into equivalent *A, E, I,* or *O* propositions.

1. Whoever is rich is a sinner.
2. The poor are lazy.
3. Most children aren't naughty.
4. Porno flicks aren't erotic.
5. Albino crows are known to exist.
6. Amateurs aren't professionals.
7. There are plenty of immodest failures.
8. Most prescription drugs are harmful.
9. Human beings are omnivorous.
10. Most movie stars aren't happy.
11. Omnivores occasionally are vegetarians.
12. None who have dry wits drink.
13. Some drinkers have wet whistles.
14. Those who forget the past suffer from amnesia.
15. Omnivores usually are not vegetarians.

2 *Existential Import*

A proposition is said to have **existential import** if its subject and predicate are taken to refer to classes that are not empty. For instance, if we assume existential import for the *A* proposition "All angels are without moral blemish," then we are assuming that there are angels, and also that there are things without moral blemish.

Syllogistic logic traditionally rested on the assumption that all the propositions to be dealt with do have existential import. In other words, syllogistic logic traditionally was restricted to categorical propositions whose terms all were taken to refer to nonempty classes.

Such a restriction severely limits the scope of syllogistic logic, since it often is quite important to reason about nonexistent entities—for one thing to make sure that they remain nonexistent. (We want to reason about World War III precisely to prevent such a disaster from occurring.) Yet if we are to retain several of its interesting and important features (and have them be valid), we must restrict the use of traditional logic to propositions that have existential import. We discuss this issue further in Section 14.

So let's assume for the moment that all the categorical propositions to be dealt with do have existential import.

3 *The Square of Opposition*

The **square of opposition** illustrates some of the more interesting features of traditional logic:

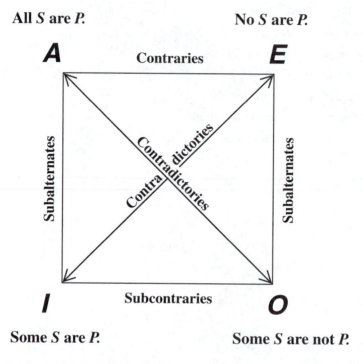

All *S* are *P*.   **No *S* are *P*.**

Some *S* are *P*.   **Some *S* are not *P*.**

(1) *Corresponding A and O propositions are contradictories.* Two propositions are **contradictory propositions** *if both cannot be true, and both cannot be false.* (So one must be true, the other false.) For instance, the *A* proposition "All humans are mortal" is true, whereas its contradictory "Some humans are not mortal," an *O* proposition, is false.

(2) *Corresponding E and I propositions also are contradictories.* Hence, both cannot be true, and both cannot be false. For example, the *I* proposition "Some humans are mortal" is true, and its contradictory, "No humans are mortal," an *E* proposition, is false.

(3) *Corresponding A and E propositions are contraries.* Two propositions are **contrary propositions** *if both cannot be true, but both may be false.* For instance, the *A* proposition, "All scientists are philosophers," is false, and its contrary "No scientists are philosophers," an *E* proposition, also is false (because some scientists are philosophers and some aren't). This is an example of contraries both of which are false. And the *A* proposition, "All humans are mortal," is true, whereas its contrary, "No humans are mortal," an *E* proposition, is false. This is an example of contraries one of which is true, one false. (But we cannot give an example of contrary propositions both of which are true, because this case cannot occur.)

(4) *Corresponding **I** and **O** propositions are subcontraries.* Two propositions are **subcontrary propositions** *if both cannot be false, but both may be true.* For instance, the **I** proposition "Some scientists are philosophers" is true, and its subcontrary, "Some scientists are not philosophers," an **O** proposition, also is true. This proposition is an example of subcontraries both of which are true. And the **I** proposition "Some humans are mortal" is true, whereas its subcontrary, "Some humans are not mortal," an **O** proposition, is false. This proposition is an example of subcontraries one of which is true, one false. (But we cannot give an example of subcontraries both of which are false, because this case cannot occur.)

(5) *Corresponding **A** and **I** propositions are subalternates.* **Subalternate propositions** are such that *if the universal member of the pair* (for instance, an **A** proposition) *is true, then so is the particular member of the pair* (for instance, the corresponding **I** proposition). The propositions "All humans are mortal," a true **A** proposition, and "Some humans are mortal," a true **I** proposition, are subalternates.

Notice that if a particular **A** proposition is *false,* nothing can be inferred as to the truth-value of its subalternate; it may be true or it may be false. For instance, the false **A** proposition "All scientists are philosophers" has as its subalternate the *true **I*** proposition "Some scientists are philosophers," while the false **A** proposition "All humans are immortal" has as its subalternate the *false **I*** proposition "Some humans are immortal." Thus, subalternation, conceived as a rule of inference, is *one-directional;* we can infer from the truth of an **A** proposition to the truth of its corresponding **I** proposition, but we cannot infer from the truth of an **I** proposition to the truth of its corresponding **A** proposition.

However, we can infer from the *falsity* of an **I** proposition to the *falsity* of the corresponding **A** proposition. For instance, if it is false that even *some* men are immortal, then it must be false that all men are immortal.

(6) Finally, *corresponding **E** and **O** propositions also are subalternates.* Hence, we can infer from the truth of an **E** proposition to the truth of its subalternate, the corresponding **O** proposition. For example, we can infer from the truth of the **E** proposition "No humans are immortal" to the truth of its subalternate, "Some humans are not immortal." But again, we cannot infer from the falsehood of an **E** proposition to the falsehood of its corresponding **O** proposition, although we can infer from the falsity of an **O** proposition to the falsity of the corresponding **E** proposition. For instance, if it is false that even some humans are not immortal, then it must be false that no humans are immortal.

The information about inferences provided by the square of opposition can also be put into tabular form, as follows (blanks indicate no valid inference possible).

A true:	*E* false	*I* true	*O* false
A false:	*E* _____	*I* _____	*O* true
E true:	*A* false	*I* false	*O* true
E false:	*A* _____	*I* true	*O* _____
I true:	*A* _____	*E* false	*O* _____
I false:	*A* false	*E* true	*O* true
O true:	*A* false	*E* _____	*I* _____
O false:	*A* true	*E* false	*I* true

Examples

(1) On the assumption that the *A* proposition "All college students are intelligent" is true (whether in fact it is or not), we can infer that

 1. "Some college students are intelligent" is true (by subalternation).
 2. "Some college students are not intelligent" is false (because "All college students are intelligent" and "Some college students are not intelligent" are contradictories).
 3. "No college students are intelligent" is false (because "All college students are intelligent" and "No college students are intelligent" are contraries).

(2) On the assumption that the *I* proposition "Some college students cheat on exams" is false, we can infer that

 1 . "No college students cheat on exams" is true (because "Some college students cheat on exams" and "No college students cheat on exams" are contradictories).
 2. "Some college students do not cheat on exams" is true (because "Some college students cheat on exams" and "Some college students do not cheat on exams" are subcontraries).
 3. "All college students cheat on exams" is false (because "Some college students cheat on exams" and "All college students cheat on exams" are related by subalternation).

(3) On the assumption that the *E* proposition "No college students cheat on exams" is true, we can infer that

 1. "Some college students cheat on exams" is false (because "No college students cheat on exams" and "Some college students cheat on exams" are contradictories).
 2. "All college students cheat on exams" is false (because "No college students cheat on exams" and "All college students cheat on exams" are contraries).
 3. "Some college students do not cheat on exams" is true (by subalternation).

(4) On the assumption that the *O* proposition "Some college students do not cheat on exams" is true, we can infer only that "All college students cheat on exams" is false.

Exercise 14-2

(1) Suppose the categorical proposition "All wars are hellish" is true. Using the machinery provided by the square of opposition, what can be inferred about the truth-values of the following?

 1. No wars are hellish.
 2. Some wars are hellish.
 3. Some wars are not hellish.

(2) Suppose "All wars are hellish" is false. Then what can be inferred about the truth-values of the preceding three propositions?

(3) Suppose "Some congressmen are sexual gluttons" is true. Then what can be inferred about the truth-values of the following?

    1. No congressmen are sexual gluttons.
    2. Some congressmen are not sexual gluttons.
    3. All congressmen are sexual gluttons.

(4) Suppose "Some congressmen are sexual gluttons" is false. Then what can be inferred about the truth-values of the following?

    1. No congressmen are sexual gluttons.
    2. Some congressmen are not sexual gluttons.
    3. All congressmen are sexual gluttons.

4   *Conversion, Obversion, Contraposition*

In this section we shall consider *operations* performed on the four propositions we have been studying. These operations are accomplished by clearly specified rules, replacing subject or predicate terms of the four proposition, and then noting the logical relationship between the new proposition and the one operated on by the rule.

Conversion

In the process of **conversion** we replace the subject of a proposition with its predicate and its predicate with its subject. For instance, "All humans are mortals" converts to "All mortals are humans," "No humans are mortals" converts to "No mortals are humans," "Some humans are not mortals" to "Some mortals are not humans," and so on.

    Not all conversions are valid. Conversion is a valid process only if used on *E* or *I* propositions. We can validly infer from "No humans are mortals" to "No mortals are humans," and from "Some humans are mortals" to "Some mortals are humans," but not from "All humans are mortals" to "All mortals are humans," and not from "Some humans are not mortals" to "Some mortals are not humans." Or from "No scientists are philosophers" to "No philosophers are scientists," but not from "All scientists are philosophers" to "All philosophers are scientists."

Conversion by limitation

In the process of **conversion by limitation** we replace the subject term of an *A* proposition with its predicate term and its predicate term with its subject term, and then change the quantity of the proposition from *A* to *I*. For instance, we can infer by conversion by limitation from the *A* proposition "All hogs are mammals" to the *I* proposition "Some mammals are hogs." Conversion by limitation is *always* a valid process.

Obversion

In the process of **obversion,** we change the quality of a proposition (from affirmative to negative or from negative to affirmative), and then replace its predicate with the negation or **complement** of the predicate.

We can obvert, say, the *E* proposition "No shadows are entities" by first changing the quality of that proposition from negative to affirmative, obtaining the proposition "All shadows are entities," and then replacing the predicate with its complement, obtaining the proposition "All shadows are nonentities." Thus "No shadows are entities" obverts to "All shadows are nonentities." Similarly, "All shadows are entities" obverts to "No shadows are nonentities." The *I* proposition "Some shadows are entities" obverts to the *O* proposition "Some shadows are not nonentities," and, likewise, "Some shadows are not entities" obverts to "Some shadows are nonentities." Obversion is *always* valid.

There is, however, an important technical difference between the notions of negation and complement, illustrated by the difference between "Some *S* are *non-P*," and "Some *S* are not *P*." The first proposition has the *I* form, because "*non-*" *is a part of the predicate term*, whereas the latter has the form of an *O* proposition, so that "not" is indeed part of the proposition's *form*. Therefore, although intuitively we know that, say "Some *S* are not non-*P*" is logically equivalent to "Some *S* are *P*," we are not so far thenceforth licensed to equate them because of this difference in form.

Contraposition

In the process of **contraposition,** we replace the subject of a proposition with the complement of its predicate and replace its predicate with the complement of its subject. Thus the contrapositive of "All humans are mortals" is "All nonmortals are nonhumans," and the contrapositive of "Some humans are not mortals" is "Some nonmortals are not nonhumans." Contraposition is valid for *A* and *O* propositions, but not for *E* and *I* propositions. Hence we can validly infer from, say, "All humans are mortals" to "All nonmortals are nonhumans," and from "Some humans are not mortals to "Some nonmortals are not nonhumans," but not from "No humans are mortals" to "No nonmortals are nonhumans," and not from "Some humans are mortals" to "Some nonmortals are nonhumans."*

Contraposition by limitation

Finally, we can validly infer from a given *E* proposition to a particular related *O* proposition by the process called **contraposition by limitation.** For instance, we can validly infer from the *E* proposition "No hems are mended" to the *O* proposition "Some unmended things are hems (not nonhems)" by contraposition by limitation.

Contraposition by limitation obviously is valid, because it is simply the combination of subalternation (of an *E* proposition) and contraposition (of the resulting *O* proposition).

Notice that conversion, obversion, and contraposition are, in effect, *equivalent inference rules;* that is, they work in both directions. For instance, we can infer from "All humans are mortals" to "All nonmortals are nonhumans" by contraposition and also from "All nonmortals are nonhumans" to "All humans are mortals." But conversion by limitation

---

*Note the comparison between contraposition in syllogistic logic and what we called contraposition in our exposition of symbolic logic. The former has the structure $(x)(Fx \supset Gx) :: (x)(\sim Gx \supset \sim Fx)$, whereas the structure of the latter is $(p \supset q) :: (\sim q \supset \sim p)$. Contraposition in syllogistic logic is thus like a quantified version of the contraposition introduced into symbolic (sentential) logic.

and contraposition by limitation are just *implicational inference rules;* that is, they work in only one direction. For instance, we can infer from "All humans are mortals" to "Some mortals are humans" by conversion by limitation, but *not* from "Some mortals are humans" to "All humans are mortals."

Examples

On the assumption that the *A* proposition "All college students are intelligent" is true, we can infer that

1. "No college students are nonintelligent" is true (by obversion).
2. "All who are nonintelligent are noncollege students" is true (by contraposition).
3. "None who are nonintelligent are college students" is true (by obversion of "All who are nonintelligent are noncollege students").
4. "Some who are intelligent are college students" is true (by conversion by limitation).
5. "Some college students are intelligent" is true (by conversion of "Some who are intelligent are college students").
6. "Some who are intelligent are not noncollege students" is true (by obversion of "Some who are intelligent are college students").
7. "Some college students are not nonintelligent" is true (by contraposition of "Some who are intelligent are not noncollege students").

Using the processes illustrated by the square of opposition, we also can infer from the truth of "All college students are intelligent" that

8. "Some college students are not intelligent" is false (because "All college students are intelligent" and "Some college students are not intelligent" are contradictories).
9. "Some who are nonintelligent are not noncollege students" is false (by contraposition of "Some college students are not intelligent").
10. "Some college students are nonintelligent" is false (by obversion of "Some college students are not intelligent").
11. "Some who are nonintelligent are college students" is false (by obversion of "Some who are nonintelligent are not noncollege students").
12. "None who are intelligent are college students" is false (because "Some who are intelligent are college students" and "None who are intelligent are college students" are contradictories).
13. "No college students are intelligent" is false (by conversion of "None who are intelligent are college students").
14. "Some college students are nonintelligent" is false (by obversion of "Some college students are not intelligent").
15. "None who are nonintelligent are noncollege students" is false (by contraposition of "No college students are intelligent").

Exercise 14-3

What can be said about the truth-values of the sentences in the following sets, assuming that the first sentence in each set is true?

(1) 1. No quitters are winners.
    2. All winners are nonquitters.
    3. Some quitters are not winners.
    4. Some winners are quitters.
    5. Some winners are nonquitters.

(2) 1. All great lovers are highly sexed.
    2. Some great lovers are highly sexed.
    3. No great lovers are highly sexed.
    4. Some highly sexed people are great lovers.
    5. No highly sexed people are great lovers.

(3) 1. No monkey wrenches are left-handed.
    2. Some left-handed things are not monkey wrenches.
    3. No left-handed things are monkey wrenches.
    4. All monkey wrenches are left-handed.
    5. Some monkey wrenches are left-handed.

(4) 1. Some SS men were not involved in atrocities.
    2. Some who were involved in atrocities were SS men.
    3. No SS men were involved in atrocities.
    4. All SS men were involved in atrocities.
    5. Some who were not involved in atrocities were SS men.

5 *Syllogistic Logic—Not Assuming Existential Import*

The logic developed so far rests on a blanket assumption of existential import. But no such assumption is made in everyday life. For instance, someone uttering the proposition "Let him who is without sin cast the first stone" does not necessarily assume that there are any human beings free from sin. Similarly, a scientist who says "All objects cooled down to absolute zero VMI conduct electricity" does not intend to imply that anything ever will be cooled down to absolute zero.

How much of the traditional logic just described is invalid if we do not make a blanket assumption of existential import? This question is best answered by implicitly assuming the translations of the *A, E, I,* and *O,* into their predicate logic forms (recall now our discussion in Chapter Seven, Sections 5 and 6):

   A $(x)(Sx \supset Px)$
   E $(x)(Sx \supset \sim Px)$
   I $(\exists x)(Sx \cdot Px)$
   O $(\exists x)(Sx \cdot \sim Px)$

It is quite simple, using our predicate logic rules, to prove that the modern *A* and *O* are contradictories, the modern *E* and *I* are contradictories, and that the rest of the tradition-al square no longer holds. So keep these translations in mind in the following discussions; they can help you more easily understand the different logical connections. Notice that the *E* in effect says that all *S* are not *P*: "All senators are not crooks" says the same thing as "No senators are crooks." Along the same lines, "No senators are not crooks" says the same thing as "All senators are *not* not crooks," that is, "All senators are crooks." Some of the following exercises use such locutions.

However, that modern syllogistic logic, first formulated in the nineteenth century by logicians such as Boole and Venn, did not have predicate logic at its disposal, and there are differences that have to be noted. If we think of modern syllogistic logic as just a sub-set of the inferences of predicate logic, then we must, to make sense of that, assume sen-tential logic, something neither Aristotle nor nineteenth-century logicians did or could do. For a further discussion, see Section 14.

A and E propositions are not contraries

We said before that two propositions are contraries if both cannot be true, but both can be false, and that *A* and *E* propositions are contraries. However, if we allow the use of empty classes, then corresponding *A* and *E* propositions both can be true, and *A* and *E* proposi-tions will not be contraries. For instance, if there are no Martians, then the *A* proposition "All Martians are immortal" and the *E* proposition "No Martians are immortal" both are true (vacuously). Recall that in the modern interpretation of universally quantified propo-sitions, the *A* and the *E* are in effect universally quantified conditionals. If you think of an expansion of these in terms of a conjunction of conditionals, each conjunct will be true because each antecedent of each conjunct is false. Hence, they are not contraries in the tra-ditional sense.*

I and O propositions are not subcontraries

We said before that two propositions are subcontraries if both cannot be false, but both can be true, and that *I* and *O* propositions are subcontraries. However, if we allow the use of empty classes, then both of two corresponding *I* and *O* propositions can be false, and so *I* and *O* propositions are not subcontraries. For example, if there are no Martians, then the *I* proposition "Some Martians are immortal" and the *O* proposition "Some Martians are not immortal" both are false. Hence they are not subcontraries in the traditional sense.[†]

But corresponding *A* and *O* propositions remain contradictories, as do corresponding *E* and *I* propositions.

Here are some more consequences of dropping the assumption of existential import.

---

*However, some texts define contraries as pairs of universal propositions that differ only in quality. According to this defini-tion, corresponding *A* and *E* propositions automatically become contraries.

†However, some texts define subcontraries as pairs of particular propositions that differ only in quality. According to this definition, corresponding *I* and *O* propositions automatically become subcontraries.

Subalternation is invalid

For instance, if there are no Martians, then the *A* proposition, "All Martians are immortal," is true (vacuously, because all of the zero number of Martians are immortal), while its subalternate "Some Martians are immortal," is false because nothing is both a Martian and immortal. So we cannot allow subalternation from an *A* to an *I* proposition. The same is true of subalternation from an *E* to an *O* proposition.

Conversion by limitation and contraposition by limitation both are invalid

For instance, if there are no Martians, then the *A* proposition "All Martians are immortal," is true, while the *I* proposition obtained from it by conversion by limitation, namely the proposition "Some immortals are Martians," is false.

To sum up, if we allow the subject or predicate terms of propositions to refer to empty classes, then subalternation, conversion by limitation, and contraposition by limitation are all invalid, *A* and *E* propositions are not contraries, and *I* and *O* propositions are not subcontraries.

Conversion of *E* and *I* propositions, obversion, and contraposition of *A* and *O* propositions all remain valid.

In the sections that follow we will no longer assume existential import.

Exercise 14-4

In this exercise, do *not* assume existential import.

(1) If it is false that all existentialists are theists, then what can be said about the truth-values of the following?

    1. No existentialists are theists.
    2. No theists are existentialists.
    3. Some nontheists are existentialists.
    4. All nonexistentialists are nontheists.
    5. Some existentialists are nontheists.
    6. Some theists are existentialists.

(2) If it is true that no existentialists are theists, then what can be said about the truth-values of the preceding propositions 2 to 6?

(3) If the proposition "All senators are promiscuous," is true, what can be inferred about the truth-values of the following?

    1. Some who are not promiscuous are senators.
    2. No senators are not promiscuous.
    3. Some senators are promiscuous.
    4. No nonpromiscuous people are senators.
    5. Some promiscuous people are senators.
    6. Some who are not promiscuous are not senators.

(4) If "No nonsenators are not promiscuous" is false, what can be inferred about the truth-values of the preceding six propositions?

(5) Suppose you know that the classes of senators, promiscuous people, nonsenators, and nonpromiscuous people all are nonempty. And suppose you know that "No nonsenators are promiscuous." What else can you infer? (Justify your answer.)

6 *Venn Diagrams*

It is both useful and informative to use **Venn diagrams** to picture categorical propositions. First, let's represent the classes denoted by the subject and predicate terms by overlapping circles, as follows:

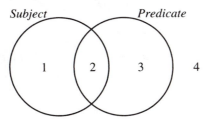

In this diagram area 1 represents the class of things that are in the subject class but not in the predicate, area 2 the class of things that are in both subject and predicate classes, area 3 the class of things that are in the predicate class but not in the subject, and area 4 the class of things that are in neither subject nor predicate classes.

Now consider the *A* proposition "All humans are mortals." This proposition asserts that the first class (things that are humans but not mortals) is empty. We can illustrate this using a Venn diagram *by shading out* area 1 (shading an area indicates that the class represented by that area is empty), as follows:

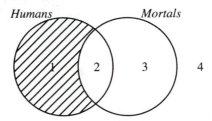

Next, consider the *E* proposition "No humans are mortal," which asserts that the class consisting of things that are both human and mortal is empty. We can diagram this proposition *by shading out* area 2 (to indicate that the class represented by this area is empty), as follows:

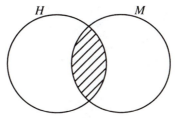

Now consider the *I* proposition "Some humans are mortal," which asserts that the class consisting of things that are both human and mortal is *not* empty, but has at least one member. We can diagram this proposition by *placing a mark (say the letter X) in area 2* (to indicate that the class represented by this area *is not* empty), as follows:

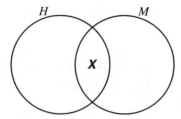

Finally, consider the *O* proposition "Some humans are not mortal," which asserts that the class consisting of things that are both human and not mortal is not empty, but has at least one member. We can diagram this proposition by placing an *X* in area 1 (to indicate that the class represented by this area is not empty), as follows:

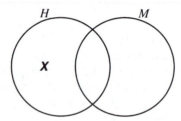

Exercise 14-5

Draw a Venn diagram for each proposition.
   Example: All millionaires are crooks.

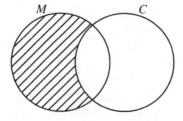

1. Most millionaires are crooks.
2. No crooks are paupers.
3. Some crooks are not millionaires.
4. No millionaires aren't crooks.
5. All environmentalists are a bit overzealous.

6. No environmentalists who tell the truth are taken seriously.
7. Some overzealous environmentalists are pretty unpopular.
8. Some mathematicians are not able to multiply.
9. No nonscientists are able to repair flush toilets.
10. Some questions are not answerable.
11. Nonfootball fans get pretty lonely in the fall.
12. Some who broadcast the news on TV are nonhigh school graduates.
13. Some Unitarians are believers in a deity.
14. No agnostics are believers in a deity.
15. There are plenty of Unitarians who are agnostics.
16. All Chicagoans are unafraid of frigid weather.
17. No comets are devoid of ice.
18. Some who believe in God are existentialists.

7 Syllogisms

A **syllogism** is a particular kind of argument containing three categorical propositions, two of them premises, one a conclusion. Here is one of the original examples (translated from the Greek and dechauvinized):

> All humans are mortal.
> <u>All Greeks are humans.</u>
> ∴ All Greeks are mortal.

The predicate of the conclusion is said to be the **major term** of the syllogism; the subject of the conclusion is said to be the **minor term;** and, finally, the **middle term** occurs once in each premise but not in the conclusion. In the argument just given, "mortal" is the major term, "Greeks" is the minor term, and "humans" is the middle term. Every syllogism has exactly three terms, each one used twice (but none used twice in the same proposition).

The **mood** of a syllogism is determined by the kind of propositions it contains. For instance, the preceding syllogism contains three *A* propositions, and so its mood is *AAA.* Similarly, the mood for the syllogism

> All morticians are philosophical.
> <u>Some sadists are morticians.</u>
> ∴ Some sadists are philosophical.

is *AII.*

The **figure** of a syllogism is determined by the position of the middle terms in its premises. There are four figures. These are easily remembered by noting the symmetrical arrangement of the middle terms. If we let *S* designate the subject of the conclusion (minor term), *P* designate the predicate of the conclusion (major term) and *M* designate the middle term, the four figures can be represented as follows:

I.	*M__P*	II.	*P__M*	III.	*M__P*	IV.	*P__M*
	S__M		*S__M*		*M__S*		*M__S*
∴	*S__P*	∴	*S__P*	∴	*S__P*	∴	*S__P*

Notice that the order of premises is important in determining the mood or the figure of a syllogism. The rule is that the predicate of the conclusion, the major term, must occur in the first premise. A syllogism with its premises in the proper order (and, of course, containing only three terms, each one appearing twice) is said to be in **standard form.**

The **form** of a syllogism is simply the combination of mood and figure. For instance, the two syllogisms just discussed have the forms *AAA-I* and *AII-I* respectively, and the syllogism

> All Greeks are mortals.
> No Greeks are humans.
> ∴ No humans are mortals.

has form *AEE-III.* (This syllogism happens to be invalid, but invalid syllogisms are still syllogisms.)

Examples

Here are more examples of syllogisms and their forms:

1. *IAO-III:*
    Some Greeks are mortals.
    All Greeks are humans.
    ∴ Some humans are not mortals.

2. *AEE-IV:*
    All mortals are Greeks.
    No Greeks are humans.
    ∴ No humans are mortals.

3. *EIO-II*
    No mortals are Greeks.
    Some humans are Greeks.
    ∴ Some humans are not mortals.

4. *AIE-I*
    All Greeks are mortals.
    Some humans are Greeks.
    ∴ No humans are mortals.

5. *EEE-III*
    No Greeks are mortals.
    No Greeks are humans.
    ∴ No humans are mortals.

6. *EIO-I*
    No Greeks are mortals.
    Some humans are Greeks.
    ∴ Some humans are not mortals.

Exercise 14-6

Using the *A, E, I, O* notation, symbolize the following arguments, put them into standard syllogistic form, and determine their mood and figure (and thus their form).

1. Some Beatles are musicians.
   <u>All musicians are rhythmic.</u>
   ∴ Some Beatles are rhythmic.

2. All things made out of grass are green.
   <u>Some things made out of grass are cigarettes.</u>
   ∴ Some cigarettes are green.

3. All homosexuals are gay.
   <u>Some homosexuals are not happy people.</u>
   ∴ Some happy people are not gay.

4. No Republicans are donkeys.
   <u>Some politicians are not Republicans.</u>
   ∴ Some politicians are donkeys.

5. All Democrats are donkeys.
   <u>Some politicians are Democrats.</u>
   ∴ Some donkeys are politicians.

6. No men not named after their fathers are juniors.
   <u>Some college students are not named after their fathers.</u>
   ∴ Some college students are not juniors.

7. All men whose sons are named after them are seniors.
   <u>No women are men whose sons are named after them.</u>
   ∴ No women are seniors.

8. No skiers are bathing lions.
   <u>All bathing lions are cool cats.</u>
   ∴ No cool cats are skiers.

9. All great chess players are geniuses.
   <u>Some geniuses are completely overlooked.</u>
   ∴ Some great chess players are completely overlooked.

10. No rules have exceptions.
    <u>Some rules are exceptional.</u>
    ∴ Some exceptional things are not exceptions.

8 Determining Syllogism Validity

A syllogism is **valid** if its form makes it impossible for the syllogism to have both premises true and its conclusion false. All other syllogisms are invalid. A valid syllogism guarantees the truth of its conclusion, provided both of its premises are true. An **invalid syllogism** may have a false conclusion even though both of its premises are true. So an invalid syllogism obviously does not guarantee anything about its conclusion, which is why we say it is invalid.

If a syllogism having a given form is a valid syllogism, then all syllogisms having that form are valid, and if a syllogism having a given form is invalid, then all syllogisms having that form are invalid.*

9 *Venn Diagram Proofs of Validity or Invalidity*

Perhaps the most common way to determine the validity or invalidity of syllogisms and of what we might call "syllogism forms" is by using Venn diagrams.

To diagram a syllogism, three overlapping circles are required, one for each term. In overlapping the three circles, seven areas are formed (plus an eighth, outside the circles):

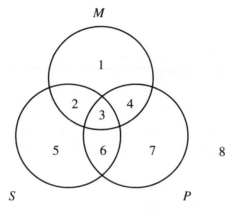

Area 1 represents the class of things that are in class *M*, but not in *S* or *P*; 2 the class of things that are in both *M* and *S* but not in *P*; 3 the class of things that are in *M*, *S* and *P*; 4 the class of things in *M* and *P* but not in *S*; and so on. The pair of areas 1 and 4, taken together, represents the class of things that are in *M* but not in *S*; the pair 3 and 6, the class of things that are in both *S* and *P*; the pair 6 and 7, the class of things in *P* but not in *M*; and so on. (We need two areas to represent these classes because in drawing a third overlapping circle we divide each of these areas into two parts.)

Now consider the syllogism

> All Greeks are mortals.
> <u>All humans are Greeks.</u>
> ∴   All humans are mortals.

---

*Except for the cases considered in Section 14 of this chapter.

In the Middle Ages, students determined the validity of a syllogistic form by reciting a chant containing a name for each of the valid moods in each figure. For instance, the name "bArbArA" occurs in the chant for the first figure, indicating that the form *AAA-I* is valid.

To diagram its first premise, "All Greeks are mortals," we shade out areas 1 and 2, to indicate that they are empty:

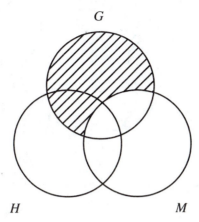

And to diagram its second premise, "All humans are Greeks," we shade out areas 5 and 6:

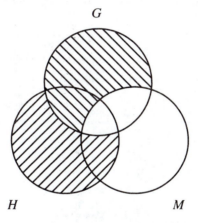

Were we now to diagram its conclusion, "All humans are mortals," we would shade out areas, 2 and 5. But in diagramming the two premises of this argument, we have already shaded out 2 and 5, and hence we have already diagrammed its conclusion. This indicates (speaking metaphorically) that the information contained in the conclusion already is contained in the premises. Hence, the syllogism, and any syllogism having the form *AAA-I,* is valid, since it cannot have true premises and a false conclusion.

Now consider the syllogism

> All Greeks are mortals.
> No humans are Greeks.
> ∴ No humans are mortals.

To diagram its first premise, we shade out areas 1 and 2, and to diagram its second premise we shade out 2 and 3, to get

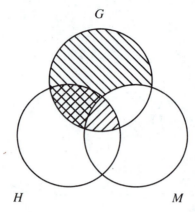

But to diagram its conclusion, we would have to shade out 3 and 6. It happens that we have shaded out 3, but we have not shaded out 6. So in diagramming the premises of this syllogism, we have not also diagrammed its conclusion. Hence, it is possible for its premises to be true and its conclusion false, and so the syllogism in question is invalid.

Examples

1.   We can diagram the premises of the syllogism

All Philadelphians are Metroliner fans.
No Metroliner fans are frequent flyers.
∴   No Philadelphians are frequent flyers.

as follows:

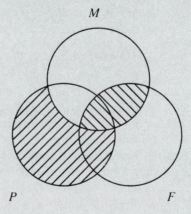

This proves that the syllogism is valid, because in diagramming its premises we have also diagrammed its conclusion.

2. We can diagram the premises of the syllogism

No doctors are in favor of smoking cigarettes.
Some cigarette smokers are doctors.
∴   Some cigarette smokers are not in favor of smoking cigarettes.

by shading out the *DF* area, then placing an *X* in area 2 to indicate that the class *CD* is not empty:

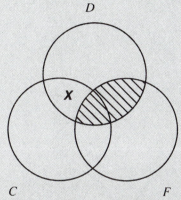

Although in diagramming the premises of this syllogism we have not quite diagrammed its conclusion (as will become evident in the next few paragraphs), we still have proved that the syllogism is valid. The reason for this is that the conclusion, "Some cigarette smokers are not in favor of smoking cigarettes," asserts that areas 2 and 5 are not both empty (that is, it asserts that either 2 or 5 has something in it), and in diagramming the premises we have placed an *X* in 2. So the premises of this argument already contain the information that is contained in the conclusion.

3. We can diagram the premises of the syllogism

No shady characters are honest.
Some shady characters are highly respected.
∴   Some who are highly respected are honest.

as follows:

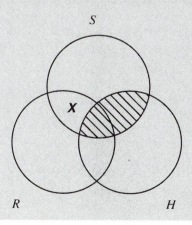

This proves that the syllogism is not valid, because in diagramming its premises we did not place an *X* in either 3 or 6, which is what would be required to diagram its conclusion.

In diagramming the premises of a syllogism, sometimes an *X* can be placed in either one of two areas. This is the case for the syllogism

> All Greeks are mortals.
> Some humans are mortals.
> ∴   Some humans are Greeks.

We diagram the first premise as follows:

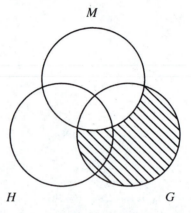

But in diagramming the second premise, the question arises as to whether to place an *X* in area 2 or in area 3. The answer is that we should not place an *X* in either area, because the premises assert only that one or the other (or perhaps both) of the classes represented by these areas has members, without indicating definitely either that the class represented by area 2 has members or that the class represented by area 3 has members. To indicate that the premises merely tell us that at least one of these classes has members, without telling us which one, we can place an *X* on the line between 2 and 3. Then the diagram will look like this:

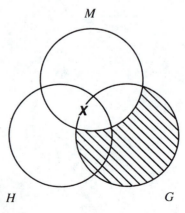

Is this syllogism valid? If it were, then in diagramming its premises, we would have placed an *X* either in 3 or in 6. Now clearly no *X* has been placed in 6. But no *X* has been placed in 3 either, for the *X* was placed on the line between 2 and 3. So we cannot guarantee the truth of the conclusion "Some humans are Greeks" on the basis of the evidence afforded by its premises, hence the syllogism is invalid. (This is the only even mildly difficult case that can arise in proving validity or invalidity using Venn diagrams, so it is worthwhile to expend a little extra effort to understand it.)

In any event, cases of this kind present no problem in practice, since all syllogisms diagrammed by placing an *X* on a line are invalid. (Similarly, all syllogisms diagrammed by doubly shading out an area are invalid.)

Sometimes it becomes clear where to place the *X* after shading in for the other premise. Always represent premises involving shading (*A* and *E* propositions) before representing a premise that requires placing an *X* (*I* and *O* propositions). So, for the valid syllogism

> Some professors are easy graders.
> All professors are teachers.
> ∴ Some teachers are easy graders.

it becomes clear where to place the *X* for the first premise once we shade for the second premise, as follows:

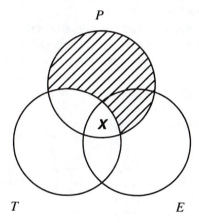

Exercise 14-7

Test the syllogisms in Exercise 14-6 for validity, using Venn diagrams as just discussed.

10 *Five Rules for Determining Validity or Invalidity*

An alternative (and much older) method for determining the validity or invalidity of syllogisms and syllogism forms is to use rules stating properties that all valid syllogisms must possess.

But before introducing a particular set of five rules of this kind, chosen from among several modestly similar sets, we must discuss the concept of **distribution.** In traditional logic texts, it is usually stated that a term in a proposition is *distributed* if (roughly) it says something about *all* members of the class designated by that term. For instance, the *A* proposition "All scientists are mathematicians" is said to distribute its subject term, because it says something about all scientists (namely that they are mathematicians), but not its predicate term, because it does not say something about all mathematicians. (It surely does not say, or imply, that all mathematicians are scientists.)

Traditional logic texts work out the distribution properties of all four kinds of categorical propositions. Letting *S* stand for subject terms and *P* for predicate terms, we can summarize the findings of the traditional logician as follows:

Table of Distribution

1. *A* propositions distribute *S*.
2. *E* propositions distribute *S* and *P*.
3. *I* propositions distribute neither *S* nor *P*.
4. *O* propositions distribute *P*.

Most students readily accept the results summarized in the first three lines of this table. But they find the idea expressed on the fourth line, that *O* propositions distribute their predicate terms, rather counterintuitive. And yet there is a certain plausibility to this idea. For instance, it seems plausible to say that the *O* proposition "Some scientists are not philosophers" distributes its predicate term, because it says of all philosophers that they are not some scientists (that is, that they are excluded from part of the class of scientists). In any event, we must say that *O* propositions distribute their predicates, or the five rules about to be presented will not function properly.*

According to these five rules for determining the validity/invalidity of syllogisms, all valid syllogisms must have

1. A middle term that is distributed at least once.
2. No term distributed in the conclusion that is not distributed in a premise.
3. At least one affirmative (nonnegative) premise.
4. A negative conclusion if one of its premises is negative, and a negative premise if the conclusion is negative.
5. One particular premise if the conclusion is particular (that is, one *I* or *O* premise if the conclusion is an *I* or *O* proposition).

Any syllogism that does not have all five of these properties is invalid. (The fifth rule is required only if we allow propositions to refer to empty classes.)†

---

*Unfortunately, the traditional characterization of the concept of distribution is not satisfactory even for *A, E,* and *I* propositions. Take the *A* proposition "All bachelors are unmarried adult males" (let's assume that "bachelor" means "unmarried adult male"). Clearly, this proposition "refers to" all bachelors, thus distributing its subject term, then it also "refers to" all unmarried adult males, thus distributing its predicate term. Hence the traditional account of distribution is inadequate. There are ways of getting around this difficulty, but they require decisions on philosophical problems beyond the scope of this text and hence are omitted.

†A sixth rule, requiring that there be exactly three terms in a valid syllogism, often is added to these five. But this rule is unnecessary because an argument that does not have exactly three terms, each one used twice, is not a syllogism according to the generally accepted definition of that term.

Examples

1. The syllogism

   Some mathematicians are scientologists.
   <u>All philosophers are mathematicians.</u>
   ∴ Some scientologists are philosophers.

violates the rule requiring that the middle term be distributed at least once, and hence is invalid.

2. The syllogism

   All hats in hand are worth two in the closet.
   <u>All bowlers in hand are hats in hand.</u>
   ∴ All things worth two in the closet are bowlers.

violates the rule requiring that no term be distributed in the conclusion that is not distributed in a premise, and hence is invalid.

3. The syllogism

   Some umbrellas in hand are not worth two in the closet.
   <u>No things worth two in the closet are better left there.</u>
   ∴ Some umbrellas in hand are not better left there.

violates the rule requiring at least one affirmative premise, and hence is invalid.

4. The syllogism

   Some shrinks are not expansive.
   <u>All who are expansive are expensive.</u>
   ∴ Some shrinks are expensive.

violates the rule requiring that the conclusion be negative, if a premise is negative, and hence is invalid. (This rule also requires that a premise be negative if the conclusion is negative.)

5. And the syllogism

   No expansive people are shrinks.
   <u>All shrinks are expensive.</u>
   ∴ Some expansive people are not expensive.

violates the rule requiring that at least one premise be particular, if the conclusion is particular, and hence is invalid.

Exercise 14-8

Put the following arguments into standard syllogistic form, and test for validity, using either the five rules of valid syllogisms or Venn diagrams. It will help you if you keep in mind the predicate logic expressions of the four categorical propositions.

1. All sinners are punished in the next life. And all nonsinners are nonmurderers. So it follows that all murderers are punished in the next life.

2. Most sinners are not murderers, since most people punished in the next life are non-murderers, and sinners are punished in the next life.

3. Eighteen-year-olds are permitted to vote. But not all who are permitted to vote in fact do vote. So there must be some eighteen-year-olds who don't exercise their right to vote.

4. Those who ignore relevant facts are likely to be mistaken. So the wise are not likely to be mistaken, because they take all known relevant facts into account.

5. Only the rich deserve the fair. So it follows that some who are handsome aren't non-rich, since some who deserve the fair aren't nonhandsome.

6. All logic classes are extremely interesting. So some classes that are harder than average are extremely interesting, since some logic classes are harder than average.

7. No logic classes are dreadfully boring, because no classes about good reasoning are boring, and all logic classes are about good reasoning.

8. All classes that are either interesting or difficult are uncrowded, because all uncrowded classes are unexciting, and all interesting or difficult ones are exciting.

9. Salespeople will do whatever is most likely to sell their product. So salespeople often will tell lies, because telling the truth often is not the best way to sell a product.

10. Because Harry enjoys himself only when he has lots of money and because Harry always enjoys going out with Jane, it follows that Harry goes out with Jane only when he has lots of money.

11. Those who live by the sword die by the sword. So all officers die with their boots on, since officers surely do live by the sword.

12. Some who live by the pen are called liars, and some are called sages. So there are people said to have great sagacity who have been referred to as frequent stretchers of the truth.

13. If to be human is to be vain, then everyone must be regularly looking in mirrors; everyone knows vanity tends to seek its own reflection.

14. We'll always have death and taxes. Right? And nobody ever gave in to either without a fight. Right? So that's why we're always fighting, fighting, fighting. Right!

15. Wet-whistled drunks all tend to be loud and shrill, which no doubt accounts for all the attention they get. Moral: Quiet people get ignored.

11 *Syllogistics Extended*

Several ways have been invented to extend the scope of syllogistic logic. Let's now consider some of these methods.

(1) *Many arguments containing four, five, and even six terms can be reduced to three terms, and thus to syllogistic form, by eliminating negation signs or by replacing terms*

with their synonyms. For instance, we eliminate a negation sign, and reduce the number of terms in the nonsyllogistic argument*

> All dentists are sadists.
> No MDs are nondentists.
> ∴ All MDs are sadists.

from four to three, by using obversion to replace its second premise with the equivalent proposition

> All MDs are dentists.

thus obtaining the valid syllogism

> All dentists are sadists.
> All MDs are dentists.
> ∴ All MDs are sadists.

Similarly, we can reduce the number of terms in the nonsyllogistic argument

> Some enclosed figures are squares.
> All triangles are enclosed figures.
> ∴ Some three-sided enclosed figures are squares.

from four to three by replacing the phrase "three-sided enclosed figures" with its synonym "triangles," thus obtaining the syllogism

> Some enclosed figures are squares.
> All triangles are enclosed figures.
> ∴ Some triangles are squares.

(2) *Many arguments that are not in syllogistic form because they contain propositions that are not categorical propositions can be translated into syllogistic form by translating the propositions they contain into categorical propositions.* Sometimes this can be accomplished by a simple change in word order. For instance, the proposition "Gamblers are all broke" may be translated into categorical form as "All gamblers are broke."

Sometimes, simply adding a suppressed quantifier will suffice to translate a proposition into categorical form. Thus, an argument containing the proposition "Men are fickle" may be translated into categorical form as "All men are fickle." And, clearly, "Every woman is mortal" can be translated into the categorical proposition "All women are mortal" and "Most gamblers are broke" into "Some gamblers are broke."

(3) *In addition, many other minor grammatical changes can be made.* For instance, we can translate the argument

> All Boy Scouts do good deeds.
> Some Girl Scouts do good deeds.
> ∴ Some Girl Scouts are Boy Scouts.

---

*Sometimes it is said that an argument of this kind is a syllogism, but not a standard form syllogism, thus taking any set of three categorical propositions to constitute a syllogism, no matter how many terms it contains.

into syllogistic form by replacing its first and second premises by the equivalent propositions "All Boy Scouts are doers of good deeds" and "Some Girl Scouts are doers of good deeds," respectively, thus obtaining the (invalid) syllogism

> All Boy Scouts are doers of good deeds.
> Some Girl Scouts are doers of good deeds.
> ∴   Some Girl Scouts are Boy Scouts.

(4) *All categorical propositions say something about classes.* Thus, technically, no *singular* proposition is a categorical proposition. Hence no syllogism can contain a singular proposition. (A **singular proposition** is a proposition one of whose terms refers to an individual rather than to a class. Thus, "Socrates is mortal," "Ada is tall," and "This man is short" all are singular propositions.)

But there are several standard ways to translate singular propositions into categorical propositions. One is simply to replace the singular term in such a proposition by a class term naming a class that can contain only one member (namely the individual referred to by the singular term). Thus, "Ada is tall" can be translated into "All members of the class whose sole member is Ada are tall." (We can also translate "Ada is tall" into "All things identical with Ada are tall," since only one thing, Ada, is identical with Ada.)

Using this method, we can translate the argument

> All persons are mortal.
> Socrates is a person.
> ∴   Socrates is mortal.

into syllogistic form as follows:

> All persons are mortal.
> All members of the class whose sole member is Socrates are persons.
> ∴   All members of the class whose sole member is Socrates are mortal.

Indeed, since we can always replace singular statements with categorical equivalents, it has become customary to treat singular propositions as categorical propositions, considering affirmative singular propositions, such as "Socrates is a person" as *A* propositions, and negative singular propositions, such as "Socrates is not mortal" as *E* propositions, without bothering to translate as we have just done. Thus, the argument

> All persons are mortal.
> Socrates is a person.
> ∴   Socrates is mortal.

is customarily treated as a syllogism, and in fact, a valid one.

(5) *Sometimes a more radical translation procedure is required to translate propositions into categorical form*, a procedure that involves the introduction of new classes. Take the proposition "We always have death and taxes." We can translate this sentence into categorical form by using the class of times (suggested by the temporal term "always," see Exercise 14-8, number 10), to obtain the categorical proposition "All times are times in which we have death and taxes." (Notice that the subject class in this case is the class of times, and the predicate class is a subclass of the class of times, namely, the class of times at which we have death and taxes.)

But, as usual, care must be used in translating. For instance, we don't want to translate the invalid argument

> Every time Anne gets an A on a logic exam she is happy.
> <u>Anne always gets A's on logic exams.</u>
> ∴   Anne always is happy.

as

> All times at which Anne gets A's on logic exams are times at which Anne is happy.
> <u>All times are times at which Anne gets A's on logic exams.</u>
> ∴   All times are times at which Anne is happy.

because the latter is a *valid* argument, and we don't want to translate invalid arguments into valid ones. The mistake was to translate the second premise, "Anne always gets A's on logic exams," so as to have Anne taking logic exams at *all* times. Clearly, what we mean when we say "Anne always gets A's on logic exams" is more accurately rendered as "All times *at which Anne takes logic exams* are times at which she gets A's." And if we correctly symbolize this premise, then the resulting argument will not even be a syllogism, much less a valid one.

12 *Enthymemes*

Arguments in daily life often omit premises everyone can be expected to know. For instance, someone might argue that Texas is larger than France, and hence, that some state in the United States is larger than France, omitting as understood that Texas is a state in the United States.

Sometimes the *conclusion* of an argument is omitted as obvious. And sometimes a premise *and* the conclusion are omitted. An example would be a mother who says, "Now, Son, it's eight o'clock, and all little boys have to go to bed at eight o'clock," thus omitting the premise that the son is a little boy, as well as the conclusion that the son has to go to bed.

An argument that omits a premise (or a conclusion) as "understood" is said to be an **enthymemic argument,** or simply an **enthymeme.**

Obviously, there is no point in declaring an argument in everyday life invalid when the addition of premises accepted by all concerned will render the argument valid. Life is short, and we have neither the time nor the inclination to be precise and complete about everything. So in determining the validity of arguments from everyday life, we should add any premises it is reasonable to assume all would concede, when such additions will make an argument in question valid.

Exercise 14-9

The following arguments are invalid as they stand. Supply a missing premise for each one that (perhaps with some arranging and synonym substitution) will turn it into a valid syllogism, and prove that the resulting syllogism is indeed valid.

1. No honest men are crooks. It follows then that no businessmen are honest.
2. Abortion takes the life of a fetus. So abortion takes the life of a human being.
3. Most adults are drug users, since caffeine and nicotine are drugs.
4. Smith must be in pretty good shape. After all, she eats plenty of brown rice.
5. Most American history textbooks conceal our theft of the American continent from the Indians. So most American history textbooks tell lies.
6. Anyone who listens to television news programs listens to very superficial accounts of the news. So you waste your time if you watch TV news programs.
7. Anyone whose primary interest is prestige or an easy life can't be a very good minister. So there must be some bishops who are pretty poor ministers.
8. Plenty of high school dropouts are smarter than lots of college graduates. So there must be an awful lot of people who never finished high school who are not incapable of holding high-level management positions.
9. Our Iranian policy was based on the judgment of some of America's best-known political scientists. So it wasn't a foolish policy.
10. No one with a scrambled brain is likely to do much good in this world. So a lot of people who have taken LSD have had it so far as being part of an effective force for good is concerned.

13 *Sorites*

Consider the argument

> All animals are life forms.
> All insects are animals.
> All bees are insects.
> ∴ All bees are life forms.

As it stands, it cannot count as a valid syllogism, because it contains four terms and three premises, and hence is not even a syllogism, much less a valid one. But clearly it is a valid argument of some sort. To bring it into the syllogistic framework, we can consider it to be an enthymematic version of a chain of two valid syllogisms. For instance, we can take the first two propositions as the premises of the valid syllogism

> All animals are life forms.
> All insects are animals.
> ∴ All insects are life forms.

and then use the conclusion of this syllogism and the third premise of our original argument as premises of the valid syllogism

> All insects are life forms.
> All bees are insects.
> ∴ All bees are life forms.

Let us refer to any argument of the kind just considered, which can be treated as a chain of enthymematic syllogisms, as a **sorites.***

Sorites can have as many premises as you wish. Here is one with four premises:

All musicians are entertainers.
All base players are musicians.
Some lead singers are base players.
No rocket scientists are entertainers.
∴   Some lead singers are not rocket scientists.

This sorites breaks down into the following chain of valid syllogisms:

All musicians are entertainers.
All base players are musicians.
∴   All base players are entertainers.

All base players are entertainers.
Some lead singers are base players.
∴   Some lead singers are entertainers.

Some lead singers are entertainers.
No rocket scientists are entertainers.
∴   Some lead singers are not rocket scientists.

Since all three of these syllogisms are valid (which the reader may want to prove), the sorites as a whole is valid.

Exercise 14-10

Translate the following sorites into standard form and determine whether they are valid or invalid.

1. Men are fickle.
   No one is disliked who is good at logic.
   Fickle people are disliked.
   ∴   No men are good at logic.

2. No skiers are nonathletic.
   Some nutritionists are skiers.
   Athletes are not brawny.
   ∴   Some nutritionists are nonbrawny.

3. Barbers are extroverts.
   No good barbers are nonbarbers.
   Some good barbers are high-strung.
   ∴   Some high-strung people are not extroverts.

---

*Originally the term "sorites" referred only to a special kind of enthymematic syllogism chain. But in recent years it has come to refer indiscriminately to all kinds.

4. No scientists are nonmathematicians.
Geologists are friendly.
No mathematicians are friendly.
∴ No geologists are scientists.

5. Occasionally, one finds a genius in graduate school.
No one can be admitted to grad school who isn't a college graduate.
People in graduate school are not college graduates.
∴ Some geniuses cannot be admitted to graduate school.

6. No one whose soul is not sensitive can be a Don Juan.
There are no profound scholars who are not great lovers of music.
Only profound scholars can be dons at Oxford.
No insensitive souls are great lovers of music.
∴ All Oxford dons are Don Juans.*

14 Technical Restrictions and Limitations; Modern Logic and Syllogistic Logic Compared

In Chapter Thirteen we pointed out that there are intuitively valid arguments that are not provable using predicate logic. One example given there was the valid argument

Art knows that he'll go either to the show or to the concert (but not to both).
Art knows that he won't go to the show.
∴ Art knows that he'll go to the concert.

Unfortunately, syllogistic logic is even less complete than predicate logic; that is, there are arguments provable using predicate logic that are not provable using syllogistic logic, even as we have extended it in Section 11. Here is a famous example.[†]

All horses are animals.
∴ All heads of horses are heads of animals.

In recent years, much work has been done in an effort to extend the scope of syllogistic logic to make it equal to that of predicate logic. No one has proved that this effort cannot succeed, but so far it has not. Indeed, a major and perhaps insurmountable hurdle is provided by relational predicate logic. Aristotelian logic simply could not handle such valid inferences as

Somebody is loved by everybody.
∴ Everybody loves somebody.

---

*Taken from C. L. Dodgson (Lewis Carroll), *Symbolic Logic* (1896), a book that, as one would expect, contains lots of cute examples.

[†]Given by Bertrand Russell, an inventor of predicate logic.

Nor could it handle an inference such as

> Bob loves Mary.
> Mary is the daughter of Sara.
> ∴   Bob loves the daughter of Sara.

let alone crucial mathematical inferences such as

> 3 is less than 5.
> 5 is less than 7.
> ∴   3 is less than 7.

Given the obvious importance of relations, it is rather amazing that no one gave a satisfactory theory of the logic of relations before Russell and Whitehead in *Principia Mathematica,* in the first decade of the twentieth century.

To see the importance of this advance, notice that Aristotle could only handle relations after a fashion. Instead of writing "Bob loves Mary," he would have to write "Bob is a Mary-lover." But doing this would not allow us to count the preceding argument about Bob and Mary as valid. To demonstrate the validity of that argument, we must be able to substitute "the daughter of Sara" for "Mary" in the second premise, using the logic of identity and definite descriptions found in Chapter Thirteen. The predicate "is a Mary-lover," however, is not amenable to substitution for "Mary," for "Mary" does not occur as a *term* in "Mary-lover," but rather as a mere part of the latter's orthography (as, for example, "Bob" in "Bobbing")!

We have said that traditional syllogistic logic could not handle relations. Its modern counterpart, of course, fares little better, even if we think of it as translated into the symbolism of predicate logic, because the issue is how to handle relational predicates in what are basically nonrelational forms.

We have mentioned that sentential logic also is not a part of traditional logic. The importance of that omission is by now quite obvious, because sentential logic is of high interest in its own right. Indeed, if we assume that we can translate modern syllogistic logic into predicate logic, our inference rules, as we know, must assume sentential logic as a part. There is thus a sense in which modern syllogistic logic cannot make sense without the assumption of sentential logic.

In Section 2 we briefly discussed the advantages and restrictions of assuming existential import. Aristotelian logic makes the assumption and modern logic does not. In the past fifty years, a considerable literature has dealt with the assumption. Despite examples from everyday life where we do reason about nonexistent entities, some philosophers and logicians have argued that Aristotelian logic is nevertheless much closer to everyday speech. This argument is part of a concerted attack on the general efficacy of symbolic logic to capture the inferences of ordinary life. As we mentioned in Chapter Seven, the utterance "All my children are upstairs asleep" would make no sense to a listener if the utterer had no children. Counting such an utterance as true, as we do without the assumption of existential import, licenses some things we want to say and do at the expense of others.

But this alleged conflict between modern and Aristotelian logic is in an important sense only apparent. If we are clear about the assumptions we make, we will be clear about which inferences we are capturing and which we are not. In that sense neither system is better than the other within the range of purposes such inferences serve. There are arguments valid in Aristotelian logic that are not valid in modern logic, but this is harmless and even useful as long as we are clear on the underlying assumptions of each logical system. The argument has in fact opened the way to a much clearer view of the relationship between modern logic and ordinary language.

In addition to being less complete than predicate logic, syllogistic logic has other difficulties. In particular, it seems to break down when applied to certain odd kinds of arguments.* A typical example is the following:

> All scientists are mathematicians.
> <u>Some brilliant scientists are not mathematicians.</u>
> ∴   No scientists are brilliant scientists.

According to the five rules for valid syllogisms, this syllogism is invalid, because it contains a term (*B*) that is distributed in the conclusion but not in a premise. And according to the Venn diagram technique, the syllogism is invalid:

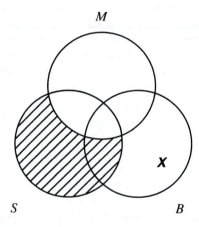

Nevertheless, this argument is valid, because its premises are contradictory,† and from contradictory statements we can prove whatever we wish. (Recall the discussion in Exercise 4-14, problem 10, both the question and its answer, and Chapter Five, Section 2.)

---

*See James W. Oliver, "Formal Fallacies and Other Invalid Arguments" *Mind*, n.s., vol. LXXVI (1967), pp. 463–478, for an excellent account of these difficulties.

†We can prove the validity of this argument using predicate logic as follows:

1. $(x)(Sx \supset Mx)$	
2. $(\exists x)[(Bx \cdot Sx) \cdot \sim Mx]$	$/\therefore (x)[Sx \supset \sim (Sx \cdot Bx)]$
3. $(Bx \cdot Sx) \cdot \sim Mx$	2 EI
4. $\sim Mx$	3 Simp
5. $Bx \cdot Sx$	3 Simp
6. Sx	5 Simp
7. $Sx \supset Mx$	1 EI
8. Mx	6,7 MP
9. $Mx \vee (x)[Sx \supset \sim (Sx \cdot Bx)]$	8 Add
10. $(x)[Sx \supset \sim (Sx \cdot Bx)]$	4,9 DS

(Notice that lines 4 and 8 explicitly contradict each other, so that any conclusion whatsoever could have been derived.)

Here is another argument that does not seem to be handled correctly either by the five rules of valid syllogisms or by Venn diagrams:

> All philosophers are tall or nontall.
> All philosophers are short or nonshort.
> ∴ Some tall-or-nontall things are short or nonshort.

Again, using either Venn diagrams or the five rules of valid syllogism, we arrive at the incorrect conclusion that this syllogism is invalid. Nevertheless, the argument is valid, this time because *its conclusion is logically true.**

Obviously, something must be done to remedy the defects in syllogistic logic illustrated by these two examples. Two remedies come to mind. One is to say simply that as *syllogistic arguments* they are invalid, although they are valid in some wider system not yet worked out. Another way is to require that the premises of a syllogism, taken together, be consistent (that is, noncontradictory), and that its conclusion not be logically true.†

But remedies of this kind are not entirely satisfactory. More work must be done on these problems before the traditional syllogistic logic will be entirely acceptable.

Exercise 14-11

1. What is lost, if anything, by restricting syllogistic logic so that it deals only with propositions having existential import? (Explain, including examples.)

2. Which of the following are *equivalence* inference rules? (Defend your answers.)
   a. Conversion
   b. Contraposition by limitation
   c. Obversion
   d. Subalternation

---

*We can prove its validity using predicate logic as follows:

1.	$(x)[Px \supset (Tx \lor \sim Tx)]$	
2.	$(x)[Px \supset (Sx \lor \sim Sx)]$	$/\therefore (\exists x)[(Tx \lor \sim Tx) \cdot (Sx \lor \sim Sx)]$
→ 3.	$\sim Tx$	AP $/\therefore \sim Tx \supset \sim Tx$
4.	$\sim Tx \lor \sim Tx$	3 **Add**
5.	$\sim Tx$	4 **Taut**
6.	$\sim Tx \supset \sim Tx$	3-5 **CP**
7.	$Tx \lor \sim Tx$	6 **Impl, DN**
→ 8.	$\sim Sx$	AP $/\therefore \sim Sx \supset \sim Sx$
9.	$\sim Sx \lor \sim Sx$	8 **Add**
10.	$\sim Sx$	9 **Taut**
11.	$\sim Sx \supset \sim Sx$	8-10 **CP**
12.	$Sx \lor \sim Sx$	11 **Impl, DN**
13.	$(Tx \lor \sim Tx) \cdot (Sx \lor \sim Sx)$ 7,12 **Conj**	
14.	$(\exists x)(Tx \lor \sim Tx) \cdot (Sx \lor \sim Sx)$	13 **EG**

(Notice that the two given premises were not used in deriving the conclusion. We didn't have to use them because the conclusion (being logically true) follows from the null set of premises.)

†The problem for traditional logic posed by logically true and logically false categorical propositions is, in fact, even broader than we have indicated. For instance, it also occurs for the notions of contraries, subcontraries, and so on. Thus, logically true *A* propositions, such as "All bachelors are unmarried," cannot have contraries, even assuming existential import. And logically false *I* propositions cannot have subcontraries. For more on these difficulties, see David Sanford, "Contraries and Subcontraries," *Noûs*, vol. 2 (1968), pp. 95–96.

3. Which of the following become invalid or, in the case of (e) and (f), false once we remove the restriction that propositions have existential import? (Defend your answers.)
    a. Contraposition
    b. Conversion by limitation
    c. Subalternation
    d. Obversion
    e. *A* and *O* propositions are contradictories
    f. *A* and *E* propositions are contraries

4. *True or False?* Since the order of premises in part determines the figure of a syllogism, changing the order of its premises may change its validity. (Defend your answer.)

5. *True or False?* If after diagramming the premises of a syllogism using a Venn diagram, we also have diagrammed its conclusion, then the syllogism is valid. (Defend your answer.)

6. When diagramming a syllogism to determine its validity, we sometimes have to place an *X* on the line between two slots. Carefully explain why. (Give an example.)

7. Carefully explain why *E* propositions distribute both their subject and predicate terms, and why *I* propositions distribute neither. (Give examples.)

8. Are singular propositions such as "Ronald Reagan is an actor" also categorical propositions? (Explain, with examples.)

9. Figure out an original example (genuinely different from the one in the text) of a valid argument, provable using the machinery of predicate logic but not of syllogistic logic; prove the argument is valid; and explain why syllogistic machinery does not permit proof.

10. Figure out an original example of a valid argument that is invalid according to the five rules of valid syllogism and Venn diagram proof procedures; prove the argument valid; and then explain why syllogistic rules go wrong. (This is a hard question.)

Key Terms Introduced in Chapter Fourteen

A proposition: (See *universal affirmative proposition.*)

Aristotelian logic: (See *syllogistic logic.*)

categorical proposition: A subject-predicate proposition that asserts, or denies, a relationship between two classes.

complement: The negation of a term. The *complement class* of a given class is the class of all things that are *not* members of the given class.

contradictory propositions: Two propositions such that if one of them is true, the other must be false, and vice versa. Corresponding *A* and *O* propositions, and *E* and *I* propositions, are contradictories.

contraposition: The rule permitting inference from a given proposition to a corresponding proposition in which the subject term has been replaced by the complement of the predicate term and the predicate term has been replaced by the complement of the subject term. For example. We can infer by contraposition from "All humans are mortals" to "All nonmortals are nonhumans." Contraposition is valid only for *A* and *O* propositions.

contraposition by limitation: The rule permitting subalternation and contraposition (of the resulting proposition) to be performed on an *E* proposition, resulting in a particular *O* proposition. For example, using contraposition by limitation we can infer from the *E* proposition "No humans are mortals" to the *O* proposition "Some mortals are not humans." Contraposition by limitation is valid only on the assumption of existential import.

contrary propositions: Two propositions such that it is not possible for both of them to be true, although it is possible for both of them to be false. Assuming existential import, corresponding *A* and *E* propositions are contraries.

conversion: The rule permitting inference from a given proposition to another proposition just like the first one, except that its subject and predicate terms have been reversed. For example, the proposition "No humans are mortals" converts to "No mortals are humans." Conversion is valid only for *E* and *I* propositions.

conversion by limitation: The rule permitting inference from an *A* proposition to the converse of a corresponding *I* proposition. For example, we can infer from "All humans are mortals" to "Some mortals are humans" by conversion by limitation. However, conversion by limitation is valid only on the assumption of existential import.

distribution: A term in a syllogism is distributed if the proposition refers to all members of the class designated by that term.

enthymemic argument (or enthymeme): An argument in which a premise, or premises, is omitted as understood. (Sometimes it is the conclusion that is omitted as understood.)

E proposition: (See *universal negative proposition*.)

existential import: A categorical proposition has existential import if it is assumed that its subject term and predicate term do not refer to empty classes.

figure: The property of a standard form syllogism determined by the positions of its major, minor, and middle terms in its premises.

Form: The property of a syllogism determined by its mood and figure.

I proposition: (See *particular affirmative proposition*.)

invalid syllogism: A syllogism that is not valid.

O proposition: (See *particular negative proposition*.)

major term: The predicate term of the conclusion of a syllogism.

middle term: The term in a syllogism that occurs once in each premise but not in the conclusion.

minor term: The subject term of the conclusion of a syllogism.

mood: The property of a standard form syllogism determined by the quality of its three propositions. For example, the syllogism

> All Greeks are mortals.
> Some humans are mortals.
> ∴ Some humans are Greeks.

has the mood *All*.

obversion: The rule permitting inference from a given proposition to a corresponding proposition in which the quality has been changed and the predicate term replaced with its complement. For example, we can infer from "All humans are mortals" to "No humans are nonmortals" by obversion. Obversion always is valid.

particular affirmative proposition: A categorical proposition having the form "Some *S* are *P*," where *S* and *P* denote classes. (Synonym: *I proposition*.)

particular negative proposition: A categorical proposition having the form "Some *S* are not *P*," where *S* and *P* denote classes. (Synonym: *O proposition*.)

predicate (or predicate term) (of a categorical proposition): The term after the copula, for instance, the word "hairsplitters" in "All logicians are hairsplitters."

quality (of a proposition): Every categorical proposition must have the quality either of being affirmative or of being negative.

quantity (of a proposition): Every categorical proposition must be either universal or particular.

singular proposition: A proposition one of whose terms refers to an individual entity rather than a class. For example, "Socrates is human" is a singular proposition.

sorites: An enthymemic version of a chain of syllogisms.

square of opposition: A diagram used to illustrate several of the inferential relationships (such as contradictoriness and contrariety) holding between categorical propositions.

standard form (of a syllogism): The form of a syllogism in which the premise placed first contains the predicate of the syllogism's conclusion.

subalternation: The rule permitting inference from an **A** proposition to a corresponding **I** proposition, or from an **E** proposition to a corresponding **O** proposition. Subalternation is valid only on the assumption of existential import.

subcontrary propositions: Two propositions such that it is not possible for both of them to be false, although it is possible for both of them to be true. Assuming existential import, corresponding **I** and **O** propositions are subcontraries.

subject (or **subject term**) **(of a categorical proposition):** The term before the copula and after the term "all," "some," or "no;" for instance, the word "logician" in "All logicians are hairsplitters." (See also *predicate*.)

syllogism: An argument containing three categorical propositions, two of which are premises and one a conclusion, such that the three propositions taken as a group contain exactly three terms, each of which occurs twice (none occurring twice in a given proposition and one of which terms occurs in each premise). The conclusion contains the minor and major terms.

syllogistic logic: The traditional logic centering on and developed from the syllogistic theory of Aristotle. The term now is often used to distinguish the traditional logic from modern symbolic logic. (Synonyms: *Aristotelian logic, traditional logic.*)

traditional logic: (See *syllogistic logic*.)

universal affirmative proposition: A categorical proposition having the form "All S are P," where S and P denote classes. (Synonym: *A proposition*.)

universal negative proposition: A categorical proposition having the form "No S are P," where S and P denote classes. (Synonym: *E proposition*.)

valid syllogism: A syllogism whose conclusion must be true if all of its premises are true. It is impossible for a valid syllogism to have true premises and a false conclusion.

Venn diagrams: Overlapping circles, used to diagram categorical propositions and categorical syllogisms without the assumption of existential import.

Part Three

Other Systems of Logic

Chapter Fifteen

Informal Fallacies

First, the bad news about fallacy theory. Although traditional syllogistic logic is incomplete, it does provide a correct account as far as it goes (with only minor changes—as noted in the previous chapter). However, traditional theories of fallacy contain serious defects that render all the various accounts unsatisfactory in one way or another. Several recent attempts have improved matters considerably, including one that is close to the heart of one of your authors,* but none has gained general acceptance. Conflicting theories abound.

Now for the good news. Even the defective traditional machinery can be quite useful for avoiding bad arguments and bad reasoning in daily life. And it can be made even more useful by adding some of the modern improvements.

1 The Nature of Fallacy

We can divide reasonings into those cases that are cogent and thus should be persuasive, and those that are fallacious and therefore should not be persuasive. **Cogent reasoning** must satisfy three conditions: (1) it must employ arguments whose premises provide good grounds for their conclusions (that is, it must use deductively or inductively valid arguments); (2) the premises must be warranted (acceptable) to the reasoner in question; and (3) the premises must contain all of the relevant information known to that reasoner. **Fallacious reasoning** is just reasoning that is not cogent, which means reasoning that either (1) does not provide sufficiently good grounds for its conclusion; (2) employs unwarranted premises; or (3) ignores or overlooks relevant information.

---

*See Howard Kahane's "The Nature and Classification of Fallacies," in J. Anthony Blair and Ralph H. Johnson, eds., *Informal Logic: The First International Symposium* (Inverness, CA: Edgepress, 1980). And for more on the use of fallacy theory in everyday reasoning, and in particular for more examples from everyday life, see Howard Kahane's *Logic and Contemporary Rhetoric*, 7th ed. (Belmont, CA: Wadsworth, 1995).

Examples

The following case of reasoning is fallacious because its premises don't provide sufficiently good grounds (in fact any grounds) for its conclusion:

1. All whole-grain cereals are nutritious.
2. Most dairy products are nutritious.
∴ 3. Most dairy products are whole-grain cereals.

Here is reasoning that (unfortunately) is fallacious because it contains an unwarranted premise:

1. Anyone who shakes hands with a chimney sweep will have good luck.
2. Dick Van Dyke shook hands with a chimney sweep.
∴ 3. Dick Van Dyke will have good luck.

And here is reasoning that is fallacious because it neglects to use all relevant information:

1. More people are employed in America today (the time was during the 1988 presidential election) than when President Reagan took office in 1981.
∴ 2. President Reagan's economic policies have been good for the working people in this country.

The most obvious of the mounds of relevant background information passed over by this argument is that there were also more people of working age in America in 1988 than in 1981. (The relevant statistics would compare percentages of workers employed in 1981 and 1988, not absolute numbers of the employed. Incidentally, note that this reasoning is enthymematic, omitting as understood the premise that increased employment is good for working people.)

It is important to notice that cogency and fallaciousness are relative to particular arguers or reasoners. What should persuade one person may be fallacious for another, because each of us has a different collection of **background beliefs** we bring to bear in assessing our reasonings. People from different places, times, or circumstances tend to acquire quite different sorts of information and, of particular importance, to construct quite different **world views** (general frameworks of background beliefs) in terms of which they evaluate the reasonings and arguments encountered in everyday life.

So long as we restrict ourselves to questions of argument validity/invalidity or inductive correctness/incorrectness, this difference in background beliefs is irrelevant. But once we move to the twin notions of cogency and fallaciousness, this difference becomes very relevant indeed, because the second and third requirements of cogent reasoning, just mentioned, require that we bring whatever relevant background information we have to bear.

It is also very important to notice that reasoning from false premises is not necessarily fallacious. Cogent reasoning requires **warranted (justified) premises,** not necessarily true ones. We don't have to know everything about a topic to reason cogently about it (a very fortunate thing indeed, given that we're all at least partly ignorant about virtually

everything). Doctors who prescribe an addictive drug believing that it is not addictive reason cogently if their acceptance of that false premise is justified by background beliefs and
experiences, for instance, by authoritative medical literature. Similarly, reasoning from a
highly confirmed scientific theory, say Newtonian mechanics, is not less cogent because
later evidence has shown that that theory, while exceedingly close to the truth, is in fact
not quite true.

Further, we often reason about what *would* happen if we did this or that, or if this or
that *were* to happen. Reasoning about what would be likely to happen if there were a third
world war is an example. We ask ourselves, what if the premise that there is a third world
war were true? And we conclude, after dragging in all sorts of scientific calculations, that
if this premise were true, the consequences would be so horrible that we must try very
hard to make sure that it becomes false, that is, to make sure that we never have a third
world war and thus never have an all-out nuclear war with all of its attending horrors.

However, even when we reason validly and from *true* premises, we may still reason
fallaciously if those premises are not warranted or if our reasoning overlooks relevant
background beliefs. In 1960 I (Kahane) made several wagers *against* John Kennedy being
elected president, based principally on the true premises that (1) Kennedy was Catholic
and (2) at that time, no non-Protestant had ever been elected president of the United
States. The mistake in this was to overlook all sorts of background knowledge about
changing conditions in America, not to mention Kennedy's charisma and Richard Nixon's
five-o'clock shadow.

Notice, by the way, that the reasoning in this case would have been just as faulty if
Kennedy had lost to Nixon in 1960. That bad reasonings sometimes yield true conclusions
does not show that they are good after all but rather just that sometimes people get lucky.

2 *Fallacy Classification*

Fallacies can be classified according to what makes reasoning fallacious (logical factors)
or what leads people to commit them (psychological factors). If we classify according to
logical factors,* we get three large fallacy classes, corresponding to the three ways in
which reasoning can go wrong. Let's call these three categories **invalid inference** or **reasoning, unwarranted (unjustified) premise,** and **suppressed (ignored) evidence.** (Note
that these categories overlap—reasoning may be invalid, contain unwarranted premises,
and ignore relevant evidence.)

Although the three broad fallacy categories just described are of great theoretical interest, experience has shown that many of the narrower traditional fallacy categories are as
useful, if not more useful, in everyday life. This is true even though the traditional categories crosscut each other, tend to be vague or ambiguous, are sometimes based on logical
and sometimes psychological factors, and do not exhaust the field (there is no guarantee
we won't encounter fallacies that don't fit any of the traditional categories).

---

*Thinking of the logical in the broad sense is often referred to as the *epistemological.*

Nevertheless, we should remember that in the last analysis, reasoning is fallacious because it violates one of the three requirements of cogent reasoning. So a complete explanation of the fallaciousness of a particular example has to show how, whatever the traditional way of describing a fallacy (*false dilemma, ad hominem argument,* and so forth), the instance in question violates at least one of the three requirements of cogent reasoning.

Bearing all this in mind, here is an alphabetical list for your perusal of some of the more frequently encountered fallacies, with examples:

- The fallacy of **ad hominem argument** (*argumentum ad hominem*) consists in irrelevantly attacking opponents rather than their arguments. *Example:* Senator Jennings Randolph responded to women who argued for passage of the Equal Rights Amendment (ERA) to the Constitution by calling them a "small band of bra-less bubbleheads." *Related fallacy:* Guilt by association—judging a person by associates or fans.

- The mistake in the case of the fallacy of **affirming the consequent** consists in reasoning from statements of the form "If A, then B" and "B" to the analogous conclusion "A." *Example:* "If it rained last night (A), then the streets were wet this morning (B). The streets were wet this morning (B). So it must have rained last night (A)." This argument overlooks other possibilities—it may have snowed and the snow melted. The point is that an argument having this form is not deductively valid, because its conclusion might be false even if both of its premises are true.

- The fallacy **appeal to authority** applies chiefly to *improper* appeals to an authority. Appeals are improper, among other cases, when there is good reason to doubt that the authorities have the information needed, or there is evidence of special interests or the like that might prejudice authoritative wisdom, or when the subject itself is controversial and competent authorities may differ on the matter. *Examples:* Taking the word of lawyers who say that no-fault insurance will raise rates and lower the quality of insurance (lawyers have an interest in insurance litigation); believing star quarterback Joe Montana when he touts Nissan autos in a TV commercial (football is his field of expertise, not autos, and he is paid handsomely for his endorsements); accepting the claim of then President Reagan—because he was president of the United States—that his "Star Wars" missile program has a good chance of success in the near future. (A large majority of experts have always been on the other side of the issue.)

- The fallacy of **appeal to ignorance** (*argumentum ad ignorantiam*) consists in arguing from the absence of proof that one's position is false to the contrary conclusion that it therefore must be correct. *Example:* Until someone has proved that ESP is impossible, we are entitled to believe it is true.

- The fallacy of **begging the question** (*petitio principii*) is committed when someone uses as a premise some form of the very thesis at issue. *Example:* Arguing that socialism is replacing capitalism because the private ownership of the means of production has become obsolete. *Related fallacy:* Evading the issue.

- Although not strictly speaking a fallacy, the linguistic device generally referred to as the fallacy of the **complex question** consists in asking a question that presupposes an incriminating answer to some other question that in fact is not asked. *Classic example:* "When did you stop beating your wife?" This implies that you once did beat your wife without explicitly saying so, making it hard to deny.

- The fallacy of **composition** (*salesperson's fallacy*) is committed when someone assumes that a whole must have some particular property because all of its parts have it. *Example:* Since each monthly payment is small, the whole price of, say, a new car is small.

- The fallacy of **denying the antecedent** is committed by those who reason from statements of the form "If A, then B" and "Not-A" to a conclusion having the analogous form "Not-B." *Example:* If today is Monday, then liquor stores are open. But today isn't Monday, so liquor stores are not open. (Liquor stores are open on other days in addition to Monday.)

- The fallacy of **division** consists in assuming that all the parts of some item have a certain property since the whole has that property. *Example:* Arguing that since a Mercedes Benz car is expensive, each part of the car is expensive. (Mercedes owners swear this is true.)

- The fallacy of **double standard** is committed when we judge the arguments or conduct of some according to higher standards than we apply in the case of others. *Example:* Holding Israel to a higher standard of conduct in the Middle East than the Palestinians, PLO, Lebanese, or Syrians.

- A term or expression is used *ambiguously* or *equivocally* in an argument when it is used in one sense in one place and in another sense in another. When we fail to notice a shift in meaning of this kind and are led to accept a conclusion that we otherwise would have denied, then we are victims of the fallacy of **equivocation.** *Example:* The sugar advertisement that argued for increased consumption of sugar on the grounds that "Sugar is an essential component of the body . . . a key material in all sorts of metabolic processes." The sugar that is essential to the body is glucose (blood sugar), while the sugar being touted in the ad was refined table sugar, that is, sucrose.

- A **false charge of fallacy** consists in accusing someone of fallacy without having good reason to do so. *Example:* Bertrand Russell was charged with *inconsistency* because soon after World War II he argued that we should nuke the Russians if they didn't behave but later argued that we had to get along with the Russians no matter what. Since he explained his mind change as due to the fact that the Soviets also had obtained nuclear weapons, he was *not* guilty of inconsistency. *Related fallacy:* Quibbling.

- The fallacy of **false dilemma** is committed by arguing from the premise that there are just two plausible solutions to a problem or issue when, in fact, there is at least one other. *Example:* Arguing that differences in behavior between the sexes are due either to heredity or to environment, neglecting the likely possibility that both of these factors play a role.

- The foolish belief that the less frequently a gambling outcome has occurred in the recent past, the more likely it is to occur now is called the **gambler's fallacy** (although in truth it should be mentioned that there are one or two other strong candidates for that honorific title). *Example:* Betting on 7 at a dice table in Atlantic City because 7 hasn't shown up for, say, seven tosses in a row at that table.

- Those who are convinced by relevant but insufficient evidence in support of a theory are guilty of the fallacy called **hasty conclusion.** *Example:* Sherlock Holmes concluding from meager clues on first meeting Dr. Watson that he was an English army doctor just back from Afghanistan. (Watson turns out to fit that description exactly, which just proves that in fiction you don't need to be smart, or even lucky, just in control of the pen!) *Variation:* Small sample.

- The fallacy of **inconsistency** consists in arguing from contradictory premises or to a contradictory conclusion. In everyday life this fallacy is often broadened to cover cases where there is no contradiction within the argument itself but there is a contradiction when commonly known and relevant facts are added. *Example:* The politician who promises all sorts of new and expensive programs in addition to the ones we already have, and then also promises to balance the budget without raising taxes. Similarly, we can extend the fallacy to cover contradictions between words and actions—between what a person says and what that person does. *Example:* Someone sitting at a bar guzzling booze and drinking to the idea of a drug-free society. (The latter kind of inconsistency is generally called *hypocrisy.*)

- The traditional name given to the fallacy now sometimes called **invalid reasoning** is **non sequitur** (literally "it does not follow")—reasoning in a way that is both deductively invalid and inductively incorrect, that is, in a way so that the premises of an argument do not lend adequate, or even any, support to its conclusion. *Example:* Fallacies of the species *affirming the consequent* and *denying the antecedent. Principal variation:* Irrelevant reason.

Exercise 15-1

Here are several very short passages. In each case, determine whether the reasoning is cogent or fallacious, and if fallacious, explain what the error consists in and provide a standard fallacy label if you know one that is appropriate. *Example:* Here is a passage to be evaluated:

> In March 1986, a Reagan administration spokesperson discussing the alleged dangers of "a communist base" in Nicaragua told members of Congress that they had to either "stand with Ronald Reagan and the resistance (the contras) or with Daniel Ortega and the communists."

And here is one person's evaluation: The implication of this passage is that we shouldn't stand with Ortega and the communists, so we should stand with Reagan and the contras. This reasoning is fallacious because one of its premises is questionable, namely that we either have to support the contras or Ortega. There were many other serious possibilities, including not supporting either side, so the argument as it stands invites us to commit the fallacy of *false dilemma.*

1. *A woman whose husband dropped evidence here and there indicating he was having an affair (which he denied) asked "Dear Abby":* Is this man a saint or a sinner? Abby's reply was "If your suspicions are correct, he's a sinner."

2. *Notice from the Hyatt Regency Hotel in New Orleans (quoted in the* Quarterly Review of Doublespeak, *July 1988):* We are pleased to confirm your reservation. It will be held on a space-available basis.

3. *Here is a reply on TV to political science professor Robert Lekachman's attack on "Reaganomics":* What do these professors know? Have they ever met a payroll?

4. *From a student exam in critical thinking:* The problem with this is that anyone can quit smoking if they have enough willpower and really want to do it.

5. *Quaker Oats box top:*

   Free Cookie Tin with two proofs of purchase and 75¢
   > See back.

6. *John S. Knight,* Detroit Free Press *(July 3, 1970):* Capitalism is the economic system in which the means of production and distribution are privately owned and operated for profit. The alternative system is called socialism, the theory of the ownership and operation of the means of production by society, with all members sharing in the work and the products.

7. *Bob Schwabach, "On Computers,"* San Francisco Chronicle (*February 24, 1986*): There aren't just a couple of brands [of IBM compatibles] for those "very low" prices; there are dozens. Do they work? Someone I know has been running one continuously for five months, and it's never missed a beat.

8. *Comment in the* Skeptical Inquirer *(Winter 1978) on astronaut Gordon Cooper's belief that some UFOs are ships from outer space:* What does Cooper do, now that he is no longer with NASA? He is currently employed, appropriately enough, by Walt Disney Enterprises.

9. *Richard H. Rovere, in his book* Senator Joe McCarthy (1959): On the Senate floor in 1950, [Senator] Joe McCarthy announced that he had penetrated "Truman's iron curtain of secrecy." He had 81 case histories of persons whom he considered to be Communists in the State Department. Of case 40, he said, "I do not have much information on this except the general statement of the agency that there is nothing in the files to disprove his Communist connections."

10. *Plato, in his* Timaeus: We must accept the traditions of the men of old time who affirm themselves to be the offspring of the gods—that is what they say—and they must surely have known their own ancestors. How can we doubt the word of the children of the gods?

11. *Overheard on the bus to Atlantic City:* I just play the quarter slots when I go to Atlantic City. That way, I don't lose too much money.

12. *American Medical Association ad against smoking:* 100,000 doctors have quit smoking cigarettes. (Maybe they know something you don't.)

13. *Lewis Carroll, in* Through the Looking Glass: "You couldn't have it if you did want it," the Queen said. "The rule is jam tomorrow and jam yesterday—but never jam *today.*"

    "It *must* come sometimes to jam today," Alice objected.
    "No it can't," said the Queen. "It's jam every *other* day: today isn't any *other* day, you know."

14. Washington Monthly *(June 1983):* According to Lou Cannon of *The Washington Post,* Fred F. Fielding recently objected to inviting Teamsters President Jackie Presser to a White House state dinner on the grounds that Presser's former Ohio local is under federal investigation for racketeering. An unnamed Reagan adviser rejected Fielding's advice by pointing out, "Teamsters are always under investigation."

15. *Private conversation:* My friend Leona has more self-control than I do. She just went to Europe for three weeks and spent only $735, not counting air fare. At least that's what she told me on the phone yesterday. So I figure she never spent more than $35 on any given day. Wow! I'd have splurged on at least one day, but apparently she didn't.

16. *Soviet sociologist Geunadi Gerasimov, quoted in the* Village Voice *(May 5, 1975):* Communism will replace capitalism because private ownership of the means of production is obsolete.

17. *Private conversation:* I asked the doctor why my mouth was so dry, and he said it was because my salivary glands are not producing enough saliva. Some doctor.

18. *Cigarette ad:* Does your cigarette taste different lately? Switch to . . .

19. *Herb Caen,* San Francisco Chronicle *(October 5, 1988):* A lot of people are living to 100 who never used to. . . .

20. *Lottery winner bragging:* I was born on July 4, so the number 74 has always been my lucky number (July being the seventh month of the year, you know). So when I realized that 74 had not shown up in the lottery in the past six months (you can bet I was paying attention), I knew 74 was due. So I bet a bundle on 74 and won! It pays to pay attention.

21. *A pamphlet mailed to voters by the Illinois Republican State Central Committee started out in large type:*
    All the murderers and rapists and drug pushers and child molesters in Massachusetts vote for Michael Dukakis.
    We in Illinois can vote against him.
    And in smaller print farther down:
    Dukakis gets the votes of all the convicts in Massachusetts prisons.

22. *Lyndon B. Johnson:* I believe in the right to dissent, but I do not believe it should be exercised.

23. *Executive to her partner:* You told me six months ago that we would lose our shirts on our line of Christmas ornaments if we didn't lower our prices. So we did lower prices and we lost a pile of dough on them anyway. You were wrong again, buster. Why do I ever think you know a thing or two about business?

24. *Bumper sticker:* America—Love It or Leave It!

25. *Although traditional Jewish practices forbid eating the meat of the pig, a large minority of Jews in Israel have developed a taste for bacon, pork, and the rest. This offended Orthodox Jews, who wanted to pass a law prohibiting the sale of these forbidden products. Rabbi Avraham Shapira, a leader of Orthodox Jews, (Fall 1985) explained:* Our law is not to forbid people to eat pork. We are very democratic here. What we want is people not to be able to sell pork. It hurts every religious man when he passes through a city in Israel and he sees a shop with pork in the window.

26. *Heard on the telephone:* A few years ago my travel agent tried to get us to take a vacation in Budapest, Hungary, because she said it was cheap and not overrun with tourists. But I was afraid of going behind the Iron Curtain, so I didn't go. So last week, I called her and said maybe I'd go now that things in eastern Europe have loosened up politically. So she said she'd look into it, but was afraid that now, if lots of

Americans were going there, it would be too crowded. So today she called back to say all the hotels in Budapest were booked solid. I was a fool to wait so long, now that so many Americans are going there.

27. **How:** Hey, what's with all this junk food you bought? You're always railing at me about eating healthily.
    Aunt: Don't fuss. It was on sale.
    How: Oh.

28. *Popular magazine article in 1874:* Louis Agassiz, the greatest scientist of his day, examined Darwin's claims for his theory of evolution very carefully and finally decided that it could not be true that man was descended from the ape and its earlier animal ancestry. Within six months the greatest German biologists, and the most learned anthropologists now living, have declared that the Darwin theory of the origin of man could not be true. In spite of the opinions of these, the . . . leading investigators of the century, the theory of Darwinism is being taught in the universities of America. There is such a thing as a little knowledge leading to a great error, and this is an example.

29. I was confident that this Star Wars business they proposed during Reagan's administration wasn't justified by scientific evidence because of what I read in the blurb I got from the Union of Concerned Scientists. Now, President Bush and his gang are backing off, so I'm even more confident.

30. *Robert Ringer in* The Tortoise Report *(September 1983), touting gold as an investment:* Two thousand years after the human flesh had disappeared, the gold that adorned it [an ancient Egyptian corpse] remained virtually unchanged. That's a real hard act for paper money to follow.

31. *An article in* New Times *(May 30, 1975, p. 13):* The Catholic Church reported its efforts to reduce the divorce rate among Catholics by instituting rules that prospective couples must satisfy to gain the Church's blessing for their marriage. A church spokesman stated that the right to marry is a natural right, but restrictions are justified when the proposed marriage "poses a threat to the common good of society."

32. *Exam question:* What is the best complete moral theory (that is, best complete set of rules to decide which actions people ought to do) that you know of?

    Student answer: I believe that every person is free to do what they want to do, so long as they do not infringe on the rights of others—the crux of my moral theory is that no person has a right to infringe on the rights of others.

33. San Francisco Examiner *(May 12, 1988, p. A-16):* Although the United States is publicly neutral in the Iran-Iraq war, the U.S. has been providing "battlefield-related intelligence" to Iraq. Asked to explain how this intelligence assistance squares with the administration's professed neutrality, Phyllis Oakley, spokeswoman for the State Department, said, "We're neutral on the outcome."

34. *Item in* Playboy *(February 1983), above a picture of Anita Bryant dancing with Russ McCraw:* Shake it, Anita! We all remember what Anita Bryant used to say about homosexuals, but here she is, discoing with gay evangelist Russ McCraw.

35. *Sigmund Freud:* Our own death is . . . unimaginable, and whenever we make the attempt to imagine it we can perceive that we really survive as spectators.

36. *Pope Pius XII (in 1944):* If the exclusive aim of nature [for sexual intercourse] or at least its primary intent had been the mutual giving and possessing of husband and wife in pleasure and delight; if nature had arranged that act only to make their personal experience joyous in the highest degree, and not as an incentive in the service of life, then the Creator would have made use of another plan in the formation of the marital act.

- A much overlooked fallacy is that of **lack of proportion**—failing to put things in proper perspective or proportion. *Example:* The great emphasis placed on the illegal drug problem in the United States by the Reagan and Bush administrations compared to their relative silence on the vastly more serious AIDS epidemic. *Variation:* Tokenism: Accepting a token gesture as though it were the genuine article.

- The device of **persuasive definition** (often discussed with fallacies, whether or not it is one) consists in defining oneself into victory. *Example:* The statement "Socialism is theft by the poor and the lazy from the rich and the industrious" is often used to argue against socialism.

- In the case of **poisoning the well** (often discussed with fallacies), the trick is to use emotively charged negative language to trash an argument before attempting to truly argue against it. *Example:* "What can we say about such a mean-spirited, selfish, inhuman system as capitalism?"

- **Provincialism** results from overstressing the importance of one's own society to the point of overlooking what is going on elsewhere that is relevant to what is at issue, or (worse) deciding what is true or false on the basis of loyalty. *Examples:* Calling the American baseball championships the World Series even though no Cuban, Japanese, or other teams are allowed to take part; claiming that American soldiers in Vietnam did not commit the atrocities that the evidence clearly proved they did, on the grounds that "Our boys couldn't do such things."

- The fallacy **questionable analogy,** or *faulty comparison,* consists in "comparing apples with oranges," that is, in reasoning by analogy when there is not a sufficient or relevant similarity between the items compared. *Humorous (and questionable?) example:* "If we have to teach the Bible account of creation along with evolution theory, we ought to have to teach the stork theory of birth along with the biological theory."

- The fallacy **questionable cause** (traditional name *post hoc, ergo propter hoc*) is committed when someone argues that something is the cause of something else without sufficient reason, usually on the basis that the first thing preceded the second in time (*post hoc, ergo propter hoc* means "after this, therefore because of this"). *Famous and no doubt apocryphal example:* Arguing that an observed correlation between fluctuations in stock prices and Olympic elk populations indicates a causal connection.

- The fallacy **questionable** or **unwarranted premise** consists in arguing from premises that should not be accepted without further justification. *Example:* Jimmy Carter: "You can trust me because I will never lie to you." *Variation:* Questionable statistics.

- Arguing that if a certain course of action is taken, it will start a slide all the way down to some horror lurking at the bottom of a slippery slope is often called, not surprisingly, the fallacy of **slippery slope.** In another variation, the fallacy is committed when someone argues that whatever would justify taking the first step along a course of action would justify every other one, but since the last step isn't justified, the first one isn't either. *Example:* Arguing that an increase in Medicare will lead to socialized medicine and eventually therefore to a completely socialistic system. *Variation:* The domino theory, popular during the Vietnam War, when it was argued that if we lost in Vietnam, then many other countries would fall like dominoes to the communists. This has recently been revived and applied to Central America.

- Arguing from relevant but insufficient evidence makes one guilty of the fallacy of **small sample.** *Example:* Predicting the outcome of a senatorial campaign on the basis of a poll of fifty-six voters.

- The fallacy **straw man** is committed when someone attacks a weakened version of an opponent's position rather than the genuine article, or attacks a weaker opponent while ignoring a stronger one. *Example:* Richard Nixon attacked his opponents, such as Helen Gahagan Douglas, by charging them with being pinko, or "soft on communism," when they were liberals. *Variation:* Exaggeration. But note that exaggeration is not fallacious when it is used for emphasis or in other ways in which it is not to be taken literally. *Example of a nonfallacious use:* "Jose Canseco and Mark McGwire are going to hit a million home runs before they're through playing baseball."

- The fallacy of **suppressed evidence** consists in the failure to apply known and relevant information to an argument. *Example:* Ex-governor of Texas John Connally, in answering a question before a congressional committee, stated that he had no significant personal interest in the oil and gas industry and cited the fact that he had made only a total of $7,240 profit from that industry, while neglecting to mention that he had received $750,000 for legal services to the foundation set up by Texas oil millionaire Sid Richardson. (Political payoffs are often disguised as other sorts of payments.) Connally's statement is said to be an "error of omission," as compared to an "error of commission," which is an outright lie.

- The fallacy **two wrongs make a right** is committed when we try to justify an apparently wrong action by charging our accusers with a similar wrong. *Example:* South Africans who answer American charges that their country is a racist society by pointing to the American treatment of blacks. Our sins don't excuse theirs. *Variations:* Many wrongs make a right, common practice, traditional wisdom, popularity.

- One of the more easily committed statistical fallacies is that of the **unrepresentative** or **biased sample,** committed when we reason from a sample to the population from which it was drawn when there is doubt that the sample is representative of the population as a whole. *Classic examples:* Sampling only the top apples from a barrel full of apples; the *Literary Digest* poll in 1936 that predicted Alf Landon would defeat Franklin Roosevelt. (The poll was based on a sample drawn from auto registration and telephone subscriber lists at a time when most Americans could not afford to own a car or a telephone.)

Exercise 15-2

Follow the instructions for Exercise 15-1.

1. The universe, like a watch, must have a maker.
2. *Article in college newspaper:* Assessment in colleges is the coming thing.

3. *Thomas O. Enders, Reagan administration official (late 1981):* There is no question that the decisive battle for Central America is under way in El Salvador. . . . If after Nicaragua El Salvador is captured by a violent minority, who in Central America would not live in fear? How long would it be before major strategic United States interests—the Panama Canal, sea lanes, oil supplies—were at risk?

4. *Subscription letter from* Intellectual Digest: Dear Former Subscriber: By 1750, humanity's fund of knowledge had doubled from what it was at the birth of Christ. It doubled again by 1900. And again by 1950. And again by 1960. And yet again by 1968. Mankind is gaining knowledge at an astonishing accelerating rate. Which means that it becomes increasingly difficult for any one individual to keep pace. And keep from becoming intellectually obsolete.

5. *Roger Magyar, "Rebuttal to Argument in Favor of Proposition 79," 1988 California Ballot Pamphlet:* Overcrowding prevents learning, incites classroom misbehavior that culminates in discourteous spectacles at graduation ceremonies, and creates an inviting atmosphere for gang violence that makes the mind-numbing consumption of drugs an understandable—though deplorable—habit.

6. *Beginning of a book review:* Erich Segal's *Love Story*—Romeo and Juliet it isn't. But who cares. It's guaranteed to give you a good cry now and then. And it couldn't have gotten off to such a flying start for nothing. Everybody is going to be reading this novel, so you better go down to your nearest bookstore and pick up a copy.

7. *Senator Sam Ervin of North Carolina (New York Times, September 30, 1970) telling how he replied to women who were in favor of the Equal Rights Amendment to the Constitution:* I tell them, "Why, ladies, any bill that lies around here for 47 years without getting any more support than this one has got in the past obviously shouldn't be passed at all. Why, I think that affords most conclusive proof that it's unworthy of consideration."

8. *Vivekananda:* There is no past or future even in thought, because to think it, you have to make it present.

9. Soon after the 1989 *Valdez* oil spill off the Alaskan coast, Exxon ran a full-page ad in the *New York Times* headlined "In World War II, We Lost 16 Times More Oil Off the East Coast." The reference was to U.S. tankers torpedoed by German submarines in 1942.

10. *John F. Kennedy:* Why, some say, the moon? Why choose this as our goal? They may [as] well ask why climb the highest mountain? Why thirty-five years ago fly the Atlantic? Why does Rice play Texas?

11. High Times *magazine interview with once-Deputy Director of the Bureau of Narcotics and Dangerous Drugs John Finlator (Fall 1974):*

    High Times: One of the excuses for keeping grass illegal is that it causes fatal car accidents.
    Finlator: I'd rather be riding with a guy who's stoned than with a guy who's drunk, or on heroin.

12. We're perfectly entitled to believe there is a God. After all, every effort by atheists to prove otherwise has failed.

13. *Paraphrase of part of a letter to the editor* (Washington Post National Weekly Edition, *March 13–19, 1989*): It's true that the Ayatollah Khomeini has gone too far with his death sentence for author Salman Rushdie (because of his outrageous book *The Satanic Verses*), but Rushdie also has gone too far by offending all Moslems. I am a strong believer in the freedom of speech. However, books like Rushdie's only create hatred and division and weaken the ties of people to each other. Therefore, his book and others like it should be abolished.

14. *Advice given to a child:* Obey the biblical dictum to do unto others as you would have them do unto you, but, of course, on the other hand, never give a sucker an even break.

15. *Nicholas von Hoffman, in the* New York Post *(October 1, 1974):* The trouble with such propositions [that there was a second murderer of John F. Kennedy] is that . . . they are seldom able to give us much of a clue as to who the "real" killer may be. It is for that reason that nobody has been able to discredit the Warren Commission report. If Lee Harvey Oswald didn't murder President Kennedy, then who did?

16. *Magazine article:* Amen, Deacon. It's time Christian people stand up for our rights. If we don't stand up for creation against evolution, we soon won't have any opportunity to worship. It'll be like Russia.

17. *From Dr. Joyce Brothers's column, in the* Houston Post *(October 3, 1976): Question:* You should be more fearful of rape at home because rapes occur more frequently in private homes than in back alleys. *Answer:* True. Studies indicate that more rapes are committed in the victim's home than in any other place. Almost half took place in either the victim's home or the assailant's; one fourth occurred in open spaces; one fifth in automobiles; one twelfth in other indoor locations.

18. *From an article claiming to prove a causal link between junk food diets and antisocial behavior, in* Moneysworth *(November 1977):* If you project a curve showing the increase in behavioral disturbances and learning disabilities over the past 25 years, you will find that it parallels the increase in the dollar value of food additives over that time.

19. *From a* New Republic *(September 5, 1983) review of the James Michener book* Iberia: Michener leads off his chapter on bullfights with an argument between your quintessential American and Spaniard about brutal sports—which the Spaniard wins by pointing out that more young men get killed and maimed every year playing American football than in the bullring.

20. *Letter in the* Huntsville *(Texas)* Item *(September 27, 1974):* The Chamber [of Commerce] proposes taxing occupancy of the hotels to build occupancy [by advertising for tourists]. If the city adopts this policy, then it should tax bank deposits and use the proceeds to advertise for more bank depositors; it should tax professors' salaries and use the proceeds to try to attract more students; it should tax retail sales and use the proceeds to advertise for more shoppers.

21. *Start of letter from Anita Bryant Ministries arguing for harsh laws against homosexuals:* "When the homosexuals burn the Holy Bible in public . . . how can I stand by silently?" Dear Friend: I don't hate the homosexuals. But as a mother, I must protect my children from their evil influence.

22. In 1978, the National Highway Traffic Safety Administration placed a value on human life, for purposes of assessing the costs to society of an accidental death, of $287,175.

23. Smoking marijuana definitely leads to heroin use. A report by the U.S. Commissioner of Narcotics on a study of 2,213 hardcore narcotic addicts in the Lexington, Kentucky, Federal Hospital shows that 70.4 percent smoked marijuana *before* taking heroin.

24. People think just because they're insured, they aren't paying for medical expenses for marginal tests and the like. But they are. One way or another, you end up paying. You pay for your insurance—directly or via your employer.

25. *Peter O'Rourke, California Office of Traffic Safety,* San Francisco Chronicle *(August 20, 1989):* It isn't that our (California) freeway system can't handle the cars; it's that congestion bottlenecks the system and prevents the smooth flow of traffic.

26. *John F. Keenan, New York Off-Track Betting Corporation chairman, responding to a question about whether licensed gambling casinos would cut into OTB revenue, in the* Washington Monthly *(August 1979):* Big business thrives on competition. When night baseball came, they didn't stop sex.

27. Hartford Courant, *"Sunday Parade" (August 20, 1972):* [There was] a judge in Salisbury, Rhodesia, who had never driven a car. Someone in his court wanted to know how [he] could rule on motor accidents without first-hand knowledge of driving. "It's really no handicap," the magistrate explained. "I also try rape cases."

28. *Newspaper article entitled "Reagan's Remedy for His 'Woman Problem'":* The Reagan administration has launched a campaign to close the political "gender gap" by attempting to improve its negative image to women. In recent days the administration has appointed two women to Cabinet positions, filed a brief supporting women's pension benefits and is hinting at taking further initiatives.

    At the same time, there is no indication that President Reagan plans to change his opposition to many fundamental rights that would strengthen women—from abortion to equal pay.

29. *From a high school civics exam:* The white settlers brought civilization to the Indians in America. So now their descendants are suing everybody in sight—total injustice, I say—even ingratitude.

30. **Congressman Frank T. Bow:** How did this so-called leak get out with regard to Kent State? [The reference was to the 1970 shootings at Kent State University.]
    FBI Director J. Edgar Hoover: That did not come from the FBI. But it did cause me great concern. The first time I knew of it was when the *Akron Beacon-Journal* had a great headline—it is part of the Knight chain of newspapers—saying "FBI: No Reason for Guard to Shoot at Kent State." I knew this was untrue. We never make any conclusions. . . . These were certainly extenuating circumstances which caused the guard to resort to the use of firearms. Perhaps they were not as completely trained as they should have been, but certainly some stated they feared for their lives and then fired; some of the students were throwing rocks and taunting the National Guardsmen.
    Congressman Bow: Do you mind this being on the record?
    Hoover: Not at all.

31. *Patient:* Doctor, my wife left me four months ago, and I've been shot ever since. I'm beginning to wonder. Will I ever pull out of this?

    Shrink: It's normal to feel a lot of anxiety and depression after a severe loss. But let me assure you that everyone does recover from this sort of thing. So you will too. Unless, of course, the trauma has been so severe that the ego is shattered.

32. *From "Intelligence Report" by Lloyd Shearer, in* Parade *magazine (November 5, 1978):* This past September, [Bob Hope] refused to cross a picket line at the Chicago Marriott Hotel, where 1500 guests were waiting for him at a dinner of the National Committee for Prevention of Child Abuse. W. Clement Stone, the insurance tycoon who contributed $2 million to the Nixon campaign fund in 1972, tried to negotiate a temporary halt of picketing so that Hope could enter the hotel. When Stone failed, Hope returned to the Drake Hotel, where he videotaped a 15-minute spot to be shown at the dinner. Hope, who belongs to four show business unions, later explained that he had crossed a picket line many years ago and subsequently had to apologize to labor leader George Meany. He promised then never to cross another.

33. *Dialog from the movie* Fun with Dick and Jane *about whether to keep the money Jane stole:*

    Jane: We've always done things the straight way.

    Dick: Yeah. Well, I'm tired of belonging to a minority group.

34. *From an interview with Ronald Reagan (taken from the* New York Review of Books):

    Mr. Otis: We would like to know . . . what the Bible really means to you.

    President Reagan: I have never had any doubt about it being of divine origin. And to those who . . . doubt it, I would like to have them point out to me any similar collection of writings that have lasted for as many thousands of years and is still the best seller worldwide. It had to be of divine origin.

35. *Henry J. Taylor, in the* Topeka Daily Capital *(July 1970):* The great Declaration of Independence begins: "When in the course of human events . . ." and for the first time in man's history announced that all rights came not from a sovereign, not from a government, but from God.

36. *Polonius in William Shakespeare's* Hamlet:

    Your noble son is mad:
    Mad call I it, for to define true madness,
    What is't but to be nothing else but mad?

37. *Editorial in the* Hartford Times *(September 11, 1970) on the topic of an extra twenty minutes of school time for teachers (the extra time was objected to by the teachers' union):* Insisting that teachers be in school [twenty minutes] longer than children may seem to some teachers like a factory time-clock operation, but it probably troubles the conscientious teacher far less than those who leave school at the final bell.

38. *Aristotle:* Oh my friends! There are no friends.

39. *Newspaper article:* Even China has safer air travel than the U.S. Proof? The 15 August 1989 accident that killed 34 people was the first in China since August 1988. During that time, there were several major accidents in the U.S. killing over 300 people.

40. *E. F. Schumacher, famous economist, in an article in* The Atlantic *(April 1979):* Fifteen months [after I had advised that rural India should have a technology inter-mediate between the hoe and the tractor,] an all-India conference on intermediate technology was arranged. (They still didn't like the term [intermediate], so they called it appropriate technology. That's all right: when I come to India and somebody says, "Oh, Mr. Schumacher, I don't believe in appropriate technology," I just look him straight in the face and say, "Oh, that's splendid. Do you believe in inappropri-ate technology?")

41. *Asked how he could support a constitutional amendment requiring balanced budg-ets while his administration had the biggest deficits in history, President Reagan replied (*New York Times, *July 29, 1982):* The budget deficits I don't think can be laid at any individual's door.

42. Atlantic *magazine article (January 1987) on the Chernobyl disaster's radioactive cloud that passed over most of Europe:* This agency [Italy's Civil Protection Agency] had arrived at its reassuring figure of twice background [radiation] by averaging the high radioactive levels of the north with those of the central and southern regions. The Civil Protection Agency's director defended himself by arguing that the author-ities in Sweden, Austria, and Switzerland had also averaged regional data.

43. *Benedetto Croce, in* Philosophy of the Practical (1966): The Inquisition must have been justified and beneficial, if whole peoples invoked and defended it, if men of the loftiest souls founded and created it severally and impartially, and its very adver-saries applied it on their own account, [funeral] pyre answering to pyre.

44. *Column by John Cunniff (July 1970):* Do Americans eat well in comparison with other nations? Millions of Americans still have poor diets, but generally speaking most Americans can afford to eat well. In the U.S. and Canada less than 20 percent of all "personal consumption expenditures" are for food. In less developed countries, the figures are much higher.

45. After the Soviet Union refused to accept a U.S. note demanding compensation for relatives of those in the Korean jet shot down by the Russians, the United States appealed to the Soviets to accept the note on grounds that it had been diplomatic common practice to do so for several centuries.

46. Hartford Courant *(December 20, 1972), in an article on the possibility of women priests in the Catholic Church:* Citing the historic exclusion of women from the priesthood, however, the study [of a committee of Roman Catholic bishops] said ". . . the constant tradition and practice, interpreted as of divine law, is of such a nature as to constitute a clear teaching of the Ordinary Magisterium [teaching authority] of the Church."

47. *St. Augustine, in* De Libero Arbitrio: See how absurd and foolish it is to say: I should prefer nonexistence to miserable existence. He who says, I prefer this to that, choos-es something. Nonexistence is not something; it is nothing. There can be no real choice when what you choose is nothing.

48. New York Times *(July 26, 1981):* [Secretary of Defense Caspar] Weinberger said [Israeli Premier Menachem] Begin's behavior [the bombing of Beirut, which killed 300 civilians] "cannot really be described as moderation," and [Deputy Secretary of

State William] Clark added that the bombing had "embarrassed and disappointed" the Administration. Mr. Begin, however, was in no mood for moralizing from Washington. "I don't want to hear anything from the Americans about hitting civilian targets," he was reported to have said. "I know exactly what Americans did in Vietnam."

49. It's all right for President Reagan to impound funds voted by the Congress. Every recent president—Carter, Ford, Nixon, Johnson—did so. In fact, Nixon did so on a grand scale.

50. *How:* Well, at least the post office is again working well, as it did years ago. We sent a whole bunch of packages and letters by regular mail across the country right before Christmas in three days.

    Aunt: What's so hot about the post office? Years ago the mailman used to get here on foot by 10 in the morning. Now they've got a young girl driving in one of those things, and she never gets here till 3 in the afternoon.

51. New York Times *(June 14, 1988, p. A1):* When several women's groups protested the Pakistani law that accords the legal testimony of women half the weight of the testimony of men, Qazi Hussain Ahmed, leader of the Islamic Party, said, "These laws do not affect women adversely. Our system wants to protect women from unnecessary worry and save them the trouble of appearing in court."

52. *William Safire in* American Heritage *magazine (December 1987):* The greatness of Lincoln was his purposefulness. He saw something that few others saw: that the democratic experiment centered on the Union and that majority rule was everything. The minute you allowed secession, you made democracy an absurdity—because what would happen would be continued subdivision.

53. *Item from newspaper report:* Accused of selling long-range supersonic bombers and refueling equipment to Libya, Soviet foreign minister Edward Shevardnadze's response was to point out in his talks with British Foreign Secretary Sir Geoffrey Howe that Britain also sold arms to Middle Eastern countries.

54. *Ronald Reagan in 1988 on why we were in the Persian Gulf (after the U.S. naval ship* Stark *was hit by Iraqi missiles):* [We're in the Gulf to answer] the call of history . . . a call to wage war against war, to stand for freedom until freedom can stand alone; to live for liberty.

55. *Paraphrase of letter to the editor* (San Francisco Chronicle, *March 31, 1988):* The *Chronicle* editorial favoring the law requiring motorcyclists to wear helmets omitted the fact that there are at least 20 times as many people killed or injured in auto accidents as there are in motorcycle accidents. And remember that it costs the same per serious injury no matter how the accident occurs. Since helmets have been proved to reduce the number of deaths and injuries in cars as well as motorcycles (the reason they're required in things like auto competitions), and indeed in lots of other kinds of competitions, why single out motorcyclists? Shouldn't you be in favor of requiring that everyone from birth wear a helmet at all times?

56. *Airplane conversation overheard during 1988 presidential campaign:*
    Male: I'm voting for Bush. Who're you voting for?
    Female: I'm for Dukakis, actually.

Male: J, you've got to be kidding. Dukakis thinks the Russian bear has become completely tame—he's against Star Wars and every other new defense system, and he wants to cut the military budget to shreds. He's completely fooled by Gorbachev. Not to mention that he's let just about every Massachusetts murderer and rapist out of jail. Don't you women pay any attention to politics?

Female: Well, I guess we just agree to disagree.

Male: Hey, just because we disagree about one thing doesn't mean we don't have a lot in common. I'll bet we agree on things like the death penalty and the abortion issue. I say the electric chair is too good for some of those bastards who rape defenseless women. I'll bet you agree with me on that one. And you've got to be against legalized abortions—killing innocent babies and all that.

Female: What can you know about abortion? You're not a woman, so what you think about abortion and rape doesn't count.

57. *Peter Singer in his* Animal Liberation (1973): The racist violates the principle of equality by giving greater weight to the interests of members of his own race when there is a clash between their interests and the interests of those of another race. The sexist violates the principle of equality by favoring the interests of his own sex. Similarly the speciesist allows the interests of his own species to override the greater interests of members of other species. The pattern is identical in each case.

58. Detroit Free Press *article by Ronald Kotulak:* If surgeons performed fewer operations more people would still be alive.

This controversial conclusion, by a public health expert from the University of California at Los Angeles, is the latest and perhaps most serious attack on the surgical field. . . .

The newest charge was made by Dr. Milton I. Roemer, professor of health-care administration at UCLA, after studying the effects of a five-week doctor strike in Los Angeles in 1976.

Roemer and Dr. Jerome L. Schwartz from the California State Department of Health found that the death rate in Los Angeles County declined significantly during the strike.

They said that fewer people had non-emergency surgery, so there was less risk of dying.

"These findings . . . lend support to the mounting evidence that people might benefit if less elective [non-emergency] surgery were performed in the United States," said Roemer. "It would appear, therefore, that greater restraint in the performance of elective surgical operations may well improve U.S. life expectancy."

59. *Shirley MacLaine* (Time, *December 7, 1987) answering charges that she and others were "getting rich" on the New Age spiritual revival:* That seems to be a concern of many journalists. But I would say we all have to decide what we're worth. . . . I think journalists who are investigating belief in the unseen have to adjust the way they are judging the issue of materialism in relation to spirituality. Anything you want to learn costs money in this world.

Exercise 15-3

1. Carefully explain when appeals to authority are legitimate and when fallacious. Give examples of each, original if possible, to illustrate your explanations.

2. *What do you think of the following argument?* The alleged fallacy of two wrongs make a right is not a fallacy. Suppose you strike me and I then retaliate. While it's true that striking someone is normally a wrong, so that in that sense two wrongs have been committed, in this case the second wrong is justified by reason of self-defense and so in this case two wrongs do indeed make a right. The point is that there is nothing wrong with fighting fire with fire, and so no such fallacy as two wrongs make a right.

3. *How about this argument?* There is no such fallacy as begging the question. After all, every deductively valid argument has its conclusion contained in its premises and so "begs the question" in some sense or other. But we don't want to call all valid deductions fallacious, do we? (This is a very difficult question.)

*Key Terms Introduced in Chapter Fifteen**

background beliefs: Beliefs we already have when we come to assess a particular argument or conclusion. (See also *world views.*)

cogent reasoning: Reasoning that (1) provides good grounds for its conclusion (is deductively valid or inductively strong), (2) contains only warranted (acceptable) premises, and (3) does not suppress (overlook or ignore) relevant information.

fallacious reasoning: Reasoning that is not cogent and thus either (1) does not provide sufficiently good evidence or grounds for its conclusion, or (2) contains an unwarranted premise, or (3) ignores (suppresses or overlooks) relevant information.

ignored evidence: (See *suppressed evidence.*)

invalid inference: Reasoning from premises that do not sufficiently support an argument's conclusion. Reasoning that is neither deductively valid nor inductively correct.

justified premise: (See *warranted premise.*)

suppressed evidence: Evidence that is relevant to an argument's conclusion but is passed over. (Synonym: *ignored evidence.*)

unjustified premise: (See *unwarranted premise.*)

unwarranted premise: A premise not justified by background beliefs. (Synonym: *unjustified premise.*)

warranted premise: A premise whose acceptance is justified by our background beliefs. (Synonym: *justified premise.*)

world views: The framework of background beliefs. The most general of a person's background beliefs. (See also *background beliefs.*)

---

*Not including the fallacy names listed in alphabetical order in the body of the text.

Chapter Sixteen

Inductive Logic

In Chapter One we divided correct arguments into two kinds, deductively valid arguments and inductively strong arguments. We now turn to an examination of inductive arguments and their role in scientific method.

However, a note of caution again is in order. Although it is true that literally nothing in philosophy is accepted by all philosophers, the material on symbolic logic presented in the first two parts of this text comes as close as anything to being generally accepted and noncontroversial. But almost all of the material to be presented now on induction and science is highly controversial, and the viewpoint expressed is just one of several.

1 *A Mistaken View of Induction and Deduction*

According to a common misconception about the distinction between deduction and induction, deductively valid reasoning involves inference from the general to the specific (particular) or from the more general to the less general, whereas inductively correct reasoning involves inference from the specific (particular) to the general, or from the less general to the more general. For example, the deductively valid argument

    1. All who attain power are corrupted by it.
∴ 2. If Jim and Tammy Bakker attained power, then they were corrupted by it.

proceeds from the general to the specific, and the inductively correct argument

    1. So far, every intelligent student has done A work in logic.
∴ 2. All intelligent students (past, present, and future) do A work in logic.

proceeds from the less general to the more general.

But only a moment's reflection is needed to see that this view of deductive and inductive reasoning is erroneous. First, deductively valid arguments do not always proceed from the general to the specific. For instance, they often proceed from the general to the equally general. An example is the argument

    1. No police officers are corruptible.
∴ 2. Anyone who is corruptible is not a police officer.

And they often proceed from the specific to the specific. An example is the following argument:

1. If Dan Rather has attained power, then he has been corrupted by it.
2. Dan Rather has attained power.
∴ 3. He has been corrupted by it.

They sometimes even proceed from the specific to the general (or the less general to the more general), although cases of this kind tend to be a bit contrived. Here are two examples:

1. John is mortal.
∴ 2. All who know John know someone who is mortal.

1. John is mortal.
2. John is not mortal or all men are mortal.
∴ 3. All men are mortal.*

Further, inductively correct arguments do not always proceed from the specific to the general. For instance, they often proceed from the specific to the specific. An example is the analogical argument

1. In 1985 Gary Kasparov defeated Anatoly Karpov for the world chess championship.
2. He did so again in 1987.
∴ 3. He'll win again next time they play for the championship.

And they often proceed from the general to the equally general:

1. All NFL teams made tons of money this year.
∴ 2. All NFL teams will make tons of money next year.

Finally, here is one that moves from the general to the specific:

1. All NFL teams made tons of money this year.
∴ 2. The San Francisco 49ers NFL team will make tons of money next year.

These examples should make clear that there is no truth to the view that deductively valid reasoning proceeds from the general to the specific, or from the more general to the less general, and inductively correct reasoning from the specific to the general, or the more specific to the less specific.

---

*This example is from Nelson Pole. "A Deductive Argument with a Specific Premise and a General Conclusion," *Notre Dame Journal of Formal Logic,* vol. XVI (1975), pp. 543–544. Pole points out that those who don't feel this argument moves from the less general to the more general (on grounds that premise 2 is as general as the conclusion) should consider the following deductively valid argument:

1. John is not mortal.
∴ 2. John is not mortal or all men are mortal.

See also Chapter 1 of Brian Skyrms, *Choice and Chance,* 3rd ed. (Belmont, CA: Wadsworth, 1985).

2 *Kinds of Inductive Arguments*

Recall that pattern, or resemblance, is the fundamental ingredient in inductive reasoning. We want our ideas about what this or that will be like in future to fit a pattern gleaned from what this or that was like in the past. (The problem, of course, is to find patterns or resemblances that fit or take account of everything we've experienced of the past.)

Inductive arguments can be divided into several different kinds.

Inductive generalization, categorical form

When we reason or argue from a premise or premises concerning particular instances, or from all examined cases of a certain kind, to a conclusion that is universal, or concerning all cases (examined or unexamined) of a certain kind, our reasoning has the form of a **categorical inductive generalization,** or **universal inductive generalization,** or **simple inductive generalization.** (These terms also apply to the conclusions of inductive generalizations.) An example is the argument

1. All examined copper things conduct electricity.
∴ 2. All copper things (examined or as yet unexamined) conduct electricity.*

Categorical inductive generalizations all have the same general form, which can be put in either one of two ways. The first way is

1. $Fa \cdot Ga^\dagger$
2. $Fb \cdot Gb$
3. $Fc \cdot Gc$

    .

    .

    .

    N. No *F* is known not to have *G.*
/∴ *N* + 1. All *F*'s are *G*'s.

And the second (equivalent) way is

1. All examined *F*'s are *G*'s.
/∴ 2. All *F*'s are *G*'s.

---

*In this case the premise of our inductive generalization is true. But the generalization would be just as inductively correct if its premise were false. The goodness of inductive reasoning depends on the connection between premises and conclusion, not on the truth of the premise. What makes an argument inductively strong is that if its premises were true, they would support acceptance of its conclusion.

†Because we are dealing with the form of categorical inductive generalizations, "*F*," "*G*," "*a*," "*b*," and "*c*" are being used as variables.

Translated into the notation of predicate logic, and letting Ex = "x is examined for the presence or absence of G," this reads

1. $(x)[(Fx \cdot Ex) \supset Gx]$
2. $(x)(Fx \supset Gx)$

Although there is much controversy over how to weigh the strength of a categorical inductive generalization, it is widely believed that the *probability*, or *degree of confirmation*, of a hypothesis, or the *evidential support* for a hypothesis, increases with each new confirming instance of it. For example, each newly examined instance of the hypothesis "All copper conducts electricity" increases the probability of that hypothesis. However, as the number of confirming instances mounts up, each new confirming instance counts less than the preceding instance. (Exactly how much less it counts is one of those things on which there is no general agreement.)

Even more controversial is the idea that the more important confirming cases are those that also disconfirm competing hypotheses. Looking out the window and finding yet another crow that's black doesn't do much, if anything, for the theory that all crows are black, given that we've already seen plenty of crows in similar circumstances. But hearing about black crows in some tropical area where crows had not previously been observed does count as good confirmation of the theory that all crows are black because, in this view, it disconfirms the competing theory that bird species in general, and thus crows in particular, vary in color from one sort of environment to another.

And some hold that the important confirmations of a theory are those that confirm consequences of the theory of a kind that hadn't been confirmed before. For example, successfully applying Newton's laws to determine the moon's gravitational force (as encountered by astronauts), tests a different consequence of Newton's laws than the usual ones about the moon's orbit or the trajectory of bullets on Earth.

Finally, some people say that there is no such thing as confirmation of a hypothesis, strictly speaking. What is often called confirmation on this view is better seen as the attempt to falsify a hypothesis; we speak (but shouldn't) about confirmation when attempts to falsify fail.

Many scientific hypotheses have the form of categorical inductive generalizations; for example, "All copper conducts electricity." But it is frequently held that the typical and important scientific hypotheses are not categorical inductive generalizations. The claim is that such categorical generalizations are characteristic of the early stages of a science, giving way fairly quickly to something more advanced and sophisticated. For example, some claim that even Galileo constructed more advanced hypotheses than the preceding one, since he constructed quantitative hypotheses. An example is the hypothesis (slightly simplified here) that the distance an object falls in free flight equals 16 times the square of the time it falls, or in symbols $S = 16t^2$. Their claim is that the mathematical equation is the standard—or at least most important—form of scientific hypothesis.

There can be no doubt that many scientific hypotheses are constructed in the form of mathematical equations. But this fact does not constitute evidence against the importance of categorical inductive generalizations in science, because mathematical equations themselves can be stated as categorical generalizations. For example, we can translate the equation $S = 16t^2$ into the categorical generalization, "All freely falling bodies are such that if S is the distance they fall, and t is the time it takes them to fall that distance, then $S = 16t^2$."

Inductive generalization, statistical form

When we reason or argue from a premise or premises concerning groups of instances to a conclusion that is statistical in form, our reasoning has the form of a *statistical inductive generalization.* An example is the argument

    1. Half of the tosses of this coin observed so far have landed heads up.
∴ 2. Half of all tosses of this coin (observed or otherwise) will land heads up.

The general form of statistical generalizations can be stated as

    1. N percent of all F's tested for G have G.
∴ 2. N percent of all F's (tested or otherwise) have G.

Statistical generalizations play an important role in science. A great many hypotheses in the social sciences (economics, sociology, and others) are statistical, and many basic hypotheses of physics itself are statistical. Two important examples are the second law of thermodynamics (the law of increasing entropy) and the gas laws. For example, the gas laws say nothing about the pressure of a gas at any given point on the surface of an enclosed container, but rather what the average, or statistical, pressure will be, calculated on the basis of the temperature and volume of the enclosed gas.

But a statistical generalization is generally not as informative or useful as the corresponding universal generalization would be. Take the statistical generalization, "One fifth of all adult Americans who smoke an average of one or more packs of cigarettes per day will die of lung cancer within 25 years." Obviously, if true, this constitutes very valuable information, for it warns those who fall into the stated category (adult Americans who smoke at least one pack per day) of their "chances" of getting lung cancer if they persist in smoking so heavily.* But it doesn't tell them that they will get lung cancer merely because they are adult Americans who smoke at least one pack of cigarettes per day.

However, suppose we discover that heavy cigarette smoking is only one of two factors leading to lung cancer, the other factor being, say, a particular abnormality in the surface tissue of the lung (let's call it "abnormality A"); that is, suppose we discover that every investigated case of heavy smoking in which abnormality A is present also is a case of lung cancer death. Then we could construct the following inductively strong argument:

    1. All heavy smokers who have been found to have abnormality A have died of lung cancer.
∴ 2. All heavy smokers who have abnormality A die of lung cancer.

The conclusion of this argument is a categorical inductive generalization concerning the connection between smoking and death by lung cancer and would be much more

---

*That their chances are one in five is significant because we know that comparatively few people who don't smoke tobacco get lung cancer.

informative and useful than the statistical generalization just cited. For if some person, say Art, were found on examination to have abnormality A, then we could present him with an argument such as

1. All heavy smokers who have abnormality A die of lung cancer.
2. Art has abnormality A.
∴ 3. If Art is (or becomes) a heavy smoker, then Art will die of lung cancer.

Surely this argument is more relevant to Art's decision about whether to smoke than the previous statistical argument linking heavy smoking and lung cancer. A corresponding statistical generalization, such as "One fifth of all heavy smokers will die of lung cancer," which when combined with the information that Art is a heavy smoker, leads to the conclusion that the chance is one in five that Art will die of lung cancer, certainly is not so informative or useful as the conclusion that Art definitely will die of lung cancer if he becomes a heavy smoker.

Thus the question naturally arises whether with sufficient knowledge we could not (at least theoretically) replace all statistical generalizations with categorical ones. It seems plausible to assume that this always can be accomplished by taking account of more and more relevant factors. For instance, knowledge that a given coin is symmetrical permits the conclusion that half of all random tosses with that coin will land heads up. But it seems plausible to assume that with better knowledge—that is, with knowledge of more relevant factors (such as the force of each toss, its starting position, wind velocity, and so on)—we could conclude that *all* tosses of a certain kind (tossed with a certain force or tossed from a certain starting position) will land heads up.

On the one hand, we cannot say ahead of time that all statistical generalizations are replaceable by categorical generalizations. In each case we must examine the world to determine whether more relevant factors exist. (Of course, simply failing to find relevant factors does not prove that none exist. We may not have been sufficiently ingenious to discover them.) So the question of whether a given statistical generalization can be replaced by a corresponding categorical generalization can be answered only by accumulating more empirical evidence to the extent that it can be answered at all.*

On the other hand, it is clear that we can regard a categorical inductive generalization as a special kind of statistical generalization, namely, the kind in which the percentage of F's tested that turn out to be G's happens to be 100 percent. In other words, we can take the basic pattern of categorical inductive generalizations to be

1. 100 percent of all F's tested for G have G.
∴ 2. 100 percent of all F's (tested or otherwise) have G.

which clearly is just a special case of the general pattern for statistical generalization.

---

*Some claim that evidence discovered by twentieth-century physicists, in particular evidence supporting the Heisenberg indeterminacy principle, provides empirical reason for believing that at least some, and perhaps all, of the ultimate laws of physics are statistical and categorical. See, for instance, Hans Reichenbach, *Rise of Scientific Philosophy* (Berkeley and Los Angeles: University of California Press, 1953), Chapter 10.

Analogies

When we infer from a premise or premises concerning particular instances (or all known instances) of a certain kind to a conclusion concerning some other particular instance of that kind, we infer **analogically,** or by **analogy.** For example, we infer analogically when we reason from the premise that a course given last year by a particular teacher was interesting to the conclusion that the course the teacher is giving this year will be interesting.

Some analogies are *stronger* than others. Analogies differ in the degree to which they support their conclusions. For one thing, the greater the number of instances mentioned in the premises, the stronger the analogy. Thus, if we reason from the fact that both of two courses taken from a particular teacher were interesting to the conclusion that the next course we take from that teacher will be interesting, our analogy is better than if we reason on the basis of only one course taken from that instructor.

Analogies also are stronger if the instances they concern are alike in more relevant ways. Thus, if we reason from the fact that the two interesting courses taken previously from a particular teacher both were logic courses to the conclusion that the next logic course we take from that teacher will be interesting, our analogy is better than if the next course happens to be ethics.

However, only *relevant* ways in which the instances are alike count. For example, it might be irrelevant if the classes both happened to meet in the same room, or at the same time of day. But it is quite difficult to know in general, or even in a particular case, exactly which things are relevant and which are not. The room in which a course is to be taught may be relevant to how interesting it will be. (For example, it will be relevant if the teacher in question dislikes large, poorly lit rooms, and the next course that teacher teaches happens to be in such a room.)

It also is important to remember that the premises supporting an analogy may be more or less *probable*. The more probable they are, obviously, the stronger the analogy. For instance, having personally taken a course from a particular instructor and having found it to be interesting and informative should count more heavily than hearing these same opinions from the grapevine.

It follows from what has just been said that what is a strong analogy for one person, given what that person knows, may be quite weak for a second, given what that second person knows. For instance, one of your authors concluded by analogy that the Woody Allen flick *What's Up Tiger Lily?* would be funny, because the other Allen films he'd seen had been funny, but other Woody Allen fans stayed away in droves, having heard, as this writer had not, what kind of movie it was (bad).

Analogies conveniently divide into two kinds, namely, **categorical analogies** and **statistical analogies.**

Valid categorical analogies have the general form

1. All *F*'s tested or observed for *G* have *G*.
∴ 2. This particular *F*, untested as yet for *G*, has *G*.

The argument discussed earlier, about taking a class from a particular teacher, is an example of a categorical analogy.

Valid statistical analogies have the general form

1. N percent (or most, or almost all) of the F's tested for G have G.
∴ 2. The probability is N percent (or the probability is high) that this particular F, as yet untested for G, has G.

Most analogies made in everyday life are statistical analogies. In daily life we rarely encounter cases in which all the known cases of a certain kind have some particular relevant property. For instance, even the best teachers are likely to teach an uninteresting class at least once, thus falsifying the premise of any *categorical* analogy whose conclusion is that their next course will be interesting, but not falsifying the premise of some *statistical* analogy whose conclusion is that their next course probably will be interesting.

It is sometimes held that analogical reasoning is not fundamental, in that any given analogy can be shown to be an enthymemic version of a categorical or statistical generalization. Take the analogy whose conclusion is that the next class taught by a particular teacher probably will be interesting. In this case, it is said, the complete form of our reasoning would be

1. Almost all classes taught so far by the teacher in question have been interesting.
∴ 2. Almost all the classes that teacher teaches are interesting.
3. This particular class will be taught by the teacher in question.
∴ 4. This particular class will probably be interesting.

Exercise 16-1

Here are three analogical arguments, each one followed by a set of five additional premises. Some of these extra premises, if added to the original analogy, increase its strength; others decrease it. State which of the extra premises increase, and which decrease the strength of the original analogy, and explain why you think so.

1. The Carnegie Hall Cinema is playing Ingmar Bergman's flick *Scenes from a Marriage* tonight. This is a serious foreign film, and the last five foreign movies I saw seemed to me to be quite good. So I expect to like *Scenes from a Marriage*.
   a. Three of the other five were also Bergman films.
   b. All five were comedies.
   c. Liv Ullmann stars in *Scenes* but wasn't in any of the other five.
   d. I saw all five on a Wednesday evening. Today is Tuesday.
   e. All five were in black and white. *Scenes* is in color.

2. They say that heart attacks run in families because of like habits and similar genes. Boy, that makes me worried! My father died of a heart attack at age 55, my mother at 31, my grandfather (father's side) at 62, his wife at 58, my other grandmother at 63, and three aunts before age 65. I should be worried—all signs point to an early heart attack.
   a. I don't smoke cigarettes; my father and his father smoked over a pack a day for many years.

b. All my close relatives ate the same sort of central European diet—lots of animal fats, pastries, highly seasoned foods; I'm a vegetarian and health nut.

c. I'm a college graduate; my father dropped out after the eighth grade and my mother finished high school, but my grandparents never even started kindergarten.

d. My father stood on his feet in a retail store for 55 to 60 hours per week for 25 years; my grandfather sat at a sewing machine. In contrast, I jog 2–5 miles every other day; I'm not sedentary as they were.

e. I remember that everyone in my family was always worried about money; we all ate well, but money for extras was very scarce. Looking back, they were all "type A" people—nervous, always in a hurry, late, tense. Now I'm a cool cat with the world's best occupation (for me)—good pay, job security, fun things to do, flexible hours, and lots of free time.

3. I recently started reading about countries that have medical care run primarily by government (socialized medicine). Finding at first that this is true in the Soviet Union, its eastern European satellites, and China, and that medical care in all these countries is extremely poor compared to that in the United States, I concluded tentatively that we don't want a medical system in the United States that is primarily run by government.

a. I then realized that none of the countries where socialized medicine produces poor results have democratic governments—governments elected by the people in genuinely free elections.

b. Pursuing the matter further, I read that in Great Britain, which has both a democratically elected government and (primarily) socialized medicine, medical care on the whole seems to be a good deal poorer for most people than it is in the United States and several European countries that, like the United States, are democratic and have medical care that is mostly in nongovernmental hands.

c. Turning to other sources, I read that in democratic Canada, medicine is mostly in the hands of the government and seems to be on the whole better than in the United States (although hard to compare because medical attention in the United States is so uneven from rich to poor compared to medical attention in Canada).

d. Next, I read that in other countries there are all sorts of variations on the government/nongovernment theme (blends of the two kinds of systems—most not being pure one way or the other), and that the quality of medical care in these other countries on average varies more with respect to national wealth and how well in general things run in that country than with respect to what sorts of medical systems they happen to have (for example, Mexico, Sweden, Japan).

e. Finally, turning to a completely different set of sources, I found that there is a great deal of difference among authorities about much of what I had previously read. One highly respected libertarian source argued that medical attention in Canada in fact is not as good on the whole as in the United States, and that anyway lots of the problems in the United States are generated by government interference (Medicare, Medicaid, and so on) in the marketplace. But another respected source argued for a generally higher level of medical attention in Canada as well as several European countries where government plays a greater role in medicine than in the United States, citing statistics concerning greater longevity, lower infant mortality, and so forth, in these other countries than in the United States in support of that claim.

Exercise 16-2

Here are some arguments containing analogical reasoning. In each case state how strong you consider the analogy, given your background information, and explain your conclusion.

1. The Christians say, "Creatures are not bound with desires unless satisfaction for those desires exists." A baby feels hunger: well, there is such a thing as food. A duckling wants to swim: well, there is such a thing as water. Men feel sexual desire: well, there is such a thing as sex. If I find in myself a desire which no experience in this world can satisfy, the most probable explanation is that I was made for another world. (C. S. Lewis, *Mere Christianity*)

2. That the aggressor, who puts himself into the state of war with another, and unjustly invades another man's right, can, by such an unjust war, never come to have a right over the conquered, will be easily agreed by all men, who will not think that robbers and pirates have a right of empire over whomsoever they have force enough to master, or that men are bound by promises which unlawful force extorts from them. Should a robber break into my house, and with a dagger at my throat, make me seal deed to convey my estate to him, would this give him any title? Just such a title by his sword has an unjust conqueror who forces me into submission. (John Locke, *Of Civil Government*)

3. If a single cell, under appropriate conditions, becomes a man in the space of a few years, there can surely be no difficulty in understanding how, under appropriate conditions, a cell may, in the course of untold millions of years, give origin to the human race. (Herbert Spencer, *Principles of Biology*)

4. "Do you think," said Candide, "that men have always massacred each other, as they do today, that they have always been false, cozening, faithless, ungrateful, thieving, weak, inconstant, mean-spirited, envious, greedy, drunken, miserly, ambitious, bloody, slanderous, debauched, fanatic, hypocritical, and stupid?"

   "Do you think," said Martin, "that hawks have always eaten pigeons when they could find them?"

   "Of course I do," said Candide.

   "Well," said Martin, "if hawks have always had the same character, why should you suppose that men have changed theirs?" (Voltaire, *Candide*)

5. We may observe a very great similitude between this earth which we inhabit and the other planets. . . . They all revolve around the sun as the earth does. . . . They borrow all their light from the sun, as the earth does. Several of them are known to revolve round their axis like the earth, and by that means, must have a like succession of night and day. . . . From all this similitude, it is not unreasonable to think that those planets may, like our earth, be the habitation of various orders of living creatures. (Thomas Reid, *Essays on the Intellectual Powers of Man*)

6. I am the father of two daughters. When I hear . . . that we can't protect freedom in Europe, in Asia, or in our own hemisphere, and still meet our domestic problems, I think it is a phony argument. It is just like saying that I can't take care of Luci because I have Lynda Bird. (President Lyndon B. Johnson, February 1968)

7. The philosopher Epicurus argued that the gods have bodies, because the gods are intelligent and all known intelligent entities (human beings) have bodies.

8. Suppose someone tells me that he has had a tooth extracted without an anesthetic, and
    I express my sympathy, and suppose I am then asked, "How do you know it hurt him?"
    I might reasonably reply, "Well, I know that it would hurt me. I have been to the den-
    tist and know how painful it is to have a toothache stopped without an anesthetic, let
    alone taken out. And he has the same sort of nervous system as I have. I infer, there-
    fore, that in these conditions he felt considerable pain, just as I should myself." (A. J.
    Ayer, "One's Knowledge of Other Minds," *Theorea,* 1953)

Inference from observed to unobservable

We have divided inductively correct inferences into three kinds, namely categorical, statistical, and analogical. But there are other useful ways to divide them.

  In particular, it is important to distinguish between reasoning from what is observed to
what is as yet unobserved *but can be observed,* and reasoning from what is observed to what
even in principle cannot be observed.

  For instance, we reason from the observed to the *observable* when we infer from the fact
that most cars of a certain kind have lasted a long time to the conclusion that a particular car
of this kind will last a long time. That a car lasts a long time is something we can directly
observe. But we reason or infer from the observed to that which even in principle *cannot be
observed* when we infer from the fact that Smith's finger was pricked by a pin, followed by
the rapid withdrawal of his hand, facial grimaces, exclamations of "ouch," and so on, to the
conclusion that Smith is in pain. In this case we cannot directly observe the thing inferred,
namely Smith's pain, for it is impossible to experience or observe directly someone else's
mental activity. In this case we must infer the unobservable pain from what we take to be
causally related to the pain, namely, the withdrawal of Smith's hand, his facial expression,
his utterances, and so on.

  Those things, like mental states, that cannot be observed directly are often called **theoretical entities,** to distinguish them from things that can be observed directly, called
observable entities. But there is a great deal of controversy about which things are, in
fact, directly observable.

  In addition, it is useful to divide the entities commonly classed as theoretical into four
kinds.

  (1) *Physical particles,* such as electrons, which many scientists claim cannot be directly observed even in principle, constitute a kind of theoretical entity, for we must infer their
existence.*

  (2) *Dispositional properties* (discussed briefly in Chapter Thirteen) constitute
another kind of theoretical entity. An example is the property of being *flammable.* We
can observe that something *burns,* but not that it is *flammable.* Similarly, we can observe
that something *bends,* but not that it is *flexible.* Burning and bending are *observable*

---

*Roughly, electrons are claimed to be unobservable because observing (in the sense of "seeing") requires the use of entities
(such as light rays) that cannot interact appropriately with something so small as an electron.

properties; flammability and flexibility are *dispositional* properties. Since dispositional properties are not directly observable, we must *infer* their existence. They constitute a kind of theoretical entity.*

(3) *Mental events* or *mental experiences* constitute still another kind of theoretical entity. However, this kind of theoretical entity is different from all others in that every given entity of this kind can be experienced by someone or other (namely, the person who "has" the mental experience), although it cannot be observed by anyone else. For instance, my pain can be (and is) experienced by me, but not by anyone else. And your pain can be (and is) experienced by you, but not by anyone else. From *your* point of view, *my* pain is theoretical, while from *my* point of view, *your* pain is theoretical. This is different from the case with respect to, say, electrons because (according to many scientists) no one can directly observe electrons. (It should be noted that, according to one philosophical theory called the *neural identity* theory, consciousness is a brain process, and therefore is observable.)

(4) Finally, many philosophers consider all *physical objects, material objects,* or *material substance* to be theoretical entities. They believe that it is what they call *sense data* that we experience directly, and not the physical objects that may be causally related to them.†
If we believe in the existence of physical objects in addition to the existence of sense data, and perhaps causally related to sense data, then this belief (if rationally founded) will be based on *inductive inferences* from what we experience, namely, sense data, to their cause, namely, physical objects.

We characterized theoretical entities as things that we cannot observe. But words such as "cannot," called *modal terms,* are notoriously tricky. In particular, the word "cannot" itself is *ambiguous*. When we say that electrons cannot be observed, we mean that it is impossible to observe them. Similarly, when we say that we cannot observe someone else's mental experiences, we mean that it is impossible for us to observe them. However, the senses of "impossible" are different in each case. In the first case we mean that it is *physically impossible* to observe electrons directly; that is, we mean that the laws of nature (the way the world happens to be) preclude our observing electrons. Or, to put it another way, we mean that it is a *contingent fact* that we cannot observe electrons. But in the second case we mean that it is *logically impossible* to observe someone else's experiences directly. We can have experiences that are just like someone else's experiences, but we cannot literally share the same experience.

---

*We omit discussion of entities such as electromagnetic fields, in particular the question whether they can be analyzed as dispositional properties of particles or constitute a separate and different set of theoretical entity.

†We cannot go into a detailed discussion concerning sense data at this point. But we can understand roughly what the philosopher who postulates the existence of sense data is talking about by thinking of a very vivid dream or hallucination concerning, say, seeing one's father, and comparing that experience with the experience of really seeing one's father. Taken alone, the dream or hallucination may be identical with the experience of really seeing one's father. Now in the dream, the experience of seeing one's father surely is mental. So when really seeing one's father, the experience (as opposed perhaps to its cause) must also be mental, since taken alone (out of context) it is identical with the mental dream experience of seeing one's father. Roughly speaking, sense data philosophers merely attach the label sense data to the content of an experience, whether of the dream–hallucination kind, or the "real" vision kind. And, of course, they attach that label to auditory experience, olfactory experience, and others, as well as to visual experience.

So before we can say what kinds of things are theoretical entities (and thus cannot be observed), we must know what kind of impossibility is appropriate. It will come as no surprise that philosophers disagree on the matter.

Exercise 16-3

In your opinion which of the following underlined terms refer to theoretical entities and which to observable ones (or both)? Explain.

1. George picked up the book on the table and observed that it had an odd red cover.
2. Opening the book, he noticed that the first sentence was about Newton's law concerning gravitational force.
3. It was, strangely, the very same sentence that started the physics text he used last year, when he first took Physics I.
4. His attention wandered from Newton to what he knew would come sooner or later, twentieth-century physics, field theories, neutrinos, and all that sort of thing.
5. Vague thoughts of dropping out of school crossed his mind, especially when he realized he also was enrolled in Chemistry I this semester.
6. He walked into the next room and picked up his chemistry text—its cover looked red, but the light was poor, so he wasn't sure.

3 *Cause and Effect*

One of the chief uses of inductive reasoning is to discover the **causes** of different kinds of things and events. Having discovered that heating a gas in a balloon always makes it expand, a budding young Robert Boyle would be justified in concluding that heating *causes* gases to expand. But what does it *mean* to say that one thing is the cause of another, or that two things are *causally related?*

Just as in the case of many other concepts, the notion of causation is really a cluster of related concepts, mostly with blurred edges. Some writers, for instance, speak of the cause of a thing or event as simply the **sufficient condition** for bringing it about. In this sense the cause of Marie Antoinette's death was being guillotined, because having one's head cut off is a sufficient condition of death.

However, some think of a cause as a **necessary condition** for bringing something about and think of the sum total of all the necessary conditions required to produce it as its complete cause. The presence of oxygen can be thought of in this way as part of the cause of the lighting of a match, even though not a complete cause. It is part of what must occur for the effect—the lighting of the match—to occur.

Note also that we often speak of causation in a statistical or probabilistic sense in cases where it isn't true that producing the cause always produces the effect, but is true that it does so in a certain percentage of cases. We say, for instance, that cigarette smoking is a **probable cause** of most cases of lung cancer, even though we know that not all people who smoke heavily for years contract that dread disease and also know that nonsmokers occasionally do so.

There is also the notion of **causal connection,** or **causal relationship,** to consider, given in particular that so many scientific discoveries are of causal relationships. Galileo's discovery of a causal connection between the time that a thing falls toward the earth and the distance it falls during that time is an example. (Note how odd it sounds to say that dropping a ball 64 feet *caused* it to fall for two seconds.)

While all of the aforementioned senses of cause are common in everyday life as well as in the sciences, another sense is the most common in everyday life and is at least not uncommon in the sciences. Central to this way of looking at causation is the notion of *human agency* (or perhaps we should say *purposive agency,* in this robotic space age). In this sense the cause of a thing or event is whatever we would need to do or change so as to bring about that thing or event.

To see how this conception of causation works, consider a simple case from everyday life, say, the lighting of a match. We know that the usual way to light a match is to strike it (on an abrasive surface), and so we would say in a given case that it was the striking of the match that caused it to light. And yet we know perfectly well that not all struck matches light—wet matches and those struck in a vacuum being cases in point. Striking a match is therefore not a sufficient condition of its lighting. And we know that matches can easily be lit without striking them, say by heating them in an oven. Thus, striking a match is not a necessary condition of its lighting either. Even so, if asked what caused a particular match to light at a certain moment, it would be perfectly right to answer that striking the match caused it to light at that moment. The reason it would be right is that striking a match is the usual way in which we get matches to light.

It is because we attach this sense of agency to most everyday talk about causes that we reject certain kinds of sufficient conditions as causes. Take a simple case, say, one in which we know that striking (heating) a well-made match in the presence of oxygen is a sufficient condition of its lighting. Letting Mx = "x is a well-made match," Hx = "x is heated to a sufficiently high temperature," Px = "x is in the presence of oxygen," and Lx = "x lights," we can symbolize the proposition that all well-made matches heated in the presence of oxygen will light as $(x)\{[(Mx \cdot Hx) \cdot Px] \supset Lx\}$. If asked why a particular match lit, we can say that it did so because it was struck (heated sufficiently) in the presence of oxygen (or say simply that it did so because it was struck—omitting reference to the presence of oxygen as understood). In other words, we can furnish an instance of the antecedent of the inductive generalization $(x)\{[(Mx \cdot Hx) \cdot Px] \supset Lx\}$ as the cause of the analogous instance of its consequent. (That is, we can furnish the instance $(Ma \cdot Ha) \cdot Pa$ of the antecedent of the generalization in question as the cause of the corresponding instance La of its consequent.

However, we cannot do this in every case. For example, the inductive generalization just referred to, namely $(x)\{[(Mx \cdot Hx) \cdot Px] \supset Lx\}$, is logically equivalent to the generalization $(x)\{[(Mx \cdot Hx) \cdot \sim Lx] \supset \sim Px\}$. But usage does not permit us to say that an instance of the antecedent of this generalization can be taken to be the cause of the analogous instance of its consequent. For example, usage does not permit us to say that oxygen was not present $\sim Pa$, because the match didn't light when heated $(Ma \cdot Ha) \cdot \sim La$. This is true in spite of the fact that if the inductive generalization is true and an instance of its antecedent is true, then the analogous instance of its consequent must be true.

There must be an important difference, then, between the cases where we say (correctly) that the match lit because it was heated in the presence of oxygen and where we say (incorrectly) that the match was not in the presence of oxygen because it was heated and didn't light. And that difference, as we stated before, is human agency. In everyday life, it's easy to make a match light by striking it (heating it), but we can't make a match not be in the presence of oxygen by striking it and having it not light.

In addition to all the preceding, causes are frequently distinguished as proximate or as remote causes. Suppose that a truck jackknifes on an icy highway, blocking three of four lanes and that a car, call it car *A*, in one of those lanes swerves into the fourth lane blocking that lane to still another vehicle, car *B*, which then slams into *A* from the rear. The ice on the road would then be said to be the **proximate cause** of the truck's accident, and a much more **remote cause** of the accident between cars *A* and *B*. In general, we refer to causes nearer to a given phenomenon as proximate and to causes more distant in the causal chain as remote, as we have done in this case.

And this suggests an important point—namely, that a given effect can be explained in terms of several different causes; which one we select usually depends on our particular interest in that effect. Thus a philosopher may be interested in the conscious willing of Smith to raise his arm, a rather remote cause of that event, whereas a biologist's interests might gravitate to attending muscle contractions, a much more proximate cause of the raised arm.

Finally, it should be noted that a good deal of discussion has gone on in the history of philosophy concerning the nature of causation in general. When we say that *A* causes *B*, or that *A*-type cases cause *B*-type cases, do we mean to assert that the occurrence of *A* necessitates the occurrence of *B*? Are there things in the universe called *necessary connections* that we discover when we find out that a particular *A* causes a certain *B*? This is an important philosophical question that has received quite different answers at the hands of different philosophers over the years. A great many of the philosophers roughly classifiable as rationalists have claimed what is called "ontological status" to necessary connections, thus thinking of causal necessity as something that exists in addition to the events that are causally connected. Empiricists, in contrast, tend to follow the lead of David Hume in thinking of causation in terms of constant conjunction between cause and effect. In the Humean analysis, the most we are justified in meaning when we say that *A* causes *B* is that whenever *A* occurs, *B* occurs. Or, to be more precise, what we mean is that whenever an *A*-like event occurs, a *B*-like event will occur (because events *A* and *B* are singular and thus cannot occur more than once). Thus, when we say that the cause of a particular well-made match's lighting is that it was struck (heated) in the presence of oxygen, most empiricists would say that this should be taken to mean that whenever a well-made match is struck in the presence of oxygen, it lights.

Note, however, that even staunch empiricists would want to somewhat qualify Hume's ideas about cause and effect. Not every constant conjunction indicates a causal connection. We don't think of night as the cause of day, or day of night, despite the (so far) constant conjunction between the two. We don't because, first, theories concerning higher-level constant conjunctions (for instance, those related to Newton's laws of motion) lead us to predict that someday Earth will stop rotating on its axis, so night will not be followed by day, and second, because we know how we could stop night from following day right now, if only we were able to exert sufficient power to stop

Earth's rotation on its axis (for example, by setting off a great many very powerful atomic bombs in just the right way). Only those constant conjunctions not counter-manded, so to speak, in this way by higher-level theories about much more general constant conjunctions are thought of as indicating causal connections.

4 Mill's Methods

The set of five methods for justifying conclusions about causes, called **Mill's Methods,**[*] were proposed as ways to both discover and justify conclusions about causal connections. We will briefly discuss three of the five methods that constitute the core of the system.

The method of agreement

The **method of agreement** is very much like inductive generalization. Here is Mill's char-acterization of this method (in his *A System of Logic*):

> If two or more instances of the phenomenon under investigation have only one circumstance in common, the circumstance in which alone all the instances agree, is the cause (or the effect) of the given phenomenon.

In other words, if we find two or more instances in which a given phenomenon, *P*, occurs, and only one other phenomenon, *Q*, is present in each instance, then we can con-clude that *P* and *Q* are causally connected (in other words, that *P* is the cause of *Q*, or *Q* of *P*). It should be noted that Mill intended us to consider only relevant circumstances—circumstances that might plausibly be the sought after cause.

Mill's example is this:

> Instances in which bodies assume a crystalline structure are found to have been preceded by instances which have in common only one antecedent, namely, the process of solidification from a fluid state.

This antecedent, therefore, is the cause of the crystalline structure. In other words, all objects observed to have a crystalline structure (*P*) have been found to have one and only one other factor in common—namely, that they have solidified from a fluid state (*Q*). Using the method of agreement, Mill concluded that having solidified from a fluid state (*Q*) is the cause of their crystalline nature (*P*). (It can't be the effect, because their fluid state precedes their crystalline state.)

The method of agreement should be familiar from its frequent use in everyday life. An example is furnished by the State Department official who discovers the source of a series of leaks to the press by noticing that only one of the many people who were privy to some

---

*After John Stuart Mill (1806–1873), who is chiefly responsible for their popularization, although not their initial formula-tion, for which much is owed to John Herschel, who in turn is fundamentally indebted to Francis Bacon and his *Novum Organon* (1620). For more on Mill's view of Mill's Methods, see his *A System of Logic* (1843).

of the items leaked had access to all of them. This is very much like the examples invented by mystery writers who, imitating reality, sometimes have their detectives find the murderer by mentally going through a list of suspects and discovering that only one (not usually the butler) could have been present at each of the slayings.

The State Department example is a typical case of the method of agreement. Among
the suspected causes (or perhaps we should say causers) of the leaks, only one had the
opportunity in each case, and so that person must be the infernal leaker. The argument's
structure is this (letting the capital letter P stand for the particular phenomenon under
investigation and the other capital letters stand for possibly relevant circumstances, and
supposing there were exactly three leaks):

> Instance One: $A, B, C, D, \ldots P$
> Instance Two: $A, L, C, Q, \ldots P$
> Instance Three: $A, B, Q, D, \ldots P$
> $\therefore$ A is the cause of P, or P of A.

Of course, as usual the greater the number of instances, the better the inference.
Similarly, the greater the number of potential common circumstances investigated, the
better the inference.

It should be obvious that Mill's method of agreement is very similar to the method of
categorical inductive generalization. The form of the latter can be rendered this way:

> 1. All examined A's are P's.
> $\therefore$ 2. All A's are P's.

This is more stringent than the method of agreement in requiring that all known cases
be included in the premises of an argument, but it is less stringent in not requiring that
there be no factor other than A that is always present when P is present. And, of course, it
doesn't justify our concluding that A causes P, a point that will be gone into later.

The method of difference

Mill's rendition of his **method of difference** is this:

> If an instance in which the phenomenon under investigation occurs and an
> instance in which it does not occur, have every circumstance in common save
> one, that one occurring only in the former, the circumstance in which alone the
> two instances differ, is the effect, or the cause, or an indispensable part of the
> cause, of the phenomenon.

In other words, if there is some factor, Q, present in an instance when P is present and
absent in an instance when P is absent, and the two instances are alike in every other (relevant) respect, then P is the cause of Q, or Q is the cause of P.

Mill's example is this:

> A man in the fullness of life is shot through the heart; he is wounded and dies.
> The wound is the only circumstance that is different; hence, his death is caused
> by the wound.

In other words, the circumstance of a man's being wounded (Q) is present in an instance when the man in question dies (P) and absent in an instance when the man is alive (nondead—absence of P), and the two instances—namely, his being wounded and dying (Q and P) and his being not wounded and not dying (absence of Q and absence of P)—are alike in every other (relevant) respect.

When used together, the methods of agreement and difference constitute a very much more powerful inductive tool than either one employed alone.* Take the example concerning the discovery of the identity of the leaker of confidential information. Using the method of agreement, it was concluded that the one person who had access to all the leaked documents must have been the guilty party. This is a perfectly good induction of some strength. But its strength would have been increased had the State Department checked and found that the person in question, call him Smith, did not have access to any of the otherwise (relevantly) similar confidential State Department documents that were not leaked to the press. Here is a table that shows how someone in the State Department might have used both the method of agreement and of difference to conclude with a good deal of strength that Smith caused the leaks:

	Jones's Access	Perez's Access	Cohen's Access	Smith's Access	Leak to Press
1.	absent	present	present	present	present
2.	absent	absent	present	present	present
3.	present	present	absent	present	present
4.	present	present	absent	absent	absent

The first three rows of this table indicate that of the possible relevant factors, only one, Smith having access to the leaked material, was present in every such case. The method of agreement tells us to conclude, therefore, that Smith was the cause of the leaks. The last two rows of the table picture the use of Mill's method of difference in this case, indicating that, although Smith had access in an instance when the material was leaked (the third row), he did not have access in an otherwise similar instance in which confidential material was not tipped off to the press (the fourth row).

It should be clear from the discussion so far that the method of agreement tells us to select as the cause of a phenomenon the one common factor in a number of otherwise different instances in which that phenomenon occurs. And the method of difference tells us to choose as the cause the one respect in which an instance where the phenomenon occurs differs from an otherwise relevantly similar instance where the phenomenon is absent.

In the cases discussed so far, Mill's methods were used to discover something *present* that caused the phenomenon in question. In the crystal case, for example, the factor present was the process of solidifying from a fluid state. But the cause of an event may be the

---

*Using both methods together in this way very much resembles the method Mill called *the method of agreement and difference*.

absence of something or other. The discovery that lack of ascorbic acid (vitamin C) causes scurvy furnishes a good example. When scurvy was a serious problem, back in the presteamboat days of sailing ships, anyone who tried to discover some factor that is always present when scurvy is present and absent when scurvy is absent was bound to have had a hard time of it. But by thinking about what might cause scurvy by its absence, it was soon discovered that absence of the intake of something found in most fruits and vegetables, in particular citrus fruits (later identified as ascorbic acid), is the cause of scurvy.

It should be noted that in using Mill's methods in a positive way, to show that a particular factor is the cause of a particular kind of circumstance, we of necessity also use them in a *negative* way, showing that the other potential factors are not the cause of that kind of circumstance. Thus, in showing that Smith was the likely source of the leaked material, we of necessity showed that the other possible candidates in fact did not cause the leaks. And in the scurvy case, since an absence of ascorbic acid intake was determined to be the cause of scurvy, all sorts of other possible candidates, for instance, various kinds of germs, were eliminated as potential causes.

The method of concomitant variation

According to the **method of concomitant variation,** if a given phenomenon varies in amount or degree in some regular way with the amount or degree of some other phenomenon, then the two factors are causally related.

Take the relationship between cigarette smoking and lung cancer. Surveys show that there is a direct relationship between smoking cigarettes and dying from lung cancer—those who smoke more cigarettes get lung cancer more often. Hence we conclude that cigarette smoking is causally related to death by lung cancer. (Notice that we cannot say that cigarette smoking is the cause of death from lung cancer, since some people who do not smoke at all die of lung cancer, indicating that there must be other causes of that disease.)

Or take the causal relationship between air pressure and the height of a column of mercury in a barometer. In this case, there is a direct quantitative relationship between the two that is so close that we use the effect (the height of the column of mercury) to measure the cause (the amount of air pressure).

Objections to Mill's Methods

Many objections have been raised against the use of Mill's Methods. The most frequent is that Mill's Methods, even when correctly applied, may lead to erroneous, even absurd, consequences. One famous example concerns the drinker who drinks scotch and soda one night, bourbon and soda the next night, gin and soda the next, and Irish whiskey and soda on the last night, each drinking bout being followed by a severe hangover. Using Mill's Methods, the drinker concludes that soda, the one common factor present on each of the four occasions, must be the cause of the hangovers.

But objections of this kind are spurious. In the drinking example, either the drinker did know that another factor, namely alcohol, was present in each case, or he did not. If he knew this, then he did not apply Mill's Methods correctly, since he knew that soda was not the only common factor. And if he did not know that alcohol was present in each case, then he was justified in applying Mill's Methods in spite of the fact that his conclusion is false and even appears ridiculous. The falsity of the conclusion is not evidence against Mill's Methods because these methods are inductive, and it is the mark of inductive methods that they sometimes yield false conclusions.

In addition, the fact that the conclusion appears ridiculous to us also is not a mark against Mill's Methods, because we know that bourbon, scotch, gin, and Irish whiskey all contain alcohol, and we know that hangovers are caused by excessive intake of alcohol. But if we did not know this (and we assume the drinker did not), then the conclusion that hangovers are caused by soda consumption would appear quite reasonable. (Incidentally, once the drinker realizes that there is another common factor, alcohol, in every case in which he had a hangover, then he can use Mill's Methods to determine which of these factors causes hangovers, simply by trying a case in which soda is present, but not alcohol, and then a case in which alcohol is present, but not soda.)

Perhaps the most important objection to Mill's Methods is that the methods of agreement and difference require the instances of the phenomenon in question to have only one other characteristic in common. In reality, this is never the case. Take Mill's own example about crystals. The phenomenon whose cause needs to be discovered is the crystalline structure of certain bodies (P). Mill says that the only thing all crystals have in common, other than being crystals, is that they have solidified from a fluid state (Q) and concludes therefore that this Q is the cause of this particular P. But in fact, there are indefinitely many other features present in every case in which P and Q are both present. For example, every crystal so far examined is smaller than a mountain, has been subjected to temperatures between zero and 100 degrees Celsius, and has been subjected to gravitational force. The fact is that we never can satisfy the method of agreement (or of difference either), as this example indicates.

Mill can be defended against this charge by pointing out that he intended us to consider only relevant common circumstances. None of the preceding bizarre circumstances count as relevant. But this only puts into sharper focus the underlying problem about how we are to decide which circumstances are relevant and which not in each case. Several solutions have been proposed, none of which have received anything like universal acceptance.* The point here is just that Mill's Methods themselves do not provide a solution.

Another objection to Mill's Methods is that the method of agreement is stated in such a way as to invite the fallacy of the small sample, or hasty conclusion. The reason this is so is that this method requires us to investigate only a minimum of two instances, which it does not require to be representative of the population from which they were drawn.

In this case Mill can be partially defended by pointing out that his examples generally concern *types* of instances, not *particular* ones. Thus, in the crystal case his evidence does in fact concern the many instances of the types being a crystal and being solidified from a fluid state.

Finally, it should be pointed out that Mill's Methods do not constitute a complete system for discovering causal connections. The method of concomitant variation, for

---

*Perhaps the most plausible is that it is our background beliefs that determine relevance. Thus, we reject being smaller than mountains as a relevant factor, because experience has never shown this to make a causal difference.

instance, deals with cases in which we observe a continual variation in both the effect whose cause we seek and in the potential cause, as in the cigarette/cancer case just mentioned. But there are several other common, indeed perhaps more common, statistical patterns. Consider a typical experiment, say, in which we expose a group of laboratory mice to a suspected carcinogen but don't expose a control group of mice. A typical result in such a case is that there is a variation in the cancer rate between the two populations, but only in the presence or the absence of the suspected carcinogen, not its variation. To cover cases like this one, we need to construct additional methods, such as the one called* the "split method of difference and concomitant variation," which deals with cases in which the effect varies in some way with the total presence or absence of the suspected causal factor.

Exercise 16-4

Show for the following whether each contains a correct use of Mill's Methods, and if so, which one(s).

1. If you heat a normally combustible item in a vacuum, or in water, or in any medium that lacks air, combustion will not take place. But if you heat such an object with air present, it will take place. So there is no question but that heating in the presence of air is the cause of combustion.

2. According to some economists, very large increases in an already huge national debt should fairly quickly lead to increases in the rate of inflation, because there should be a corresponding increase in the money supply. So the Reagan administration ran the biggest budget deficits in U.S. peacetime history. By 1985 the national debt was out of sight, and yet inflation was down several percentage points.

3. Smith reasoned that if strong labor unions demanding and getting high salaries are the primary cause of inflation, then less well-organized industries should have little or no price inflation. But on checking, he discovered that the industries studied did suffer from price inflation, although their prices rose more slowly than did those of industries having strong, well-organized unions.

4. Being told by a health enthusiast that my extreme lethargy might be caused by low blood sugar, I took his advice and stopped eating snacks high in carbohydrates and low in protein and almost immediately felt better.

5. Prison experience unquestionably boosts the chance that an offender will break the law again. In one experiment, conducted by the California Youth Authority, a group of convicted juvenile delinquents were given immediate parole and returned to their homes or foster homes, where they got intensive care from community parole officers. After five years, only 28 percent of this experimental group have had their paroles revoked, compared to 52 percent of a comparable group that was locked up after conviction. (*Time*, March 24, 1967)

---

*By its inventor Thomas R. Grimes. See his article "A Sixth Mill's Method," *Teaching Philosophy*, vol. 10 (June 1987), pp. 123–127.

6. I'm satisfied that smoking marijuana does not by itself lead one to try heroin. For one thing, I know quite a few people who have been smoking the stuff for years, but have never tried heroin.

7. Louis Pasteur's theory that vaccination with anthrax virus produces immunity to anthrax disease was confirmed by an interesting experiment. Over twenty farm animals were vaccinated with the virus, and then these animals, plus a like number not so vaccinated, were given a normally fatal dose of anthrax germs. None of the vaccinated animals contracted the disease; all those not vaccinated contracted it.

8. Mr. Joule of Manchester conclusively proved that friction is the cause of heat by expending exact quantities of force by rubbing one substance against another, and showed that the heat produced was exactly greater or less in proportion as the force was greater or less. (W. S. Jevons)

9. If a man's destiny is caused by the star under which he is born, then all men born under that star should have the same fortune. However, masters and slaves and kings and beggars are born under the same star. (Pliny the Elder, *Natural History*)

10. It once was assumed that large brains (relative to body weight) are the cause of great intelligence, because the brains of several known geniuses had, after their deaths, turned out to be much larger than average. But when the brain of Anatole France was examined after his death, it was discovered to be quite small relative to his overall body size. However, his brain contained an unusually large number of deep furrows (resulting in a much larger than usual outer surface), as did the brains of several other geniuses when examined after their deaths. So rather than brain size, it would appear that it is the amount of outer brain surface that leads to genius in human beings.

11. All children up to fifth grade in a certain California elementary school were given a standard IQ test, which teachers were told was a test designed to predict which students would have the largest intellectual growth in the following two years. After the test was administered, teachers were given the names of students selected at random (some had scored high and some low), but were told that these students had scored high on the test and therefore could be expected to "spurt" ahead academically in the following year. During the next two years, students were given follow-up IQ tests, and it was found that in some grades—especially the first and second—those designated as likely fast learners improved more than did those not so designated. Since the "spurters" were chosen at random, it was concluded that a teacher's expectations are a causal factor in improving student IQ. (From Robert Rosenthal and Lenore F. Jacobson, "Teacher Expectations for the Disadvantaged," *Scientific American,* April 1968)

12. I placed two silver dimes next to this bar, and they moved toward it. I then tried a few paper clips, a teaspoon, some nails, and a small pair of scissors, and they all moved toward it. So I tried a one-ounce liquor glass, a couple of envelopes, a half-gallon carton of milk, and a spool of thread; none moved toward the bar. Obviously, this wonderful bar attracts all metals, but nothing else.

13. A researcher noticed that several victims of keratitis (a kind of blindness) were deficient in riboflavin. So he examined others suffering from the disease, and they too were low on that nutrient. Finding no other likely cause for the disease, the researcher theorized that keratitis is caused by a lack of riboflavin and confirmed his hunch by giving keratitis victims large doses of riboflavin and observing that the keratitis was cured.

Exercise 16-5

True or False? Explain your answers.

1. An inductively strong argument can have true premises and a false conclusion.
2. Although false that induction goes from the particular to the general while deduction goes the other way, still it's true that induction goes from the less general to the more general, whereas deduction goes just the other way.
3. There is no such thing as a correct statistical inductive generalization.
4. We can regard a categorical inductive generalization as a special kind of statistical generalization in which the ratio of examined *F*'s that are *G*'s is 100 percent.
5. The same hypothesis may be highly probable (highly confirmed), given one set of evidence, while disconfirmed by another.
6. One way to state the pattern or form of correct categorical inductive generalizations is this:
   1. All examined *F*'s are *G*'s.
   ∴ 2. All *F*'s are *G*'s.
7. The greater the number of instances mentioned in the premises of an analogical argument, the higher their degree of support for its conclusion.
8. The greater the difference between items mentioned in the premises of an analogical argument, the lower their degree of support for the conclusion.
9. It has been claimed that analogies are just enthymematic versions of categorical or statistical inductions.
10. Theoretical entities are entities referred to in as yet unsupported scientific theories. After such a theory receives sufficient confirmation, its formerly theoretical entities are then considered existent, not theoretical, entities.
11. The property of being water soluble is a dispositional property, hence also a theoretical one.
12. The physically impossible violates at least one law of nature, whereas the logically impossible violates at least one law of logic.
13. What Mill's method of agreement requires is that we find at least two occurrences of some phenomenon, *P*, that are also occurrences of some phenomenon, *Q*; finding them, we're entitled to assert that *P* is (probably) the cause of *Q*.
14. The main problem with Mill's method of agreement is that all examined instances of a phenomenon never have only one other factor in common.
15. Mill's Methods can be used negatively to discover that one phenomenon, *P*, is not the cause of another, *Q*, by finding an instance of *P* that is not an instance of *Q*.

5 *Inductive Probability*

The premises of a strong inductive argument make its conclusion *probable*. Probabilities and sentences about probabilities play an important role both in everyday life and in science, as the following examples illustrate:

1. The probability of getting a seven with an honest pair of dice is 1/6.
2. Art will probably beat Charles at squash this afternoon.
3. We'll probably have rain tomorrow.
4. The probability that a given American male will die of lung cancer in the next year is 0.0008.
5. The theory of relativity is more probable on today's evidence than on the evidence available in 1919.
6. The probability that a given birth will be a male birth equals 0.51.

The variety of probability we are concerned with here is probability in the sense of *degree of support* or *degree of confirmation,* and is commonly referred to as "inductive" or "logical" probability. An argument is inductively strong if and only if the conclusion of the argument is inductively probable, given the argument's premises.

Unlike validity, inductive strength comes in degrees. The more probable an inductive argument's conclusion is relative to its premises, the stronger the argument. The probability here is conditional, the conclusion is probable relative to the argument's premises. Thus a conclusion that is probable relative to one set of premises may be improbable relative to a different set of premises. Stated formally, the expression $P(p/q)$ is shorthand for "the (inductive) probability of p, given q." If we let q represent the conjunction of an argument's premises and p the conclusion of the argument, then in order for an argument to be strong $P(p/q)$ must be greater than .5. However, to be inductively strong $P(p/q)$ must also be less than the maximum degree of probability, namely 1. If $P(p/q) = 1$ the argument is valid, not inductively strong, since in this case there is no possibility that the premises could be true and the conclusion false.

The Probability Calculus

Let's now consider how, given certain probabilities, other probabilities can be calculated from them. The **probability calculus** has been constructed to answer this question.

Some pairs of propositions are such that the truth of one of them has an *effect* on the probability of the other. For example, if it is true that I have already drawn an ace from a deck of cards (without putting it back into the deck) then the proposition that I will get an ace on the next draw is less likely to be true.

But other pairs of propositions are bearing on each other. For example, the proposition that I have drawn an ace from a deck of cards and put the ace back into the deck has *no* effect on the proposition that I will get an ace on the next draw. (The cards don't "know" that an ace was picked on the first draw.) If two propositions are such that the truth of one has no effect on the probability of the second, they are said to be **independent propositions.**

In addition, some pairs of propositions are such that it is *logically possible* for both of them to be true. For example, it is logically possible for it to be true that a die will land with face six up on its first throw and also true that it will land with face six up on its second throw.

But other pairs of propositions are such that it is not logically possible for both to be true. For example, it is not logically possible for face five *and* face six to turn up on a single throw of a die. If two propositions are such that it is not logically possible for both to be true, they are said to be **mutually exclusive propositions.**

We can write the basic rules of the probability calculus as follows:

1.   Restricted Conjunction Rule

If p and q are independent propositions, then $P(p \cdot q) = P(p) \times P(q)$.

For instance, if the probability of getting a six on a given throw $(p) = 1/6$, and the probability of getting a six on some other throw $(q) = 1/6$, then since p and q are independent of each other, the probability of getting sixes on both throws equals the probability of getting a six on the first throw *times* the probability of getting a six on the second throw. Thus, the probability of getting sixes on both throws equals $1/6 \times 1/6$, or $1/36$.

2.   General Conjunction Rule

$P(p \cdot q) = P(p) \times P(q, \text{given } p)$

For instance, if the probability of picking a spade on a second draw, *given that a spade was picked on the first draw* (and not replaced) $= 12/51,$* then the probability that spades will be drawn on both the first and second draws $= 1/4 \times 12/51 = 1/17$.

Notice that if $P(q, \text{given } p) = P(q)$, then the two conjunction rules both yield the same result. In fact, this is the case in which p and q are independent of each other.

3.   Restricted Disjunction Rule

If p and q are mutually exclusive propositions, then $P(p \vee q) = P(p) + P(q)$.

For example, if the probability of getting a five on a given throw of a die $= 1/6$, and the probability of getting a six on a given throw of that die $= 1/6$, then the probability of getting a five *or* a six on a given throw of the die $= 1/6 + 1/6 = 2/6 = 1/3$.

4.   General Disjunction Rule

$P(p \vee q) = P(p) + P(q) - P(p \cdot q)$

For instance, if the probability of getting a six on any given throw of a die $= 1/6$, then the probability of getting at least one six out of two throws (that is, a six on the first throw or a six on the second) $1/6 + 1/6 - (1/6 \times 1/6) = 2/6 - 1/36 = 11/36$.

Notice that if p and q are mutually exclusive, then $P(p \cdot q) = 0$, and then the two disjunction rules yield the same result.

In addition, it is customary to assume that the probability of a *contradiction* $= 0$, and the probability of a *logical truth* $= 1$. In symbols, this reads

---

*Because 12 spades remain out of 51 cards.

5. $P(p \cdot \sim p) = 0$

6. $P(p \vee \sim p) = 1$

It follows from this that the probability of $\sim p = 1 - P(p)$; that is,

7. $P(\sim p) = 1 - P(p)$

7   *Bayes' Theorem*

We have now, in effect, provided seven rules for calculating complicated probabilities from simpler ones. But one further kind of complicated probability needs mentioning, namely, what is sometimes called an **inverse probability.**

Suppose we know that 90 percent of the families in a certain city own a television set and that among these 10 percent also own a computer. Suppose we also know that among the 10 percent who don't own a TV set, 20 percent do own a computer. What is the probability that a family owning a computer also owns a TV set?

To deal with this problem, let $P(p)$ = the probability that a given family owns a computer, and $P(q)$ = the probability that a given family owns a TV set. Then, in our example,

$$P(q) = 0.9 \qquad\qquad\qquad\qquad P(p, \text{given } q) = 0.1$$
$$P(\sim q) = 0.1 \qquad\qquad\qquad\qquad P(p, \text{given } \sim q) = 0.2$$

(The probabilities on the left are sometimes called *prior probabilities* and those on the right *conditional probabilities,* or *forward probabilities.*) We want to calculate the probability that a given computer-owning family also owns a TV set, in symbols $P(q, \text{given } p)$, and for this purpose we can use a simplified version of **Bayes' Theorem,** namely*

$$P(q, \text{given } p) = \frac{P(q) \times P(p, \text{given } q)}{[P(q) \times P(p, \text{given } q)] + [P(\sim q) \times P(p, \text{given } \sim q)]}$$

Plugging in values from the case at hand, we get

$$P(q, \text{given } p) = \frac{0.9 \times 0.1}{(0.9 \times 0.1) + (0.1 \times 0.2)} = \frac{0.09}{0.11} = \frac{9}{11}$$

Bayes' Theorem is intuitively plausible. In our example, common sense says the probability that a computer family also is a television set family should depend on, first, the

---

*The general form of Bayes' Theorem is

$$P(q, \text{given } p) = \frac{P(q) \times P(p, \text{given } q)}{[P(q_1) \times P(p, \text{given } q_1)] + \ldots + [P(q_n) \times P(p, \text{given } q_n)]}$$

We use the general formula when there are more than two values for q to consider.

prior probability that a family owns a television set and, second, the conditional probability that a family owning a television set also owns a computer. And this is what Bayes' Theorem calculates.*

Bayes' Theorem is clearly legitimate in cases, such as the preceding, where the relevant prior probabilities are known (in our example, presumably known by statistical inductions from samples). But objections have been raised against the use of Bayes' Theorem when prior probabilities are not known (a common kind of case). Some answer such objections by saying that in the absence of reasons for preferring one value over another, all prior probabilities will be considered equal.

In addition to questions about the applicability of Bayes' Theorem when prior probabilities are not known, questions have been raised as to the applicability of the probability calculus in general. An important argument often raised in support of the probability calculus is that using any other calculation rules leads to clearly unacceptable results, in particular making possible what is called a "Dutch book."

The term comes from gambling. Gamblers who are sufficiently careless or ignorant in placing a series of bets may find that no matter what happens, the bookie must win. When this happens, they're said to have a **Dutch book** made against them. Obviously, any system of rules for calculating odds that might lead gamblers to allow a Dutch book to be made against them is not an acceptable system. It turns out that any system that deviates from the standard probability calculus is susceptible to a Dutch book (can have a Dutch book made against it). Thus many writers would say that only the standard calculus is acceptable as a measure of inductive probability.

Exercise 16-6

Use the probability calculus to determine the following probabilities, showing enough work to justify your answers.

1. What is the probability of getting (a) an even number face up on a given throw of a symmetrical die; (b) an odd number?

2. What is the probability of getting (a) two heads in a row with a symmetrical coin; (b) three heads in a row?

---

*We can prove Bayes' Theorem, in the sense that it can be derived from a few of the other rules for calculating probabilities. Here is a proof of the simplified version of Bayes' Theorem:

1. $P(q, \text{given } p) = \dfrac{P(p \cdot q)}{P(p)}$ From general conjunction rule

2. $P(q, \text{given } p) = \dfrac{P(p \cdot q)}{P[(p \cdot q) \vee (p \cdot \sim q)]}$ Because p is logically equivalent to $(p \cdot q) \vee (p \cdot \sim q)$

3. $P(q, \text{given } p) = \dfrac{P(p \cdot q)}{P[(p \cdot q) + (p \cdot \sim q)]}$ From restricted disjunction rule

4. $P(q, \text{given } p) = \dfrac{P(q) \times P(p, \text{given } q)}{P(q) \times P(p, \text{given } q) + [P(\sim q) \times P(p, \text{given } \sim q)]}$ From general conjunction rule

3. Suppose it's as likely that a person be born on one day as on another. Then what is the probability that two people chosen at random both were born on April 19? (Forget about leap year.)

4. What is the probability of getting an even number or a number less than 3 (or both) with a standard six-sided die on a single toss?

5. Using a pair of symmetrical dice, what is the probability of getting (a) two sevens on the first two tosses; (b) any combination of sevens and elevens on the first two tosses?

6. Alpha Alpha Alpha fraternity has a blind date affair each month with Phi Phi Phi sorority. The custom is to randomly pair ten members of each group with ten of the other. What is the probability that Babs, a member of Phi Phi Phi, will be paired with the same guy on the next two dates?

7. What is the probability of getting *at least* two heads out of three with a symmetrical coin?

8. What is the probability of getting exactly two heads out of three with a symmetrical coin?

9. Suppose you draw two cards from a standard deck, replacing the first one before drawing the second. What is the probability that you'll get (a) two aces; (b) at least one ace; (c) two spades; (d) at least one spade?

10. Suppose you draw two cards from a standard deck, not replacing the first one before drawing the second. What is the probability that you'll get (a) two aces; (b) at least one ace; (c) two spades; (d) two black aces?

8 *Induction Is Unjustified—The Old Riddle of Induction*

Recall that the characteristic mark of all inductive (nondeductive) reasoning is a "gap" between premises and conclusion. As soon as this gap was realized,* the question of *how any inductive argument can be justified* was raised; that is, the question was raised about the *rationality* of the acceptance of hypotheses on inductive grounds.

Unfortunately, a good answer to this question has been hard to come by. A great many solutions to the problem of induction have been proposed, most of which can be classified into four categories.

1. The most obvious thought is that we are justified in using induction because it "works." All science is based on inductive conclusions of some sort or other, and everyone knows how successful science is. Everyone knows that the scientific method, which uses induction, *works.*

Unfortunately, this obvious solution to the problem is not satisfactory. It simply isn't true that we know that induction works or is successful. At best, what we know is that it

---

*The philosopher David Hume was the first person to perceive it clearly and to try to bridge it. See *A Treatise of Human Nature*, Book 1, Part IV, Section 1; and *An Enquiry Concerning Human Understanding*, Section V.

has worked, or *has been successful.* But will it be successful in the future? We don't know. Indeed, the problem seems to be that we haven't the slightest reason to think induction will be successful in the future.

It often is claimed that in fact we do have a very good reason for thinking that induction will be successful in the future, namely its success in the past. But only a little thought is needed to see that this reason will not do, because to argue that induction will be successful because it *has* been successful is to argue *inductively.* (The premise of such an argument is, "Induction has been successful [on the whole] up to now," and its conclusion is, "Induction always will be successful [on the whole]." Clearly, this argument itself is an inductive argument.) So when we argue this way, we use induction to justify itself, which means that we argue circularly, and hence, fallaciously.

2.   Perhaps the most popular solutions to the problem of induction are those that use some principle concerning the *uniformity of nature,* such as the principle that *every event has a cause.*

For instance, if we assume that nature is uniform, then we can reason inductively from the fact that all examined pieces of copper are uniform with respect to conductivity to the conclusion that all pieces of copper (examined or as yet unexamined) are uniform with respect to the conducting of electricity.

But solutions of this kind are unsatisfactory. First, even if nature is uniform, there is no guarantee that the particular uniformities we have observed up to a given time will hold in the future; the true uniformities of nature may be more complex or subtle. And second, the assumption that every event has a cause, or that nature is uniform, itself can be challenged. Why assume that nature is uniform? Again, there seems to be no answer. (Remember that we cannot argue that the assumption that nature is uniform has been fruitful in the past, and hence is likely to be fruitful in the future, for such an argument would be an inductive argument, and we cannot use induction to justify a principle of uniformity and then use that principle to justify the use of induction.)

3.   Some philosophers have proposed justifications based on the so-called self-corrective nature of induction.* For example, suppose we conclude that half of 10,000 tosses of a coin will land heads up, on the basis of the evidence that half of the first 100 tosses of this coin landed heads up. Suppose this conclusion is false. Then we can "correct" it simply by observing larger and larger coin-tossing samples, basing our conclusion about the relative frequency of heads in the total series of 10,000 tosses on the relative frequency of heads in the largest sample we have at any given time. If we continue the process long enough, at some point we must reach the correct value. Hence, it is claimed, we are justified in using inductive reasoning in such cases because the process is self-correcting; repeated applications must get us closer and closer to the truth.

Suppose, for instance, that one half of 10,000 tosses of a coin in fact will land heads up. If we get heads on exactly half of the first 5,000 tosses, then we know with deductive certainty that the relative frequency of heads compared to total tosses in the entire series

---

*See, for instance, Charles Peirce, "Induction as Experimental and Self-Correcting," *Collected Papers of Charles Sanders Peirce,* vol. VI, Charles Hartshorne and Paul Weiss, eds. (Cambridge, Mass.: Harvard University Press, 1935). Reprinted in Edward H. Madden, *The Structure of Scientific Thought* (Boston: Houghton Mifflin, 1960), pp. 296–298.

of 10,000 tosses must be somewhere between 1/4 and 3/4.* Hence our prediction that half of the 10,000 tosses will be heads cannot be off by more than ±1/4.

Now suppose that after 8,000 tosses the observed relative frequency of heads is still 1/2. Then we know at this point that the relative frequency of heads in the total series of 10,000 tosses must be somewhere between 2/5 and 3/5.† Hence at this point our prediction that half of the 10,000 tosses will be heads cannot be off by more than ±1/10. So we are getting closer and closer to the correct value (no matter what that value happens to be), since the *largest possible error* in our predictions keeps getting smaller and smaller.

The trouble is that our predictions get closer and closer to the correct value because larger and larger portions of the series concern *past tosses* and are incorporated into our *evidence,* whereas smaller and smaller portions of the series concern *future tosses.* At no point do we have any guarantee that we are getting any closer to the actual relative frequency of heads among future (unexamined) tosses of the coin. But if the self-corrective claim is to have any force, it must apply to predictions about the future (or the as yet unexamined past).

The situation is even worse for infinitely long series, since the relative frequency of any given finite portion of an infinite series is compatible with any relative frequency whatever in the infinite series. For instance, even if every one of millions of tosses of a coin lands heads up, the *limit* of such an infinite series of tosses (assuming an infinite series of tosses is possible) still might equal zero. Hence, for an infinite series, inductive practices embody no self-corrective feature whatever.

We must conclude, then, that we cannot justify the use of induction on the grounds that it is self-correcting.

4.   Finally, there are the so-called dissolutions of the problem of induction, according to which the very problem itself is a pseudoproblem.‡ We shall consider two of the many solutions of this kind. In the first, it is claimed that it is not rational to doubt the principles of inductive reasoning because these principles themselves *determine* (in part) what it means to be rational. In other words, if we doubt the rationality (the reasonableness) of the use of induction, then we simply don't know what it means to be rational.

Unfortunately, this argument is defective. Were we to find ourselves in a community in which it is considered rational to believe everything said by the oldest member of the community, it would be reasonable to inquire if it *really* is rational to do so. And if the reply were that what it *means* to be rational is to believe the oldest member of the community, then it would be perfectly proper to ask *why* we should be rational. Put into this context, the problem of induction is that we seem to have no answer to the question "Why be rational?" either for the peculiar concept of rationality in the imaginary community just described or for the concept of rationality in the real community.

According to the second kind of "dissolution" of the problem, there is no problem of justifying the use of inductive principles because *no justification is possible,* and if none

---

*If the 5,000 remaining tosses all are tails, then the relative frequency will be 1/4, and if they all are heads, then the relative frequency will be 3/4.

†If the 2,000 remaining tosses all are tails, then the relative frequency will be 2/5, and if they all are heads, then the relative frequency will be 3/5.

‡See, for instance, A. J. Ayer, *Language, Truth and Logic* (New York: Dover, 1952), pp. 49–50.

is possible, then none can be required. Two kinds of arguments have been presented in support of this claim.

First, it has been argued that such a justification would have to be either *inductive* or *deductive.* An inductive justification would be circular, since it would use the very principles of reasoning we are trying to justify. And we could never construct a valid deductive justification, because it is impossible to prove deductively that nature is uniform, or that every event has a cause, or that the future will resemble the past.*

But this argument is defective. It is true that metaphysical assumptions, such as the uniformity of nature, cannot be proved deductively. But a deductive justification does not necessarily require that any such principle be proved. Perhaps other kinds of assumptions can be proved that will justify the use of induction.[†]

Second, it has been argued that just as the theorems in an axiom system cannot all be proved (without circularity or infinite regress), so also all principles of *reasoning* or *inferring* cannot be justified (without circularity or infinite regress). Hence we should not be surprised that no justification of induction is possible.

Clearly, there is something to this last argument. It is true that we cannot justify every principle of reasoning any more than we can prove every theorem. And it may well be that the basic inductive principle will be among those that remain forever unjustified and hence remain forever as a kind of primitive inference rule. But the argument in question does not prove this. All that it proves is that some principle or other will remain unjustified. It does not prove induction is that principle.

However, recognition of the important fact that some principle or other must remain unjustified may make it more tolerable that as yet no one seems to have been able to justify the basic principle of induction.

9   *Not All Instances of Theories Confirm Them— The New Riddle of Induction*

Perhaps the most curious of the objections raised against our account of scientific method is the one posed by Nelson Goodman's so-called new *riddle of induction.*

The old riddle, you will recall, has to do with justifying induction and inductive inferences in general, and in particular with justifying the belief that generalizations are confirmed by their instances (as, say, the generalization "All dogs have tails" is confirmed by finding an instance of it—namely, a dog with a tail). The new riddle, according to Goodmanites, has to do with distinguishing those generalizations that *are* confirmed by their instances from those that are not.

---

*What is often meant by such an argument is that metaphysical principles of this kind are not *theorems of logic,* or *deductively obtainable from the null set of premises,* or *knowable prior to any particular empirical observations.*

[†]For instance, the pragmatic justification presented by Hans Reichenbach in *The Theory of Probability* (Berkeley: University of California Press, 1949), pp. 469–482, is based on an attempt to prove deductively that if any method of predicting the future is successful, then the use of induction will be successful.

To see the difference between these two kinds of cases, consider the following example. Suppose 100 emeralds, all of them green, are observed for color. This would usually be considered good evidence for the hypothesis or generalization (H-1) "All emeralds are green." But now let's introduce a new color term, "grue," referring to all things examined for color *before* a particular time *t*, say January 1, 2101, that are green, and to other things just in case they are blue. Then emeralds, for instance, will be "grue" just in case they either are green and the time in question is before time *t* or are blue and the time in question is at *t* or after. An emerald examined now and found to be green would thus be "grue," but one examined in the twenty-second century and found to be green would not be "grue" (it would, however, be *bleen*, that is, it would be either examined before time *t* and blue, or not so examined and green).

All of the 100 green emeralds observed in our hypothetical example are "grue," as well as green, since they're green and the time is prior to time *t*. So according to what has been said so far about confirmation, it would seem that the 100 observed "grue" emeralds constitute confirming instances of the hypothesis (H-2): "All emeralds are grue," just as these same emeralds, being green, confirm (H-1): "All emeralds are green." But (H-1) and (H-2) *conflict* with each other, because according to (H-1), emeralds observed after time *t* will be green while according to (H-2), they will be blue. In fact, of course, no one would accept (H-2) no matter how many confirming cases we find in its favor. Goodman's problem is to find some way to distinguish "grue-like" illegitimate predicates and hypotheses from legitimate green-like ones, so that hypotheses like (H-1) will be confirmed by their instances while those like (H-2) will not.

Most of the proposed solutions to this problem are seriously defective. Rudolf Camap, for example, argued that terms such as "grue" are what he called "positional," meaning that they are terms whose definitions in part refer to individual objects, or to individual places or times. But Camap's solution is unsatisfactory, in particular because lots of "good" predicates are positional and in fact are used in acceptable generalizations all the time. Some examples given by Goodman are "Ming," "Arctic," and "Pleistocene." Generalizations like "All Ming vases are expensive" would usually be held to be confirmed by their instances (in this case, by particular Ming vases that are expensive).

The interesting thing about Goodman's riddle is that an obvious answer lies right at hand, and was proposed soon after Goodman formulated the problem; indeed, it must have occurred independently to countless readers of the literature since then. Take our two competing hypotheses (H-1) "All emeralds are green," and (H-2) "All emeralds are grue." The first contains the "good" term "green," the second the "bad" term "grue." What is good about the former but bad about the latter? The first thought many of us have is that all green things *resemble* each other in a certain way, namely, by being green in color, while there is no such color resemblance uniting all grue things, since items that are grue prior to time *t* are green, while those that are grue after time *t* are blue. What the term "green" *means* requires all items referred to by that predicate to resemble each other in color— share a common color—namely, green. But what the term "grue" means does not require this; prior to time *t* grue things are green, after time *t* they are blue. By simply saying that only those generalizations containing terms such as "green" are confirmed by their instances, the problem would seem to be solved. That is, it seems as though we can quite easily solve the problem by rejecting all generalizations containing terms, such as "grue," that select classes of items that do not necessarily all resemble each other in some relevant way. One idea behind inductive reasoning is, after all, to find items that resemble each other in some specified way that also share some other common property. In the case of (H-1): "All emeralds are green," we find stones that resemble each other in being beryl silicates (and thus emeralds)* and discover that they also share the common property of being green. In the case of (H-2) "All emeralds are grue," there also is a shared common property, namely, that of being grue, but that is not a *resembling* property—not all grue things resemble each other in the appropriate way.

Perhaps the main reason why this obvious solution to the grue problem has not settled the matter is that Goodman provided what most writers on the subject have accepted as a conclusive objection to it. Goodman argued that, given any two things, however different they may seem, we can always invent a property they both share, as we did in inventing the property of being grue. That is, he argued that all grue things do in fact share a common property, namely, that of being grue, and thus do in fact resemble each other (since they all are grue). We've noticed that all emeralds have resembled each other by being green, perhaps, because "green" is a term we've become familiar with through long use—it has become well *entrenched* in our language. But we've failed to notice that all emeralds so far encountered have resembled each other by being grue, perhaps because we're not familiar with and haven't used the term "grue"—it hasn't become entrenched in our language.

Underlying Goodman's view on the grue question is an extreme version of a very old philosophical position called **nominalism** (something some of the nonnominalistic writers on the subject seem to have overlooked). In its extreme form, nominalism says that "there is nothing common to a class of particulars called by the same name other than that they *are* called by the same name."[†] That is why Goodman says that just as green things resemble each other in being green so also grue things *equally* resemble each other in being grue.[‡]

But suppose we reject the nominalist's view and accept the commonsense, everyday idea of resemblance that makes it wrong to speak of "grue" things as resembling each other just as much as do green things. (This is in fact what the vast majority of philosophers have done over the ages.) Then the Goodman problem fails to get off the ground,[§] and our account of the philosophy of science remains intact.

---

*Goodman's choice of example was unfortunate in that according to one common definition of *emerald* a nongreen beryl silicate would not be an emerald.

[†]A. D. Woozley in his article "Universals," in the *Encyclopedia of Philosophy*, edited by Paul Edwards (New York: Collier Macmillan, 1967). Woozley's article also contains an excellent rebuttal of this extreme form of nominalism (in the opinion of Kahane).

[‡]Goodman's basic nominalistic principle is that there are individual things in the world, and sums of individual things, but no general properties. (See his article "A World of Individuals" in *The Problem of Universals* [Notre Dame, IN: Notre Dame University Press, 1956].) But he is quickly led to the version of nominalism Woozley discussed, and without doubt believes that any two things (for example, any two grue emeralds) may resemble each other just as much as any other two things (for example, any two green emeralds).

[§]There are, of course, some wrinkles to take care of. For example, Goodman argues that lots of acceptable terms, such as "electrical conductor," are not resembling terms in the everyday sense; we therefore have to show what the resemblances might be like in these cases. See Howard Kahane's article "Pathological Predicates and Projections" (*American Philosophical Quarterly*, vol. 8 (1971), pp. 171–178), for more on this, and also for some other thoughts on the grue problem and how to solve it, as well as for a bibliography on the subject.

Key Terms Introduced in Chapter Sixteen

analogical inference: An inductive inference from particular instances to a conclusion concerning some other particular instance. An example is the inference from the evidence that three English suits wore well to the conclusion that some other English suit will wear well.

Bayes' Theorem: The simplified version is

$P(q,$ *given* $p) =$

$$\frac{P(q) \times P(p, \text{ given } q)}{[P(q) \times P(p, \text{ given } q)] + [P(\bar{q}) \times P(p, \text{ given } \bar{q})]}$$

The completely general version is

$P(q_1,$ *given* $p) =$

$$\frac{P(q_1) \times P(p, \text{ given } q_1)}{[P(q_1) \times P(p, \text{ given } q_1)] + \ldots + [P(q_1) \times P(p, \text{ given } q_1)]}$$

categorical analogy: Inductive inference from the evidence that all tested *F*'s are *G*'s to the conclusion that some as yet untested *F* is a *G*.

categorical inductive generalization: An inductive inference from particular instances to a universal conclusion. An example is the inference from the evidence that all observed ravens are black to the categorical generalization that all ravens are black. (Synonyms: *universal inductive generalization, inductive generalization.*)

causal connection (or relationship): A certain kind of constant conjunction between two sorts of things (for instance, between putting sugar in coffee and having the coffee taste sweet).

cause and effect: A kind of causal connection in which the earlier of a pair of causally connected items is said to be the cause and the later the effect.

dispositional property: An unobservable property or power. An example is the property of being flexible.

Dutch book: A series of bets placed so that a gambler must lose, no matter what the outcomes of the individual bets.

general conjunction rule: The rule that $P(p \cdot q) = P(p) \times P(q, \text{ given } p)$.

general disjunction rule: The rule that $P(p \vee q) = P(p) + P(q) - P(p \cdot q)$.

independent propositions: Propositions such that the truth of one has no effect on the probability of the second—for example, the proposition that I have drawn an ace from a deck of cards and put the ace back in and the proposition that I will draw an ace on the next draw.

inverse probabilities: Backward probabilities. *Example:* The inverse probability of *p*, given *q* is $P(q, \text{ given } p)$.

method of agreement: One of Mill's Methods, namely, the method of inferring that if *P* is the only factor present in every observed occurrence of *Q*, then *P* and *Q* are causally related.

method of concomitant variation: One of Mill's Methods, namely, the method of inferring that if a given phenomenon varies in some regular way with some other phenomenon, then the two phenomena are causally related.

method of difference: One of Mill's Methods, namely, the method of inferring that whatever is present when *Q* is present, and absent when *Q* is absent, is causally related to *Q*.

Mill's Methods: Methods for finding (or confirming) causal relationships, championed by the nineteenth-century philosopher John Stuart Mill.

mutually exclusive propositions: Propositions that are such that it is not logically possible for both to be true—for example, the proposition that the next coin toss will land on heads and the proposition that the next coin toss will land on tails.

necessary condition: A part of what is required in order to produce a thing or event (or, in some cases, all of what is required). *Example:* The presence of oxygen is a necessary condition for the lighting of a match. (See also *sufficient condition.*)

observable entity: That which can be experienced or observed directly. (Antonym: *theoretical entity.*)

probability calculus: A set of rules for calculating probabilities from initial probabilities. For instance, the restricted disjunction rule is a member of this set, and allows us to calculate, say, that the probability of getting a red jack or black queen with an ordinary card deck is 1/26 + 1/26 = 2/26 = 1/13.

probable cause: Causation in the statistical sense, used when we have just a statistical connection between cause and effect. *Example:* Cigarette smoking is a probable cause of most cases of lung cancer among cigarette smokers.

proximate cause: A cause relatively close in a causal chain to an effect. *Example:* A muscle twitch that causes someone's arm to rise. (See also *remote cause.*)

remote cause: A cause relatively distant in a causal chain from an effect. *Example:* The willing that causes someone's arm to move. (See also *proximate cause.*)

restricted conjunction rule: The rule that if *p* and *q* are independent events, then

$P(p \cdot q) = P(p) \times P(q)$.

restricted disjunction rule: The rule that if *p* and *q* are mutually exclusive events, then

$P(p \vee q) = P(p) + P(q)$.

simple inductive generalization: (See *categorical inductive generalization.*)

statistical analogy: Inductive inference from the evidence that *N* percent of the tested *F*'s are *G*'s to the conclusion that the probability is *N* percent that some as yet untested *F* is a *G*.

statistical inductive generalization: An inductive inference from particular instances to a statistical conclusion. An example is the inference from the evidence that half of all tosses with this coin so far landed heads up to the statistical conclusion that half of all tosses with this coin will land heads up.

sufficient condition: Whatever is sufficient to bring about a particular event. *Example:* Chopping off Marie Antoinette's head was a sufficient condition to cause her death. (See also *necessary condition.*)

theoretical entity: Postulated entity that cannot be experienced or observed directly. (Antonym: *observable entity.*)

universal inductive generalization: (See *categorical inductive generalization.*)

Chapter Seventeen

Axiom Systems

One way to *systematize* a given area of knowledge is to use an **axiom** system.

1 *The Nature of an Axiom System*

An axiom system has three main elements: symbols (or words), formulas, and inference rules. Symbols divide into **defined symbols,** for which explicit definitions are presented, and **primitive (undefined) symbols,** for which no definitions are presented. For instance, in an axiom system for anthropology we might introduce the terms "parent" and "male" as primitives, and then define the term "father" to mean "male parent." Symbols also divide into **logical symbols,** such as "and," "not," "some," and so on, and **extralogical** or **nonlogical symbols,** which vary depending on the area of knowledge to be systematized.

Formulas break down into sentences and sentence forms (or functions).* They also divide into **axioms,** for which no justification is provided within the system, and **theorems,** which can be derived from the axioms by means of the inference rules of the system. Indeed, one of the main reasons for constructing axiom systems is to derive theorems from axioms.

Formulas also can be divided into **well-formed formulas,** such as $p \supset q$ and $\sim [(A \vee B) \supset \sim C]$, and those that are not, such as $(pq \vee$ and $AB) \vee$. (This distinction will be explained in more detail later.) And finally, inference rules divide into **primitive inference rules,** for which no justification is provided within the system, and **derived inference rules,** for which a justification is provided.

Of course, not every system need have all these elements. For instance, we can have an axiom system without defined symbols or derived rules. But to be complete, an axiom system must have symbols, formulas, and inference rules.

One of the primary motives for constructing axiom systems is *rigor.* We want symbols precisely defined, and theorems rigorously proved. Consequently, it might be supposed that to include *undefined* symbols, *unproved* axioms, and *unjustified* inference rules is to

---

*This is not quite true for what are called *uninterpreted* systems, because it is inappropriate to speak of the formulas of such systems as sentences or sentence forms.

settle for something less than the ideal. But this is an illusion. It is impossible to define all symbols, prove all sentences, or justify all inference rules within a given system, except either circularly or by an infinite (and useless) series of definitions or proofs. (For example, it would be useless to define "automobile" as "car" and then to define "car" as "automobile." And it would be useless to attempt to present an infinite series of definitions, because, to understand it, one would have to run through the entire series, something it is impossible to do.) So we must settle for at least some undefined symbols, unproved axioms, and unjustified inference rules.*

Of course, undefined symbols must be understood, and the axioms and inference rules must be acceptable. Clearly, some symbols will not do as primitives in a rigorous system. But the question of *which* symbols and which axioms and inference rules are acceptable as primitives is in dispute. For instance, some claim that the axioms of an axiom system for deductive logic must be *intuitively acceptable,* or *self-evidently true,* whereas others say that, theoretically, any theorems of logic can be axioms, the choice being made to obtain the smallest possible set of axioms from which all theorems can be derived. But all agree that (other things being equal) it is desirable to have very few axioms or primitive rules of inference and very few undefined symbols.

Note that the undefinability *within a system* of all terms of that system does not entail the inherent *undefinability* of any terms of that system. It may be that no terms are undefinable.

Most of us are familiar with at least one axiom system, Euclidean geometry, although it is normally presented only in a semirigorous form. (For instance, usually only a partial list of inference rules is provided.) But it is clear how such a system can be made more rigorous, and so we can take Euclidean geometry as our model of an axiom system.

2 *Interpreted and Uninterpreted Systems*

An **uninterpreted axiom system** is one in which the primitive symbols not only are not defined *within* the system, but are given no meaning or interpretation whatsoever. (Of course, those who construct uninterpreted axiom systems generally have particular interpretations in mind. For instance, anyone who constructs an uninterpreted axiom system for sentential logic obviously has sentential logic in mind; otherwise there would be no point in calling it an uninterpreted system *for sentential logic.*)

The point of an uninterpreted system is to enable us to concentrate on form or structure without being distracted by content and to make it less likely that we will tacitly use knowledge not contained in the axioms of the system. For example, dealing with an uninterpreted axiom system for geometry makes it less likely that we will tacitly appeal to geometric intuitions not explicitly stated in the axioms and inference rules of the system. (In fact, Euclid himself made tacit use of information about geometry not explicitly stated in his system.)

---

*It is sometimes possible to reduce the number of axioms to zero by increasing the number of primitive inference rules. But we can never reduce the number of axioms *and* primitive inference rules in a given system to zero.

An **interpreted axiom system** is one for which all the primitive terms are assigned a meaning or interpretation. In some axiom systems the formulas, when interpreted, are sentences; in others they are sentence forms.

Notice that it is one thing to define a term within a system, and another to assign a meaning to a primitive term. A term defined within a system is defined by the primitive terms of the system (or other terms so defined). Primitive terms are assigned meanings in other ways. For example, in applied geometry the primitive term "straight line" may be taken to refer to the path of a light ray.

Although there is some dispute about which terms are usable as primitives, other things being equal, terms whose meanings we clearly understand (however we obtain this understanding) are preferable to those that are vague or figurative.

3 *Properties of Axiom Systems*

Good axiom systems themselves have several important properties, in particular *consistency* and *completeness*.

Consistency

The most important requirement for an acceptable axiom system is *consistency*. An axiom system is **consistent** if and only if (iff) contradictory formulas cannot be derived from its axioms by means of its rules of inference. An axiom system that fails to satisfy this requirement, so that a contradiction is derivable as a theorem, is said to be *inconsistent* and is obviously unsatisfactory.

Example

A system containing the two axioms

> (A1) $p \supset {\sim} p$
> (A2) p

plus the two inference rules

> (R1) If p and $p \supset q$, then we can infer q. (Modus Ponens)
> (R2) If p and q, then we can infer $p \cdot q$. (Conjunction)

is inconsistent, since we can derive a contradiction in such a system, as follows:

> 1. $p \supset {\sim} p$ **Axiom**
> 2. p **Axiom**
> 3. ${\sim} p$ 1,2 **MP**
> 4. $p \cdot {\sim} p$ 2,3 **Conj**

The general procedure for proving that an axiom system is *inconsistent* is the same as the one for proving a set of premises inconsistent, namely, the derivation of an explicit contradiction. But failure to derive a contradiction does not prove that a given axiom system is consistent, for we may have failed through lack of ingenuity. Instead, the general procedure for proving that an axiom system is consistent is to prove that a formula exists that is not derivable as a theorem of that system. This proves that a given axiom system is consistent because inconsistent systems permit the derivation of any and every expressible formula (since a *contradiction* logically entails any and every expressible formula). Hence if there is some formula that cannot be derived as a theorem, then no contradiction can be derived either, and the system must be consistent.*

Expressive completeness

An axiom system is **expressively complete** if its language is rich enough to express everything that the system is intended to express. For example, the usual axiom systems for Euclidean geometry are expressively complete, because they permit every statement (true or false) concerning geometry. But an axiom system for Euclidean geometry would be expressively incomplete if, say, it contained no method for stating sentences about circles.

Completeness

There is another kind of completeness, more frequently discussed in the literature than expressive completeness and much more difficult to state. This kind concerns the *provability* or *derivability* of formulas. Perhaps the best criterion we can give for this kind of completeness is that an axiom system is **complete** in this sense iff all of the formulas we *desire to* prove as theorems of the system in fact are provable as theorems of that system.

Although it is quite difficult to state precisely what this kind of completeness consists of *in general,* it is less difficult to characterize it for *desire* of the more important kinds of axiom systems:

(1) An axiom system for sentential logic is complete iff every tautologous sentence or sentence form expressible in the system is provable as a theorem of the system.

(2) In Chapter Five sentences that can be known to be true by means of logic alone were called *theorems of logic.* Adopting this terminology, we can say that an axiom system for predicate logic is complete iff every theorem of logic is provable as a theorem of that system. (Notice that we cannot use the same criterion of completeness for predicate logic that we used for sentential logic, because many theorems of predicate logic are not tautologies.)

(3) An axiom system for *arithmetic* is complete iff every sentence expressible in the system is such that either it or its negation is a theorem of the system. To see that this criterion is adequate, consider several kinds of typical sentences of arithmetic.

---

*This criterion of consistency, known as "Post's consistency criterion" after its inventor E. L. Post, works only for complete systems. Incomplete systems that also are inconsistent may be such that there are no formulas expressible in the system that are not provable.

First, consider *unquantified* sentences, such as $2 + 2 = 4$, $7 + 1 = 3$, and so on. Clearly, every such sentence is either true, in which case it is a theorem of arithmetic, or false, in which case its negation is a theorem of arithmetic. (An example of the latter would be the sentence $\sim (7 + 1 = 3)$, which is a theorem of arithmetic.)

Next, consider *quantified* sentences, such as $(x)(y)[(x + y) = (y + x)]$, $\sim (x)(x = x)$, and so on. Once again, it is clear that every such sentence is either true, in which case it is a theorem of arithmetic, or false, in which case its negation is a theorem of arithmetic.

Notice that the kind of completeness required of an axiom system for arithmetic is stronger than that required for sentential or predicate logic. We cannot require such a strict kind of completeness for logic, because axiom systems for logic contain either *contingent sentences* or *contingent sentence forms*, and neither they nor their negations are theorems of logic.

Axiom independence

An axiom of a given system is **independent** of the other axioms iff it cannot be derived from them by using the inference rules of that system. Otherwise an axiom is dependent.

Example

Assume that the eighteen rules of inference for sentential logic are (rewriting the first eight as their test statement forms) adopted as an axiom system. We can show that $(p \supset q) \equiv (\sim q \supset \sim p)$, contraposition, is not independent by deriving it from the other rules, as follow:

→ 1.	$p \supset q$	**AP**
2.	$\sim p \vee q$	1 **Impl**
3.	$q \vee \sim p$	2 **Comm**
4.	$\sim \sim q \vee \sim p$	3 **DN**
5.	$\sim q \supset \sim p$	4 **Impl**
6.	$(p \supset q) \supset (\sim q \supset \sim p)$	1–5 **CP**
→ 7.	$\sim q \supset \sim p$	**AP**
8.	$\sim \sim q \vee \sim p$	7 **Impl**
9.	$\sim p \vee \sim \sim q$	8 **Comm**
10.	$\sim p \vee q$	9 **DN**
11.	$p \supset q$	10 **Impl**
12.	$(\sim q \supset \sim p) \supset (p \supset q)$	7–11 **CP**
13.	$[(p \supset q) \supset (\sim q \supset \sim p)] \cdot$ $[(\sim q \supset \sim p) \supset (p \supset q)]$	6,12 **Conj**
14.	$(p \supset q) \equiv (\sim q \supset \sim p)$	13 **Equiv**

Naturally, the preceding proof does *not* use Contraposition, since that would make the proof viciously circular, and hence useless.

We can prove that a given axiom is *dependent* by deriving it from the other axioms of a system. But failure to find such a proof does not constitute a proof that an axiom is independent; we may simply have overlooked the proof.

To prove that an axiom is *independent* of a given set of axioms, it suffices to show that there is some characteristic or property possessed by every axiom in the given set and also possessed by every formula derivable from that set of axioms, which is not possessed by the axiom in question. This proves independence because any particular axiom that does not have a property possessed by every formula derivable from a given set of axioms itself cannot be derivable from that set and hence, itself must be independent of that set.

Decision procedure

A **decision procedure** is a mechanical method for determining in a finite number of steps whether or not a given formula is a theorem of an axiom system. For example, truth table analysis is a decision procedure for sentential logic, because it enables us to determine in a finite number of steps whether or not a given formula is a tautology and hence, a theorem of sentential logic.

The existence of a decision procedure for a given axiom system renders all questions about the theorems of that system *routinely* answerable, without the need for ingenuity in the construction of proofs. This has the advantage that all questions and disputes about whether a particular formula is a theorem of the system can be settled by the mere manipulation of symbols of the kind that computers can be programmed to perform.

Axiom systems for which there is no decision procedure are generally of more interest to logicians and mathematicians, because questions and disputes about alleged theorems of these systems, even if in principle soluble, require genius (or a good deal of luck) for their solution. Indeed, many such questions may go unanswered forever.

4   *Outline of an Axiom System for Sentential Logic*

Object language–metalanguage

We now present the bare outline of an axiom system for sentential logic. However, to do so, we must *talk about* that system. Since there is a sense in which that axiom system itself constitutes a language, we need some other language to talk about it. And since the sentential logic axiom system, "SL" for short, is the *object* of discussion, we can refer to it as the **object language,** and refer to the language used to talk about SL as the **metalanguage.**

The terms "object language" and "metalanguage" are relative. For instance, if we use German to talk about English, then German is the metalanguage. But if we use English to talk about German, then English is the metalanguage. Of course, the same language can be both object and metalanguage. For instance, in an English grammar class conducted in English, English is used to talk about itself, and hence is both object and metalanguage. (However, problems arise when we use a language to talk about its own *semantic* properties. The liar paradox discussed in Chapter Thirteen is an example.)

Quotation marks often are used to distinguish between *talk about* (or *mention of*) a language and *use of* a language. For instance, we can use English sentences to talk about, or mention, the state of Kansas. But we also can talk about, or mention, the *words used* to talk about the state of Kansas (recall the discussion in Chapter Two, Section 8). In talking about the state of Kansas, we use its English name without quotes; in talking about the word that is the name of the state, we put that word, "Kansas," in quotes. Thus we can say that "Kansas" has six letters, whereas Kansas is a state roughly in the center of the continental United States. We can also go one step further and talk about the name of the name of Kansas. Thus, we can say that "'Kansas'" contains quotation marks, whereas "Kansas" does not, and that "Kansas" is the name of a state, whereas Kansas is not (since it *is* a state). In other words, the device of quotation marks provides a convenient and automatic way for generating names of linguistic entities.

Another device used for generating names of linguistic entities is boldface and lightface type. For instance, we can use the term *w* in the object language SL and **w** in the metalanguage when we wish to talk about "*w*."

From the point of view of logic, many other methods for naming words would do just as well as the preceding two. For instance, we might refer to the word "Kansas" by the name "Art." And then we could say (truthfully) that Art has six letters, the first one "K," the second "a," and so on. But such a notation would be inconvenient to say the least.

We shall adopt ordinary English (suitably fortified with special terms to refer to the symbols of SL) as the metalanguage both of SL and of itself. But in our informal exposition, we also shall refer to many terms and expressions of SL and its metalanguage simply by placing them in quotation marks.

Syntax, semantics, pragmatics

The **syntactic properties** of a language are its *structural* properties, that is, those properties it has in abstraction from the meanings of its terms (other than the logical terms). For instance, the English sentence "John is tall" has the syntactic property of containing ten letters. And the sentence "Art is handsome and Betsy is smart" has the syntactic property of being a *conjunction*.

The **semantic properties** of a language are those properties that it possesses by virtue of the *meanings* of its terms. For instance, English has the semantic property of containing sentences stating arithmetic truths, such as "2 plus 2 equals 4," a semantic property that SL lacks. And the sentence "Snow is white" has the semantic property of containing a color term, namely the term "white." (Notice that uninterpreted systems have no semantic properties whatsoever, because their symbols have no meanings.)

The **pragmatic properties** of a language are those that it has in relation to its speakers (or users). For example, the English sentence "Snow is white" has the pragmatic property of *being believed* by many English-speaking people. And English itself has the pragmatic property of being spoken by most citizens of the United States.

Another way to look at the difference between syntax, semantics, and pragmatics is to say that the syntax of a language concerns the relationships between the elements of the language (such as letters, words, sentences, and so on), semantics the relationships between the elements of a language and the things that the language can talk about, and pragmatics the relationships between the elements of a language, the things it talks about, and the users of the language.

Little will be said here about the pragmatic properties of SL. However, bear in mind that in considering only the syntax and semantics of a language we are abstracting from the total language-use situation, which by its very nature must include language users. A "language" that no one ever uses or understands is no language at all.

Similarly, we should bear in mind that in discussing the syntax of an interpreted system, we are abstracting not only from its pragmatic properties, but also from its semantic properties.*

The symbols of SL

An axiom system for sentential logic can be either interpreted or uninterpreted.[†] The axiom system SL, to be outlined here, is an interpreted system. This means that although the primitive terms are not defined in the system, they are taken to have their usual meanings.

All the symbols of SL are primitive symbols. Among these symbols we distinguish *logical primitives* and *extralogical primitives*. (But there is no indication *within* SL whether a symbol is a logical or extralogical primitive. This distinction is made in the metalanguage. Recall the discussion in Chapter Thirteen, Section 7, of the *logical* and the *descriptive*.)

SL contains exactly four logical primitives, namely "~," " ⊃," "(," and ")," in boldface type (the last two to be used as left- and right-hand parentheses respectively).

In addition, SL contains indefinitely many *sentence variables,* **p, q, r,** and so on, as extralogical primitives.

Notice that the usual logical connectives " · ," " ∨ ," and " ≡ " do not occur in SL. They are omitted to simplify the number of primitive symbols and the number of axioms. However, their counterparts will be introduced later as *defined* terms in the metalanguage.

Definition of **wff**

Among all possible finite strings of terms of SL, some are *well-formed,* such as $((p \supset q) \supset p)$, $(p \supset \sim q)$, and so on, and some not, such as $(pp \supset \sim)$, $)(((p,$ and others. Intuitively, it is clear that all of the well-formed formulas ("*wff*" for short) of SL are sentence forms. So we could define "*wff* of SL" to mean "sentence form of SL." This would be a *semantic* definition of *wff*. But we cannot always provide semantic definitions of *wff*. For instance, we cannot do so for uninterpreted axiom systems, since they do not have semantic properties. The definition of *wff* for an uninterpreted system must therefore be *syntactic*. And since we want SL to serve as an example, we shall provide a purely syntactic definition of "*wff* of SL."

Of course, the definition of *wff* occurs in the metalanguage, not in SL itself. So we need to introduce certain terms into the metalanguage to talk about the formulas of the object language SL. For this purpose we introduce into the metalanguage the symbols *P, Q, R,* and so on, as *formula variables,* that is, as symbols in the metalanguage for which formulas in the object language can be substituted. Thus, in a given use, a formula variable denotes any formula of the object language (subject to the usual rule concerning the use of variables, which requires that in a single context every occurrence of a given variable must denote the same formula).

---

*However, in syntactic analyses, we generally do not abstract from the meanings of the logical terms of a system. This fact is frequently overlooked.

[†]Although some would deny that it makes sense to speak of an uninterpreted axiom system for any given area.

We also introduce the symbols "⊃," "~," "(," and ")," in lightface type, and stipulate (roughly) that these symbols denote the boldface type symbols "**⊃**," "**~**," "**(**," and "**)**" of the object language. (We also have available in the metalanguage the lightface type symbols *p, q, r,* and so on, that is, symbols that name particular formulas of the object language. However, these symbols are not used in the definition of *wff*.)

Finally, to facilitate talk about the object language, we introduce the symbols "∨," "~," and "≡" as *defined terms* of the metalanguage:

(D1): "$(P \lor Q)$" is defined as an abbreviation for "$(\sim P \supset Q)$."

(D2): "$(P \cdot Q)$" is defined as an abbreviation for "$\sim (\sim P \lor \sim Q)$."

(D3): "$(P \equiv Q)$" is defined as an abbreviation for "$(P \supset Q) \cdot (Q \supset P)$."

These defined terms are sometimes useful in talking about the *wff*s of SL, but they are not used in the definition of "*wff* of SL" itself.

We now are ready to define the terms of SL:

1. All sentence variables of SL are *wff*s of SL.
2. If a formula *P* is a *wff* of SL, then so is $\sim (P)$.
3. If *P* and *Q* are *wff*s of SL, then so is $(P \supset Q)$.

We further state that no formula is a *wff* of SL unless it is according to lines 1 through 3 (just given).

This definition provides an effective mechanical procedure for recognizing the *wff*s of SL. If a formula is a *wff* of SL, repeated application of the preceding definition will reveal this fact.* An infinite number of formulas of SL are *wff*s according to this definition.

To illustrate how this definition works, consider the formula $(\sim (p \supset p) \supset q)$. According to line 1 of the definition, *p* and *q* both are *wff*s. Therefore, according to line 3, $(p \supset p)$ is a *wff*; and according to line 2, $\sim (p \supset p)$ is a *wff*. Consequently, according to line 3 $(\sim (p \supset p) \supset q)$ is a *wff*.

The axioms and inference rules of SL[†]

We stipulate three *wff*s as the axioms of SL:

(A1): $(p \supset (q \supset p))$

(A2): $((p \supset (q \supset r)) \supset ((p \supset q) \supset (p \supset r)))$

(A3): $((\sim q \supset \sim p) \supset ((\sim q \supset p) \supset q))$

We also stipulate two rules of inference for SL. However, these two rules are formulated in the *metalanguage,* not in SL itself:

(R1): If $(P \supset Q)$ and *P* are either axioms or theorems of SL, then *Q* may be inferred from them.

---

*However, it does not provide an effective mechanical procedure for determining in general *whether* a formula is a *wff* of SL; that is, it does not provide a method for determining that a non-*wff* is not a *wff* of SL. But such a procedure can be provided.

†For details of a system just like SL, see Elliot Mendelson, *Introduction to Mathematical Logic* (Princeton, NJ: Van Nostrand, 1964).

(R2):   If P is an axiom or theorem of SL, then any *wff* may be substituted for any variable in P, provided that the substitution is made for every occurrence of that variable in P.

(R1) already is familiar, since it is simply Modus Ponens. **(R2)** also should be familiar, since it simply states *explicitly* the rule of substitution *used implicitly* in the sentential and predicate logics presented earlier. For instance, **(R2)** permits inferences from $(p \supset (q \supset p))$ to $(r \supset (q \supset r))$ and to $((s \supset t) \supset (q \supset (s \supset t)))$, and so on.

We now define a proof of SL as a sequence of *wffs*, all of which are axioms of SL or are inferable from the axioms by repeated applications of **(R1)** and/or **(R2)**. For example, all sequences of *wffs* of the object language having the forms

$$(P \supset (O \supset P))$$
$$(\sim P \supset (Q \supset \sim P))$$

are proofs of SL. An example would be the sequence of formulas

$$(p \supset (q \supset p))$$
$$(\sim p \supset (q \supset \sim p))$$

which constitutes a proof of SL because the second *wff* follows from the first by an application of **(R2)**, and the first is an axiom of SL.

Another example of a proof having this form is the following sequence of formulas:

$$(p \supset (q \supset p))$$
$$(\sim (r \supset s) \supset (q \supset \sim (r \supset s)))$$

which also constitutes a proof because the second *wff* follows from the first by an application of **(R2)**.

Proofs of SL tend to be quite long and very difficult to construct, which is the price we have to pay for having so few axioms and inference rules. The following is a more complex proof of SL:

$$(p \supset (q \supset p))$$
$$(p \supset ((q \supset p) \supset p))$$
$$((p \supset (q \supset r)) \supset ((p \supset q) \supset (p \supset r)))$$
$$((p \supset ((q \supset p) \supset p)) \supset ((p \supset (q \supset p)) \supset (p \supset p)))$$
$$((p \supset (q \supset p)) \supset (p \supset p))$$
$$(p \supset p)$$

This constitutes a proof of SL because the first and third lines are axioms of SL, the second line follows from the first by **(R2)**, the fourth line from the third by **(R2)**, the fifth line from the second and fourth by **(R1)**, and the sixth line from the first and fifth by **(R1)**.

We now define a **theorem of SL** as a *wff* for which a proof can be given in SL. Thus, the *wff* $(\sim p \supset (q \supset \sim p))$ is a theorem of SL, since it follows from the axiom $(p \supset (q \supset p))$ by an application of **(R2)**, and consequently a proof for it can be given in SL. (Of course, the *fact* that it is a theorem of SL, and the *fact* that the two preceding formulas constitute a proof of SL, cannot be stated within SL itself, but must be stated in the metalanguage.)

Properties of SL

Earlier, we discussed the properties, such as completeness, consistency, expressive completeness, and so on, that we want axiom systems to possess. The question arises as to which of these properties are possessed by SL, and the answer is that SL possesses all of them.

It has been proved that SL is complete (in the sense that every tautology is a theorem of SL), consistent, and expressively complete. In addition, it has been proved that there is a decision procedure for SL (namely, truth table analysis), and that its axioms are independent.*

5 *Axiom Systems for Predicate Logic*

Axiom systems for first-order predicate logic are quite similar to those for sentential logic. (Indeed, to be complete, a system for predicate logic must contain a system for sentential logic as a part.) Let's briefly examine a particular system of this kind, which we'll call "QL" (for quantifier logic).

The symbols of QL

The primitive symbols of QL will be those of SL plus a set of predicate symbols **F, G, H,** and so on, a set of variables **x, y, z,** and so on, and the symbol **U,** used to denote the *universal quantifier.*

In addition, we introduce the symbol *U* into the metalanguage to denote the symbol *U* of the object language, the symbol *u* as a metalanguage variable ranging over the object language variables **x, y, z,** and also the symbol "∃," which is introduced by means of the following definition:

" (∃u)**P** " is defined as an abbreviation for "~ (Uu) ~ P."

Let's take infinitely many formulas as axioms of QL, and introduce five axiom patterns in the metalanguage, using the letters *P, Q,* and *R* as formula variables, as before, and the letters *u* and *w* as metalinguistic variables ranging over the object language individual variables **x, y, z,** and so on:

(A1): $(P \supset (Q \supset P))$

(A2): $((P \supset (Q \supset R)) \supset ((P \supset Q) \supset (P \supset R)))$

(A3): $((\sim Q \supset \sim P) \supset ((\sim Q \supset P) \supset Q))$

(A4): $(Uu)(P \supset Q) \supset (P \supset (Uu)Q)$, where *P* contains no free occurrence of the variable *u*.

(A5): $(Uu)P \supset Q$, where *Q* results from *P* by the replacement of all free occurrences of *u* in *P* by *w*, and *w* occurs free in *Q* at all places at which *u* occurs free in *P*.†

The Inference Rules of QL

We introduce (into the metalanguage) two rules of inference for QL:

(R1):   If $(P \supset Q)$ and P are either axioms or theorems of QL, then Q may be inferred from them.

(R2):   If P is an axiom or theorem of QL, then $(Uu)P$ may be inferred from P.*

Properties of QL

It has been proved that QL is complete (in the sense that all sentence forms expressible in QL that are theorems of logic are provable as theorems of QL), consistent, and expressively complete. In addition, it has been proved that the axioms of QL are independent. However, not only is there no known decision procedure for QL, but it has been proved that there cannot be such a decision procedure.[†] This fact is of vital importance because the existence of a decision procedure for predicate logic would make possible the construction of a machine capable of answering all questions about predicate logic in a purely mechanical way.

6 *Other Kinds of Axiom Systems*

Some philosophers have held that axiom systems are the ideal way to systematize in the *sciences,* just as in logic or mathematics, although as a matter of fact very few axiom systems for science have been attempted.

(1) As stated previously, we want an axiom system for arithmetic to be complete in a different sense than is required for logic. The difference stems from the fact that (roughly) systems for logic can express *contingent* sentences while those for arithmetic cannot. And since they cannot, all their well-formed formulas that are sentences will be either *truths of arithmetic* or *negations of truths of arithmetic.* Hence, to be complete, an axiom system for arithmetic must be such that every sentence expressible in the system is either a theorem of that system or the negation of a theorem of that system.

(2) There are axiom systems for sentential and predicate logic that have been proved to be complete. Unfortunately, not only has no completeness proof been discovered for arithmetic, but it has been proved that *there cannot be a complete axiom system for all of arithmetic.*[‡] No matter how many axioms and theorems such a system contains, we can always find some truth of arithmetic that is not a theorem

---

*(R2) of QL corresponds to the rule **UG** introduced in Chapter Nine. Because QL contains infinitely many axioms, it doesn't have to contain a rule of inference similar to the **(R2)** of SL.

[†]The proof was first given by Alonzo Church. For details on this and related topics, see S. C. Kleene, *Introduction to Meta-Mathematics* (New York: Van Nostrand, 1952).

[‡]More precisely, what has been proved is that there cannot be a complete and consistent axiom system for arithmetic. Obviously, an inconsistent system could be constructed that would be complete, but such a system would be worthless. The famous proof that arithmetic is essentially incomplete is by Kurt Gödel. For details, see S. C. Kleene, *Introduction to Meta-Mathematics.*

of that system. Indeed, having found such a truth, it won't help matters to add it to the list of axioms of the system, for it has been proved that no matter how many times we do this, there will always be other truths of arithmetic discoverable that are still not axioms or theorems of the system.

The proof that we cannot have a complete axiom system for arithmetic is widely regarded as one of the most important proofs about arithmetic ever constructed.

(3) It also has been proved that *there can be no decision procedure for axiom systems for arithmetic.* Thus, just as in the case of predicate logic, we can never construct a computer that will solve all the problems of arithmetic in a purely mechanical way.

(4) Perhaps there is some consolation in the fact that proofs of consistency have been constructed for axiom systems for certain parts of arithmetic, and that decision procedures also have been devised for portions of arithmetic.

7 *Objections to Axiom Systems*

Finally, let's note that some philosophers are less than enthusiastic concerning the construction of axiom systems. One reason for this lack of enthusiasm is that the construction of an axiom system (at least for logic) involves a certain amount of *vicious circularity.*

Take an axiom system for predicate logic. Suppose we want to prove that such a system is *consistent.* The trouble is that a proof of consistency (in the metalanguage) unavoidably uses the very "tools of reasoning" (such as Modus Ponens) that are taken as inference rules in the system itself. Now if these "tools of reasoning" themselves are consistent, then a proof that the object language system is consistent is worthwhile. However, if they are inconsistent, then such a proof is worthless. So no progress is made by constructing a consistency proof, since we have to believe ahead of time in the consistency of the very rules of inference that the consistency proof establishes as consistent.*

Key Terms Introduced in Chapter Seventeen

axioms: Underived formulas for which no justification is provided within the system.

complete (axiom system): An axiom system is complete iff all the formulas we *desire to* prove as theorems of the system in fact are provable as theorems of that system.

consistent (axiom system): An axiom system is consistent iff contradictory formulas cannot be derived from its axioms by means of its rules of inference.

decision procedure: A decision procedure is a mechanical method for determining in a finite number of steps whether or not a given formula is a theorem of an axiom system.

---

*The same is true for the *axioms* of the system. Indeed, to be precise, we should speak of the consistency of the rules of inference *and* axioms taken as a unit.

defined symbols: Symbols for which explicit definitions are presented.

derived inference rules: The rules of an axiom system for which a justification is provided by using other rules in the system.

expressively complete: An axiom system is expressively complete iff its language is rich enough to express everything that the system is intended to express.

extralogical or **nonlogical symbols:** Symbols other than logical symbols. The meaning of these symbols will vary depending on the area of knowledge to be systematized.

independent (axiom system): An axiom of a given system is independent of the other axioms if it cannot be derived from them by using the inference rules of that system.

interpreted axiom system: An axiom system for which all of the primitive terms are assigned a meaning or interpretation.

logical symbols: Symbols that represent logical operators such as "and," "not," "some," and so on.

metalanguage: When talking about the properties of a particular language the metalanguage is the language that is used to talk about the object language.

object language: When talking about the properties of a particular language the object language is the language that is the object of discussion.

pragmatic properties: The pragmatic properties of a language are those that it has in relation to its speakers (or users). For example, the English sentence "Snow is white" has the pragmatic property of *being believed* by many English-speaking people. And English itself has the pragmatic property of being spoken by most citizens of the United States.

primitive inference rules: Rules in an axiom system for which no justification is provided within the system.

primitive (undefined) symbols: Symbols for which no definitions are presented.

semantic properties: The semantic properties of a language are those properties that it possesses by virtue of the *meanings* of its terms.

syntactic properties: The syntactic properties of a language are its *structural* properties, that is, those properties it has in abstraction from the meanings of its terms (other than the logical terms).

theorems: Formulas that can be derived from the axioms by means of the inference rules of the system.

uninterpreted axiom system: An axiom system in which the primitive symbols not only are not defined *within* the system, but are given no meaning or interpretation whatever.

well-formed formulas (*wffs*): A string of symbols that is properly put together according to the "gramatical" rules of a system. For example, strings such as $p \supset q$ and $\sim [(A \vee B) \supset \sim C]$ are well-formed formulas in sentential logic, whereas $(pq \vee$ and $AB) \vee$ are not.

Chapter Eighteen

Alternative Logics

The predicate logic developed earlier in this text, many claim, cannot adequately capture the logical structure of many valid arguments. To correct this deficiency, alternative systems of logic have been devised. In this chapter we will briefly introduce three such systems: modal logics, deontic logics, and epistemic logics.

1 Modal Logic

Modal logic is designed to express the logic structure of sentences that contain **modal terms,** that is, terms such as "possible," "necessary," and their variants.* To extend sentential logic to handle modal sentences, we must add at least one symbol denoting a modal term. Let's introduce the diamond symbol "$\Diamond$" as the **possibility operator,** used to symbolize sentences expressing possibilities. For instance, using the possibility operator, we can symbolize "A is possible" as $\Diamond A$.

Examples

Here are some basic sentences that can be symbolized using the possibility operator (letting S = "Snow is white"):

Symbolization	English Sentence
1. $\Diamond S$	1. It's possible that snow is white.
2. $\Diamond \sim S$	2. It's possible that snow isn't white.
3. $\sim \Diamond S$	3. It's not possible that snow is white.
4. $\sim \Diamond \sim S$	4. It's not possible that snow isn't white.

---

*For more details on modal logic than are presented in this book, see G. E. Hughes and M. J. Cresswell, *Introduction to Modal Logic* (London: Methuen, 1968) and (particularly for the so-called Lewis systems) C. I. Lewis and C. H. Langford, *Symbolic Logic*, 2nd ed. (New York: Dover, 1959).

After one modal symbol has been introduced, others can be defined in terms of it. For instance, we can define the **necessity operator** "$\Box$" by the following definition:

$$\Box p = df \sim \Diamond \sim p*$$

To say, for instance, that it's not possible that snow *isn't* white, in symbols $\sim \Diamond \sim S$, is, after all, to say exactly that it's necessary that snow *is* white. $\Box S$, then, has the same meaning as $\sim \Diamond \sim S$.

Similarly, to say that it's impossible that snow is white is to say that it's necessary that snow isn't white. So the formula $\sim \Diamond S$, is logically equivalent to $\Box \sim S$.

In fact, as should now be apparent, the possibility and necessity operators are linked in exactly the same way as are the existential and universal quantifiers of predicate logic.

Examples

Here are four logical equivalences relating the existential and universal quantifiers and the analogous equivalences relating the possibility and necessity operators:

Quantifier Equivalences   **Modal Equivalences**

1. $(x)p :: \sim (\exists x) \sim p$ 1. $\Box p :: \sim \Diamond \sim p$
2. $(\exists x)p :: \sim (x) \sim p$ 2. $\Diamond p :: \sim \Box \sim p$
3. $(x) \sim p :: \sim (\exists x)p$ 3. $\Box \sim p :: \sim (\Diamond)p$
4. $(\exists x) \sim p :: \sim (x)p$ 4. $\Diamond \sim p :: \sim \Box p$

2 *Strict Implication*

There are different kinds of possibilities and necessities. For instance, we might mean by "necessarily *p*" that *p* is **logically necessary** (true because of the laws of logic) or that it is **physically necessary** (true because of the laws of nature). Modal logic systems have been developed to capture the ideas of logical necessity, logical possibility, and logical impossibility. In particular, a modal logic seems to be needed to capture the concepts of **logical entailment** (or **logical implication**) and **logical equivalence.**

Take the notion of logical implication, or entailment. If *p* logically implies *q*, we can't symbolize that fact as $p \supset q$, because $p \supset q$ is too weak. It might be true, for instance, simply because *p* is false, and not because its truth logically implies the truth of *q*.

But by using modal operators, we can symbolize statements of logical implication quite easily. For *p logically implies q if, and only if, $p \supset q$ is a theorem of logic*, and thus

---

*We introduce the symbol "$= df$" to abbreviate "is defined as."

necessarily true.* Letting the symbol "$\Rightarrow$" stand for logical implication, or as it is usually called, **strict implication,** we can introduce the following definition:

$$(p \Rightarrow q) = df \,\square\, (p \supset q)$$

Examples

Here are some sentences and their correct symbolizations, using first the necessity operator and then the symbol for strict implication:

1. $(A \cdot B)$ logically entails A.
   $\square\, [(A \cdot B) \supset A]$
   $(A \cdot B) \Rightarrow A$

2. $(B \supset C)$ logically implies $(\sim C \supset \sim B)$.
   $\square\, [(B \supset C) \supset (\sim C \supset \sim B)]$
   $(B \supset C) \Rightarrow (\sim C \supset \sim B)$

3. $[A \vee (B \cdot C)]$ entails $[(A \vee B) \cdot (A \vee C)]$.
   $\square\, \{[A \vee (B \cdot C)] \supset [(A \vee B) \cdot (A \vee C)]\}$
   $[A \vee (B \cdot C)] \Rightarrow [(A \vee B) \cdot (A \vee C)]$

4. $(A \supset B)$ logically implies $(B \supset A)$.
   $\square\, [(A \supset B) \supset (B \supset A)]$
   $(A \supset B) \Rightarrow (B \supset A)$

(Of course, this last sentence is false, but we must be able to symbolize false sentences, also.)

It is important that the difference between "$\Rightarrow$" and "$\supset$" be grasped quite clearly, and that it be understood why "$\supset$" does not capture the sense of logical implication. Take the modal sentence "'Anna is smart' logically implies 'Bob is bombastic,'" Letting A = "Anna is smart" and B = "Bob is bombastic," we can symbolize the sentence as "$A \Rightarrow B$." Now if A and B both are true, then $A \supset B$ will be true. But $A \Rightarrow B$ is false, no matter what the truth values of A and B, since A does not logically imply B. That is, $A \Rightarrow B$ is false because "A /$\therefore$ B" is not a valid deductive argument (even if A and B both happen to be true).[†]

Now let's introduce a symbol for logical equivalence, bearing in mind that two sentences are *logically equivalent* if, and only if, they logically imply each other. Letting the symbol "$\Leftrightarrow$" represent logical equivalence, we can introduce the following definition:

$$p \Leftrightarrow q = df (p \Rightarrow q) \cdot (q \Rightarrow p)$$

---

*Or in the case of sentence forms, if and only if all its substitution instances are true.

[†]This account of the logical necessity captured by the "$\Rightarrow$" symbol avoids the controversy over semantic analytic truths. Most philosophers want the notion of logical implication to be wide enough to make, say, "(Art is a bachelor) $\Rightarrow$ (Art is unmarried)" a true modal statement, but some do not.

Examples

Here are some equivalences and their translations using the symbol for logical equivalence:

1. $(A \cdot B)$ is logically equivalent to $(B \cdot A)$.

    $(A \cdot B) \Leftrightarrow (B \cdot A)$
2. $(A \supset B)$ is logically equivalent to $(\sim B \supset \sim A)$.

    $(A \supset B) \Leftrightarrow (\sim B \supset \sim A)$
3. $(A \cdot B)$ is logically equivalent to A.

    $(A \cdot B) \Leftrightarrow A$

(Of course, this last sentence is false.)

3 *Modal Axioms*

The philosopher C. I. Lewis constructed the first axiom systems for sentential modal logic. Indeed, he constructed several nonequivalent modal systems.

The fact that *nonequivalent* systems have been proposed and argued about illustrates a difference in status between the ordinary truth-functional logic and non–truth-functional modal logic; modal logic is much more controversial than ordinary truth-functional logic. It is true that some argue against sentential or predicate logic on the grounds that they cannot adequately handle some of the non–truth-functional sentences of natural languages. But no one would argue that any of the axioms of an axiomatized sentential or predicate logic are *false*. Yet that is precisely the situation for modal logic. Modal axioms have been proposed whose very truth is in question.

Let's now examine the Lewis modal axioms (passing over the technical details of his systems). Here are eleven of his axioms, used by Lewis in developing his modal systems S1 through S5 (along with some of their sentential logic analogs):*

Modal Axiom	**Sentential Logic Analog**	
(1) $(p \cdot q) \Rightarrow (q \cdot p)$	$(p \cdot q) \supset (q \cdot p)$	(Comm)
(2) $(p \cdot q) \Rightarrow p$	$(p \cdot q) \supset p$	(Simp)
(3) $p \Rightarrow (p \cdot p)$	$p \supset (p \cdot p)$	(Taut)
(4) $[(p \cdot q) \cdot r] \Rightarrow [p \cdot (q \cdot r)]$	$[(p \cdot q) \cdot r] \supset [p \cdot (q \cdot r)]$	(Assoc)
(5) $p \Rightarrow \sim \sim p$	$p \supset \sim \sim p$	(DN)
(6) $[(p \Rightarrow q) \cdot (q \Rightarrow r)] \Rightarrow (p \Rightarrow r)$	$[(p \supset q) \cdot (q \supset r)] \supset (p \supset r)$	(HS)

---

*With minor changes.

(7) $[p \cdot (p \Rightarrow q)] \Rightarrow q$ $[p \cdot (p \supset q)] \supset q$ **(MP)**
(8) $\Diamond (p \cdot q) \Rightarrow \Diamond p$
(9) $(p \Rightarrow q) \Rightarrow (\sim \Diamond q \Rightarrow \sim \Diamond p)$
(10) $\Box p \Rightarrow \Box \Box p$
(11) $\Diamond p \Rightarrow \Box \Diamond p$

The system S1 contains the first seven axioms (axiom (5) incidentally, can be derived from the others and is thus superfluous); S2 the first seven plus (8); S3 the first seven plus (9); S4 the first seven plus (10); and S5 the first seven plus (11). It has been proved that every theorem of S1 is a theorem of S2, every theorem of S2 a theorem of S3, and so on (but not vice versa). Thus, as you go up the Lewis modal ladder, the systems get stronger and stronger. (The problem is just how strong the *right* system should be.)

Axiom (10) has generated a great deal of controversy. Take as an example the necessary sentence "Snow is white or it isn't." Clearly, that sentence is necessary, since it is a logical truth. But is it *necessary* that it is necessary? Opinions seem to differ. (It should also be noted that adoption of S5 leads to the interesting consequence that all modal propositions will be either necessarily true or necessarily false, a consequence that some find unacceptable.)

4 *Modal Theorems*

There is a very close resemblance between the theorems (counting axioms as theorems) of modal logic and the theorems of sentential logic that correspond to the valid argument forms discussed in Part One. With three exceptions, these theorems parallel one another. For instance, corresponding to the theorem we might by extension call *Modus Ponens,* namely, $[p \cdot (p \supset q)] \supset q$, is the modal theorem $[p \cdot (p \Rightarrow q)] \Rightarrow q$. The three exceptions are *Implication, Exportation,* and one version of *Equivalence.* (In particular, $(p \Rightarrow q) \Leftrightarrow (\sim p \vee q)$, the modal parallel to *Implication, is not* a modal theorem.) However, for each of these there are slightly altered parallels. Thus, for *Implication* there is $(p \Rightarrow q) \Rightarrow (\sim p \vee q)$, for *Exportation* there is $[(p \cdot q) \Rightarrow r] \Leftrightarrow [p \Rightarrow (q \supset r)]$, and for *Equivalence* there is $(p \Leftrightarrow q) \Rightarrow (p \cdot q) \vee (\sim p \cdot \sim q)]$.

Here are some other interesting theorems of modal logic, all provable in S5, although some are not provable in S4, S3, S2, or S1, and thus are controversial:

1. $(p \Rightarrow q) \Rightarrow (p \supset q)$
2. $(p \Leftrightarrow q) \Rightarrow (p \equiv q)$
3. $(p \Leftrightarrow q) \Leftrightarrow (p \Leftrightarrow q)$
4. $(p \Rightarrow q) \supset (p \Rightarrow q)$
5. $\Diamond p \Rightarrow \sim \Diamond \sim \Diamond p$
6. $\Box \Box p \Rightarrow \Box \Box \Box p$
7. $\Diamond p \Rightarrow \Diamond \Diamond p$

8. $\square\,(p \cdot q) \Leftrightarrow (\square\,p \cdot \square\,q)$
9. $\lozenge\,(p \vee q) \Leftrightarrow (\lozenge\,p \vee \lozenge\,q)$
10. $\lozenge\,(p \cdot q) \Rightarrow (\lozenge\,p \cdot \lozenge\,q)$ (But not vice versa.)
11. $(\lozenge\,p \vee \lozenge\,q) \Rightarrow \lozenge\,(p \vee q)$ (But not vice versa.)

5 *Modal Paradoxes*

When he developed his modal systems, Lewis pointed out that there are apparently para-doxical theorems in modal logic analogous to the alleged paradoxes of material implica-tion.* One example is this theorem:

$$\sim \lozenge\,p \Rightarrow (p \Rightarrow q)$$

But Lewis felt that this theorem is acceptable, despite its apparent paradoxicality. For it merely states the principle behind the rule of indirect proof (reductio ad absurdum)—that what is contradictory (not possible) logically implies anything and everything.

Another theorem that appears paradoxical is this one:

$$\square\,p \Rightarrow (q \Rightarrow p)$$

Lewis felt this theorem also is acceptable, because it merely states the principle that we can deduce a tautology (necessarily true sentence) from any sentence whatever, which must be accepted since a tautology can be deduced even from the null set of premises.

6 *A Philosophical Problem*

At the beginning of this chapter we introduced the topic of modal logic by saying that it is *claimed* by many that we need a special logic to deal with sentences containing modal terms. The word "claimed" was inserted because some deny that a special modal logic is needed at all.[†]

One objection is that if "$\square\,p$" *means* the same as "*p* is a theorem of logic," or "*p* is provable," then the statements of modal logic all become statements expressible in the *metalanguage* of any given system without the need to introduce special modal symbols.[‡] But lurking behind the dispute is the more serious question of exactly what necessity, pos-sibility, and so on, consist of. One view is that necessity is a purely linguistic concept. A theorem is provable, according to this view, precisely because of linguistic conventions. That is, a theorem is true just because of the meanings of its terms. (This theory is con-

---

*Recall our brief discussion on page 305.

[†]See, for instance, Gustav Bergmann, "The Philosophical Significance of Modal Logic," *Mind*, vol. 69 (1960), pp. 466–485.

[‡]Another is that in any event the term "modal *logic*" is a misnomer because the axioms of modal logic are not *logical* truths, containing as they do nonlogical constants such as "$\square$" and "$\lozenge$."

sistent with the view that theorems of logic and logical truths are provable from the null set of premises precisely because they are empty of factual content.)

On the other side are those who insist that necessity is more than merely linguistic, that necessities are real and independent of language conventions or even the existence of language users.

Those who hold the latter view tend to accept the principle that $\Box p \Rightarrow \Box \Box p$ (sometimes called the *axiom of reiterated necessity*). Those who hold the former view (that necessity is essentially linguistic) deny that principle, because if "$\Box p$" *means* the same as "*p* is a theorem of logic," then the axiom of reiteration would appear false. (To be true, it would have to be the case that the statement "*p* is a theorem of sentential logic" is itself a theorem of sentential logic, which it is not.)

7 *Modal Predicate Logic*

So far, we have been discussing modal extensions of sentential logic, a fairly controversial topic. Now let's very briefly discuss modal *predicate* systems, an even more controversial area.

There are two important problems with modal predicate logic systems, in addition to the ones it inherits from modal sentential logic. The first concerns the validity in modal logic of the four quantifier rules, as well as the rule of *identity* (π**ID**).*

Consider the following argument (where *a* = "the number of planets"):

1. $(x)[(x = 9) \supset \Box (x > 7)]$ p
2. $a = 9$ p /∴ $\Box (a > 7)$
3. $(a = 9) \supset \Box (a > 7)$ 1 **UI**
4. $\Box (a > 7)$ 2,3 **MP**

It appears that both premises are true, and the conclusion false (since it isn't necessary that the number of planets be greater than seven). And yet the conclusion follows from the premises by the normal inference rules of predicate logic (in this case **UI** and **MP**).

Examples of this kind have elicited several different responses. One, of course, is simply to reject modal predicate logic entirely, as ill conceived. Another is to devise restrictions on the four quantifier rules (as well as the rule of identity, to handle related problems arising from the use of that rule). For instance, we seem able to block undesirable consequences of the kind just illustrated by placing a new restriction on the general schema for **UI**:[†]

$(u)(\ldots u \ldots)$
/∴ $(\ldots w \ldots) \ldots$

Proviso: No *u* free in . . . *u* . . . is within the scope of a necessity operator, unless (. . . *w* . . .) is necessary [that is, unless $\Box$ (. . . *w* . . .)].

---

*See for instance, W. V. Quine, "Notes on Existence and Necessity," *Journal of Philosophy*, vol. 40 (1943), pp. 113–127.

[†]See Richard L. Purtill, *Logic for Philosophers* (New York: Harper & Row, 1971), pp. 289–291.

This seems to eliminate the troublesome use of **UI** in the preceding example because the *x* in the phrase "*x* > 7" on line 1 is within the scope of a necessity operator. (But it doesn't rule out the legitimate use of **UI** in the inference from, say, $(x)[(x = 9) \supset \Box (x > 7)]$ to $(3^2 = 9) \supset \Box (3^2 > 7)$, because the latter is necessarily true.)

Finally, another way out of the problem is to argue that despite appearances, rule **UI** is universally valid in modal predicate logic. Take the example in question. Either *a* (the expression "the number of planets") designates the number 9, or it does not. If it does, then premise 2 is true. *But so is the argument's conclusion,* since the number 9 necessarily is greater than 7. So if *a* designates the number 9, the argument in question does not take us from true premises to a false conclusion, and we haven't proved the inference pattern invalid.

Now suppose that *a* does *not* designate the number 9. Then premise 2 is false, since it asserts that *a* is identical with the number 9, which must be false if *a* does not designate the number 9. (Obviously, only the number 9 is identical with the number 9, so if *a* does not designate that number, what it does designate cannot be identical with the number 9.) So if *a* does not designate the number 9, one of the premises is false, we have not gone from true premises to a false conclusion, and thus have not proved that the argument schema is invalid in modal predicate logic. It may well be valid after all.

A second important problem for modal predicate logic is simply to decide which of the many plausible candidates should be accepted as *theorems* of modal predicate logic. Let's end our very brief discussion of modal logic by listing a few theorem candidates, then explaining why some of them are controversial (letting *p* and *q* be any well-formed formulas and "(u)" and "$(\exists u)$" be, respectively, any universal or existential quantifiers):

(A) $(\exists u) \Box p \Rightarrow \Box (\exists u)p$
(B) $\Diamond (u)p \Rightarrow (u) \Diamond p$
(C) $(\exists u) \Diamond p \Leftrightarrow \Diamond (\exists u)p$
(D) $\Box (u)p \Leftrightarrow (u) \Box p$
(E) $\Box (u)(p \supset q) \supset \Box [(u)p \supset (u)q]$
(F) $(u) \Box (p \supset q) \supset \Box [(u)p \supset (u)q]$

The first two of these formulas, while intuitively unobjectionable, are interesting because they generally are believed not to hold in the opposite direction. Take the reverse of (A), namely $\Box (\exists u)p \Rightarrow (\exists u) \Box p$, and consider the substitution instance $\Box (\exists x)Nx \Rightarrow (\exists x) \Box Nx$, where Nx = "*x* is the number of planets." The antecedent of this expression states that necessarily some *x* is the number of planets, which is true, because even if there were no planets, there still would of necessity be some number of planets (namely, zero). But the consequent of this expression seems to be false, because there is no number that *necessarily* is the number of planets (since the actual number of planets is a contingent and not a necessary fact—logic does not dictate that there be exactly nine planets).

Now consider the reverse of (B), namely, $(u) \Diamond p \Rightarrow \Diamond (u)p$, and consider the substitution instance $(x) \Diamond Nx \Rightarrow \Diamond (x)Nx$, where again Nx = "*x* is the number of planets." The antecedent of this expression states that given any *x*, it is possible that *x* is the number of planets, which is true because logic does not require that there be any certain number of planets (instead of nine there might have been eight or seven or a million, so far as logic is concerned). But the consequent of this expression is false because it is not possible that *every* number be the actual number of planets.

While (A) and (B), just given, are generally accepted, and their reverses generally rejected, (C) seems more problematic. Consider, for instance, the substitution instance $(\exists x) \diamond Fx \Leftrightarrow \diamond (\exists x)Fx$, where Fx = "x is on fire."* If we suppose that $(\exists x) \diamond Fx$ translates back into English as "There is something that may be on fire" and $\diamond (\exists x)Fx$ as "There may be something on fire," then clearly the two do not strictly imply each other. So if we want to accept (C) as a legitimate modal theorem, we must find some other translation for the substitution instance in question.[†]

Theorem (D), given earlier, is also extremely controversial. Specifically, the controversy centers on a particular consequence of (D), namely, the formula $(u) \Box p \Rightarrow \Box (u)p$, called the **Barcan Formula.**[‡]

At first glance, this formula seems acceptable. But consider one of its instances, say the sentence $(x) \Box Tx \Rightarrow \Box (x)Tx$, where Tx = "x is triangular." In the actual universe, the antecedent of this statement is false, and hence the whole statement is true. But logical principles have to be valid in all possible universes, not just the real one. So imagine a universe containing nothing but trilaterals. Then, since all triangles are necessarily also trilaterals, the left-hand side of the Barcan substitution instance, namely, $(x) \Box Tx$, will be true. But the right-hand side, namely, $\Box (x)Tx$, appears to be false. Even though *in fact* all x's would be triangular in the world we have just imagined, it wouldn't be *necessary* that all things in that universe be triangular; it *might* have contained some squares, circles, or other nontriangles.

Hence it is argued that the Barcan Formula is not acceptable. (Since the Barcan Formula can be derived as a theorem in any modal predicate logic containing the Lewis system S5 as its sentential component, those who reject the Barcan Formula also have to reject S5. Conversely, those who accept the Barcan Formula are almost certainly committed to accepting S5.)

8 Epistemic Logic: The Logic of Knowledge and Belief

In discussing the limitations of predicate logic (Chapter Thirteen), we pointed out that it is not clear whether predicate logic can adequately handle sentences containing so-called belief contexts, such as the sentence "Art believes he'll go to the show." Attempts to develop a logic of knowledge and belief, an **epistemic logic,** are intended to extend predicate logic so that it can deal with such cases.

---

*The example is from W. Kneale and M. Kneale, *The Development of Logic* (London: Oxford University Press, 1962), p. 615.
[†]For instance, see Purtill, pp. 263–265.
[‡]After Ruth Barcan Marcus, See her article "A Functional Calculus of First Order Based on Strict Implication," *Journal of Symbolic Logic,* vol. II (1946), p. 2.

The application of the standard rules of predicate logic to epistemic contexts is in doubt, just as is their application in modal contexts. Here is an example in which the rule of *identity*, **ID**, seems to fail when used in an epistemic context:

1. Art believes that Mark Twain wrote *Huckleberry Finn*.   p
2. Mark Twain = Samuel Clemens.   p
3. Art believes that Samuel Clemens wrote *Huckleberry Finn*.   1,2 **ID**

If we let Bxy = "x believes that y," t = "Mark Twain," c = "Samuel Clemens," h = "*Huckleberry Finn*," a = "Art," and Wxy = "x wrote y," then we can symbolize the preceding argument as

1. $Ba (Wth)$ p
2. $t = c$ p
3. $Ba (Wch)$ 1,2 **ID**

The problem with this example is this: Suppose Art happens to be ignorant of the fact that Mark Twain and Samuel Clemens are the same person. Then it seems possible for premises 1 and 2 of this argument both to be true when the conclusion 3 is false. If so, then it is possible to go from true premises to a false conclusion by the rule of *identity*, something no valid system may permit.

Now let's look at an example where it is claimed that the quantifier rule **EG** gets us into trouble:*

1. Philip is unaware that Tully denounced Cataline.   p
2. Some x is such that Philip is unaware that x denounced Cataline.   1 **EG**

Letting Uxy = "x is unaware that y," and using other obvious abbreviations, we can symbolize this argument as

1. $Up (Dtc)$ p
2. $(\exists x)Up(Dxc)$ 1 **EG**

Suppose we assume that Philip really is not aware that Tully denounced Cataline, but is aware that Cicero did, even though (unknown to Philip) Tully = Cicero. Then, it has been argued, although 1 is true, 2 is false. For who is the x who denounced Cataline without Philip learning of that fact? Tully, that is, Cicero? No, because this would conflict with the fact that the statement "Philip is unaware that Cicero denounced Cataline" is false. Hence the inference from 1 to 2, it is claimed, is invalid.

Finally, consider one more example. Suppose it is true that some little child, say Virginia, believes that Santa Claus comes down her chimney every Christmas bringing toys. Then using rule **EG**, we can construct the following apparently invalid argument (letting Cx = "x comes down Virginia's chimney on Christmas," g = "Virginia," and c = "Santa Claus"):

---

*The example is from W. V. Quine, "Notes on Existence and Necessity," *Journal of Philosophy*, vol. 40 (1943), pp. 117–118. Quine claims that this example shows rule **EG** must be restricted in epistemic contexts.

1. *Bg(Cc)*
2. (∃x)*Bg(Cx)*   1 **EG**

Again, we seem hard pressed to find an *x* that would make 2 a true statement. In particular, Santa Claus does not seem to be such an *x*, because, sad to relate, Virginia, there *is* no Santa Claus.

We can't go into all the claims and counterclaims on this topic, but let's briefly look into a line of reasoning that parallels the defense (discussed on page 432) of the use of **UI** in modal contexts.

Consider again the argument.

1. *Ba(Wth)*   p
2. *t = c*   p
3. *Ba(Wch)*   1,2 **ID**

Either *c* designates the person Mark Twain or it does not. Suppose it does. (We're assuming, of course, that the term *t* designates the person Mark Twain.) Then if premise 1 is true (if Art believes the person Mark Twain wrote *Huckleberry Finn*), then so is the conclusion true (that Art believes the person Sam Clemens (also known as Mark Twain) wrote *Huckleberry Finn*). We thus will have moved from true premises to a true conclusion, and so the argument will be valid. Therefore this case can't be an example of the failure of **ID** in epistemic contexts.

Now suppose *c* does not designate the person Mark Twain. Then the second premise of this argument, which states that *t = c*, will be false (given that *t* does designate Mark Twain). We thus will not have moved from true premises to a false conclusion, and so this case can't be an example of the failure of **ID** in epistemic contexts.

In like manner, it is claimed, all the varied examples alleged to illustrate the validity of rule **ID** in epistemic contexts can be successfully rebutted.

It also is claimed that some (but not all) of the alleged counterexamples to the legitimacy of rule **EG** in epistemic contexts can be easily disposed of. Recall the one just given about Philip being unaware that Tully denounced Cataline:

1. *Up(Dtc)*   p
2. (∃x)*Up(Dxc)*   1 **EG**

It was objected that although 1 is true, 2 is false, since there seems to be no *x* who denounced Cataline without Philip learning of that fact.

But surely, if there is no such *x*, then premise 1 is false (and so we will not have moved from true to false). After all, for Philip to be unaware that Tully was the denouncer, there must be an *x*, namely Tully, whose actions Philip is unaware of; if there is no such *x*, then Philip can't be unaware of his actions, and premise 1 will be false. (What is true, of course, is that Philip is unaware that the person he knows as Cicero also was known as Tully.)

9   *Epistemic Theorems*

A second problem for epistemic logic, again paralleling modal predicate logic, is the difficulty in deciding which epistemic statements we want to be theorems of epistemic logic.

Here are a few of the obvious candidates (letting *Kap* = "*a* knows that *p*"; and *Bap* = "*a* believes that *p*"):

(1) *Kap ⊃ Bap*
(2) *Ka ~ p ⊃ ~ Bap*
(3) *~ Kap ⊃ Ba ~ p*
(4) *Kap ⊃ p*
(5) *Bap ⊃ p*
(6) *Kap ⊃ KaKap*
(7) *Bap ⊃ BaBap*
(8) *Bap ⊃ KaBap*
(9) *Kap ⊃ BaKap*

Of these, (3) and (5) clearly are inadmissible. From the fact that Art doesn't know that Sophia is the capital of Bulgaria, it doesn't follow that he believes it *isn't* the capital of Bulgaria. So (3) must be rejected. And from the fact that Johnny believes Santa Claus comes down his chimney, it doesn't follow that Santa actually does so. So (5) must be rejected.

However, (1) clearly is acceptable; you can't know something without believing it. But all the others, however plausible they may initially appear, are open to doubt, or at least some have thought so.

Take (6), often called the **KK thesis,** according to which if you know something, it follows that you know you know that thing. One argument against the KK thesis is this:* For a person *a* to know something, *a* must *understand* that thing. Hence, to know *p*, *a* has to understand *p*. But for *a* to know that *a* knows *p*, *a* must understand not only *p* but also the sentence "*Kap.*" It seems possible for *a* to understand *p*, but not understand "*Kap,*" and hence possible that *a* knows *p*, but does not know that *a* knows *p*.

Since similar remarks seem to apply to believing, formulas (7), (8), and (9) also appear fairly doubtful.

Now let's consider (2), which states that if *a* knows ~ *p*, then *a* doesn't believe *p*. If knowing *p* entails believing *p*, and if no one can believe contradictory propositions, then (2) has to be accepted. But there are those who claim that it is possible to believe contradictory propositions. And if this is possible, then (2) must be rejected, because then someone might know ~ *p* and still believe *p*.

Finally, a few might reject even (4), which says that if you know *p*, then *p* must be the case. The idea behind this formula is that one cannot know something that is false. But some pragmatists† have denied that one cannot know something that is false, because their pragmatic explication of the concept of knowledge does not make the truth of a sentence a necessary condition for knowing that sentence.

---

*The argument is given by Arthur C. Danto in "On Knowing That We Know," in Avrum Stroll, ed., *Epistemology* (New York: Harper & Row, 1967), pp. 32–53.

†For instance, Robert, J. Ackermann, who in effect argued against the validity of (4) in his paper "A Pragmatic Analysis of Knowledge," delivered to the American Philosophical Association, Western Division, May 1972. Ackermann argued along pragmatist lines that because we can never be sure a statement is true and hence (if truth is a component of knowledge) can never know that we know anything whatever, it is useless to make truth a component of knowledge. He thus advised that we adopt a conception of knowledge that has no truth component, using the word "true" to refer to very highly confirmed theories, making it possible to know *x* in some cases even though *x* later turns out to be false.

10 *Deontic Logic*

Predicate logic, modal logic, and epistemic logic all can be said to be **operator logics,** because they deal with operators (we called them quantifiers when we discussed predicate logic) that bind parts of expressions. Recently, attempts have been made to develop a similar system for another area of philosophy, namely, certain kinds of reasoning in ethics. The result is **deontic logic,** which deals with the ethical notions of permission, obligation, and the like.

Several different deontic systems have been proposed. Most of them are fairly similar. To illustrate the problems and complexities they all face, let's concentrate on part of a typical system, namely, the one proposed by Nicholas Rescher (which we will refer to as RDL, for "Rescher's deontic logic").*

RDL has seven axioms, written in the notation of modal predicate logic together with one new operator. The new operator is the **permission operator,** defined as

$$P\,(p\,/c) = df\,(\text{Action } p \text{ is permitted in circumstance } c)$$

Here are the axioms of RDL:

(1) $P\,(p \vee \sim p/c)$
(2) $P\,(p \vee q\,/c) \Rightarrow [P\,(p/c) \vee P\,(q/c)]$
(3) $(p \Rightarrow q) \Rightarrow [P\,(p/c) \Rightarrow P\,(q/c)]$
(4) $P\,(p \cdot q/c) \Rightarrow P\,(p/c \cdot q)$
(5) $[P\,(p/c) \cdot P\,(q/c \cdot p)] \Rightarrow P\,(p \cdot q/c)$
(6) $P\,(p/c \cdot \sim c) \Rightarrow P\,(p/d)$
(7) $P\,(p/d) \Rightarrow P\,(p/c \vee \sim c)$

All these axioms have an initial plausibility. The first says that tautologies are always permitted, which sounds fairly trivial but surely not fallacious; the second that $(p \vee q)$'s being permitted in some circumstance c is logically equivalent to either p's being permitted in that circumstance or q's being so permitted; the third that if p entails q, then that entails that p's being permitted in some circumstance c in turn entails that q is permitted in that circumstance; and so on.

From the axioms, many plausible permission theorems can be derived. For instance, here is a proof that $P\,(p/c) \vee P\,(\sim p/c)$, or in English that in any circumstance either p is permitted or $\sim p$ is permitted (important because it ensures that in every circumstance there is *something that* you're permitted to do):

1. $P\,(p \vee \sim p/c)$ **Axiom (1)**
2. $P\,(p \vee \sim p/c) \Leftrightarrow [(p/c \vee P\,(\sim p/c)]$ **Axiom (2)**
3. $\{P\,(p \vee \sim p/c) \Rightarrow [P\,(p/c) \vee P\,(\sim p/c)]\} \cdot$
    $\{[P\,(p/c) \vee P\,(\sim p/c)] \Rightarrow P\,(p \vee \sim p/c)\}$ 2 **Strict Equiv.**[†]

---

*In his article "An Axiom System for Deontic Logic," *Philosophical Studies*, vol. 9 (1958), pp. 24–30.
[†]The modal equivalent of $(p \equiv q) :: (p \supset q) \cdot (q \supset p)$.

4. $P (p \vee \sim p/c) \Rightarrow [P (p/c) \vee P (\sim p/c)]$ 3 **Simp**
5. $P (p/c) \vee P (\sim p/c)$ 1,4 **Strict MP**∗

Here are some other plausible theorems:

(8) $\sim P (p/c) \Rightarrow P (\sim p/c)$
(9) $P (p \cdot q/c) \Rightarrow [P (p/c) \cdot P (q/c)]$
(10) $P (p \cdot q/c) \Rightarrow [P (p/c) \cdot P (q/c \cdot p)]$
(11) $P (p/c) \cdot P (q/c \cdot p)] \Rightarrow P (q/c)$
(12) $P (p/c \cdot q) \Rightarrow P (p \vee \sim q/c)$
(13) $[P (p/c) \cdot \sim P (q/c)] \Rightarrow P (p \cdot \sim q/c)$
(14) $P (p/c) \Rightarrow [P (q/c) \vee P (p/c \cdot \sim q)]$

In addition, Rescher introduces several other deontic operators, defined in terms of the permission operator. For instance, he defines the **obligation operator** as

$$O (p/c) = df \sim P (\sim p/c)$$

This says that "*p* is obligatory in circumstance *c*" means the same as "$\sim p$ is not permitted in circumstance *c*." Some theorems concerning this operator are

(15) $O (p/c) \Rightarrow P (p/c)$
(16) $O (p \cdot q /c) \equiv [O (p/c) \cdot O (q /c)]$
(17) $(p \Rightarrow q) \Rightarrow [O (p/c) \Rightarrow O (q /c)]$
(18) $[O (p/c) \vee O (q/c)] \Rightarrow O (p \vee q /c)$ (But not vice versa.)

11   *Problems with Deontic Systems*

There is a great deal of controversy concerning most of the axioms proposed for deontic systems. For instance, one objection raised against RDL is that axioms (3) and (5) (plus appropriate rules and theorems of modal logic), yield the following theorem:[†]

$$[P (p/c) \cdot P (\sim p/c \cdot p)] \Rightarrow P (q/c)$$

This theorem states that permission to do *p* in *c* and permission to do $\sim p$ in $c \cdot p$ entails permission to do any *q* whatever in *c*. Thus, if one is permitted to smoke and permitted to not smoke in the circumstance that one is smoking in a railroad smoking car, one is permitted to do anything (murder, for instance) in that smoking car.

Obviously, this theorem is not acceptable if it yields such results, so Rescher replaced Axiom (5) with what he called "A5∗":

$$A5∗ \; \{[P (p/c) \cdot P (q /c \cdot p)] \cdot \Diamond (p \cdot q)\} \Rightarrow P (p \cdot q /c)$$

∗The modal equivalent of $p, p \supset q / \therefore q$.

[†]For proof, see Alan Ross Anderson, "On the Logic of Commitment," *Philosophical Studies*, vol. X (1959), pp. 23–27.

Since p · ~ p is not possible, the counterexample just discussed cannot be derived in RDL when A5* replaces A5.

But other suspicious theorems can be derived. For example, from A5* plus A3 we can derive the following theorem:*

$$\{[P\,(p/c) \cdot P\,(q/c \cdot p)] \cdot \Diamond\,(p \cdot q)\} \Rightarrow [P\,(p/c) \cdot P\,(q/c)]$$

But if c is, for instance, the circumstance of being in an honors program, p the action of taking Philosophy 1H, and q the action of taking Philosophy 2H, where 1H is a prerequisite for 2H, then this theorem yields an unacceptable result. For it says that if one is permitted to take Philosophy 1H, in the circumstance that one is in the honors program, and permitted to take Philosophy 2H, in the circumstance of being in the honors program and having taken Philosophy 1H, and if it is possible to take both 1H and 2H, then all this entails that in the circumstance of being an honors student one is permitted to take 1H, and in the same circumstance (with or without the added circumstance of having taken 1H) one is permitted to take 2H. This is unacceptable of course, since in the example only those honors students who take 1H are permitted to take 2H.

In addition to objections to its axioms, RDL has been objected to because one of its *definitions* seems to yield questionable consequences. The definition objected to[†] is the one defining the obligation operator:

$$O\,(p/c) = df \sim P\,(\sim p/c)$$

For this definition (plus several RDL axioms) yields the following theorem:

$$O\,(p/d) \Rightarrow O\,([\,p/c \lor \sim c)$$

And this entails (using Castañeda's example, if feminists will permit it) that if in the circumstance that you're married to Jane you ought to support her, then this entails that you ought to support her in any circumstance ($c \lor \sim c$). But surely we can't accept this result, and so we must reject either the definition of obligation (as Castañeda suggests) or else one of the axioms used in the proof.

Objections of the kind just discussed have led some to reject deontic logic, as some reject modal or epistemic logic. Some even claim, though for other reasons, that these operator systems, unlike predicate logic, are not real *logic* systems at all.

But whatever the merits of this last claim, this much seems certain. It would be very useful indeed if we had generally acceptable modal, epistemic, and deontic rules, so that when philosophers argued about ethics, or whatever, they could say (as Leibniz hoped we might some day be able to) "Come, let us calculate."

---

*For more on this counterexample, see John Robinson, "Further Difficulties for Conditional Permission in Deontic Logic," *Philosophical Studies,* vol. XVIII (1967), pp. 27–30.

[†]By Hector-Neri Casteñeda, "The Logic of Obligation," *Philosophical Studies,* vol. X (1959), pp. 17–23.

Key Terms Introduced in Chapter Eighteen

Barcan Formula: The disputed modal theorem $(u) \Box\, p \Rightarrow \Box\, (u)\, p$.

deontic logic: A logic that deals with the ethical notions of obligation, permission, and so on.

epistemic logic: A logic designed to deal with statements containing epistemic contexts. *Example:* Enrique believes that now is the time to sell real estate.

KK thesis: The thesis that if someone knows some x, then that person knows he or she knows x.

logical entailment: An implication that is a theorem of logic. (Synonyms: *logical implication, strict implication.*)

logical equivalence: An equivalence that is a theorem of logic.

logical Implication: (See *logical entailment.*)

logical necessity: A statement that is true because of the laws of logic—a theorem of logic. *Example:* "It will rain or it won't."

modal logic: A logic designed to handle statements and arguments containing modal operators, such as "It is necessary that _____ ."

modal terms: Terms (operators) expressing necessity, possibility, and so on.

necessity operator: The symbol "$\Box$," used to express the concept of necessity.

obligation operator: The operator "O," used to express obligation.

operator logic: A logic dealing with operators that bind all or parts of expressions.

permission operator: The operator "P," used to express permission.

physical necessity: A statement that is true because of the laws of nature. *Example:* "All copper conducts electricity."

possibility operator: The symbol "$\Diamond$," used to express possibilities.

strict implication: (See *logical entailment.*) The symbol "$\Rightarrow$" is used to express strict implication.

Answers to Even-Numbered Exercise Items

Exercise 1-1

2. This is a *description* of how the speaker spent her summer vacation, not an argument.

4. At the present rate of consumption, the oil will be used up in 20–25 years (premise). And we're sure not going to reduce consumption in the near future (premise). So we'd better start developing solar power, windmills, and other "alternative energy sources" pretty soon (conclusion).

6. *Conjecture*, not an argument.

8. Don't be fooled by the "thus" in this passage. This is an explanation, not an argument.

10. To be sustained under the Eighth Amendment, the death penalty must "comport with the basic concept of human dignity at the core of the Amendment"; the objective in imposing it must be "consistent with our respect for the dignity of other men" (premise). [The death penalty] has as its very basis the total denial of the wrongdoer's dignity and worth (premise). The taking of life "because the wrongdoer deserves it" surely must fail (conclusion).

12. Every event must have a cause (premise). An infinite series of causes is impossible (premise). There must be a first uncaused cause of everything: God (conclusion).

14. Not an argument.

Exercise 1-2

(2) 1. McDonald's serves lobster or McDonald's serves hamburgers.

    2. It's not true that McDonald's serves lobster.

∴ 3. McDonald's serves hamburgers .

(4) 1. If McDonald's serves lobster, then McDonald's is a restaurant.

    2. It's not true that McDonald's serves lobster.

∴ 3. McDonald's is a restaurant.

(6) 1. If McDonald's sells auto parts, then McDonald's is an auto parts store.

    2. It's not true that McDonald's sells auto parts.

∴ 3. McDonald's is an auto parts store.

Exercise 1-3

2. Yes, because the premises of such an argument show only that the conclusion is *probably* true.

4. Yes, if one or more of its premises are false.

6. No. A deductively valid argument with true premises guarantees the truth of its conclusion.

8. No, because a sound argument is one that is valid and has all true premises, and a valid argument containing all true premises must have a true conclusion.

10. Yes, so long as it is possible for them all to be true.

12. No.

14. Here are five—"therefore," "thus," "so," "hence," and "consequently."

Exercise 2-1

2, 4, 6, 10, and 12 are correctly symbolized by the dot; 8 is not.

Exercise 2-2

2. The horseshoe ⊃

4. The first tilde

6. The second horseshoe

8. The tribar ≡

10. The tribar ≡

Exercise 2-3

2. $(J \lor A) \cdot \sim (J \cdot A)$ (J = "Michael Jordan is the greatest basketball player ever to play the game"; A = "Kareem Abdul Jabbar is the greatest basketball player ever to play the game")

4. $C \lor N$ (C = "It's going to snow on Christmas eve"; N = "It's going to snow on New Year's eve")

6. $(T \lor \sim T) \cdot \sim (T \cdot T)$ (T = "This sentence is true"; $\sim T$ = "This sentence is not true").

8. $(A \lor C) \cdot \sim (A \cdot C)$ (A = "The A's are going to win the World Series this year"; C = "The Cleveland Indians are going to win the World Series this year")

10. $(A \lor L) \cdot \sim (A \cdot L)$ (A = "Anita Hill told the truth about Clarence Thomas"; L = "The lie detector test is totally unreliable"

12. $I \lor S$ (I = "The gunman was insane," S = "The gunman was experiencing a severe emotional disturbance")

Exercise 2-4

2. $\sim (S \lor A)$, or $\sim S \cdot \sim A$

4. $\sim (H \lor P)$, or $\sim H \cdot \sim P$

6. $\sim (E \lor C) \cdot \sim O$

8. $(M \lor D) \cdot \sim (M \cdot D)$

10. $\sim (D \lor H) \cdot (P \cdot C)$

12. $(U \cdot I) \lor C$

14. $(D \cdot I) \cdot \sim (S \lor B)$

Exercise 2-5

2. $\sim J \supset \sim H$, or $H \supset J$, or $\sim H \lor J$

4. $\sim (R \lor A)$, or $\sim R \cdot \sim A$

6. $R \supset A$, or $\sim A \supset \sim R$

8. $\sim P \supset \sim A$ or $P \lor \sim A$

10. $\sim C \supset A$, or $A \lor C$

Exercise 2-6

2. $H \supset (L \cdot M)$
4. $(L \vee M) \supset G$
6. $\sim(T \vee A) \supset \sim G$
8. $L \supset (H \vee A)$

10. $(L \cdot P) \supset W$
12. $W \supset [(L \cdot P) \cdot M]$
14. $\sim(M \vee P) \cdot [(T \cdot A) \supset G]$

Exercise 2-7

2. $\sim E \supset \sim B$
4. $B \supset (M \cdot S)$
6. $(M \vee B) \supset \sim E$
8. $\sim M \supset D$
10. $\sim G \supset \sim D$
12. $\sim C \supset (B \cdot \sim L)$
14. $(M \cdot \sim B) \cdot \sim F$
16. $(\sim M \cdot S) \supset \sim B$

18. $(\sim M \cdot \sim B) \supset (\sim S \vee F)$
20. $\sim G \supset (D \vee E)$
22. $(\sim M \supset \sim W) \cdot B$
24. $W \equiv (B \cdot O)$
26. $(T \cdot S) \vee \sim D$
28. $(T \cdot S) \supset (N \supset \sim D)$
30. $\sim[(R \vee S) \vee G]$,
    or $(\sim R \cdot \sim S) \cdot \sim G$

Exercise 2-8

2. Sheila likes neither Johnny Depp nor Ellen de Generes.
4. Sheila doesn't like Johnny Depp and she doesn't like Ellen de Generes either. (Or you could use the answer from number 2)
6. If Sheila likes Russell Crowe, she's no pacifist.
8. If Sheila likes both Russell Crowe and Ted Kennedy, she's no pacifist.
10. If Sheila is a pacifist, then she doesn't like Russell Crowe or Ted Kennedy.
12. If Sheila likes either Russell Crowe or Ted Kennedy, yet she's a pacifist, then she's got a twisted sense of humor.
14. If the economy is in a recession, then you shouldn't buy real estate or common stocks.
16. If demand is high and interest rates are low, then unless you are a knowledgeable investor you should buy real estate.
18. You should buy stocks or bonds if and only if you are a knowledgeable investor (or a psychic) and the economy is not in a recession.
20. Unless you are a knowledgeable investor, you should not buy stocks or bonds; rather, you should invest in a mutual fund.
22. If you are not a knowledgeable investor, then you should not buy stocks or bonds, unless you are a psychic.
24. If the economy is in a recession and interest rates are low and you are neither a knowledgeable investor nor a psychic, then you should invest in real estate.

Exercise 2-9

2. *NKab*
4. *ANab*
6. *CKabNc*
8. *EaKbNc*

10. *CaKKbcc*
12. *CKAabcd*
14. *EAabKAcdNe*

Exercise 2-10

2. Inclusive: "Brenda jogs or pumps iron every day." Exclusive: "Either you're with me or you're against me."
4. "But," "however," and many others.
6. Compound. It is the negation of the atomic sentence "Archie Leach is a public figure."
8. Compound—it could be symbolized as $(\sim N \cdot \sim B) \cdot \sim W$

Exercise 3-1

2. True: $A \equiv (C \vee B)$
           T T F T T

4. True: $\sim [C \vee (D \vee E)]$
           T FF F F F

6. False: $\sim [(A \cdot \sim B) \supset (C \cdot \sim D)]$
           F TFFT T FFTF

8. True: $\sim (C \cdot D) \vee \sim (\sim C \cdot \sim D)$
           T FFF TF TFTTF

10. True: $A \supset [(B \supset C) \supset (D \supset E)]$
           T T TFF T FT F

12. False: $[(A \supset \sim B) \vee (C \cdot \sim D)] \equiv [\sim (A \supset D) \vee (\sim C \vee E)]$
           TF FT F FFTF F T T TFF T TFTF

14. False: $[A \supset (\sim A \vee A)] \cdot \sim [(A \cdot A) \supset (A \cdot A)]$
           T T FTTT FF TTT T TTT

Exercise 3-2

2. True. Because $\sim C$ is true, $Q \vee \sim C$ is also true.
4. False. A biconditional is true only if the two component sentences have the same truth value.
6. False. Because $\sim A$ is false, $\sim A \supset D$ is true. This tells us that $R \supset (\sim A \supset D)$ is true.
8. We can't tell in this case. We can tell that $C \supset Q$ is true, but that is all.
10. True. Because C is false, $\sim (C \cdot R)$ must be true. That's all we need to know to tell that the entire disjunction is true.
12. False, because the consequent is false and the antecedent is true. The antecedent is true because both conditionals in its antecedent and consequent are true due to the falsity of D.

Exercise 3-3

2. B, F
4. A, B, E, F

Exercise 3-4

2. a, d
4. a, c, l
6. a, d, f, n
8. a, d, k, o

10. a, d, f, n
12. a, d, f, g, n
14. a, b, i, j

Exercise 3-5

2. $p, p \supset q, \sim p \supset q, p \supset \sim q, \sim p \supset \sim q$
4. $p, \sim p, \sim (p \lor q)$
6. $p, p \equiv q, p \equiv \sim q, (p \cdot q) \equiv r, (p \cdot q) \equiv \sim r, (p \cdot q) \equiv \sim q$
8. $p, p \supset q, \sim p \supset q, \sim (p \equiv q) \supset r$
10. $p, \sim p, \sim (p \supset q), \sim [(p \equiv q) \supset r]$
12. $p, \sim p, \sim (p \supset q), \sim [(p \cdot q) \supset r], \sim [p \supset (q \lor r)], \sim [(p \cdot q) \supset (r \lor q)], \sim [(p \cdot q) \supset (r \lor s)]$

Exercise 3-6

2. Tautology

p	$\sim (p \equiv \sim p)$
T	T T F F T
F	T F F T F

4. Tautology

p	q	$p \supset (p \lor q)$
T	T	T T T T T
T	F	T T T T F
F	T	F T F T T
F	F	F T F F F

6. Contingent

p	q	$p \equiv (q \lor p)$
T	T	T T T T T
T	F	T T F T T
F	T	F F T T F
F	F	F T F F F

8. Contingent

p	q	$(q \supset p) \supset (p \supset q)$
T	T	T T T T T T T
T	F	F T T F T F F
F	T	T F F T F T T
F	F	F T F T F T F

10. Contingent

p	q	$(q \lor p) \supset (p \supset q)$
T	T	T T T T T T T
T	F	F T T F T F F
F	T	T T F T F T T
F	F	F F F T F T F

12. Contingent

p	q	r	$p \supset [q \supset (p \supset r)]$
T	T	T	T T T T T T T
T	T	F	T F T F T F F
T	F	T	T T F T T T T
T	F	F	T T F T T F F
F	T	T	F T T T F T T
F	T	F	F T T T F T F
F	F	T	F T F T F T T
F	F	F	F T F T F T F

14. Tautology

p	q	r	s	$\{p \supset [(q \lor r) \lor (s \lor \sim q)]\} \lor \sim p$
T	T	T	T	T T T T T T T F T T F T
T	T	T	F	T T T T T T F F T T F T
T	T	F	T	T T T T F T T T F T T F T
T	T	F	F	T T T T F T F F F T T F T
T	F	T	T	T T F T T T T T T F T F T
T	F	T	F	T T F T T T F T T F T F T
T	F	F	T	T T F F F T T T T F T F T
T	F	F	F	T T F F F T F T T F T F T
F	T	T	T	F T T T T T T T F T T T F
F	T	T	F	F T T T T T F F F T T T F
F	T	F	T	F T T T F T T T F T T T F
F	T	F	F	F T T T F T F F F T T T F
F	F	T	T	F T F T T T T T T F T T F
F	F	T	F	F T F T T T F T T F T T F
F	F	F	T	F T F F F T T T T F T T F
F	F	F	F	F T F F F T F T T F T T F

Exercise 3-7

2. Not logically equivalent.

p q	p ∨ q	p
T T	T T T	T
T F	T T F	T
F T	F T T	F
F F	F F F	F

(arrow over final p)

4. Not logically equivalent.

p	p	p ∨ ~ p
T	T	T T F T
F	F	F T T F

6. Logically equivalent.

p	p · ~ p	p ≡ ~ p
T	T F F T	T F F T
F	F F T F	F F T F

8. Not logically equivalent.

p q	p ∨ ~ q	p · ~ q
T T	T T F T	T F F T
T F	T T T F	T T T F
F T	F F F T	F F F T
F F	F T T F	F F T F

10. Not logically equivalent.

p q	p ⊃ ~ q	p · q
T T	T F F T	T T T
T F	T T T F	T F F
F T	F T F T	F F T
F F	F T T F	F F F

12. Not logically equivalent.

p q	p ∨ q	p ∨ (q ⊃ q)
T T	T T T	T T T T T
T F	T T F	T T F T F
F T	F T T	F T T T T
F F	F F F	F T F T F

14. Not logically equivalent.

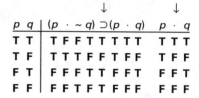

p q	(p · ~ q) ⊃ (p · q)	p · q
T T	T F F T T T T T	T T T
T F	T T T F F T F F	T F F
F T	F F F T T F F T	F F T
F F	F F T F T F F F	F F F

16. Logically equivalent.

p q	p ⊃ (q ⊃ p)	q ⊃ (p ⊃ q)
T T	T T T T T	T T T T T
T F	T T F T T	F T T F F
F T	F T T F F	T T F T T
F F	F T F T F	F T F T F

18. Not logically equivalent.

p q	~ (p · ~ q)	(~ p · ~ q) ∨ (p ∨ q)
T T	T T F F T	F T F F T T T T T
T F	F T T T F	F T F T F T T T F
F T	T F F F T	T F F F T T F T T
F F	T F F T F	T F T T F T F F F

20. Not logically equivalent.

	↓	↓
p q r	(p · q) ∨ (q · r)	(~ p · ~ q) ∨ (~ q · ~ r)
T T T	T T T T T T T	F T F F T F F T F F T
T T F	T T T T T F F	F T F F T F F T F T F
T F T	T F F F F F T	F T F T F F T F F F T
T F F	T F F F F F F	F T F T F T T F T T F
F T T	F F T T T T T	T F F F T F F T F F T
F T F	F F T F T F F	T F F F T F F T F T F
F F T	F F F F F F T	T F T T F T T F F F T
F F F	F F F F F F F	T F T T F T T F T T F

Exercise 3-8

2. Valid. Line 1 is the only line where all the premises are true, and on this line the conclusion is true as well.

	↓	↓		
p q r	r ⊃ p	p ⊃ (q · r)	r	/∴ q
T T T	T T T	T T T T T	T	T
T T F	F T T	T F T F F	F	T
T F T	T T T	T F F F T	T	F
T F F	F T T	T F F F F	F	F
F T T	T F F	F T T T T	T	T
F T F	F T F	F T T F F	F	T
F F T	T F F	F T F F T	T	F
F F F	F T F	F T F F F	F	F

4. Valid.

	↓		↓
p q r	(p · q) ⊃ r	p	/∴ q ⊃ r
T T T	T T T T T	T	T T T
T T F	T T T F F	T	T F F
T F T	T F F T T	T	F T T
T F F	T F F T F	T	F T F
F T T	F F T T T	F	T T T
F T F	F F T T F	F	T F F
F F T	F F F T T	F	F T T
F F F	F F F T F	F	F T F

6. Valid.

p q r	p ⊃ q	~ (r · q)	r	/∴ ~ p
T T T	T T T	F T T T	T	F T
T T F	T T T	T F F T	F	F T
T F T	T F F	T T F F	T	F T
T F F	T F F	T F F F	F	F T
F T T	F T T	F T T T	T	T F
F T F	F T T	T F F T	F	T F
F F T	F T F	T T F F	T	T F
F F F	F T F	T F F F	F	T F

8. Invalid. On the fifth line the premises are all true and the conclusion false.

p q r	p ∨ r	p ⊃ ~ q	q	/∴ ~ r
T T T	T T T	T F F T	T	F T
T T F	T T F	T F F T	T	T F
T F T	T T T	T T T F	F	F T
T F F	T T F	T T T F	F	T F
F T T	F T T	F T F T	T	F T
F T F	F F F	F T F T	T	T F
F F T	F T T	F T T F	F	F T
F F F	F F F	F T T F	F	T F

10. Valid.

p q r	(p · q) ∨ r	~ p	/∴ r
T T T	T T T T T	F T	T
T T F	T T T T F	F T	F
T F T	T F F T T	F T	T
T F F	T F F F F	F T	F
F T T	F F T T T	T F	T
F T F	F F T F F	T F	F
F F T	F F F T T	T F	T
F F F	F F F F F	T F	F

12. Valid.

p q r	(p · q) ∨ r	~ (p ∨ q)	/∴ r
T T T	T T T T T	F T T T	T
T T F	T T T T F	F T T T	F
T F T	T F F T T	F T T F	T
T F F	T F F F F	F T T F	F
F T T	F F T T T	F F T T	T
F T F	F F T F F	F F T T	F
F F T	F F F T T	T F F F	T
F F F	F F F F F	T F F F	F

14. Valid.

p q r	p ∨ (~q · r)	q ⊃ ~p	/∴ ~q
	↓	↓	↓
T T T	T T F T F T	T F F T	F T
T T F	T T F T F F	T F F T	F T
T F T	T T T F T T	F T F T	T F
T F F	T T T F F F	F T F T	T F
F T T	F F F T F T	T T T F	F T
F T F	F F F T F F	T T T F	F T
F F T	F T T F T T	F T T F	T F
F F F	F F T F F F	F T T F	T F

16. Invalid. On lines 11, 12, and 15 the premises are true and the conclusion is false.

p q r s	p ⊃ q	r ⊃ s	q ∨ s	/∴ p ∨ r
	↓	↓	↓	↓
T T T T	T T T	T T T	T T T	T T T
T T T F	T T T	T F F	T T F	T T T
T T F T	T T T	F T T	T T T	T T F
T T F F	T T T	F T F	T T F	T T F
T F T T	T F F	T T T	F T T	T T T
T F T F	T F F	T F F	F F F	T T T
T F F T	T F F	F T T	F T T	T T F
T F F F	T F F	F T F	F F F	T T F
F T T T	F T T	T T T	T T T	F T T
F T T F	F T T	T F F	T T F	F T T
F T F T	F T T	F T T	T T T	F F F
F T F F	F T T	F T F	T T F	F F F
F F T T	F T F	T T T	F T T	F T T
F F T F	F T F	T F F	F F F	F T T
F F F T	F T F	F T T	F T T	F F F
F F F F	F T F	F T F	F F F	F F F

18. Invalid, as shown by line 12.

p q r s	p ⊃ q	r ⊃ s	q ∨ r	/∴ p ∨ s
	↓	↓	↓	↓
T T T T	T T T	T T T	T T T	T T T
T T T F	T T T	T F F	T T T	T T F
T T F T	T T T	F T T	T T F	T T T
T T F F	T T T	F T F	T T F	T T F
T F T T	T F F	T T T	F T T	T T T
T F T F	T F F	T F F	F T T	T T F
T F F T	T F F	F T T	F F F	T T T
T F F F	T F F	F T F	F F F	T T F
F T T T	F T T	T T T	T T T	F T T
F T T F	F T T	T F F	T T T	F F F
F T F T	F T T	F T T	T T F	F T T
F T F F	F T T	F T F	T T F	F F F
F F T T	F T F	T T T	F T T	F T T
F F T F	F T F	T F F	F T T	F F F
F F F T	F T F	F T T	F F F	F T T
F F F F	F T F	F T F	F F F	F F F

20. Valid.

p q r s	p ⊃ (q ⊃ r)	/∴ (~ r · s) ⊃ (q ⊃ ~ p)
	↓	↓
T T T T	T T T T T	F T F T T T F F T
T T T F	T T T T T	F T F F T T F F T
T T F T	T F T F F	T F T T F T F F T
T T F F	T F T F F	T F F F T T F F T
T F T T	T T F T T	F T F T T F T F T
T F T F	T T F T T	F T F F T F T F T
T F F T	T T F T F	T F T T T F T F T
T F F F	T T F T F	T F F F T F T F T
F T T T	F T T T T	F T F T T T T T F
F T T F	F T T T T	F T F F T T T T F
F T F T	F T T F F	T F T T T T T T F
F T F F	F T T F F	T F F F T T T T F
F F T T	F T F T T	F T F T T F T T F
F F T F	F T F T T	F T F F T F T T F
F F F T	F T F T F	T F T T T F T T F
F F F F	F T F T F	T F F F T F T T F

Exercise 3-9

2. Inconsistent.

		↓	↓
p q		p ≡ q	p ≡ ~q
T T		T T T	T F F T
T F		T F F	T T T F
F T		F F T	F T F T
F F		F T F	F F T F

4. Consistent, as shown by the seventh line.

		↓	↓	↓
p q r		p ⊃ q	~q v ~r	r · ~p
T T T		T T T	F T F F T	T F F T
T T F		T T T	F T T T F	F F F T
T F T		T F F	T F T F T	T F F T
T F F		T F F	T F T T F	F F F T
F T T		F T T	F T F F T	T T T F
F T F		F T T	F T T T F	F F T F
F F T		F T F	T F T F T	T T T F
F F F		F T F	T F T T F	F F T F

6. Consistent, as shown by the third, fifth, seventh, and eighth lines.

		↓	↓	↓
p q r		(p · q) ⊃ ~r	p ⊃ r	q ⊃ r
T T T		T T T F F T	T T T	T T T
T T F		T T T T T F	T F F	T F F
T F T		T F F T F T	T T T	F T T
T F F		T F F T T F	T F F	F T F
F T T		F F T T F T	F T T	T T T
F T F		F F T T T F	F T F	T F F
F F T		F F F T F T	F T T	F T T
F F F		F F F T T F	F T F	F T F

8. Inconsistent.

		↓		↓	↓
p q r		p ≡ ~q	p	q v r	~r
T T T		T F F T	T	T T T	F T
T T F		T F F T	T	T T F	T F
T F T		T T T F	T	F T T	F T
T F F		T T T F	T	F F F	T F
F T T		F T F T	F	T T T	F T
F T F		F T F T	F	T T F	T F
F F T		F F T F	F	F T T	F T
F F F		F F T F	F	F F F	T F

10. Inconsistent.

		↓	↓	
p q r	(p ⊃ q) ∨ (p ⊃ r)	~ (q ∨ r)	p
T T T	T T T T T T T	F T T T	T
T T F	T T T T T F F	F T T F	T
T F T	T F F T T T T	F F T T	T
T F F	T F F F T F F	T F F F	T
F T T	F T T T F T T	F T T T	F
F T F	F T T T F T F	F T T F	F
F F T	F T F T F T T	F F T T	F
F F F	F T F T F T F	T F F F	F

Exercise 3-10

2. $V(A) = F, V(B) = T$
4. $V(N) = T, V(R) = T, V(L) = T$ or F
6. $V(A) = F, V(B) = T, V(C) = T, V(D) = T$
    $V(A) = F, V(B) = T, V(C) = F, V(D) = T$
    $V(A) = F, V(B) = T, V(C) = T, V(D) = F$
    $V(A) = F, V(B) = F, V(C) = T, V(D) = T$
    $V(A) = F, V(B) = F, V(C) = F, V(D) = T$
8. $V(A) = F$
10. $V(A) = T, V(B) = T, V(C) = F, V(D) = F$
    $V(A) = F, V(B) = F, V(C) = T, V(D) = T$
    $V(A) = F, V(B) = F, V(C) = F, V(D) = T$
    $V(A) = F, V(B) = T, V(C) = F, V(D) = T$
    $V(A) = F, V(B) = T, V(C) = T, V(D) = T$
12. $V(A) = T, V(B) = T, V(C) = T, V(D) = F$
14. $V(A) = F, V(B) = F, V(C) = F, V(D) = F, V(E) = T, V(F) = T$
16. $V(D) = F, V(L) = F, V(R) = F$
    $V(D) = F, V(L) = F, V(R) = T$
18. $V(A) = T, V(B) = T, V(C) = T, V(D) = T, V(E) = F, V(F) = F$
20. $V(N) = F, V(P) = T$ or $F, V(Q) = F, V(R) = T, V(S) = F, V(T) = T, V(W) = F$

Exercise 3-11

2. $V(F) = T, V(G) = F, V(H) = F$
4. $V(F) = F, V(G) = T, V(H) = F$
6. $V(A) = F, V(B) = F, V(C) = F, V(D) = T$
8. $V(A) = T, V(B) = T, V(C) = F, V(D) = T, V(E) = T, V(F) = F$

Exercise 3-12

2. Suppose we have an argument:

> Bob loves Mary if and only if Mary loves Bob.
> Bob does not love Mary.
> Therefore, Mary loves Bob.

This is clearly invalid. Thus, if we take the form of the argument to be

$$p \equiv q$$
$$\sim p$$
$$\therefore q$$

and assign $V(q) = $ **F**, and $V(p) = $ **F**, the second premise is true and the conclusion false. Under these conditions, we want $V(p \equiv q) = $ **T**; this is the only way to capture the invalidity of this argument form. By varying the negations of the second premises and conclusion in the original argument, we can easily get all four lines of the table for the tribar.

4. There is no way to determine a line from this argument. If we assign $V(p \# q) = $ **F**, then we know either $V(p) = $ **F** or $V(q) = $ **F**, but we do not have enough information to tell which one that is. This shows a limitation on the intuitively valid arguments we can use to justify truth tables. Suppose that our # is actually the dot. Even though the argument in question is obviously valid—if two statements are true, then surely their conjunction is—that argument alone does not tell us enough to say which line of the table we have.

6. To answer this one correctly, we must really mind our p's and q's! It seems obvious that we must assign $V(q) = $ **F** and thus $V(p) = $ **T**, to get the conclusion false and the second premise true. But now under those conditions, $V(p * q) = $ **T**. Notice the occurrence of $\sim q$ on the right side of the *. What we have learned is that when the left side of a * statement is true, and the right side is true—$V(\sim q) = $ **T**!— then the whole * statement is true. Thus we have the *first line* of the truth table for *, where its left and right sides are both true, and not the second, as it might seem from the assignment of $V(p) = $ **T** and $V(q) = $ **F**. To see that clearly, consider the following invalid argument:

> If Bob loves Mary, then Mary does not love Bob.
> Bob loves Mary.
> Therefore, Mary loves Bob.

If we symbolize its form as

$$p \supset \sim q$$
$$p$$
$$\therefore q$$

we immediately see that when we have $V(q) = $ **F** and $V(p) = $ **T**, we want the first premise to be true. But the first premise is true when its antecedent and its consequent are both true, $V(\sim q) = $ **T**. We do not want to say that a horseshoe statement is true when $V(p) = $ **T** and $V(q) = $ **F**! We must be very careful about how our variables function in these argument forms.

Exercise 3-13—Exercises over Chapter Three

2. Yes. Every compound sentence is a substitution instance of more than one form. For example, $A \vee B$ is a substitution of both p and $p \vee q$.

4. The argument must be valid, because there is no possibility of true premises and a false conclusion.

6. The argument is valid. If one of the premises is a contradiction, it is not possible for all the premises to be true—so, of course, it is impossible for all the premises to be true and the conclusion false.

8. At least one of the premises must be false.

Exercise 4-1

(2)	4. 1,2 **HS**		(8)	6. 1,3 **HS**
	5. 3,4 **MT**			7. 5,6 **MP**
(4)	4. 2,3 **MP**			8. 2,4 **DS**
	5. 1,4 **MT**			9. 7,8 **MT**
(6)	5. 3,4 **HS**		(10)	6. 3,4 **HS**
	6. 2,5 **HS**			7. 5,6 **MP**
	7. 1,6 **MP**			8. 1,7 **MP**
				9. 2,8 **MP**

Exercise 4-2

(2)	3. R	1,2 **MP**	(12)	5. $\sim T$	1,4 **DS**
(4)	3. $L \supset (R \cdot W)$	1,2 **HS**		6. $\sim (L \vee M)$	3,5 **MP**
(6)	4. N	1,3 **DS**		7. R	2,6 **DS**
	5. G	2,4 **MP**	(14)	5. $P \cdot Q$	2,4 **MP**
(8)	4. $\sim H$	2,3 **DS**		6. $R \vee (T \cdot S)$	1,5 **MP**
	5. G	1,4 **DS**		7. R	3,6 **DS**
(10)	5. $\sim D$	2,4 **DS**			
	6. $A \supset B$	3,5 **MP**			
	7. C	1,6 **MP**			

Exercise 4-3

(2)	2. 1 **Simp**		(8)	4. 2 **Simp**
(4)	4. 1,2,3 **CD**			5. 1,3 **HS**
(6)	4. 2,3 **DS**			6. 4,5 **MP**
	5. 1,4 **MP**			7. 2 **Simp**
	6. 2,5 **MT**			8. 6,7 **Conj**

(10) 4. 2 **Simp**
      5. 1,4 **MT**
      6. 3,5 **DS**
(12) 5. 1,4 **HS**
      6. 2 **Add**
      7. 5,6 **MP**
      8. 3,7 **DS**
      9. 2,8 **Conj**

(14) 5. 2 **Simp**
      6. 2 **Simp**
      7. 3,5 **DS**
      8. 1,4,7 **CD**
      9. 6,8 **DS**

Exercise 4-4

(2) 2. $(A \equiv B) \supset B$
(4) 2. $\sim C$
     3. $\sim B$
(6) 2. $A \vee D$
     4. A

(8) 1. $T \cdot S$
     2. $[(T \cdot S) \vee U] \supset \sim L$
     6. $\sim G$
     7. T

Exercise 4-5

(2) 3. $(R \vee S) \supset T$ 2 **Simp**
     4. T 1,3 **MP**
     5. $T \vee L$ 4 **Add**
(4) 3. B 1 **Simp**
     4. C 2,3 **MP**
(6) 3. A 2 **Simp**
     4. B 1,3 **MP**
     5. $B \vee D$ 4 **Add**
(8) 5. $\sim B \cdot C$ 1,4 **MP**
     6. C 5 **Simp**
     7. D 2,6 **MP**
     8. $\sim B$ 5 **Simp**
     9. E 3,8 **DS**
    10. $D \cdot E$ 7,9 **Conj**
(10) 4. $L \vee R$ 1 **Add**
     5. $\sim T$ 3,4 **MP**
     6. $\sim R$ 2,5 **DS**
     7. $\sim R \vee B$ 6 **Add**
(12) 4. $\sim (R \cdot A)$ 2,3 **MT**
     5. E 1,4 **DS**
     6. $E \cdot \sim D$ 3,5 **Conj**

(14) 3. $A \vee \sim D$ 1 **Add**
      4. $R \cdot S$ 2,3 **MP**
      5. $(R \cdot S) \vee B$ 4 **Add**
(16) 5. $\sim R$ 1,3 **MT**
      6. Z 4,5 **DS**
      7. $\sim M \cdot \sim N$ 2,5 **MP**
      8. $(\sim M \cdot \sim N) \cdot Z$ 6,7 **Conj**
(18) 5. B 1,4 **DS**
      6. $\sim C$ 2,4 **MT**
      7. $B \cdot \sim C$ 5,6 **Conj**
      8. $D \cdot \sim C$ 3,7 **MP**
      9. D 8 **Simp**
(20) 6. $\sim (D \cdot E)$ 2 **Simp**
      7. $\sim A$ 4,6 **DS**
      8. $\sim A \cdot \sim (D \cdot E)$ 6,7 **Conj**
      9. $B \supset \sim D$ 1,8 **MP**
     10. $B \vee E$ 5,6 **MP**
     11. $\sim D \vee F$ 3,9,10 **CD**

Exercise 4-6

(2)		
	3. $\sim\sim B$	2 **DN**
	4. $\sim\sim A$	1,3 **MT**
	5. A	4 **DN**
(4)	2. $\sim J \cdot \sim K$	1 **DeM**
	3. $\sim K$	2 **Simp**
(6)	4. $\sim (J \cdot K)$	2 **DeM**
	5. H	1,4 **DS**
	6. $\sim\sim H$	5 **DN**
	7. $\sim A$	3,6 **DS**
(8)	4. $\sim W \vee \sim\sim Z$	3 **DeM**
	5. $\sim\sim X$	2 **DN**
	6. $\sim\sim W$	1,5 **MT**
	7. $\sim\sim Z$	4,6 **DS**
	8. Z	7 **DN**

(10)		
	4. $\sim\sim A \cdot \sim B$	2 **DeM**
	5. $\sim B$	4 **Simp**
	6. $\sim C$	1,5 **MP**
	7. D	3,6 **DS**
(12)	4. $\sim A \vee \sim\sim B$	1 **DeM**
	5. $\sim\sim A \cdot \sim\sim C$	3 **DeM**
	6. $\sim\sim A$	5 **Simp**
	7. $\sim\sim B$	4,6 **DS**
	8. B	7 **DN**
	9. $\sim\sim C$	5 **Simp**
	10. C	9 **DN**
	11. $B \cdot C$	8, 10 **Conj**
	12. D	2,11 **MP**

Exercise 4-7

(2)		
	4. 1 **DN**
	5. 3 **Comm**
	6. 4,5 **MT**
	7. 2 **DeM**
	8. 6,7 **DS**
(4)	3. 1 **Assoc**
	4. 2 **Dist**
	5. 4 **Simp**
	6. 4 **Simp**
	7. 3,5 **DS**
	8. 7 **Comm**
	9. 6,8 **Conj**
	10. 9 **Dist**
(6)	3. 1 **Equiv**
	4. 2 **DeM**
	5. 4 **Add**
	6. 5 **Impl**
	7. 2 **Impl**
	8. 6,7 **HS**
	9. 8 **Exp**
	10. 9 **Impl**
	11. 10 **Taut**

(8)		
	3. 2 **Comm**
	4. 3 **Assoc**
	5. 4 **Impl**
	6. 1 **Contra** and **DN** (twice)
	7. 5,6 **HS**
	8. 7 **Impl**
	9. 8 **Assoc**
	10. 9 **Comm**
	11. 10 **DN**
	12. 11 **Impl**
	13. 12 **Impl**
(10)	3. 1 **Equiv**
	4. 3 **Impl**
	5. 4 **DeM**
	6. 5 **Impl** (twice)
	7. 6 **DN**
	8. 7 **DeM** (twice)
	9. 8 **DN** (twice)
	10. 9 **Assoc**
	11. 2 **DeM**
	12. 10,11 **DS**
	13. 12 **Comm**
	14. 13 **Dist**
	15. 14 **Simp**
	16. 15 **Tau**

Exercise 4-8

(2)	3. ~ (R · S)	1 **DeM**		(10)	3. ~ R ∨ S	1 **Impl**
	4. ~ A	2,3 **MT**			4. ~ R ∨ T	2 **Impl**
(4)	3. ~ B ∨ ~ ~ C	2 **DeM**			5. (~ R ∨ S) · (~ R ∨ T)	3,4 **Conj**
	4. ~ B ∨ C	3 **DN**			6. ~ R ∨ (S · T)	5 **Dist**
	5. B ⊃ C	4 **Impl**			7. R ⊃ (S · T)	6 **Impl**
	6. A ⊃ C	1,5 **HS**		(12)	3. ~ C ∨ ~ A	2 **DeM**
(6)	4. ~ H ∨ ~ G	2 **DeM**			4. A	1 **Simp**
	5. ~ ~ H	3 **DN**			5. ~ ~ A	4 **DN**
	6. ~ G	4,5 **DS**			6. ~ C	3,5 **DS**
	7. ~ F	1,6 **MT**			7. B ⊃ C	1 **Simp**
(8)	2. (M ⊃ N) · (N ⊃ M)	1 **Equiv**			8. ~ B	6,7 **MT**
	3. N ⊃ M	2 **Simp**		(14)	4. ~ A	1,3 **DS**
	4. ~ N ∨ M	3 **Impl**			5. ~ A ∨ ~ ~ B	4 **Add**
					6. ~ (A · ~ B)	5 **DeM**
					7. ~ C	2,6 **MP**

Exercise 4-9

(2)	2. ~ ~ A ∨ B	1 **DN**		(12)	2. ~ ~ B ⊃ ~ A	1 **Contra**
	3. ~ A ⊃ B	2 **Imp**			3. B ⊃ ~ A	2 **DN**
(4)	2. ~ A ∨ ~ B	1 **Add**		(14)	2. (A · B) ⊃ C	1 **Exp**
	3. ~ (A · B)	2 **DeM**			3. (B · A) ⊃ C	2 **Comm**
(6)	2. ~ A ∨ ~ B	1 **DeM**			4. B ⊃ (A ⊃ C)	3 **Exp**
	3. A ⊃ ~ B	2 **Imp**		(16)	2. A · (B ∨ C)	1 **Dist**
(8)	2. ~ (~ A ∨ B)	1 **Imp**			3. B ∨ C	2 **Simp**
	3. ~ ~ A · ~ B	2 **DeM**		(18)	2. C ∨ (A · B)	1 **Comm**
	4. ~ B	3 **Simp**			3. (C ∨ A) · (C ∨ B)	2 **Dist**
(10)	2. A ∨ ~ {~ [L ∨ (~ M ≡ R)]}	1 **Add**			4. C ∨ A	3 **Simp**
	3. ~ {~ [L ∨ (~ M ≡ R)]} ∨ A	2 **Comm**		(20)	2. ~ A ∨ ~ A	1 **Imp**
					3. ~ A	2 **Taut**

Exercise 4-10

(2)	3. ~ A	1,2 **MT**		(10)	3. A ∨ ~ B	2 **Add**
	4. ~ A ∨ ~ B	3 **Add**			4. C	1,3 **MP**
(4)	4. A ∨ B	3 **Add**			5. C ∨ ~ B	4 **Add**
	5. C	1,4 **MP**			6. ~ B ∨ C	5 **Comm**
	6. C ∨ E	5 **Add**		(12)	5. ~ B	1,2 **MT**
	7. F	2,6 **MP**			6. ~ B · C	3,5 **Conj**
(6)	3. A ∨ B	1 **Add**			7. (~ B · C) ∨ D	6 **Add**
	4. (A ∨ B) ∨ C	3 **Add**			8. E	4,7 **MP**
	5. D	2,4 **MP**				
(8)	5. A ∨ B	3 **Add**				
	6. C	1,5 **MP**				
	7. C ∨ B	6 **Add**				
	8. D ∨ F	2,7 **MP**				
	9. D	4,8 **DS**				

Exercise 4-11

(2) 3. $A \vee (B \vee C)$ 1 **Assoc**

4. A 2,3 **DS**

(4) 3. $[(A \cdot B) \vee C] \cdot$
$[(A \cdot B) \vee D]$ 1 **Dist**

4. $(A \cdot B) \vee C$ 3 **Simp**

5. $A \cdot B$ 2,4 **DS**

6. A 5 **Simp**

(6) 2. $[(A \cdot B) \vee C] \cdot$
$[(A \cdot B) \vee D]$ 1 **Dist**

3. $(A \cdot B) \vee D$ 2 **Simp**

4. $D \vee (A \cdot B)$ 3 **Comm**

5. $(D \vee A) \cdot (D \vee B)$ 4 **Dist**

6. $D \vee A$ 5 **Simp**

(8) 3. $C \cdot (A \vee B)$ 1 **Comm**

4. $(C \cdot A) \vee (C \cdot B)$ 3 **Dist**

5. $\sim C \vee \sim A$ 2 **Comm**

6. $\sim (C \cdot A)$ 5 **DeM**

7. $C \cdot B$ 4,6 **DS**

(10) 2. $(\sim R \cdot A) \vee$
$\sim (R \vee Q)$ 1 **Assoc**

3. $(\sim R \cdot A) \vee$
$(\sim R \cdot \sim Q)$ 1 **DeM**

4. $\sim R \cdot (A \vee \sim Q)$ 3 **Dist**

5. $\sim R$ 4 **Simp**

(12) 3. $[(D \cdot F) \vee (A \cdot B)]$
$\vee (B \cdot C)$ 1 **Comm**

4. $(D \cdot F) \vee [(A \cdot B)$
$\vee (B \cdot C)]$ 3 **Assoc**

5. $(A \cdot B) \vee (B \cdot C)$ 2,4 **DS**

6. $(B \cdot A) \vee (B \cdot C)$ 5 **Comm**

7. $B \cdot (A \vee C)$ 6 **Dist**

8. B 7 **Simp**

Exercise 4-12

(2) 4. $[(A \vee B) \supset C] \cdot$
$[C \supset (A \vee B)]$ 2 **Equiv**

5. $C \supset (A \vee B)$ 4 **Simp**

6. $\sim A \cdot \sim B$ 1,3 **Conj**

7. $\sim (A \vee B)$ 6 **DeM**

8. $\sim C$ 5,7 **MT**

9. $\sim C \vee \sim D$ 8 **Add**

10. $\sim (C \cdot D)$ 9 **DeM**

(4) 3. $(S \vee \sim R) \cdot (S \vee T)$ 1 **Dist**

4. $S \vee \sim R$ 3 **Simp**

5. $\sim \sim S \vee \sim R$ 4 **DN**

6. $\sim S \supset \sim R$ 5 **Impl**

7. $R \supset \sim R$ 2,6 **HS**

8. $\sim R \vee \sim R$ 7 **Impl**

9. $\sim R$ 8 **Taut**

(6) 5. $\sim (B \vee D)$ 3,4 **MT**

6. $\sim B \cdot \sim D$ 5 **DeM**

7. $\sim B$ 6 **Simp**

8. $\sim A$ 1,7 **MT**

9. $\sim D$ 6 **Simp**

10. $\sim C$ 2,9 **MT**

11. $\sim A \cdot \sim C$ 8,10 **Conj**

12. $\sim (A \vee C)$ 11 **DeM**

(8) 3. $\sim C \cdot \sim \sim A$ 2 **DeM**

4. $\sim C$ 3 **Simp**

5. $[(A \cdot B) \supset C] \cdot$
$[C \supset (A \cdot B)]$ 1 **Equiv**

6. $(A \cdot B) \supset C$ 5 **Simp**

7. $\sim (A \cdot B)$ 4,6 **MT**

8. $\sim A \vee \sim B$ 7 **DeM**

9. $\sim \sim A$ 3 **Simp**

10. $\sim B$ 8,9 **DS**

(10) 4. $(W \cdot Y) \vee$
$(\sim W \cdot \sim Y)$ 1 **Equiv**

5. $\sim (W \cdot Y)$ 2 **DeM**

6. $\sim W \cdot \sim Y$ 4,5 **DS**

7. $\sim Y$ 6 **Simp**

8. $\sim Y \vee \sim Z$ 7 **Add**

9. $\sim (Y \cdot Z)$ 8 **DeM**

10. $\sim X$ 3,9 **MT**

(12) 3. $\sim R \supset \sim P$ 1 **Contra**

4. $\sim R \supset (\sim R \supset S)$ 2,3 **HS**

5. $(\sim R \cdot \sim R) \supset S$ 4 **Exp**

6. $\sim R \supset S$ 5 **Taut**

7. $\sim \sim R \vee S$ 6 **Impl**

8. $R \vee S$ 7 **DN**

(14) 3. ~ (A ∨ C) 1 **Comm**
   4. ~ (~ ~ A ∨ C) 3 **DN**
   5. ~ (~ A ⊃ C) 4 **Impl**
   6. ~ B 2,5 **MT**

Exercise 4-13

(2) 3. (S ∨ ~ R) · (S ∨ T) 1 **Dist**
   4. S ∨ ~ R 3 **Simp**
   5. ~ R ∨ S 4 **Comm**
   6. R ⊃ S 5 **Impl**
   7. ~ S ⊃ ~ R 6 **Contra**
   8. R ⊃ ~ R 2, 7 **HS**
   9. ~ R ∨ ~ R 8 **Impl**
   10. ~ R 9 **Taut**

(4) 4. D ⊃ C 3 **Contra**
   5. B ∨ C 1,2,4 **CD**
   6. ~ ~ B ∨ C 5 **DN**
   7. ~ B ⊃ C 6 **Impl**
   8. ~ B ⊃ B 2,7 **HS**
   9. ~ ~ B ∨ B 8 **Impl**
   10. B ∨ B 9 **DN**
   11. B 10 **Taut**

(6) 4. (D · B) ⊃ W 2 **Exp**
   5. (B · D) ⊃ W 4 **Comm**
   6. B ⊃ (D ⊃ W) 5 **Exp**
   7. D ⊃ (D ⊃ W) 1,6 **HS**
   8. (D · D) ⊃ W 7 **Exp**
   9. D ⊃ W 8 **Taut**
   10. D ⊃ (W ⊃ S) 1,3 **HS**
   11. (D · W) ⊃ S 10 **Exp**
   12. (W · D) ⊃ S 11 **Comm**
   13. W ⊃ (D ⊃ S) 12 **Exp**
   14. D ⊃ (D ⊃ S) 9,13 **HS**
   15. (D · D) ⊃ S 14 **Exp**
   16. D ⊃ S 15 **Taut**

(8) 3. ~ (R ∨ S) ∨ T 2 **Impl**
   4. (~ R · ~ S) ∨ T 3 **DeM**
   5. T ∨ (~ R · ~ S) 4 **Comm**
   6. (T ∨ ~ R) ·
    (T ∨ ~ S) 5 **Dist**
   7. T ∨ ~ R 6 **Simp**
   8. ~ R ∨ T 7 **Comm**
   9. R ⊃ T 8 **Impl**
   10. [K · (L ∨ M)] ⊃ R 1 **Exp**
   11. [(L ∨ M) · K] ⊃ R 10 **Comm**
   12. (L ∨ M) ⊃ (K ⊃ R) 11 **Exp**
   13. ~ (L ∨ M) ∨ (K ⊃ R) 12 **Impl**
   14. (~ L · ~ M) ∨ (K ⊃ R) 13 **DeM**
   15. (K ⊃ R) ∨ (~ L · ~ M) 14 **Comm**
   16. [(K ⊃ R) ∨ ~ L] ·
    [(K ⊃ R) ∨ ~ M] 15 **Dist**
   17. (K ⊃ R) ∨ ~ M 16 **Simp**
   18. ~ M ∨ (K ⊃ R) 17 **Comm**
   19. M ⊃ (K ⊃ R) 18 **Impl**
   20. (M · K) ⊃ R 19 **Exp**
   21. (M · K) ⊃ T 9,20 **HS**
   22. (K · M) ⊃ T 21 **Comm**
   23. K ⊃ (M ⊃ T) 22 **Exp**

(10) 5. C ∨ A 2 **Comm**
   6. ~ ~ C ∨ A 5 **DN**
   7. ~ C ⊃ A 6 **Impl**
   8. ~ C ⊃ B 1,7 **HS**
   9. ~ C ∨ D 4 **Comm**
   10. C ⊃ D 9 **Impl**
   11. C ⊃ B 3,10 **HS**
   12. B ∨ B 1,5,11 **CD**
   13. B 12 **Taut**

(12)   2. $(\sim A \vee A) \supset (\sim \sim A \vee \sim A)$ 1 **Impl** (twice)
        3. $\sim (\sim A \vee A) \vee (\sim \sim A \vee \sim A)$ 2 **Impl**
        4. $(\sim \sim A \cdot \sim A) \vee (\sim \sim A \vee \sim A)$ 3 **DeM**
        5. $(A \cdot \sim A) \vee \sim (\sim A \cdot A)$ 4 **DeM** and **DN**
        6. $\sim (\sim A \cdot A) \vee (A \cdot \sim A)$ 5 **Comm**
        7. $[\sim (\sim A \cdot A) \vee A] \cdot [\sim (\sim A \cdot A) \vee \sim A]$ 6 **Dist**
        8. $\sim (\sim A \cdot A) \vee A$ 7 **Simp**
        9. $(\sim \sim A \vee \sim A) \vee A$ 8 **DeM**
       10. $(A \vee \sim A) \vee A$ 9 **DN**
       11. $(\sim A \vee A) \vee A$ 10 **Comm**
       12. $\sim A \vee (A \vee A)$ 11 **Assoc**
       13. $\sim A \vee A$ 12 **Taut**
       14. $A \vee \sim A$ 13 **Comm**

(14)   3. $\sim A \vee B$ 1 **Impl**
        4. $(\sim A \vee B) \vee D$ 3 **Add**
        5. $\sim A \vee (B \vee D)$ 4 **Assoc**
        6. $(B \vee D) \vee \sim A$ 5 **Comm**
        7. $\sim C \vee D$ 2 **Impl**
        8. $(\sim C \vee D) \vee B$ 7 **Add**
        9. $\sim C \vee (D \vee B)$ 8 **Assoc**
       10. $\sim C \vee (B \vee D)$ 9 **Comm**
       11. $(B \vee D) \vee \sim C$ 10 **Comm**
       12. $[(B \vee D) \vee \sim A] \cdot [(B \vee D) \vee \sim C]$ 6,11 **Conj**
       13. $(B \vee D) \vee (\sim A \cdot \sim C)$ 12 **Dist**
       14. $(\sim A \cdot \sim C) \vee (B \vee D)$ 13 **Comm**
       15. $\sim (A \vee C) \vee (B \vee D)$ 14 **DeM**
       16. $(A \vee C) \supset (B \vee D)$ 15 **Impl**

Exercise 4-14

2. Equivalence argument forms may be used on parts of lines because in doing so we replace part of a line with another formula having the same truth-value, so that the truth-value of the whole line remains the same. *Example:* Using **Taut** on $A \supset B$ to get $(A \cdot A) \supset B$ cannot result in a sentence with a different truth-value.

4. Because some substitution instances of some invalid argument forms are valid, since they also are substitution instances of some valid argument form or other. *Example:* The valid argument $A \supset B, A / \therefore B$, a substitution instance of the invalid form $p, q / \therefore r$, also is a substitution instance of the valid argument form Modus Ponens.

6. It shows that some of the rules can be used to deduce the rest. Logicians have been interested in finding such a set (or sets) of rules in their study of *axiomatic* systems for logic. Such systems are analogous to axiom systems in geometry, where we adopt a list of such axioms and then prove theorems from them.

8. There have been many discussions about the importance of negation by philosophers and logicians—there is general agreement that negation expresses something very basic logically such that no other expressions can replace it.

10. Any statement whatever can be joined with a given premise p, using **ADD**, and then that statement will follow by **DS** if we also have $\sim p$ as a premise. This very important idea, which we use in the next chapter in discussing Indirect Proof, illustrates that from a contradiction, one can prove anything—which is why contradictions as premises are to be avoided!

Exercise 5-1

(2) → 2. *A*   **AP /∴ C**
     3. *B · C*   1,2 **MP**
     4. *C*   3 **Simp**
     5. *A ⊃ C*   2–4 **CP**

(4) → 3. *A*   **AP /∴ ~ B**
     4. *B ⊃ C*   1,3 **MP**
     5. *~ B*   2,4 **MT**
     6. *A ⊃ ~ B*   3–5 **CP**

(6) → 3. *A*   **AP /∴ C**
     4. *B*   2,3 **MP**
     5. *B ⊃ C*   1,3 **MP**
     6. *C*   4,5 **MP**
     7. *A ⊃ C*   3–6 **CP**

(8) → 3. *A · B*   **AP /∴ D**
     4. *C*   1,3 **MP**
     5. *B*   3 **Simp**
     6. *B · C*   4,5 **Conj**
     7. *D*   2,6 **MP**
     8. *(A · B) ⊃ D*   3–7 **CP**

(10) → 3. *A*   **AP /∴ B ⊃ D**
     4. *B ⊃ C*   1,3 **MP**
     5. *B ⊃ D*   2,4 **HS**
     6. *A ⊃ (B ⊃ D)*   3–5 **CP**

(12) → 4. *~ B*   **AP /∴ F**
     5. *~ B ∨ ~ C*   4 **Add**
     6. *~ (B · C)*   5 **DeM**
     7. *~ A*   1,6 **MT**
     8. *D*   3,7 **DS**
     9. *E · F*   2,8 **MP**
     10. *F*   9 **Simp**
     11. *~ B ⊃ F*   4–10 **CP**
     12. *~ ~ B ∨ F*   11 **Impl**
     13. *B ∨ F*   12 **DN**

(14) → 2. *D*   **AP /∴ D · G**
     3. *G*   1,2 **MP**
     4. *D · G*   2,3 **Conj**
     5. *D ⊃ (D · G)*   2–4 **CP**
  → 6. *D · G*   **AP /∴ D**
     7. *D*   6 **Simp**
     8. *(D · G) ⊃ D*   6–7 **CP**
     9. *[D ⊃ (D · G)] ·*
        [(D · G) ⊃ D]   5,8 **Conj**
     10. *(D · G) ≡ D*   9 **Equiv**

Exercise 5-2

(6) → 4. *D*   **AP /∴ S**
     5. *B ⊃ W*   2, 4 **MP**
     6. *B*   1, 4 **MP**
     7. *W ⊃ S*   3, 6 **MP**
     8. *W*   5, 6 **MP**
     9. *S*   7, 8 **MP**
     10. *D ⊃ S*   4–9 **CP**

(8) → 3. *K*   **AP /∴ M ⊃ T**
    → 4. *M*   **AP /∴ T**
     5. *(L ∨ M) ⊃ R*   1, 3 **MP**
     6. *M ∨ L*   4 **Add**
     7. *L ∨ M*   6 **Comm**
     8. *R*   5, 7 **MP**
     9. *R ∨ S*   8 **Add**
     10. *T*   2, 9 **MP**
     11. *M ⊃ T*   4–10 **CP**
     12. *K ⊃ (M ⊃ T)*   3–11 **CP**

(14) → 3. *A ∨ C*   **AP /∴ B ∨ D**
     4. *B ∨ D*   1, 2, 3 **CD**
     5. *(A ∨ C) ⊃ (B ∨ D)*   3–4 **CP**

Exercise 5-3

(2)
→	3. ~ A	AP /∴ A
	4. B	1,3 MP
	5. ~ ~ A ∨ ~ B	2 DeM
	6. A ∨ ~ B	5 DN
	7. ~ B	3,6 DS
	8. B · ~ B	4,7 Conj
	9. A	3–8 IP

(4)
→	3. B	AP /∴ ~ B
	4. ~ A	2,3 MP
	5. ~ B · C	1,4 DS
	6. ~ B	5 Simp
	7. B · ~ B	3,6 Conj
	8. ~ B	3–7 IP

(6)
→	4. ~ C	AP /∴ C
	5. ~ ~ A	2,4 MT
	6. A	5 DN
	7. A · B	3,6 Conj
	8. C	1,7 MP
	9. C · ~ C	4,8 Conj
	10. C	4–9 IP

(8)
→	4. ~ (C ∨ D)	AP /∴ C ∨ D
	5. ~ C · ~ D	4 DeM
	6. ~ C	5 Simp
	7. A ∨ D	3,6 MP
	8. ~ D	5 Simp
	9. A	7,8 DS
	10. B	2,9 MP
	11. B ⊃ C	1,9 MP
	12. C	10,11 MP
	13. C · ~ C	6,12 Conj
	14. C ∨ D	4–13 IP

(10)
→	3. ~ (C ⊃ D)	AP /∴ C ⊃ D
	4. ~ (~ C ∨ D)	3 Imp
	5. ~ ~ C · ~ D	4 Dem
	6. ~ ~ C	5 Simp
	7. C	6 DN
	8. D ∨ ~ (A ∨ B)	1,7 MP
	9. ~ D	5 Simp
	10. ~ (A ∨ B)	8,9 DS
	11. ~ A · ~ B	10 Dem
	12. ~ A	11 Simp
	13. ~ B	11 Simp
	14. B	2,12 MP
	15. B · ~ B	13,14 Conj
	16. C ⊃ D	3–15 IP
	17. ~ D ⊃ ~ C	16 Contra

Exercise 5-4

(2) *Without* **IP**:

4.	$(H \cdot A) \supset B$	1 **Exp**
5.	$(A \cdot H) \supset B$	4 **Comm**
6.	$A \supset (H \supset B)$	5 **Exp**
7.	$H \supset (H \supset B)$	3,6 **HS**
8.	$(H \cdot H) \supset B$	7 **Exp**
9.	$H \supset B$	8 **Taut**
10.	$\sim C \supset (B \vee H)$	2 **Comm**
11.	$\sim C \supset (\sim \sim B \vee H)$	10 **DN**
12.	$\sim C \supset (\sim B \supset H)$	11 **Impl**
13.	$(\sim C \cdot \sim B) \supset H$	12 **Exp**
14.	$(\sim C \cdot \sim B) \supset B$	9,13 **HS**
15.	$\sim C \supset (\sim B \supset B)$	14 **Exp**
16.	$\sim C \supset (\sim \sim B \vee B)$	15 **Impl**
17.	$\sim C \supset (B \vee B)$	16 **DN**
18.	$\sim C \supset B$	17 **Taut**
19.	$\sim \sim C \vee B$	18 **Impl**
20.	$C \vee B$	19 **DN**

(2) *With* **IP**:

→ 4.	$\sim (C \vee B)$	**AP** /∴ $C \vee B$
5.	$\sim C \cdot \sim B$	4 **DeM**
6.	$\sim C$	5 **Simp**
7.	$H \vee B$	2,6 **MP**
8.	$\sim B$	5 **Simp**
9.	H	7,8 **DS**
10.	A	3,9 **MP**
11.	$A \supset B$	1,9 **MP**
12.	B	10,11 **MP**
13.	$B \cdot \sim B$	8,12 **Conj**
14.	$C \vee B$	4–13 **IP**

(4) *Without* **IP**:

5.	$\sim (R \supset M) \vee L$	1 **Impl**
6.	$\sim (\sim R \vee M) \vee L$	5 **Impl**
7.	$(\sim \sim R \cdot \sim M) \vee L$	6 **DeM**
8.	$L \vee (\sim \sim R \cdot \sim M)$	7 **Comm**
9.	$(L \vee \sim \sim R) \cdot$ $(L \vee \sim M)$	8 **Dist**
10.	$L \vee \sim \sim R$	9 **Simp**
11.	$\sim (P \supset R) \vee L$	3 **Impl**
12.	$L \vee \sim (P \supset R)$	11 **Comm**
13.	$L \vee \sim (\sim P \vee R)$	12 **Impl**
14.	$L \vee (\sim \sim P \cdot \sim R)$	13 **DeM**
15.	$(L \vee \sim \sim P) \cdot$ $(L \vee \sim R)$	14 **Dist**
16.	$L \vee \sim R$	15 **Simp**
17.	$\sim \sim L \vee \sim R$	16 **DN**
18.	$\sim L \supset \sim R$	17 **Impl**
19.	$\sim \sim R \vee L$	10 **Comm**
20.	$\sim R \supset L$	19 **Impl**
21.	$\sim L \supset L$	18,20 **HS**
22.	$\sim \sim L \vee L$	21 **Impl**
23.	$L \vee L$	22 **DN**
24.	L	23 **Taut**

(4) *With* **IP**:

→ 5.	$\sim L$	**AP** /∴ L
6.	$\sim (R \supset M)$	1,5 **MT**
7.	$\sim (\sim R \vee M)$	6 **Impl**
8.	$\sim \sim R \cdot \sim M$	7 **DeM**
9.	$\sim \sim R$	8 **Simp**
10.	$\sim (P \supset R)$	3,5 **MT**
11.	$\sim (\sim P \vee R)$	10 **Impl**
12.	$\sim \sim P \cdot \sim R$	11 **DeM**
13.	$\sim R$	12 **Simp**
14.	$\sim R \cdot \sim \sim R$	9,13 **Conj**
15.	L	5–14 **IP**

Exercise 5-5

(2)
→ 4.	$\sim (G \cdot \sim I)$	**AP** /∴ $G \cdot \sim I$
5.	$\sim G \vee \sim \sim I$	4 **DeM**
6.	H	2 **Simp**
7.	$I \supset F$	2 **Simp**
8.	$\sim F$	3,6 **MP**
9.	G	1,8 **DS**
10.	$\sim I$	7,8 **MT**
11.	$\sim G \vee I$	5 **DN**
12.	$\sim G$	10,11 **DS**
13.	$G \cdot \sim G$	9,12 **Conj**
14.	$G \cdot \sim I$	4–13 **IP**

(4)
→ 4.	$\sim T$	**AP** /∴ T
5.	$\sim S$	2,4 **MT**
6.	$T \supset R$	1,5 **DS**
7.	$(T \supset R) \cdot \sim (T \supset R)$	3,6 **Conj**
8.	T	4–7 **IP**

(6)
→ 3.	B	**AP** /∴ C
4.	$\sim B \vee \sim A$	2 **DeM**
5.	$\sim \sim B$	3 **DN**
6.	$\sim A$	4,5 **DS**
7.	$D \cdot C$	1,6 **MP**
8.	C	7 **Simp**
9.	$B \supset C$	3–8 **CP**
10.	$\sim C \supset \sim B$	9 **Contra**

(8)
→ 4.	C	**AP** /∴ E
5.	$(A \vee \sim B) \vee \sim C$	1 **Assoc**
6.	$\sim \sim C$	4 **DN**
7.	$A \vee \sim B$	5,6 **DS**
8.	$\sim \sim B \cdot \sim \sim D$	3 **DeM**
9.	$\sim \sim B$	8 **Simp**
10.	A	7,9 **DS**
11.	$D \supset E$	2,10 **MP**
12.	$\sim \sim D$	8 **Simp**
13.	D	12 **DN**
14.	E	11,13 **MP**
15.	$C \supset E$	4–14 **CP**

(10)
→ 3.	$\sim T$	**AP** /∴ T
4.	$\sim S$	2 **MT**
5.	$T \cdot R$	1,4 **DS**
6.	T	5 **Simp**
7.	$T \cdot \sim T$	3,6 **Conj**
8.	T	3–7 **IP**

(12)
→ 3.	$M \cdot H$	**AP** /∴ $N \cdot K$
4.	$(M \cdot H) \supset (N \cdot \sim L)$	2 **Exp**
5.	$N \cdot \sim L$	3,4 **MP**
6.	N	5 **Simp**
7.	$\sim L$	5 **Simp**
8.	H	3 **Simp**
9.	$H \vee K$	8 **Add**
10.	$L \vee K$	1,9 **MP**
11.	K	7,10 **DS**
12.	$N \cdot K$	6,11 **Conj**
13.	$(M \cdot H) \supset (N \cdot K)$	3–12 **CP**

(14)
→ 4.	$D \cdot H$	**AP** /∴ F
5.	D	4 **Simp**
6.	$E \supset F$	1, 5 **MP**
7.	$G \supset \sim H$	3, 5 **MP**
8.	H	4 **Simp**
9.	$E \vee G$	2,8 **MP**
10.	$F \vee \sim H$	6,7,9 **CD**
11.	$\sim \sim H$	8 **DN**
12.	F	10,11 **DS**
13.	$(D \cdot H) \supset F$	4–12 **CP**
14.	$D \supset (H \supset F)$	13 **Exp**
15.	$\sim (H \supset F) \supset \sim D$	14 **Contra**
16.	$\sim (\sim F \supset \sim H) \supset \sim D$	15 **Contra**

Exercise 5-6

(2)
1. $A \cdot B$ — AP /∴ A
2. A — 1 **Simp**
3. $(A \cdot B) \supset A$ — 1–2 **CP**

(4)
1. $A \supset (B \supset C)$ — AP /∴ $(A \supset B) \supset (A \supset C)$
2. $A \supset B$ — AP /∴ $A \supset C$
3. A — AP /∴ C
4. B — 2,3 **MP**
5. $B \supset C$ — 1,3 **MP**
6. C — 4,5 **MP**
7. $A \supset C$ — 3–6 **CP**
8. $(A \supset B) \supset (A \supset C)$ — 2–7 **CP**
9. $[A \supset (B \supset C)] \supset [(A \supset B) \supset$
   $(A \supset C)]$ — 1–8 **CP**

(6)
1. $A \vee B$ — AP /∴ $[(A \supset C) \cdot (B \supset C)] \supset C$
2. $(A \supset C) \cdot (B \supset C)$ — AP /∴ C
3. $A \supset C$ — 2 **Simp**
4. $B \supset C$ — 2 **Simp**
5. $C \vee C$ — 1,3,4 **CD**
6. C — 5 **Taut**
7. $[(A \supset C) \cdot (B \supset C)] \supset C$ — 2–6 **CP**
8. $(A \vee B) \supset \{[(A \supset C) \cdot$
   $(B \supset C)] \supset C\}$ — 1–7 **CP**

(8)
1. $A \equiv B$ — AP /∴ $\sim A \equiv \sim B$
2. $(A \supset B) \cdot (B \supset A)$ — 1 **Equiv**
3. $A \supset B$ — 2 **Simp**
4. $B \supset A$ — 2 **Simp**
5. $\sim B \supset \sim A$ — 3 **Contra**
6. $\sim A \supset \sim B$ — 4 **Contra**
7. $(\sim A \supset \sim B) \cdot (\sim B \supset \sim A)$ — 5,6 **Conj**
8. $\sim A \equiv \sim B$ — 7 **Equiv**
9. $(A \equiv B) \supset (\sim A \equiv \sim B)$ — 1–8 **CP**
10. $\sim A \equiv \sim B$ — AP /∴ $A \equiv B$
11. $(\sim A \supset \sim B) \cdot (\sim B \supset \sim A)$ — 10 **Equiv**
12. $\sim A \supset \sim B$ — 11 **Simp**
13. $\sim B \supset \sim A$ — 12 **Simp**
14. $B \supset A$ — 12 **Contra + 2DN**
15. $A \supset B$ — 13 **Contra + 2DN**
16. $(A \supset B) \cdot (B \supset A)$ — 14,15 **Conj**
17. $A \equiv B$ — 16 **Equiv**
18. $(\sim A \equiv \sim B) \supset (A \equiv B)$ — 10–17 **CP**
19. $(A \equiv B) \supset (\sim A \equiv \sim B) \cdot$
    $(\sim A \equiv \sim B) \supset (A \equiv B)$ — 9,18 **Conj**
20. $(A \equiv B) \equiv (\sim A \equiv \sim B)$ — 19 **Equiv**

Exercise 5-7

(2)   4. $\sim \sim A$ 3 **DN**
       5. B 1,4 **DS**
       6. $\sim B$ 2,4 **DS**
       7. $B \cdot \sim B$ 5,6 **Conj**

(4)   4. $\sim (R \vee S)$ 1 **DeM**
       5. $\sim (S \vee T)$ 3,4 **MP**
       6. $\sim S \cdot \sim T$ 5 **DeM**
       7. $\sim S$ 6 **Simp**
       8. $\sim S \cdot T$ 2,7 **DS**
       9. T 8 **Simp**
      10. $\sim T$ 6 **Simp**
      11. $T \cdot \sim T$ 9,10 **Conj**

(6)   5. $(L \vee K) \supset (L \vee K)$ 1,2 **HS**
       6. $(H \vee \sim H) \supset (H \cdot \sim H)$ 1,4 **HS**
       7. $\sim (H \vee \sim H) \vee (H \cdot \sim H)$ 6 **Impl**
       8. $(\sim H \cdot \sim \sim H) \vee$
          $(H \cdot \sim H)$ 7 **DeM**
       9. $(\sim H \cdot H) \vee (H \cdot \sim H)$ 8 **DN**
      10. $(H \cdot \sim H) \vee (H \cdot \sim H)$ 9 **Comm**
      11. $H \cdot \sim H$ 10 **Taut**

(8)   7. B 6 **Simp**
       8. $\sim C$ 4,7 **MP**
       9. $B \cdot A$ 3,8 **DS**
      10. A 9 **Simp**
      11. $\sim A$ 6 **Simp**
      12. $A \cdot \sim A$ 10,11 **Conj**

(10)   4. $\sim \sim A \cdot \sim [C \supset (B \cdot D)]$ 3 **DeM**
       5. $\sim \sim A$ 4 **Simp**
       6. $\sim \sim C \cdot \sim (A \vee \sim D)$ 2 **DeM**
       7. $\sim (A \vee \sim D)$ 6 **Simp**
       8. $\sim A \cdot \sim \sim D$ 7 **DeM**
       9. $\sim A$ 8 **Simp**
      10. $\sim A \cdot \sim \sim A$ 5,9 **Conj**

Exercise 5-8

2 and 6 are valid argument forms; 4 is an invalid argument form.

Exercise 5-9

(2)   2. A **AP** $/ \therefore \sim A$
       3. $A \vee B$ 2 $\vee$ **I**
       4. $\sim (A \vee B)$ 1 **R**
       5. $(A \vee B) \cdot \sim (A \vee B)$ 3,4 $\cdot$ **I**
       5. $\sim A$ 2–5 $\sim$ **I**
       6. B **AP** $/ \therefore \sim B$
       7. $A \vee B$ 6 $\vee$ **I**
       8. $\sim (A \vee B)$ 1 **R**
       9. $(A \vee B) \cdot \sim (A \vee B)$ 7,8 $\cdot$ **I**
      10. $\sim B$ 6–9 $\sim$ **I**
      11. $\sim A \cdot \sim B$ 5,10 $\cdot$ **I**

(4)   2. $\sim (\sim A \vee \sim B)$ **AP**
                       $/ \therefore \sim \sim (\sim A \vee \sim B)$
       3. $\sim A$ **AP** $/ \therefore \sim \sim A$
       4. $\sim A \vee \sim B$ 3 $\vee$ **I**
       5. $(\sim A \vee \sim B) \cdot$
          $\sim (\sim A \vee \sim B)$ 2,4 $\cdot$ **I**
       6. $\sim \sim A$ 3–5 $\sim$ **I**
       7. A 6 $\sim$ **E**
       8. $\sim B$ **AP** $/ \therefore \sim \sim B$
       9. $\sim A \vee \sim B$ 8 $\vee$ **I**
      10. $(\sim A \vee \sim B) \cdot$
          $\sim (\sim A \vee \sim B)$ 2,9 $\cdot$ **I**
      11. $\sim \sim B$ 8–10 $\sim$ **I**
      12. B 11 $\sim$ **E**
      13. $A \cdot B$ 7,12 $\cdot$ **I**
      14. $(A \cdot B) \cdot \sim (A \cdot B)$ 1,13 $\cdot$ **I**
      15. $\sim \sim (\sim A \vee \sim B)$ 2,6–7,11–14 $\sim$ **I**
      16. $\sim A \vee \sim B$ 15 $\sim$ **E**

(6)
2. ~ B   AP /∴ ~ A
3. A   AP /∴ ~ A
4. B   1,3 ⊃ I
5. B · ~ B   2,4 · I
6. ~ A   3–5 ~ I
7. ~ B ⊃ ~ A   2,6 ⊃ I

(8)
2. ~ A   AP /∴ ~ ~ A
3. A   1,2 ∨ E
4. A · ~ A   2,3 · I
5. ~ ~ A   2–4 ~ I
6. A   5 ~ E

(10)
2. A   1 · E
3. B   1 · E
4. B · A   2,3 · I

(12)
2. A · B   AP /∴ C
3. A   2 · E
4. B ⊃ C   1,3 ⊃ E
5. B   2 · E
6. C   4,5 ⊃ E
7. (A · B) ⊃ C   2–6 ⊃ I

(14)
4. ~ (B ∨ D)   AP /∴ ~ ~ (B ∨ D)
5. B   AP /∴ ~ B
6. B ∨ D   5 ∨ I
7. (B ∨ D) · ~ (B ∨ D)   4,6 · I
8. ~ B   5–7 ~ I
9. A   AP /∴ ~ A
10. B   1,9 ⊃ E
11. B · ~ B   8,10 · I
12. ~ A   9–11 ~ I
13. C   3,12 ∨ E
14. D   2,13 ⊃ E
15. B ∨ D   14 ∨ I
16. (B ∨ D) · ~ (B ∨ D)   4,15 · I
17. ~ ~ (B ∨ D)   4,8,12–16 ~ I
18. B ∨ D   17 ~ E

Exercise 6-1

(2)
✔ 1. $p \supset q$ p
✔ 2. $q \supset (r \cdot p)$ p
3.   p   p /∴ r
4.   ~ r   Negation of conclusion

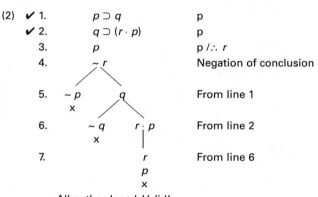

5.   ~ p   q   From line 1
6.   ~ q   r · p   From line 2
7.   r   From line 6

All paths closed. Valid!

(4)
✔ 1. $(p \cdot q) \supset r$ p
2.   p   p /∴ q ⊃ r
✔ 3.   ~ (q ⊃ r)   Negation of conclusion
4.   q   From line 3

✔ 5.   ~ (p · q)   r   From line 1
6. ~ p   ~ q

All paths closed. Valid!

(6) ✔ 1. $p \supset q$ p
     ✔ 2. $\sim (r \cdot q)$ p
        3. r p /∴ $\sim p$
        4. $\not{+} \not{+} p$ Negation of conclusion

        5. $\sim r$ $\sim q$ From line 2
                   x
        6. $\sim p$ q From line 1
                          x   x
              All paths closed. Valid!

(8) ✔ 1. $p \vee q$ p
     ✔ 2. $p \supset \sim r$ p
        3. r p /∴ $\sim q$
        4. $\not{+} \not{+} q$ Negation of conclusion

        5. $\sim p$ $\sim r$ From line 2
                                   x
        6. p q From line 1
              x   *

              Invalid. Open branches. In the branch marked with *, let $V(p) = \mathbf{F}$
                                                                          $V(q) = \mathbf{T}$
                                                                          $V(r) = \mathbf{T}$

(10) ✔ 1. $(p \cdot q) \vee r$ p
        2. $\sim p$ p /∴ r
        3. $\sim r$ Negation of conclusion

     ✔ 4. $p \cdot q$ r From line 1
                   | x
        5. p From line 4
                    q
                    x
              All paths closed. Valid!

(12) ✔ 1. $(p \cdot q) \vee r$ p
     ✔ 2. $\sim (p \vee q)$ p /∴ r
        3. $\sim r$ Negation of conclusion
        4. $\sim p$ From line 2
                        $\sim q$

     ✔ 5. $p \cdot q$ r From line 1
                   | x
        6. p From line 5
                    q
                    x
              All paths closed. Valid!

(14) ✔ 1. $p \lor (\sim q \cdot r)$ p
   ✔ 2. $q \supset \sim p$ p /∴ ~ q
      3.   ≁ ≁ q   Negation of conclusion

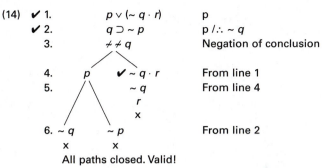

      4.   p   ✔ ~ q · r   From line 1
      5.   ~ q   From line 4
                      r
                      x

      6. ~ q   ~ p   From line 2
        x   x
      All paths closed. Valid!

(16) ✔ 1. $p \supset q$ p
   ✔ 2. $r \supset s$ p
   ✔ 3. $q \lor s$ p /∴ p ∨ r
   ✔ 4. $\sim (p \lor r)$ Negation of conclusion
      5.   ~ p   From line 4
                ~ r

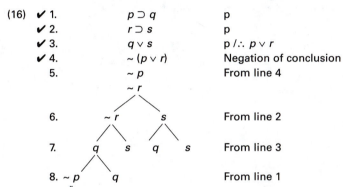

      6.   ~ r   s   From line 2

      7.   q   s   q   s   From line 3

      8. ~ p   q   From line 1
          *

      Invalid. Open branches. In the branch marked with *, let V(p) = **F**
                                                    V(q) = **T**
                                                    V(r) = **F**

(18) ✔ 1. $p \supset q$ p
   ✔ 2. $r \supset s$ p
   ✔ 3. $q \lor r$ p /∴ p ∨ s
   ✔ 4. $\sim (p \lor s)$ Negation of conclusion
      5.   ~ p   From line 4
                ~ s

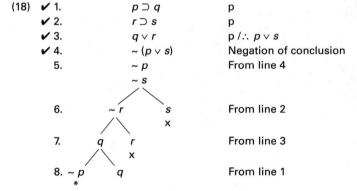

      6.   ~ r   s   From line 2
                        x

      7.   q   r   From line 3
                x

      8. ~ p   q   From line 1
          *

      Invalid. Open branches. In the branch marked with *, let V(p) = **F**
                                                    V(q) = **T**
                                                    V(r) = **F**
                                                   V(s) = **F**

(20) ✔ 1. $p \supset (q \supset r)$ $p / \therefore (\sim r \cdot s) \supset (q \supset \sim t)$
      ✔ 2. $\sim [(\sim r \cdot s) \supset (q \supset \sim t)]$ Negation of conclusion
        3.   ✔ $\sim r \cdot s$ From line 2
              ✔ $\sim (q \supset \sim t)$
        4. $\sim r$ From line 3
                  s
        5. q From line 3
                  t

        6. $\sim p$ $q \supset r$ From line 1
              *

Invalid. Open branches. In the branch marked with *, let $V(p) = $ **F**
                                                           $V(q) = $ **T**
                                                           $V(r) = $ **F**
                                                           $V(s) = $ **T**
                                                           $V(t) = $ **T**

Exercise 6-2

(2) ✔ 1. $p \equiv q$
     ✔ 2. $p \equiv \sim q$

       3. p $\sim p$ From line 1

                     q $\sim q$

       4. p $\sim p$ p $\sim p$ From line 2
              $\sim q$ q $\sim q$ q
                x   x   x   x

                    Inconsistent.

(4) ✔ 1. $p \supset q$
     ✔ 2. $\sim q \vee \sim r$
     ✔ 3. $r \cdot \sim p$
       4. r From line 3
                                 $\sim p$
       5. $\sim q$ $\sim r$ From line 2
                                         x
       6. $\sim p$ q From line 1
                   *   x

Consistent. In the branch marked with *, let $V(p) = $ **F**
                                               $V(q) = $ **F**
                                               $V(r) = $ **T**

(6) ✔ 1. $(p \cdot q) \supset \sim r$

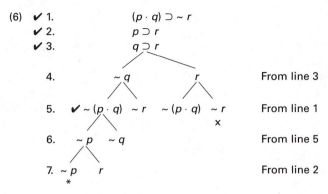

              Consistent. In the branch marked with *, let $V(p) =$ **F**

                                                                 $V(q) =$ **F**

(8) ✔ 1. $p \equiv \sim q$

      2. p

    ✔ 3. $q \lor r$

      4. $\sim r$

      5. q r From line 3

                           x

      6. p $\sim p$ From line 1

           $\sim q$ q

           x   x

       Inconsistent.

(10) ✔ 1. $(p \supset q) \lor (p \supset r)$

    ✔ 2. $\sim (q \lor r)$

      3. p

      4. $\sim q$ From line 2

              $\sim r$

      5.   ✔ $p \supset q$ ✔ $p \supset r$ From line 1

      6. $\sim p$ q $\sim p$ r From line 5

          x   x   x   x

       Inconsistent.

Exercise 6-3

(1) Given the form is invalid, we want to get a case of a false conclusion and true premises. So, if $V(q) =$ **F**, then to get the first premise true we must assign $V(p) =$ **F**. Under those conditions, which are given in the fourth line of the truth table, we want $V(p\,?\,q) =$ **T**.

(2) Since $V(p\,?\,q) =$ **T** only in the fourth line, we know the tree rule for $p?q$ must be

$$p\,?\,q$$
$$\sim p$$
$$\sim q$$

and for $\sim (p\,?\,q)$ our rule must be $\sim (p\,?\,q)$

$$p \qquad q$$

(3) Here is the tree:

✔ 1. $p \supset (q \supset r)$
✔ 2. $r \equiv \sim (\sim p \mathbin{?} \sim r)$ p
✔ 3. $\sim (\sim p \vee \sim q)$ p /∴ $\sim [\sim p \mathbin{?} (\sim q \vee \sim r)]$
✔ 4. $\neq \neq [\sim p \mathbin{?} (\sim q \vee \sim r)]$ Negation of conclusion

   5.   p   From line 3
                          q
✔ 6. $\neq \neq p$ From line 4
                          $\sim (\sim q \vee \sim r)$

   7.   q   From line 6
                          r

   8. $\sim p$ ✔ $q \supset r$ From line 1
                x

   9. $\sim q$ r   From line 8
                        x

   10.   r $\sim r$ From line 2
                    ✔ $\sim (\sim p \mathbin{?} \sim r)$ $\neq \neq (\sim p \mathbin{?} \sim r)$
                                                            x

   11. $\sim p$ $\sim r$ From line 10
                     x   x

         Valid! All paths closed.

Exercise 7-1

   2. *Bb*   6. *Gr · Pr*
   4. $\sim Mj \cdot \sim Mr$ or $\sim (Mj \vee Mr)$ 8. $\sim Mc \supset \sim Mk$

Exercise 7-2

   2.   (1) *x* is bound.
         (2) *a* is an individual constant; *F* and *G* are property constants.
         (3) No free variables; *a* is within the scope of the (*x*) quantifier.
   4.   (1) *y* and the first *x* variable (not counting the *x* that is part of the quantifier) are
             bound; the second *x* variable is free.
         (2) No individual constants; *F, G,* and *D* are property constants.
         (3) Free *x* variable is within the scope of the (*y*) quantifier.
   6.   (1) The first *x* variable and the *y* variable are bound. The last 2 *x* variables are free.
         (2) *F, G,* and *D* serve as property constants; *a* as an individual constant.
         (3) The two free *x* variables are within the scope of the (*y*) quantifier. The individual
             constant, *a*, is within the scope of the (*x*) quantifier.

Exercise 7-3

   2. $(x)(Ex \supset Cx)$ 8. $(x)[Cx \supset (Nx \cdot Ex)]$
   4. $(x)(Ex \supset \sim Cx)$ 10. $(x)[Ex \supset (Nx \vee \sim Cx)]$
   6. $(x)[(Ex \cdot Cx) \supset Nx]$ 12. $(x)[Mx \supset (Cx \cdot \sim Nx)]$
                                                    14. $(x)(Ex \supset Nx) \supset (x)(Ex \supset \sim Mx)$

Exercise 7-4

2. $(x)(Px \supset \sim Ix)$

4. $\sim Ir \supset \sim (x)(Px \supset Ix)$

6. $(Ib \lor \sim Ir) \supset [\sim (x)(Px \supset \sim Ix) \cdot \sim (x)(Px \supset Ix)]$

8. $(x)(Sx \supset \sim Lx)$

10. $(x)(Lx \supset \sim Px)$

12. $\sim (x)(Sx \supset Lx) \supset \sim (x)(Sx \supset \sim Px)$

14. $(x)(Px \supset \sim Sx) \supset (\sim La \supset Sa)$

16. $(\sim Pa \cdot \sim La) \supset [\sim (x)(Sx \supset Px) \cdot \sim (x)(Sx \supset Lx)]$

Exercise 7-5

2. $(\exists x)(Ax \cdot \sim Ox)$

4. $(\exists x)(Ex \cdot Ox)$

6. $(\exists x)(Ax \cdot Px) \cdot (\exists x)(Ax \cdot Tx)$

8. $(\exists x)(Tx \cdot \sim Px)$

10. $(\exists x)(Rx \cdot Sx)$

12. $(\exists x)(Rx \cdot Fx)$

14. $(x)[(Rx \cdot Fx) \supset \sim Dx]$

Exercise 7-6

2. $(x)[(Ax \cdot Px) \supset Mx]$
(Ax = "x is an animal," Px = "x has a pouch," Mx = "x is a marsupial")

4. $(x)[(Ax \cdot \sim Px) \supset \sim Mx]$

6. $(x)[(Wx \lor Bx) \supset (Mx \cdot \sim Kx)]$
(Wx = "x is a wombat," Bx = "x is a bandicoot," Kx = "x is well known")

8. $(x)[Mx \supset (Cx \cdot Fx)] \supset (x)[Ox \supset (Cx \cdot Fx))$
(Cx = "x is cute," Fx = "x is furry," Ox = "x is an opossum")

10. $(x)[(Ax \lor Rx) \supset \sim Mx]$
(Ax = "x is an aardvark," Rx = "x is an armadillo")

12. $(x)[Ax \supset (\sim Mx \cdot \sim Rx)$
(Rx = "x is a reptile")

14. $(\exists x)[(Px \cdot Cx) \cdot \sim Tx]$
(Px = "x is a physician," Cx = "x is competent," Tx = "x is tactful")

16. $\sim (x)[(Sx \cdot Fx) \supset Hx]$
(Sx = "x is a soldier," Fx = "fought in Iraq," Hx = "x is a hero")

18. $(\exists x)(Gx \cdot Cx) \cdot (\exists x)(Bx \cdot Cx)$
(Gx = "x is a Girl Scout," Bx = "x is a Boy Scout," Cx = "x is to be congratulated by Bush")

20. $\sim (x)(Dx \supset Sx) \cdot \sim (x)(Rx \supset Sx)$
(Dx = "x is a Democrat," Rx = "x is a Republican," Sx = "x supported the president's tax plan")

Exercise 7-7

2. Some TV newscasters are not political experts.

4. All TV newscasters are not political experts. Or, No TV newscasters are political experts.

6. Anyone who is a political expert but doesn't have a pleasant personality is not a TV newscaster. Or, No political expert lacking a pleasant personality is a TV newscaster.

8. Some TV newscasters either have pleasant personalities or are political experts.

10. If Dan Rather is a TV newscaster, then not all TV newscasters with pleasant personalities are political experts.

12. If all TV newscasters have pleasant personalities and are political experts, then it's not true that either Dan Rather or Barbara Walters are TV newscasters.

Exercise 7-8

2. $(Fa \lor Ga) \lor (Fb \lor Gb)$

4. $[Fa \cdot (Ga \lor Ha)] \lor [Fb \cdot (Gb \lor Hb)]$

6. $\sim (Fa \cdot Ga) \lor \sim (Fb \cdot Gb)$

8. $\sim [(Fa \lor Ga) \lor (Fb \lor Gb)]$

10. $[Fa \supset \sim (Ga \cdot Ha)] \cdot [Fb \supset \sim (Gb \cdot Hb)]$

12. $[(Fa \cdot Ga) \supset (Ha \cdot Ka)] \cdot [(Fb \cdot Gb) \supset (Hb \cdot Kb)]$

14. $\sim \{\sim [(Fa \cdot Ga) \cdot \sim (Ha \cdot Ka)] \cdot \sim [(Fb \cdot Gb) \cdot \sim (Hb \cdot Kb)]\}$

Exercise 7-9

(Using obvious abbreviations)

2. $(x)[(Sx \cdot Fx) \supset \sim Rx]$

4. $(x)(Hx \supset Px)$

6. $(x)(Dx \supset Sx)$

8. $\sim Qj \supset (x)(Fx \supset Rx)$

10. $\sim (x)(Ex \supset Px) \supset (x)(Ex \supset Dx)$

12. $(x)[Rx \supset (\sim Tx \supset Px)]$

Exercise 7-10

(Using obvious abbreviations, except where noted otherwise.)

2. $(x)(Sx \supset Lx)$

4. $\sim (x)(Lx \supset Gx)$ Or $(\exists x)(Lx \cdot \sim Gx)$
   (Lx = "x glitters," Gs = "x is gold")

6. $(\exists x)(Cx \cdot \sim Sx)$
   (Cx = "x is a cigar," Sx = "x is significant" —the import of Freud's remark)

8. $(x)[(Px \cdot Cx) \supset Dx]$

10. $(x)[(Wx \cdot \sim Mx) \supset Bx]$

12. $(\exists x)[(Bx \cdot Sx) \cdot Cx]$

14. $(\exists x)[(Cx \cdot Sx) \cdot \sim Bx]$

16. $(\exists x)(Sx \cdot \sim Lx) \supset (\exists x)[(Px \cdot \sim Bx) \cdot Sx]$
    (Lx = "x succeeds in life")

18. $(x)(Sx \supset Bx) \supset (x)[(Px \cdot \sim Sx) \supset \sim Lx]$

20. $\sim (\exists x)Sx \supset [(\exists x)(Px \cdot \sim Lx) \cdot (\exists x)(Px \cdot Lx)]$

Exercise 8-1

2. True:

   Domain: Unrestricted

   $Ax = x$ is an NBA basketball player
   $Bx = x$ is more than 6 feet tall

   English: Some NBA basketball players
   are not more than 6 feet tall.

   False:

   Domain: Positive Integers

   $Ax = x > 4$
   $Bx = x > 3$

   English: There are positive integers that
   are greater than 4 and not greater than 3.

4. True:

   Domain: Unrestricted

   $Ax = x$ is a bachelor
   $Bx = x$ wants to marry

   English: Not every bachelor wants
   to marry.

   False:

   Domain: Positive Integers

   $Ax = x > 4$
   $Bx = x > 3$

   English: Not every positive integer
   greater than 4 is greater than 3

6. True:

   Domain: Positive Integers

   $Ax = x > 2$
   $Bx = x > 3$
   $Cx = x > 5$

   English: There are positive integers that
   are greater than 2 and 3 but not greater
   than 5.

   False:

   Domain: Unrestricted

   $Ax = x$ is an argument
   $Bx = x$ has inconsistent premises
   $Cx = x$ is valid

   English: Some arguments with
   inconsistent premises are invalid.

8. True:

   Domain: Unrestricted

   $Ax = x$ is a whale
   $Bx = x$ is a mammal
   $Cx = x$ lives in the sea

   English: If all whales are mammals,
   then some mammals live in the sea.

   False:

   Domain: Positive Integers

   $Ax = x < 0$
   $Bx = x$ is odd
   $Cx = x$ is even

   English: If all positive integers less than
   2 are odd, then some odd positive
   integers are even.

Exercise 8-2

(Assume the domain of discourse to be positive integers.)

2. *Ax = x* is an even number
   Bx = x is an integer

   1. All even positive integers are integers.
   2. <u>Some positive integers are not even.</u>
   ∴ Some positive integers are not integers

4. *Fx = x > 3*
   Gx = x > 2
   Ex = x > 0

   1. Every positive integer greater than 3 is greater than 2.
   2. <u>Every positive integer not greater than 3 is greater than 0.</u>
   ∴ Every positive integer not greater than 2 is not greater than 0.

6. *Px = x* is prime
   Qx = x > 2
   Rx = x is odd

   1. Every prime positive integer greater than 2 is odd.
   2. <u>Some positive integers greater than 2 are not odd.</u>
   ∴ Some positive integers are not prime and not greater than 2.

8. *Mx = x* is prime
   Nx = x > 2
   Px = x is odd
   Qx = x divisible by 1

   1. Every prime number greater than 2 is odd.
   2. <u>Every number not divisible by 1 is not odd.</u>
   ∴ Every number divisible by 1 is both prime and greater than 2.

10. *Ax = x > 10*
    Bx = x > 9
    Cx = x > x

    1. There are positive integers that are either greater than 10 or not greater than 9.
    2. <u>Every positive integer that is both greater than 10 and not greater than 9 is greater than itself.</u>
    ∴ There is at least one positive integer that is greater than itself.

Exercise 8-3

(2) 1. (*Aa* ⊃ *Ba*) · (*Ab* ⊃ *Bb*)
         F T T   T   T   T T
                     ↓   ↓
     2. ~ *Aa* ∨ ~ *Ab* /∴ ~ *Ba* ∨ ~ *Bb*
         T F   T F T   F T F F T

                                    ↓
(4)   1.   (Fa ⊃ Ga) · (Fb ⊃ Gb)
                F   T   F   T   T   T   T

                                    ↓
         2.   (~ Fa ⊃ Ea) · (~ Fb ⊃ Eb)
                T   F   T   T   T   F   T   T   T

                                    ↓
       /∴   (~ Ga ⊃ ~ Ea) · (~ Gb ⊃ ~ Eb)
              T   F   F   F   T   F   F   T   T   F   T

                                    ↓
(6)   1.   [(Pa · Qa) ⊃ Ra] · [(Pb · Qb) ⊃ Rb]
                F   F   T   T   F   T   T   T   F   F   T   F

                                    ↓
         2.   (Qa · ~ Ra) ∨ (Qb · ~ Rb)
                T   T   T   F   T   F   F   F   T   F

                                    ↓
         3.   (Pa · ~ Ra) ∨ (Pb · ~ Rb)
                F   F   T   F   T   T   T   T   F

                                    ↓
       /∴   (~ Pa · ~ Qa) · (~ Pb · ~ Qb)
              T   F   F   F   T   F   F   T   F   T   F

                                    ↓
(8)   1.   [Ma ⊃ (Na ⊃ Pa)] · [Mb ⊃ (Nb ⊃ Pb)]
                F   T   F   T   F   T   F   T   T   T   T

                                    ↓
         2.   (~ Qa ⊃ ~ Pa) · (~ Qb ⊃ ~ Pb)
                T   F   T   T   F   T   F   T   T   F   T

                                    ↓
       /∴   [Qa ⊃ (Ma · Na)] · [Qb ⊃ (Mb · Nb)]
              F   T   F   F   F   F   T   F   F   F   T

                                    ↓
(10)   1.   (Aa ∨ ~ Ba) ∨ (Ab ∨ ~ Bb)
                T   T   F   T   T   T   T   F   T

                                    ↓   ↓   ↓
         2.   [(Aa · ~ Ba) ⊃ Ca] · [(Ab · ~ Bb) ⊃ Cb]   /∴ Ca ∨ Cb
                T   F   F   T   T   F   T   T   F   F   T   T   F   F   F   F

Exercise 8-4

(Assume the domain of discourse to be positive integers.)

2.   Rx = x is even
     Mx = x is odd

   1. Some positive integers are even or odd.

   2. Every positive integer that is odd is not even.

4. $Bx = x$ is even
   $Kx = x < 0$

   1. Some positive integers are even.

   2. No positive integers are less than 0.

   3. Every positive integer less than 0 is not even.

6. $Dx = x$ is even
   $Fx = x$ is odd
   $Gx = x$ is prime

   1. It is not true that all even positive integers are either not odd or are prime.

   2. Some odd positive integers are even or not prime.

8. $Fx = x$ is divisible by 4
   $Gx = x$ is even

   1. Every positive integer divisible by 4 is even.

   2. Not all even positive integers are divisible by 4.

   3. There is a positive integer that is divisible by 4 and even.

Exercise 9-1

(2)
   3. $Ax \vee (Bx \cdot \sim Cx)$ 1 **UI**
   4. Cx 2 **UI**
→ 5. Dx **AP /∴** Ax
   6. $Cx \vee \sim Bx$ 4 **Add**
   7. $\sim Bx \vee Cx$ 6 **Comm**
   8. $\sim Bx \vee \sim \sim Cx$ 7 **DN**
   9. $\sim (Bx \cdot \sim Cx)$ 8 **DeM**
  10. Ax 3,9 **DS**
  11. $Dx \supset Ax$ 5–10 **CP**
  12. $(\exists x)(Dx \supset Ax)$ 11 **EG**

(4)
   4. $Ab \supset Bb$ 2 **UI**
   5. $(Ab \supset Bb) \supset Ab$ 3 **UI**
   6. Ab 4,5 **MP**
   7. Bc 1,6 **MP**

(6)
   4. $Rx \supset \sim Gx$ 1 **UI**
   5. $Bx \vee Gx$ 2 **UI**
   6. Rx 3 **UI**
   7. $\sim Gx$ 4,6 **MP**
   8. Bx 5,7 **DS**
   9. $(y)By$ 8 **UG**

(8)
   4. $(Rb \cdot Ab) \supset Tb$ 1 **UI**
   5. Rb 3 **UI**
   6. $Rb \cdot Ab$ 2,5 **Conj**
   7. Tb 4,6 **MP**
   8. $Tb \cdot Rb$ 5,7 **Conj**

Exercise 9-2

(2)
   4. Invalid. Quantifier must be removed first.

   5. Invalid. The (x) quantifier did not quantify the whole line.

   6. Invalid. Antecedent of line 5 does not match line 3.

   7. Invalid. Can't universally generalize from a constant.

(4)
   5. Invalid. Can't use **UG** to bind a variable that is free in a line that is justified by **EI**. In this case y is free in line 2.

(6)
   4. Invalid. The (x) quantifier does not quantify the whole line.

   5. Invalid. Can't replace a variable with a constant when using **EI**.

   9. Invalid. Can't universally generalize from a constant.

Exercise 9-3

(2) 3. $Fx \supset Gx$ 1 UI
     4. $Gx \supset Hx$ 2 UI
     5. $Fx \supset Hx$ 3,4 HS
     6. $\sim Hx \supset \sim Fx$ 5 Contra
     7. $(z)(\sim Hz \supset \sim Fz)$ 6 UG

(4) 4. $\sim Gx$ 3 EI
     5. $Ax \supset Fx$ 2 UI
     6. $Fx \supset Gx$ 1 UI
     7. $Ax \supset Gx$ 5,6 HS
     8. $\sim Ax$ 4,7 MT
     9. $(\exists x) \sim Ax$ 8 EG

(6) 4. $\sim Ox$ 2 EI
     5. $Rx \supset Ox$ 1 UI
     6. $\sim Rx \supset Px$ 3 UI
     7. $\sim Rx$ 4,5 MT
     8. Px 6,7 MP
     9. $(\exists z) Pz$ 8 EG

(8) 4. Rx 1 EI
     5. $\sim Gx \supset \sim Rx$ 2 UI
     6. Mx 3 UI
     7. $Rx \supset Gx$ 5 Contra
     8. Gx 4,7 MP
     9. $(\exists x) Gx$ 8 EG
    10. $(\exists x) Mx$ 6 EG
    11. $(\exists x) Gx \cdot (\exists x) Mx$ 9, 10 Conj

(10) 3. $Mx \cdot Lx$ 2 EI
      4. $Kx \supset \sim Lx$ 1 UI
      5. Lx 3 Simp
      6. $\sim \sim Lx$ 5 DN
      7. $\sim Kx$ 4,6 MT
      8. Mx 3 Simp
      9. $Mx \cdot \sim Kx$ 7,8 Conj
     10. $(\exists x)(Mx \cdot \sim Kx)$ 9 EG

(12) 4. $Rx \cdot Kx$ 2 EI
      5. $Lx \supset \sim Kx$ 1 UI
      6. $(\sim Lx \cdot Rx) \supset Bx$ 3 UI
      7. Kx 4 Simp
      8. $\sim \sim Kx$ 7 DN
      9. $\sim Lx$ 5,8 MT
     10. Rx 4 Simp
     11. $\sim Lx \cdot Rx$ 9,10 Conj
     12. Bx 6,11 MP
     13. $(\exists x) Bx$ 12 EG

Exercise 9-4

2. Correct.
4. Incorrect. Correct use would result in $(y)(Ry \cdot \sim Ky)$.
6. Correct.

8. Correct.
10. Incorrect. Correct use would result in $\sim (\exists x)(Fx \supset Gx)$.

Exercise 9-5

(2) 2. $Hx \supset \sim Kx$ 1 UI
     3. $\sim Hx \vee \sim Kx$ 2 Impl
     4. $\sim (Hx \cdot Kx)$ 3 DeM
     5. $(y) \sim (Hy \cdot Ky)$ 4 UG
     6. $\sim (\exists y)(Hy \cdot Ky)$ 5 QN

(4) 2. $(x) \sim Fx$ 1 QN
     3. $\sim Fa$ 2 UI
     4. $\sim Fa \vee Ga$ 3 Add
     5. $Fa \supset Ga$ 4 Impl

(6) 3. $(\exists y) \sim Cy$ 2 EG
     4. $\sim (y) Cy$ 3 QN
     5. $\sim (\exists x)(Ax \cdot Bx)$ 1,4 MT
     6. $(x) \sim (Ax \cdot Bx)$ 5 QN
     7. $\sim (Ax \cdot Bx)$ 6 UI
     8. $\sim Ax \vee \sim Bx$ 7 DeM
     9. $Ax \supset \sim Bx$ 8 Impl
    10. $(x)(Ax \supset \sim Bx)$ 9 UG

(8)
3. $(\exists x) \sim (Hx \lor Kx)$ 1 **QN**
4. $\sim (Hx \lor Kx)$ 3 **EI**
5. $\sim Hx \cdot \sim Kx$ 4 **DeM**
6. $\sim Kx$ 5 **Simp**
7. $(\sim Kx \lor Lx) \supset Mx$ 2 **UI**
8. $\sim Kx \lor Lx$ 6 **Add**
9. Mx 7,8 **MP**
10. $(\exists z)Mz$ 9 **EG**

(10)
→ 3. $\sim (\exists x)Sx$ **AP**
4. $\sim (\exists x)Rx$ 1,3 **MT**
5. $(x) \sim Rx$ 4 **QN**
6. $\sim Rx$ 5 **UI**
7. $Tx \supset Rx$ 2 **UI**
8. $\sim Tx$ 6,7 **MT**
9. $(x) \sim Tx$ 8 **UG**
10. $\sim (\exists x)Tx$ 9 **QN**
11. $\sim (\exists x)Sx \supset \sim (\exists x)Tx$ 3–10 **CP**
12. $(\exists x)Tx \supset (\exists x)Sx$ 11 **Contra**

(12)
4. $Ix \cdot \sim Hx$ 2 **EI**
5. $\sim Fx \lor Gx$ 3 **UI**
6. $Gx \supset Hx$ 1 **UI**
7. $Fx \supset Gx$ 5 **Impl**
8. $Fx \supset Hx$ 6,7 **HS**
9. $\sim Hx$ 4 **Simp**
10. $\sim Fx$ 8,9 **MT**
11. Ix 4 **Simp**
12. $Ix \cdot \sim Fx$ 10,11 **Conj**
13. $(\exists x)(Ix \cdot \sim Fx)$ 12 **EG**

(14)
3. $(\exists x) \sim (Fx \supset Gx)$ 1 **QN**
4. $\sim (Fx \supset Gx)$ 3 **EI**
5. $\sim (\sim Fx \lor Gx)$ 4 **Impl**
6. $\sim \sim Fx \cdot \sim Gx$ 5 **DeM**
7. $\sim Gx$ 6 **Simp**
8. $(x) \sim (\sim Gx \cdot Hx)$ 2 **QN**
9. $\sim (\sim Gx \cdot Hx)$ 8 **UI**
10. $\sim \sim Gx \lor \sim Hx$ 9 **DeM**
11. $Gx \lor \sim Hx$ 10 **DN**
12. $\sim Hx$ 7,11 **DS**
13. $(\exists x) \sim Hx$ 12 **EG**

(16)
→ 3. Fx **AP** $/\therefore \sim Lx$
4. $(\exists x)Fx$ 3 **EG**
5. $(\exists x)(Gx \cdot Hx)$ 1,4 **MP**
6. $Gy \cdot Hy$ 5 **EI**
7. Hy 6 **Simp**
8. $Hy \lor Ky$ 7 **Add**
9. $(\exists x)(Hx \lor Kx)$ 8 **EG**
10. $(x)Lx$ 2,9 **MP**
11. Lx 10 **UI**
12. $Fx \supset Lx$ 3–11 **CP**
13. $(x)(Fx \supset Lx)$ 12 **UG**

(18)
3. $Px \supset (Ax \lor Bx)$ 1 **UI**
4. $(Bx \lor Cx) \supset Qx$ 2 **UI**
→ 5. $Px \cdot \sim Ax$ **AP** $/\therefore Qx$
6. Px 5 **Simp**
7. $Ax \lor Bx$ 3,6 **MP**
8. $\sim Ax$ 5 **Simp**
9. Bx 7,8 **DS**
10. $Bx \lor Cx$ 9 **Add**
11. Qx 4,10 **MP**
12. $(Px \cdot \sim Ax) \supset Qx$ 5–11 **CP**
13. $(x)[(Px \cdot \sim Ax) \supset Qx]$ 12 **UG**

(20)
→ 2. $\sim (\exists x)Cx$ **AP** $/\therefore$ $\sim (\exists x)Ax \lor Cx$
3. $(x) \sim Cx$ 2 **QN**
4. $\sim Cx$ 3 **UI**
5. $(Ax \lor Bx) \supset (Cx \cdot Dx)$ 1 **UI**
6. $\sim (Ax \lor Bx) \lor (Cx \cdot Dx)$ 5 **Impl**
7. $(\sim Ax \cdot \sim Bx) \lor (Cx \cdot Dx)$ 6 **DeM**
8. $[(\sim Ax \cdot \sim Bx) \lor Cx] \cdot [(\sim Ax \cdot \sim Bx) \lor Dx]$ 7 **Dist**
9. $(\sim Ax \cdot \sim Bx) \lor Cx$ 8 **Simp**
10. $\sim Ax \cdot \sim Bx$ 4,9 **DS**
11. $\sim Ax$ 10 **Simp**
12. $\sim Ax \cdot \sim Cx$ 4,11 **Conj**
13. $(x) \sim (Ax \lor Cx)$ 12 **DeM**
14. $(x)(\sim Ax \cdot \sim Cx)$ 13 **UG**
15. $\sim (\exists x)(Ax \lor Cx)$ 14 **QN**
16. $\sim (\exists x)Cx \supset \sim (\exists x)(Ax \lor Cx)$ 2–15 **CP**
17. $(\exists x)(Ax \lor Cx) \supset (\exists x)Cx$ 16 **Contra**

Exercise 10-1

2. ~ Mbc
4. ~ (∃x) (Px · Mbx)
6. Abs ⊃ Ake
8. (∃x)[(Wx · Bxd) · ~ Idx]
10. (∃x) ~ Pxf ⊃ (~ Pjf ∨ ~ Pkf)

12. (∃x)(Cx · Ex) ⊃ ~ (∃x)(Px · Sxeg)
14. ~ (∃x)(Mxa · Llx)
16. Lpm ⊃ (∃x)(Mxa · Lpx)
18. Hca ⊃ (∃x)(Sx · ~ Qx)
20. (x)(Sxach ⊃ Tx) ⊃ Hca

Exercise 10-2

2. (∃x)(∃y)Sxy
    (Saa ∨ Sab) ∨ (Sba ∨ Sbb)
4. (x)(∃y)Sxy
    (Saa ∨ Sab) · (Sba ∨ Sbb)
6. ~ (∃x)(y)Sxy
    ~ [(Saa · Sab) ∨ (Sba · Sbb)]

8. (∃x)(y)Syx
    (Saa · Sba) ∨ (Sab · Sbb)
10. ~ (x)(∃y)Sxy
    ~ [(Saa ∨ Sab) · (Sba ∨ Sbb)]
12. (x)(y)(Sxy ⊃ Sxx)
    [(Saa ⊃ Saa) · (Sab ⊃ Saa)]
    · [(Sba ⊃ Sbb) · (Sbb ⊃ Sbb)]

Exercise 10-3

2. ~ (∃x)[Sx · (y)Kxy]
4. ~ (∃x){Sx · (y)[(Ey · Txy) ⊃ Pxy]}
6. (x){(Gx · Sx) ⊃ (∃y)[(Dy · Cy) · Txy]}
8. (∃x)(Sx · ~ Bx) · (∃x)(Cx · ~ Bx)
10. (x){Sx ⊃ (∃y)[(Cy · Tjy) · Txy]}
12. (x)(Qx ⊃ Dx) · (x)(Ex ⊃ Dx) or
    (x)[(Qx ∨ Ex) ⊃ Dx]
14. (x){(Bx · Cx) ⊃ (y)[(Dy · Cy) ⊃ Hxy]}
16. (x) [(Gx · Sx) ⊃ (y)[(By · Cy) ⊃ ~Txy]]

18. (x){(Ex · ~ Pmx) ⊃ (y)[(Ey · Tjy) ⊃ Dxy]}
20. (∃x){[(Dx · Cx) · (y)[(By · Cy) ⊃ Ixy]}
22. (x)(Kjx ⊃ Kmx) · (x)[(Px · Kjx) ⊃ Kmx]
24. (x)[(Cx · ~ Gx) ⊃ ~Tmx]
26. (x){[(Ex · Tjx) · ~ Dx] ⊃ Pjx}
28. (x){(Gx · Sx) ⊃ (y)[(Cy · ~ Dy) ⊃ ~Txy]}
30. (x){(Cx · Tmx) ⊃ (y){[(Cy · Tjy) · Pjy] ⊃
    (Hxy · Ixy)}}

Exercise 10-4

2. ~ (x)(∃y)[(Px · Cy) ⊃ Ayx] or (∃x)[Px · (y)(Cy ⊃ ~ Ayx)]
    (Px = "x is a place"; Cx = "x is a cheater"; Axy = "x is at y")
4. ~ (∃x)(Px · Mxh)
    (Px = "x is a place"; Mxy = "x is more beautiful than y"; h = "Hawaii")
6. (x){Px ⊃ (∃y)[(Ty · Axy) · Fxy]}
    (Tx = "x is a time"; Px = "x is a person"; Axy = "x is alive at y"; Fxy = "x must face reality at y")
8. (x)[Tx ⊃ (∃y)(Py · Fyx)]
    (Tx = "x is a time"; Px = "x is a person"; Fxy = "you can fool x at y")
10. ~ (∃x)(Tx · (∃y)(Py · ~ Ryx))
    (Tx = "x is a time"; Px = "x is a person"; Rxy = "x can still reform at y")
12. (x)[Tx ⊃ (∃y)(Dy · Wryx)]
    (Tx = "x is a time"; Dx = "x is a designer dress"; Wxyz = "x wears y at z"; r = Hillary
    Rodham Clinton)
14. ~ (∃x)[(Tx ∨ Px) · ~ (∃y)(Hy · Ayx)]
    (Tx = "x is a time"; Px = "x is a place"; Hx = "x is an instance of honesty"; Axy = "x is at
    y") (See Chapter Thirteen, Section 4, for a discussion of second-order predicate logic and
    properties of items such as honesty.)

Exercise 10-5

2. $(x)(y)[(Px \cdot Py) \supset (Lxy \supset Bxy)]$ or $(x)\{Px \supset (y)[(Py \cdot Lxy) \supset Bxy]\}$
   (Px = "x is a person"; Lxy = "x laughs after y"; Bxy = "x laughs better than y")

4. $(x)\{Cx \supset [Rx \cdot (y)(Py \supset \sim Hxy)]\}$
   (Cx = "x is a cult"; Rx = "x is a religion"; Px = "x is power"; Hxy = "x has y)

6. $(x)[Gx \supset (y)(Ryx \supset Ly)]$ (Gx = "x is a government"; Rxy = "x runs y"; Lx = "x is a liar")

8. $(x)\{[Px \cdot (\exists y)(Cy \cdot Wxy)] \supset (\exists z)(Hzx \cdot \sim Lz)\}$
   (Px = "x is a person"; Cx = "x is a crown"; Wxy = "x wears y"; Hxy = "x is y's head";
   Lx = "x lies easy")

10. $(x)(y)[(Px \cdot Ay) \supset Oxy]$
    (Px = "x is a good professional"; Ax = "x is an amatuer"; Oxy = "x can outperform y")

12. $(x)[(Px \cdot Hgx) \supset Hxx]$ (g = God; Px = "x is a person"; Hxy = "x helps y")

14. $(x)[Px \supset (y)(Lxy \supset Txyx)]$
    (Px = " x is a person"; Lxy = "x learns y"; $Txyz$ = "x teaches y to z")

16. $(x)(y)[(Vx \cdot My) \supset (z)(Tz \supset Ryxz)]$
    (Vx = "x is virtue"; Mx = "x is money"; Tx = "x is a time; $Rxyz$ = "x is more respectable
    than y at z")

18. $(x)[Px \supset \sim (\exists y)(Ty \cdot Bxya)]$
    (Px = " x is a person"; Tx = "x is a time ; a = "the American public"; $Bxyz$ = "x went
    broke at y underestimating the intelligence of z")

20. $(x)[(Gx \cdot Wsx) \supset \sim Dsx]$ $\cdot$ $(x)[(Ex \cdot \sim Wsx) \supset Dsx]$ or, perhaps
    $(\exists x)[(Gx \cdot Wsx) \cdot \sim Dsx]$ $(\exists x)[(Ex \cdot \sim Wsx) \cdot Dsx]$
    (s = "the speaker" Gx = "x is good"; Ex = "x is evil"; Wxy = "x wants to do y"; Dxy =
    "x does y")

Exercise 10-6

2. $(x)\{[Cx \cdot (\exists y)(Vy \cdot \sim Cxy)] \supset Lx\}$
   (Cx = "x is a candidate"; Vx = "x is a potential voter"; Cxy = "x caters to y"; Lx = "x will
   lose")

4. $(\exists x)(\exists y)[(Px \cdot Dy) \cdot Exy] \supset (x)[Px \supset (\exists y)(Dy \cdot Hxy)]$
   (Px = "x is a politician"; Dx = "x is demogoguery"; Exy = "x engages in y"; Hxy = "x has
   to engage in y")

6. $(x)\{(Px \cdot Bxg) \supset (y)(z)[(Cyg \cdot Tz) \supset Oxyz]\}$
   (Px = "x is a person"; Bxy = "x believes in y"; Cxy = "x is a commandment of y"; Tx = "x
   is a time"; $Oxyz$ = "x obeys y at z"; g = "God")

8. $(x)[Px \supset (\exists y)(\exists z)[(Dy \cdot Tz) \cdot Bxyz]$
   (Px = "x is a person"; Dx = "x is a scientific discovery"; Tx = "x is a time"; $Bxyz$ = "x has
   benefited from y at z")

10. $(x)(y)[(Px \cdot Dyn) \supset Bxy] \supset (\exists x)(\exists y)[(Px \cdot Gy) \supset Oxyn]$
    (Px = "x is a person"; Dxy = "x is a discovery of y"; Bxy = "x has benefited from y";
    Gx = "x is a debt of gratitude"; $Oxyz$ = "x owes y to z"; n = Newton)

12. $(x)\{Px \supset (\exists y)(\exists z)[(Py \cdot Mz) \cdot Oxzy]\} \supset \sim (\exists x)[Px \cdot (y)(Dy \supset Fxy)]$
    (Px = "x is a person"; Mx = "x is money"; $Oxyz$ = "x owes y to z"; Dx = "x is a debt"; Fxy
    = "x is free of y")

14. $(x)[\{Px \cdot \sim (\exists y)(\exists z)[(My \cdot Sz) \cdot Pxyz]\} \supset (y)\{Py \cdot (\exists z)(\exists u)[(Mz \cdot Su) \cdot Pyzu] \supset Lxy]$ (Px = "x is
    a person"; Mx = "x is money"; Sx = "x is a scientist"; $Pxyz$ = "x pays y to z"; Lxy = "x
    looks down on y")

Exercise 10-7

2. Some people believe in God.
4. Not everyone believes in God.
6. Anyone who doesn't vote is disenfranchised.
8. Not all nonvoters are disenfranchised.
10. Some people don't have any redeeming features.

12. All redeeming features are lacked by somebody (or other).
14. No one has any redeeming features.
16. If Art doesn't vote, then if everyone who doesn't vote is disenfranchised, then Art is disenfranchised.
18. Anyone who votes is the master of someone who doesn't vote.

Exercise 10-8

(2) 1. $(Faa \lor Fab) \cdot (Fba \lor Fbb)$
          T T F T F T T
   /∴ $(Faa \cdot Fab) \lor (Fba \cdot Fbb)$
          T F F F F F T

(4) 1. $[(Fa \supset Gaa) \lor (Fa \supset Gab)] \cdot [(Fb \supset Gba) \lor (Fb \supset Gbb)]$
          T T T   T T F   F   T T T   T T T   F   F
   /∴ $[(Fa \supset Gaa) \cdot (Fa \supset Gab)] \lor [(Fb \supset Gba) \cdot (Fb \supset Gbb)]$
          T T T   F T F   F   F T T   T F T   F   F

(6) 1. $[(Faa \supset Gaa) \lor (Fab \supset Gab)] \cdot [(Fba \supset Gba) \lor (Fbb \supset Gbb)]$
          T T   T T T   F   F   T T   T T T   F   F
     2. $[(Gaa \supset Haa) \lor (Gab \supset Hab)] \cdot [(Gba \supset Hba) \lor (Gbb \supset Hbb)]$
          T F   F T F   T   F   T T   F F T   F   T   F
   /∴ $(Faa \supset Haa) \lor (Fab \supset Hab)] \cdot [(Fba \supset Hba) \lor (Fbb \supset Hbb)]$
          T F   F F T   F   F   F T   F F F   T   F   F

(8) 1. $[(Faaa \cdot Faab) \cdot (Faba \cdot Fabb)] \lor [(Fbaa \cdot Fbab) \cdot (Fbba \cdot Fbbb)]$
          T T T T T T T   T   F   F F F F F F
   /∴ $[(Faaa \lor Faab) \cdot (Faba \lor Fabb)] \cdot [(Fbaa \lor Fbab) \cdot (Fbba \lor Fbbb)]$
          T T T T T   T T F F   F   F F F F F

Exercise 10-9

(2) 1. Inference to line 4 violates the second restriction on **EI.**

   2. Inference to line 6 is invalid, because the *x* on line 6, supposedly obtained by **EG,** is in fact free.

(4) 1. Inference to line 3 is invalid because the *y* on line 3 that replaces the *x* on line 1 is not free.

   2. Inference to line 5 is invalid because if *Fy* is substituted for *p* in a given use of **MP,** we cannot also substitute *Fx* for *p* in that same use.

   3. Inference to line 8 violates the restriction on **EG,** since there are not 2 *y* variables free in line 7 corresponding to the 2 *w* variables free in $(Fw \supset Gw)$.

   4. Inference to line 9 is invalid because the scope of the $(\exists w)$ quantifier has been extended to cover *Gy.*

(6) 1. Inference to line 3 is invalid because the (*y*) quantifier dropped by **UI** does not quantify the whole line.

   2. Assuming that line 3 had been obtained by a valid use of **UI,** line 6 would be valid because the use of **UG** on that line quantifies the *y* variable introduced free by **UI** and not the *a* constant free in the assumed premise (line 4) within whose scope this use of **UG** lies.

   3. The inference to line 8 is invalid, because the **EG** is done only to part of line 7.

Exercise 10-10

(2)
2. $(y)(Fay \cdot Fya)$ — 1 **UI**
3. $Faa \cdot Faa$ — 2 **UI**
4. Faa — 3 **Taut**

(4)
3. $\sim Fx$ — 2 **EI**
4. $Fx \lor (\exists y)Gy$ — 1 **UI**
5. $(\exists y)Gy$ — 3,4 **DS**
6. Gy — 5 **EI**
7. $(\exists x)Gx$ — 6 **EG**

(6)
2. $(y)(Fwy \supset Gyw)$ — 1 **EI**
3. $Fwz \supset Gzw$ — 2 **UI**
4. $(\exists y)(Fyz \supset Gzy)$ — 3 **EG**
5. $(x)(\exists y)(Fyx \supset Gxy)$ — 4 **UG**

(8)
2. $(y) \sim Fxy$ — 1 **EI**
3. $\sim Fxa$ — 2 **UI**
4. $(\exists x) \sim Fxa$ — 3 **EG**
5. $\sim (x)Fxa$ — 4 **QN**

(10)
2. $(y)(\sim Axy \supset Ayx)$ — 1 **EI**
3. $\sim Axx \supset Axx$ — 2 **UI**
4. $\sim \sim Axx \lor Axx$ — 3 **Impl**
5. $Axx \lor Axx$ — 4 **DN**
6. Axx — 5 **Taut**
7. $(\exists y)Axy$ — 6 **EG**
8. $\sim (y) \sim Axy$ — 7 **QN**
9. $(\exists x) \sim (y) \sim Axy$ — 8 **EG**
10. $\sim (x)(y) \sim Axy$ — 9 **QN**

(12)
3. $(y) \sim (\exists x) \sim Bxy$ — 2 **QN**
4. $(y)(x) \sim \sim Bxy$ — 3 **QN**
5. $(y)(Cw \supset \sim Byw)$ — 1 **EI**
6. $Cw \supset \sim Byw$ — 5 **UI**
7. $(x) \sim \sim Bxw$ — 4 **UI**
8. $\sim \sim Byw$ — 7 **UI**
9. $\sim Cw$ — 6,8 **MT**
10. $(\exists y) \sim Cy$ — 9 **EG**
11. $\sim (y)Cy$ — 10 **QN**

Exercise 10-11

(2)
2. $Fx \cdot (y)(Gy \supset Hxy)$ — 1 **EI**
3. Fx — 2 **Simp**
4. $(y)(Gy \supset Hxy)$ — 2 **Simp**
5. $Ga \supset Hxa$ — 4 **UI**
6. $Fx \cdot (Ga \supset Hxa)$ — 3,5 **Conj**
7. $(\exists x)[Fx \cdot (Ga \supset Hxa)]$ — 6 **EG**

(4)
3. $(\exists y)Ay$ — **AP**
    $/\therefore \sim Gx$
4. Ay — 3 **EI**
5. $(\exists x)Ax$ — 4 **EG**
6. $\sim (\exists y)Gy$ — 2,5 **MP**
7. $(y) \sim Gy$ — 6 **QN**
8. $\sim Gx$ — 7 **UI**
9. $(\exists y)Ay \supset \sim Gx$ — 3–8 **CP**
10. $(x)[(\exists y)Ay \supset \sim Gx]$ — 9 **UG**

(6)
3. $\sim (\exists x)(y) \sim Fxy$ — **AP**
    $/\therefore (\exists x)(y) \sim Fxy$
4. $(x) \sim (y) \sim Fxy$ — 3 **QN**
5. $(x)(\exists y)Fxy$ — 4 **QN**
6. $(x)(\exists y)Gxy$ — 1,5 **MP**
7. $(y) \sim Gxy$ — 2 **EI**
8. $(\exists y)Gxy$ — 6 **UI**
9. Gxy — 8 **EI**
10. $\sim Gxy$ — 7 **UI**
11. $Gxy \cdot \sim Gxy$ — 9,10 **Conj**
12. $(\exists x)(y) \sim Fxy$ — 3–11 **IP**

(8)
3. $Ax \cdot (y)[(Ay \cdot Bxy) \supset Cxy]$ — 2 **EI**
4. $Ax \supset (\exists y)(Ay \cdot Bxy)$ — 1 **UI**
5. Ax — 3 **Simp**
6. $(\exists y)(Ay \cdot Bxy)$ — 4,5 **MP**
7. $Ay \cdot Bxy$ — 6 **EI**
8. $(y)[(Ay \cdot Bxy) \supset Cxy]$ — 3 **Simp**
9. $(Ay \cdot Bxy) \supset Cxy$ — 8 **UI**
10. Cxy — 7,9 **MP**
11. $\sim (\exists x)(\exists y)[(Ax \cdot Ay) \supset Cxy]$ — **AP**
    $/\therefore (\exists x)(\exists y)[(Ax \cdot Ay) \supset Cxy]$
12. $(x) \sim (\exists y)[(Ax \cdot Ay) \supset Cxy]$ — 11 **QN**
13. $(x)(y) \sim [(Ax \cdot Ay) \supset Cxy]$ — 12 **QN**
14. $(y) \sim [(Ax \cdot Ay) \supset Cxy]$ — 13 **UI**
15. $\sim [(Ax \cdot Ay) \supset Cxy]$ — 14 **UI**
16. $\sim [\sim (Ax \cdot Ay) \lor Cxy]$ — 15 **Impl**
17. $\sim \sim (Ax \cdot Ay) \cdot \sim Cxy$ — 16 **DeM**
18. $\sim Cxy$ — 17 **Simp**
19. $Cxy \cdot \sim Cxy$ — 10,18 **Conj**
20. $(\exists x)(\exists y)[(Ax \cdot Ay) \supset Cxy]$ — 11–19 **IP**

(10) →3. ~ (x)(Dx ⊃ Ex)   **AP**
           /∴ ~ ~ (∃x)[Dx · (~ Ax ∨ ~ Bx)]
        4. ~ ~ (∃x)(Cx · Dx)   2,3 **MT**
        5. (∃x)(Cx · Dx)   4 **DN**
        6. Cx · Dx   5 **EI**
        7. Ax ⊃ (Bx ⊃ ~ Cx)   1 **UI**
        8. Cx   6 **Simp**
        9. ~ ~ Cx   8 **DN**
       10. (Ax · Bx) ⊃ ~ Cx   7 **Exp**
       11. ~ (Ax · Bx)   9,10 **MT**
       12. ~ Ax ∨ ~ Bx   11 **DeM**
       13. Dx   6 **Simp**
       14. Dx · (~ Ax ∨ ~ Bx)   12,13 **Conj**
       15. (∃x)[Dx · (~ Ax ∨ ~ Bx)]   14 **EG**
       16. ~ ~ (∃x)[Dx ·
           (~ Ax ∨ ~ Bx)]   15 **DN**
      17. ~ (x)(Dx ⊃ Ex) ⊃ ~ ~ (∃x)[Dx ·
          (~ Ax ∨ ~ Bx)]   3–16 **CP**
      18. ~ (∃x)[Dx · (~ Ax ∨ ~ Bx)] ⊃
          (x)(Dx ⊃ Ex)   17 **Contra**
                                            + 2 **DN**

(12)   4. Dz · (∃x)[(Ex · Fx) · Bzx]   2 **EI**
       5. (∃x)[(Ex · Fx) · Bzx]   4 **Simp**
       6. (Ew · Fw) · Bzw   5 **EI**
       7. Ew · Fw   6 **Simp**
       8. Fw   7 **Simp**
       9. Fw ⊃ Aw   3 **UI**
      10. Aw   8,9 **MP**
      11. (∃y)(Ay · Bzy) ⊃ Cz   1 **UI**
      12. Bzw   6 **Simp**
      13. Aw · Bzw   10,12 **Conj**
      14. (∃y)(Ay · Bzy)   13 **EG**
      15. Cz   11,14 **MP**
      16. Dz   4 **Simp**
      17. Cz · Dz   15,16 **Conj**
      18. (∃x)(Cx · Dx)   17 **EG**

(14) →3. ~ (x)(y) ~ Axy   **AP**
           /∴ (x)(y) ~ Axy
        4. (∃x) ~ (y) ~ Axy   3 **QN**
        5. (∃x)(∃y)Axy   4 **QN**
        6. (∃y)Axy   5 **EI**
        7. Axy   6 **EI**
        8. Axy ∨ Bxy   7 **Add**
        9. (∃y)(Axy ∨ Bxy)   8 **EG**
       10. (∃x)(∃y)(Axy ∨ Bxy)   9 **EG**
       11. (∃z)Cz   1,10 **MP**
       12. Cz   11 **EI**
       13. (y)(Cz ⊃ ~ Cy)   2 **UI**
       14. Cz ⊃ ~ Cz   13 **UI**
       15. ~ Cz ∨ ~ Cz   14 **Impl**
       16. ~ Cz   15 **Taut**
       17. Cz · ~ Cz   12,16 **Conj**
       18. (x)(y) ~ Axy   3–17 **IP**

Exercise 10-12

(2) →1. ~ (x)(Gx ≡ Gx)   **AP**
          /∴ (x)(Gx ≡ Gx)
       2. (∃x) ~ (Gx ≡ Gx)   1 **QN**
       3. ~ (Gx ≡ Gx)   2 **EI**
       4. ~ [(Gx ⊃ Gx) ·
          (Gx ⊃ Gx)]   3 **Equiv**
       5. ~ (Gx ⊃ Gx)   4 **Taut**
       6. ~ (~ Gx ∨ Gx)   5 **Impl**
       7. (~ ~ Gx · ~ Gx)   6 **DeM**
       8. (x)(Gx ≡ Gx)   1–7 **IP**

(4) →1. (∃x)(y)Fxy   **AP**
          /∴ (y)(∃x)Fxy
       2. (y)Fxy   1 **EI**
       3. Fxy   2 **UI**
       4. (∃x)Fxy   3 **EG**
       5. (y)(∃x)Fxy   4 **UG**
       6. (∃x)(y)Fxy ⊃
          (y)(∃x)Fxy   1–5 **CP**

(6)
1. $(x)Fx \lor (x)Gx$ **AP** $/\therefore (Fx \lor Gx)$
2. $\sim Fx$ **AP** $/\therefore Gx$
3. $(\exists x)\sim Fx$ 2 **EG**
4. $\sim(x)Fx$ 3 **QN**
5. $(x)Gx$ 1,4 **DS**
6. Gx 5 **UI**
7. $\sim Fx \supset Gx$ 2–6 **CP**
8. $\sim\sim Fx \lor Gx$ 7 **Impl**
9. $Fx \lor Gx$ 8 **DN**
10. $(x)(Fx \lor Gx)$ 9 **UG**
11. $[(x)Fx \lor (x)Gx] \supset (x)(Fx \lor Gx)$ 1–10 **CP**

(8)
1. $(\exists x)(Fx \cdot Gx)$ **AP** $/\therefore (\exists x)Fx \cdot (\exists x)Gx$
2. $Fx \cdot Gx$ 1 **EI**
3. Fx 2 **Simp**
4. $(\exists x)Fx$ 3 **EG**
5. Gx 2 **Simp**
6. $(\exists x)Gx$ 5 **EG**
7. $(\exists x)Fx \cdot (\exists x)Gx$ 4,6 **Conj**
8. $(\exists x)(Fx \cdot Gx) \supset [(\exists x)Fx \cdot (\exists x)Gx]$ 1–7 **CP**

(10)
1. $(x)Fx \cdot P$ **AP** $/\therefore (x)(Fx \cdot P)$
2. $(x)Fx$ 1 **Simp**
3. Fx 2 **UI**
4. P 1 **Simp**
5. $Fx \cdot P$ 3,4 **Conj**
6. $(x)(Fx \cdot P)$ 5 **UG**
7. $[(x)Fx \cdot P] \supset (x)(Fx \cdot P)$ 1–6 **CP**
8. $(x)(Fx \cdot P)$ **AP** $/\therefore (x)Fx \cdot P$
9. $Fx \cdot P$ 8 **UI**
10. Fx 9 **Simp**
11. $(x)Fx$ 10 **UG**
12. P 9 **Simp**
13. $(x)Fx \cdot P$ 11,12 **Conj**
14. $(x)(Fx \cdot P) \supset [(x)Fx \cdot P]$ 8–13 **CP**
15. $7 \cdot 14$ 7,14 **Conj**
16. $[(x)Fx \cdot P] \equiv (x)(Fx \cdot P)$ 15 **Equiv**

(12)
1. $(x)(P \supset Fx)$ **AP** $/\therefore P \supset (x)Fx$
2. P **AP** $/\therefore (x)Fx$
3. $P \supset Fx$ 1 **UI**
4. Fx 2,3 **MP**
5. $(x)Fx$ 4 **UG**
6. $P \supset (x)Fx$ 2–5 **CP**
7. $(x)(P \supset Fx) \supset [P \supset (x)Fx]$ 1–6 **CP**
8. $P \supset (x)Fx$ **AP** $/\therefore (x)(P \supset Fx)$
9. P **AP** $/\therefore Fx$
10. $(x)Fx$ 8,9 **MP**
11. Fx 10 **UI**
12. $P \supset Fx$ 9–11 **CP**
13. $(x)(P \supset Fx)$ 12 **UG**
14. $[P \supset (x)Fx] \supset (x)(P \supset Fx)$ 8–13 **CP**
15. $7 \cdot 14$ 7,14 **Conj**
16. $(x)(P \supset Fx) \equiv [P \supset (x)Fx]$ 15 **Equiv**

(14)
1. $(\exists x)(P \cdot Fx)$ **AP** $/\therefore P \cdot (\exists x)Fx$
2. $P \cdot Fx$ 1 **EI**
3. P 2 **Simp**
4. Fx 2 **Simp**
5. $(\exists x)Fx$ 4 **EG**
6. $P \cdot (\exists x)Fx$ 3,5 **Conj**
7. $(\exists x)(P \cdot Fx) \supset [P \cdot (\exists x)Fx]$ 1–6 **CP**
8. $P \cdot (\exists x)Fx$ **AP** $/\therefore (\exists x)(P \cdot Fx)$
9. P 8 **Simp**
10. $(\exists x)Fx$ 8 **Simp**
11. Fx 10 **EI**
12. $P \cdot Fx$ 9,11 **Conj**
13. $(\exists x)(P \cdot Fx)$ 12 **EG**
14. $[P \cdot (\exists x)Fx] \supset (\exists x)(P \cdot Fx)$ 8–13 **CP**
15. $\{(\exists x)(P \cdot Fx) \supset [P \cdot (\exists x)Fx]\} \cdot \{[P \cdot (\exists x)Fx] \supset (\exists x)(P \cdot Fx)\}$ 7,14 **Conj**
16. $(\exists x)(P \cdot Fx) \equiv [P \cdot (\exists x)Fx]$ 15 **Equiv**

(16) ⊢→ 1. (∃x)(Fx ⊃ P)   AP /∴ (x)Fx ⊃ P
    ⌐→ 2. (x)Fx   AP /∴ P
     | 3. Fx ⊃ P   1 EI
     | 4. Fx   2 UI
     ⌊   5. P   3,4 MP
         6. (x)Fx ⊃ P   2–5 CP
         7. (∃x)(Fx ⊃ P) ⊃ [(x)Fx ⊃ P]   1–6 CP
    ⌐→ 8. ~ (∃x)(Fx ⊃ P)   AP /∴ ~ [(x)Fx ⊃ P]
     | 9. (x) ~ (Fx ⊃ P)   8 QN
     | 10. ~ (Fy ⊃ P)   9 UI
     | 11. ~ (~Fy ∨ P)   10 Impl
     | 12. ~ ~Fy · ~ P   11 DeM
     | 13. Fy · ~ P   12 DN
     | 14. Fy   13 Simp
     | 15. (x)Fx   14 UG
     | 16. ~ P   13 Simp
     | 17. (x)Fx · ~ P   15,16 Conj
     | 18. ~ ~ (x)Fx · ~ P   17 DN
     | 19. ~ [~ (x)Fx ∨ P]   18 DeM
     ⌊ 20. ~ [(x)Fx ⊃ P]   19 Impl
        21. ~ (∃x)(Fx ⊃ P) ⊃ ~ [(x)Fx ⊃ P] 8–20 CP
        22. [(x)Fx ⊃ P] ⊃ (∃x)(Fx ⊃ P)   21 Contra
        23. {(∃x)(Fx ⊃ P) ⊃[(x)Fx ⊃ P]} ·
             {[(x)Fx ⊃ P] ⊃ (∃x)(Fx ⊃ P)}   7,22 Conj
        24. (∃x)(Fx ⊃ P) ≡ [(x)Fx ⊃ P]   23 Equiv

Exercise 10-13

(2)   2. (x) ~ Fx   1 QN   (8) ⌐→ 2. ~ (∃x)(Ax ⊃ Gx)   AP
       3. ~ Fa   2 UI | /∴ (∃x)(Ax ⊃ Gx)
       4. ~ Fa ∨ Ga   3 Add | 3. (x) ~ (Ax ⊃ Gx)   2 QN
       5. Fa ⊃ Ga   4 Impl | 4. (x) ~ Ax   1 QN
(4)   3. Fy ∨ (∃x)Gx   1 UI | 5. ~ Ax   4 UI
       4. ~ Fy   2 UI | 6. ~ (Ax ⊃ Gx)   3 UI
       5. (∃x)Gx   3,4 DS | 7. ~ (~ Ax ∨ Gx)   6 Impl
(6) ⌐→ 3. ~ (x)Hx   AP /∴ (x)Hx | 8. ~ ~ Ax · ~ Gx   7 DeM
      | 4. (∃x) ~ Hx   3 QN   ⌊   9. ~ ~ Ax   8 Simp
      | 5. ~ Hx   4 EI   10. ~ Ax · ~ ~ Ax   5,9 Conj
      | 6. Ka ⊃ (y)Hy   2 UI   11. (∃x)(Ax ⊃ Gx)   2–10 IP
      | 7. (y)Hy   1,6 MP
      | 8. Hx   7 UI
      ⌊ 9. Hx · ~ Hx   5,8 Conj
        10. (x)Hx   3–9 IP

(10)

→ 4.	~ [(∃x)Gx · (∃x)Mx]	**AP** /∴ (∃x)Gx · (∃x)Mx
5.	~ (∃x)Gx ∨ ~ (∃x)Mx	4 **DeM**
6.	Rx	1 **EI**
7.	~ Gx ⊃ ~ Rx	2 **UI**
8.	~ ~ Rx	6 **DN**
9.	~ ~ Gx	7,8 **MT**
10.	~ ~ (∃x)Mx	3 **DN**
11.	~ (∃x)Gx	5,10 **DS**
12.	(x) ~ Gx	11 **QN**
13.	~ Gx	12 **UI**
14.	~ Gx · ~ ~ Gx	13,9 **Conj**
15.	(∃x)Gx · (∃x)Mx	4–14 **IP**

Exercise 10-14

(2)

→ 2.	~ (x)(∃y)Fxy	**AP** /∴ (x)(∃y)Fxy
3.	(∃x)(y) ~ Fxy	2 **QN** (twice)
4.	(y) ~ Fxy	3 **EI**
5.	(x)Fxy	1 **EI**
6.	Fxy	5 **UI**
7.	~ Fxy	4 **UI**
8.	Fxy · ~ Fxy	6,7 **Conj**
9.	(x)(∃y)Fxy	2–8 **IP**

(4)

→ 3.	~ (∃x)(∃y)Gxy	**AP** /∴ (∃x)(∃y)Gxy
4.	(x)(y) ~ Gxy	3 **QN** (twice)
5.	Fx	2 **EI**
6.	Fx ⊃ (∃y)Gxy	1 **UI**
7.	(∃y)Gxy	5,6 **MP**
8.	Gxy	7 **EI**
9.	~ Gxy	4 **UI** (twice)
10.	Gxy · ~ Gxy	8,9 **Conj**
11.	(∃x)(∃y)Gxy	3–10 **IP**

(6)

→ 2.	~ (x)[(∃y)Ay ⊃ ~ Gx]	**AP** /∴ (x)[(∃y)Ay ⊃ ~ Gx]
3.	(∃x) ~ [(∃y)Ay ⊃ ~ Gx]	2 **QN**
4.	~ [(∃y)Ay ⊃ ~ Gx]	3 **EI**
5.	~ [~ (∃y)Ay ∨ ~ Gx]	4 **Impl**
6.	(∃y)Ay · Gx	5 **DeM DN**
7.	(∃y)Ay	6 **Simp**
8.	Ay	7 **EI**
→ 9.	~ (∃x)Ax	**AP** /∴ (∃x)Ax
10.	(x) ~ Ax	9 **QN**
11.	~ Ay	10 **UI**
12.	Ay · ~ Ay	8,11 **Conj**
13.	(∃x)Ax	9,12 **IP**
14.	~ (∃y)Gy	1,13 **MP**
15.	(y) ~ Gy	14 **QN**
16.	~ Gx	15 **UI**
17.	Gx	6 **Simp**
18.	Gx · ~ Gx	16,17 **Conj**
19.	(x)[(∃y)Ay ⊃ ~ Gx]	2–8,13–18 **IP**

Exercise 11-1

2. The inference to line 5 is invalid, because it violates the fourth restriction on **UG**; to each x free in (Px ⊃ Lxx) there does not correspond a y free in Py ⊃ Lxy.

(No answers are provided for the other items in this exercise set, because the importance of the questions lies in the way students explain and defend their answers.)

Exercise 11-2

(2)
```
   →  2. Flag a
      3. (x)Fxb              1 EI Flag b
      4. Fab                 3 UI
      5. (∃y)Fay             4 EI
      6. (x)(∃y)Fxy          2–5 UG
```
(4)
```
      3. Fa                  2 EI Flag a
      4. Fa ⊃ (∃y)Gay        1 UI
      5. (∃y)Gay             3,4 MP
      6. (∃x)(∃y)Gxy         5 EG
```

(6)
```
   →  2. Flag a
    → 3. (∃y)Ay              CP /∴ ~ Ga
      4. Ab                  3 EI
      5. (∃x)Ax              4 EG
      6. ~ (∃y)Gy            1,5 MP
      7. (y) ~ Gy            6 QN
      8. ~ Ga                7 UI
      9. (∃y)Ay ⊃ ~ Ga       3–8 CP
     10. (x)[(∃y)Ay ⊃ ~ Gx]  2–9 UG
```

Exercise 12-1

(2)
```
      1.      (x)[Fx ⊃ (y)Gy]      p
      2.      Fa                   p /∴ (x)Gx
    ✔ 3.      ~ (x)Gx              Denial of conclusion
    ✔ 4.      (∃x) ~ Gx            3 FC2
      5.      ~ Gb                 4 FC4
    ✔ 6.      Fa ⊃ (y)Gy           1 FC5
    ✔ 7.      Fb ⊃ (y)Gy           1 FC5

    ✔ 8.   ~ Fa      (y)Gy         6 FC3
      9.    x

     10.   ~ Fb        (y)Gy       7 FC3
     11.    Ga
           Gb   8 FC4
                       Ga          10 FC4
     12.    x           Gb
     13.                 x
```
Valid. All paths close.

(4)
```
    ✔ 1.      (∃x)Fx                      p
      2.      (x)(~ Gx ⊃ ~ Fx)            p
      3.      (x)Mx                       p /∴ (∃x)Gx · (∃x)Mx
    ✔ 4.      ~ [(∃x)Gx · (∃x)Mx]         Denial of conclusion
    ✔ 5.      ~ (∃x)Gx ∨ ~ (∃x)Mx         4 FC3
    ✔ 6.      (x) ~ Gx ∨ (x) ~ Mx         5 FC2
      7.
              (x) ~ Gx    (x) ~ Mx        6 FC3

      8.        Fa          Fa            1 FC4
      9.       ~ Ga        ~ Ma           7 FC5
     10.        Ma          Ma            3 FC5
     11.                     x

            ~ ~ Ga    ~ Fa                2 FC5
     12.      x         x
```
Valid. All paths close.

(6) ✔ 1. $(x)(Ax \supset Fx)$ p
   ✔ 2. $(\exists x)Fx \supset \sim (\exists y)Gy$ p /∴ $(x)[(\exists y)Ay \supset \sim Gx]$
   ✔ 3. $\sim (x)[(\exists y)Ay \supset \sim Gx]$ Denial of conclusion
   ✔ 4. $(\exists x) \sim [(\exists y)Ay \supset \sim Gx]$ 3 **FC2**

5.   ✔ $\sim (\exists x)Fx$ ✔ $\sim (\exists y)Gy$ 2 **FC3**
6. $(x) \sim Fx$ $(y) \sim Gy$ 5 **FC2**
7.   ✔ $\sim [(\exists y)Ay \supset \sim Ga]$ 4 **FC4** $\sim [(\exists y)Ay \supset \sim Ga]$ 4 **FC4**
8. $\sim Fa$ 6 **FC5** $\sim Ga$ 6 **FC5**

9.   ✔ $Aa \supset Fa$ 1 **FC5** $Aa \supset Fa$ 1 **FC5**

10. $\sim Aa$ Fa 9 **FC3** $(\exists y)Ay$ 7 **FC3**
                                                  ✔ $\sim \sim Ga$

11.   ✔ $(\exists y)Ay$ ×   7 **FC3** Ga 10 **FC2**
            $\sim \sim Ga$ ×

12. Ga 11 **FC2**
13. Ab 11 **FC4**
14. $\sim Fb$ 6 **FC5**
15.   ✔ $Ab \supset Fb$ 1 **FC5**

16. $\sim Ab$ Fb 15 **FC3**
17.   ×   ×

Valid. All paths close.

(8) 1. $(x) \sim Fxx$ p
  ✔ 2. $\sim (x)Gx \supset (\exists y)Fya$ p /∴ $(\exists z)(Gz \cdot Fzz)$
  ✔ 3. $\sim (\exists z)(Gz \cdot Fzz)$ Denial of conclusion
  4. $(z) \sim (Gz \cdot Fzz)$ 3 **FC2**

5.   ✔ $\sim \sim (x)Gx$ $(\exists y)Fya$ 2 **FC3**
6. $(x)Gx$ 5 **FC2**
7. Ga 6 **FC5**
         $\sim Faa$ 1 **FC5**
      $\sim (Ga \cdot Faa)$ 4 **FC5**

8. $\sim Ga$ $\sim Faa$
       ×   ↑

Invalid. Open path.

Let $V(Faa) = $ **F** and $V(Ga) = $ **T**. The expansions give us $\sim Faa$ for the first premise, $\sim Ga \supset$ $Fyaa$ for the second premise, and $Ga \cdot Faa$ for the conclusion; thus true premises, false conclusion.

(10)   1. $(x)(\exists y)(Fx \cdot Gxy)$ p /∴ $(\exists y)(x)(Fx \cdot Gxy)$
       ✔ 2. $\sim (\exists y)(x)(Fx \cdot Gxy)$ Denial of conclusion
        3. $(y) \sim (x)(Fx \cdot Gxy)$ 2 FC2
        4.   ✔ $\sim (x)(Fx \cdot Gxa)$ 3 FC5
                    ✔ $(\exists y)(Fa \cdot Gay)$ 1 FC5
       ✔ 5. $(\exists x) \sim (Fx \cdot Gxa)$ 4 FC2
        6.   ✔ $Fa \cdot Gab$ 4 FC4
                    ✔ $\sim (Fc \cdot Gca)$ 5 FC4
        7. Fa 6 FC3
                    Gab 6 FC3

        8. $\sim Fc$ $\sim Gca$

        9. $(\exists y)(Fb \cdot Gby)$ 1 FC5
            $(\exists y)(Fc \cdot Gcy)$
            ✔ $\sim (x)(Fx \cdot Gxb)$ 3 FC5
            ✔ $\sim (x)(Fx \cdot Gxc)$
       10. $(\exists x) \sim (Fx \cdot Gxb)$ 9 FC2
            $(\exists x) \sim (Fx \cdot Gxc)$ 9 FC2

                        .
                        .
                        .

We must now do a new round of **FC4** steps on 10, to new constants. This will necessitate a new round of **FC5** steps and so on . . . so the argument's invalidity is not decidable by the tree.

Exercise 13-1

(2) → 4. $a = b$ AP /∴ $\sim (a = b)$
       5. $Pa \supset Qa$ 1 UI
       6. $Qa \supset Ra$ 2 UI
       7. $Pa \supset Ra$ 5,6 HS
       8. Pa 3 Simp
       9. Ra 7,8 MP
      10. $\sim Rb$ 3 Simp
      11. $\sim Ra$ 4,10 ID
      12. $Ra \cdot \sim Ra$ 9,11 Conj
      13. $\sim (a = b)$ 4–12 IP

(4) → 4. $a = b$ AP /∴ $\sim (a = b)$
       5. $Fa \supset (\exists y)Gya$ 1 UI
       6. $(\exists y)Gya$ 2,5 MP
       7. Gya 6 EI
       8. $\sim Gyb$ 3 UI
       9. $\sim Gya$ 4,8 ID
      10. $Gya \cdot \sim Gya$ 7,9 Conj
      11. $\sim (a = b)$ 4–10 IP

(6) → 2. $\sim (\exists y)[\sim (y = z) \cdot Fyz]$ AP /∴ $\sim \sim Gz$
       3. $(y) \sim [\sim (y = z) \cdot Fyz]$ 2 QN
       4. $(y)\{[\sim Fwy \supset (w = y)] \cdot Gw\}$ 1 EI
       5. $[\sim Fwz \supset (w = z)] \cdot Gw$ 4 UI
       6. $\sim [\sim (w = z) \cdot Fwz]$ 3 UI
       7. $(w = z) \vee \sim Fwz$ 6 DeM, DN
       8. $\sim (w = z) \supset \sim Fwz$ 7 DN, Impl
       9. $\sim Fwz \supset (w = z)$ 5 Simp
      10. $\sim (w = z) \supset (w = z)$ 8,9 HS
      11. $(w = z) \vee (w = z)$ 10 Impl, DN
      12. $w = z$ 11 Taut
      13. Gw 5 Simp
      14. Gz 12,13 ID
      15. $\sim \sim Gz$ 14 DN
      16. $\sim (\exists y)[\sim (y = z) \cdot Fyz] \supset \sim \sim Gz$ 2–15 CP
      17. $\sim Gz \supset (\exists y)[\sim (y = z) \cdot Fyz]$ 16 Contra + 2 DN
      18. $(x)\{\sim Gx \supset (\exists y)[\sim (y = x) \cdot Fyx]\}$ 17 UG

(8)			(10)		
4. $Fx \cdot Mx$	3 **EI**		4. $(\exists x)(Ax \cdot Bx)$	1 **QN**	
5. $Fx \supset (x = a)$	1 **UI**		5. $Ax \cdot Bx$	4 **EI**	
6. Fx	4 **Simp**		6. $\sim(x = a) \supset \sim Ax$	2 **UI**	
7. $x = a$	5,6 **MP**		7. Ax	5 **Simp**	
8. $Mx \supset (x = b)$	2 **UI**		8. $\sim\sim Ax$	7 **DN**	
9. Mx	4 **Simp**		9. $\sim\sim(x = a)$	6,8 **MT**	
10. $x = b$	8,9 **MP**		10. $x = a$	9 **DN**	
11. $a = b$	7,10 **ID**		11. $\sim[(x \neq b) \cdot Bx]$	3 **UI**	
			12. $\sim(x \neq b) \vee \sim Bx$	11 **DeM**	
			13. Bx	5 **Simp**	
			14. $\sim\sim Bx$	13 **DN**	
			15. $\sim(x \neq b)$	12,14 **DS**	
			16. $x = b$	15 **DN**	
			17. $a = b$	10,16 **ID**	

Exercise 13-2

2. $(x)[(Sx \cdot Px) \supset (x = r)]$

4. $(x)(y)\{[(Fx \cdot Rx) \cdot (Fy \cdot Ry)] \cdot (x \uparrow y)\} \supset (z)\{(Fz \cdot Rz) \supset [(z = x) \vee (z = y)]\}$

6. $(Pr \cdot Sr) \cdot (x)[(Px \cdot Sx) \supset (x = r)]$

8. $(x)\{[Px \cdot (x \neq a)] \supset Cax\}$

10. $(x)\{[Cx \cdot (x \neq z)] \supset Kzx\}$

Exercise 13-3

2. $Sb \cdot (x)\{[Sx \cdot (x \neq b)] \supset Ibx\}$
   (Sx = "x is a student"; Ixy = x is more intelligent than y"; b = "Bonny")

4. $\sim(\exists x)\{[(Rx \cdot (x \neq r)] \cdot Ex\} \cdot \sim Er$
   (Rx = "x is a rule"; Ex = "x is an exception"; r = "this rule")

6. $(\exists x)\{\{Cx \cdot (y)[Cy \supset (y = x)]\} \cdot (x = k)\}$, or just $Ck \cdot (y)[Cy \supset y = k]$
   (Cx = "x is currently world chess champion"; k = "Gary Kasparov")

8. $(\exists x)(\exists y)\{\{[(Mx \cdot My) \cdot (x \neq y)] \cdot (Lxy \cdot Lyx)\} \cdot (z)\{Mz \supset [(x = z) \vee (y = z)]\}\}$
   (Mx = "x is a Maine senator"; Lxy = "x likes y")

10. $\sim(x)(Sx \supset Bcx) \supset (\exists y)\{(Sy \cdot Byc) \cdot (z)[(Sz \cdot Bzc) \supset (z = y)]\}$
    (Sx = "x is a sprinter"; Bxy = "x is a better sprinter than y"; c = "Carl Lewis")

Exercise 13-4

2. Asymmetrical, intransitive, irreflexive

4. Asymmetrical, transitive, irreflexive

6. Symmetrical, transitive, totally reflexive

8. Nonsymmetrical, nontransitive, nonreflexive

Exercise 13-5

2. Some say that the levels-of-language theory solves this paradox. We can think of a bibliography as a very long conjunction, each entry in the bibliography being a conjunct of that conjunction. Suppose (N) is a bibliography of this kind. Then, on the levels-of-language theory, no conjunct in (N) can refer to itself—to talk of (N) itself, we need to go one flight up, to a higher-level language, where we can have a bibliography listing all bibliographies on a lower level. So in the levels-of-language theory, there cannot be a bibliography that lists all bibliographies that do not list themselves, nor indeed a bibliography that does list itself.

4. Some claim the simple theory of types solves this paradox. For in that theory, a class must be of a higher type than its members; thus, there is neither a class of all classes that are members of themselves nor of all classes that are not.

Exercise 13-6

2. (Not appropriate to answer.)
4. (Not appropriate to answer.)
6. (1) Observed—manifest
   (2) Solubility—dispositional
   (3) Green—both
   (4) Teachable—dispositional

   (5) Dangerous—dispositional
   (6) Dependable—dispositional
   (7) Character—dispositional

Exercise 14-1

2. All poor are lazy.
4. No porno flicks are erotic.
6. No amateurs are professionals.
8. Some prescription drugs are harmful.

10. Some movie stars are not happy.
12. No persons who have dry wits are drinkers.
14. All persons who forget the past are sufferers from amnesia.

Exercise 14-2

(2)
1. Can't infer to the truth-value of "No wars are hellish."
2. "Some wars are hellish" could be either true or false (because if one of two contraries is false, the other sometimes is true, sometimes false).
3. "Some wars are not hellish" is true (because "All wars are hellish" and "Some wars are not hellish" are contradictories).

(4)
1. "No congressmen are sexual gluttons" is true (because "Some congressmen are sexual gluttons" and "No congressmen are sexual gluttons" are contradictories.)
2. "Some congressmen are not sexual gluttons" is true (because "Some congressmen are sexual gluttons" and "Some congressmen are not sexual gluttons" are sub-contraries).
3. "All congressmen are sexual gluttons" is false (because its subalternate, "No congressmen are sexual gluttons", is false).

Exercise 14-3

(2)   2, 4—True; 3, 5—False
(4)   2, 3—Indeterminate; 4—False; 5—True

Exercise 14-4

(2)   2—True; 3, 4, 5—Indeterminate; 6—False
(4)   1–5—Indeterminate; 6—True

Exercise 14-5

2.

4.

6.

8.

10.

12.

14.

16.

18.

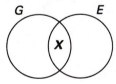

Exercise 14-6

2. *AII-III*
4. *EOI-I*
6. *EOO-I*
8. *EAE-IV*
10. *EIO-III*

Exercise 14-7

2. Valid

8. Invalid

4. Invalid

10. Valid

6. Invalid

Exercise 14-5

2.

12.

4.

14.

6.

16.

8.

18.

10.

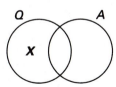

Exercise 14-6

2. *All-III*
4. *EOI-I*
6. *EOO-I*
8. *EAE-IV*
10. *EIO-III*

Exercise 14-7

2. Valid

8. Invalid

4. Invalid

10. Valid

6. Invalid

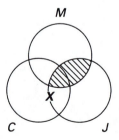

Exercise 14-8

(2) 1. Some people punished in the next life are not murderers.
   2. All sinners are punished in the next life.
∴ 3. Some sinners are not murderers.

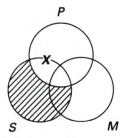

Invalid. Violates rule 1.

(4) 1. All who ignore the facts are likely to be mistaken.
   2. All who are wise are not those who ignore the facts.
∴ 3. All who are wise are not likely to be mistaken.

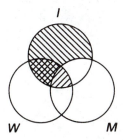

Invalid. Violates rule 2.

(6) 1. All logic classes are extremely interesting.
   2. Some logic classes are harder than average.
∴ 3. Some classes that are harder than average are extremely interesting.

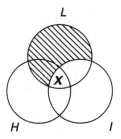

Valid.

(8)   1. All classes that are exciting are crowded.
         2. All classes that are interesting or difficult are exciting.
    ∴   3. No classes that are interesting or difficult are crowded.

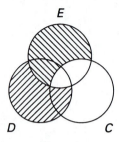

         Invalid. Violates rules 2 and 4.

(10)   1. All times that Harry enjoys himself are times when Harry has lots of money.
         2. All times Harry goes out with Jane are times that Harry enjoys himself.
    ∴   3. All times Harry goes out with Jane are times when Harry has lots of money.

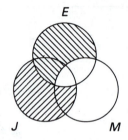

         Valid.

(12)   1. Some who live by the pen are called liars.
         2. Some who live by the pen are called sages.
    ∴   3. Some who are called sages are called liars.

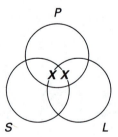

         Invalid. Violates rule 1.

(14) 1. All times when we have death and taxes are times when we fight.
      2. All times are times when we have death and taxes.
   ∴ 3. All times are times when we fight.

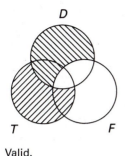

Valid.

Exercise 14-9

(2) 1. Abortion takes the life of a fetus.
     2. Anything that takes the life of a fetus takes the life of a human being.
  ∴ 3. Abortion takes the life of a human being.

(4) 1. Smith eats plenty of brown rice.
     2. Anyone who eats plenty of brown rice is in pretty good shape.
  ∴ 3. Smith is in pretty good shape.

(6) 1. Anyone who listens to television news programs listens to very superficial accounts of the news.
     2. Anyone who listens to very superficial accounts of the news, wastes one's time.
  ∴ 3. Anyone who listens to television news programs wastes one's time.

(8) 1. Some high school dropouts are smarter than lots of college grads.
     2. Anyone who's smarter than lots of college grads is capable of holding a high-level management position.
  ∴ 3. Some high school dropouts are capable of holding a high-level management position.

(10) 1. Some who've taken LSD have scrambled brains.
     2. No one with a scrambled brain is likely to do good in this world.
  ∴ 3. Some who've taken LSD are not likely to do good in this world.

Exercise 14-10

(2) 1. All skiers are athletes.
     2. Some nutritionists are skiers.
∴   3. Some nutritionists are athletes.

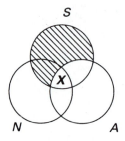

Valid.

     1. Some nutritionists are athletes.
     2. No athletes are brawny.
∴   3. Some nutritionists are not brawny.

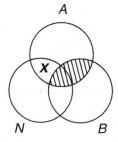

Valid.

(4) 1. All scientists are mathematicians.
     2. No mathematicians are friendly.
∴   3. No scientists are friendly.

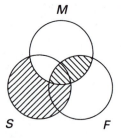

Valid.

1. No scientists are friendly.
2. All geologists are friendly.
∴ 3. No geologists are scientists.

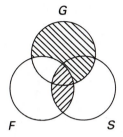

Valid.

(6) 1. All profound scholars are great lovers of music.
2. All Oxford dons are profound scholars.
∴ 3. All Oxford dons are great lovers of music.

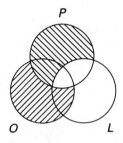

Valid.

1. No insensitive souls are great lovers of music.
2. All Oxford dons are great lovers of music.
∴ 3. No Oxford dons are insensitive souls.

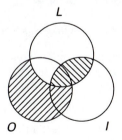

Valid.

1. No insensitive souls are Don Juans.
2. No Oxford dons are insensitive souls.
∴ 3. All Oxford dons are Don Juans.

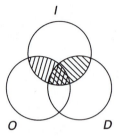

Invalid: *OD* slot is not completely shaded out. Violates rules 3 and 4.

(There are other possibilities, all invalid. A complete proof would cover all these possibilities. But it is clear the sorites is invalid, because one of its premises is negative and yet its conclusion is affirmative.)

Exercise 14-11

2. *a* and *c,* because they work in both directions.
4. False. The order of the premises makes no difference to validity.
6. Because sometimes a premise tells us that one of the two classes is nonempty, but does not tell us which one.
8. Yes, they can be interpreted as categorical propositons where the subject class has only one member. "Bill Clinton jogs" can be translated into "All members of the class whose sole member is Bill Clinton, jog."
10. (Not appropriate to answer.)

Exercise 15-1

2. **Inconsistency:** A reservation that will be held only on a space-available basis is not a reservation.
4. **Begging the question:** The question is whether smokers will have enough willpower to quit.
6. **False dilemma:** There are other alternatives not considered, such as various combinations of capitalism and socialism.
8. **Ad hominem argument:** Attacking Cooper himself (the implication of his working for Walt Disney) rather than his belief.
10. **Begging the question:** The question is whether they are in fact the children of the gods.
12. **No fallacy:** If you're still smoking cigarettes, maybe they do know something you don't. Medical doctors are legitimate authorities on the subject of the health dangers in nicotine.
14. **Irrelevant reason:** But it would be a reason, if true, for not inviting other Teamster presidents to dinner at the White House.
16. **Begging the question:** The question was whether the private ownership of the means of production was in fact obsolete.
18. **Irrelevant reason** (and for those who don't smoke—**complex question**): This slogan, used with variations by several brands over the years, gives no reason for switching to the touted brand rather than any other, or better yet, quitting.
20. **Gambler's fallacy:** The odds remain the same no matter what the recent pattern of winning numbers happens to be. (The laws of nature that determine which number will be selected aren't influenced by which numbers have recently come up.)
22. Elsewhere I stated my opinion that this is an example of the fallacy of **inconsistency**, but

it seems to me now that I was mistaken. A right need not ever be exercised. *Analogy:* I believe in the right of those in perfect health who are enjoying life to the fullest to commit suicide, but I do not believe this right should be exercised.

24. **False dilemma:** Another alternative would be to work to make America more as you may desire it to be.

26. **Affirming the consequent:** Budapest hotels may have been booked solid because of an influx of non-American tourists, for example, from West Germany (this happened to be the fact of the matter).

28. **Appeal to authority:** Since authorities differed on the matter in those days, the wise person either held no opinion on the matter or else delved into it a bit themselves. (Also perhaps suppressed evidence, namely the readily available evidence that a great many authorities accepted Darwin's theory.)

30. **Irrelevant reason:** A classic example. That a particular $100 bill you have in your pocket won't exist a few years down the road whereas the gold in a tiny nugget worth $100 at today's prices in all probability will exist thousands of years from now is not the slightest reason for investing in gold.

32. **Begging the question:** Which rights others have must be determined by a moral theory of some kind or other, which needed to be provided if a complete moral theory was to be presented.

34. **False charge of fallacy:** Since Bryant had publicly expressed a change of heart on the matter of homosexuals, she was not being hypocritical or inconsistent. (This is one of those cases where relevant background information is crucial.)

36. **False dilemma:** The Creator might have meant sexual intercourse to serve both of these functions. (Indeed, some biologists see sexual intercourse as having several functions, one being the obvious one of reproduction and another being to keep males attached to the females who bear their children.)

Exercise 15-2

2. **Popularity:** The implication is that because it is the coming thing (i.e., becoming popular), it should be instituted in this college.

4. **Questionable statistics:** How could anyone make more than a very general guess at these statistics?

6. **Popularity** (or **appeal to authority** of the crowd): But for those who have learned from experience that what is popular is generally interesting for them, this may not be fallacious. The same is true for those who like to keep up with what is fashionable in order to sound interesting at parties and such.

8. **Equivocation:** What is the "it" you have to make present? Not the past but rather just thoughts of the past.

10. **Begging the question** or **questionable analogy:** The reasons for sending men to the moon were different from those for climbing the highest mountain and surely different from those for flying the Atlantic in the 1920s.

12. **Appeal to ignorance:** Atheists could equally well argue against belief in God on the grounds that every effort to prove otherwise have failed. (Note, however, that plenty of theologians have, of course, argued we can and have proved there is a God while no one has proved there is no God.)

14. **Inconsistency:** Unless you don't want others to give you an even break?

16. **Slippery slope:** The context of the item was the teaching of "creation science" in public schools. But if not taught there, that would still be a far cry from the suppression of religion that has marked the Soviet regime in Russia, and would constitute no serious reason for supposing that we are moving anywhere near that kind of suppression in the countries in the West.

18. **Questionable cause:** We have all sorts of background knowledge indicating this correlation is an accidental one, and several other much better candidates, to mention only one better diagnosis of these matters (which suggests the fallacy of **questionable statistics**).

20. This is a good example to chew around, because there are all sorts of relevant factors to consider and background beliefs to be brought to bear. The implication is that just as we shouldn't tax these other items for the stated purposes, so also we shouldn't tax hotels to build occupancy. To start with, is this a case of **questionable analogy?** The hotels taxed directly benefit by increased occupancy. Would, for instance, college professors receive increased salaries if taxes taken from their salaries did in fact increase college enroll-ments? And isn't the point of increasing hotel occupancy by taxes that the economy of a place in general is increased by increases in tourism? Further, is this a case of **irrelevant reason?** Whether or not we should, say, tax bank deposits would seem to be irrelevant to whether we should or shouldn't tax hotel rooms to increase occupancy.

22. **Questionable statistics:** Even supposing it makes sense to place an economic value on human life (granting that the attempt to do so is inevitable), can we possibly calculate it down to an exact dollar figure?

24. The question is whether there is **suppressed evidence**, namely that you pay less when your employer pays than when you pay directly. (This obviously is a much disputed point, because, on the one hand, it has been argued that your employer of necessity lowers your salary to cover the increase in health insurance costs, while, on the other hand, it is argued that as an individual you can't get health insurance at the low group rate obtained by your employer.)

26. **Questionable analogy:** Sex and baseball are much different and not in competition with each other (at least in most cases!), while one kind of gambling clearly is in competition with other kinds. (But I doubt we needed this spelled out.)

28. **Tokenism:** Also perhaps for some **begging the question,** for instance as to whether being against abortion is bad for women, as women's rights activists generally claim.

30. **Inconsistency:** Hoover said that the FBI never draws conclusions and then he drew a conclusion.

32. **Inconsistency** (between words and actions): While allowing a 15-minute tape to be shown wasn't exactly crossing a picket line, it's in the same spirit. The point of Hope's not crossing a picket line was to show solidarity with ordinary laborers—in this case, by depriving those inside of the benefit of Hope's entertainment. (People who sneak out of obligations in this way are derisively called "legalists.")

34. **Traditional wisdom:** Earth no doubt was believed to be flat for many more thousands of years by a majority of people. Or perhaps **irrelevant reason,** just as most people having believed that Earth is flat for most of human history is irrelevant to the question whether it is indeed flat.

36. **Begging the question:** Of course Shakespeare knew very well what he was doing.

38. **No fallacy,** certainly not the fallacy of **inconsistency.** Aristotle was trying to point out the unfortunately true fact that friendship has its limits.

40. **Equivocation** and **persuasive definition:** His answer is a good one only if "inappropriate technology" is taken in its usual literal sense, whereas the Indians were using it to mean what Schumacher meant by "intermediate technology."

42. **Common practice:** That others did this is no justification.

44. **Irrelevant reason:** That we can afford to eat well does not prove we do in fact eat well. But perhaps this is not completely irrelevant since we can assume most people want to eat well if they can afford to do so.

46. **Traditional wisdom:** We can't dismiss every attempt at change by arguing that the tradi-tional way is best because traditional. This is just a way of begging the question.

48. **Two wrongs make a right:** American wrongdoings in Vietnam can't justify Israeli wrong-doings, if they were, in Lebanon.

50. **Irrelevant reason:** That my aunt's mail route was changed so that she receives her mail in the afternoon instead of morning says nothing about the general efficiency of the post office in delivering mail.

52. **Slippery slope:** One wonders whether Safire would argue that the American revolution-ary war, which after all was a war of secession—a civil war—also must of necessity lead to further subdivisions.

54. **Begging the question:** Was this the "call of history"? As politicians often do, President Reagan was engaging in "mom and apple pie" rhetoric—generalities everyone agrees to that mask the issues on which there is controversy—the questions at issue, such as the advisability of having U.S. warships in the Persian Gulf at that time.

56. **Straw man:** Male took George Bush TV commercial falsehoods for truths about Michael Dukakis's political record. Also **poisoning the well.** "He's completely fooled by Gorbachev." "What can you know about abortion? . . . "

58. **Questionable cause** and **suppressed evidence:** It was much more plausible to believe that the reduction in deaths was caused by delaying nonemergency but still risky operations on otherwise terminally ill patients, such as cancer victims, than by avoiding unnecessary operations that might have resulted in deaths. (This doesn't mean that there are no such unnecessary operations; it just means that even if there were none, and even no botched ones, we still could temporarily reduce the number of deaths by postponing risky nonemergency operations.)

Exercise 15-3

(Not appropriate to provide answers.)

Exercise 16-1

2. Neutral: c; Decrease: a,b,d,e

Exercise 16-2

2. Strong analogy: It calls our attention to a feature of military conquest we might otherwise overlook, and the one analogical instance it presents is convincing.

4. Although weak in itself because it has only one analogical instance, it is still very strong, because it is enthymematic for an analogy that mentions the constant nature of as many animals as we wish, since all are constant.

6. Weak analogy: LBJ taking care of daughters and the U.S. government protecting freedom everywhere are two vastly different undertakings depending on totally different factors, namely, Johnson's economic position and the power of the United States relative to its enemies.

8. Although weak in itself, because it has only one analogical instance, it still is very strong because it is enthymematic for an analogy that mentions lots of cases where we note a correlation between our inner sensations and overt appearance and behavior. However, this argument from analogy to the existence of other streams of consciousness notoriously differs from most cases in that we can never check up directly to see if our conclusion is correct, because we cannot experience another person's experience (behaviorists and others obviously disagree in one way or another). (This last point is relevant also to question 7.)

Exercise 16-3

2. Theoretical

4. Attention—theoretical; neutrinos—probably theoretical

6. Both: ". . . looked red"—observable; ". . . he wasn't sure" that it was red—theoretical

Exercise 16-4

2. Concomitant variation (negative)

4. Difference

6. Agreement (negative)

8. Concomitant variation

10. Agreement (negative) and agreement (positive)

12. Agreement and difference

Exercise 16-5

2. False
4. True
6. True
8. True
10. False
12. True
14. True

Exercise 16-6

2. a. $p = 1/2 \times 1/2 = 1/4$
   b. $p = 1/2 \times 1/2 \times 1/2 = 1/8$

4. Probability of even number $= 3/6$
   Probability of number less than 3 $= 2/6$
   Probability of even number less than 3 $= 3/6 \times 2/6 = 1/6$
   Probability of either even number or number less than 3 (or both) $=$
   $3/6 + 2/6 - 1/6 = 4/6 = 2/3$

6. $P(p \cdot q) = P(p) \times P(q) =$ or $P(p \cdot q) =$
   (This item is ambiguous.)

8. Probability of *HHT* or (*HTH* or *THH*) $= 1/2 \times 1/2 \times 1/2 = 1/8$
   Probability of exactly two heads out of three $= 1/8 + 1/8 + 1/8 = 3/8$

10. a. Probability of ace on first draw $= 1/13$
    Probability of ace on second draw $= 3/51$
    Probability of two aces in a row $= 1/13 \times 3/51 = 1/221$

    b. Probability of at least one ace $= 1/13 + 3/51 - 1/221 = 29/221$

    c. Probability of first spade $= 1/4$
    Probability of second spade $= 12/51$
    Probability of two spades $= 1/4 \times 12/51 = 1/17$

    d. Probability of first black ace $= 1/26$
    Probability of second black ace $= 1/51$
    Probability of two black aces $= 1/26 \times 1/51 = 1/1326$

Bibliography

The following is a selected list of books and articles dealing with material covered in this book. Starred items are mentioned in the body of the text.

Parts One and Two

Bird, Otto. *Syllogistics and Its Extensions.* Englewood Cliffs, NJ: Prentice-Hall, 1964.

Bochenski, I. M. *A History of Formal Logic.* (trans. and ed. Ivo Thomas). New York: Chelsea, 1970.

*Carroll, Lewis (C. L. Dodgson). *Symbolic Logic and the Game of Logic.* New York: Dover, 1958.

*Church, Alonzo. *Introduction to Mathematical Logic.* Princeton, NJ: Princeton University Press, 1956.

*Copi, Irving. *Symbolic Logic,* 7th ed. New York: Macmillan,1986.

*Dodgson, C. L. (Lewis Carroll). *Symbolic Logic.* 1896.

*Fitch, Frederick B. *Symbolic Logic.* New York: The Ronald Press, 1952.

*Jeffrey, Richard. *Formal Logic: Its Scope and Limits,* 1st and 3rd eds. New York: McGraw-Hill, 1967, 1991.

Kleene, Stephen C. *Mathematical Logic.* New York: Wiley, 1967.

Kneale, W., and M. Kneale. *The Development of Logic.* Oxford, UK: Clarendon Press, 1962.

Kuhn, T. S. *The Structure of Scientific Revolutions.* 2nd ed. Chicago: University of Chicago Press, 1970.

Lemmon, E. J. *Beginning Logic.* (revised by G. N. D. Barry). Indianapolis: Hackett, 1978. (Originally published London: Thomas Nelson, 1965.)

*Oliver, James W. "Formal Fallacies and Other Invalid Arguments." *Mind,* n.s., vol. 76 (1967).

*Purtill, Richard L. *Logic for Philosophers.* New York: Harper & Row, 1971.

Reichenbach, Hans. *Elements of Symbolic Logic.* New York: Macmillan, 1947. (Reprinted by Dover.)

*Russell, Bertrand. "Mr. Strawson on Referring," in *My Philosophical Development.* London: Allen and Unwin, 1959.

*Russell, Bertrand. "On Denoting." *Mind,* n.s., vol. 14 (1905). Reprinted in Robert C. Marsh, ed., *Logic and Knowledge.* New York: Macmillan, 1956.

*Russell, Bertrand. "The Philosophy of Logical Atomism." *Logic and Knowledge,* ed. Robert C. Marsh. New York: Macmillan, 1956.

*Russell, Bertrand. *Principles of Mathematics.* Cambridge, UK: Cambridge University Press, 1903.

*Russell, Bertrand, and Whitehead, A. N. *Principia Mathematica,* abridged ed. Cambridge, UK: Cambridge University Press, 1962.

*Sanford, David. "Contraries and Subcontraries." *Nous,* vol. 2 (1968).

Stevenson, Charles L. "If-iculties." *Philosophy of Science,* vol. 41 (1970).

*Strawson, P. F. "On Referring." *Mind,* n.s., vol. 59 (1950).

*Suppes, Patrick. *Introduction to Logic.* Princeton, NJ: Van Nostrand, 1957.

*Tarski, Alfred. "Semantic Conception of Truth." *Philosophy and Phenomenological Research,* vol. 4 (1944).

*Thomason, Richmond H. *Symbolic Logic.* Toronto: Macmillan, 1970.

*Wittgenstein, Ludwig. *Tractatus Logico Philosophicus.* New York: Harcourt Brace, 1922.

Part Three

*Anderson, Allan Ross. "On the Logic of Commitment." *Philosophical Studies,* vol. 10 (1959).

*Ayer, A. J. *Language, Truth and Logic.* New York: Dover, 1952.

*Barker, Stephen. *Elements of Logic,* 5th ed. New York: McGraw-Hill, 1989.

*Baum, Robert. *Logic,* 2nd ed. New York: Holt, Rinehart and Winston, 1981.

*Bergmann, Gustav. "The Philosophical Significance of Modal Logic." *Mind,* n.s., vol. 69 (1960).

*Blair, J. Anthony, and Johnson, Ralph H. *Informal Logic: The First International Symposium.* Inverness, CA: Edgepress, 1980.

*Cadwallader, Eva H. "Christine Ladd-Franklin's Antilogism." *Newsletter on the Teaching of Philosophy,* Fall 1980.

*Carnap, Rudolf. *The Continuum of Inductive Methods.* Chicago: University of Chicago Press, 1952.

*Carnap, Rudolf. *Logical Foundations of Probability,* 2nd ed. Chicago: University of Chicago Press, 1962.

*Carnap, Rudolf. "On the Application of Inductive Logic." *Philosophy and Phenomenological Research,* vol. 8 (1947).

*Castañeda, Hector-Neri. "The Logic of Obligation." *Philosophical Studies,* vol. 10 (1959).

Church, Alonzo. *Introduction to Mathematical Logic.* Princeton, NJ: Princeton University Press, 1956.

Cohen, Morris R., and Ernest Nagel. *An Introduction to Logic.* New York: Harcourt, 1962.

*Copi, Irving. *Introduction to Logic,* 7th ed. New York: Macmillan, 1986.

Copi, Irving. *Symbolic Logic,* 6th ed. New York: Macmillan, 1982.

*Danto, Arthur C. "On Knowing That We Know." In Avrum Stroll, ed., *Epistemology.* New York: Harper & Row, 1967.

Eaton, Ralph M. *General Logic.* New York: Scribner's, 1931.

*Gensler, Harry. "Star Test." *Notre Dame Journal of Formal Logic,* vol. 14 (1973).

*Gierre, Ronald. *Understanding Scientific Reasoning,* 2nd ed. New York: Holt, Rinehart and Winston, 1984.

*Goodman, Nelson. *Fact, Fiction, and Forecast,* 3rd ed. Indianapolis: Bobbs-Merrill, 1973.

*Hempel, Carl. *Philosophy of Natural Science.* Englewood Cliffs, NJ: Prentice-Hall, 1966.

*Hempel, Carl. "Studies in the Logic of Confirmation." *Mind,* n.s., vol. 54 (1945).

*Hume, David. *An Enquiry Concerning Human Understanding.*

*Hume, David. *A Treatise of Human Nature.*

*Kahane, Howard. "Baumer on the Confirmation Paradoxes." *British Journal for the Philosophy of Science,* vol. 18 (1967).

*Kahane, Howard. "Eliminative Confirmation and Paradoxes." *British Journal for the Philosophy of Science,* vol. 20 (1969).

*Kahane, Howard. "Hempel and Goodman on the Ravens." (Private paper)

*Kahane, Howard. *Logic and Contemporary Rhetoric,* 5th ed. Belmont, CA: Wadsworth, 1988.

*Kahane, Howard. "Pathological Predicates and Projection." *American Philosophical Quarterly,* vol. 8 (1971).

*Kleene, S. C. *Introduction to Meta-Mathematics.* New York: Van Nostrand, 1964.

*Marcus, Ruth Marcan. "A Functional Calculus of First Order Based on Strict Implication." *Journal of Symbolic Logic,* vol. II (1946).

*Mendelson, Elliot. *Introduction to Mathematical Logic,* 2nd ed. Princeton, NJ: Van Nostrand, 1979.

*Mill, John Stuart. *Systems of Logic,* 1843.

Nagel, Ernest. *The Structure of Science.* New York: Harcourt, 1961.

Orwell, George. "Politics and the English Language," in *Shooting an Elephant and Other Essays.* New York: Harcourt Brace, 1945.

*Peirce, Charles. "Induction as Experimental and Self-Correcting." *Collected Papers of Charles Sanders Peirce,* vol. VI, ed. Charles Hartshorne and Paul Weiss. Cambridge, MA: Harvard University Press, 1935.

*Pole, Nelson. "A Deductive Argument with a Specific Premise and a General Conclusion." *Notre Dame Journal of Formal Logic,* vol. XVI (1975).

*Popper, Karl. *The Logic of Scientific Discovery.* New York: Basic Books, 1959.

*Quine, Willard V. *From a Logical Point of View.* Cambridge, MA: Harvard University Press, 1953.

*Quine, Willard V. "Notes on Existence and Necessity." *Journal of Philosophy,* vol. 40 (1943).

*Ramsey, Frank. *The Foundations of Mathematics.* London: Routledge & Keegan Paul, 1931.

*Reichenbach, Hans. *Nomological Statements and Admissible Operations.* Amsterdam: North Holland Publishers, 1954.

*Reichenbach, Hans. *Rise of Scientific Philosophy.* Berkeley: University of California Press, 1951.

*Reichenbach, Hans. *The Theory of Probability.* Berkeley: University of California Press, 1949.

Reichman, William J. *Use and Abuse of Statistics.* New York: Oxford University Press, 1962.

*Rescher, Nicholas. "An Axiom System for Deontic Logic." *Philosophical Studies,* vol. IX (1958).

*Robison, John. "Further Difficulties for Conditional Permission in Deontic Logic." *Philosophical Studies,* vol. XVIII (1967).

*Ruby, Lionel. *The Art of Making Sense,* 2nd ed. New York: Lippincott, 1954.

Salmon, Wesley C. *The Foundations of Scientific Inference.* Pittsburgh: University of Pittsburgh Press, 1967.

*Skyrms, Brian. *Choice and Chance,* 3rd ed. Belmont, CA: Wadsworth, 1985.

*Suppes, Patrick. *Introduction to Logic.* Princeton: Van Nostrand, 1957.

*von Wright, G. H. *Logical Problems of Induction,* 2nd rev. ed. New York: Barnes & Noble, 1965.

*Woozley, A. D. "Universals." *Encyclopedia of Philosophy,* ed. Paul Edwards. New York: Collier Macmillan, 1967.

Special Symbols

Symbol	Introduced on Page	Symbol	Introduced on Page
∴	2	C	51
.	24	E	51
~	29	::	105
(), [], {}	30	(x)	169
∨	32	$(\exists x)$	169
⊃	38	=	283
≡	40	≠	284
¬	50	$\bar{P}$	308
∧	50	◇	425
&	50	□	426
→	50	⇒	427
↔	50	⇔	427
N	51	$P\ (p/c)$	427
K	51	$O\ (p/c)$	428
A	51		

Index

absorption, 127, 149
accidentally bound variables, 261–265
accounting, in predicate logic truth trees, 280–281
Ackermann, Robert J., 436
Addition (Add)
  in indirect proofs, 137
  in proofs generally, 96–99
  strategy rules and, 102–105
  as valid implicational argument form, 96, 98
  weakening effect of using, 118–119
ad hominem arguments, 360
affirming the consequent, 360
affirmo, 316
agreement, method of, 391–392
Akron Beacon-Journal, 370
alternation, in Polish notation, 51
alternative logics
  deontic, 437–439
  epistemic, 433–436
  modal. *See* modal logic
American Heritage, 373
American Medical Association, 363
American Philosophical Quarterly, 408
analogical inference, 409
analogies, in inductive logic, 382–386
analysis, truth table, 56, 87
Anderson, Alan Ross, 438
Animal Liberation, 374
antecedents
  in conditional sentences, 37
  defined, 52
  denying, 361

AP (Assumed Premise). *See* Assumed Premise (AP)
appeals to authority, 360
appeals to ignorance, 360
A propositions
  as categorical propositions, 316–319
  contraposition and conversion in, 323–326
  defined, 352
  distribution and, 340
  existential import of, 326–329
  obversion in, 323–326
  square of opposition and, 320–323
  as syllogisms, 331–333
  Venn diagrams of, 329–331, 335, 339
argumentem ad ignorantiam, 360
argument forms
  deductive, 7–8
  defined, 16, 124
  invalid. *See* invalid argument forms
  in proofs generally, 88–90
  valid. *See* valid argument forms
arguments, introducing, 1–17
  conclusions. *See* conclusions of arguments
  consistency of, 12–13
  context of discovery and justification, 15–17
  deduction vs. induction, 5–8
  defined, 16, 88
  elements of, 1–4
  inductive. *See* inductive arguments
  invalidity of. *See* invalidity

key terms, 16–17
philosophical discussions, 16
premises. *See* premises of arguments
soundness of, 11–12
syllogisms. *See* syllogisms
truth and validity, 8–11
validity generally. *See* validity
validity vs. consistency of, 13–14
argumentum ad hominem, 360
Aristotelian logic
  defined, 352
  predicate logic vs. syllogistic logic, 348–350
  symbolic logic vs., 22
  universal quantifiers in, 171
arithmetic, 414–415, 422–423
Association (Assoc), 108, 110
Assumed Premise (AP)
  in axiom systems, 415
  in conditional proofs, 125–131
  defined, 149
  in indirect proofs, 135–136
  in proving premises inconsistent, 142
  quantifier rules and, 208–209
  in strategy for relational predicate logic proofs, 245
  in theorems of predicate logic, 247–250
  Universal Generalization and, 206–207
asymmetrical relations, 292, 314
Atlantic, The, 372
"at least," symbolizing, 286
"at most," symbolizing, 286

511